COLLABORATIVE CONSULTATION IN THE SCHOOLS

Effective Practices for Students with Learning and Behavior Problems

Second Edition

Thomas J. Kampwirth
California State University–Long Beach

Merrill
Prentice Hall

Upper Saddle River, New Jersey
Columbus, Ohio

Library of Congress Cataloging-in-Publication Data

Kampwirth, Thomas J.
  Collaborative consultation in the schools: effective practices for students with learning
and behavior problems/ Thomas J. Kampwirth.–2nd ed.
    p. cm.
  Includes bibliographical references and index.
  ISBN 0-13-096852-8 (pbk.)
  1. Educational counseling–United States. 2. Group work in education–United States.
3. Learning disabled children–Services for–United States. 4. Problem children–Services
for–United States. 5. School management and organization–United States. I. Title.

LB1027.5.K285 2003
371.9—dc21   2001059616

Vice President and Publisher: Jeffery W. Johnston
Editor: Allyson P. Sharp
Editorial Assistant: Penny Burleson
Production Editor: Sheryl Glicker Langner
Production Coordinator: Tiffany Kuehn, Carlisle Publishers Services
Design Coordinator: Diane C. Lorenzo
Cover Designer: Jason Moore
Cover art: Super Stock
Production Manager: Laura Messerly
Director of Marketing: Ann Castel Davis
Marketing Manager: Amy June
Marketing Coordinator: Tyra Cooper

This book was set in Garamond and GillSans by Carlisle Communication, Ltd. It was printed and bound
by Maple Vail Book Manufacturing Group. The cover was printed by Phoenix Color Corp.

Pearson Education Ltd.
Pearson Education Australia Pty. Limited
Pearson Education Singapore Pte. Ltd.
Pearson Education North Asia Ltd.
Pearson Education Canada, Ltd.
Pearson Educación de Mexico, S.A. de C. V.
Pearson Education–Japan
Pearson Education Malasia Pte. Ltd.
Pearson Education, *Upper Saddle River, New Jersey*

Merrill
Prentice Hall

10 9 8 7 6 5 4 3 2 1
ISBN 0-13-096852-8

This text is dedicated to our children and grandchildren.
May their dreams come true.

About the Author

*T*homas Kampwirth is professor emeritus in the Department of Educational Psychology, Administration, and Counseling at California State University–Long Beach. He has taught in the areas of special education and school psychology since 1971. He was coordinator of the school psychology program at CSULB for 25 years. He is a consulting school psychologist for the alternative and correctional educational system operated by the Orange County Department of Education in California.

He has served as a special education teacher and a school psychologist in numerous districts in Illinois, Arizona, and California. His research interests include aptitude-treatment interactions and consultation processes. Dr. Kampwirth received his doctorate in school psychology from the University of Illinois in 1968.

Preface

This book was written to fill the needs of two different groups: university students and practitioners in the schools. The students are likely to be doing work in special education, school psychology, school counseling, or educational administration. The practitioners are currently employed in these professions and are being asked more and more to help others, usually teachers or parents, solve teaching/learning and behavior management problems. In this book, I present the consultation process as a collaborative, problem-solving endeavor designed to assist consultees in their work with students who have, or are at risk for, school adjustment or learning problems. In addition, I include a chapter on ethics and advocacy and a chapter on systems-level consultation designed to improve service delivery to students and teachers in a whole school or district.

Consultation as a service delivery system in the public schools has increased in popularity over the past decade. Prior to 1990, most special and general educators were still expected to deal on their own with whatever problems they experienced in their teaching or management of children; indeed, those who sought help may have been regarded as unable to deal with the job of teaching and subtly, or overtly, rejected by their peers or supervisors. To an even greater extent, parents in the United States, since the decline of the extended family configurations that were prevalent before the Second World War, have been expected to raise their children without much assistance from others. The "village" that it takes to raise a child had disappeared and been replaced by neighbors known only slightly and relatives who lived far away. Only people with large financial resources could access relatively expensive professional help for their children who needed it. Most parents, including those with children with disabilities, were left to their own resources.

In today's schools, we are fortunate to have experienced a change in attitudes about the value of team building and collaborative assistance. Part of the credit for this change should be given to the field of special education, which, as a result of P.L. 94-142, first implemented in 1977, established the need for team conferences (IEP meetings) to discuss the needs of, and solutions for, the learning and behavior/adjustment problems of students with disabilities. Since that time, teacher assistance teams, student study teams, and a host of other formal or semiformal team arrangements have been developed and have proven their effectiveness in meeting the needs of students who require some degree of assistance to be successful in school. These team interactions also meet the needs of teachers and parents in their efforts to teach or parent effectively.

Beyond what takes place in team meetings, there remains a real need for everyday assistance for both special education teachers who are providing direct teaching services to students with disabilities and general educators who are charged with teaching mainstreamed or included students with disabilities, in addition to a large cadre of other at-risk students. This text is primarily devoted to helping those who assist these special and general educators to deal with the everyday, ongoing challenges presented by these students. Largely because of increased inclusion and a seemingly growing number of at-risk youth, school personnel have learned the value of collaborative work as opposed to isolated work. In a school with a collaborative work ethic, the administration supports teachers who freely seek help from others, join in groups to discuss common or individual problems, and admit that they need help. Job descriptions and expectations have changed accordingly. Special education teachers are increasingly leaving their resource rooms and special day classes and are spending part, if not all, of their school days in general education classes. School psychologists are learning alternative ways of assessing students, which include more time observing in the classes and more time talking with the teachers about the referrals and appropriate interventions that can be utilized in general education classes. School counselors are more likely to see if they can deal with some referrals through consultation with teachers and parents in conjunction with individual or group counseling efforts. Mentor teachers, vice-principals, and others who may have the opportunity to assist teachers and parents are also seeing their roles expand to include consultation.

UNIQUE ASPECTS OF THIS TEXT

This text differs in two major ways from others that are devoted to consultation in the schools. The first difference is the inclusion of five extended case studies. Two of these are about students who manifest behavior problems, two are in regard to students with learning (achievement) problems, and the fifth is a study of a systems-change effort. The second difference is the inclusion of separate chapters on students' learning and behavior problems. These problems are the main reasons for referral to a school consultant, whether that person has a primary position as a special education teacher, a school counselor, a school psychologist, a mentor teacher, or a vice-principal. Thus, it is important to have fundamental information about the probable causes and possible solutions to these problems.

This text has a number of strengths: (1) It is written in a user-friendly fashion. The author is very experienced in the practice of school consultation and has utilized his experiences to keep the situations described and interventions discussed at a very practical level. There is a bit of folk wisdom permeating these pages, a kind of common sense that may be lacking in some other texts that take perhaps too much of a seemingly impractical research-oriented perspective. Practitioners know that consultation is not an easy process to implement; this text presents the rough with the smooth and, because of this, lets future consultants know what the realities of the public schools are. (2) Each chapter has a number of student activities embedded in the narrative. These are intended to focus readers' attention on key aspects of the material and to give them a chance to practice the skills being discussed and to interact with others regarding the critical issues that are presented. (3) There are a number of figures and tables that serve a variety of purposes, such as models of forms, examples of paperwork that are used, and material cited from the work of others.

In this second edition I have added a set of objectives for each chapter which serve as guides to what the chapter covers. Also, this second edition has nearly twice the number of activities as did the first edition. There are also many more specific suggestions about interventions, especially in Chapter 5. The addition of a whole chapter on ethics and advocacy (Chapter 4) is not common among texts on consultation, in spite of the importance of these issues; I hope you will find it enlightening.

ORGANIZATION

Chapter 1 presents an overview of school consultation as practiced by internal (i.e., regularly employed personnel) consultants. It defines terms and discusses the characteristics of consultation that are collaborative in nature; major focus points and questions about them; and the benefits and effectiveness of school consultation. I consider the consultee as a variable and explore information about consultation in culturally and linguistically diverse settings. The chapter concludes with a statement of philosophy about the educational placements of students with disabilities.

Chapter 2 presents a brief overview of various models and functional aspects that apply to school consultation. The behavioral and mental health models are discussed in some detail. There is also information about the roles, skills, and activities of consultants; student study team functions; and information about the development and conduct of inservice training.

Chapter 3 presents an extended discussion of the communication and interpersonal skills needed for effective consultation and reviews resistance to consultation and power dynamics in the consultative process.

Chapter 4 is devoted to issues of ethics and advocacy. In addition to a general overview of ethical issues, the chapter includes a review of the CEC ethical code and the standards of practice development for special educators. Case studies are presented to show how to apply the code and standards to situations that can occur in schools. A separate discussion of advocacy indicates how this potentially sensitive area can be utilized in a collaborative manner.

Chapter 5 is the heart of this text. Here I present generic models of the consultation process along with the solutions-oriented consultation system (SOCS), a 10-step practical model designed to guide school-based consultants through the often confusing stages that are necessary for comprehensive consultation work.

Chapter 6 reviews students' behavior/adjustment problems. I discuss reasons for these problems, terminology, and diagnostic methods including functional assessment, observation, interviews, rating scales, and charting methods. I also include general ideas for modifying classroom behavior.

Chapter 7 contains two extended case studies about two students who manifest behavior/adjustment problems and demonstrate how SOCS can be used to guide consultants' work.

Chapter 8 reviews learning/achievement problems among students and offers ideas for the diagnosis and remediation of these problems.

Chapter 9 consists of two case studies about students who manifest poor school achievement. Again, I use SOCS as the conduct guide for the consultation.

Chapter 10 is concerned with systems-change efforts. Reform and the revitalization of our public schools are topics of considerable importance as we move toward the achievement of GOALS 2000 and the "No child left behind" federal education bill approved by President George W. Bush in 2002. This chapter deals with systems-change ideas and presents a case study showing how a major change in service delivery to students with disabilities can be achieved.

ACKNOWLEDGMENTS

I would like to thank the reviewers of the manuscript for their constructive comments: Donna Kearns, University of Central Oklahoma; Mark P. Mostert, Old Dominion University; Qaisar Sultana, Eastern Kentucky University; and Diana T. Woodrum, West Virginia University.

Discover the Companion
Website Accompanying This Book

THE PRENTICE HALL COMPANION WEBSITE:
A VIRTUAL LEARNING ENVIRONMENT

Technology is a constantly growing and changing aspect of our field that is creating a need for content and resources. To address this emerging need, Prentice Hall has developed an online learning environment for students and professors alike—Companion Websites—to support our textbooks.

In creating a Companion Website, our goal is to build on and enhance what the textbook already offers. For this reason, the content for each user-friendly Website is organized by topic and provides the professor and student with a variety of meaningful resources. Common features of a Companion Website include:

FOR THE PROFESSOR—

Every Companion Website integrates **Syllabus Manager**™, an online syllabus creation and management utility.

- **Syllabus Manager**™ provides you, the instructor, with an easy, step-by-step process to create and revise syllabi, with direct links into Companion Website and other online content without having to learn HTML.

- Students may logon to your syllabus during any study session. All they need to know is the Web address for the Companion Website and the password you've assigned to your syllabus.

- After you have created a syllabus using **Syllabus Manager**™, students may enter the syllabus for their course section from any point in the Companion Website.

- Clicking on a date, the student is shown the list of activities for the assignment. The activities for each assignment are linked directly to actual content, saving time for students.

- Adding assignments consists of clicking on the desired due date, then filling in the details of the assignment—name of the assignment, instructions, and whether it is a one-time or repeating assignment.

- In addition, links to other activities can be created easily. If the activity is online, a URL can be entered in the space provided, and it will be linked automatically in the final syllabus.

- Your completed syllabus is hosted on our servers, allowing convenient updates from any computer on the Internet. Changes you make to your syllabus are immediately available to your students at their next logon.

FOR THE STUDENT—

- **Topics Overviews**—outline key concepts in topic areas.
- **Characteristics**—General information about each topic/disability covered on this website.
- **Read About It**—A list of links to pertinent articles found on the Internet that cover each topic.
- **Teaching Ideas**—Links to articles that offer suggestions, ideas, and strategies for teaching students with disabilities.
- **Web Links**—A wide range of websites that provide useful and current information related to each topic area.
- **Resources**—A wide array of different resources for many of the pertinent topics and issues surrounding Special Education.
- **Electronic Bluebook**—send homework or essays directly to your instructor's email with this paperless form.
- **Message Board**—serves as a virtual bulletin board to post—or respond to—questions or comments to/from a national audience.
- **Chat**—real-time chat with anyone who is using the text anywhere in the country—ideal for discussion and study groups, class projects, etc.

To take advantage of these and other resources, please visit the *Collaborative Consulatation in the Schools: Effective Practices for Students with Learning and Behavior Problems,* Second Edition, Companion Website at

www.prenhall.com/kampwirth

Contents

CHAPTER 2

Models and Functional Aspects of Consultation   41

CHAPTER 3

Communication and Interpersonal Skills   101

CHAPTER 4

Ethics and Advocacy in School Consultation   159

CHAPTER 5

The Process of Consultation   177

CHAPTER 6

Consulting About Students with Behavior Problems 225

CHAPTER 7

Case Studies in Consultation: Behavior Problems in the Classroom 277

CHAPTER 8

Consulting About Students with Academic Learning Problems 311

CHAPTER 9

Case Studies in Consultation: Academic Learning Problems in the Classroom   349

CHAPTER 10

Systems-Level Consultation: The Organization as the Target of Change   383

CHAPTER I

Overview of School-Based Consultation

OBJECTIVES

1. Orient the reader to the field of consultation as it is practiced in the schools.

2. Define terms that are common in the field, while highlighting the differences and similarities between the terms "consultation" and "collaboration," and then showing how these two terms can be used together to describe a method of consultation that validates the concept of collaboration.

3. Indicate how collaborative consultation is becoming a significant role for many school personnel, especially special educators, but also school psychologists, speech and language specialists, and school counselors.

4. Highlight the central purpose of consultation, which is to develop, monitor, and evaluate interventions for students with behavior and learning problems.

5. Explain the different forms consultation takes, as well as the relationship between the process and the content of consultation.

6. Respond to frequently asked questions regarding consultation.

7. Discuss consultation in relation to issues of diversity.

8. Explicate a philosophy regarding inclusion of students with disabilities.

You are the newly appointed resource specialist, school psychologist, or counselor at Alpha School, a K–6 school in the Alpha–Beta K–12 school district. Your job includes being a consultant to teachers, parents, and others about student learning and behavior/adjustment problems. Mrs. Jones, an experienced third-grade teacher, stops you in the hallway one day in early October and says, "You've got to do something about Johnny B. He really needs a lot of help." How would you proceed?

Ms. Simpson is a first-year teacher at Alpha School. She is teaching sixth grade, although her student teaching was limited to kindergarten and grade four. She is referring four students, whom she states are all virtually nonreaders. What do you think about this referral, and how might you proceed?

Ms. Nguyen, principal of Martin Luther King, Jr. High School, wants you to explain your role as a consultant to the teachers. Consider how you might prepare a two-minute presentation at the next teacher staff meeting regarding the meaning of school-based consultation. Take your presentation from the perspective of a special education teacher, or school counselor, or school psychologist.

How you might proceed is a function of many variables, such as your personal philosophy of professional practice; the expectations of your supervisors and coworkers; and factors such as caseload, established precedents, your reinforcement history, and your training. I believe that a consultation-based service delivery model is, for most referrals and most constituents (that is, teachers, parents, and other consultees), an appropriate and useful approach when used with other service requirements of your position as a special education teacher, school psychologist, or school counselor.

CONSULTATION AND COLLABORATION: DEFINITIONS, DISTINCTIONS, AND CHARACTERISTICS

The terms *consultation* and *collaboration* have been discussed in many different ways by various authorities. *Webster's College Dictionary* (1997) defines *consult* as seeking guidance or information, or to give professional or expert advice. A *consultant* is a person who gives such advice. *Consultation* is the act of consulting; a meeting for deliberation or discussion (p. 284). The word *collaborate* means to work, one with another; cooperate (p. 257). Four key concepts are mentioned: *information seeking* or *giving, discussion, expert,* and *working together.* This book discusses these four concepts, among many others.

The *Webster's* (1997) definitions of *consultation* and *collaboration,* although generic, are not precise enough for our purposes. Writers in the field of consultation have worked to refine the definitions of consultation and collaboration from the perspectives of the public schools. Figure 1.1 contains examples of definitions of consultation, collaboration, and collaborative consultation taken from the current literature. Essentially, most writers believe that the term *consultation* should be reserved for instances where one person, the consultant, develops interventions for referral problems with a consultee who is primarily, if not solely, responsible for carrying out the recommended interventions. The term *collaboration* (or *collaborative*) is reserved for those instances in which two or more people agree to work together (i.e., both take somewhat equal responsibility for the implementation of the interventions). Team teaching might be an example of collaboration between a regular and special education teacher. A collaborative might also be an agreement among representatives of different agencies to work together to seek common solutions to shared problems. An example might be the probation department working with the public schools and the local mental health agency to institute programs aimed at reducing youth violence.

This author's preference is to combine the essence of what is embodied in the terms *collaborative* and *consultation.* This has led to the following definition which supports the content and purpose of this book: *Collaborative consultation is a process in which a trained, school-based consultant, working in an egalitarian, non-hierarchical relationship with a consultee, assists that person in her efforts to make decisions and carry out plans that will be in the best educational interests of the students.* All the terms in this definition are found in the other definitions listed in Figure 1.1, with the exception of *egalitarian* and *non-hierarchical.* These refer to the author's belief that consultees, who are usually teachers or parents, are much more likely to engage in the consultation process when they believe they have an amount of input into the planning process that is at least equal to that of the consultant.

Figure 1.1

Definitions/descriptions of *consultation, collaboration,* and *collaborative consultation*

Included below are definitions or descriptions of the words *consultation* and *collaboration* and the term *collaborative consultation.* The purpose of presenting three different sets of definitions/descriptions is to assist the reader in understanding how these terms are related and how they differ.

Definitions/descriptions of *consultation:*
Consultation is a process that has the following six characteristics: (1) it is a helping or problem-solving process; (2) it occurs between a professional helpgiver and a helpseeker who has responsibility for the welfare of another person; (3) it is a voluntary relationship; (4) the helpgiver and helpseeker share in solving the problem; (5) the goal is to help solve a current work problem of the helpseeker; and (6) the helpseeker profits from the relationship in such a way that future problems may be handled more sensitively and skillfully. (Parsons & Meyers, 1984, p. xii)

Teacher consultation is a problem-solving process which takes place over a period of time and has a number of stages. During this process, the consultant assists the consultee (e.g., the classroom teacher) in maximizing the educational development of his or her pupils. Consultation focuses on a current work problem of the consultee. The process is differentiated from both supervision and counseling in that the interchange is collaborative, there is an emphasis on the consultee's equal role in contributing to the problem resolution, and the consultee is free at all times to accept or reject the solutions recommended during consultation. (Aldinger, Warger, & Eavy, 1991, p. 2)

Human services consultation . . . is engaged primarily for the purpose of assisting consultees to develop attitudes and skills that will enable them to function more effectively with a client which can be an individual, group or organization for which they have responsibility. (Brown, Pryzwansky, & Schulte, 2001, p. 6)

School consultation is a voluntary process in which one professional assists another to address a problem concerning a third party. (Friend & Cook, 2000, p. 73)

The following are definitions/descriptions of *collaboration:*

Collaboration refers to two or more people working together, using systematic planning and problem-solving procedures, to achieve desired outcomes. (Curtis & Stollar, 1995, p. 52)

Interpersonal collaboration is a style for direct interaction between at least two coequal parties voluntarily engaged in shared decision making as they work toward a common goal. (Friend & Cook, 2000, p. 6)

Collaboration involves interaction between two or more equal parties who voluntarily share decision making in working toward a common goal.(Fishbaugh, 1997, p. 6)

Effective collaboration consists of designing and using a sequence of goal-oriented activities that result in improved working relationships between professional colleagues. (Cramer, 1998, p. 6)

The following are definitions/descriptions of *collaborative consultation:*

Collaborative school consultation is interaction in which school personnel and families confer, consult, and collaborate as a team to identify learning and behavioral needs, and to plan, implement, evaluate, and revise as needed the educational programs for serving those needs. (Dettmer, Dyck, & Thurston, 1999, p. 6)

Collaborative consultation is an interactive process that enables groups of people with diverse expertise to generate creative solutions to mutually defined problems. The outcome is enhanced and altered from original solutions that group members tend to produce independently. (Idol, Nevin, & Paolucci-Whitcomb, 2000, p. 1)

ACTIVITY 1.1

Speak to several people outside your field of professional interest, asking them what images or expectations come to mind when they hear the word *consultant.* What percentage of people use the word *expert?* How often do they mention the concept of collaboration?

ACTIVITY 1.2

After reviewing the definitions of consultation and collaboration in this chapter, identify the key activities that are common to both, and ways in which they appear to be different.

COLLABORATIVE CONSULTATION AS AN EXPANDED ROLE

Collaboration and consultation are not necessarily interchangeable because consultation is not always collaborative. Consultation is a generic term, defined, as we have seen above, with some variations in emphasis or style but generally consistent with the *Webster's* definition.

Brown et al. (2001) suggest that it may be inappropriate to use the two terms to refer to the same process since a common meaning of collaboration includes the fact that two or more people provide *direct* service, whereas consultation traditionally is considered an *indirect* service. I believe that both terms have evolved sufficiently to allow them to be used together, with the collaborative part referring to mutual problem solving by equal partners and the consultation part referring to the third-party interaction. Whether or not the person identified as the consultant actually does some part of the direct service to the client seems moot. Pryzwansky (1977) has described a model (referred to as collaboration) wherein the consultee and the consultant assume joint responsibility for all aspects of the process, including shared implementation. Actually, in school consultation, the consultee usually does most of the in-classroom or on-the-playground implementation, and the parent as consultee does most of the at-home implementation. This reality fits the concept of collaborative consultation described herein, and the author's definition of collaborative consultation presented above.

Collaboration refers to a very specific kind of consultation, one characterized by "a reciprocal arrangement between individuals with diverse expertise to define problems and develop solutions mutually" (Pugach & Johnson, 1988, p. 3), and defined as egalitarian and non-hierarchical by this author. Defined in this way, collaboration may seem very different from forms of consultation practiced in the business, medical, or military arenas because it is not clear from this definition that any one person is the expert. Resolution of this dilemma revolves around the belief that consultation can take place between or among two or more people, with the role of expert shifting periodically among the partners in this enterprise. For example, a Student Study Team (SST) meeting might involve the regular education teacher as an expert in curriculum and teaching method, the counselor as an expert in explaining how a client's withdrawn apathetic approach to tasks stems from family dynamics, the psychologist or special education teacher as an expert in suggesting a contingency reinforcement plan or a memory-enhancing system that the teacher might use to increase content retention, the student's mother as an expert in reviewing how she assists the student with his academic work, and the student as an expert in reviewing his interests and preferred learning styles and reinforcers. As these participants collaborate with one another in understanding a problem and designing a program, they are sharing their expertise, with each party contributing a varying amount depending on the nature of the referral.

This philosophy also extends to plan implementation. Although the primary person carrying out the plan is usually the classroom teacher, either general or special education, the other team members contribute their expertise in ways appropriate to their training and experience. In the case just described, plan implementation might involve the counselor working with the parents in regard to family dynamics, the psychologist or special education teacher observing the teacher who is trying new methods in order to provide feedback, and the student contributing by self-monitoring and helping the consultee fine-tune the classroom reinforcement system. This example demonstrates how expertise and mutual assistance are the two major components of a consultation model that has come to be known as collaborative (Friend & Cook, 2000; Idol, 1990; Idol, Nevin, & Paolucci-Whitcomb, 2000).

Throughout this book there are many other examples of how this model can be effective with a wide variety of school referral problems.

In spite of its apparent common-sense appeal, the model is not easy to implement for a number of reasons, one of which is the fact that school-based personnel have either not been trained in this model or would rather emphasize different models of functioning. Another reason is that not all consultees are willing to, or have been trained to, work in a collaborative fashion. Kurpius (1991) discusses how the culture of an organization may be either open or closed to change and how this variable interacts with an organization's need to change, which Kurpius refers to as equilibrium-disequilibrium. This same model may be applied to individual consultees, with the addition of another variable that has to do with a desire to, or willingness to, participate in collaborative efforts, which to some extent is the result of exposure to this model and training in how it is conducted. West & Idol (1989) have developed an entire inservice and preservice curriculum for teaching collaborative skills to teachers, support staff, and administrators.

Figure 1.2 gives a personal view of the author regarding the collaborative consultation method.

Figure 1.2

Collaborative consultation: Rationale, limitations, and suggestions—a personal view

In my way of conducting collaborative consultation, I give a lot of emphasis to the possibility that the consultee can, and should be strongly encouraged to, come up with their own solutions to the referral problems. Some individuals apparently believe that this is not an appropriate approach. After all, if the consultee knew a solution to his referral question, why wouldn't he just implement it and save time and energy? Also, if the consultee's referral has been sent to you for your assistance, doesn't he have a right to expect that you will have, and impart to him, expert knowledge?

My experience has taught me that consultees, both teachers and parents, when faced with relatively difficult problems in learning and/or behavior, sometimes get confused, or stuck, in their thinking. They probably have tried some solutions, and when these haven't worked, they've experienced some sort of breakdown in their usually dependable problem-solving strategies, and they feel as though they don't know what to do next. Or, they have an idea but they just aren't sure about it, and they would like to discuss their idea with someone else. This someone else becomes their consultant. Hopefully, this person will acknowledge the consultee's experience and expertise by doing at least these two things:

1. Ask the consultee to review what she has done to improve the situation so far, and how these efforts have worked.
2. Encourage the consultee to tell the consultant what she (the consultee) wants to do next. Use such questions as "Given what you've told me, and in light of your understanding of the problem at this time, what would you like to try next?" "You've tried a number of things so far. What are you thinking of doing tomorrow?" "So far you've felt like what you've tried just hasn't been the best solution. What's next? What do you want to try now?"

Figure 1.2 *continued*

I refer to this effort at intervention development by consultees as the ACCEPT method, ACCEPT being an acronym that acknowledges the consultant's philosophy about the consultee's contributions, and stands for the following behaviors which, to me, are at the heart of collaborative consultation:

A *Acknowledging* the consultee's predominant role in carrying out the planned interventions, usually in his classroom (or home), in the context of that setting, and in his style.

C *Commenting* positively on the efforts the consultee has made to date in trying to solve the problem, and the effort he is expending now on behalf of the student.

C *Convincing* the consultee that he has good ideas to offer, and that you, the consultant, would like to hear them.

E *Expecting* that the consultee will come up with ideas if encouraged to do so.

P *Pointing* out possibilities for effective interventions based on the consultee's ideas. This involves taking his ideas and helping him think through the pros and cons of these ideas and the details of implementation. In this way, you provide your content expertise in the context of his ideas. When collaborative consultation is working well, the consultant's role is that of *facilitator* of the consultee's ideas.

T *Treating* him as an equal. One of the hallmarks of a collaborative model is that it brings adults together in an atmosphere of mutual respect. Both are equally expert, both need help from the other, and both give ideas and contribute to the final solutions.

LIMITS TO A COLLABORATIVE CONSULTATION MODEL:
This model does not always work as planned. Some consultees seem bereft of ideas, or appear to be too irritated by the problem to be able to think clearly. Some get in a punishment mode, particularly in regard to serious behavior problems, and they are not able to think positively. Some always prefer to think that someone else (e.g., special education, or a more restrictive setting) should take over the student and solve their problem that way. Others are simply deferential to the consultant; they cannot get over the "consultant-as-expert" idea. They assume it's easier to get you to solve the problem, to determine the interventions and their implementation. That way, if it doesn't work, guess who's to blame? Lastly, some are too inexperienced, or at least act that way, and they simply need more direct help.

SUGGESTIONS:
Collaborative consultation sometimes seems to break down because the ideas from the consultee are inappropriate, weak, or too few in number. Some people have only one tool; if that doesn't work, they give up. (This, by the way, is common among some who advocate an expert role. They have essentially one way of doing things, and if it doesn't work they too seem bereft of further ideas.)

When you sense that any of the above are true, the collaboratively-oriented consultant most certainly can suggest interventions. My opinion is that it is best to come up with two or three viable interventions, hopefully based on "best practices," and to ask the consultee what s/he thinks of each of them.

Which of the ideas is s/he attracted to? Which does s/he seem able and willing to do? The interventions you suggest should meet at least the following criteria:

1. *Treatment acceptability:* If the teacher doesn't accept an intervention as something she is willing to do, you either have to be a good salesperson and convince her of its merits, or forget about it; she won't do it. Or she will agree to try the intervention, give it a half hearted try, claim it didn't work (it probably didn't), and require you to come up with another idea. You don't know what interventions meet the criteria of treatment acceptability until you suggest them.
2. *Treatment validity:* Is there research support for the idea? "Best practices" are those that have at least some degree of support, either from the literature or from your own experience or knowledge base.
3. *Treatment ethics:* The concern here is about the appropriateness of an intervention from the standpoint of the students' best interests; their dignity as people; probable benefits versus risks; and an orientation toward replacement of, rather than suppression of, challenging behaviors.
4. *Treatment integrity:* Was the treatment implemented correctly? This, of course, won't be known until the treatment is tried.
5. *Treatment effectiveness:* Is the treatment working? By what standards? Does it need to be changed? Again, these answers aren't known until the treatment has been tried for sufficient time to determine its effectiveness.

It is also important to stick to the referral and not to wander off in other directions. It may be tempting to think that a given consultee needs help in many areas which s/he may not be aware of. Except in serious cases (abusive behavior toward students; chaotic, dangerous classroom management practices; personal problems that are impacting the classroom), it is best to establish well-defined goals relative to the referral problem and work toward solving them and let other issues emerge as the consultee feels the necessity for dealing with them. Remember that change is difficult; overwhelming a consultee with your ideas about how to make the classroom or home perfect may be regarded as intrusive and perhaps overwhelming. No one wants assistance from an intrusive person who wants to tell other people what to do. Do a good job helping him with his current concerns and he will get back to you later about other things, or you can bring them up at some later point.

Lastly, but nonetheless importantly, consider the role of family and culture: Interventions that are selected need to be sensitive to the student's cultural background. This issue is discussed in more depth later in this chapter.

RECENT TRENDS IN THE TRAINING
OF SCHOOL CONSULTANTS

The past decade has seen a tremendous increase in the number of special education teacher training programs that require coursework in consultation. Yocum and Cossairt (1996) conducted a nationwide survey of special education teacher training programs and found that 63 percent offered a course in consultation, with the collaborative model mentioned most frequently (50 percent) as the preferred model taught. Two other models mentioned were the behavioral model (taught in 13 percent of the programs) and the education/training model, an eclectic, expert-based approach (taught in 10 percent of the programs).

For school psychologists, consultation training has been a relatively recent phenomenon. University coursework has steadily increased since 1980 but is still not found in all training programs. In 1981, Meyers, Wurtz, and Flanagan (1981) found that only 40 percent of school psychology training programs offered at least one course in consultation. School psychologists traditionally have been taught that their major function is to accept referrals, provide assessment, decide eligibility for special education, and then repeat the process with the next referral (Gutkin & Curtis, 1990; Zins, Curtis, Graden, & Ponti, 1988). This refer–test–place model is still practiced by many school psychologists, who feel comfortable with both the philosophy and the practice of searching for intrachild deficiencies. Others would like to try more consultation-centered activities but feel that they are prohibited by the practices and habits of those with whom they work. Increasingly, however, school psychology is moving toward a consultation-based service delivery model (Graden, Zins, & Curtis, 1988; Gutkin & Curtis, 1999; Stoner, Shinn, & Walker, 1991). I hope this change will take place more rapidly as part of the school restructuring that is becoming necessary as we enter the twenty-first century (Bahr, 1996; Futrell, 1989).

School counselors, like school psychologists, have traditionally operated from a direct service philosophy. Consultation training in their programs has paralleled that of school psychologists, though possibly somewhat more slowly. Brown, Spano, and Schulte (1988) found that, at the master's level, only about 20 percent of the programs require a course in consultation. Thus, it is not surprising to find that most currently employed school counselors have learned their consultation skills in conferences, workshops, and conventions in a fashion similar to that of other current school consultants.

ACTIVITY 1.3

Interview people employed in the schools as special education teachers, school psychologists, or school counselors regarding their training in consultation. How much did they receive? Is it proving valuable to them? What additional training did they wish they had received, or wish they could get now?

DEFINING CHARACTERISTICS OF CONSULTATION

The following assumptions about the nature and characteristics of consultation follow from the definition offered above:

1. The consultant is a trained professional. Generally this includes such people as special education teachers, mentor teachers, school counselors and psychologists. It may of course refer to any person, including regular education teachers, who perform the services indicated by the definition. Such individuals can appro-

priately serve as consultants in matters in which they have expertise, such as curriculum, teaching methods, and behavior management.

2. Authentic, honest communication is essential for successful consultation.

3. The nature of the referral problem influences the roles of the consultant and the consultee, and thus the process in which they engage. Chapter 2 lists consultants' roles and activities; it is common for practitioners to shift among them.

4. While consultation can be initiated by either the consultant or the consultee, both must make a valid effort to engage in the process if consultation is to occur. The real power in the consultation process rests with the consultee since she is primarily responsible for carrying out the jointly agreed-on interventions.

5. Task-content variables and the process of consultation interact and must be considered simultaneously. This is especially true in a collaborative consultation approach in which non-hierarchical, egalitarian positions are occupied by both the consultee and the consultant, who are both involved in idea generation within a problem-solving context.

6. Systemic variables impinge on the consultant, consultee, and student and must be considered as integral parts of the process. Unlike medical consultants, who work out of their own offices and are responsible only to legal and ethical codes, school consultants and consultees always operate within a larger set of variables, including not only legal and ethical codes but also societal expectations, cultural norms, district and school-level guidelines, and family concerns. Further, the interventions discussed, particularly at group meetings (SST, etc.), are immediately available for scrutiny by others in the meeting.

7. Consultation is governed by certain ethical guidelines that influence consultant roles as well as the process of consultation. Chapter 4 discusses ethical and advocacy issues in consultation. Practical examples demonstrating the influence of these factors appear in Chapters 7 and 9.

8. One goal of collaborative consultation is to improve the functioning of the client while enhancing the functioning of the consultee.

9. Another goal of collaborative consultation is to find ways to ensure student success in the general education classroom as often as possible.

10. There is an emphasis on observation and interview as assessment methods.

11. Collaborative consultation seeks solutions, not labels. While realizing that some students may benefit from special education and related services in specialized settings, most students who manifest learning and/or behavior or adjustment problems may benefit more in the long run from being maintained in the regular track with tailored and specified instruction and behavior management strategies that can be delivered by general educators with the assistance (i.e., consultation) of those able to provide those services.

12. School consultants must be experts in process (the "how" of consultation; see Chapter 5), but not necessarily in content (the actual interventions that are discussed and selected). This means that the collaboratively-minded consultant must be

adept at encouraging teachers and parents to develop plans and interventions that make sense in the context of their classrooms and homes. The consultant's job is to facilitate the thinking of these "primary care providers" (i.e., parents and teachers serving as consultees) so these individuals can feel empowered to carry out their ideas about how to best assist the student, under the guidance and encouragement of the consultant.

13. Problem solving is the primary goal of consultation. Consultants are employed for the express purpose of solving the learning and behavior problems exhibited by schoolchildren. Generically, *problem solving* refers to any set of steps or procedures intended to assist the consultee in dealing with referred students (Dougherty, 2000). This process may take many forms or styles, depending on the nature of the problem, the philosophical beliefs of both consultant and consultee, the constraints or limitations of the setting, and so on. The steps in problem solving are discussed in detail in Chapter 5.

14. Occasionally consultees may bring information into the discussion that is more closely related to their personal lives and problems than to the learning or behavior problems of the referred student. The consultant has to be careful not to confuse the consultative relationship by taking on the role of a counselor to the consultee. Decisions about the relevance of any particular piece of information are not always easy to make, but it is usually best to gently steer the conversation back to the appropriate work-related problem. Of course, if the consultant perceives that the consultee does have a personal problem that should be dealt with, whether it is affecting the referral problem or not, she may refer the consultee to a resource where he can get whatever help is needed. Because it is possible for a consultee to have personal issues that interfere with his ability to view the referral problem objectively, the consultant may need to mention any concerns she has to the consultee in a helpful and positive way (Caplan & Caplan, 1993).

ACTIVITY 1.4
Discuss the characteristics presented above in small groups. Do the groups believe these are essential characteristics? What others might they add?

CONSULTATION AS THE PLANNING, MONITORING, AND EVALUATING OF INTERVENTIONS

Some school-based consultants describe themselves as interventionists (Sprick, Sprick, & Garrison, 1994). The preference for this name comes from the belief that the main purpose of consultation is to develop interventions that the consultee and/or others can implement as part of the problem-solving process. While it is true that the development of interventions is a key goal of the problem-solving process, in the collaborative consultation model the consultant may not be the prime developer of whatever interventions are finally implemented. The consultee may be the person who develops the intervention, with some assistance and facilitation from the consultant.

Caplan (1964) described three levels of intervention: primary (prevention), secondary (corrective), and tertiary (remedial). In the primary stage steps are taken to ensure that students are unlikely to develop learning or behavioral difficulties. Standards, appropriate curriculum and teaching methods, and interventions as common as classroom rules are all part of primary prevention. Secondary refers to actions taken when a student appears to be having difficulties. Student Study Team (SST) meetings, parent conferences, in-class modifications, and other mild forms of intervention are common during this stage. In the tertiary condition, the referral problems are very serious, major steps need to be taken (e.g., special education eligibility, possible service delivery in settings other than general education, suspensions), and those concerned with the student's welfare need to consult with each other and collaboratively develop plans that are in the best educational interest of the student. In a school setting, most referrals for consultant assistance are either secondary or tertiary, which is unfortunate. More emphasis on preventive programs, especially for students who are at risk, has been recommended in the human services field for decades (Meyers & Nastasi, 1999). However, pressures to deal with currently severe problems, combined with inadequate staffing ratios, have slowed the move to a prevention-oriented service delivery approach. Bergan (1995) comments that this may be true partly because no specific funding exists for consultation (or primary prevention) services while funds do exist for placing and supporting students in special education services.

Once plans have been developed and are being implemented, the role of the collaborative consultant becomes largely one of monitor. The teacher or parent consultee will need some assistance in the area of treatment integrity (Gresham, 1989; Witt, 1990), and possibly treatment ethics. Ongoing evaluations of the effectiveness of the interventions are also necessary. Details about this process are presented in Chapter 5.

ACTIVITY 1.5

Reflect on your experiences in the school. How were interventions for students with disabilities and other at-risk students developed? Who monitored their implementation? How were they evaluated? Did these processes seem well structured or rather casual?

THE TRIADIC NATURE OF CONSULTATION

The most common form of consultation in schools consists of interactions among a consultant, the consultee(s), and a student. As Figure 1.3 shows, the consultant and the consultee freely interact in a non-hierarchical, reciprocal relationship. To some extent this reciprocity can also occur between the consultee and the student, although a teacher–student relationship usually is more constrained than the one that

Figure 1.3

The triadic nature of consultation

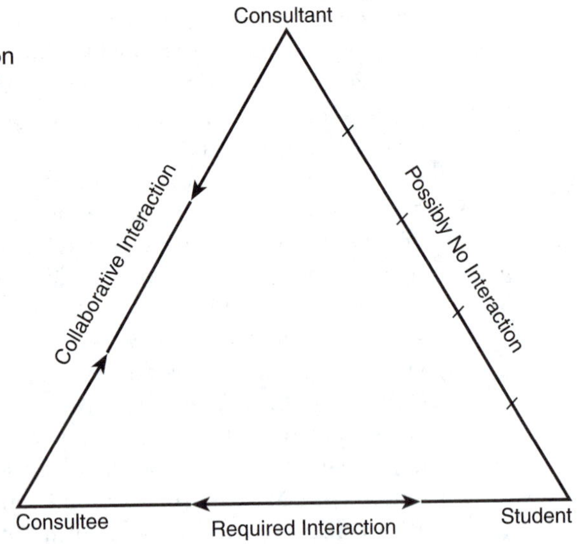

should exist between the consultant and the consultee. However, the consultant may never have any direct interaction with the student. For example, in the vignette in the beginning of the chapter, Mrs. Jones asks the consultant for help in dealing with a student. Because the teacher has presented a poorly defined problem, the consultant may spend considerable time talking with Mrs. Jones but may never talk with or observe the student. It is certainly possible, and in most cases desirable, for the consultant to have some degree of relationship with the student, if only to observe her in the classroom or on the playground. It is not, however, necessary.

VARIATIONS ON THE TRIADIC MODEL

Although the triad presented in Figure 1.3 is the most common conceptualization of consultative interactions in schools (Dougherty, 2000; Friend & Cook, 2000; Tharp, 1975), there are many possible variations. For example, there may be multiple consultants, such as a school psychologist, a resource specialist, a mentor teacher, a nurse, and a counselor. These ancillary personnel are expected to play consultant roles at SST meetings and at other case conferences, including the individualized educational program (IEP) team meeting. There may also be multiple consultees. A resource specialist may meet with all five of a student's high school teachers to talk about ways to accommodate his learning disabilities in classes in which he is mainstreamed. A school psychologist may consult with a student's teachers or parents who have different needs and perspectives about the student's learning or behavior problems. Lastly, there may be more than one student involved. A school counselor, serving as a consultant, may be asked to work with a teacher (consultee) regarding a group of schoolchildren who exhibit hostile, scapegoating behaviors toward other children or who manifest learning problems, as in the third vignette at the beginning

Figure 1.4

A quadratic model of collaborative consultation

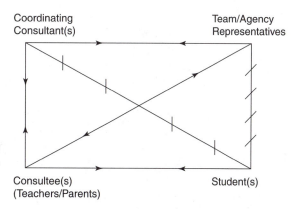

Coordinating Consultant(s)

Team/Agency Representatives

Consultee(s) (Teachers/Parents)

Student(s)

of the chapter. Even an entire system (such as a grade-level team, a whole school, or a whole district) can stand in the place of the student in Figure 1.3.

Figure 1.4 represents a quadratic model, which illustrates collaborative consultation where the number of involved parties has increased to include constituent individuals or teams that may either be from within an individual school or district or may be from outside the school or district. In Figure 1.4 one corner is represented by a "Coordinating Consultant(s)," a person or persons who, formally or informally, directs the efforts of the whole group. Another corner is represented by the consultee(s), who is usually the involved teacher(s) and/or parents. The third corner represents the targeted student(s), and the fourth corner represents other consulting teams or agencies. Lines between each of the corners indicate the type of interaction, with arrows indicating direct, usually face-to-face interactions, and slashed lines indicating little, if any, direct interaction. Issues concerning larger groups, as well as collaboratives, where (possibly) groups from within and outside the school are involved in change efforts, are discussed in Chapters 3 and 10.

THE ROLE OF PROCESS AND CONTENT EXPERTISE IN CONSULTATION

People in general usually relate the concept or practice of consultation to activities carried out by skilled businesspeople, engineers, and medical professionals, and the public tends to think of consultation in terms of expertness. In the business world, a consultant may be hired to solve a particularly tricky problem in production, merchandising, or taxes. The hiring firm expects that the consultant will have expertise in the area and will come up with a solution that has a good chance of working well. For this level of "expert consultation," business executives expect to pay well (Lippitt & Lippitt, 1986).

One might expect that successful consultants working in the schools with teachers and parents should also adopt a stance of expertise. I take the position that expertness should be expected in the area of process and that it is highly desirable but not sufficient in the area of content. By *process,* I mean the interactions that occur between the consultant and the consultees through which a behavior or a learning problem is approached and solved; it is concerned with *how* one acts as a consultant. *Content* refers to the actual ideas that the consultees will implement, such as a contract method, cooperative learning, a parent conference, or the use of stickers or stars as reinforcers; it represents the *what* people will do as a result of consultation. Collaborative consultation requires expertise in process; without such expertise, the process disintegrates, resistance increases, and consultees become dissatisfied with the consultative approach for dealing with their students' difficulties in learning and/or behavioral adjustment. As indicated by the definitions and discussion presented above, the collaborative approach depends on a degree of mutual expertise in problem solving, resulting in content decisions that are jointly generated and approved by both the consultant and the consultee(s) within a non-hierarchical, reciprocal relationship (Friend & Cook, 2000; Idol, Nevin, and Paolucci-Whitcomb, 2000).

Among human services personnel, particularly in the schools, there is a general consensus that the expert model, defined as one in which a consultant, sometimes from outside the local school or district, unilaterally decides which interventions it would be most appropriate for a teacher or parent to use, has limitations that make it less than ideal. For example, an outsider (unlike a business consultant) cannot always indicate the best way to solve a problem because the outsider may not understand the interpersonal, ecological, and other dynamics that exist in a school or a school district. Further, in both schools and the business world, people tend to be more likely to implement changes that they have been involved in discussing and creating (Comer, 1993; Rappaport, 1981; Weiss, 1993).

ACTIVITY 1.6

Discuss the role of process versus content. Do you think a school consultant needs to have a set of interventions for every problem or issue a teacher or parent can describe? How might you deal with a consultee who insists on your having answers for every problem?

FREQUENTLY ASKED QUESTIONS ABOUT SCHOOL CONSULTATION

Direct and Indirect Benefits

What direct and/or indirect benefits can be expected from the consultation model discussed in this text?

A number of benefits can accrue from a consultation-based service delivery program. *Direct benefits* include the following:

- The development of closer working relationships between regular and special educators and others who serve in a collaborative consultant mode.

- The assistance given to consultees in their efforts to deal with the learning and behavior difficulties that some students present.

- The generation of ideas that more readily occurs when two or more people are involved in problem solving.

- The likelihood that important underlying (often systemic) issues will be raised through the discussion of individual student problems.

- The feeling of a professional, collaborative approach to problem solving engineered by a person identified as a school-based consultant.

- The improved services given to referred students that derives from the increased attention to academic and social needs, rather than placement-driven labels or categories.

Other direct benefits include a reduction in referrals for special education eligibility determination (Ponti, Zins, & Graden, 1988; Ritter, 1978; Villa, Thousand, Nevin, & Malgeri, 1996) even though requests for consultative assistance increase (Grubb, 1981; Rosenfield & Gravois, 1996; Zins, 1992). This is regarded as good news by many who argue in favor of the consultative approach to service delivery, although others believe it will become good news only when the system-generated pressure to place students in categorical programs diminishes (Marks, 1995). There is evidence that districts that have adopted a consultation-based approach to dealing with referrals, rather than a refer–test–place model, place fewer students in special education separate classroom programs (Villa, Thousand, Nevin, & Melgeri, 1996).

Indirect benefits include the following:

- The learning that goes on while dealing with the needs of a referred student (which can often be used with other students).

- The information traded among consultees based on their experiences with the consultant.

- The development of teachers' beliefs that they are part of a communicating team of professionals, which alleviates one of the more common causes of teacher stress—the feeling that teaching is an isolated profession.

- Potential spin-offs, such as the generation of ideas for inservice meetings or for development and implementation of school or district-wide programs, or extra-district collaboratives (see Chapter 7).

Equivalent benefits can be observed when parents are involved as consultees. They can learn new ways of dealing with their child, have a chance to be heard by a professional from the school, and get to understand and contribute to the school's perspective on their child's problems and progress. Indirect benefits include less tension about child rearing, a feeling that the parents are considered part of the solution instead of part of the problem, and a chance to build their repertoire of child-rearing skills (Christenson, 1995; Turnbull & Turnbull, 1997).

School Consultation as a Service Delivery System of Choice

Why has collaborative consultation emerged as a service delivery system of choice?

During the past 20 years there has been an increase in the use of collaborative consultation in the schools. Idol, Nevin, and Paolucci-Whitcomb (2000) indicate that the term *collaborative consultation* was first used by them (Idol, Poalucci-Whitcomb & Nevin, 1986) to refer to a model of consultative interactions that are not so much dependent on the superior knowledge base of the consultant as they are on shared expertise, a confluence of ideas generated in an atmosphere of non-hierarchical cooperation. As such they were utilizing the concept of empowerment (Rappaport, 1981), which posits that change is most likely to occur when it comes from the ideas and experiences of those closest to the problem and those most likely to implement whatever changes (i.e., interventions) are proposed. This is not to imply that the collaboratively-oriented school consultant does not need knowledge about teaching methods, curriculum, behavior management, disabilities, culture, and a host of other areas that interact in the process of teaching. What it does imply is that the consultant does not need to act like the "expert" who is there to tell a teacher or parent what to do, without considering the opinions and ideas of these individuals. As the information in Figure 1.2 indicates, there are exceptions to this general rule of practice, especially occurring with new teachers or those who are unable to think of interventions that are likely to be successful. In these instances the collaborative consultant adopts more of the expert stance and suggests possible interventions.

Apparent Slowness of Adoption of Collaborative Consultation

If this model of collaborative consultation is so powerful, why hasn't it emerged as a dominant model of service delivery for at-risk students? One of the reasons consultation is emerging slowly is the usual reason for the slowness of change in schools and other large-scale bureaucratic organizations: habit strength. In regard to an approach to responding to the needs of students referred for learning and/or behavior problems, there are many who continue to prefer the long-established model of refer–test–place, which has dominated the special education–school psychology partnership for many years (Ysseldyke, 1986). In the refer–test–place model, a student is referred, and some degree of effort is made to resolve the problem through suggestions generated by the Student Study Team. A few weeks go by, during which the problem doesn't resolve easily, and the team decides to generate an assessment plan to determine if the student is eligible for services as a student with a disability. The most likely category the student will be eligible for is learning disabilities, simply because it comprises over 50 percent of those eligible for special education services, and the odds are about three out of four that if an assessment plan is generated and the assessment takes place the student will be found eligible for such services (Ysseldyke, 1986; Ysseldyke, Vanderwood, & Shriner, 1997). The student will most likely be given services in a Special Education Resource Room program for one or two periods a day with, as indicated above, dubious results. One of the goals of the collaborative consultation movement is to dramatically change this picture. This text, along with those of Dettmer, Dyck, & Thurston (1999), Friend & Cook (2000), and Idol, Nevin, & Paolucci-Whitcomb (2000), among others, advocate for a different approach, one where the process of collaborative consultation assumes a much stronger role, with the goals being to forestall placements outside the general education track as often as possible and to increase both special and general educators' ability and willingness to accommodate to the needs of at-risk students through jointly designed interventions. In this way the practice of collaborative consultation may serve to enhance the probability of there one day being one system of education for all students instead of the two-tiered (regular and special education) system that has prevailed for so long (Stainback, Stainback, & Forest, 1989; Wang, Reynolds, & Walberg, 1986; Will, 1986).

Another reason that prevents this model from being fully utilized is that it requires changing to a system that might involve relatively prolonged, intensive efforts to accommodate to students' needs with interventions at the regular classroom level. To some teachers, administrators, and parents, this seems unnecessarily burdensome and possibly futile. The fairly well-ingrained idea that special education is good for students with mild to moderate levels of disability is difficult to overcome. The limited evidence for the success of pull-out programs (Affleck, Madge, Adams, & Lowenbraun, 1988; Powers, 2001; Reynolds, 1989; Wang, Reynolds, & Walberg, 1986) is not acknowledged; habits resist incompatible data.

A third reason for the seemingly slow adoption of a collaborative consultation model has to do with the research base for this model. As discussed below, the research on the effectiveness of consultation is just emerging; most practitioners may not be aware of it. Until the research evidence becomes common knowledge, or, what is more likely, until a cadre of special education teachers and other school personnel are adequately trained in consultation and bring this training to their own practice in the schools, the change process is likely to remain slow. What is needed for consultation to become the service delivery system of choice is a philosophical shift from the still-dominant refer–test–place model to one that operates under the belief that for most students with mild to moderate difficulties, and for some with more severe disabling conditions in learning or behavior, the regular classroom may be the most appropriate and least restrictive setting *if the general education teachers can be given support, primarily through a well-organized system of collaborative consultation.* Ysseldyke and Marston (1999) present evidence from five different projects throughout the United States (Minnesota, Florida, Iowa, Illinois, and Kansas) that have demonstrated that alternatives to the refer–test–place model can have the beneficial effects of reducing dependence on special education placement and empowering general education teachers to provide effective programming within their classrooms.

Last, since there is no one way to practice consultation, it is not clear what a person means by consultation until she describes it in some detail or you see her doing it. Current practice varies across a wide range of philosophies, roles, and activities. The different models discussed in Chapter 2 indicate some of the variations currently practiced in the schools.

RESEARCH ON THE EFFECTIVENESS
OF SCHOOL CONSULTATION

As previously stated, one of the reasons consultation is somewhat slow to emerge as a dominant model of service delivery is because of the limited amount of compelling research evidence that supports it. In public education it is often necessary to try programs or approaches that may not have much empirical support because they are too new to have been studied in any depth. Consultation as a service delivery model is currently in this position. It has grown out of a relatively new disaffection with older models of service delivery, primarily the refer–test–place and pull-out models previously discussed, but it does not yet have a compelling body of support in the research literature (Hughes, 1994).

As many teachers and educational pundits have observed, public education sometimes seems fad-oriented. Teachers are used to hearing about wonderful new ways of teaching, assessing, and managing classrooms—supposedly successful methods that hold great promise when described by their advocates. Once these new ideas catch on and are supported by some degree of administrative support, they seem to gain strength simply because people come to believe in them, not because they have an impressive array of data to support them (Sarason, 1982; 1991).

The problem isn't due to a paucity of research studies. Brown, Pryzwansky, and Schulte (2001) indicate that from 1978 to 1985 about 173 data-based consultation studies were referenced in *Psychological Abstracts*. More recently, Idol, Nevin, and Paolucci-Whitcomb (2000) studied articles having to do only with collaborative consultation between the years of 1994 to 1997 and found 52 citations. Gutkin and Curtis (1999) review a number of studies conducted primarily in the areas of school psychology and special education, most of which reported at least partially successful outcomes.

Henning-Stout (1993) divides the research on consultation into process studies and outcome studies. *Process* refers to what consultants do and whether consultees believe it was worth doing. *Outcome* focuses on what effect the consultation has on students' learning and behavior/adjustment problems. Generally, research in both areas demonstrates that consultation has positive effects on consultees and students. Some process studies indicate that consultation is likely to be received favorably if consultees believe they are involved in plan development (Reinking, Livesay, & Kohl, 1978), if they are asked rather than told what to do (Bergan & Neumann, 1980), and if they are involved in the development of interventions (Curtis & Van Wagener, 1988). All of these findings support the collaborative consultation model. Alderman and Gimpel (1996) found that teacher consultees believe that the most effective consultation includes (1) personal support with contact and listening, (2) suggestions that have been proven to work, and (3) suggestions that are practical and part of a plan. The collaborative model stresses these approaches.

Typical outcome research findings include those of Bergan and Tombari (1976), who provided one of the first pieces of empirical evidence regarding the conditions under which consultation is likely to be effective. They found that the consultant's ability to determine the relevant problem is a good predictor of consultation success.

Other outcome studies have shown that the introduction of a consultation service delivery approach in a district results in fewer requests for special education assessment for students who are at risk (Ritter, 1978) and a greater tendency among general educators to try to solve learning and behavior/adjustment problems within the general education class (Ponti et al., 1988; Rosenfield & Gravois, 1996). Chalfant and Pysh (1989) utilized a Teacher Assistance Team (TAT) approach, similar to an SST approach. They worked with first-year teachers and found that, with TAT consultations, only 21 percent of at-risk students needed to be referred for special education services. Yocum and Staebler (1996) found that, after the introduction of a collaborative consultation model of prereferral intervention, the accuracy of referrals for special education, defined as the ratio of the number of students assessed to the number of students found eligible for services, increased from 61 percent during the first year of the model to 83 percent during the fourth year. Unfortunately, Yocum and Staebler (1996) did not indicate if there was a significant drop in the number of students referred for assessment over the four years of their study.

Researchers and authorities agree that the research base demonstrating the effectiveness of consultation is not yet secure. Gresham and Kendell (1987), for example, point out that the amount of research is certainly not adequate and that most of it does not address real needs or practices of school-based consultants. This may be due to the fact that many practitioners do not read the literature to learn what the research demonstrates. Moreover, the abstract and sometimes artificial nature of research (e.g., analogue studies) leads consultants and consultees to doubt its practicality in determining what they should do in real cases.

Hughes (1994) believes that the available research on the effectiveness of consultation is not very strong. Much of what exists is based on somewhat irrelevant outcomes (such as teacher attitude and process refinements) instead of essentials (such as improved student achievement or behavior). Especially lacking are follow-up data. Most studies provide summative evaluations at some designated end point but do not go back later to see if the effects are still extant or if they have dissipated since the end of the study. Hughes summarizes her concern by noting that the question "Does consultation work?" should be replaced with a more refined question, such as "What consultation approaches result in what effects with which clients and consultees?" (Hughes, 1994, p. 82).

In an effort to approach this refined perspective, Conoley, Conoley, Ivey, and Scheel (1991) asked 37 teachers to read a description of a school-aged student who presented with a behavior problem and to state their opinions about the case. They were all then given the same standard intervention, which was described in a way that either matched their beliefs, mismatched their beliefs, or was unrelated. The researchers found that, when the rationale for using the standard intervention matched the belief system of the teachers, they were more likely to accept it and believe in its value.

Gutkin (1993a) indicates that most of the research literature is based on what graduate students, acting in a consultation role, do in contrived situations (Pryzwansky, 1986). Gutkin comments, "Consistent with Gendlin's suggestion that we create a 'bank of clearly successful cases' (1986, p. 131) as a means for improving the psychotherapy research literature, a parallel data base of successful consultation interactions would likewise be extremely useful. Case studies and small-*n* methodologies would seem to be the keys to reaching this modest but important goal" (Gutkin, 1993b, p. 238). This book includes cases for analysis that meet Gendlin's (1986) call for "a bank of . . . cases." As you will find, not all of the cases presented in Chapters 7, 9, and 10 of this text are "clearly successful." *Success* is an elastic term that stretches from total to partial. The cases in this book demonstrate that range of success and clarify why some cases are more successful than others.

The search for the keys to effectiveness in consultation continues. Periodicals such as *Journal of Educational and Psychological Consultation, Exceptional Children, School Psychology Review, Journal of Learning Disabilities, Professional Psychology, Journal of Special Education, Remedial and Special Education, Teaching Exceptional Children, Journal of Counseling and Development, Journal of School Psychology,* and *School Psychology Quarterly* contain articles devoted to the scientific study of all aspects of consultation, including process and outcome studies.

ACTIVITY 1.7

How might you structure a research study to answer some questions you have about consultation? What are some unresolved issues that need more research? Why is meaningful research on consultation difficult to do?

THE CONSULTEE AS AN ADULT LEARNER–COLLABORATOR

Beginning school-based consultants need to learn that dealing with adults in the schools, as well as parents of referred students, is very different from, and often more challenging than, dealing with the students themselves. Most school personnel currently being asked to serve as school consultants were originally trained to provide direct services to students. Many of these consultants, especially those who entered the field before the 1980s, probably were not trained specifically in consultation, especially in collaborative techniques. As a result, they may be uncomfortable with the role of consultant, particularly when consultees resist (see Chapter 3). Of course, it is also possible that many of these experienced school personnel not only have mastered collaborative consultation skills but also are responsible for the move toward this productive way of working together to solve student learning and behavior/adjustment problems.

Consultants need to appreciate that adult consultees differ in learning styles, willingness to participate in the process, ability to carry out plans, and perspectives on problems. As the three vignettes in the beginning of this chapter suggest (and as the case studies in Chapters 7, 9, and 10 show in detail), the school consultant must be ready to deal with many different types of consultees among both teachers and parents. The ability to understand the consultee in the same way that a teacher or assessor tries to understand a student may determine a consultant's degree of success. Having all the expert content knowledge in the world in the areas of curriculum, teaching methods, and behavior management is of no use if the consultant does not know how to relate it to the consultee as an adult learner–collaborator.

One problem of some consultants is their tendency to consult as if their consultees are school-age students. Possibly they confuse consultation with their basic role, direct contact with children as students, consultees, or people referred for assessment, the one they came into the schools to practice. Whatever its source, this approach will fail because adults and children expect and react to interactions in very different ways.

Adults prefer to be self-directed; they do not want or expect to be told what to do unless they directly ask for this assistance. They prefer to be active contributors to the interactive process known as consultation; they do not prefer to be passive participants mandated to accept transmitted expertise from others (Cobern, 1993). Adults prefer to believe that they are able to solve their own problems with some facilitative (collaborative) help from the consultant. On the other hand, students expect to be told what to do in school. If they are not given firm direction from adults, students will provide direction for themselves and others, to the possible dismay of the teacher. Students have a limited range of experience on which to draw, while adults have real experiences as teachers or parents and have developed the frame of reference that they bring into a consultative relationship. This experience, coupled with the nature of the student's need and the approach of the consultant, determines how consultees want to solve the problem. Installed, other-directed solutions that fail to consider a consultee's experience, position, and points of view may gain surface acquiescence and possibly admiration but may also be honored in promises rather than execution.

A consultee's ownership of a solution drives her desire to make it successful (Rappaport, 1981). The consultant may actually direct how the consultee sees the problem and what should be done about it. However, whether or not consultees carry out the plan may depend on the consultant's skill in getting them to believe that they have had a central voice in the problem's conceptualization and solution.

 ACTIVITY 1.8

As an adult person, how do you like to be approached regarding a work-related issue? Do you prefer that others tell you what to do, or would you rather figure out answers for yourself with or without benefit of assistance from others? Are you more likely to implement your own ideas or those suggested to you by others?

Training Consultees to Understand the
Nature of Collaborative Consultation

Brown et al. (1995) give an example of a statement that a collaboratively oriented consultant might make to a parent consultee as an overture for collaboration:

Consultant: It is important for you to recognize how important you are in this process. Sometimes people involved in consulting relationships look to the consultant for "answers" and when they do that, they disregard their own ability and knowledge. My view of consultation is that we are equals. As parents, you know your child far better than I can and that knowledge is far more important in the success of this process than all the things I've learned about children. But if we combine the things I've learned about working with children with what you know about your own child, then I am confident that our work together can be successful. (p. 213)

Many veteran special education teachers have not been exposed to formal training in a collaborative model; rather, they were taught how to provide direct teaching services to children who had a variety of learning or behavior problems and to do it in a special education setting. Changes are occurring in this area as special educators move toward making the Regular Education Initiative (Will, 1986) a reality. An early example of these changes was described by Brann, Loughlin, and Kimball (1991). They used cooperative teaching, a model of service delivery designed to integrate classrooms of regular and special education students. They found that as involved teachers worked to reduce potential barriers to this program, their belief in the value of this sort of collaborative enterprise was validated. Givens-Ogle, Christ, and Idol (1991) reviewed the steps they took to implement collaborative consultation training among 13 resource specialist teachers who used this model to mainstream a greater percentage of their special education students into general education classes. After receiving administrative support, principals discussed the proposal at their schools. Thirteen principals received sufficient support from their staffs to move forward with twenty-five weeks of training for three hours per week followed by a two-day school-site team training seminar, which emphasized West & Idol's (1989) collaborative training modules. Although West & Idol caution that this was more of a case study than a research project, they presented some heartening results: Many of the elementary students they worked with, both mildly disabled and at-risk, were able to return to regular classwork successfully. The program was an example of the resource/consulting teacher model (see Chapter 3). More recently, Villa et al. (1996), using a rationale for a statewide effort of training in collaboration defined as "positive social interdependence," describe a program of collaborative interactions that resulted in a major increase in successful inclusion of students in the state of Vermont, where 83 percent of students with disabilities were included in general education classrooms, contrasted with 36 percent nationwide.

Zins (1993) has reviewed the literature regarding the training of consultees in the consultation process. He stresses the need for specific skill training in the processes of consultation. Among these skills are (1) understanding what consultation is, (2) learning how to present information, (3) learning about the consultant and how he functions, and (4) learning what to expect from consultation (Sandoval, Lambert, & Davis, 1977). Kratochwill, Van Someren, and Sheridan (1989) have presented a competency-based model for teaching interview skills to school consultants. Chapter 3 has information about interview skills and activities designed to build skills in this area.

Expectations and Preferences of Consultees

The primary variables that influence school consultation are the setting, the problem, the student, the people surrounding the situation (such as peers, parents, administrators, and other staff), the consultant, and the consultee. Effective consultation depends on the consultant's ability to understand the drives, concerns, needs, and interests of the consultee. Given time factors, the inability to gather detailed information about each consultee, and consultees' appropriate reticence about divulging personal information, the consultant must make do with whatever information she can gather and inferences she can draw about the consultee's dynamics. Because of our inability to ever fully grasp some of these complexities, consultation is at best an inaccurate science. It may be more properly considered an art (Idol et al., 2000).

Two consultee variables have been studied somewhat extensively: expectations and preferences (Brown et al., 2001). *Expectations* are what a person believes is likely to happen in a given situation. What does a consultee expect to happen in consultation? Naturally, this varies among consultees. Sources of this variation include preconceived notions, recent experiences, overheard experiences of other consultees, and basic personality factors such as openness and optimism. *Preferences* are what a consultee wants to happen which may not be the same as what he believes will happen. In school consultation, there is evidence that teacher consultees prefer consultation to psychometry as a role for psychologists (Gutkin, 1980; Gutkin & Ajchenbaum, 1984; Gutkin & Bossard, 1984). There is also some evidence that teacher consultees have preferences about how they want to be worked with in consultation. Coleman (1976), Wenger (1979), and Hughes and DeForest (1993) report that teachers prefer collaborative methods to expert-oriented consultation, and Weiler (1984) has found the same result when parents are the consultees.

In a study that divides teacher consultees according to experience (preservice versus experienced) and level (elementary versus secondary), Morrison, Walker, Wakefield, and Solberg (1994) found that elementary and preservice secondary teachers prefer a collaborative approach to consultation, whereas experienced secondary teachers prefer to work alone in solving classroom problems. Most of the interactions indicate a preference for collaboration or independent solution generation rather than an expert model.

Consideration of parents and families as variables in the consultation process is discussed in Chapters 3 and 5.

Useful Generalizations About Dealing with Consultees

The following suggestions are essential for success as a school-based consultant. Dettmer, Dyck, and Thurston (1999) and Friend and Cook (2000) offer many additional tips.

Make the consultee comfortable with you. Chapter 3 delineates the communication and interpersonal skills that enhance this possibility.

Make it clear that you prefer to work collaboratively. You should not tell the consultee what to do but should help him come up with practical solutions that have a high probability of success in his classroom or home. Be prepared to switch roles from time to time: Collaboration assumes that consultant and consultee may shift leadership roles in the development of interventions. Consultants need to listen to the expertise and ideas of the consultee to understand that person's point of view. When consultees believe that their ideas are important and are being considered, they are more likely to listen carefully to the consultant's ideas and are more likely to put the collaboratively developed ideas into practice. To assist in knowing whether an intervention is acceptable to a teacher–consultee, Witt and Elliott (1985) developed the Intervention Rating Profile, a 15-item scale designed to get teachers' opinions about the acceptability of proposed interventions. In order to measure the degree with which you are utilizing a collaborative approach, Erchul (1987) provided the Consultant Evaluation Form, a 12-question rating form that includes items pertaining to collaboration in the consultant–consultee interaction.

The following is a possible way to introduce the idea of collaborative consultation to a consultee with whom you have not previously worked.

"Hello, Mr. Sanchez, I'm Ms. Washington. I'm the new resource teacher here at ABC School. I'm pleased to meet you. I know you're anxious to tell me about Isaiah, and I'm anxious to get going with our discussion also, but I'd like to start by mentioning two important items. The first has to do with the way I like to be of assistance as a consultant. I prefer to work in what is known as a collaborative model. By this I mean that we problem solve together and try to come up with interventions that are appropriate for your classroom. I'm not the expert, by any means; in fact, in your classroom, you're the expert. I'm here primarily to get your insights and ideas about the problems and possible solutions. Through our discussions, I'm sure we can come up with some good ideas.

Now, the other thing I need to mention is confidentiality. When I work with consultees in the schools, I regard everything they tell me as confidential; that is, it stays between us. I don't talk to the principal or other teachers about the details of our discussions or about what I observe in your classroom. You, however, are free to tell anyone else about our work together. Naturally, in team meetings we will both be sharing information we have discussed about Isaiah and other students. There are only three exceptions to this confidentiality: If you tell me about anyone who is being abused, is abusing others, or is threatening others, I am obligated to report it. Is this information clear? Do you have any questions? No? Okay, let's start with you telling me about Isaiah. I'll be keeping notes just to help me keep the facts straight."

Don't waste people's time. Most school-based consultation sessions need to occur in 10 to 15 minutes because teachers are too busy to devote much more than that amount of time to a single consultative meeting. Brown, Pryzwansky, and Schulte (2001) describe the 15-minute consultation, acknowledging that school-based consultants do not have the luxury of time available to consultants in the business world. Exceptions may occur during a first meeting (when a student's background is reviewed), when the consultant is engaged in a group consultation regarding a particularly difficult situation (perhaps as part of an SST or IEP meeting), or when the consultant is doing system-improvement work. Longer sessions may also occur with parents.

Think constantly about solutions. Some consultants take pleasure in "admiring the problem"—acting as if the problem is amazing, inexplicable, or even amusing. They shake their heads and make mouth noises that punctuate the seriousness of the problem while stalling for time in hopes that someone else will solve the problem or it will go away. A competent consultant categorizes the nature of the problem, gathers the necessary data, synthesizes the information, and then leads the consultee to consider strategies for intervention. These activities represent the "directive" nature of collaborative consultation.

Try to get inside the consultee's world. Observation in a classroom, a playground, or a lunchroom can give the consultant a good picture of the setting of the problem and may lead to a focused discussion of practical interventions. It also shows consultees that the consultant is really interested in seeing the problem from their perspective—in other words, "walking in their shoes."

Stay with the situation until it is resolved. A competent consultant knows that problems are rarely solved after one consultation session. Often the first session is devoted to establishing rapport, discussing how to think about the problem, considering what data to gather and how to gather it, reviewing the student's history, and discussing tentative solutions. This session does not usually involve the development of substantive or final solutions to the problem. Follow-through is necessary. One of the requirements of most initial consultation sessions is that the consultant and consultee set another time to meet again for further discussion. The exception is when the situation is finally resolved to everyone's satisfaction or when there is mutual agreement that it might be best to put the case aside for a while.

Make every effort to understand the current pressures on teacher and parent consultees. Americans demand more from their public schools every day. The constant cry for accountability, tougher standards, more discipline, higher technology, and (for students with disabilities) greater opportunities for mainstreaming and inclusion can easily overwhelm even experienced teachers (Harvard School of Education, 1993; Johnson & Johnson, 1980; National Council on Education Standards and Testing, 1992; Stainback, Stainback, & Forest, 1989). Sensitivity to a teacher's burden of stress is certainly necessary.

CONSULTATION IN CULTURALLY AND LINGUISTICALLY DIVERSE SETTINGS

The public schools in late twentieth-century America are extremely diverse. In many urban and some suburban areas, Caucasian students are no longer the majority they were 50 years ago. Thus, schools have had to reconsider some of the basic ideas that have sustained them throughout their history and come to grips with the new America. Eurocentrism, Americanization (a belief in the melting-pot idea associated with cultural homogeneity), and similar notions are giving way to ideas about the positive values of multiculturalism, cultural pluralism, and bilingual education (Banks, 1993).

Pena (1996) has issued a call for more effective leadership and consultation to deal with issues of multiculturalism in the schools. He particularly recommends a more proactive preventive philosophy in dealing with students who demonstrate behavior and achievement needs. Consultation is much better designed to deal with these issues than is a refer–test–place, psychoeducational model of school practice. The latter waits to take action after the problem is established; the former seeks ways of improving school services and the delivery of these services before predictable problems arise.

A growing literature relates consultation to multi- or crosscultural issues, which is reflective of the fact that many school-based consultants deal daily with crosscultural issues. Sue and Sue (1990) point out some of the ways in which people from different cultures react differently from one another—for example, in language (including paralanguage behaviors such as inflections, use of hands, loudness, and nonverbal communication), time orientation, and proxemics (personal space). Tobias (1993) warns against "Western chauvinism," a tendency for native-born Anglo-Americans to devalue or discredit the contributions, values, or abilities of those from other countries, ethnic groups, or cultures.

Dettmer et al. (1999) discuss approaches suggested by Cross (1988), Huff and Telesford (1994), and Lynch and Hansen (1992) that consultants should use when dealing with parents from culturally diverse groups:

1. Acknowledge cultural differences; they can affect parent–teacher (and consultant) interactions.

2. Examine your own cultural beliefs and ways of responding.

3. Realize that group interactions and ways of responding (such as etiquette and patterns of responding) vary across cultural groups.

4. Try to understand a student's behavior as a function of her culture.

5. Find ways to validate culturally specific ideas.

6. Learn about backgrounds and beliefs regarding schooling, disability, and child rearing.

7. Realize that many families are not used to a collaborative approach.

8. Be familiar with some words and forms of greetings that are common to the families you will be dealing with.

9. Locate members of the family's background or culture who can mediate between the constituent parties (e.g., an older sibling, or a minister).

10. For students who recently arrived from a non–English-speaking country, learn important words and phrases to assist the student's very early adjustment to the classroom.

Pinto (1981) believes that effective crosscultural consultation occurs when the consultant has knowledge of cultural differences, accepts (empathizes with) them, is able to contrast them with his own values, and adapts appropriately. Pinto (1981) refers to this style of consulting as *Client-Centered Adaptive,* meaning that the method (i.e., style, process) used by the consultant is congruent with the comfort level and preferences of the consultee. This approach is clearly in line with the collaborative consultant model emphasized in this text. Brown (2001) and Srebalus and Brown (2001) have expanded on Pinto's ideas regarding the *Client-Centered Adaptive* approach to consultation by giving examples of how time orientation, personal space, eye contact, and other subtleties can make a difference in how the consultant will be regarded and valued. Further, in the area of content, as opposed to process, a school-based consultant needs to consider cultural values and norms when discussing interventions. Generalizations regarding potentially unacceptable interventions are risky, since a consultee's degree of acculturation and desire to comply interact with her sense of the necessity for interventions and the practicality of them. The issue of treatment acceptability needs to be carefully explored when dealing with consultees of a racial/ethnic group different from that of the consultant.

For example, Gibbs (1980) has written about differences between African-American and Caucasian consultees, and has made three formulations: "(a) there are ethnic (e.g., black-white) differences in the initial orientation to the consultant-consultee relationship; (b) these differences are along the dimension of interpersonal *versus* instrumental competence; and (c) these differences have significant implications for the implementation of the consultation process and its outcome" (p. 195). Gibbs believes that African-American consultees focus on "interpersonal competence," which she defines as "a measure of the ability of the individual [the consultant] to invoke positive attitudes and to obtain favorable responses to his actions" (p. 199). She believes that Caucasian consultees prefer to focus on "instrumental competence," which is "a measure of the degree of effectiveness with which a goal or task is accomplished by the individual" (p. 199). Gibbs describes five stages in the consultation process in which the consultant and consultee evaluate each other in terms of their compatibility. Most of this occurs at the entry level, although it could occur at any time in the process.

Unfortunately, Gibbs's (1980) conceptualization does not seem to have considered moderating variables such as social class, age, gender, experience, or the degree to which a consultant has used Pinto's (1981) *Client-Centered Adaptive* style of responding. In an effort to validate Gibbs's ideas, Duncan and Pryzwansky (1988) asked 124 experienced African-American female teachers to observe African-American and Caucasian consultants on a videotape and rate their effectiveness. Preferences for the race of the consultant were not observed. There was a general preference for the instrumentally oriented consultants, contrary to what Gibbs's ideas predict.

In another study, Naumann, Gutkin, and Sandoval (1996) asked college students to listen to audiotapes of consultation sessions with a school psychologist as the consultant and a kindergarten teacher as the consultee. The referral problem was a child's failure to speak in class. Information given to the raters included the race of the consultant and the race of the child, in each case either African-American or Euro-American. After listening to the tapes, each rater responded to questionnaires that measured intervention acceptability and consultant credibility. There were no significant effects for either consultant race or child race. Although a study of this type precludes significant generalization, it does raise some doubt about generalizations concerning the effects of race in either the consultant or the client. The race of the consultee was not a variable in this study; if it had been, this variable may have interacted with either consultant or client. As previously mentioned, generalizations across racial/ethnic groups may need to be reexamined in light of the consultant's growing knowledge of individual consultees' approaches to interpersonal relationships and acceptability of interventions.

Goh (1993) has indicated that, when compared to a traditional psychoeducational model for dealing with the learning and adjustment problems of minorities (test the student, find something "wrong" with him, find a label that fits, and then place the student in a special education setting), a crossculturally sensitive consultation model has more potential for avoiding the over-identification of these students. Rosenfield (1995) and Behring and Ingraham (1998) mention some of the areas that consultants need to be aware of when dealing with crosscultural issues, including bilingual education, acculturation, and cultural identity. Banks (1993) indicates two of the reasons parents from diverse groups may not seem interested in collaborating with school personnel regarding the needs of and plans for their children: (1) coping with the everyday demands of making a living puts such a degree of stress on the parent(s) that the idea of attending meetings and brainstorming with degree-laden teachers and specialists is not appealing; and (2) some parents did not have good experiences while in school, and discussing similar problems their own children are now manifesting recalls those experiences they would just as soon forget.

Clearly, more needs to be known about a consultant and a consultee than their race or ethnicity in order to determine the likelihood of an effective consultation process or content match.

ACTIVITY 1.9

Students from many different racial or ethnic groups might wish to comment on the content of this previous section. Which has more influence on a person's communication style, her ethnicity or her social class? How do people vary in their preferences for interpersonal relations? Are these variations a function of ethnicity, cultural expectations, or other variables?

THE EDUCATIONAL PLACEMENT OF STUDENTS WITH DISABILITIES

The following comments were recently overheard in three different SST meetings at Hilltop Junior High:

"It sounds like this student might have a learning disability. We better get an assessment plan and advise the parents of their rights."

"I don't know how he can keep up in general education. I'd better see him in my resource room two or three periods a day."

"He sounds disturbed. There may even be some autism or schizoid tendencies in his withdrawal patterns. I'll put him in one of my counseling groups and advise the parents to seek outside help."

These statements should sound familiar to experienced school personnel: they were made by a school psychologist, a resource specialist, and a school counselor— all well-meaning and experienced professionals. Notice that each of the statements implies some degree of "savior" behavior, the idea that someone recognizes a problem and decides to "save" the student by taking the student away from the general education program, at least for part of the day. For almost 40 years, statements like these, and a concomitant belief in the saving value of special education, have been the traditional responses of professionals who are confronted with children who exhibit noticeable difficulties in learning or behavior (Cole & Siegel, 1990; Smith, 2001). Such judgments and recommendations will probably never go away completely because there are times when these actions prove to be valuable for some students. I hope, however, that these steps will be taken only after determined efforts have been made to ameliorate the problem in the general education setting through a consultative approach.

I believe that all children belong in the general education program until it is demonstrated that such placement is harmful to their welfare or to the welfare of others (Yell, 1995). This belief is in accord with the mandates of the courts' rulings in *Daniel R. R. v. State Board of Education* (1989), and in *Board of Education v. Holland* (1992). In *Daniel R. R.,* the court indicated a two-part test for determining compliance with the requirement for placement in a Least Restrictive Environment:

> First, we ask whether education in the regular classroom, with the use of supplementary aids and services, can be achieved satisfactorily for a given child. If it cannot and the school intends to provide special education or to remove the child from regular education, we ask, second, whether the school has mainstreamed the child to the maximum extent appropriate. (p. 1,048)

In *Holland* the court said:

> Thus the decision as to whether any particular child should be educated in a regular classroom setting all of the time, part of the time, or none of the time, is necessarily an inquiry into the needs and abilities of one child, and does not extend to a group or category of handicapped children. (p. 878)

It follows that ancillary personnel, such as those engaged in consultative responsibilities, should not search for intrachild deficits and treat them somewhere else but should find ways of modifying and improving the general education program to enhance educational opportunities for these students.

At the present time, it is clear that not all special education teachers, school psychologists, counselors, and others engaged in these activities agree with this new philosophy; there is still a fairly strong belief in categorical pullout programs, in counseling as a remedy for behavior/adjustment problems, and in the need to find intrachild deficiencies (Cobb, 1990; Kaufmann & Hallahan, 1995; Woody, LaVoie, & Epps, 1992). The major professional organization devoted to issues of students with disabilities, the Council for Exceptional Children, supports the full inclusion of students with disabilities into general education as a "meaningful goal," but continues to advocate for a continuum of services and supports that includes separate classrooms for some students with severe disabilities. Fuchs and Fuchs (1994) indicate that a radical shift to full inclusion of all students with disabilities may be putting philosophy and desire ahead of technology and practicality. They suggest a respect for special education's traditions and values while seeking to strengthen the mainstream as well as other education placements in a continuum of services.

In spite of the commonplace nature of the statements quoted at the beginning of this section, it is clear that the picture is changing, that most special educators now favor the inclusion movement. Conferences, workshops, journal publications, and textbooks all attest to the fact that school psychologists, special education teachers, school counselors, and other school-based consultants are being trained in newer modes of service delivery which are compatible with the idea of regular education being the placement of choice. Collaborative consultation is, and will continue to be, a major activity for special educators and other school personnel who are in a position to assist teachers in dealing with students who present with learning and/or behavior adjustment challenges (Aldinger, Warger, & Eavy, 1992; Brown et al., 2001; Dougherty, 2000; Dettmer, Dyck, & Thurston, 1999; Friend & Cook, 2000; Graden, Zins, & Curtis, 1988). The reason for this shift in roles is not difficult to understand. There has been an increasing amount of criticism of traditional diagnosis (Figueroa, 1990; Howell & Hazelton, 1999; Shinn, Nolet, & Knutson, 1990; Ysseldyke & Marston, 1999); there have been concerns about the effectiveness of special education programs, both self-contained and resource rooms (Dunn, 1968; Fuchs & Fuchs, 1994; Graden, Zins, Curtis, & Cobb, 1988; Idol, Nevin, & Paolucci-Whitcomb, 2000; Johnson, 1969; Shinn, 1986; Ysseldyke & Marston, 1999); and there is an increasing call for students to stay in regular education programs with the assistance of ancillary personnel and support services (Curtis & Meyers, 1988; Forness & Kavale, 1991; Gresham, 1999; Kern & Dunlap, 1999; Will, 1986; Wisniewski & Alper, 1994).

Among the benefits of inclusion are at least the following:

1.   Students with disabilities are able to feel that they are part of the normal environment. They are able to think of themselves as being "regular" rather than "special."

2.   Students with disabilities who engage in behaviors regarded as detrimental to school success may benefit from other students' modeling of appropriate behav-

iors. Sometimes this can work the other way around: Students without identified disabilities whose behavior is inappropriate may observe prosocial behaviors exhibited by students with disabilities.

3. Students without disabilities are exposed to those with disabilities and may develop more positive images of individuals with disabilities. Instead of thinking of students with disabilities as being somewhere else in the educational system, they are now able to see these students as part of the general education program and to that extent as "regular" instead of otherwise.

4. Students without disabilities may be able to exercise the human tendency to help others who need it (for example, academically or socially); likewise, students with a disability may be able to contribute to the class in ways not previously considered.

5. Inclusion is becoming more efficient and less disruptive to all concerned. In pull-out programs, students often leave the class at crucial times and miss out on the regular curriculum. This results in a very scattered school day.

6. The broader community will soon include today's students. These students will bring the idea of inclusion to their adult lives and will look for ways to ensure that those with disabilities are treated equally, as is their right.

The 1980s and 1990s have been characterized by an immense increase in awareness about, and implementation of, inclusion in regular programming for students with disabilities (Fuchs & Fuchs, 1994; Heward, 2000; Johnson & Johnson, 1980; Mastropieri & Scruggs, 2000; Stainback et al., 1989). General educators have sometimes felt that the prospect of a marriage of special and general education, as envisioned by the full inclusion movement, was exciting to the bride (special education) but somehow failed to include a serious invitation to the groom (general education). Additionally, some general educators are concerned that they are overburdened with too many issues and demands and cannot keep up with the pressures they already have. They believe that adding the time it takes to collaborate in planning for students with disabilities is neither practical nor fair (Kaufmann & Hallahan, 1995; Zigmond & Baker, 1995). Since the courts have not tended to agree or be concerned with these arguments, citing the law as having precedence over the objections of some general educators, the inclusion movement has progressed, prompting general educators to seek ways to make it work. Inservice training, workshops on curriculum modification, teaching methods, co- or team-teaching, peer tutoring, group work, and other modifications are now becoming commonplace in schools that have embraced the inclusion philosophy.

Collaborative consultation is the key to the effectiveness of the inclusion movement. The activities of school consultants in their efforts to move the inclusion agenda forward by helping general educators accommodate students with disabilities may determine the success of this movement (Dettmer et al., 1999; Friend & Cook, 2000; Idol, Nevin, & Paolucci-Newcomb, 2000; Tiegerman-Farber & Radziewicz, 1998).

ACTIVITY 1.10

Those familiar with full inclusion should talk about their experiences with it, and especially how they think a school consultant could be of use to a general education teacher in the cases with which they are familiar. What were the issues that could have (or did) make the inclusion difficult, and how were potentially difficult situations handled?

SUMMARY

This chapter has defined the concept of collaborative consultation and offered some background information about it. Consultation can be an effective intervention for problem solving about students' learning and behavior/adjustment problems. It provides a method for affecting system-wide change in methods of service delivery to students and bridges gaps among teachers, parents, and ancillary personnel. It also serves efforts to keep students in regular education and return those in special education to the regular track as soon as is sensible.

Merely talking about problems does not solve them. However, many educators and parents have come to the conclusion that not enough collaborative problem solving is practiced before students are referred for special education and related services or before any effort is made to return them to the general track. Special education teachers and ancillary personnel, such as psychologists and counselors, should devote more time to the collaborative consultation activities described in this book. This would represent a healthy step away from the tendency to treat a referral as permission to find something wrong with a student and to treat that problem somewhere other than the regular class.

REFERENCES

Affleck, J. Q., Madge, S., Adams, A., & Lowenbraun, S. (1988). Integrated classroom versus resource model: Academic viability and effectiveness. *Exceptional Children, 54,* 339–348.

Alderman, G. L., & Gimpel, G. A. (1996). The interaction between type of behavior problem and type of consultant: Teachers' preferences for professional assistance. *Journal of Educational and Psychological Consultation, 7*(4), 305–314.

Aldinger, L., Warger, C., & Eavy, P. (1991). *Strategies for teacher collaboration.* Ann Arbor, MI: Exceptional Innovations.

Bahr, M. W. (1996). Are school psychologists reform-minded? *Psychology in the Schools, 33,* 295–307.

Banks, C. A. M. (1993). Parents and teachers: Partners in school reform. In J. A. Banks & C. A. M. Banks (Eds.), *Multicultural education: Issues and perspectives* (2nd ed., pp. 332–352). Boston: Allyn & Bacon.

Behring, S., & Ingraham, C. (1998). Culture as a central component of consultation: A call to the field. *Journal of Educational and Psychological Consultation, 9*(1), 57–72.

Bergan, J. R. (1995). Evolution of a problem-solving model of consultation. *Journal of Educational and Psychological Consultation, 6,* 111–124.

Bergan, J. R., & Neumann, A. J., III. (1980). The identification of resources and constraints influencing plan design in consultation. *Journal of School Psychology, 18,* 318–323.

Bergan, J. R., & Tombari, M. L. (1976). Consultant skill and efficiency and the implementation and outcomes of consultation. *Journal of School Psychology, 14,* 3–14.

Board of Education v. Holland, 786 F. Supp. 874 (E.D. Cal. 1992).

Braaten, B., Mennes, D., Brown, M., & Samuels, H. (1992). A model of collaborative service for middle school students. *Preventing School Failure, 36*(3), 10–15.

Brann, P., Loughlin, S., & Kimball, W. (1991). Guidelines for cooperative teaching between general and special education teachers. *Journal of Educational and Psychological Consultation, 2*(2), 197–200.

Brown, D. (2001). An eclectic, culturally sensitive approach to consultation in mental health settings. In S. Salvador (Ed.), *Counseling and psychotherapy: A practical guidebook for trainees and new professionals.* Boston: Allyn & Bacon.

Brown, D., Pryzwansky, W., & Schulte, A. (2001). *Psychological consultation* (5th ed.). Boston: Allyn & Bacon.

Brown, D., Pryzwansky, W., & Schulte, A. (1995). *Psychological consultation* (3rd ed.). Boston: Allyn & Bacon.

Brown, D., Spano, D. B., & Schulte, A. C. (1988). Consultation training in master's level counselor education programs. *Counselor Education and Supervision, 27,* 323–330.

Caplan, G. (1964). *Principles of preventive psychiatry.* New York: Basic Books.

Chaplan, G., & Caplan, R. B. (1993). *Mental health consultation and collaboration.* San Francisco: Jossey-Bass.

Chalfant, J., Pysh, M. (1989). Teacher assistance teams: Five descriptive studies on 96 teams. *Remedial and Special Education, 10* (6), 49–58.

Christenson, S. L. (1995). Supporting home-school collaboration. In A. Thomas & J. Grimes (Eds.), *Best practices in school psychology—III.* Washington, DC: NASP.

Cobb, C. T. (1990). School psychology in the 1980s and 1990s: Context for change and definition. In C. Reynolds & T. B. Gutkin (Eds.), *The handbook of school psychology* (pp. 21–32). New York: Wiley.

Cobern, W. (1993). Constructivism. *Journal of Educational and Psychological Consultation, 7*(1), 105–112.

Cole, E., & Siegel, J. (1990). *Effective consultation in school psychology.* Toronto: Hogrefe & Huber.

Coleman, S. (1976, August). *Developing collaborative-process consultation: Teacher and participant-observer perceptions and outcome.* Paper presented at the American Psychological Association Convention, Washington, DC.

Comer, J. P. (1993). *School power: Implications of a preventive project.* New York: Free Press.

Cramer, S.F. (1998). *Collaboration: A success strategy for special educators.* Boston: Allyn & Bacon.

Cross, T. (1988). Services to minority populations: What does it mean to be a culturally competent professional? *Focal Point, 2,* 1–3.

Curtis, M. J., & Meyers, J. (1988). Consultation: A foundation for alternative services in the schools. In J. L. Graden, J. E. Zins, & M. J. Curtis (Eds.), *Alternative educational delivery services: Enhancing instructional options for all students* (pp. 35–48). Washington, DC: NASP.

Curtis, M. J., & Stollar, S. A. (1995). Best practices in system-level consultation and organizational change. In A. Thomas and J. Grimes (Eds.), *Best practices in school psychology* (3rd ed., pp. 51–58). Washington, DC: National Association of School Psychologists.

Curtis, M. J., & Van Wagener, E. (1988). *An analysis of failed consultation.* Paper presented at the annual meeting of the National Association of School Psychologists, Chicago.

Daniel R. R. v. State Board of Education, 874 F. 2d. 1036 (1989).

Dettmer, P., Dyck, N., & Thurston, L. (1999). *Consultation, collaboration and teamwork* (3rd. ed.). Boston: Allyn & Bacon.

Dettmer, P., Thurston, L., & Dyck, N. (1993). *Consultation, collaboration and teamwork.* Boston: Allyn & Bacon.

Dougherty, A. (2000). *Psychological consultation and collaboration in school and community settings* (3rd ed.). Pacific Grove, CA: Brooks/Cole.

Duncan, C., & Pryzwansky, W. B. (1988). Consultation research: Trends in doctoral dissertations, 1978–1985. *Journal of School Psychology, 26,* 107–119.

Dunn, L. (1968). Special education for the mildly handicapped: Is much of it justifiable? *Exceptional Children, 35,* 5–22.

Erchul, W. P. (1987). A relational communication analysis of control in school consultation. *Professional School Psychology, 2,* 113–124.

Figueroa, R. A. (1990). Best practices in the assessment of bilingual children. In A. Thomas & J. Grimes (Eds.), *Best practices in school psychology—II.* Washington, DC: NASP.

Fishbaugh, M. S. (1997). *Models of collaboration.* Boston: Allyn & Bacon.

Forness, S. R., & Kavale, K. (1991). School psychologists' roles and functions: Integration into the regular classroom. In G. Stoner, M. R. Shinn, & H. M. Walker (Eds.), *Interventions for achievement and behavior problems.* Washington, DC: NASP.

Friend, M., & Cook, L. (2000). *Interactions: Collaboration skills for school professionals* (2nd ed.). New York: Longman.

Fuchs, D., & Fuchs, L. S. (1994). Inclusive schools movement and the radicalization of special education reform. *Exceptional Children, 60*(4), 294–309.

Futrell, M. (1989). Mission not accomplished: Educational reform in retrospect. *Phi Delta Kappan, 71*(1), 9–14.

Gendlin, E. T. (1986). What comes after traditional psychotherapy research? *American Psychologist, 41,* 131–136.

Gibbs, J. T. (1980). The interpersonal orientation in mental health consultation: Toward a model of ethnic variations in consultation. *Journal of Community Psychology, 8,* 195–207.

Givens-Ogle, L., Christ, B., & Idol, L. (1991). Collaborative consultation: The San Juan District project. *Journal of Educational and Psychological Consultation, 2*(3), 267–284.

Goh, D. S. (1993, April). *Advancing toward a theory of cross-cultural consultation: Discussion of symposium papers.* Paper presented at the meeting of the National Association of School Psychologists, Washington, DC.

Graden, J. L., Zins, J. E., & Curtis, M. J. (1988). *Alternative educational delivery systems: Enhancing instructional options for all students.* Washington, DC: NASP.

Graden, J. L., Zins, J. E., Curtis, M. J., & Cobb, C. T. (1988). The need for alternatives in educational services. In J. L. Graden, J. E. Zins, & M. J. Curtis (Eds.), *Alternative educational delivery systems: Enhancing instructional options for all students.* Washington, DC: NASP.

Gresham, F. M. (1989). Assessment of treatment integrity in school consultation and prereferral intervention. *School Psychology Review, 18,* 37–50.

Gresham, F. M. (1999). Non-categorical approaches to K-12 emotional and behavioral difficulties. In D. J. Reschly, W. D. Tilly, & J. P. Grimes (Eds.), *Special Education in Transition* (pp. 107–138). Longmont, CO: Sopris West.

Gresham, F. M., & Kendell, G. K. (1987). School consultation research: Methodological critique and future research directions. *School Psychology Review, 16,* 306–316.

Grubb, R. (1981). Shaping the future of school psychology: A reaction. *School Psychology Review, 10,* 243–259.

Gutkin, T. B. (1980). Teacher perceptions of consultation services provided by school psychologists. *Professional Psychology, 11,* 637–642.

Gutkin, T. B. (1993a). Conducting consultation research. In J. E. Zins, T. R. Kratochwill, & S. N. Elliott (Eds.), *Handbook of consultation services for children* (pp. 227–248). San Francisco: Jossey-Bass.

Gutkin, T. B. (1993b). Moving from behavioral to ecobehavioral consultation: What's in a name? *Journal of Educational and Psychological Consultation, 4,* 95–99.

Gutkin, T. B., & Ajchenbaum, M. (1984). Teachers' perception of control and preferences for consultation services. *Professional Psychology: Research and Practice, 15*(4), 565–570.

Gutkin, T. B., & Bossard, M. D. (1984). Impact of consultant, consultee, and organizational variables in teachers' attitudes toward consultation services. *Journal of School Psychology, 22*(3), 251–258.

Gutkin, T. B., & Curtis, M. J. (1990). School based consultation: Theory and techniques. In C. Reynolds & T. B. Gutkin (Eds.), *The handbook of school psychology* (pp. 577–613). New York: Wiley.

Gutkin, T. B., & Curtis, M. J. (1999). School-based consultation theory and practice: The art and science of indirect service delivery. In C. R. Reynolds & T. B. Gutkin (Eds.), *The handbook of school psychology* (3rd ed., pp. 598–637). New York: Wiley.

Harvard School of Education. (1993). The push for new standards provokes hype and fear—and both are justified. *Harvard Education Letter, 9*(5), 1–5.

Henning-Stout, M. (1993). Defining human service consultation. In J. E. Zins, T. R. Kratochwill, & S. N. Elliott (Eds.), *Handbook of consultation services for children* (pp. 15–45). San Francisco: Jossey-Bass.

Heward, W. L. (2000). *Exceptional children: An introduction to special education*. Upper Saddle River, NJ: Merrill/Prentice Hall.

Howell, K. W., & Hazelton, S. C. (1999). Curriculum-based evaluation: Finding solutions to educational problems. In D. J. Reschly, W. D. Tilly, & J. P. Grimes (Eds.), *Special education in transition* (pp. 233–258). Longmont, CO: Sopris West.

Huff, B., & Telesford, M.C. (1994). Outreach efforts to involve families of color. In the Federation of Families for Children's Mental Health'. *Focal Point,* 10, 180–184.

Hughes, J. (1994). Back to basics: Does consultation work? *Journal of Educational and Psychological Consultation,* 5(1), 77–84.

Hughes, J., & DeForest, P. (1993). Consultant directiveness and support as predictors of consultation outcomes. *Journal of School Psychology, 31,* 355–373.

Idol, L. (1990). The scientific art of classroom consultation. *Journal of Educational and Psychological Consultation, 1*(1), 3–22.

Idol, L., Nevin, A., & Paolucci-Whitcomb, P. (2000). *Collaborative consultation* (3rd ed.). Austin, TX: Pro-Ed.

Idol, L., Paolucci-Whitcomb, P., & Nevin, A. (1986). *Collaborative consultation*. Austin, Texas: PRO-ED.

Johnson, D. W., & Johnson, R. T. (1980). Integrating handicapped students into the mainstream. *Exceptional Children, 47,* 90–98.

Johnson, J. L. (1969). Special education and the inner city: A challenge for the future or another means for cooling the mark? *Journal of Special Education, 3,* 241–251.

Kaufmann, J., & Hallahan, D. (1995). *The illusion of full inclusion*. Austin, TX: Pro-Ed.

Kern, L. & Dunlap, G. (1999). Developing effective program plans for students with disabilities. In D. J. Reschly, W. D. Tilly, & J. P. Grimes (Eds.), *Special education in transition* (pp. 213–232). Longmont, CO: Sopris West.

Kratochwill, T. R., Van Someren, K. R., & Sheridan, S. M. (1989). Training behavioral consultants: A competency-based model to teach interview skills. *Professional School Psychology, 4,* 41–58.

Kurpius, D. J. (1991). Why collaborative consultation fails: A matrix for consideration. *Journal of Educational and Psychological Consultation,* 2(2), 193–195.

Lippitt, G., & Lippitt, R. (1986). *The consulting process in action* (2nd ed.). San Diego, CA: University Associates.

Lynch, E. W., & Hansen, M. J. (1992). *Developing cross-cultural competence: A guide for working with young children and their families*. Baltimore: Paul H. Brooks.

Marks, E. S. (1995). *Entry strategies for school consultation*. New York: Guilford.

Mastropieri, M. A., & Scruggs, T. E. (2000). *The inclusive classroom: Strategies for effective instruction*. Upper Saddle River, NJ: Merrill/Prentice Hall.

Meyers, J., & Nastasi, B. K. (1999). Primary prevention in school settings. In C. Reynolds & T. Gutkin (Eds.), *Handbook of school psychology* (3rd ed.), (pp. 764–799). New York: Wiley.

Meyers, J., Wurtz, R., & Flanagan, D. (1981). A national survey investigating training occurring in school psychology programs. *Psychology in the Schools, 18,* 297–302.

Morrison, G. M., Walker, D., Wakefield, P., & Solberg, S. (1994). Teacher preferences for collaborative relationships: Relationship to efficacy for teaching in prevention-related domains. *Psychology in the Schools, 31,* 221–231.

National Council on Education Standards and Testing. (1992). *Raising standards for American education*. Washington, DC: U.S. Government Printing Office.

Naumann, W. C., Gutkin, T. B., & Sandoval, S. R. (1996). The impact of consultant race and student race on perceptions of consultant effectiveness and intervention acceptability. *Journal of Educational and Psychological Consultation,* 7(1), 151–160.

Parsons, R. D., & Meyers, J. (1984). *Developing consultation skills*. San Francisco: Jossey-Bass.

Pena, R. A. (1996). Multiculturalism and educational leadership: Keys to effective consultation. *Journal of Educational and Psychological Consultation,* 7(4), 315–326.

Pinto, R. F. (1981). Consultant orientations and client system perceptions. In R. Lippitt & G. Lippitt (Eds.), *Systems thinking: A resource for organization diagnosis and intervention* (pp. 57–74). Washington, DC: International Consultants Foundation.

Ponti, C. R., Zins, J. E., & Graden, J. L. (1988). Implementing a consultation-based service delivery system to decrease referrals for special education: A case study of organizational considerations. *School Psychology Review, 17,* 89–100.

Powers, K. (2001). Problem solving student support teams. *The California School Psychologist, 6,*19–30.

Pryzwansky, W. B. (1977). Collaboration or consultation: Is there a difference? *Journal of Special Education, 1,* 179–182.

Pryzwansky, W. B. (1986). Indirect service delivery: Considerations for future research in consultation. *School Psychology Review, 15,* 479–488.

Pugach, M. C., & Johnson, L. J. (1988). Rethinking the relationship between consultation and collaborative problem solving. *Focus on Exceptional Children, 21*(4), 1–8.

Rappaport, J. (1981). In praise of paradox: A social policy of empowerment over prevention. *American Journal of Community Psychology, 9,* 1–25.

Reinking, R. J., Livesay, G., & Kohl, M. (1978). The effects of consultation style on consultee productivity. *American Journal of Community Psychology, 6,* 283–290.

Reynolds, M.C. (1989). An historical perspective: The delivery of special education to mildly disabled and at-risk students. *Remedial and Special Education, 10*(6), 7–11.

Ritter, D. R. (1978). Effects of a school consultation program upon referral patterns of teachers. *Psychology in the Schools, 15,* 239–243.

Rosenfield, S. (1995). The practice of instructional consultation. *Journal of Educational and Psychological Consultation, 6*(4), 317–327.

Rosenfield, S., & Gravois, T. (1996). *Instructional consultation teams.* New York: Guilford Press.

Sandoval, J., Lambert, N. M., & Davis, J. M. (1977). Consultation from the consultee's perspective. *Journal of School Psychology, 15*(4), 334–342.

Sarason, S. B. (1982). *The culture of the school and the problem of change* (2nd ed.). Boston: Allyn & Bacon.

Sarason, S. B. (1991). *The predictable failure of educational reform.* San Francisco: Jossey-Bass.

Shinn, M. R. (1986). Does anyone care after the refer-test-place sequence: The systematic evaluation of special education program effectiveness. *School Psychology Review, 15*(1), 49–58.

Shinn, M. R., Nolet, V., & Knutson, N. (1990). Best practices in curriculum-based measurement. In A. Thomas & J. Grimes (Eds.), *Best practices in school psychology*—II (pp. 237–308). Washington, DC: NASP.

Smith, D. D. (2001). *Introduction to special education* (4th ed.). Boston: Allyn & Bacon.

Sprick, R., Sprick, M., & Garrison, M. (1994). *Interventions.* Longmont, CO: Sopris West.

Srebalus, D. J., & Brown, D. (2001). *Becoming a skilled helper.* Boston: Allyn & Bacon.

Stainback, S., Stainback, W., & Forest, M. (Eds.). (1989). *Educating all students in the mainstream of education.* Baltimore: Brookes.

Stoner, G., Shinn, M. R., & Walker, H. M. (1991). *Interventions for achievement and behavior problems.* Silver Springs, MD: NASP.

Sue, D. W., & Sue, D. (1990). *Counseling the culturally different: Theory and practice* (2nd ed.). New York: Wiley.

Tharp, R. (1975). The triadic model of consultation. In C. Parker (Ed.), *Psychological consultation: Helping teachers meet special needs* (pp. 135–151). Minneapolis, MN: Leadership Training Institute/Special Education.

Tiegerman-Farber, E., & Radziewicz, C. (1998). *Collaborative decision making: The pathway to inclusion.* Upper Saddle River, NJ: Merrill/Prentice Hall.

Tobias, R. (1993). Underlying cultural issues that affect sound consultant/school collaboratives in developing multicultural programs. *Journal of Educational and Psychological Consultation, 4*(3), 237–251.

Turnbull, A. P., & Turnbull, H. R. (1997). *Families, professionals, and exceptionality: A special partnership* (3rd ed.). Upper Saddle River, NJ: Merrill/Prentice Hall.

Villa, R., Thousand, J., Nevin, A., & Malgeri, C. (1996). Installing collaboration for inclusive schooling as a way of doing business in public schools. *Remedial and Special Education, 17,* 169–181.

Wang, M. C., Reynolds, M. C., & Walberg, H. J. (1986). Rethinking special education. *Educational Leadership, 44,* 26–31.

Webster's college dictionary. (2nd ed.). (1997). New York: Random House.

Weiler, M. B. (1984). *The influence of contact and setting on the ratings of parents for models of consul-*

tation. Unpublished master's thesis, North Carolina State University, Raleigh.

Weiss, C. H. (1993). Shared decision making about what? A comparison of schools with and without teacher participation. *Teachers College Record, 95,* 69–92.

Wenger, R. D. (1979). Teacher response to collaborative consultation. *Psychology in the Schools, 16,* 127–131.

West, J. F., & Idol, L. (1989). *Collaboration in the schools: Communicating, interacting and problem-solving*. Austin, TX: Pro-Ed.

Will, M. (1986). Educating children with learning problems: A shared responsibility. *Exceptional Children, 51,* 411–415.

Wisniewski, L., & Alper, S. (1994). Including students with severe disabilities in general education settings. *Remedial and Special Education, 15*(1), 4–13.

Witt, J. C. (1990). Face-to-face verbal interaction in school-based consultation: A review of the literature. *School Psychology Quarterly, 5,* 199–210.

Witt, J. C., & Elliott, S. N. (1985). Acceptability of classroom management strategies. In T. R. Kratochwill (Ed.), *Advances in school psychology* (Vol. 4, pp. 251–288). Hillsdale, NJ: Lawrence Erlbaum Associates, Inc.

Woody, R. H., LaVoie, J. C., & Epps, S. (1992). *School psychology: A developmental and social systems approach*. Boston: Allyn & Bacon.

Yell, M. L. (1995). Least restrictive environment, inclusion, and students with disabilities: A legal analysis. *Journal of Special Education, 28,* 389–404.

Yocum, D. J., & Cossairt, A. (1996). Consultation courses offered in special education teacher training programs: A national survey. *Journal of Educational and Psychological Consultation, 7*(3), 251–258.

Yocum, D. J., & Staebler, B. (1996). The impact of collaborative consultation on special education referral accuracy. *Journal of Educational and Psychological Consultation, 7*(2), 179–192.

Ysseldyke, J. (1986). Current practice in school psychology. In S. Elliott & J. Witt (Eds.), *The delivery of psychological services in the schools*. Hillsdale, NJ: Lawrence Erlbaum Associates.

Ysseldyke, J. E., & Marston, D. (1999). Origins of categorical special education services in the schools and a rationale for changing them. In D. J. Reschly, W. D. Tilly, & J. P. Grimes (Eds.), *Special education in transition* (pp. 1–18). Longmont, CO: Sopris West.

Ysseldyke, J. E., Vanderwood, M., & Shriner, J. (1997). Changes over the past decade in special education referral to placement probability: An incredibly reliable practice. *Diagnostique, 23*(1), 193–202.

Zigmond, N., & Baker, J. M. (1995). Current and future practices in inclusive schooling. *Journal of Special Education, 29,* 245–250.

Zins, J. E. (1992). Implementing school-based consultation service: An analysis of 5 years of practice. In R. K. Conyne & J. O'Neil (Eds.), *Organizational consultation: A casebook* (pp. 50–79). Newbury Park, CA: Sage.

Zins, J. E. (1993). Enhancing consultee problem-solving skills in consultative interactions. *Journal of Counseling and Development, 72,* 185–190.

Zins, J. E., Curtis, M. J., Graden, J. L., & Ponti, C. R. (1988). *Helping students succeed in the regular classroom*. San Francisco: Jossey-Bass.

CHAPTER 2

Models and Functional Aspects of Consultation

OBJECTIVES

1. Present information on two theoretical models of consultation: behavioral and mental health.

2. Review a wide variety of functional models of consultation.

3. Specify what consultants do: their roles, skills needed, and activities performed.

4. Indicate the similarities and differences between individual and team-based consultation.

5. Discuss how teams in schools work collaboratively toward common purposes.

6. Present ideas about consulting with parents and families.

7. Give a framework for the development and implementation of staff development activities.

Mrs. Smith, Billy's mother, calls you because of her concerns about the quality of instruction Billy is receiving in his first-grade class. Billy, who has Down syndrome, has presented with many acting-out problems, although his behavior has recently begun to improve. He is served by the general education teacher, yourself (his special education teacher), and a part-time aide; and he has been included in most of the activities of the regular first grade. What model of consultation do you think would be useful to follow in this case? What skills will you bring to bear on this situation?

José is a junior in a comprehensive high school. He has been referred to the counselor numerous times over the past two years because of his academic apathy, inability to stay awake in class, and general disinterest in school. José has been identified as a student with academic promise. You (the school counselor) would like to heighten the awareness of the teachers and José's parents and develop a plan for dealing with José's situation. How could you do this collaboratively?

Elise, a ninth grader with a learning disability in reading and writing, is in danger of failing her general education classes in English and social studies. Her teachers are having her use only the regular texts (which she has a difficult time reading) because she has insisted that she does not want to appear "retarded" in front of her friends. You are the special education teacher consultant in this school. How might you deal with this issue?

A RATIONALE FOR A MODEL

A model is a way of conceptualizing or approaching a problem. A consultant is always, if only unwittingly, following a model. Some consultants follow a particular model very closely because they believe it is the most appropriate way of thinking about and solving the referral problem. Others may have only a vague notion of what the various models are; these consultants tend to follow a generalized problem-solving scheme: identifying the problem, brainstorming reasons for and solutions to the problem, deciding on possible steps to take, and encouraging the consultee to follow through. This process is then recycled until the problem is solved (Gutkin & Curtis, 1999). Some authors have commented on a discrepancy between what some consultants and consultees call their *theoretical base* and their actual behavior, which may not seem to be driven by that base (Argyris, 1991; Senge, 1990).

Kurpius, Fuqua, and Rozecki (1993) encourage consultants to strive toward some conceptual understanding of the meaning and purpose of consultation by asking questions that define the parameters of their beliefs. Such questions might include the following:

- What model(s) of consultation do I prefer?
- How do I define consultation to myself and others?
- How do I determine what approach would be most efficient and effective in any given situation?
- How will I reconcile my beliefs with those of the consultee if we differ?
- What theories of learning and instruction do I believe are most appropriate, given the nature of the classrooms I will be serving?
- What recommendations for common problems arise from my theoretical position?
- How does my view of inclusive education influence my recommendations?

These are difficult questions, and certainly this list is not exhaustive. In every consultation case that arises in the schools these questions are being answered, if only implicitly, through a study of the actual behaviors of the consultant and consultee. Generally, however, neither the consultant nor the consultee verbalizes them.

TYPES OF MODELS

Dougherty (2000) identifies five consultation models—generic, behavioral, mental health, organizational, and collaborative—and indicates some of the similarities and differences among them. Brown, Pryzwansky, and Schulte (2001) devote a chapter to each of their four models: behavioral, organizational, Adlerian (which is based on the social psychology of Alfred Adler; see Ansbacher & Ansbacher, 1956), and mental health. West and Idol (1987) review several others, including collaborative, process, clinical, program, and education/training. This chapter will review two models, behavioral and mental health, that are regarded as theoretical because they derive from well-established theories of human behavior, and some of the practical, non-theoretical models discussed by West and Idol (1987), among others. Organizational consultation is presented in Chapter 10 because it relates most closely to system change issues. Collaboration as a model of consultative functioning was discussed in Chapter 1.

TWO THEORETICAL MODELS

Behavioral Model

The behavioral model is built on the theories of learning that have been adapted by behaviorists such as Skinner, Bandura, and Meichenbaum (Conoley & Conoley, 1992). Essentially, a behaviorist believes that behaviors are a function of the contingencies that control them (i.e., their antecedents and consequences). One looks to these environmental stimuli when trying to understand why behaviors exist and how they can be altered (Skinner, 1969).

Behaviorism has progressed in many ways over the seventy years of its existence. During the 1980s and 1990s, for example, there has been an increasing interest in what is known as cognitive behavior modification, which differs from more traditional thinking in its emphasis on internal, cognitive events. Traditional behaviorism was not concerned with internal events primarily because they could not be observed and counted. Now, however, it is widely recognized that ignoring internal mediating events leaves a gap in behaviorists' ability to understand the wellsprings of human behavior (Alberto & Troutman, 1999; Kaplan, 1995, 2000; Meichenbaum, 1977; Schloss & Smith, 1998).

Another major change has been formulated by Bandura (1977), who believes that social learning, or learning by observing models, is a major force in one's learning history. Using role models or rehearsing specific behaviors under conditions of positive reinforcement are some of the behavior change techniques suggested by Bandura's work.

It is clear that behavioral consultation is moving forward to embrace newer conceptualizations and applications. Kratochwill, Sladeczek, and Plunge (1995) provide a brief review of the evolution of behavioral consultation.

Basic Concepts in Behavioral Consultation   Dougherty (2000) suggests the following definition of behavioral consultation: "a relationship whereby services consistent with a behavioral orientation are provided either indirectly to a client or a system, [or] directly by training consultees to enhance their skills with clients or systems" (p. 279).

In traditional behavior modification, social learning and the newer cognitive emphasis, the basic paradigm one uses to analyze behaviors consists of antecedents, behaviors, and consequences. This ABC model has been expanded by some writers (Kanfer & Saslow, 1969) but is still useful in its original format as developed by Skinner (1969).

Antecedents are events that precede, and are believed to be functionally connected to, the behavior that follows the antecedents' occurrence. Antecedents can be either external or internal. Examples of external antecedents are a teacher's direction to a student to do something, the behavior of the child sitting next to a target student, or a fire-drill alarm. Internal antecedents include hunger, anger over a preceding event, or self-talk.

These examples of external and internal antecedents are what Herbert (1978) refers to as proximal rather than distal. According to Herbert, "proximal antecedents are close in time to the actual behavior" while distal refers "to the more distant (historical) events in the client's life" (p. 56). As with most variables that exist on a continuum, it is not always easy or practical to make the distinction between identifying any given antecedent as distal or proximal. In spite of this, the distinction is valuable because it reminds observers that any behavior may be a function of antecedents that occurred years earlier rather than simply those events that are currently happening. Distal antecedents include child-rearing practices, a history of gang-related activity in a child's family, events seen on television, habit strength, memories of a situation similar to a current situation, and so on. In fact, what often appears to be the immediate (proximal antecedent) cause of a child's misbehavior may not be the main reason for the observed behavior. By knowing a child's history and, when possible, something of the child's inner life through counseling or reflective listening techniques, one may come to understand the distal antecedents of that child's behavior. Gutkin has emphasized this point, suggesting that behavioral consultation needs to attend more seriously to distal antecedents by becoming "ecobehavioral," by looking at the larger picture of a student's life and history rather than just at immediate prompting events (Gutkin, 1993).

ACTIVITY 2.1

List, either by yourself or in a class group, all the antecedent reasons you can think of for classroom misbehavior (however defined). In other words, what prompts misbehavior in school? Determine which antecedents are distal and which are proximal.

ACTIVITY 2.2

Repeat Activity 2.1, this time focusing on academic learning problems. What are some reasons for poor academic performance? Which seem to be biological and which are environmental?

Consequences (defined here as the effects of a behavior on the student) are ordinarily regarded as the events that follow a behavior. These can be positive, neutral, or negative (or aversive). It is the effect on a student that determines whether a consequence is positive, neutral, or negative, not the intention of the person who delivers the consequence. The student determines the effect, which might be the opposite of that designed or caused by the person or environmental event that delivers the consequence to the student. For example, teachers (and parents) often warn children not to tip their chairs back because they might fall. If they do fall, the effect may be positive from the point of view of the adult since it validates the adult's ability to predict events. Or it may be negative, if the child is hurt and the adult feels sorry for him. From a child's point of view, the effect may be negative if he gets hurt, or it may be positive if he obtains some sort of pleasure from disrupting a classroom or obtaining approval from his peers, even if he does get hurt.

Walker and Shea (1999) discuss four kinds of consequences: positive reinforcement, negative reinforcement, extinction, and punishment. They point out, as I have mentioned, that the consequence intended by the "contingency manager" (parent, teacher, and so on) may not be the one that actually occurs in the mind of the student since the positive or negative value of a consequence is always determined by the student, as the example of chair tilting indicates.

Another example is the intended use of extinction. For example, a teacher decides to ignore the verbal outbursts of Billy, a student with autism, believing that the outbursts are partially a function of the fact that they gain so much attention. After one week of ignoring this behavior, its incidence has tripled. The teacher is now considering either a punishment consequence ("Billy, when you scream, you must go to time-out") or a return to her previous method, which was an attempt to interpret the communicative intent of the verbal outbursts (e.g., "Billy, tell or show me what you want"). Actually, the student may have interpreted the teacher's comments as a punishment consequence. Thus, the fact that the outbursts are now being "ignored" seems to the student to be a toleration of them by the teacher, or an ignoring of the interpretation of the communicative intent, and so their incidence has increased.

This latter situation is an example of an unwitting consequence: one that occurs without our planning for it or wanting it. For instance, a teacher who believes that he is positively reinforcing students by verbally praising them may find that some of his students don't seem to want or like this praise. From their perspective, which may arise from sociocultural norms, praise from a teacher, at least in public, is aversive and therefore a punishment instead of a positive reinforcement.

Given these examples, how does one know whether an adult or peer's response to a targeted behavior is reinforcing or punishing? The answer lies only in a careful study of the data. Is the targeted behavior decreasing as a function of the consequences it elicits? If so, then these consequences are having the desired effect. Are positive behaviors increasing as a result of the responses that follow these behaviors? If so, then you are probably providing the appropriate consequences (i.e., reinforcing contingencies).

Elements of a Behavioral Approach to Consultation   According to Dougherty (2000), a behavioral approach to consultation has three elements:

1. A behavioral orientation is required. This means that the focus should be on behaviors that are either observable to the teacher or parent or reportable by the student. Hypothetical constructs and pseudo-explanatory concepts and labels, such as attention deficit/hyperactivity disorder (ADHD) or Conduct Disorder or others listed in the DSM-IV (American Psychiatric Association, 1994), are not regarded as constructive except for purposes of communication among experts. It is not valuable to state that a student acts in a certain way because he has a mental illness or disease, as popular and seductive as that approach may be. The behaviorist does not say that a student is

out of her seat and running around the room because she has ADHD. Rather, the behaviorist is inclined to say that the student engages in an excessive amount of out-of-seat behavior (operationally defined and usually determined in relation to a norm for a given classroom or other setting), which you can call ADHD if you want. ADHD cannot be treated, but out-of-seat behavior may be treatable, either by a contingency change procedure or through medication. If medication is used, the behaviorist believes that the prescribing physician must also be a behaviorist because the physician is treating the behaviors (out-of-seat and possibly others). To learn if drug therapy has been successful, a behaviorist counts the occurrence and duration of out-of-seat behavior or some other targeted behavior. The behaviorist (and the physician–behaviorist) share the same goal: to reduce the frequency of symptoms because, as the behaviorist believes, the symptom is the disease (Ullmann & Krasner, 1965).

2.   Behavioral consultation, when used as part of a case study and in a collaborative rather than an expert fashion, is usually an indirect service-delivery method. A consultant observing a student is being passively direct because such observation does not involve interaction with the student. The behavioral consultant, therefore, does not deal directly with the student but directly with the consultee, as demonstrated by Figure 1.3, which shows the triadic nature of consultation.

3.   Direct training is given to consultees when it is clear that they need assistance in performing the behaviors needed to carry out a behavioral plan. For example, some teachers don't know how to use contingency contracts or how to be consistent and contingently appropriate in their use of praise. The behavioral consultant teaches these skills directly to consultees. In turn, the consultee (teacher or parent) directly teaches prosocial behavior to the student.

Lutzker and Martin (1981) describe six elements of a behaviorally oriented problem-solving sequence:

1.   The problem must be described in behavioral terms. For example, if the referring teacher says that she would like help with a student because he has ADHD, the behavioral consultant asks the teacher to describe the behaviors that concern her. This discourages reliance on nonfunctional terminology and allows the consultant and the consultee to communicate more productively. Some teachers and parents will need help on "staying behavioral" because they have not been taught to do so.

2.   The behaviorist wants to obtain a functional assessment of the target behavior(s). This means that she asks the referring teacher to describe the (at least, suspected) antecedents and consequences of the behavior and to give a topological overview of the behavior itself. This overview consists of describing the motor and verbal behavior of the student, the frequency of the targeted behavior, the duration of episodes (such as crying or tantrums), the intensity of the behavior, and any other factors that will help the consultant understand the nature of the referral problem. The consultee will also be asked to speculate as to the motivation behind the behavior: Why does the student do it? What is he trying to get or avoid with the behavior? Usually the consultant will also want to observe these behaviors

unobtrusively. Functional assessment, and its follow-up activity, functional analysis, are described further in Chapter 6.

3.   After the nature of the referral behaviors has been well established, the consultant and the consultee will decide which behaviors to work on in what order. This sometimes requires negotiation between the consultant and the consultee because of differing values and pressures.

4.   The generation of behavioral objectives is the next step. Here the consultant and the consultee agree about what they want to see in terms of change. Must the student give up all instances of the referred behavior, or will an 80 percent reduction be acceptable? How will we know when the prosocial replacement behaviors we will teach have reached a suitable level? It is always a good idea to agree about the specifics of a planned behavior change. Differences between the parties may be avoided if both the consultant and the consultee know what their mutual objectives are.

5.   The program is then ready to be designed and implemented. A typical initial step is to be sure that a baseline of frequency, intensity, and so on has been obtained. The intervention is then put into place, and data about the important topological features continue to be gathered. If it appears that the selected intervention is not having a desirable effect, the consultant and the consultee need to confer and make appropriate changes.

6.   During the course of the intervention(s) and after the program has been completed, it is appropriate to evaluate the program. Because behavior modification activities are complicated to implement in a classroom, and because antecedents and consequences are truly difficult to predict and control, it is not surprising to achieve results somewhat different from those you planned for in step 4.

Stages in the Behavioral Consultation Model   Bergan (1977) and Bergan and Kratochwill (1990) have delineated four stages that form the structure of the behavioral consultation model: problem identification, problem analysis, plan implementation, and problem evaluation. The following is a description of the activities carried on during these stages and an indication of some of the objectives that underlie each stage (Gutkin & Curtis, 1999; Martens, 1993).

In *problem identification*, the consultant receives and discusses a referral with the consultee and attempts to clarify its nature. Is it primarily a behavior/adjustment problem or a learning problem? What do the terms used by the consultee to describe the problem mean operationally? The objectives of this stage are to assess the nature of the consultee's concerns; prioritize problems; select target behavior(s); make an initial estimate of the problem's seriousness; decide on tentative goals; discuss the antecedents, sequences (i.e., how the behavior unfolds in time), and consequences; discuss possible data-collection ideas; and set a next meeting date.

In *problem analysis*, the consultant delves further into the nature of the problem, usually by observing it directly, conducting a functional assessment if appropriate, and brainstorming possible interventions. The objectives are to analyse the data; solidify goals; verify antecedents, behavioral sequences, and consequences; and design and get agreement about the intervention plan. If the behavioral consultation is being conducted in the collaborative mode, the consultee makes the final determination about what to implement and how to do it, with the guidance and facilitation of the consultant. They also discuss ongoing data collection methods, and schedule the next interview and/or observation.

In *plan implementation,* the consultee proceeds with the appropriate interventions. The consultant's main objectives in this stage are to monitor what the consultee is doing (to ensure treatment integrity), suggest modifications as appropriate, and reinforce the consultee for their efforts.

For *problem evaluation,* Bergan (1977) suggests three steps: evaluating goal attainment, evaluating plan effectiveness, and planning postimplementation. The goals should have been established during the problem identification stage and should have flowed naturally from the nature of the problem. The primary objective of this stage is to determine how well the goals have been met. Continuation, modification, or termination of the plan are determined in this stage. A plan may look elegant and may have worked elsewhere, but the consultant and the consultee have to determine how well it has worked in the present case, which is always different in important, if subtle, ways from all other instances of similar problems.

Postimplementation planning refers to a discussion of how to proceed after the current consultative relationship is terminated. What steps should be taken to ensure that the problem won't recur? In school consultation, consultants should learn to expect recurrence of problems from certain students and from certain teachers. Some cases continually resurface due to students' home conditions; serious learning disabilities; or other biophysical, psychodynamic, or classroom ecological influences. Sometimes postimplementation simply means putting a partially successful case on the back burner, sometimes because a "tincture of time" is useful, sometimes because the pressure of other cases forces you into this situation.

If the consultant wishes to do a detailed analysis of the content of the interviews between the consultant and the consultee in an effort to evaluate their effectiveness, they can use the Consultation Analysis Record (CAR) (Bergan & Tombari, 1975), which involves coding tape-recorded consultation interactions according to the interview procedures described by Bergan (1977). The structure of the CAR technique is reviewed in the material on communication skills in Chapter 3.

Kratochwill and Bergan (1990) elaborate on the steps a consultant should take to implement the four stages I have described. Their set of suggested interview procedures and objectives is the most detailed of any model and certainly should be studied by all school-based consultants.

ACTIVITY 2.3

A teacher tells you that she is concerned about a student who is anxious. What else do you, as a behaviorally oriented consultant, want to know about the child? What are the behaviors of anxiety? Which can be treated, the anxiety or the behaviors? How might a traditional behaviorist differ from a cognitively oriented behaviorist in his approach to this problem?

ACTIVITY 2.4

Form teams of two (dyads). Member A thinks of a social relationship problem she has observed in a student. Member B acts as a consultant and tries to get functional information about the problem from the consultee. The consultant asks for a behavioral definition of the social relationship problem and gets information about the antecedents and consequences, frequency of occurrence, durations, intensities, and so on. Then reverse roles, seeking a behavioral definition concerning academic underachievement.

ACTIVITY 2.5

In dyads, the consultee lists five behavior or learning problems of a student. The consultant helps the consultee prioritize these concerns, and together they agree about what concerns to address first. They select one of the behavior or learning problems and do a functional assessment, obtaining as much information as they can about the problem, using only the interview process.

ACTIVITY 2.6

As a class, define behavioral objectives for the following: excessive talking out, gum chewing in class, and low academic productivity. Define these activities more accurately by inventing baseline data before establishing behavioral objectives. Add a time line to your plan.

Current Thinking About the Behavioral Model   Bergan (1995) has updated the behavioral model of consultation since its inception about twenty-five years ago. He points to a wide literature that supports this highly structured approach and indicates how it has assisted consultants and consultees in defining problems that can be operationalized and solved. He specifically indicates a problem-centered approach, which is not always evident in approaches taken by consultants who follow other theoretical or functional models. This approach avoids the focus on a referred student's negative behavior and instead asks questions that focus on a program of possible skill development. For example, instead of asking "What's wrong with Johnny?" the consultant asks "What would you like to see Johnny accomplish in the area of skill development this year?" While it is likely that referral questions may contain some explication of what a student is doing wrong (such as variations on "He won't behave or do his work"), this is not necessarily the problem the consultant should work on. Rather, it is more appropriate to stress the teaching goal for the student (such as "What social or academic skills does the student need to work on, and how can we arrange the environment, broadly defined, to see that this happens?").

The behavioral approach has considerable surface appeal in addition to a solid track record of empirical validation. Nevertheless, many teachers do not use behavioral approaches. Indeed, some teachers and administrators want nothing to do with them. Axelrod, Moyer, and Berry (1990) point to a number of reasons why this is so. Some teachers balk at this approach because data have to be kept, a teacher may have to change her own behavior, and programs need to be individualized. Also, reinforcement is often misinterpreted as bribery. Some teachers believe in the "Protestant ethic," by which they mean that students should do work because they are told to; thus, bribing them is unnecessary, even immoral. Such teachers believe that this approach may be all right for rats and pigeons but not for people.

Finally, most teachers have not been trained in behavioral techniques, and a "behavior mod" zealot may turn them off by conveying a superior attitude. Given the rich data base that supports the behavioral approach, it is not surprising that those who have studied and applied it successfully might be evangelistic in their efforts to get others to use behavioristic methods. Astute behaviorally oriented school consultants need to guard against this attitude or impression. They need to remember that teachers usually don't read the *Journal of Applied Behavioral Analysis,* may not be at all impressed with studies done under controlled conditions (which classrooms are not), and are primarily concerned with the students in their classrooms, not others who seem to live in laboratories somewhere else.

Kratochwill and Van Someren (1995) have also indicated reasons why behavioral consultation is not always successful in the schools. Among the reasons they discuss are a lack of specific training of consultants, little training of consultees for their roles in consultation, difficulties in identifying target behaviors, acceptability of behavioral techniques, and potential problems in consultant–consultee relationships.

Witt, Gresham, and Noell (1996) are concerned about the behavioral model for different reasons, one being the underlying assumptions of this form of consultation. They believe that the standard behavioral model relies too much on teacher (consultee) opinion, teacher reports of treatment integrity, and teacher analysis of the success of treatment. In their provocative article, they promote an alternative that they refer to as "behavior analytic." In this approach, which relies on functional analysis (see Chapter 6) rather than the behavioral model's problem analysis, the consultant conducts mini-tests of environmental variables so that factors maintaining or suppressing target behaviors can be isolated. In functional analysis, the reason for the behavior is important; it may not be in behavioral consultation. Erchul and Schulte (1996), although agreeing with many of the points made by Witt et al. (1996), offer a lively rejoinder, pointing out that, while teacher opinion (for example, about the severity of behaviors before, during, and after a behavioral intervention) may sometimes be an undependable measure of reality, it may well be the best measure available. These differences of opinion create fertile ground for empirical studies.

Bergan (1995) has pointed to an area of development in behavioral consultation that currently receives more emphasis: family involvement. Recognition of the central role of family-centered contingencies in the lives of children has prompted current behaviorists, such as Kramer (1990) and Sheridan and Kratochwill (1992), to expand their ideas about behavioral applications with families. This aspect of the behavioral model is referred to as *conjoint behavioral consultation* (Sheridan & Colton, 1994; Sheridan, Kratochwill, & Bergan, 1996). In this system, both parents and teachers serve as consultees, thus increasing the complexity of the consultant's data-gathering and communication efforts. In one example of this approach, Colton and Sheridan (1998) report on a conjoint project utilizing the efforts of both parents and teachers in a collaborative effort to modify the play behaviors of three boys with ADHD. By utilizing a 15-day social-skills training program with four components (coaching and role playing, self-monitoring, home-school communications, and positive reinforcement) which was individually tailored for each student, they were able to demonstrate a marked reduction in the negative behaviors associated with ADHD and an increase in positive behaviors displayed by all three boys which held up at follow-up for two of the three boys. I hope that methods characterized by conjoint efforts between school personnel and parents will have more far-reaching results than interventions designed to touch only on the student's hours in school.

Summary of the Behavioral Model   Henning-Stout (1993) has summarized the basic tenets of the behavioral approach:

1. All behaviors are learned.
2. The establishment, maintenance, and change of social behavior can be explained through the observation of functional interactions of the individual, his or her behavior, and the environment.
3. Assessment, intervention, and evaluation of the intervention's effectiveness are directly linked.
4. Behaviors of focus must be observable, measurable, and quantifiable.
5. Environmental antecedents provide powerful points for initiating change.
6. Because learning histories vary, intervention is necessarily idiosyncratic.
7. Understanding and intervening with any behavior is guided and modified according to systematically collected data reflecting the frequency, intensity, or duration of that behavior.
8. For one person's behavior to be changed, behaviors in other individuals interacting within the environment of focus must also be modified. (pp. 25–26)

This brief overview of the behavioral model presents a foundation for understanding and appreciating the contributions of this model to the consultation process. You may detect considerable overlap between what has been presented here as the behavioral model and what is presented later in Chapter 5 as an ecobehavioral model (Gutkin & Curtis, 1999). The ecobehavioral model is a blend of the behavioral model and a more generic problem-solving model presented earlier by Gutkin (1993) and Gutkin and Curtis (1982, 1999). Readers intending to pursue the behavioral approach to consultation should review the primary sources of information to obtain a more thorough understanding of the methods used by behaviorally oriented consultants (Alberto & Troutman, 1999; Bergan, 1977; Bergan & Kratochwill, 1990; Elliott & Busse, 1993; Gresham & Davis, 1988; Gutkin & Curtis, 1999; Kazdin, 1984; Kratochwill & Bergan, 1990; Kratochwill, Elliott, & Rotto, 1995; Martens, 1993; Meichenbaum, 1977; Sheridan et al., 1996; Sugai & Tindal, 1993; Witt & Elliott, 1983; Zirpoli & Melloy, 2001).

Mental Health Model

The mental health model is based on psychodynamic theories of human interaction (Conoley & Conoley, 1992; Erchul, 1993). It was primarily developed by Gerald Caplan, M.D. His seminal text, *The Theory and Practice of Mental Health Consultation* (Caplan, 1970), reviews the many intricacies of this complex model. In 1993, Dr. Caplan and Ruth Caplan authored an updated text on the mental health model, which added the word "collaboration" to the title: *Mental Health Consultation and Collaboration*.

In strong contrast to the behavioral model, which emphasizes contingencies of reinforcement, modeling, and self-reinforcement, the mental health model stresses intrapsychic feelings and shows how they affect interpersonal relationships. Caplan based his ideas largely on his work as a consulting psychiatrist in Israel after the Second World War. His task was to assist the staffs of relocation centers and orphanages for children displaced by the war to deal effectively with the wide array of emotional and behavioral problems exhibited by these children. He discovered that (1) there was not nearly enough time for the professional staff to provide the individual therapy desirable, (2) the caretaking staff needed assistance in dealing with the extremity of the emotional problems of the children, (3) the caretaking staff did not possess the necessary skills to deal with a wide range of behavior management problems, (4) some staff seemed to fall into stereotypic belief systems that resulted in faulty child-rearing methods, (5) staff could improve both their attitudes toward their work and their methods of dealing with their clients if given time to express their needs and concerns, and (6) the mental health staff profited from visiting the institutions in which the caretaker staff did their work rather than requiring that the caretakers come to the mental health staff offices. Caplan presented many of these ideas in his earlier works on preventive psychiatry (Caplan, 1964).

Although the primary distinguishing factor in mental health consultation is its emphasis on intra- and interpersonal variables, it does not ignore environmental influences. Caplan makes many references to the importance of the ecological context in which behavior unfolds, such as communication patterns between the client and the consultee and organizational and community influences on the behavior of both clients and caregiver-consultees.

Every school-based consultant needs to be sensitive to one of Caplan's discoveries: when outsiders (consultants) enter the world of insiders (consultees), they need to understand that they are entering a world different from their own, one that has its own norms, beliefs, habits, and ways of doing things. No matter how expert a consultant may be, the consultee is largely responsible for the way in which an intervention is finally put into effect. Therefore, Caplan and Caplan (1993) stress the need for a collaborative approach to consultation. They discuss the problems that arise when the consultant attempts to take over a case and assume the expert role. This may reduce the consultee's involvement in the case and his subsequent willingness to generate or follow through on solutions to the referral problems.

Key Concepts of the Mental Health Model   Caplan and Caplan (1993, pp. 21–23) list fourteen basic characteristics of their mental health model. The following list adapts five of these characteristics as they apply to school consultation:

1. The relationship between the consultant and the consultee is coordinate and non-hierarchical. Throughout this book I emphasize this basic tenet of the collaborative model. Even though the consultee has referred the problem to the consultant and might therefore be thought of as the dependent person in the dyad, the working relationship established in the collaborative model soon clarifies an "equal-partners" dyad.

2. Consultation is usually conducted as a short series of interviews. In public schools there is no time for many lengthy sessions between a consultant and a consultee. While it may be true in extreme cases that weekly meetings occur for some months, the usual case involves between two and five meetings, some of which may be brief phone conversations. Because of the large number of students needing the services of those staff who deliver consultative services, there is necessarily a premium on time efficiency. It follows that there is little inclination to develop any sort of dependency relationship between a consultant and a consultee.

3. The consultant does not get involved in the personal problems of the consultee. If it is clear that the consultee is undergoing some sort of emotional conflict that impedes her ability to carry out a consultation plan, the consultant should make an appropriate referral to another source for counseling. It is clearly best not to confuse the consultation role with counseling, even though it is often tempting to do so. As I indicated in the various definitions of consultation presented in Chapter 1, the process of consultation should be centered around work-related problems, not the intrapersonal issues of the consultee.

4. A long-term goal of all consultation is to improve the on-the-job functioning of the consultee. Toward that goal, the consultant attempts to give the consultee skills, knowledge, confidence, and a sense of objectivity that the consultee may be lacking and that will be useful in future cases that the consultee might have to deal with.

5. Caplan intends his model to be used primarily for mental health problems. However, the ideas discussed in his work can apply to any behavior or learning problem a student is experiencing.

Types of Mental Health Consultation   Caplan and Caplan (1993) discuss four types of consultation: client-centered case, consultee-centered case, program-centered administrative, and consultee-centered administrative. The first two types concern individual client (or small-group) issues, and the latter two are system-oriented. Another way to divide the four types is in terms of focus: on the consultee or on the client (or the program in the case of the program-centered administrative type). The following section breaks down these groupings according to type, purpose, and example.

Type: Client-centered case consultation

Purpose: The consultant deals directly with a client (student) in order to provide some service (such as assessment or treatment) or to develop ideas that a consultee can use when working with the client. The consultant has little direct interaction with the consultee. This seems to be the least pure form of collaborative consultation. The consultant is acting as an expert in the areas of assessment or therapy with the client and then passing on information that will assist the consultee in the performance of her responsibilities vis-à-vis the client. Caplan and Caplan (1993) point out that this form of consultation is in the "traditional type of specialist consultation of medical practice" (p. 19), and as such has only limited applicability to the central theme of this text: collaborative interactions.

School-based example: A teacher refers a student to the resource specialist or school psychologist because of learning problems. This specialist takes the student from the regular education classroom, does some assessment work, and writes a report for the teacher telling him what he should do to help the student.

Type: Consultee-centered case consultation

Purpose: The consultant deals directly with the consultee in order to assist the consultee in formulating a plan for dealing with the client. The consultant has little or no direct interaction with the client. This is the model described by the triangle pictured in Figure 1.3.

School-based example: The resource teacher meets with the regular education teacher, assists her in making a plan for helping a student, and monitors the plan as it unfolds. In this situation the consultant may never meet directly with the student; meeting is optional, depending on the situation.

Type: Program-centered administrative consultation

Purpose: The consultant evaluates a policy or program and develops a plan for improving it.

School-based example: A reading expert, possibly from outside the district, is brought in to evaluate a district's reading program and to develop a set of guidelines for improving it.

Type: Consultee-centered administrative consultation

Purpose: A consultant works with a group of consultees to help them develop better ways of managing their program.

School-based example: The consultant meets with elementary school principals (consultees) to review their schoolwide behavior management methods and to help them develop better plans that will meet their needs as well as those of their students.

Each of these four types are commonly used in the schools. The first two, which focus on individual student cases, are by far the most common, especially for internal, school-based consultants such as school counselors, special education teachers, and school psychologists. The last two tend to be relegated to external consultants or to administrators within the district, if only because of tradition. There is no reason why school-based consultants cannot perform these administrative consultation functions. Most of this text is devoted to individual or small-group consultation work; Chapter 10 focuses on the last two (administrative) types of consultation.

The Four "Lacks" of Consultees   Caplan and Caplan (1993) point out four "lacks" that may explain why a consultee has difficulty dealing with a client: *knowledge, skill, confidence,* and *objectivity*. In a situation in which *knowledge* is lacking, the consultee simply needs to know more about a targeted student or about techniques that can be used to assist the student. In school-based consultation, this lack occurs with some frequency. Some teachers do not know much about a student's background or about cultural factors that may be influential. Some teachers take pride in never reading the cumulative folders of their new students; others have not read psychological or medical reports that are already in the file. The consultee may not have a good grounding in various ways to teach reading or other academic subjects or how to question students in order to develop their critical thinking skills. As Sandoval (1996) indicates, "Some consultees are a *tabla rasa* and need to be helped to gain knowledge" (p. 93). Later in this chapter I will expand on the idea that one of the roles of school consultants is that of teacher. Consultee-centered consultation is a good place to use this role. To whatever extent is necessary, the school consultant needs to impart information to the consultee in order to help her deal more effectively with the student, hoping that these facts or insights will be used with other students as appropriate. Many topics designed to increase the knowledge base of consultees can be delivered in staff development forums, which are discussed later in this chapter.

A lack of *skill* is diagnosed when the consultee has the requisite knowledge but doesn't seem to know how to apply it successfully. The best way to diagnose this condition is to watch the consultee apply his knowledge to solve a particular problem. The consultant may observe that the consultee knows what to do but not how to do it. An example might be the use of contingency contracts. The consultee has written a good contract but does not enforce it consistently or tries to demand more than the contract calls for before delivering the specified reinforcer. Another example is communication skills. Most teachers know about reflective or active listening yet may never have practiced these skills; therefore, they misapply them without knowing they are doing so. Once again the role of the consultant is to help the consultee perfect his skills so that he can function more effectively with his current and future students.

The third lack is *confidence*. Some teachers and parents simply lack confidence to try things they know how to do or could easily learn. They may have tried specific tactics in the past and believed they were not successful, or they may be currently dealing with what appears to be a more difficult or threatening situation and are fearful of trying something and possibly failing. Consider a successful teacher who takes on a new challenge of teaching a class for emotionally disturbed students. The behaviors of these students frighten the teacher. During the first few weeks, the teacher seems reluctant to implement the behavior management techniques that have always worked in the past and were part of the reason he was nominated for this position. He would benefit from having someone observe the interactions in the class and assist him in gaining more confidence in his ability to redirect these students.

According to Caplan and Caplan (1993), the fourth lack, *objectivity*, is the most common "in a well-organized institution or agency" (p. 107). If consultees have the knowledge, skill, and confidence it takes to deal with their work-related problems but are still having difficulty, they may be letting subjective perceptions and judgments impair their ability to deal with issues involving students who present with difficult problems. The Caplans indicate five connected reasons for a lack of objectivity: direct personal involvement, simple identification, transference, characterological distortions, and theme interference (Caplan & Caplan, 1993, p. 108). The most important of these is theme interference, and it is a good example of the psychodynamic roots of the mental health model.

In *theme interference,* the consultee sees something in the behavior of the student that reminds her of some unresolved conflict in her own life. Knowledge of this conflict may not be available to the consultee on a conscious level; hence, she is blocked from realizing what is going on and why the behavior bothers her so much or why she seems unable to deal with it. The consultant knows, or at least suspects, that theme interference is occurring when an otherwise objective, reasonable consultee is suddenly upset about and unable to deal effectively with a problem that doesn't seem all that difficult to an objective observer. The lack of objectivity leads to faulty tactics, overreactions, and an inability to separate the student from his behavior.

The consultant's role in theme interference reduction is to help the teacher (or parent or administrator) to see the case in more objective terms, to reassess the behaviors of concern, and to see that the student does not represent some example of the general theme that underlies the consultee's lack of objectivity. This process is common in school-based consultation. It sometimes becomes clear to the consultant that progress is stymied because the teacher may have curious misperceptions about the reasons for, or meaning of, the student's behavior. The best tactic at this point is to stick to the facts, review possible tactics, point out that the feared outcome of the student's behavior is not as likely as some other outcomes that the teacher can control, and hope that the teacher has enough confidence to follow the consultant's lead and try things she may initially fear are doomed to fail.

ACTIVITY 2.7

A teacher consultee tells you that he expects the student to be loud and sarcastic because he has seen many children from similar home backgrounds "and they all act like that." Assume that you understand this to be a case of theme interference. How would you, as a consultant, get this consultee to understand that this line of reasoning may be coloring his expectations? How might you get the consultee to be more objective in dealing with the client? Do you think it may be a simple case of a lack of knowledge, as suggested by Sandoval (1996)?

ACTIVITY 2.8

Select one of Caplan's four lacks. Specify the way in which that lack manifests itself among a group of teacher consultees. Design an inservice or staff development meeting to assist consultees with this lack. For example, if you select *skill*, develop a workshop to teach the deficit skill (such as communicating with teenage girls who use an abrasive communication style).

It is interesting to note that Caplan refers to objectivity as a possible lack on the part of consultees. However, though Caplan doesn't address it, it certainly may be a lack on the part of a school consultant, as could any of the other three lacks. All consultants need to continually look at their own behavior and question themselves about the possibility that the plans they suggest are a result of their own lack of objectivity. There is no doubt that each of us has his or her own personal baggage, beliefs that may not be appropriate, specific ideas that we like even though they may not be the most appropriate for any given situation, and so on. Sometimes we learn about this from our consultees, who question our ideas based on the objective facts. Self-reflection can go a long way toward guarding against this possibility, as can review of your work with other competent practitioners in the schools.

Certainly a consultant's lack of objectivity, which may be misinterpreted as some lack within the consultee, can lead to resistance from the consultee. Alternatively, a school consultant may not have fully adopted his current role expectations or may not have separated emotionally from his previous work, perhaps as a resource room teacher. He may find himself over identifying with a teacher consultee and wish to rescue that teacher by offering to take a student who manifests learning or behavior-adjustment problems out of the mainstream and do individual work with the student as he used to do. As Marks (1995) indicates, it is hard to be a true facilitator if your desire is to be a rescuer.

ACTIVITY 2.9

Caplan talks about theme interference as a lack on the part of the consultee. However, consultants may also allow this lack to affect their work. List some common themes among school-based consultants that may interfere with their abilities to have objective, compassionate dealings with students or consultees.

In regard to the issue of one's own lacks, it is important to note that not all likely candidates for the position of school-based consultant should be asked to do the job. Holland (1966), in discussing one's vocational choice, points out that those who prefer routine and wish to avoid conflict or the pressure of being assertive may have a very difficult time being a consultant because consultation is not routine, may involve some degree of confrontation, and requires the ability to be assertive. Lacks in these areas should be remediated if possible or lead to a decision to move to some other aspect of schoolwork that does not depend on these skills or on the communication or interpersonal skills discussed in Chapter 3.

Three lacks—skills, knowledge, and confidence—are a reality in the schools (as they are in most settings related to human services work, including parenting), but the fourth lack—objectivity—which the Caplans believe is the most common, does not seem to be as insidious as they suggest. Gutkin (1981) has found that loss of objectivity related to theme interference is actually the least common of the problems that teachers manifest compared to possible lacks of skill, knowledge, or confidence. Sandoval (1996) gives examples of how a consultant worked with teachers of students with physical disabilities to help them to reconceptualize their "themes" about the abilities and limitations of students with these disabilities. The "themes" these teachers held were reconceptualized as lacks in the area of knowledge.

Current Approaches to the Mental Health Model   Caplan's model has been modified since its original description in 1970, and some of his basic tenets have been revised to bring them into line with behavioral–ecological views. Hodges and Cooper (1983) have reconceptualized Caplan's four lacks and four types of consultation into three newer models of consultation that are well designed for use by school consultants.

The *educational* model presumes that the teacher is lacking knowledge or skill, and the solution is to teach these skills, commonly through inservice or staff development sessions. When working with individuals, the consultant can model a new or different way of dealing with a student.

The *individual-process* model assumes that the teacher is having difficulty because of personality issues, biases, or detrimental beliefs. Today students with disabilities are more often included in general education classes and settings, and it is not uncommon for general education teachers to continue to resist this movement because of biases against the notion of inclusion or because they believe it will be detrimental to students or to their ability to teach. These problems are similar to theme interference issues. Suggested tactics to deal with problems in this area include inservice staff development on issues related to inclusion and ways to make it work, strength building, and other strategies to improve personal functioning (Joyce & Showers, 1995).

The s*ystems-process* model is espoused by Hodges and Cooper and is related to Caplan's administrative consultation types. Here the consultant tries to work with the whole system (for example, the school, the district, or another administrative configuration) in an effort to effect change that will in turn influence the lives of the consultees and the students within the system.

Marks (1995) has recently modified the Parsons and Meyers (1984) systemic approach, which is based on four targets: *direct service to the client* (similar to Caplan's client-centered consultation), *indirect service to the client* (a bridge between client-centered and consultee-centered consultation), *direct service to the consultee* (similar to Caplan's consultee-centered consultation), and *direct service to the organization* (where the system or organization becomes the client, similar to Hodges and Cooper's systems-process model). Parsons and Meyers believe that it was appropriate to think of all problems (referrals) as indications of systemic (level 4) problems, with the system being the first consideration for intervention. Marks believes that a holistic approach that conceptualizes consultation at any of Parsons and Meyers' levels can lead to a systemic impact. Marks correctly points out that, for internal school-based consultants, starting at the level of the referral (usually level 1 in Parsons and Meyers's scheme), the consultant can effect changes that begin to spread upward through the system. According to Marks, the internal consultant should look for opportunities to make each consultation case have implications for system improvement that go beyond one teacher and one classroom and become part of a pattern of changes that influence the way in which a district delivers its services.

Caplan, Caplan, and Erchul (1995) have presented their views on the importance of the shift to a collaborative model for school consultants who want to use a mental health approach. The Caplans continue to believe that the term *consultant* should refer to an outside expert who has psychological distance from the consultee and the situation in the school. Schools, however, have embraced the idea that internal staff (counselors, special education teachers, psychologists, mentor teachers) should do consultation. I am convinced that this school consultation should be collaborative consultation since it is an indirect service delivered in a non-hierarchical atmosphere of collaboration among experts from diverse fields. The two terms (*consultation* and *collaboration*), although they define specialized purposes (see definitions in Chapter 1), fit together well when the interaction among school personnel fits the description previously presented.

ACTIVITY 2.10

Can a consultant use ideas from behaviorism and the Caplan model in the same case? Can a person be both a psychodynamicist and a behaviorist? Discuss these questions in regard to a sample case, such as that of a student referred for acting-out behavior. See Maital (1996) for a discussion of this possibility.

Summary of the Mental Health Model   The mental health model espoused by Caplan (1970) and Caplan and Caplan (1993) is not as commonly used in the schools as is the behavioral model. The mental health model is important because it serves to emphasize aspects of interpersonal and intrapersonal relationship factors that are not regarded as important in the behavioral model. The four lacks, especially the first three (knowledge, skill, and confidence), need to be addressed. The fourth lack, objectivity, seems (fortunately) not as common as Caplan suggests. The variations of Hodges and Cooper (1983); Parsons and Meyers (1984); Marks (1995); and Meyers, Brent, Faherty, and Modafferi (1993) seem to have more appeal and practical utility.

Caplan, Caplan, and Erchul (1995) have provided some contemporary views of mental health consultation. Brown et al. (2001) provide a more extensive review of these modifications than are found in this text.

FUNCTIONAL ASPECTS OF CONSULTATION

Functional Models of School Consultation

The process of consultation in the schools is continually evolving. Current beliefs have prompted individuals to develop working models of service delivery for consultation that vary depending on the philosophies, policies, practices, and goals of those charged with implementing services. Some of these models are based on theories of human behavior and derive their operations from these theories (see above: behavioral and mental health models), while many others borrow from theoretical positions but also depend on notions of human behavior, influence, and, to some extent, values that are not specifically tied to well-developed theoretical positions. They may be more appropriately thought of as functional or eclectic in their formulations and derivations.

West, Idol, and Cannon (1989) discuss 11 consultation models that range in theoretical base from strong (such as behavioral and mental health) to vague (such as education/training and expert):

1. *Mental health* (see above).
2. *Behavioral* (see above).
3. *Human relations.* The focus is on people's needs, attitudes, group processes, and so on. This approach is very helpful when dealing with issues of full inclusion or schoolwide policies in which attitudes can make significant differences in whether or not a new method will have a positive outcome (see Chapter 3 material on interpersonal skills).
4. *Organizational thinking.* After an organization is analyzed, training consists of helping personnel work together as a whole. At the district or local school level, it is helpful when people can take the broader view of change efforts and think through the effects at all levels (see Chapter 10).
5. *Education/training.* The consultant works directly on solving immediate problems. This is usually an expert model, and inservice or staff development activities (discussed later in this chapter) often apply.
6. *Expert.* Consultees are told what to do about students with difficulties, often by someone outside the school. To the extent that these interventions require adherence to a model not accepted by the consultee (e.g., behavior modification is still not accepted by many teachers because they regard it as "bribery," Grieger, 1977) or is seen as a "top-down" innovation, it likely will be either passively accepted or rejected outright (Sarason, 1990). This is often the fate of recommendations written by psychologists and speech therapists in their reports required by the special education assessment

process, especially if these recommendations have not been constructed in consultation with those expected to carry them out (Gutkin & Curtis, 1999).

7. *Clinical.* The consultant provides a diagnosis of the student and tells the consultee what to do with the information (similar to Caplan's client-centered consultation system; see above). This is a variant of the *expert* model.

8. *Program.* This is similar to organizational thinking but emphasizes the evaluation of programs.

9. *Advocacy.* The consultant advocates for the needs of the student, which may conflict with the needs of the school, but which still may be in the best interest of the student. Issues concerning advocacy are discussed in Chapter 4.

10. *Process.* This is similar to organizational thinking but emphasizes understanding how a system works, both interpersonally and in terms of product development (see Chapter 10).

11. *Collaborative consultation.* This model was discussed in detail in Chapter 1.

Heron and Harris (1987) and Dettmer, Dyke, and Thurston (1999) discuss the following additional models:

Stephens (systems) model. This is a fairly standard problem-solving approach that grew out of Stephens's (1977) directive teaching ideas. It is similar to the diagnostic–prescriptive approach to learning disabilities treatment that has been popular for many years. Implementation of the model requires five phases: assessment, specification of goals, determining interventions, implementation and measurement of progress, and evaluation. Strengths of this generic model include a highly structured format, a collaborative rather than expert approach, and an evaluation component. Possible weaknesses are that it seems time-consuming and may be too elaborate for many relatively simple issues. Baer and Richards (1980) provide an example of this model, demonstrating that the contingency developed as the intervention in their study (i.e., increased recess time) was effective in increasing the percentage of accuracy in both math and English assignments.

Resource/consulting teacher (R/ct) program model. The evolution of the function of the resource specialist in the public schools has been characterized by a reduction in the practice of sending most students identified as having disabilities to pull-out programs where they were given direct services by the RSP teacher to more current models that emphasize mainstreaming and inclusion. The R/ct model, developed by Idol, Paolucci-Whitcomb, and Nevin (1986), works as a bridge between these two models: The resource consultant offers direct service to referred students through tutoring and small-group instruction (similar to that in most special education resource rooms) but also offers indirect service through the consultation process to teachers who have mainstreamed or included students in their classrooms. This is one of the most common ways in which resource specialists and special day-class teachers are moving toward a consultation-based mainstreaming-emphasis model of service delivery for students identified as having disabilities. Its strengths include flexibility of programming depending on the needs of the students and other programming considerations, and opportunities for close communication between general educators and special educator–consultants. Possible problems are attributable to excessive case loads, insufficient time to plan, and role confusion. West and Idol (1990) have made suggestions for finding time for general and special educators to plan for collaboration using this R/ct model, including the following:

1. Specifying times to meet outside of classroom time.
2. Having someone else teach the class for one hour a week, which is then devoted to planning time.
3. Meeting during regularly scheduled whole school activities.
4. Periodically providing substitute teachers.

The case presented in Chapter 10 of this text utilizes certain aspects of the R/ct model as a solution to the challenge from a pull-out program to one emphasizing a consultation approach.

School consultation committee model. This model differs from the others in that most of the work is done through a committee. In many schools this committee (SST, SGT, TAT, and so on) is a general education function designed to deal with referrals, make recommendations, and (hopefully) forestall unnecessary referrals for special education assessment and likely placement. Knopf and Batsche (1997) found a 67 percent drop in special education placements through their Project ACHIEVE, which relied somewhat on a team consultation model among other components. Dettmer et al. (1999) point out that when the process is a committee function, responsibilities sometimes get diffused, confidentiality is harder to ensure, and the process is very time consuming. Ironically, in order to deal with the problem of time limitations, committees sometimes operate on strict time frames such as those suggested by Sprick, Sprick, and Garrison (1994), restricting the easy flow of ideas that is helpful to the problem-solving process. More information about this SST model is presented later in this chapter.

Vermont consulting teacher model. This model arose from a collaboration among local school districts, the Vermont Department of Education, and the University of Vermont (Heron & Harris, 1987). Teachers receive advanced coursework in behavioral analysis and student assessment at the university (or in local workshops) and are assisted at the local level by a consulting teacher. Services are performance-level rather than diagnostic-label driven. A strength of this model is the requirement that teachers take coursework at the university. Another is that parents must have input regarding proposed plans before they are put into effect. This aspect of the Vermont model predates what has recently become a popular modification of behavioral consultation known as conjoint (i.e., with parents) behavioral consultation (Sheridan, Kratochwill, & Bergan, 1997). A possible weakness of this model is that the consultants may be considered outsiders; they are often not regular employees of the district. Knight et al. (1981) did an evaluation of the effectiveness of this model over a four-year period and found the experimental schools indicated significantly greater gains in achievement than those using a more traditional special-education service-delivery model.

The problem-solving model. Over the past ten years a number of states have developed a set of decision-making alternatives for placing students in special education services. Through a variety of waivers obtained from government agencies, personnel in at least five states have implemented what is generally known as a problem-solving model, which is to be distinguished from a model heavily dependent on formal, norm-based psychometry, particularly the aptitude–achievement discrepancy model. In the problem-solving model, a team attempts to help a general education teacher in devising interventions which are closely monitored by a school-based consultant and evaluated primarily through curriculum-based measures. A student becomes eligible for special education only if interventions at the general education level prove insufficient. One of the strengths of this model is its emphasis on evaluating ecological variables such as school and class environment, curriculum, and instructional methodology. Ysseldyke and Marston (1999) and Powers (2001) review the generally positive results emanating from this alternative model.

Collaborative consultation model. This is the most widely known of the models discussed. Since 1990, it has been emphasized throughout the educational and psychological literature as the model of choice (Aldinger, Warger, & Eavy, 1992; Brown et al., 2001; Cole & Siegal, 1990; Conoley & Conoley, 1992; Dougherty, 2000; Friend & Cook, 2000; Pugach & Johnson, 1995; Reyes & Jason, 1993; West & Idol, 1990). Its leading spokespeople are Idol, Paolucci-Whitcomb, and Nevin (1986); Idol, Nevin, and Paolucci-Whitcomb (2000); Pugach and Johnson (1995); and Thomas et al. (1995). The key components of this model are shared decision making and an emphasis on mutuality in all stages of the process. The definition of collaborative consultation given by Idol, Nevin, and Paolucci-Whitcomb (2000) is contained in Chapter 1. Here is a brief overview of the components that form the model's skills, knowledge base, and attitudes:

1. *Interpersonal, communicative, interactive, and problem-solving skills.* Effective consultants need to demonstrate interpersonal intelligence (Armstrong, 1994; Gardner, 1983): the ability to be sensitive to verbal and nonverbal behavior, to interpret subtle behavioral cues, and to respond effectively to feelings as well as words. Also included in this area are interpersonal attitudes. Idol, Nevin, and Paolucci-Whitcomb (2000) have listed 11 attitudes, including (3) behave with integrity, (5) take risks, and (9) respond proactively. The ability to work with others in groups, where many decisions about school-based problems are discussed (such as SSTs and IEPs), as well as in informal chats, is also necessary. Lastly, the effective collaborative consultant needs to have a firm problem-solving structure from which to operate. This ensures a steady progression toward goals based on a continuing accumulation of data.

2. *The knowledge base.* Idol, Nevin, and Paolucci-Whitcomb (2000) suggest 12 modules, or essential components of an underlying knowledge base, including

(1) knowledge of the elements of effective instruction, (5) ability to observe and interpret instructional environments, and (10) knowledge of effective classroom management and discipline.

These skills, knowledge, and attitudes make up what Idol (1990) referred to as the "artful base" of school-based collaborative consultation.

Roles, Skills, and Activities of School-Based Consultants

Professionals engaging in school-based consultation have as their primary role the responsibility of providing assistance to other school personnel and parents regarding issues involving students' learning and behavior/adjustment problems. This primary role requires skills in communication, interpersonal effectiveness, and problem solving (Dougherty, 2000), which are manifested in a wide range of activities. This chapter delineates the additional roles of school-based consultants, the skills they need to be effective in these roles, and some of the numerous activities they engage in while carrying out these roles.

Roles   The word *roles* refers to the perceived purposes or reasons for the existence of a job. People are employed, generally, to engage in role-specific behavior, which is often spelled out in a job description provided to a prospective employee. Increasingly, job descriptions for special education teachers, school counselors, and school psychologists refer to consultation as an expected role. In some states, this expectation is spelled out in laws or regulations. For example, in its Education Code, the state of California defines the role of resource teachers in part as the "Provision of consultation, resource information, and material regarding individuals with exceptional needs to their parents and to regular staff members" (Hinkle, 2001, p. 4–22 (3)). That same document also spells out an expectation that school psychologists will provide "consultative services to parents, pupils, teachers, and other school personnel" (p. A-28 (b)). Additionally, school counselors are expected to offer "counseling and consultation with parents and staff members on learning problems and guidance programs for pupils (p. A-27 (4)). Most other states have established similar legislative bases for the roles of school-based consultants.

The following are some of the roles that have been found appropriate for school-based consultation:

1. *Information delivery.*   The consultant gives consultees information, ideas, facts, opinions, and food for thought about students' learning and behavior/adjustment problems. For example, consultants may provide an explanation, in practical terms, of the meaning of an information-processing deficit manifested by a student identified as having a learning disability, or they may review methods of teaching sight vocabulary to students who are not profiting from whatever methods are currently being used.

ACTIVITY 2.11

Evaluate various models of SST that are being used in local districts or that are described in the literature. Have teams of five to seven people act out the ways in which these meetings are held. Discuss the merits of each system.

2. *Coordination/facilitation/teaching.* The consultant develops collaborative ways of facilitating planning for targeted students. An example is organizing a structured meeting of the regular education teachers of a targeted student to discuss ways of accommodating learning tasks to the student's abilities. Consultants need to think of themselves as "habit-change coordinators"—persons who recognize that, to change the behavior of targeted students, the adults who control contingencies and activities need to change the way they respond to these students. This involves changing the behaviors (habits) of the adults who provide direct services (teaching, parenting) to students.

3. *Indirect service provision.* The school-based consultant acts indirectly in the service of students by working directly with teachers and parents, who in turn (for the most part) are the direct service providers to the students. The vignettes at the beginning of this chapter show the need for this type of service. Although some part of the program developed for a student may involve direct services on the part of the consultant (such as counseling or specific skill development), it is generally understood that the primary service providers are the general education or special day-class teacher, the parents, or an outside agency.

The development of this indirect service role marks a watershed in the conceptualization of the work of many people who service students in the schools. Most people now being asked to engage in this role were originally trained to give direct service to students through teaching, counseling, assessment, or therapy (speech and language, occupational or physical, and so on). Their role has expanded to include the indirect service of consultation, which is usually carried out in the triadic model discussed in Chapter 1. Because of this shift from direct to indirect service, there may be some role confusion within schools and in the thinking of these newly ordained consultants. For example, consultants need to realize that they probably will have considerably less direct contact with the referred students compared to what they used to have. Their primary interaction with the student will now be through observation, usually in the consultee's classroom or on the playground. As you may know, students currently in university training programs are being specifically taught how to provide the indirect services discussed in this text. Many more experienced special education teachers are now developing these skills through various staff development, conference workshop, or self-training methods.

A number of writers have identified valuable and practical roles for school-based consultants. Lippitt and Lippitt (1986) have discussed five: (1) *objective observer-reflector,* in which the consultant passively observes the process of interaction between consultees and/or students and helps consultees understand how and why problems (or progress) may be occurring; (2) *process counselor,* which adds to the observer-reflector by actively engaging consultees in a discussion of their processes; (3) *fact finder,* which consists of gathering data and interpreting it in the interests of problem identification and resolution; (4) *trainer/educator,* in which the consultant presents technical information about behavior and learning processes, problems, and solutions; and (5) *advocate,* wherein the consultant presents specific ideas about how to deal with students who manifest behavior or learning problems, usually based on a point of view favored by the consultant. This last role is sometimes played by consultants who have strong beliefs and wish to have consultees buy into these beliefs. The desire to advocate for one's favorite approach to problem solving must be tempered with the overriding need to collaborate. As Abiden (1982) has indicated, pushing one's own ideas about how others should behave may be the "zenith of stupidity" in consultation, particularly in school consultation.

What determines which of the numerous roles is best to use in any given situation? Experience is the best determinant, but other variables may also be influential. Your values, theoretical predispositions, and skills; consultee preferences, expectations, and skills; time pressures; and supervisor expectations all combine to help determine the role that best fits. Choosing the proper role and knowing when to shift roles often determines one's degree of success as a school-based consultant.

Skills/Knowledge   To carry out the roles I have described, the school consultant needs to be skillful in a number of areas. Bradley (1994) has listed some of the essential skills and necessary components of the knowledge base for school consultants. These include the ability to examine the personal characteristics of consultees (including preferences and expectations) and to understand how the values and attitudes of consultees interact to affect the collaborative process; knowledge about communication dynamics, including the interactive process, problem-solving skills, and interpersonal skills; knowledge of stages in the consultative process as well as teaching and behavior management strategies and methodologies that may be valuable to consultees; and awareness of various models of consultation service delivery. Here is a sample of the skills identified by Bradley and others as crucial to the practice of school-based consultation:

1.   *Communication.*   Consultants spend much of their time simply talking and listening. Teachers, parents, bus drivers, administrators, and others need someone to talk to when they are unable to solve the puzzles created by students who aren't being successful in school. Because this is such a key role for the consultant, there is an expanded discussion of communication skills in Chapter 3.

2.   *Problem solving.*   The consultant engages consultees in the process of problem definition, analysis, and solution seeking. He interprets and breaks down barriers, encourages participation in the collaborative problem-solving process, facilitates the development of plans, and monitors implementation of these activities. Pugach and Johnson (1995) point out that the facilitative problem-solving role differs substantially from the way in which an expert may give advice because

facilitation specifically focuses on helping consultees develop their own ideas and skills. Being facilitative, rather than taking over problems for consultees, is one of the most challenging tasks for beginning consultants to learn. This is what a somewhat experienced consultant says about learning to be facilitative:

> In my early perception of consulting I viewed myself as the expert. Experience has taught me I am not. Expert language is usually understood by very few. Knowing how to frame good questions is an invaluable tool. I used to think I knew what was best for the child. Experience again has shown me that this is not so—we must all get our respective "what's bests" on the table and mediate. I felt that I needed to have all the workable solutions to the problem at hand, but this was assuming too much. I thought everyone likes and respects the "expert" and wants his or her help. I now perceive my task as one of earning the right to become part of the planning for any child. This means that I must be as knowledgeable as possible, not only in my own field, but about the total environment (physical and mental) of each child. I am still learning that effective intervention takes time and careful planning. (unknown author, cited in Dettmer, Thurston, & Dyck, 1993, p. 12)

Facilitation requires the ability to get people with different perspectives to work together. Being able to sit in on a teacher–parent conference and keep the conversation issue-oriented and directed toward solutions can make an immense difference in a student's life.

3. Plan development and implementation and progress evaluation. Closely related to facilitative problem solving is the expectation that the consultant will be able to assist with the actual development of an intervention plan, follow through with some degree of implementation monitoring, and assist with ongoing evaluation of the intervention. Dougherty (2000) has indicated that school consultants need to have these skills:

- Convincing people to accept them in the consultative role.
- Clarifying and defining the problem.
- Evaluating factors contributing to the problem.
- Interpreting data.
- Analyzing the forces that are related to nonproductive behavior of students and teachers.
- Developing plans with consultees through a collaborative process.
- Monitoring the implementation of these plans.
- Evaluating the success of these plans.

4. Interpersonal effectiveness. A basic question for consultants to answer is "If I have met once with a consultee, will he or she want to meet with me again?" A large part of this answer will be determined by the interpersonal skills of the consultant. Because this set of skills is so important, I have given detailed attention to it in Chapter 3.

West and Cannon (1988) asked acknowledged experts in the field of consultation to rate critical consultation skills. This resulted in a list of forty-seven skills in eight categories. Listed below are those eight categories, each with one representative skill:

Consultation theory and models. Match consultation approaches to specific consultation situations, settings, and needs.

Research. Translate relevant consultation research findings into effective school-based consultation practice.

Personal characteristics. Be caring, respectful, empathic, congruent, and open in consultation interactions.

Interactive communication. Use active, ongoing listening and responding skills to facilitate the consultation process (for example, acknowledging, paraphrasing, reflecting, clarifying, elaborating, and summarizing).

Collaborative problem solving. Evaluate intervention alternatives to anticipate possible consequences, narrow and combine choices, and assign priorities.

Systems change. Develop the role of change agent (such as implementing strategies for gaining support and overcoming resistance).

Equity issues and values. Advocate for services that accommodate the educational, social, and vocational needs of all students with or without disabilities.

Evaluation. Ensure that persons involved in planning and implementing the consultation process are also involved in its evaluation.

ACTIVITY 2.12

Some people can understand models better if they are pictured rather than defined with words only. Select one of the numerous models discussed in this chapter and draw a picture to help explain how the model works. You may wish to go to some of the original sources to get more specifics about each model before you try to represent it with a drawing.

Activities What does a school consultant do to operationalize the roles and skills we have just discussed? What are the actual, observable behaviors of school consultants? Here is a sample of the major activities of consultants, many of which have been alluded to in the discussion of roles and skills.

Conducting interviews or facilitating discussions. This is the primary activity of consultants, and Chapter 3 devotes considerable space to it. Group-oriented interview procedures, such as those found in SST and IEP meetings, are discussed later in this chapter and in Chapter 5.

Observing interactions. It is quite common for a consultant to be asked to take a look at a student, at the interactions of a number of students, or at classroom or playground dynamics. These activities are discussed in Chapter 5 and 6 (for behavior-related issues) and 8 and 9 (for teaching-learning issues).

Reviewing records. All students have information collected in their cumulative folders, and all students found eligible for special education and related services have a separate file of information that should be accessible to school consultants working in their behalf. Taking time to review a student's records to determine what others have said and done about her is essential.

Coordinating services. Although not a consultation activity per se, coordinating services may assist the case carrier (for students identified as exceptional) in processing the steps needed to provide services for these students or to direct the implementation of interventions for nonexceptional targeted students. Whenever there are more than two people involved in an intervention, someone must take charge of the process to see that all parties are fulfilling their roles. Otherwise, plans can go awry and confusion can develop. A consultant may be involved in face-to-face interactions, phone calls, faxes, e-mail, in-house memos, and so on. In complex cases especially, it is important to leave a paper trail attesting to everyone's efforts. Special education due process hearings, mediations, and court cases are sometimes won or lost on the strength of documented efforts (Prasse, 1986).

Keeping accurate records. Closely related to coordinating services is keeping track of your own efforts in some permanent fashion. For example, when a consultant meets with a teacher, a parent, or an administrator about a student, he should keep a written record of that interaction and provide a copy of it to the person with whom he met or place it in a central information location where others can see it, such as a running log of events that may be housed in the student's school records or special education file. Forms for this purpose are presented in Chapters 3 and 5.

In an effort to describe the various activities consultants engage in, along with other dimensions of their work, Blake and Mouton (1976) developed a Consulcube, a model of conceptualizing consultation into three dimensions: units of change (such as individuals or organizations), focal issues (such as power/authority or goals/objectives), and kinds of interventions (the roles or activities consultants engage in when trying to effect change in individuals or groups). Each kind of intervention can be translated into a role or an activity such as the following:

Acceptant. Here the consultant plays a somewhat passive role: listening, clarifying, supporting, and assisting the consultee to help understand the problems and her reactions to them without taking over or giving much direct help. It is a soft-touch approach to consultation, perhaps too close to what some writers have referred to as "feel-good" consultation.

Catalytic. This is somewhat similar to Block's (1981) "pair-of-hands" model in that the consultant takes an active part in obtaining data that help clarify the problem for the consultee. A school-based consultant might do some curriculum-based assessment of a client in order to assist the consultee to better understand the learning needs or progress of a student; or she might make a phone call to a parent, a task the consultee could do but for various reasons has not, thus blocking progress; or she might develop a contingency contract to show as an example for the consultee to consider.

Confrontation. Confrontation can assist the consultee in clarifying his conceptualization of the problem and breaking through thinking patterns that may not be objective. Consultees sometimes are not consistent; they say one thing but do another. Or they may adopt a strategy that is in their best interests rather than those of clients. Be careful with confrontation: On the one hand, a point has to be made; on the other hand, if you make it too strongly, you run the risk of alienating the consultee and destroying the relationship. The cases presented in Chapters 7 and 9 give examples of confrontation in the consultation process.

Prescriptive. This is the standard expectation of some consultants: They will give the consultee a prescription that will be accepted and carried out faithfully. It is similar to what Block (1981) calls the expert role. It is suitable for collaboratively minded school-based consultants only in an emergency or when the consultee is too inexperienced, immature, or perhaps overwhelmed to develop his ideas with the facilitative help of the consultant.

Theory and principles. Here the consultant provides some instruction to the consultee that may be applicable to a given case. For example, the consultant may teach the consultee about behavior modification techniques, review and rehearse methods useful in teaching academic content, or suggest communication methods useful for defusing conflict situations.

The Blake and Mouton (1976) conceptualization of types of interventions was written in the mid-1970s before the development of collaboration as an intervention-generating style of interaction. Given the current predominance of collaboration and its obvious advantages for school consultants, I believe it should be added to the Blake and Mouton (1976) conceptualization of interventions.

TWO SETTINGS FOR CONSULTATION: INDIVIDUAL AND TEAM-BASED

School consultants work with individual consultees and with teams of other consultants and consultees. Chapter 1 presents information about individual consultee work, in which the consultant accepts a referral from the consultee, meets individually with him, and together they work out a plan for understanding and dealing with the referral. Although there are variations in this scenario (such as two consultants or consultees, more than one client, and so on), generally this one-on-one model has been the most common form of school consultation (Brown et al., 2001; Dougherty, 2000; Friend & Cook, 2000; Thomas et al., 1995). It is popular and practical simply because it involves the least number of individuals. Excessive reliance on team-based meetings is often regarded as impractical and/or frustrating in schools because of the conflicting demands and time limits of team members who sometimes express conflicting, unresolvable opinions.

However, it is widely recognized that individual consultation by itself has serious limitations (Dettmer, Dyck, & Thurston, 1999; Evans, 1990; Friend & Cook, 2000; Rosenfield, 1987; Rosenfield & Gravois, 1996; Thomas, Correa, & Morsink, 1995). Recently school consultants have been emerging from this one-on-one micro level, recognizing that they should be working in and through teams more than they may have in the past. This change in emphasis has come about for a variety of reasons, including the following:

- If more people collaborate on a problem, it may result in a wider diversity of ideas about how to solve the problem (Cramer, 1998; DeBoer, 1995).

- Special education regulations require prereferral interventions, which are often, though not necessarily, developed in the context of a team meeting and are referred to variously as student study teams, teacher assistance teams, school guidance teams, school consultation teams, instructional consultation teams, intervention teams, and so on (Allen & Graden, 1995; Basham et al., 2000; Bay et al., 1994; Friend & Cook, 2000; Idol et al., 2000; Rosenfield & Gravois, 1996; Ross, 1995; Thomas et al., 1995).

- There is a current emphasis on school reform and restructuring, which depends on teamwork. Teams provide possibilities for change within a context of ownership and empowerment that is not available to individuals (Basham et al., 2000; Maeroff, 1993; Sarason, 1990).

- Ideas generated in a team spread throughout the team and often beyond in a ripple effect that has a potential impact on the larger environment of the school or district (Dettmer et al., 1999; Thomas et al., 1995). Chapter 10 is devoted to issues of system-level improvement through consultation with teams of constituents at the local school or district level.

In this section we are concerned with issues involving team approaches to dealing with referrals of individual children or small groups of children. We will first discuss the team that is primarily designed to deal with students referred for learning and behavior/adjustment problems, called the student study team (SST) throughout this book. Later we will discuss a broader concept of teaming that goes beyond the tightly focused meetings that constitute SST work and is devoted to the much larger issue of school reform.

Student Study Teams

The SST is essentially a general education function designed to assist teachers (and parents) in working out ways to more effectively meet their teaching and behavior management responsibilities to students. The membership of an SST usually reflects constituencies beyond that of general education, such as special education and ancillary services. The SST usually consists of a facilitator or leader (who may or may not be a school administrator), a recorder (someone assigned to keep notes on the procedures), the referring teacher(s), another teacher or two from the general education staff, a special education teacher, and possibly some ancillary staff (such as the school counselor or the school psychologist). Preferably, staff with interest or expertise in the problems being discussed is asked to participate when appropriate. Parents should be invited and encouraged to attend. Students may also be invited if the group believes that their presence will be helpful to the student concerned and the process.

SSTs mean various things throughout the country. There is no one format or approach that defines the activities of these teams. Indeed, they can have different approaches and styles in different schools within a district. What they do share is a common philosophy or purpose: to work together to solve learning and behavior/adjustment problems of students. According to Meyers, Valentino, Meyers, Boretti, and Brent (1996), educators believe that SSTs should have at least the following goals:

1. Help at-risk students and their teachers by providing alternatives in terms of teaching and behavior management strategies.
2. Prevent learning problems and unnecessary placement in special education.
3. Delineate and clarify suggestions for teachers.
4. Approach school problems by using teamwork and brainstorming.
5. From an administrative standpoint, provide a method for tracking cases and coordinating services.

To meet these goals, the SST usually meets on a weekly basis for varying amounts of time per student (depending on the complexity of the problem), and varying numbers of times concerning any given student. Examples of variations on this basic theme were presented earlier in this chapter in Functional Models of School-Based Consultation.

Districts and local educational agencies have developed myriad forms for SSTs to use to keep track of the proceedings, data, and plans that the teams discuss or develop. Figure 2.1 gives an example.

After the team meets and discusses the areas listed in Figure 2.1, action is taken as specified on the form for the period indicated, and the team meets again on the date listed as "next meeting date" unless some contingency suggests the need for an earlier meeting. Once again the team discusses the target student, this time possibly using a slightly altered form designed for the second and all further meetings regarding this student. An example of a follow-up meeting form is shown in Figure 2.2.

A copy of each form containing the information gathered and decisions made should be sent to each participant and all others mentioned on the forms. In the interests of economy, a single copy of the forms intended for use by all involved

Figure 2.1

SST information and planning form: Initial referral

Student: **Date:**   **Referring teacher:**

Age: **Grade:**   **Parent(s):**

Reason for referral:

Brief history (family, health, school):

Student assets or strengths:

Interventions tried, with results to date:

Questions to be answered:

Possible solutions (include resources needed, personnel involved, time commitment, locations of services, time lines):

Today's plan (include who, what, when, where, how):

Next meeting date:

Participants:

---

school personnel may be kept in a confidential place within the school. School personnel will be informed of this procedure. Obviously, whoever is the recorder will need to be given time to put his notes in good order for appropriate distribution.

The Importance of Structure

Schools have generally come to understand the need for providing a good deal of structure in these team meetings. Poorly organized meetings tend to be inefficient

Figure 2.2

SST information and planning form: Follow-up meeting

Student: **Date:**   **Referring teacher:**
Follow-up meeting #_____
Results of interventions:
Current status/continuing concerns:
Today's plan:
Next meeting date:
Participants:

and unproductive; busy teachers and others resent having to attend them. Elements of structure include having a set schedule for when the team will be meeting and who will be on it, with at least a week's notice given to expected attendees, along with the names of the students to be discussed. At least a week is needed to inform parents so that they can make arrangements if they plan to attend. In addition, the referring teacher and others who have information to contribute need time to prepare themselves and gather relevant data. Consideration needs to be given to time constraints: How long will the team meet and how much time will be devoted to each student? Although it is possible to spend one full hour on one student, this is rarely necessary. A more typical structure is to set the meeting for one hour, to discuss three or four students, and to select time allotments based on the leader's estimate of the amount of time needed at this meeting for each student. Usually the team leader will prepare an agenda for the following week at the end of each weekly meeting.

Figure 2.3 is an example of an agenda announcing an SST meeting for an elementary school.

The amount of time devoted to a given student (in Figure 2.3, 15 or 30 minutes) may not seem like enough to allow the team to fully discuss the status and needs of the student and those interacting with him. The choice is either to have a structured

Figure 2.3

SST meeting agenda

> **Memo to School Staff**
> **October 5, 2001**
> **SST Agenda for October 12, 2001—Smith School**
>
> 7:45—Sammy Wilson (initial meeting). Teacher: Persill; Ancillary to attend: Falama, Kampwirth, Jackson
>
> 8:00—Shawna Cutrell (follow-up #4). Teacher: Zill; Ancillary to attend: Kampwirth, Peterson
>
> 8:15—Bill Loftus (follow-up #1). Teacher: Simpson; Ancillary to attend: none; Student Bill Loftus will attend
>
> 8:45—Adjourn

time limit or to run the risk of talking excessively and thereby ruining any chance for other students to be discussed. There had been a tendency in the past to allow participants to say their piece, no matter the time cost. Currently, however, this is not common practice. As Rosenfield and Gravois (1996) point out, time is a most precious resource. In their efforts to introduce instructional consultation teams (IC-teams) to schools, they have had to confront this problem. They provide suggestions for facilitators to use to keep members of IC-teams on track.

Each SST needs to decide on its parameters based on the needs and norms of the school culture. However, all team members should be informed that, whatever structure is decided on, it should be taught in a staff development format, and parents should be informed of the structure when they attend their first SST. It is possible to put time limits on each of the separate elements of the SST meeting (see Figure 2.1), such as one minute for a statement of the reason for referral; three minutes for the family, health, and school history; and so forth.

Sprick, Sprick, and Garrison (1994) recommend seven structured steps to be used by an intervention planning team in a 25-minute session. Background for the problem is done in six minutes, goal building has two minutes, indicating behaviors of concern gets four minutes, determining consequences for irresponsible behavior is done in two minutes, brainstorming proactive strategies is done in four minutes, detailing the plan is covered in three minutes, and final details (which include the development of an evaluation plan) are given four minutes. Following this whirlwind of activity, the interventionist fills out an intervention summary form that spells out the responsibilities of all concerned. Although this hectic approach to consultation may seem unsettling to those used to a more casual process of events, it may be a useful antidote to those committees that can never get anywhere in the time allotted and thereby demonstrate the need for more structure in their deliberations.

However, in selected cases, it may be unduly rigid to impose an arbitrary set of limits; some students have a much more involved history and present with many more challenges than do others. Different teachers may have tried many interesting interventions before coming to SST, and these take time to be discussed. The development of plans in some cases is more involved than it is in others. All of these reasons, in addition to not wanting to rush parents who probably are not used to such a structured situation, argue against the predetermination of rigid time lines for any given segment of the SST plan. A total time limit, however, is recommended; your agenda is useless without it.

Meyers et al. (1996) point out that, in spite of the many real and potential advantages of an SST system, not all educators who participate are convinced that it is a useful expenditure of their time and effort. Prereferral intervention team members have indicated the following weaknesses of this teaming effort:

1. Insufficient teacher involvement/participation in the process.
2. Lack of respect for the teachers by some team members.
3. Meetings not held with sufficient frequency or consistency.
4. Inconsistent attendance by some team members.
5. Insufficient follow-up.
6. Process too slow and possibly delaying the provision of needed services (such as special education).
7. No solutions to problems.
8. Reluctance to refer to special education.
9. Problem with group process.
10. Consultation not provided sufficiently.
11. Consultation ideas difficult to implement.

Meyers et al. indicate that some respondents saw the strengths of the teams in the opposite of several of these problems. Obviously, the list contains a depressing reality: Not all efforts at team problem solving are effective. The variation across schools and districts can be immense. It is important to remember that the potential for team collaboration is positive; but poorly conducted team meetings, an inability or unwillingness to deal with predictable sources of resistance, and a lack of regard for some of the issues raised in this list will negate that positive potential and cause dissension and discouragement among the team members.

Further comments about SSTs appear in Chapter 5 in the description of how the SST can be used in the solutions-oriented consultation system (SOCS).

Beyond SST Reform as a Basis for Integrating a Teaming Philosophy

Over the past decade it has become clear that a team approach to assisting all students to become better learners has become part of the zeitgeist known as *reform* or *restructuring*. National leaders have formulated three major reform statements: *America*

2000, Goals 2000, and the *No Child Left Behind Act.* The first of these was proposed by the first Bush (1991) administration and consisted of six goals:

1. By the year 2000, every child in the United States will begin school ready to learn.
2. High school graduation rates in the United States will increase to at least 90 percent by the year 2000.
3. All students in fourth, eighth, and twelfth grades will be tested for progress in key subjects.
4. U.S. students will rank first in the world in science and mathematics achievement.
5. Every adult will be a skilled, literate worker and citizen.
6. Every school will be drug-free and will provide a climate in which learning can occur.

Many people welcomed these goals from our national leaders but were concerned that they might prove to be only rhetoric because no explicit promise for funding was attached to them nor did they address specifics about how to overcome the daunting problems still in existence when they were written (Halpern, 1992; Howe, 1991).

In 1994 President Clinton signed a federal school reform package (*Goals 2000*) that consisted of the same six goals plus two others:

1. The teaching force will have access to programs for continued self-improvement of professional skills.
2. Every school will promote partnerships that increase parent involvement and participation.

This more inclusive version of national standards is monitored by the National Educational Goals Panel and the National Council on Education Standards and Testing. The panel consists of government officials, both federal and state; the council is composed of government officials as well as leaders from business, education, and other arenas. Title III of the 1994 legislation provides funding in the form of federal grants to the states for reform efforts designed to meet the eight goals (Shriner, Ysseldyke, & Thurlow, 1996).

In January 2002, President George W. Bush signed into law, the *No Child Left Behind Act,* another far reaching piece of federal legislation. The requirements of this legislation are to require annual testing in reading and math of all students in grades three through eight, and to provide additional funds to support schools that are underachieving in a consistent pattern.

All this federal interest in our public schools stems from the fact that many Americans, both in and out of government, are concerned about problems that seem to be increasing: declining SAT scores, lowered international opinion about our graduates and their ability to compete in a global marketplace, increased drug use, gang activity, violence invading the schools, and an increase in students who are at risk for school failure and lifelong economic and personal–social problems (California Department of Justice, 1993; Chicago Public Schools, 1994). Educators know that lofty goals from the federal level do not necessarily lead to meaningful change at the local school level. It is still up to the local level to provide the planning that will earn the federal money and the implementation that will result in an effective use of the money.

Fundamental to all reform efforts is a belief that educators need to work more closely with each other and with representatives from the broader community, including parents, community leaders (such as police and mental health agencies), colleges and universities, and the business world (Goodlad, 1988). General and special educators focus primarily on in-school efforts to achieve the goals of reform by learning how to work more closely together (collaboratively) in the interests of students at risk for academic difficulties.

Curriculum is an area in which educators can get together to discuss a unified approach for dealing with diversity among learners. Knowledge of curriculum reveals some of the complexities that make current efforts at reform so difficult to achieve. To some people, curriculum reform means striving toward tougher standards for all students, a return to basics, annual high-stakes testing, and a kind of uniformity that some believe used to be the American standard. It often includes reference to phonics as an icon and a sure cure for education's ills (O'Neil, 1990; Shepard, 1987). Taking the opposite view are many urban and special educators, who predict that these tougher standards will lead to more student failure because they do not take into account the diversity among learners, including children with disabilities (Carnine & Kameenui, 1990). Trying to find some middle ground requires collaborative skills of the highest order.

The area of student adjustment also has two strong camps. One believes that the schools must not tolerate disruptive behavior, that students who choose to disturb the learning of others, willingly or otherwise, should be educated elsewhere, although where is not always described (Gallup, 1994; U.S. General Accounting Office, 1995). The other camp believes the schools are far too quick to ignore their responsibilities to disturbed or disturbing students. This camp believes that causes for disruptive behavior may lie in the ways in which schools and some classrooms operate (Alberto & Troutman, 1999; Sidman, 1989; Zirpoli & Melloy, 2001) and that we have a responsibility to these students in settings other than self-contained classes because these placements remove them from the opportunity to learn better behavior from students in the mainstream. Certainly, these students do not belong in the streets (Eitzen, 1992; Noddings, 1992).

Whatever the specific area of concern (curriculum, behavior problems, cultural diversity, physical-plant use, expertise sharing, decision-making systems, materials sharing, and so on), all can be discussed in an atmosphere that encourages shared problem solving. The older top-down, hierarchical, authoritarian administrative models are mostly passé. The challenge now is for educators, including teachers, ancillary staff, and administration, to realize that the newer models of shared governance, site-based, community-organized, and collaborative schools are not easy to develop or implement; it takes a new degree of commitment to make these models work.

CONSULTING WITH PARENTS AND FAMILIES

Consultation with parents is increasingly recognized as a valuable, indeed essential, responsibility of the school-based consultant (Brown et al., 2001; Dettmer et al., 1999; Marks, 1995; O'Shea et al., 2001; Sheridan, 1993; Sheridan et al., 1996; Turnbull & Turnbull, 1997). It is a truism that students identified as disabled and others at risk for school failure need to be served from a base broader than the one that occurs during the six hours of the school day. Aside from eight hours for sleep, there are another ten hours in a schoolchild's life. What goes on during those ten hours can make a significant difference in how well students achieve and behave in school (Booth & Dunn, 1996; Children's Defense Fund, 1999; Epstein, 1995; Hanson & Carta, 1996)).

Schools have traditionally believed in the value of school–home links; for students with disabilities, these links are required by the Individuals with Disabilities Education Act (IDEA). For at-risk students, more schools are reaching out with a variety of approaches and philosophies to embrace the family as a critical component in dealing with the challenges associated with the needs of these students (Berger, 1995; Buzzell, 1996; Swap, 1987). The benefits of parent consultation and/or collaboration include at least the following (Christenson & Cleary, 1990):

- For students, improved grades, attitudes, and school attendance.
- For teachers, improved attitudes and better parent and principal ratings.
- For parents, more interaction with children in a more productive way.
- More parental cooperation with school personnel in solving children's learning and behavior/adjustment problems.

The question for the school-based consultant is rarely as simple as "Should we contact the parents about this problem?" More likely questions center around issues of when the parents should be contacted, by whom, how often, and with what agenda, goals, or offers to assist.

When. In the solutions-oriented consultation system (SOCS) process discussed in Chapter 5, there are suggested specific entry points for interaction with parents. However, the process also allows this interaction to be continuous, preferably starting with a teacher who contacts the parents of a targeted student and continuing throughout the entire SOCS process, with the contact made by the consultant, the teacher, or both.

By whom. There are no formal rules as to who is the best person to be in contact with parents about their children. Traditionally, the classroom teacher has been the primary contact person, and this remains generally true when students have been identified as disabled and are being served primarily by a special education teacher. In today's more collaborative methods of serving the needs of identified disabled students, parent contact may be shared equally by either the regular or the special education teacher. Circumstances and need can determine the pattern (Dettmer et al., 1999; Thomas et al., 1995).

How often. Again, the answer depends largely on circumstances. School personnel try to balance the need to communicate with the parent's right to privacy; certainly it doesn't help to intrude into family life when it isn't appreciated. The sensitive consultant will determine the amount of parent contact necessary and the parents' willingness to engage in these contacts. Of course, the parents can take the lead by contacting school personnel whenever they want. Most parents do not abuse this privilege.

An agenda for parent consultation. The school-based consultant or teacher who contacts the parents needs to have a predetermined, specific agenda to govern her consultative interactions. Here are some topics to think about before contacting the parents:

- What exactly do I want to convey? What is the problem or issue? How can I frame it in an objective manner without stirring up parent defensiveness? A main purpose of the first contact is information trading. What information do I want to give, and what do I want to get?

- Just who is this parent? Do I know her? What is the family structure? Who lives at home? What are their resources?

- How can I frame my concern as an invitation for the parent to work with me? What positive things can I say about his child? How can I express my concerns in language he can understand? For most parents, use the language of laypeople; avoid jargon and technical terms.

- Assuming a positive, or at least neutral, response from the parent, what can I suggest as a next step? What do I want her to do? Shall I invite her in for a conference? Shall I give her a specific task? How can I suggest we collaborate?

- In the case of a family in which a language other than mine is spoken, who can translate for me? What implications does this have for the nature of the phone contact?

The consultant also needs to consider this information:

1. Each family constructs its own reality; members may not see the problem as you do.

2. Many families do not have the amount or type of education you have; be careful not to talk down to people.

3. Some families are not forthcoming about themselves or their customs, values, or beliefs. Be alert for their unwillingness to share much about themselves while you try to remain objective about the facts and the need to take some action.

4. Some families may not know how to solve educationally related problems. They accept problems as a part of life and may not share your desire to do something about it. While recognizing this value difference, try to indicate why their assistance would be helpful and show or tell them specific things they can do to assist in problem remediation.

5.   Parents generally appreciate being asked to collaborate in problem solving (Sheridan, 1993; Thomas et al., 1995; Turnbull & Turnbull, 1997). They may respond positively and with many good ideas if asked for their advice about the referral problem. Others express a belief that you as the educator know best what to do. Many parents put the same amount of faith in educators that they do in physicians. While I am not advocating a doctor–patient expert model, I believe that the sensitive consultant needs to understand that not all parents are able or willing to collaborate beyond a willingness to listen and participate as doers rather than planners.

6.   Establish goals and explain what is needed, who will do it, when it needs to be done, where it will be done, and how we will know if it has been successful.

7.   Assume, until evidence indicates otherwise, that all families want to be an integral part of the problem-solving process, and be ready to join with them in this spirit. Think of the family as the best possible case manager for the child, and respect members' desire to have that distinction.

8.   Last but not least, remember that consultation, whether with teachers or parents, is not about winning arguments or gaining some tactical advantage as in a debate. It is also not about blaming or a search for intrachild (or intrafamily) deficits. It is about problem solving. Seeley (1985) reminds us that learning is not produced by schools but is obtained by students who have supportive assistance from their schools, parents, and communities. This is a positive and constructive frame of mind to bring to parent consultation work.

After a first contact by phone, it is likely that the parents will come to the school for a discussion. (This is not to imply that home visits by the consultant or the teacher are undesirable. In fact, they can be constructive and instructive. However, always let the parents take the lead in inviting you.) The teacher or school-based consultant may conduct the meeting by himself or may coordinate a visit with all involved persons, which may include representatives from community agencies. Naturally, the parents need to be informed about the participants and asked if they want to invite others. Parents will sometimes bring in members of their extended family, including younger siblings of the referred student. Depending on the situation this creates, it may be a good idea to arrange for child care during the conference. Naturally, if the parents speak a language other than those of the other team members, a translator is necessary.

The nature of the discussion in this meeting varies according to the referral problem, the needs of the participants, time constraints, and other factors. Leadership of the school-based team, at least for the purposes of this meeting, needs to be determined in advance, as do the goals and agenda for the meeting. The following are suggested steps for the conduct of the meeting:

1.   Secure a comfortable, attractive room for the meeting. It should reflect the seriousness and importance of the meeting and should be free from distractions. Refreshments, though optional, are always appreciated. A recorder of important information should be assigned, especially when the information relates to plan development.

2.   The person conducting the meeting should be alerted to the arrival of the parents by the secretary at the front office and should come out to greet the parents, lead them to the meeting room, offer them seats, and conduct the introductions of all team members. Having name cards in front of all participants may be a good idea, especially in large meetings. Remember, parents may be overwhelmed by a crowd of strangers. Whether or not the student attends the conference depends on factors such as the student's age, his ability to attend to the content of the meeting, the parents' wishes, and so on. One factor to consider is the sensitive nature of the information to be delivered. If the committee believes that the student may not be able to comfortably integrate the complexity or personal nature of the information, it is better to inform the student about the essential substance of the meeting in a private setting with the parent and a faculty or staff member well-known to the student.

3.   Some small talk designed to establish rapport and help the parents to relax may be useful. Then the team leader should announce the purpose and goals of the meeting, asking the parents to give their input regarding these issues.

4.   The problem should be stated in behavioral terms, avoiding jargon and disease-oriented terminology. For example, it is better to say "We are concerned about Billy's high level of activity and his apparent inability or unwillingness to approach his assignments in a calm and task-oriented way" rather than "Observation of Billy suggests ADHD, probably stemming from some form of cerebral deficit or other constitutional dysfunction. Do others in Billy's family find it hard to concentrate?" Frame the issues in a way that suggests an educational approach will be useful, even if you believe and ultimately suggest that some medical advice may also be helpful. Again, get the parents' opinions about the nature of the problem. Do they see it at home? How does it manifest itself there? Have they tried specific approaches to deal with it? How have these approaches worked? What are they doing about it now? Some of this information may be expanded on later through the use of a questionnaire or rating scale which the parent will fill out with the assistance of the school staff, usually a school psychologist.

5.   Analyze the problem to the depth necessary to develop a set of goals and interventions. Keep the parent input coming, being sure to add their comments to whatever written documentation is being developed. Develop only as many goals as are necessary and possible to attain, at least in the foreseeable future. These goals must be stated in language that describes specific behaviors. "Billy will increase the amount of time he is seated in his desk and actively working on his assignments" is preferable to "Billy will improve his behavior and reduce his hyperactivity." Each goal should be accompanied by one or more interventions that may be implemented by a variety of team members, including the parents, and Billy himself. The who, what, when, where, and how questions mentioned previously need to be answered here. Loose ends need to be tied, or people will get frustrated later when the plan unravels due to poor planning.

It is best in a group meeting when the parents are in attendance for the consultant and other team members to be ready to suggest a variety of interventions that may be useful. This is done because parents ordinarily do not know enough about school or classroom procedures to make practical suggestions. Additionally, most parents expect the school team to know what to do; they would find it odd to be asked by the team what the team should do in school. Again, however, I am not implying that the school representatives will decide the goals and interventions; some parents have strong and often valuable ideas in regard to both these issues, especially goals. Encourage parental participation and input, being ready to indicate when their suggestions are useful and offering modifications as needed.

6. Assuming that the parents (or the student) will have a role in the implementation of the selected interventions, you must be sure that they are able to do their part in carrying them out. Earlier in this chapter a discussion of Caplan's (1970) mental health theory of consultation was presented, in which he points out that consultees (in this case, including parents) may have certain *lacks* that prevent them from effectively carrying out the interventions. He has identified these as *skill* (not knowing how to carry out the interventions), *knowledge* (not knowing what interventions are appropriate), *confidence* (knowing what to do and how to do it but not being able to because of fear of one's own incompetence or another psychological block, such as "My child won't like me if I get firm with him about his behavior"), and *objectivity* (not being able to see the problem objectively; being defended against seeing the truth of what others see).

At the point of assigning responsibilities to the parents, remember that you may be asking them to engage in behaviors or undertake activities with which they are unfamiliar or uncomfortable. Christenson (1995) suggests that the school team should ask the parents "What resources or support would you like to have as you try this idea?" Sometimes parents don't know how to answer because they haven't experienced this sort of question before. It may be good to suggest ways in which the school can help, at least informing the parents of the school team's intention of following up on plan implementation. Do this in a way that suggests that you are there to help, not to spy on or pressure the parents. Black (1998) discusses the following six kinds of family involvement that should be encouraged:

a. *Effective parenting*—Meeting students' basic needs for food, safety, and physical and emotional well-being.

b. *Consistent communication between families and school*—Phone calls are returned, report cards are evaluated, and conferences are attended. It is not uncommon in special education for there to be a daily log sent back and forth between parents and families.

c. *Volunteer service*—Many parents are eager to help out at school; They only need to be asked. Others can't because of other commitments. It is sometimes refreshing and illuminating to see how families can be of direct or indirect help at school if their help is solicited in a positive—"We need you"—manner.

d. *Support via home learning*—Homework assistance and trips to the library and other sources of cultural enrichment are examples of ways families can support the school's efforts and can provide an enjoyable outing for parents and their children, which oftentimes are relatively inexpensive.

e. *Decision-making efforts by family members and school personnel*—It is increasingly common for parents to belong to PTAs, site-based management teams, and other avenues of increased collaboration between home and school.

f. *Collaboration efforts*—Beyond those between home and school, the family may become involved with other community agencies, both professional/legal and voluntary that may be of assistance to the educational needs of their students.

7. It is now time to bring the meeting to a close. It is a good idea to briefly summarize the purpose, the goals and interventions developed, and the team members' responsibilities. If a written document is ready at this time, copies can be given to relevant personnel. The parents are thanked for their participation, and a plan for the next follow-up procedure is established.

The plan is then implemented, problems are worked out according to the steps in the SOCS (see Chapter 5), and ongoing evaluation indicates what activities, including future meetings, are needed.

ACTIVITY 2.13

Effective parent–school consultant teams depend on a framework such as the one I have just mentioned and considerable practice. Working in teams of varying sizes, with different members taking turns at various roles and using the following problems, rehearse (role-play) consultation meetings. After each rehearsal, discuss your adherence to the steps and considerations just listed. In addition to other topics of your choosing, deal with the following situations:

1. Third-grade boy, poor reader, starting to act aggressively toward others. Intact family.

2. Fifth-grade girl, very poor academically, little parent contact over the past two years. Single mother, works full time.

3. High-school sophomore, refuses to go to his resource class anymore. Says he's "sick of being one of those geeks." Parents cooperative but seem to be losing control of their son at home.

4. Twelve-year-old with severe developmental disabilities. Parents want him fully included in the regular sixth-grade class, preferably without an aide, since none of the regular education students have aides.

5. Seventh-grade girl, long history of antisocial and withdrawn behavior, has told her friends of her suicide ideation. Parents to date have denied any problem.

Further discussion of issues relating to parents and families in the consultation process can be found throughout this book. Chapter 1 presents information about the consultee as an adult learner–collaborator and as a variable in the consultation process. Certainly the information presented there applies to parents as consultees. Resistance to consultative efforts by parents and families is discussed in Chapter 3. Consultation with families is discussed throughout Chapter 5, especially in step 4 of the SOCS; and the participation of families is a major part of each of the five case studies (see Chapters 7, 9, and 10).

ACTIVITY 2.14

Review why consultation as a service-delivery model has been slow to develop. Dettmer et al. (1999) suggest four reasons for this: lack of understanding about roles, lack of framework for consultation, lack of assessment and support for consultation, and lack of preparation for the roles. Which of these reasons stands out in the local school districts with which you are familiar?

INSERVICE/STAFF DEVELOPMENT ACTIVITIES OF CONSULTANTS

Providing inservice training is a role related to three of Blake and Mouton's (1976) types of interventions (catalytic, prescriptive, and theory and principles). Its value has been noted by many researchers, including Darling-Hammond (1997, 1999), who recently demonstrated the connection between teacher training in effective teaching tactics and improved student achievement. School consultants are increasingly being asked to become involved in staff and professional development among personnel in a school, a district, or a larger administrative unit. Such training includes providing information about students' learning and behavior/adjustment difficulties, laws relating to special education, teaching techniques, the development of behavior support systems, parent conferencing, mediation and due process procedures, strategies and tactics for inclusion, assessment, and other topics of particular interest regarding students who are disabled or at risk. A school district may use both school-based and external consultants to provide training in skills or in team building. A school consultant may be giving a workshop one week and taking one from someone else the next week; collaborative models of team functioning often lead to this sort of parity among team members.

The purpose of inservice/staff development (ISD) is to provide activities that will enhance the skill and knowledge base of team members who collaborate for the educational welfare of students. It can consist of any formally established approach that has an agenda, a structured set of goals and activities, and a method of evaluation. The time period can vary considerably. For example, ISD can be a brief half-hour, one-time meeting of a team or a larger staff group in which the consultant presents some new information, or it can be a semester-long, three-hour-per-week seminar devoted to a thorough explication of enduring issues relevant to public education. It may occur in the teacher's lounge or in a separate facility rented specifically for the purpose. It is not devoted to clinical (that is, one child) issues as are most individual consultation meetings or team meetings such as SSTs or IEPs.

Since ISD involves formal preparation and activities beyond those typically provided by a school-based consultant, it requires administrative sanction and support. Indeed, the impetus for ISD usually comes from the administration, which responds to a felt or expressed need of the staff and discusses it with important constituents (such as teachers, parents, aides, itinerant staff, and so on) before determining content, format, and other details of the proposed ISD program. Assuming that there is a consensus about the importance of whatever topic is being discussed, the administrator or some designee (very likely the school-based consultant) is asked to engage in a series of logical steps designed to organize and carry out the ISD program. The following steps are typical of such a planning effort.

Identify Needs

Generally, there are two sources of needs: those determined by the service providers and those determined by their supervisors. For example, teachers who are service providers might feel a need for more approaches to teaching reading. Their principals might think there is a greater need for these teachers to learn curriculum-based assessment methods. Whose needs shall be met? Probably the best answer is "both." Each group in the school may believe that others have a need for learning certain information or skills; this belief may not be shared by those others. Negotiating the content of ISD can be a delicate matter.

The best approach to determining needs is to conduct both formal needs assessments and informal discussions among the staff. Formats for needs determination include questionnaires, surveys, checklists, interviews, and other sources of input, such as supervisors' formal evaluations of teachers. Figure 2.4 is an example of a combined checklist/open-ended survey of regular education teachers' needs in mainstreaming/inclusion.

ACTIVITY 2.15

Discuss class members' experiences with ISD. What types have they participated in? What formats have they observed? Who decided the content? What input did students have concerning goals/objectives, presenters, purposes, and so on? What were the strengths and weaknesses of the activities?

Figure 2.4

Needs/interests for staff development

Teachers: Please indicate your interest in each of the listed topics by ranking them in order of importance to you. Then at the bottom of the sheet, tell us what specific information you would like to gain in the course of our ISD services this year. Please return these forms by Friday, September 6, to Dr. Kampwirth's box. Thanks.

_____ Teaching phonics-within-literacy skills to slower learners.

_____ Effective positive discipline tactics for students who are disruptive.

_____ Teaching to different learning styles (such as "frames of mind").

_____ Alternative assessment methods (such as CBM, authentic, portfolio, etc.).

_____ Different methods for development of cooperative groups.

Please indicate your ideas about what you would like to have presented during our ISD this year:

ACTIVITY 2.16

Working in teams of three to five people, develop ISD programs to meet a mutually agreed-on need of teachers, such as those suggested in this chapter. Go through the steps indicated and lay out ideas about how you could develop an effective ISD program.

Setting Goals and Expectations

Based on the information gathered in needs determination, the ISD planning team generates a set of goals/expectations that are both skill- and knowledge-based. They may determine that teachers need/want more about classroom management, varied ways of teaching reading, parent conferencing, and math games and activities. They decide that they can meet these needs in the context of the four teacher/staff development days that are allocated for the year in addition to some follow-up activities designed to reinforce the material presented at the all-day workshops. They specify the order in which these topics will be presented. For example, in the Appleton Elementary District (K–8) the teachers seem most concerned about behavior management, so the ISD planning team has scheduled that topic for the first day. The team then goes back to the Appleton teachers with another needs survey instrument asking for more specific needs in this area. Based on this refined set of ideas, the team decides what it will plan to offer. These are the goals/expectations for this first workshop:

- Increase knowledge about reasons for poor behavior (guest speaker).
- Generate ideas about proximal and distal causes for behavioral challenges.
- Teach the basics of four different approaches to behavior management (guest speaker).
- By grade levels, discuss the possible use of these four methods, using case examples provided by the teachers.
- In small groups (three to five people), discuss approaches to dealing with common behavioral challenges experienced by each group member.

Presenting the ISD

If teachers have a say in determining both the general and specific parameters of the ISD, they are more likely to be willing participants in the ISD presentations. Teachers are practical people; they know that they alone will be facing the class at 9:00 Monday morning, and what they get in ISD better be useful then. They want to learn about proven techniques (i.e., best practices) that are directly applicable or can be easily adapted to their situations. The way in which presenters bring information and provide chances for rehearsal of new or challenging skills largely determines their acceptance and ultimate use. For example, ideas or skill demonstrations presented by "one of our own" teachers or others from the district are especially appreciated, partly because they come from a peer, and partly because the approach demonstrates to the participants that the ISD planners are sensitive to local talent. Principals and ancillary staff (school consultants) should be alert for good examples of teaching or behavior management that can be presented at an ISD related to those skills (Brandt, 1989).

Hall and Hord (1987) have provided an interesting perspective on the point of view of the participants as a factor in determining content and method in ISD. Their concerns-based adoption model (CBAM) emphasizes that change is a process rather than an event; it is a personal experience for each of the participants that is determined by individual perceptions. Hall and Hord call these perceptions, or developmental stages in readiness and openness to change, "stages of concern." These stages can be informally measured by asking teachers how they feel about potential changes or new program ideas. Hall and Hord have identified three stages: *self-concerns*, wherein the participants are somewhat interested in a new idea or approach but may be defensive if they feel it will upset what they are used to doing; *task concerns*, manifested by some degree of acceptance of a change but with concerns about its implementation; and *impact concerns*, which occur when the idea is accepted and implemented and the staff cooperates to see how it can best serve the needs of the students. By being sensitive to the stages among ISD participants, the presenters can modify their materials to meet these concerns. A more detailed explication of Hall and Hord's (1987) CBAM ideas is presented in Chapter 10.

Follow-Up, Monitoring, and Evaluation

One of the criticisms of ISD is that it too often consists of a one-shot burst of interest and energy that quickly fades because nothing is done to ensure its maintenance. Follow-up and monitoring of its effects need to be part of the total ISD package. This is a valuable role for the school consultant. How and to what extent this is done is a function of time, accessibility, and interest, issues that usually can be worked out to some degree. Like so many things, following up is a question of values: If the need to follow up is considered important, people find time to do it. Classroom visits to observe a new skill that is being implemented, meetings with small groups of teachers to discuss their use of the skill, brief refresher seminars, and reports of successes at weekly staff meetings are some of the ways in which districts monitor skills applications. Whatever can be done to reduce isolation in teachers' efforts to learn new skills can be effective; learners, either children or adults, like to know that they are sharing the experience of learning with others. The support they give each other has ramifications for staff morale and for the collaborative team-building efforts so necessary in this era of school reform. Whatever administrators can do to encourage the use of new skills will be noticed by the staff. Release time for planning and consultation, public recognition of efforts, private conferences for reinforcement, and so on are all ways in which administrators can show their acknowledgment of efforts at service delivery improvement.

Scriven's (1967) model of formative and summative evaluation has proven useful in many ways in the field of consultation, including ISD. Formative evaluation, sometimes referred to as process evaluation, is used to monitor the use of a new or ongoing procedure as it is being implemented. A school-based consultant adopts this method as he watches teachers use a new procedure and consults with them about it. Summative evaluation is used at the end of a procedure to measure its final value; for example, how well are our third-graders reading after three years of a phonics-based approach to literacy development? What has been the effect on discipline referrals since the incorporation of some new method of behavior management? Answering these questions, either qualitatively or quantitatively, is the purpose of a summative evaluation.

Is ISD effective? The answer depends on a number of factors, especially your definition of *effective*. There may be many reactions to and effects of ISD, some directly related to its purposes, some indirect but by no means less important. Perhaps the Appleton district's one-day inservice on behavior management was not well received for a variety of reasons, but the discussions it generated led to a different format for approaching discipline, quite unexpectedly, and this new format is proving to be successful. Because individuals disagreed so much about the proposed "return to phonics" workshop, the subsequent series of small-group discussions about methods of teaching reading have resulted in a modified phonics-with-whole-language approach that most people are happy with. These spinoff benefits, including the fact that teachers can find a forum for discussion among themselves about how to solve their problems and issues, are possible only in systems that are open to collaborative approaches to decision making. Administrative nay-saying about these spinoff effects are certain to put a chill on the creative interests and commitments of teachers who manifest interest in change at the task and impact concerns levels. Chapter 10 contains a case study where ISD was used as part of the district's approach to implementing the development of a consultation-based service delivery system for special education.

Figure 2.5 is a modification and summary of the steps presented by King et al. (1977) which are needed for planning, programming, presenting, and evaluating ISD activities.

Figure 2.5

Planning, programming, presenting, and evaluating inservice staff development activities

1. Establish a planning committee for the delivery of ISD.
   Constituents should include teachers, ancillary staff, and administrators.

2. Identify needs and desires.
   Whose are they? Administration? Those of the presenter? Staff?
   Recipients of the ISD need input into its contents. To get this input use surveys, questionnaires, and so on.
   Know your audience: What do they want and need?

3. Examine feasibility and assign priorities.
   Review requests for content. This should be done by the planning committee.
   Consider the goals of the school and financial possibilities, especially if outside presenters will be used.

4. Obtain commitment from administration and others.
   Does the administration support it, philosophically and financially?
   Do the staff who will be involved in presenting the ISD support it?

5. Planning and programming.   Have the committee discuss at least these issues:
   Purpose and desired outcomes.
   Dates, times, and locations.
   Review expectations with presenters.
   Will the participants need information about the topic prior to the meeting?

Figure 2.5   *continued*

> Detail expenses.
> Prepare announcements: What, who, where, when? Make
> the announcements attractive.
> Arrangements for outside presenters (hotel, transportation,
> and so on).
> Preparations for "The Day":
> Furniture arranged.
> Procedure for signing in participants (name tags? group
> assignments?).
> Refreshments: What are they and who is responsible?
> Materials needed: A-V, handouts, activity materials.
> Develop a final check-off sheet specifying activities, timing,
> responsible persons, and so on.
>
> 6. Presenting the ISD.
>   Who will give the opening remarks: Administration? Bargaining agent representa-
>   tive? Principal? Planning committee chair?
>   Presenters utilize a blend of different teaching approaches (little lecture with
>   visual backup; activities such as demonstrations, role-playing, small-group
>   discussion; aim for maximal audience involvement).
>   Be alert to audience reactions; set breaks.
>
> 7. Evaluation.
>   Prepare materials in advance; perhaps distribute them in advance.
>   Keep them simple; blend check marks with open-ended questions.
>   Design it so it will tell you what you want to know.
>
> 8. Follow-up.
>   How can you be sure there will be some retention of material or behavior change
>   on the part of the participants as a result of the ISD?
>   Send letters to presenters thanking them and informing them of the participants'
>   evaluations.

SUMMARY

This chapter has summarized two theoretical models of consultation that are relatively well-known and well respected (behavioral and mental health), as well as
other functional models, roles, skills, activities, and inservice delivery functions of
school-based consultants.

The behavioral model is the more common of the two theoretical models and
has been far more researched. I make numerous references to this model in the
chapters that follow, particularly in Chapter 6, which is about students who present

with behavior disorders. Although the behavioral model is currently dominant, the Caplans' ideas, contained in the mental health model, especially about consultee lacks, should certainly be studied since problems in consultee functioning, which may not be obvious to the untrained person, often contribute to the behavior or learning problem of the referred student. The school-based consultant should be aware of the principles that underlie each of these models because each contains ideas and insights that are useful in the consultation process.

Roles, skills, and activities of school-based consultants that are applicable to both individual consultation (that is, consultant and consultee alone) or consultation conducted in larger groups or teams were reviewed. Although individual consultation is still very common, it is increasingly important for consultants to recognize the value of using consultation with larger teams of people, including SST and other teams that deal with issues of reform or restructuring of service delivery to students. This chapter also examined a number of functional models of consultation, which are characterized by their ready applicability in the schools and their generally favorable research support. Consulting with families was reviewed, as well as inservice and staff development techniques which were presented as valuable activities for both internal and external consultants.

REFERENCES

Abiden, R. R. (1982). A psychosocial look at consultation and behavior modification. *Psychology in the Schools, 9,* 358–364.

Alberto, P. A., & Troutman, A. C. (1999). *Applied behavioral analysis for teachers.* Upper Saddle River, NJ: Merrill/Prentice Hall.

Aldinger, L., Warger, C., & Eavy, P. (1992). *Strategies for teacher collaboration.* Ann Arbor, MI: Exceptional Innovations.

Allen, S. J., & Graden, J. L. (1995). Collaborative problem solving for intervention design. In A. Thomas & J. Grimes (Eds.), *Best practices in school psychology—III* (pp. 667–678). Washington, DC: NASP.

American Psychiatric Association. (1994). *DSM-IV: Diagnostic and Statistical Manual of Mental Disorders.* Washington, DC: Author.

Ansbacher, H. L., & Ansbacher, R. R. (Eds.). (1956). *The individual psychology of Alfred Adler.* New York: Basic Books.

Argyris, C. (1991). Overcoming client-consultant defensive routines that erode credibility: A charge for the 90's. *Consulting Psychologist's Bulletin, 43,* 30–35.

Armstrong, T. (1994). *Multiple intelligences in the classroom.* Alexandria, VA: Association for Supervision and Curriculum Development.

Axelrod, S., Moyer, L., & Berry, B. (1990). Why teachers do not use behavior modification procedures. *Journal of Educational and Psychological Consultation, 1*(4), 309–320.

Baars, B. (1986). *The cognitive revolution in psychology.* New York: Guilford.

Backer, T. E., & Glaser, E. M. (1979). *Portraits of 17 organizational consultants.* Los Angeles: Human Interaction Research Institute.

Baer, G. G., & Richards, H. C. (1980). An interdependent group-oriented contingency system for improving academic performance. *School Psychology Review, 9,* 190–193.

Bandura, A. (1977). *Social learning theory.* Upper Saddle River, NJ: Prentice Hall.

Basham, A., Appleton, V., & Dykeman, C. (2000). *Team building in education: A how-to guidebook.* Denver: Love Publishing.

Bay, M., Bryan, T., & O'Connor, R. (1994). Teachers assisting teachers: A prereferral model for urban educators. *Teacher Education and Special Education, 17,* 10–21.

Bergan, J. R. (1977). *Behavioral consultation.* Upper Saddle River, NJ: Merrill/Prentice Hall.

Bergan, J. R. (1995). Evolution of a problem-solving model of consultation. *Journal of Educational and Psychological Consultation, 6* (2), 11–124.

Bergan, J. R., & Kratochwill, T. R. (1990). *Behavioral consultation and therapy.* New York: Plenum.

Bergan, J. R., & Tombari, M. L. (1975). The analysis of verbal interactions occurring during consultation. *Journal of School Psychology, 13,* 209–226.

Berger, E. H. (1995). *Parents as partners: Families and schools working together.* Upper Saddle River, NJ: Merrill/Prentice Hall.

Black, S. (1998). Parent support. *The American School Board Journal, 185*(4), 50–52.

Blake, R. E., & Mouton, J. S. (1976). *Consultation.* Reading, MA: Addison-Wesley.

Block, P. (1981). *Flawless consulting.* Austin, TX: Learning Concepts.

Booth, A., & Dunn, J. F. (Eds.). (1996). *Family-school links: How do they affect educational outcomes?* Mahway, NJ: Erlbaum.

Bradley, D. F. (1994). A framework for the acquisition of collaborative consulation skills. *Journal of Educational & Psychological Consultation, 5,* 51–68.

Brandt, R. S. (1989). *Coaching and staff development.* Alexandria, VA: Association for Supervision and Curriculum Development.

Brann, P., Loughlin, S., & Kimball, W. (1991). Guidelines for cooperative teaching between general and special education teachers. *Journal of Educational and Psychological Consultation, 2*(2), 197–200.

Brown, D., Pryzwansky, W., & Schulte, A. (2001). *Psychological consultation* (5th ed.). Boston: Allyn & Bacon.

Brown, D., Spano, D. B., & Schulte, A. C. (1988). Consultation training in master's level counselor education programs. *Counselor Education and Supervision, 27,* 323–330.

Bush, G. (1991). *America 2000: An educational strategy.* Washington, DC: U.S. Department of Education.

Buzzell, J. B. (1996). *School and family partnerships.* Albany, NY: Delmar.

California Department of Justice, Division of Law Enforcement. (1993). *Profile 1992.* Sacramento: Author.

Caplan, G. (1964). *Principles of preventive psychiatry.* New York: Basic Books.

Caplan, G. (1970). *The theory and practice of mental health consultation.* New York: Basic Books.

Caplan, G., & Caplan, R. (1993). *Mental health consultation and collaboration.* San Francisco: Jossey-Bass.

Caplan, G., Caplan, R., & Erchul, W. (1995). A contemporary view of mental health consultation: Comments on "types of mental health consultation" by Gerald Caplan (1963). *Journal of Educational and Psychological Consultation, 6*(1), 23–30.

Carnine, D., & Kameenui, E. J. (1990). The general education initiative and children with special needs: A false dilemma in the face of true problems. *Journal of Learning Disabilities, 23*(3), 141–144, 148.

Chicago Public Schools, Bureau of Safety and Security. (1994). *Annual report.* Chicago: Author.

Children's Defense Fund. (1999). *The state of America's schoolchildren yearbook.* Washington, DC: Author.

Christenson, S. L. (1995). Best practices in supporting home-school collaboration. In A. Thomas & J. Grimes (Eds.), *Best practices in school psychology—III* (pp. 253–268). Washington, DC: NASP.

Christenson, S. L., & Cleary, M. (1990). Consultation and the parent-educator partnership: A perspective. *Journal of Educational and Psychological Consultation, 1*(3), 219–241.

Cole, E., & Siegal, J. (1990). *Effective consultation in school psychology.* Toronto: Hogrefe & Huber.

Colton, D. L., & Sheridan, S. M. (1998). Conjoint behavioral consultation and social skills training: Enhancing the play behavior of boys with attention deficit hyperactivity disorder. *Journal of Educational and Psychological Consultation, 9*(1), 3–28.

Conoley, J. C., & Conoley, C. W. (1992). *School consultation: A guide to practice and training* (2nd ed.). Upper Saddle River, NJ: Merrill/Prentice Hall.

Cramer, S. F. (1998). *Collaboration.* Boston: Allyn & Bacon.

Darling-Hammond, L. (1997). Principals and teachers must devise new structures to meet the challenges of education in the 21st century. *Principal, 77*(1), 5–11.

Darling-Hammond, L. (1999). Target time towards teachers. *Journal of Staff Development, 20*(2), 31–41.

DeBoer, A. (1995). *Working together.* Longmont, CO: Sopris West.

Dettmer, P., Dyck, N., & Thurston, L. P. (1999). *Consultation, collaboration, and teamwork.* Boston: Allyn & Bacon.

Dettmer, P., Thurston, L. P., & Dyck, N. (1993). *Consultation, collaboration, and teamwork for students with special needs.* Boston: Allyn & Boston.

Dougherty, A. (2000). *Consultation: Practice and perspectives* (3rd ed.). Pacific Grove, CA: Brooks/Cole.

Eitzen, D. (1992). Problem students: The sociocultural roots. *Phi Delta Kappan, 73,* 584–590.

Elliott, S. N., & Busse, R. T. (1993). Effective treatments with behavioral consultation. In J. E. Zins, T. R. Kratochwill, & S. N. Elliott (Eds.), *Handbook of consultation services for children* (pp. 179–203). San Francisco: Jossey-Bass.

Epstein, J. L. (1995). School/family/community partnerships: Caring for the children we share. *Phi Delta Kappan, 76*(9), 701–712.

Erchul, W. P. (1993). *Consultation in community, school, and organizational practice: Gerald Caplan's contributions to professional psychology.* Washington, DC: Taylor & Francis.

Erchul, W. P., & Schulte, A. C. (1996). Behavioral consultation as a work in progress: A reply to Witt, Gresham, and Noell. *Journal of Educational and Psychological Consultation, 7*(4), 345–354.

Evans, R. (1990). Making mainstreaming work through prereferral consultation. *Educational Leadership, 47,* 73–77.

Friend, M., & Cook, L. (2000). *Interactions: Collaboration skills for school professionals* (3rd ed.). New York: Longman.

Futrell, M. (1989). Mission not accomplished: Educational reform in retrospect. *Phi Delta Kappan, 71*(1), 9–14.

Gallesich, J. (1982). *The profession and practice of consultation: A handbook for consultants, trainers of consultants and consumers of consultation services.* San Francisco: Jossey-Bass.

Gallup, A. M. (1994). *Results of the annual Gallup Poll.* Lincoln, NE: Gallup Organization.

Gardner, H. (1983). *Frames of mind: The theory of multiple intelligences.* New York: Basic Books.

Givens-Ogle, L., Christ, B., & Idol, L. (1991). Collaborative consultation: The San Juan District project. *Journal of Educational and Psychological Consultation, 2*(3), 267–284.

Goodlad, J. I. (1988). School-university partnerships for educational renewal: Rationale and concepts. In K. A. Sirotnik & J. I. Goodlad (Eds.), *School-university partnerships in action* (pp. 205–225). New York: Teachers College Press.

Graden, J. L., Zins, J. E., & Curtis, M. J. (1988). *Alternative educational delivery systems: Enhancing instructional options for all students.* Washington, DC: NASP.

Gresham, F. M., & Davis, C. J. (1988). Behavioral interviews with teachers and parents. In E. S. Shapiro & T. R. Kratochwill (Eds.), *Behavioral assessment in schools: Conceptual foundations and practical applications* (pp. 455–493). New York: Guilford Press.

Grieger, R. M. (1977). Teacher attitudes as a variable in behavioral consultation. In J. Meyers, R. Martin, & I. Hyman (Eds.), *School consultation: Readings about preventive techniques for pupil personnel workers* (pp. 137–148). Springfield, IL: Thomas.

Gutkin, T. B. (1981). Relative frequency of consultee lack of knowledge, skill, confidence, and objectivity in school settings. *Journal of School Psychology, 19,* 637–642.

Gutkin, T. B. (1993). Moving from behavioral to ecobehavioral consultation: What's in a name? *Journal of Educational and Psychological Consultation, 4*(1), 95–99.

Gutkin, T. B., & Curtis, M. J. (1982). School-based consultation: Theory and techniques—Intervention in the schools. In C. R. Reynolds & T. B. Gutkin (Eds.), *The handbook of school psychology* (pp. 796–828). New York: Wiley.

Gutkin, T. B., & Curtis, M. J. (1999). School-based consultation: Theory, techniques, and research. In T. B. Gutkin & C. R. Reynolds (Eds.), *The handbook of school psychology* (3rd ed., pp. 598–637). New York: Wiley.

Hall, G., & Hord, S. (1987). *Change in schools: Facilitating the process.* Albany: State University of New York Press.

Halpern, A. S. (1992). Transition: Old wine in new bottles. *Exceptional Children, 58*(3), 202–211.

Hanson, M. J., & Carta, J. J. (1996). Addressing the challenges of families with multiple risks. *Exceptional Children, 62*(3), 201–212.

Henning-Stout, M. (1993). Theoretical and empirical bases of consultation. In J. E. Zins, T. R. Kratochwill, & S. N. Elliott (Eds.), *Handbook of consultation services for children* (pp. 15–45). San Francisco: Jossey-Bass.

Herbert, M. (1978). *Conduct disorders of children and adolescents: A behavioral approach to assessment and treatment.* New York: Wiley.

Heron, T. E., & Harris, K. C. (1987). *The educational consultant* (2nd ed.). Boston: Allyn & Bacon.

Hinkle, P. (2001). *California special education programs: A composite of laws.* Sacramento: California Department of Education.

Hodges, W. F., & Cooper, S. (1983). General introduction. In S. Cooper & W. F. Hodges (Eds.), *The mental health consultation field* (pp. 19–25). New York: Human Services Press.

Holland, J. L. (1966). *Psychology of vocational choice.* Waltham, MA: Blaisdell.

Howe, H., II. (1991). America 2000: Bumpy ride on four trains. *Phi Delta Kappan, 73*(3), 192–203.

Idol, L. (1990). The scientific art of classroom consultation. *Journal of Educational and Psychological Consultation, 1*(1), 3–22.

Idol, L., & West, J. F. (1992). *Effective instruction for difficult-to-teach students.* Austin, TX: Pro-Ed.

Idol, L., Nevin, A., & Paolucci-Whitcomb, P. (2000). *Collaborative consultation* (3rd ed.). Austin, TX: Pro-Ed.

Idol, L., Paolucci-Whitcomb, P., & Nevin, A. (1986). *Collaborative consultation.* Rockville, MD: Aspen.

Jacob-Timm, S., & Hartshorne, T. (1994). *Law and ethics for school psychologists* (2nd ed.). Brandon, VT: CPPC.

Joyce, B., & Showers, B. (1995). *Student achievement through staff development: Fundamentals of school renewal* (2nd ed.). White Plains, NY: Longman.

Kanfer, F., & Saslow, G. (1969). Behavioral diagnosis. In C. M. Franks (Ed.), *Behavior therapy: Appraisal and status* (pp. 417–444). New York: McGraw-Hill.

Kaplan, J. (1995). *Beyond behavior modification: A cognitive-behavioral approach to behavior management in the schools* (3rd ed.). Austin, TX: Pro-Ed.

Kaplan, J. (2000). *Beyond functional assessment: A social-cognitive approach to the evaluation of behavior problems in children and youth.* Austin, TX: Pro-Ed.

Kazdin, A. E. (1984). *Behavior modification in applied settings* (2nd ed.). Homewood, IL: Dorsey.

Keith-Spiegel, P., & Koocher, G. P. (1985). *Ethics in psychology.* Hillsdale, NJ: Erlbaum.

King, J. C., Hayes, P. C., & Newman, I. (1977). Some requirements for effective inservice. *Phi Delta Kappan, 58,* 686–687.

Knight, M. T., Meyers, H. W., Paolucci-Whitcomb, P., Hasazi, S. E., & Nevin, A. (1981). A four-year evaluation of consulting teacher service. *Behavioral Disorders, 6,* 92–100.

Knopf, H. M., & Batsche, G. M. (1997). *Project ACHIEVE: Background Information.* Unpublished manuscript.

Kramer, J. J. (1990). Training parents as behavior change agents: Successes, failures and suggestions for school psychologists. In T. B. Gutkin & C. R. Reynolds (Eds.), *Handbook of school psychology* (2nd ed., pp. 685–702). New York: Wiley.

Kratochwill, T. R., & Bergan, J. R. (1990). *Behavioral consultation in applied settings: An individual guide.* New York: Plenum.

Kratochwill, T. R., Elliott, S. N., & Rotto, P. C. (1995). Best practices in school-based behavioral consultation. In A. Thomas & J. Grimes (Eds.), *Best practices in school psychology—III* (pp. 519–537). Washington, DC: NASP.

Kratochwill, T. R., Sladeczek, I., & Plunge, M. (1995). The evolution of behavioral consultation. *Journal of Educational and Psychological Consultation, 6*(2), 145–157.

Kratochwill, T. R., & Van Someren, K. R. (1995). Barriers to treatment success in behavioral consultation: Current limitations and future directions. *Journal of Educational and Psychological Consultation, 6*(2), 125–143.

Kratochwill, T. R., Van Someren, K. R., & Sheridan, S. M. (1989). Training behavioral consultants: A competency-based model to teach interview skills. *Professional School Psychology, 4,* 41–58.

Kurpius, D. J. (1991). Why collaborative consultation fails: A matrix for consideration. *Journal of Educational and Psychological Consultation, 2*(2), 193–195.

Kurpius, D. J., Fuqua, D., & Rozecki, T. (1993). The consulting process: A multidimensional approach. *Journal of Counseling and Development, 71,* 601–606.

Lippitt, G., & Lippitt, R. (1986). *The consulting process in action* (2nd ed.). San Diego: University Associates.

Lutzker, J., & Martin, J. (1981). *Behavioral change.* Pacific Grove, CA: Brooks/Cole.

Maeroff, G. I. (1993). Building teams to rebuild school. *Phi Delta Kappan, 75,* 512–519.

Maital, S. L. (1996). Integration of behavioral and mental health consultation as a means of overcoming resistance. *Journal of Educational and Psychological Consultation, 7*(4), 291–303.

Marks, E. S. (1995). *Entry strategies for school consultation.* New York: Guilford.

Martens, B. K. (1993). A behavioral approach to consultation. In J. E. Zins, T. R. Kratochwill, & S. N. Elliott (Eds.), *Handbook of consultation services for children* (pp. 65–86). San Francisco: Jossey-Bass.

Meichenbaum, R. (1977). *Cognitive-behavior modification: An integrative approach.* New York: Plenum.

Meyers, B., Valentino, C. T., Meyers, J., Boretti, M., & Brent, D. (1996). Implementing prereferral intervention teams as an approach to school-based consultation in an urban school system. *Journal of Educational and Psychological Consultation, 7,* 119–149.

Meyers, J., Brent, D., Faherty, E., & Modafferi, C. (1993). Caplan's contributions to the practice of psychology in the schools. In W. P. Erchul (Ed.), *Consultation in community, school, and organizational practice: Gerald Caplan's contributions to professional psychology* (pp. 99–122). Washington, DC: Taylor & Francis.

Meyers, J., Wurtz, R., & Flanagan, D. (1981). A national survey investigating training occurring in school psychology programs. *Psychology in the Schools, 18,* 297–302.

National Association of School Psychologists. (1992). *Principles for professional ethics.* Silver Spring, MD: Author.

Newman, J. L. (1993). Ethical issues in consultation. *Journal of Counseling and Development, 72,* 148–156.

Noddings, N. (1992). *The challenge to care in the schools: An alternative approach to education.* New York: Teachers College Press.

O'Neil, J. (1990). Drive for national standards picking up steam. *Educational Leadership, 48* (5), 4–8.

O'Shea, D., O'Shea, L., Algozzine, R., & Hammitte, D. (2001). *Families and teachers of individuals with disabilities.* Boston: Allyn & Bacon.

Parsons, R. D., & Meyers, J. (1984). *Developing consultation skills.* San Francisco: Jossey-Bass.

Powers, K. (2001). Problem solving student support teams. *The California School Psychologist, 6,* 19–30.

Prasse, D. P. (Ed.). (1986). Litigation and special education. *Exceptional Children, 52,* 311–390.

Pryzwansky, W. B. (1977). Collaboration or consultation: Is there a difference? *Journal of Special Education, 1,* 179–182.

Pryzwansky, W. B. (1993). Ethical consultation practice. In J. E. Zins, T. R. Kratochwill, & S. N. Elliott (Eds.), *Handbook of consultation services for children* (pp. 329–350). San Francisco: Jossey-Bass.

Pugach, M. C., & Johnson, L. J. (1988). Rethinking the relationship between consultation and collaborative problem-solving. *Focus on Exceptional Children, 21*(4), 1–8.

Pugach, M. C., & Johnson, L. J. (1995). *Collaborative practitioners, collaborative schools.* Denver: Love Publishing.

Reyes, O., & Jason, L. A. (1993). Collaborating with the community. In J. E. Zins, T. R. Kratochwill, & S. N. Elliott (Eds.), *Handbook of consultation services for children* (pp. 305–316). San Francisco: Jossey-Bass.

Rosenfield, S. A. (1987). *Instructional consultation.* Hillsdale, NJ: Erlbaum.

Rosenfield, S. A., & Gravois, T. A. (1996). *Instructional consultation teams: Collaborating for change.* New York: Guilford Press.

Ross, R. P. (1995). Implementing intervention assistance teams. In A. Thomas & J. Grimes (Eds.), *Best practices in school psychology—III* (pp. 227–238). Washington, DC: NASP.

Sandoval, J. (1996). Constructivism, consultee-centered consultation, and conceptual change. *Journal of Educational and Psychological Consultation, 7,* 89–90.

Sandoval, J., Lambert, N. M., & Davis, J. M. (1977). Consultation from the consultee's perspective. *Journal of School Psychology, 15*(4), 334–342.

Sarason, S. B. (1990). *The predictable failure of school reform: Can we change before it's too late?* San Francisco: Jossey-Bass.

Schloss, P., & Smith, M. (1998). *Applied behavioral analysis.* Boston: Allyn & Bacon.

Schulte, A. C., & Osborne, S. S. (1993, April). What is collaborative consultation? The eye of the beholder. In D. Fuchs (Chair), *Questioning popular beliefs about collaborative consultation.* Symposium presented at the annual meeting of the Council for Exceptional Children, San Antonio.

Scriven, M. (1967). The methodology of evaluation. In R. Tyler, R. Gagne, & M. Scriven (Eds.), *Perspectives of curriculum evaluations* (AERA Monograph Series on Curriculum Evaluation) (pp. 39–83). Chicago: Rand-McNally.

Seeley, D. S. (1985). *Education through partnership.* Washington, DC: American Enterprise Institute for Public Policy Research.

Senge, P. (1990). *The fifth dimension.* New York: Doubleday.

Shepard, L. (1987). The new push for excellence: Widening the schism between regular and special education. *Exceptional Children, 53,* 327–329.

Sheridan, S. M. (1993). Models for working with parents. In J. Zins, T. R. Kratochwill, & S. N. Elliott (Eds.), *Handbook of consultation services for children.* San Francisco: Jossey-Bass.

Sheridan, S. M., & Colton, D. L. (1994). Conjoint behavioral consultation: A review and case study. *Journal of Educational and Psychological Consultation, 5*(3), 211–228.

Sheridan, S. M., & Kratochwill, T. R. (1992). Behavioral parent-teacher consultation: Conceptual and research considerations. *Journal of School Psychology, 30,* 117–139.

Sheridan, S. M., Kratochwill, T. R., & Bergan, J. R. (1996). *Conjoint behavioral consultation: A procedural manual.* New York: Plenum.

Shriner, J. G., Ysseldyke, J. E., & Thurlow, M. L. (1996). Standards for all American students. In E. L. Meyen, G. A. Vergason, & R. J. Whelan (Eds.), *Strategies for teaching exceptional children in inclusive settings* (pp. 53–80). Denver: Love Publishing.

Sidman, M. (1989). *Coercion and its fallout.* Boston: Authors Cooperative.

Skinner, B. (1969). *Contingencies of reinforcement: A theoretical analysis.* Upper Saddle River, NJ: Prentice Hall.

Snow, D. L., & Gersick, K. E. (1986). Ethical and professional issues in mental health consultation. In F. V. Mannino, E. J. Trickett, M. F. Shore, M. G. Kidder, & G. Levin (Eds.), *Handbook of mental health consultation* (DHHS Publication No. ADM 86-1446) (pp. 393–431). Washington, DC: U.S. Government Printing Office.

Sprick, R., Sprick, M., & Garrison, M. (1994). *Interventions.* Longmont, CO: Sopris West.

Stephens, T. M. (1977). *Teaching skills to children with learning and behavior disorders.* Upper Saddle River, NJ: Merrill/Prentice Hall.

Stoner, G., Shinn, M. R., & Walker, H. M. (1991). *Interventions for achievement and behavior problems.* Silver Spring, MD: NASP.

Sugai, G., & Tindal, G. (1993). *Effective school consultation: An interactive approach.* Pacific Grove, CA: Brooks/Cole.

Swap, S. M. (1987). *Enhancing parent involvement in the schools.* New York: Teachers College Press.

Thomas, C. C., Correa, V. I., & Morsink, C. V. (1995). *Interactive teaming: Consultation and collaboration in special programs.* Upper Saddle River, NJ: Merrill/Prentice Hall.

Turnbull, A. P., & Turnbull, H. R. (1997). *Families, professionals, and exceptionality: A special partnership* (3rd ed.). Upper Saddle River, NJ: Merrill/Prentice Hall.

U.S. General Accounting Office. (1995). *School safety: Promising practices for addressing school violence* (GAO/HEHS-95-106). Washington, DC: Author.

Ullmann, L., & Krasner, L. (1965). *Case studies in behavior modification.* New York: Holt, Rinehart, & Winston.

Walker, J. E., & Shea, T. M. (1999). *Behavior management: A practical approach for educators* (7th ed.). Upper Saddle River, NJ: Merrill/Prentice Hall.

West, J. F., & Cannon, G. S. (1988). Essential collaborative consultation competencies for regular and special educators. *Journal of Learning Disabilities, 21,* 56–63.

West, J. F., & Idol, L. (1987). School consultation: An interdisciplinary perspective on theory, models, and research. *Journal of Learning Disabilities, 20*(7), 388–408.

West, J. F., & Idol, L. (1990). Collaborative consultation in the education of mildly handicapped and at-risk students. *RASE: Remedial and Special Education, 11*(1), 22–31.

West, J. F., Idol, L., & Cannon, G. (1989). *Collaboration in the schools: Communicating, interacting, and problem-solving.* Austin, TX: Pro-Ed.

Will, M. (1986). Educating children with learning problems: A shared responsibility. *Exceptional Children, 52*(5), 411–415.

Witt, J. C., & Elliott, S. N. (1983). Assessment in behavioral consultation: The initial interview. *School Psychology Review, 12,* 42–49.

Witt, J. C., Gresham, F. M., & Noell, G. H. (1996). What's behavioral about behavioral consultation?

Journal of Educational and Psychological Consultation, 7(4), 327–344.

Yocum, D. J., & Cossairt, A. (1996). Consultation courses offered in special education teacher training programs: A national survey. *Journal of Educational and Psychological Consultation, 7*(3), 251–258.

Ysseldyke, J., & Marston, D. (1999). Origins of categorical special education services in schools and a rationale for changing them. In D. Reschly, W. D. Tilly, & J. P. Grimes (Eds.), *Special education in transition: Functional assessment and noncategorical programming.* Longmont, CO: Sopris West.

Zins, J. E. (1993). Enhancing consultee problem-solving skills in consultative interactions. *Journal of Counseling and Development, 72,* 185–190.

Zins, J. E., Curtis, M. J., Graden, J. L., & Ponti, C. R. (1988). *Helping students succeed in the regular classroom.* San Francisco: Jossey-Bass.

Zirpoli, T. J., & Melloy, K. J. (2001). *Behavior management: Applications for teachers.* Upper Saddle River, NJ: Merrill/Prentice Hall.

CHAPTER 3

Communication and Interpersonal Skills

OBJECTIVES

1. Review the elements of effective communication skills.

2. Provide a set of activities designed to assist the reader in developing a communication style that is likely to result in personal acceptance by consultees and the development of effective interventions.

3. Review the nature, types, and causes of resistance to consultation, along with suggestions for dealing proactively with resistance, both individual and systemic.

4. Analyze the nature of interpersonal skills as they apply to the practice of consultation.

5. Discuss the nature of power in interpersonal relationships, and how consultants can ethically develop and maintain a collaboratively oriented power base.

6. Provide a set of activities designed to assist consultants in practicing skills of interpersonal relations, including relationship building, relating to a consultee's affective needs, and developing a power base.

Ms. Baker, a third-grade teacher, was asked to comment on her work with Mrs. Osprey, who is the resource specialist–consultant at her school. Ms. Baker said she greatly enjoyed her work with the consultant because she thought that Mrs. Osprey listened to her ideas, knew how to help her describe the problem accurately, and helped out not by taking over her job but by showing her how to deal with the problem more effectively. Together they clarified issues regarding a schedule for Mrs. Osprey's direct work in Ms. Baker's class. Ms. Baker would gladly welcome help from the consultant again.

Mr. Cook (a seventh-grade teacher–consultee), commenting on his work with Dr. Tilly, the school psychologist (the consultant) at Williams Junior High, said that he was not happy with his recent consultation experience. He thought that Dr. Tilly acted like he knew everything, didn't listen well, rushed to conclusions based on previous cases that he wanted to brag about, and implied that the consultee should have been able to solve the problem without having referred it to the consultant. The consultee has decided not to bother with this process in the future. The consultant was heard to comment that he had just finished successfully helping Mr. Cook with a very complicated problem.

This chapter discusses and analyzes the subcomponents of communication and interpersonal skills separately. However, you should recognize that these skills continually interact during the consultation process. As the vignettes above indicate, two interdependent phenomena occur simultaneously as the consultant and the consultee deal with one another. In the first case, the consultant's effective and positive communication and interpersonal skills made Ms. Baker feel that consultation was a very useful experience, one that she wants to repeat. In the second case, Mr. Cook left the consultation experience with the exact-opposite feeling. We can imagine that Dr. Tilly needs to improve his communication and interpersonal skills. In both cases, the consultees were influenced by the way in which they and their consultants were communicating (verbally and nonverbally) with each other and the way in which they were relating (bonding, distancing, merging, dissolving, accepting, resisting) as the consultation sessions proceeded.

When school-based consultants enter into a consultation role with consultees, they need to remember that they are playing multiple subroles and engaging in many activities that are essential to the consultative function, such as gathering and considering data, generating plans, identifying resources, teaching skills, encouraging, clarifying, modifying plans, and so on. Embedded in all these general subroles are communication and interpersonal skills. The third primary skill needed by school-based consultants, problem solving, is considered in Chapter 5.

COMMUNICATION SKILLS

The following skills are among the many needed for effective communication.

Attending

Nothing is more annoying in a conversation than having a listener who isn't paying attention. It's demeaning to feel that you are talking to someone who doesn't care enough to pay attention to what you are saying. Attending skills are characterized by good facial mannerisms such as eye contact, head nods, and squinting or lifting of the eyebrows as appropriate. Egan (1998) has suggested the acronym of SOLER (straight, open, lean, eye contact, relaxed) as the key elements of body posture that imply that your attention is with the speaker. By *straight*, Egan means the need to face the listener squarely. *Open* refers to a posture in which your arms and legs are relaxed, not crossed or turned away from the listener. *Lean* means to bend forward slightly as if you are approaching your consultee in a positive way. Good *eye contact* means that at least 50 percent of the time you are looking at the speaker. When she is talking to you, your eye contact should be closer to 100 percent. *Relaxed* means that you are able to do each of the four behaviors just mentioned in such a way that they do not appear artificial or stilted. It is probably the most important of the five SOLER keys.

Consultants need to be careful not to let personal habits interfere with their communication style and detract from it. Some people squint too much, twirl their hair, look at their nails, or look at the clock or their watch every 30 seconds. All of this tells the listener that they aren't paying attention, possibly because they are bored.

Effective body language is necessary for anyone who wishes to convey the idea that he really cares about what another person is saying. It is one of the nonverbal aspects of communication, which often carries a more important message than the verbal aspects do. Other nonverbal factors include the *setting* in which consultation is held (the consultee's classroom versus your formal office), *time allotted* (allow enough time; don't act as if you would rather be elsewhere), and *image generation*

ACTIVITY 3.1

In teams of two (dyads), have one person try to speak to another who seems bored, disinterested, distant, or otherwise nonattending, perhaps behaving as others have done to you. Discuss how this makes the speaker feel. Then have one of the partners try the SOLER skills, modifying them until they feel comfortable both to the speaker and the listener.

(avoid acting or dressing in a superior manner or acting as if you are doing the consultee a favor to talk to her).

Attending is both physical and psychological. It isn't happening if it doesn't look like it is; that is why the SOLER skills, or some modification of them (Carkhuff & Pierce, 1975), are essential. Beyond these surface appearances, however, are the more important internal attending skills, which require a balance among listening to the words the consultee is using; translating them according to your experiences and preferred theories; and blocking out your urges to interrupt, pass judgment, or rush to a conclusion. Urging your consultee to cut to the chase is a good fantasy but will give him the clear impression that he and his perceptions of the problem and possible solutions are not important.

Active Listening

Active, or reflective, listening as a communication skill has gained in popularity since the 1970s because of the works of Carkhuff (1969), Ginott (1972), and Gordon (1974). Active listening shows the speaker that you have heard both the subject content and the emotional content of her message. The active listener reflects back the speaker's words in such a way that the speaker knows that her words have been accurately heard and that the listener has understood the feelings behind the words. A more passive listener may be listening, but rarely gets really involved in the content of the message. This passive style has its uses, especially if the listener senses that the speaker just wishes to "vent" for awhile.

Gordon (1974, pp. 48–49) has presented twelve "roadblocks" to active listening. These are methods or tactics that have the effect, wittingly or otherwise, of blocking communication. They are presented here with examples of what a consultant might say to demonstrate each one. Of course, using these roadblocks will likely spoil a consultation relationship. Imagine how you would feel if any of the following statements were made to you!

1. *Ordering, commanding, directing.* "Never mind what might happen; just ignore the student when he acts out. You have to do it; it's a 'best practice'."
2. *Warning, threatening.* "If you don't use some different tactic in regard to the student, I won't be responsible for the consequences."

3. *Moralizing, preaching, giving "shoulds" and "oughts."* "You shouldn't allow your personal feelings to enter into it. You ought to be able to deal with the student more objectively."

4. *Advising, offering solutions or suggestions.* "Well, be that as it may, it would be best to do it my way. I've seen it work before in other classes; it ought to work for you."

5. *Teaching, lecturing, giving logical arguments.* "Of course positive reinforcement works. Haven't you read the literature? It's worked on much tougher kids than your student, so it should work here, too."

6. *Judging, criticizing, disagreeing, blaming.* "Your teaching methods won't work with these inner-city kids. Didn't they tell you that at your teacher's college?"

7. *Name calling, stereotyping, labeling.* "You're like a lot of beginning teachers I've seen. You're afraid that if you're firm, the kids won't like you. I call that being wishy-washy."

8. *Interpreting, analyzing, diagnosing.* "You know, when you don't engage in the interventions we've discussed, I begin to wonder what there is about you that's behind this resistance."

9. *Praising, agreeing, giving positive evaluations.* "Well, anyone as bright as you who's been to Euphoric U. ought to be able to figure out how to work with these students with ADHD."

10. *Reassuring, sympathizing, consoling, supporting.* "First of all, it's not the end of the world. These are tough kids. We all know that. Just keep a stiff upper lip, don't let them see you cry, and I'm sure you'll make it to Thanksgiving."

11. *Questioning, probing, interrogating, cross-examining.* "Why do you think the student is misbehaving? No, why do you really think she is? Now look at your reactions to her. What's behind that? Is there something else?"

12. *Withdrawing, distracting, being sarcastic, humoring, diverting.* "This is a tough one. Tell me, how's it going with the others? Surely they can't all be ruining your career. Ha, ha; just kidding."

ACTIVITY 3.2

Review Gordon's (1974) 12 roadblocks to active listening. Think of a comment that a child or an adult might make that has embedded feelings not directly expressed (for example, "Oh my God! My mother-in-law is coming over this weekend!"). Invent responses that would fit each of the 12 roadblocks Gordon describes. Do you know anyone who uses some or all of these roadblocks?

Bolton (1986) has grouped Gordon's 12 roadblocks into three categories: *sending solutions* (numbers 1 through 5), *judging* (numbers 6 through 9), and *avoiding others' concerns* (numbers 10 through 12). Miller (1996) mentions nine common stereotypes of ineffective communication styles:

Florist: avoids issues by using flowery euphemisms.

Detective: skirts issues by persistently prying with questions.

Magician: dismisses issues by pretending they are not there.

Drill sergeant: avoids conflict by barking orders.

Foreman: clouds issues with compulsive business.

Hangman: induces guilt to avoid confronting problems.

Guru: covers issues by giving a cliché for every occasion.

Swami: smoke-screens issues by predicting dismal outcomes.

Sign painter: dismisses problems by tacking labels onto them.

Subskills of active listening include the use of *prompts,* such as "You're feeling angry because Mrs. Brown has said some things that you don't think are fair." Generally these responses make the speaker feel that you have really been attending to his message, not just to his words, and that you want to hear more about it. *Clarification-seeking* and *summarizing* are other subskills of active listening. Here are some examples of clarification-seeking:

"I'm not sure that I understand what is happening between you two. Could you tell me more about it?"

"Tell me more about his rudeness to the other children. Just what does he say to them?"

"So what you're telling me is that only the cold-stare technique seems to be having any effect. Is that correct?"

The following are examples of summarizing:

"Now, let me summarize to be sure I'm hearing everything you've told me."

"OK, here's what I'm hearing: _____. Are those the main points?"

Being Empathic

Empathy is implied by active listening, but I highlight it because it is crucial to the consultant's general style and demeanor. Teachers and parents expect professionals in the field of education to be empathic. They want educators to listen to their concerns, to understand them at a level greater than just the word meanings alone, and not to cut them off before they have expressed themselves. Indeed, empathy is one of the most important, and often one of the most difficult, skills and attitudes that school consultants need to possess.

ACTIVITY 3.3

In dyads, person A speaks to person B about some real or imagined trauma that she remembers from her childhood. Person B puts a mark on a piece of paper every time he feels like commenting instead of listening until person A has told her whole story. Reverse the roles. How did person A feel when she found that she could tell her whole story without being interrupted? How many times did person B have to mark his paper because he felt like commenting or questioning person A?

Being Assertive

The consultant needs to be assertive in her response style. Dettmer, Dyck, and Thurston (1999) have discussed seven basic aspects of an assertive communication style, which are listed below with an example of each:

Use an "I" message instead of a "you" message: "I'm concerned about our lack of progress. What do you think is preventing Maria from progressing?"

Say "and" instead of "but": "Your firmness was really needed there, and your efforts at controlling the whole group have really improved."

State behavior objectively: "What I saw when I was in your room was that Joanne twice hit other children, but not hard or with what I would call an attempt to harm them. Is this usually the way she interacts with others?"

Name your own feelings: "I just wanted to tell you how thrilled I am with the way you deal with the 'fearsome foursome.' You are providing the curriculum and methods that encourage attending and responding from them as well as the others. It's great to watch it working so well."

Say what you want to happen: "We've discussed your approach to the 'fearsome foursome' previously. We had agreed that you would separate them and assign them to the same group only rarely. We know that doing this reduces the number of disruptions. I believe you ought to be implementing that intervention. What do you think?"

Express concern for others: Acknowledging the realities for teachers and parents is a method used by collaboratively minded consultants to indicate that they are empathic (see above) and are trying to demonstrate that they have concern for these realities. This statement was used by the author when talking with a teacher in a self-contained class for students with emotional disturbance: "Bill, teaching your students is one of the toughest jobs on this campus. People aren't exactly waiting in line to take your class. It's draining; it's frustrating. I admire you for being as patient as you are when so many of your students are having a bad time of it all at once."

Use assertive body language: Consider your regard for, and willingness to work closely with, individuals who have trouble establishing and maintaining eye contact, slouch, mutter, seem very unsure of anything, and act like they would rather be somewhere else. Most people would rather spend their professional hours with people who reflect the opposite picture to the one I've just painted. They admire and tend to follow the reasoning and ideas of people who have some degree of "command presence," a term used in the military to refer to an image that indicates confidence and authority, necessary traits in officers. Obviously, a collaboratively minded school consultant isn't operating from the hierarchical stance that military life requires; these consultants use their assertive body language to convey the image that the referral problem will be solved, that they and the consultee can work together to solve it, and quitting is not a viable option.

As simple as these suggestions may seem, some consultants find them increasingly difficult to practice when the consultation relationship starts to falter, possibly due to uncooperative behavior from the consultee. Some consultees seem to project a passive resistance that is hard to pin down. Sometimes the consultant simply has to "call the game," a phrase used by Berne (1964) to refer to a confrontative tactic in which one party informs the other that she detects a failure to progress because of some resistance on the part of the other, and she wants to know what's behind it. Here the consultant needs to use an assertive style that lets the consultee recognize the consultant's concerns and perceptions without blaming or accusing. Further information about, and ideas to remedy, resistance in consultation are developed later in this chapter.

Questioning

This is the most important and most delicate skill in the consultative interaction because questions, by their very nature, can be both inviting and threatening. Their primary purpose, of course, is to gain information; but the manner in which they are used may often have unfortunate consequences, particularly if the consultee suspects that the point of a question is other than what its surface content implies. One of the most important realities in a consultative relationship is that the consultee is seeking help in regard to a work-related problem. This can result in the (usually unstated) belief that he is therefore in a "one-down" position relative to the consultant. After all, he is seeking help; and in the cultures in which most of us were raised, seeking help is a way of appearing unable to handle our own affairs or deal with our own work-related responsibilities. It is therefore incumbent on the consultant to ask questions in such a way that the consultee is not threatened by the questions and, by extension, the consultation process.

Questions serve three main purposes: to gather information and data, to seek opinions, and to detect attitudes. The first purpose is the most important and ostensibly the one that underlies most questions. The other two purposes may be more covert: The consultant gets information about the subjective realities that may be coloring the interactions between the consultee and the student but are not spoken about objectively. For example, consider a teacher–consultee who has implemented a behavior management program that he does not want to use because he believes it is either too labor-intensive or simply won't work. His responses to the consultant's questions about how it is working will give the consultant a pretty good idea that the consultee doesn't want to continue with this strategy. As a consultant, when you get this feeling, it is best to inquire about it, using the assertive response styles previously discussed. Consider the following interchange between a consultant and a consultee about a token-economy system:

Consultant:	Bill, tell me how the point system is working for Allen.
Consultee:	Yeah, well, we're doing it. I don't know. He might be getting better.
Consultant:	You sound a little unsure. Is the frequency of yelling out decreasing since you started using the point system?
Consultee:	Oh, I don't know. I'm too busy to be doing all this charting and whatever. He's probably better. I'm going to go back to using the sentence-writing strategy. [This is a punishment tactic in which the client writes "I must not talk out in class" fifty times for every time he talks out. It is this consultee's favorite technique; he's well known for it.] Allen needs to know that I mean business.

It seems clear that the consultee has not bought into the point system. It's possible not enough groundwork was laid, he does not have the skills necessary to do it, or he may be philosophically opposed to rewarding students for expected behavior. For whatever reason, the information-seeking questions have revealed opinions and attitudes that need to be worked on before progress can be expected to occur.

There are three excellent sources of detailed information about the questioning process in consultation, all of them found in the counseling literature: Cormier and Cormier (1985, summarized in some depth in Kurpius & Rozecki, 1993), Egan (1998), and Benjamin (1987).

Benjamin (1987) indicates that there are three format considerations in the questioning process: open/closed, direct/indirect, and single/multiple. An open question is designed to gain maximum information over a relatively broad scope. "Tell me about Jane's progress over the past two months" is quite open since it asks for (apparently) any kind of information over a long period of time in any area that strikes the consultee as important. A closed question, however, asks for brief answers to highly focused questions, such as "Tell me how often Bill hit others on the playground today during the morning recess" or "Tell me how many words José read correctly in this week's one-minute assessment." Note that neither of these "questions" ends with a question mark.

A direct question is a straight request for information: "How do you like teaching students who have learning disabilities?" or "How many words did José get right on the one-minute assessment?" An indirect question seeks information in a more subtle fashion: "I'd sure like to know how it must be to work with these kids all day long" or "It must be frustrating dealing with parents who don't respond to their children's needs." Note that these indirect questions, like those concluding the paragraph above, do not have question marks; they seem to lie somewhere between a statement and a direct question. Most people understand that when a speaker uses this indirect style, she expects the listener to respond as if a question had been asked. Some consultees aren't naturally forthcoming; they seem reticent about speaking their minds unless they know, by a direct interrogatory, that they are expected to respond with something other than a yes or no. Only your experience with them tells you what you can expect in this regard. Consider the following "fencing match" between a consultant using a series of direct questions and a consultee who acts guarded in his response style:

Consultant:	So how's it going with Shaquelle?
Consultee:	Fine.
Consultant:	Is he getting to school more often now?
Consultee:	I guess so.
Consultant:	Has his responsiveness to you increased?
Consultee:	Hard to tell.

The consultant will sense that the consultee seems to be avoiding a meaningful discussion through the use of noncommittal and vague responses. Given a conversation like that, the consultant has reason to be concerned about the quality of the professional, communicative relationship between himself and the consultee. In that case, the consultant may shift to a more indirect method of asking for information, such as the following: "I know you've been concerned with Shaquelle's apparent disinterest in school, and you've tried some interventions. Tell me how you see the picture now." This addition of a "prefatory statement" (Friend & Cook, 2000) is useful for establishing a context for the question, and reminding the consultee of the steps already taken or suggested.

Single questions such as "What do you do when Omar gets into his dawdling mode?" seem to enhance the communication process much more than do multiple questions, such as "What do you do when Omar gets into his dawdling mode? Do you get after him right away or wait awhile? How do you know when to intervene? Some people react too quickly I think; what do you think?" Confronted with that barrage of multiple questions, most consultees probably, and correctly, ask you to wait until they can answer one question before you ask another.

Courtroom lawyers know that it is best to only ask questions to which they already know the answers. They ask for specific information in each question in order to guard against the possibility that the witness may go too far in responding to a vague question and thereby spoil the direction in which the lawyer wanted him to go. Lawyers don't want surprises. In school consultation we do not have this artificial constraint impeding us, and we very often want the chips to fall where they may since we know that this tells us about the consultee's opinions and attitudes. Still, it is generally best to focus our questions for a number of reasons. First, we get the kind of information we're after. Second, our time is usually limited, and although we might like to spend more time with each consultee, we and they usually don't have that luxury. Third, by being focused we give the consultee the impression that we are efficient and competent. Finally, it is dangerous to be casual in our choice of questions with some consultees because they take that as an excuse to ramble. There are definitely times to ask "How's it going?" but we are likely to make more specific progress if we ask "In regard to the extinction plan, can you give me an example of when it seemed to work?" When the consultee has responded to that single, direct, and closed question, then you may want to ask "And can you give me an example of when it didn't?"

ACTIVITY 3.4

Class members should list examples of poor questioning techniques that they have encountered. Discuss why these techniques were poor, why they were used, and what effect they had on the communication process. Class members should suggest ways to improve these techniques.

For example, a consultant is concerned about the appropriateness of a given curriculum for an included student. She says to the teacher, "Can't you find something more appropriate for Billy to do?" Instead of using this confrontive technique, how might she have begun the discussion of the curriculum?

ACTIVITY 3.5

In teams of three, have partner A ask a very general, broad, open question, such as "Well, how's it going?" Partner B should focus the question, such as "How does the rules-ignore-praise plan seem to be working?" Partner C should turn it into a closed question, such as "Since implementing the R.I.P. program, what has been the frequency per day of Billy's loud outbursts?" Team members should take turns practicing the different ways of asking questions and reflect on how they would feel as a consultee if they were asked questions in the various styles possible.

ACTIVITY 3.6

In teams of three, generate some realistic topics for a consultant–consultee interchange. Then have member A play the role of the consultant, member B the consultee, and member C an observer. The consultant conducts the interview for about five minutes, while the consultee responds. The observer then comments on the interview (positive criticism mainly) using the following criteria:

Was some degree of rapport established?
Did the interview flow well?

Was there a good balance between open and closed questions, and direct and indirect questions?

Were single questions primarily used?

Were questions posed in such a way that the consultee didn't appear to be threatened by them?

If most of the answers were positive, the consultant did a good job. Change roles until each partner has had a chance to play each role.

ACTIVITY 3.7

Videotape a simulated consultative interaction, preferably with a consultee with whom you are not familiar. When reviewing the tape, respond to the questions presented in Activity 3.6. Note your body language and nonverbal communication efforts. Were you aware of them? Do you believe they add to or detract from your interviewing skills?

A Behavioral Approach to Communication

Bergan (1977) and Kratochwill and Bergan (1990) have made major contributions to the development of the behavioral approach to consultation, which was discussed in Chapter 2. An integral component of the behavioral approach is the use of an interview method designed to gather information and clarify issues during each of the four stages of the behavioral approach: problem identification, problem analysis, plan implementation, and problem evaluation (Martens, 1993). Behaviorists believe that it is necessary to have a formal structure for interviewing consultees for the following reasons:

- It facilitates discussion. By having a structured system, the consultant knows what steps she should follow and in what sequence.

- The structure allows the consultant to influence not only the flow of the conversation but the consultee's verbal behavior as well. Erchul (1987) has indicated that consultees perceive controlling consultants (that is, those with high dominance scores on personality inventories) as more effective. (*Note:* For a lively discussion of the research that supports consultant dominance of the communication process, see Gutkin, 1999, and Erchul, 1999).

- Progress in refining the process of consultation can only be made if there is control of the relevant variables, one of which is the method of interviewing.

Bergan (1977) describes *three dimensions of the communication process* in behavioral consultation, all of which apply to the information-gathering process. The first is *content,* which has seven areas: (1) background-environmental, (2) setting factors, (3) the parameters of the client's behavior, (4) special characteristics of the client, (5) the content of the observations, (6) efforts made to correct the problem to date and suggestions for future efforts, and (7) other. These seven areas should be covered in the initial formal interview with the consultee, although data about them may not be readily available. For example, consultees may not have gathered any real data about the incidence of a challenging behavior; they may just know that it is a problem, at least to them. Also, it may not be best to establish any firm future plan until the consultant has made an observation. In the case of the seventh category (other), this may involve information that the consultee doesn't have, which will have to be obtained from further observation or from others (for example, is the student supposed to be wearing glasses?).

Bergan's second dimension consists of *five verbal processes: specification* ("Tell me more about. . . ."), *evaluation* ("How do you feel about. . . ?"), *inferences* ("It seems to me. . . ."), *summarizations* ("Let's review my understanding of what's going on."), and *validation* ("Can we conclude . . . ? It seems to me. . . ."). Although some of these examples are stated in the indirect question mode, they could easily be turned into direct questions as long as they serve the purpose of clarification, which is a type of information seeking.

The third dimension consists of *two types of leads* that the consultant uses: *elicitors* and *emitters.* The elicitor is a question; the emitter is a statement of fact. Both may be used to gather information. This is obvious in the case of the elicitor (for example, "Tell me how often. . . .") but less obvious in the case of an emitter (for example, "Every time Billy threatens the other children, they give him a wide berth. It seems like it works for him.").

Figure 3.1 gives examples of how the three dimensions operate together in the verbal content categories labeled "parameters of the client's behavior" and "special characteristics of the client," the verbal processes of specification and summarization, and both elicitor and emitter leads.

Bergan (1977), Kratochwill and Bergan (1990), and Brown, Pryzwansky, and Schulte (2001) give more examples of questions and statements that exemplify Bergan's three dimensions of communication. Benes, Gutkin, and Kramer (1991) have done a microanalysis of consultee and consultant verbal and nonverbal behavior using Bergan's consultation analysis record (1977) to measure the verbal aspects of the conversations and another coding system to measure nonverbal (affective) aspects of the conversation—specifically, consultant and consultee voice cues or intonation, facial cues, and body cues. Although their results are not generalizable (they used only two graduate students as their consultants), they do point the way toward a potentially sophisticated method of analyzing the verbal and nonverbal aspects of the communication dyad so common to consultation.

ACTIVITY 3.8

Make up questions and statements about a mythical case and then analyze them according to Bergan's three dimensions. Review occasions when the consultant may want to use different parts of each of these dimensions.

Figure 3.1

Examples of Bergan's three dimensions of communication

Content: Parameters of the client's behavior

Process: Specification

Leads:

> *Elicitor:* "Can you estimate how often Diego has had these behavioral episodes and how long they last?"
>
> *Emitter:* "I'm curious about the ways his behavior has increased since you started the intervention."

Process: Summarization

Leads:

> *Elicitor:* "Let's see if I have this right. Every time Susan puts her head down on her desk, do you start the timer?"
>
> *Emitter:* "OK, so what happens is that Devore gives you a dirty look whenever you prompt him to get busy."

Content: Special characteristics of the client

Process: Specification

Leads:

> *Elicitor:* "What effect do you think Sam's hearing disorder has on his adjustment?"
>
> *Emitter:* "Being the middle child in a family can be hard on some children."

Process: Summarization

Leads:

> *Elicitor:* "Given Sally's dependency on you, which we've seen for months, what steps do you think are appropriate at this time?"
>
> *Emitter:* "It seems like we have good news: The distractible behavior of both of your ADHD children has decreased."

The Interview

All of the communication skills we have discussed are used in an interview format, which may be informal or formal. Informal interviews are more common. They consist of those numerous occasions when the consultant and the consultee meet in the hallway or the teacher's lounge and spend a relatively unstructured (but not purposeless) five minutes or so talking about a student. Formal interviews are planned in advance, are held at a specified time and place, have a definite agenda and set of goals, and may occur in a group or team setting (for example, an SST).

In responding to a referral, the consultant has the option of making the first meeting with the consultee either formal or informal. This choice depends on a number of factors, including the consultant's relationship with the consultee, the amount of information already known about the client, the apparent severity of the problem, and school or district policies. When it is the consultant's choice to decide how to proceed, it is generally best to schedule an informal meeting first, simply to find out how severe the referral problem is. Sometimes this informal meeting is all that is necessary: The consultee may leave with the information or idea that she needs in order to deal effectively with the problem without any further assistance. Usually, however, the result of this first (informal) meeting is the decision to either direct this referral to the SST or to some other ancillary consultant, or to meet again in a formal way.

When setting up a formal interview, it is important to establish a non-hierarchical, collaborative relationship at the outset. You can do this by having the consultee establish the time and place of the meeting. Since teacher–consultees have a fairly rigid daily schedule compared to that of most school consultants, this flexibility on the part of the consultant should be expected. These meetings usually take place in the consultee's classroom and, of course, at a time when the students are elsewhere.

The consultant should have at least a semi-structured set of questions to ask during the formal interview. I suggest "semi-structured" because the flow of the interview may suggest times when a formally structured plan, such as is suggested by the behaviorists, may prove to be too rigid at a time when flexibility may be more appropriate. The nature of the questions depends on the nature of the referral. In the case of behavior problem referrals, the consultant will want to know about type, frequency, duration, impact, and goals of the behaviors in addition to information about antecedents, consequences, and the sequence of actions that constitute the behavior problem. Dettmer, Dyck, and Thurston (1999) have provided a set of questions, thoughts, facilitative comments, and factors to look for during each of the ten steps they have outlined in their consultation process. Similar information is available in Chapter 5 of this book in the description of the ten-step solutions-oriented consultation system.

Taking Notes, Keeping Track

It is important for the consultant to take notes during a formal interview. Since some consultees may be disconcerted by your note keeping, it is necessary for you to explain why you will be doing so, especially if this is the first formal interview you have had with a particular consultee. Your reasons will probably include at least the following:

1. It is important that you keep information accurately since many situations are complicated.
2. You are dealing with many student–teacher–parent issues at the same time, and it is easy to get cases confused as the weeks go by if you don't keep fairly detailed notes.
3. You will probably be writing a report on this referral at some point, especially if it becomes a referral for special education eligibility consideration, and your notes are necessary for this purpose.

It is important for the consultee to understand that your note taking isn't part of some devious plot to undermine his security as a teacher. My experience is that teacher and parent consultees seem favorably impressed when they see that I am keeping notes; one teacher commented that she wished her physician seemed as interested in what she had to say as I did!

As the interview progresses, it usually becomes clear that additional information will be needed in order to understand and deal with the problem. Some of this information will be obtained by the consultee, and some by the consultant. Some may come from conversations with others (such as parents, last year's teacher, the counselor, outside agency personnel, and so on); and some will be obtained through observation by the consultee, the consultant, or both. The "wh" issues (who, what, when, where) need to be settled before the interview is concluded so that both parties know their respective responsibilities in regard to the next steps.

It is a good idea to give the consultee a copy of your notes, either the ones you wrote during the interview or a more polished and summarized version that you can prepare as soon as the interview is completed. Not only does this give the consultee the impression that you and he have covered important issues, but it also shows that you regard him as a full partner in the process. This report or summary should also include each partner's responsibilities regarding the "wh" questions.

Figures 3.2 and 3.3 are examples of summary notes given to consultees after a first consultation meeting with a consultant. These summary statements were generated from the notes the consultant took during the interview with the consultee. Both are good examples of solutions-oriented collaborative consultations.

Dettmer et al. (1999) present an example of a consultation log in which one records the date, participants, and topic of each consultation meeting, along with other information such as the general topic of concern, the purpose of the meeting, a brief summary of what transpired, steps agreed on (by whom and when), and follow-up plans. Conoley and Conoley (1992) suggest the use of progress notes with these sections: nature of the problem, with whom discussed, possible strategies, interventions tried and degree of success, current plans, and other comments.

Figure 3.2

Summary notes from a first consultation meeting (Billy)

Consultee (teacher): Ms. Sallie

Grade: 5 (and RSP)   **Room:** 14

Consultant: Ms. Morrison, RSP teacher

Student referred: Billy Appleby

Student's birthdate: 5-20-91

Date: 9-26-01

School: Jefferson

Parent: Mrs. Appleby

Age: 10-4

Reason for referral: Billy isn't completing his work in any subjects in his main-streamed fifth-grade class with Ms. Sallie. He dawdles, plays with toys, talks to and bothers others, and alternates between being the class clown and playing the role of the tough guy (e.g., "You can't make me"). Ms. Sallie is suggesting a self-contained class for him.

Background information: Billy is the second of three children of parents who were divorced in June 2000. His schoolwork started to fall off last year (mother's report). Mom now works full time. Father has moved to another state. Billy is doing well in his one period of special education with me.

Solutions that have been tried and results: Billy has been kept after school, made to take work home, been moved nearer the teacher, and been put on a behavior contract. His mother has also tried tutoring him at home. The contract has helped somewhat but probably needs to have stronger contingencies. Otherwise, he just seems to be getting worse.

Tentative ideas that were discussed: Review behavior contract (consultant and consultee); conference with mother; conference with Billy; counseling for Billy; use Billy as a tutor, dependent on increased productivity of work (possibly in a different special education class); get Billy a tutor from an upper grade; get Billy an in-class study-buddy; I'll assess further to determine specific skill deficiencies in the content areas; increased consultation time between Ms. Sallie and me.

Today's plan: Consultant will arrange a conference with Billy and then with his mom. Consultee will review behavior contract with Billy, seeking input from him on more effective reinforcers. Consultee will review Billy's day with him at the close of every day for one week; a note will be sent home to Mom summarizing each day. I'll do an additional assessment within a week. I'll contact Mr. Pruzek (school psychologist) about possible counseling.

Next meeting date: 10-4-01 at 10:30, Ms. Sallie's room.

cc: Mr. Poplar, Principal; Mrs. Appleby; Mr. Pruzek, counselor.

Figure 3.3

Summary notes from a first consultation meeting (Joshua)

Consultee (teacher): Ms. Hedy   **Date:** 9-4-01

Grade: 2 (Spec. ed; SDC)   **Room:** 8   **School:** Carver

Consultant: Dr. Kampwirth, School Psychologist

Student: Joshua McCovey   **Age:** 8-1   **Parent:** Mrs. Mays (MGP)

Student's birthdate: 8-6-1993

Reason for referral: We discussed three concerns: (1) Joshua's failure to complete his work in all areas; (2) his disruptive behavior, defined as bothering others, which draws your attention away from your teaching and his peers' learning; and (3) your concern about his low level of academic skills.

Background information: Joshua was apparently sent by his mother last year to live with his grandmother, Mrs. Mays. His father visits him occasionally, but is not a dependable source of parenting for Joshua. Joshua was seen by the counselor last year because of loud, disruptive behavior in the classroom. The counselor put Joshua on a behavioral contract, but it had little apparent success. Joshua has been identified as a student with an emotional disturbance, and was placed in the self-contained special education class in May 2001.

Interventions that have been tried and success to date: You have been giving him the services of your aide for 25 minutes a day of individualized reading assistance, along with Sam and Danielle. It is too early to tell if this is having a worthwhile effect. You have been keeping him after school on some of the days when he hasn't finished his work. Again, it's too early to notice any effect, though you suspect that he enjoys this extra time at school. You have moved his seat in an effort to reduce his disruptiveness. Not much change is noted as a result of this. You are also implementing a Colored Card system, which apparently hasn't had enough time to have an effect as yet.

Tentative ideas that were discussed: You've considered time-out, but aren't sure yet if you want to try this. You've decided to stop the staying-after-school plan, since it may be reinforcing to him. You want to help him keep his work area clean by instituting an "Area Clean-up Time" for the whole class just before dismissal. We might want to consider reinstituting the counseling services again.

Today's plan: We agreed for now to continue his reading work with the aide. We also thought it worthwhile to try a very brief (60 seconds or so) time-out to the "no-work desk" contingent on his bothering others. These tactics are designed to increase his skills, bolster his work productivity, and remind him of his behavioral obligations toward others. These seem to be excellent goals to have for your work with Joshua. These interventions will be continued for at least two weeks to determine their effectiveness.

    Also, we discussed some other ideas about his disruptiveness. I'll visit on Wednesday morning to observe him. Let's both be thinking about ways to improve his task attendance and good student behaviors. It's your choice on the time-out procedure; I think it's worth a try.

I had mentioned to you that I would look into criteria for getting assistance in the Reading Recovery program. I also mentioned talking with Joshua's grandmother about her helping him at home. We'll do more with this idea when we meet next. Also, I'll put a note in the counselor's (Mr. Galindo) box about our next meeting time and encourage him to come. Also, you agreed to ask Ms. Marks, the school psychologist, about developing a functional behavioral assessment on Joshua.

Next meeting date: 10-4-01 at 3:00 in Ms. Hedy's room.

cc: Mr. Poplar, Principal; Mr Galindo, Counselor; Ms. Marks, School Psychologist

Controlling the Consultative Interaction

To what extent should the consultant attempt to control the flow of conversation in consultation? Behaviorists (Bergan, 1977; Erchul, 1987; Erchul & Martens, 1997; Kratochwill & Bergan, 1990) believe that it is appropriate and necessary for the consultant to structure verbal interactions in order to gather the required information as efficiently as possible. Erchul (1987), for example, concluded that dominance (defined as the ratio between attempts to control an interaction by the consultant and consultee's yielding such control) and consultee's perceptions of consultant effectiveness were positively related and approached statistical significance (p <.08). Gutkin (1999) has pointed out some inconsistencies in the Erchul (1987) article, as well as other articles (Erchul & Chewning, 1990; Witt, Erchul, McKee, Pardue, & Wickstrom, 1991) purporting to demonstrate the advantages of dominance or other aspects of control on the part of consultants. Witt et al. (1991) provide some evidence that if consultants control the conversation during consultation, consultees are more willing to cooperate in gathering baseline data and in carrying out treatment plans. Unfortunately, this study only used as consultants individuals who adhered to a behavioristic model, so there is no way to know if the consultees would have responded similarly to a more collaborative model of verbal interaction. DeForest and Hughes (1992), Hughes and DeForest (1993), Maitland et al. (1985), and Schowengerdt et al. (1976) have demonstrated the effectiveness of a collaborative approach through studies that point to the importance of interpersonal skills that have the effect of making the consultee feel supported in his efforts. Other studies (Babcock & Pryzwansky, 1983; Pryzwansky & White, 1983) have shown potential consumers of school consultation services to have a clear preference for a collaborative relationship rather than one dominated by consultant control of the process. Those who favor a more collaborative mode are comfortable with letting the consultee give direction to the conversation based on her needs and interests as long as the conversation is goal-directed (Friend & Cook, 2000; Thomas, Correa, & Morsink, 1995). Safran (1991) summarizes his review of the communication process in consultation:

Overall, it is my conclusion that communication research in school-based consultation has largely been conceptualized as a linear interaction between parties or as addressing questions colored by functionalist and behaviorist thinking. Although these conceptualizations of the problem-solving process allow researchers to optimalize experimental control of the variables and produce "clean data," the process often becomes isolated from the realities of school life. For example, Bergan's analysis of the verbal interaction process, although of great value strictly on a content level, omits such factors as personality, interpersonal affect, domineeringness, and school organization. In addition, the interpretavist perspective, which places its highest priority on collaboration and a purist "negotiated understanding" of the system (Daniels & DeWine, 1991), may be incompatible with empirical paradigms that dominate school psychology and special education research. (pp. 366–367)

Potential Difficulties in Communication

It is not uncommon in interpersonal communications for people to miscommunicate, to talk past each other, to simply disagree, and possibly to slip into an argument that may disrupt, if not destroy, the consultative process. Although consultants cannot control the reactions of consultees, they can avoid behaviors on their part that may lead to poor communication and problem-solving breakdowns. Pugach and Johnson (1995) discuss several barriers to effective communication:

1. *Advice.* Eventually, consultants do give advice, if only as a confirmation or facilitation of a consultee's thinking about his own problem-solving efforts. When teachers and parents are stuck for ideas, the consultant should certainly be able to suggest a number of alternative interventions, hopefully based on best practices. The error is in giving your advice before the consultee has had a chance to explore his own thinking about solutions; in giving your advice too quickly, before you have a good grasp of the problem and/or before the consultee is ready for it; or because it is your favorite technique. Our "quick fixes" often do not meet the criteria of treatment acceptability or treatment validity (see Chapter 5).

2. *False reassurances.* Some consultants, in an effort to relieve the stress of a consultee, make it sound like the referral issue is really quite simple and may resolve itself, or will quickly be improved. This may serve to minimize the consultee's feelings and devalue her concerns. It may also set up a feeling within herself that she must be incompetent to be worried about something so trivial. Finally, it may set up a situation where time proves that the consultee was right about the seriousness of a problem, thus indicating a lack of competence on the part of the consultant. The false reassurance is similar to one of Gordon's (1974) roadblocks to effective communication.

3. *Misdirected questions.* This happens for one of two reasons: (1) the consultant has his own agenda and seems determined to force it on the consultee, attempting to have the problem fit a predetermined notion the consultant has formed about the problem or (2) the consultant's listening skills are so poorly developed that he has no idea that he is interrupting or asking irrelevant questions. Here is an example of this latter problem:

Consultant: So, Ms. Ortiz, tell me about Alphonso.

Ms. Ortiz: Well, his reading is really quite poor. He—

Consultant (Interrupting):	Oh, like so many of those second-language boys. By the way, does he have a brother in the fourth grade? I think I know him.
Ms. Ortiz:	Well, yes he does. But Alphonso is really almost a non-reader—
Consultant (Interrupting again):	Well, here's what we have to do. Can you get me his cumulative folder? Put it in my mailbox. Now, if he's like his brother, well, you tell me. Does he have ADHD?

Here the consultant is flying off in all directions, lacking focus and sensitivity to the needs and interests of the consultee. Somehow the question of how to get help for Alphonso in reading has become a family-related problem, epidemic among English-language learners, and possibly associated with ADHD. One wonders if this consultant will ever begin to problem solve about Alphonso's reading problem.

4. *Wandering interaction.* This is similar to the issue of misdirected questions, but here the consultant seems to be the person with ADD. She can't remember what was told to her a few minutes ago, gets cases mixed up, and seems unable to focus on what is relevant.

5. *Interruptions.* Just as the consultee is getting to the heart of the concern, the consultant breaks in to ask questions or to make comments that frustrate the efforts of the consultee to tell her story. This sort of consultant impulsivity breaks the flow of the interaction and suggests that trying to problem solve with this consultant is not worth the effort.

6. *Cliches.* The use of cliches tends to diminish the stature of the person to whom they are directed. To refer to a student as a "shady eighty," a reference to one for whom there are lowered academic expectations because his or her I.Q. is in the eighties, or to imply that parentage is the root of a student's problems, as in "The apple doesn't fall far from the tree," not only implies lowered expectations for the student but may cause the teacher–consultee to give up trying to implement accommodations in behalf of the student.

7. *Credibility gap.* This is the most subtle of the communication problems. It involves the usually unspoken belief on the part of one or both parties that they shouldn't take the consultation process seriously because the other party isn't (a) competent, (b) in a position to collaborate, or (c) of any real help. This can occur when a consultee has been so uncooperative in the past that the consultant enters a dyadic interaction with little hope for a positive outcome. It can also occur if a consultee has no faith that the consultant can grasp the significance of a problem or can help construct meaningful interventions. In either case, the lack of faith precludes success because collaboration cannot operate in a climate of little faith in each other.

Evaluating Your Communication Skills

Many of the skills I have mentioned do not come easily or naturally to those wishing to become school-based consultants. It is important that all consultants periodically evaluate themselves either by self-analysis or by asking others, usually consultees, to evaluate them. West, Idol, and Cannon (1989) have provided a self-assessment device that includes factors such as personal characteristics, interactive communication, and collaborative problem solving, among others. The consultant rates himself on the numerous items that are included under each factor. For example, under *personal characteristics* is "maintain positive self-concept and enthusiastic attitude throughout the consultation process." Under *interactive communication* is "give and solicit continuous feedback that is specific, immediate, and objective." And under *collaborative problem solving* is "evaluate intervention alternatives to anticipate possible consequences, narrow and combine choices, and assign priorities."

Both beginning and experienced consultants will do well to occasionally have their efforts at consultation evaluated by their consultee(s). Feedback of this sort can help the consultant to understand how others perceive both the consultant personally and her effectiveness. Conoley and Conoley (1982) have provided a self-analysis form that could easily be used by others to evaluate the consultant. In their later book, Conoley and Conoley (1992) provide a consultant trainee evaluation form that could easily be modified to suit the purposes of the experienced consultant. Marks (1995) gives an example of a method of analyzing a taped transcript of a consultation session according to Carkhuff's (1969) two major categories: responding and personalizing. By engaging in this level of self-analysis, along with the more objective feedback provided by their consultees, consultants can develop the feeling of confidence that comes from the awareness that they are effective communicators.

ACTIVITY 3.9

Devise a self-analysis method that includes at least the following dimensions for evaluating your communication skills:

Listens without interrupting

Accepts consultee's point of view

Identifies important points

Summarizes, paraphrases, clarifies

Interprets nonverbal language to self and possibly to consultee

Pursues issues assertively

Reinforces consultee's efforts

RESISTANCE

During the interview, the consultant must be aware of resistance tactics that may be used, wittingly or otherwise, by consultees with an agenda that differs from yours. These disruptive, nonproductive activities delay progress or, at worst, completely thwart the spirit and purpose of consultation. Because of the pervasive nature of resistance to change, including the kinds of changes that are often required if consultation is to be successful, I discuss resistance in terms of its types, causes, and ways of dealing with it.

A consultee's behavior, like that of everyone else, has one of two functions: to get something or to avoid something. Those who decide that they don't want something develop an ability not to get it. If consultees or clients don't want to engage in the changes intended by a consultative effort, they usually find some way to avoid that effort. We call these avoidance tactics *resistance*.

Resistance seems to occur in just about all change efforts. It appears to be a natural reaction to self-initiated change efforts as well as those we perceive as being suggested or directed by others (Carner & Alpert, 1995; Piersal & Gutkin, 1983; Resnick & Patti, 1980; Wagner, 1998; Wickstrom & Witt, 1993).

Resistance is an effort to avoid what one doesn't want from the environment. It occurs when a consultee feels either threatened by proposed changes in his work environment, as would be necessary if he needed to change his behavior in order to affect a change in a student's behavior, or if he believes that his ideas were not given appropriate consideration.

Gallesich (1982) states, "Resistance to consultants is a natural phenomenon. The integration of any new person into an ongoing social structure unbalances it, creating reactions and forcing members to make adjustments" (p. 279). Gallesich reminds us that resistance can be healthy or unhealthy. A healthy form of resistance might occur when the changes being suggested are really counterproductive and the consultee resists on that basis. Unhealthy resistance might take the form of blocking needed changes that would benefit the student or the system but would be inconvenient for the consultee to perform, or would be alien to the consultee's beliefs or accustomed ways of behaving. Another example of unhealthy resistance would be when the consultee is angry or fearful about a proposed change (innovation; intervention) and does not express this anger directly, but rather does so indirectly by subtly sabotaging or ignoring the recommended intervention. An example of sabotage is given in Activity 3.10.

ACTIVITY 3.10

Mrs. Provo, the third-grade teacher of Ahmad, agreed with the resource specialist to try a "Good Behavior Card" for Ahmad just so she could end the conference. This consists of putting a card on the corner of a student's desk that has target positive behaviors written on it, which the teacher is to check off as they occur. Mrs. Provo thought the idea added too much extra work for her, but she did it, although with a tone of voice and attitude that made Ahmad feel more like he was being punished than rewarded.

1. Analyze the dynamics behind this situation.

2. How might the consultant handle this situation once it becomes clear that Mrs. Provo is being passively resistant to the intervention?

Gross (1980) views resistance "as a normal coping behavior having as its purpose the preservation of the organism rather than the obstruction of change" (p. 1). These two effects may occur together: The organism, defective or perfect, is preserved as change is obstructed. Here, again, resistance can be seen as healthy or otherwise.

Wickstrom and Witt (1993) define resistance as follows:

> Within the context of the consultant–consultee relationship, resistance includes those system, consultee, consultant, family and client (that is, student) factors that interfere with the achievement of goals established during consultative interactions. Resistance, then, is *anything* that impedes problem-solving or plan implementation and, ultimately, problem resolution, including both passive and active components of an ecology that functionally operate to get in the way of intervention planning, implementation, or outcome. (p. 160)

This is a broad definition of resistance that goes beyond the belief that resistance is always and only something that exists in the behavior of the consultee. I, along with Wickstrom and Witt, take the view that systemic factors, governmental regulations, well-accepted school norms, and even subtle hints from administrators can be the sources of resistance that impede the consultative process.

Types of Resistance

All experienced consultants have their own lists of behaviors they have observed that demonstrate resistance. Here are some of the most common types of resistance.

The Direct Block   The consultee tells the consultant, usually directly, that she isn't going to engage in the consultation process or in the suggestions that have emerged from the consultation. There are some teachers who have no interest in consultation, ignore any efforts to get them to change their minds, and simply stonewall the whole process. Or they may engage in the process up to the point of implementation and then decide that they don't want to participate any longer. Fortunately, this response style is not common in today's schools.

"Yes, but. . . ."   The consultee always seems to have some reason not to try anything. Although he may agree that an idea has merit, he concludes that it is not worth trying because it might not work. He may give some of the following reasons:

"I tried it before with a different student, and it didn't work."

"Somebody else said she tried it, and it didn't work."

"The problem is too serious."

"This student has [some disability], and this needs to be treated elsewhere."

"I don't have the time."

"This is a bad time to be trying something new."

All of these reasons (excuses) for not implementing a change effort may have some truth. Only an analysis of the situation can determine what part is truth and what part is an excuse or stalling tactic.

"I did it, but it didn't work."   The consultee has (or claims to have) tried the recommendations and found them wanting. You often don't find out that resistance is involved until you inquire about the effectiveness of the intervention. If the consultee calls you to tell you that an intervention isn't working and asks for further help, she probably isn't resisting. Resistance occurs after a plan has been developed, time has gone by, and the consultee supposedly has tried the plan and been unsuccessful but hasn't bothered to tell you about it. Of course, it is entirely possible that the recommendations haven't been successful for a variety of reasons other than resistance, When you look into the situation and see if the consultee is eager to move forward or not, you will have a better sense of whether the problem is resistance or something else. Naturally, it is necessary to investigate to determine if there was treatment integrity: that is, was the treatment carried out as intended (Gresham, 1989; Kratochwill, Sheridan, & Van Someren, 1988)?

Friend and Bauwens (1988) list other types of resistance common to school consultation: the *reverse,* in which the consultee agrees to planned interventions but does not follow through or does them in a manner that is unlikely to work (as in the example in Activity 3.10); the *projected threat,* in which the consultee refuses to cooperate because some person (principal, parent, perhaps even the student) won't like it; the *guilt trip,* manifested by a consultee who acts as though the extra burden of the intervention is excessive; and *tradition,* in which history is invoked as an argument against trying anything new or different.

Whatever the type of resistance, it is necessary to investigate both the causes and possible ways of working with the resistance in order to reduce or eliminate it.

Causes of Resistance

Any threat to the status quo can cause some people to put up defensive barriers and to find many reasons to resist. The following are among the most common causes for resistance.

Habit Strength   Teaching and parenting are supported in part by the usefulness of habit, or consistency. Teachers and parents tend to do today what they did yesterday, last week, and last year. Each of us has a relatively limited supply of reactions to standard situations; these reactions survive for the most part because they work in some fashion. A consultant is usually called in because the consultee's habitual reactions to the referral situation aren't working. Thus, trying to get the consultee to try new approaches is to some extent a question of appreciating the strength of the consultee's habits and suggesting a new behavior with which the consultee has a good chance of being successful. For example, a consultee's usual reaction to the disruptive behavior of a student is a mild reprimand, a cold stare, a brief talk with the offending student after class, a punishment consequence (perhaps having the client write class rules a number of times), and then a conference with the parents, usually in that order. Imagine that your consultee tried these tactics with a client, then redid them more strongly, but to little avail. Because she has used up her habit repertoire, she refers the client to the school's SST, and you proceed with your consultative efforts. You may find that the only kinds of suggestions that she will come up with, or will accept from you, are those closely related to the five habitual ideas she has already tried. Success in this case might well depend on the consultant's ability to structure recommendations that are similar to, or compatible with, these five habitual responses yet have a better chance of working than those the consultee has already tried. It is also possible that the consultant can get the consultee to reframe the problem, to think about it differently, and on that basis to accept ideas that she may not have thought of herself.

Threat to Role Image or Security   A consultee who has referred a student because he is not being successful with that student may feel that he has demonstrated some degree of incompetence by having made the referral. Like all professionals, teacher consultees have an image of themselves as being generally competent. Students with moderate-to-severe learning or behavior problems may threaten this image. Having to ask someone else for assistance puts the consultee in a "one-down" position, which can lead to the types of resistance we have discussed. Being one down can lead to what Wickstrom and Witt (1993) call *psychological reactance:* the tendency of people to fight back against any perception that their freedom as individuals to act is being abridged (by the student) or being overruled (by the types of interventions that may be suggested).

An example is the case of a veteran teacher (Mrs. Jones) who has a good reputation for dealing with difficult students. She now gets the most troublesome student she has ever had, one who has caused her to lose her professional demeanor in front of her class and who definitely threatens her security and comfort level as a teacher. Needing to refer this student erodes Mrs. Jones's self-image further. Defensiveness may accompany this situation as she tries to project her belief that she has tried everything, that the problem lies within the student, and that she shouldn't have to try anything else. She believes that special education (or suspension or movement to a different classroom) is needed.

Your success as a consultant in this case depends on your ability to develop a positive rapport with Mrs. Jones—to convince her that you appreciate what she has done and that it would be helpful to try some new tactic with the student, if only for the sake of your relationship, or because a reframing or variation of her own good ideas might work, or in the interest of gathering data.

Too Much Work   Consultants need to be sure that the ideas they and the consultee have discussed are not really too labor-intensive. It is common to find that resistance develops after the consultee tries the suggested intervention; only then does it become clear that it really is too much work, or at least appears to be. Interventions that derive from the behavior modification approach seem to some consultees to be too much work when they involve cumbersome ways of data collection, awkward timing of reinforcement delivery, or dealing with the bookkeeping that seems to be part of token systems.

Philosophical Belief Conflicts   In school-based consultation, we need to recognize that each participant in a collaborative consultation team has an implicit philosophy or set of beliefs and values that governs his practice and views regarding the needs and welfare of students. One of the sources of philosophical dispute that is currently in the schools has to do with the concept and practice of full inclusion of students with disabilities in general education classes (Stainback & Stainback, 1984). Others, such as the responsibilities of general education teachers for dealing with students who have mild-to-moderate disabling conditions (such as learning disabilities and behavior disorders, including ADD and ADHD), are more common sources of disputes. To what extent should a teacher–consultee vary her approach for a student? At what point does the consultee have a right to say "You're asking too much of me. The other students are suffering. A student like this is what resource rooms or special education day classes are for."

Naturally, there is no answer without knowledge of a specific case. There is, however, recognition, shared by most school personnel, that we are in a period with a wider span of adjustments and an increased use of accommodations within the general education track for students who may well have been exiled to special education, possibly for their entire educational career, only a decade ago (Heward, 2000). Although some teachers and other professionals (Hallahan & Kauffman, 1995; Kauffman, Gerber, & Semmel, 1988; Smelter, Bradley, & Yudewitz, 1994) caution against total participation in this current thinking, most special and regular educators maintain a cautiously benevolent attitude toward the inclusion movement (see Chapter 1).

Another philosophical belief that many teachers and parents apparently have is that positive reinforcement is akin to bribery. They do not believe that students ought to be given special recognition or rewards for "doing what they are supposed to be doing." They seem to maintain a puritan ethic that requires, but does not reinforce, perfection in behavior. Perhaps a gentle reminder would be helpful that the first dictionary definition of bribery implies a payment to someone in authority for something that is illegal or immoral. Using inducements (a second definition of a bribe) such as free time, stickers, or social praise for students who need an extra boost hardly seems to fit the first dictionary definition of bribery (*Webster's,* 1997).

Poor Planning/Delivery   Certainly there exists the possibility that consultation is being resisted because it has been poorly designed, either at the conceptual level (that is, not well explained as a service delivery model) or at the case level (when an actual case is being poorly managed by the consultant). It is easy to understand resistance if a consultant new to a school does not engage in the entry steps discussed in Chapter 5 or those mentioned by Dougherty (2000) and Marks (1995), if there is a perception on the part of potential consultees that this method does not have the support of the principal or the teacher's union, or if the new consultant is brusque or heavy-handed in his approach. Some specific steps to take to ensure competent delivery of consultative services are:

1. Establish rapport before discussing interventions. Getting to know the teacher or parent beyond surface appearances is not always easy in schools because of the busy schedules all professionals (and parents) have. Still, it doesn't take long to convey to people the idea that you are interested in what they have to say, that you are particularly interested in what they have done to date about the concerns they have, and that you are interested in their ideas about what to do next.

2. Do not get caught up in the "I'm in a rush; tell me what to do" syndrome that seems to characterize many "hallway" referrals that occur in schools. Be firm about the process that has been established for accessing your services and, with some exceptions based on emergencies, stick to it. Your staff will regard you as more professional if you indicate that you believe their issue is important enough to set aside time for a meaningful discussion.

3. Keep notes. (Examples of how to do this were previously presented.)

A problem for some consultants is that they may be too attached to a particular approach that isn't working. Consultants need to know when flexibility is more important than firmness. Maital (1996) presents an interesting scenario showing how a combination of a behavioral and a mental health approach in the same case resulted in an effective solution. The consultee was dealt with in a consultee-centered (mental health model) manner, while the actual problems presented by the client were handled in a behavioral fashion.

Psychological Deficits Within the Consultee   There are times when a consultee will not participate in the consultation process for reasons that are not clear. She may vacillate between compliance and refusal or may work very hard at the interventions for a period of time and then ignore them inexplicably. Such behavior may signal the presence of some disturbed intrapsychic activity that should be dealt with outside the consultative interactions, preferably in a therapeutic setting. This is a matter of some delicacy. One would want to have evidence from situations outside of the consultative interactions that verify these concerns. Common indicators of stress that may be leading to impaired functioning are a long-term change in mood from well-modulated to depressed or angry; rapid, inexplicable mood shifts; overreaction to mild setbacks; and comments that indicate that the person is "on the edge" emotionally (Maslach, 1982; Sapolsky, 1994; Selye, 1993). Caplan and Caplan (1993) have discussed manifestations of psychological deficits under their "lack of objectivity" condition, which was discussed briefly in Chapter 2.

Lack of Skills   Imagine that, in the course of discussing the disruptive behavior of a student, a consultee mentions the use of a contract. The consultant agrees that this would be a good idea and encourages the consultee to do it. The consultee, Mr. Smith, has never written a contract before; he's just heard about it. In the course of their quickly terminated conversation, the consultee doesn't tell the consultant that he needs help in designing a contract. A week goes by; nothing happens. The consultant inquires about the situation, and the consultee states that he hasn't had time to look into it. Another week goes by: same thing. By now the consultant is convinced that the consultee is resisting, for unknown reasons, so she confronts him mildly. At this point it becomes clear that the consultee doesn't know how to write or implement contracts but was shy about admitting it. Caplan and Caplan (1993) refer to skill deficits as one of the four "lacks" found in some consultees (see Chapter 2).

The case of Mr. Smith may not really demonstrate resistance; but to the consultant, resistance appears to be involved until she learns that the problem involves a skill deficit. My point is that the consultant has to be sure that the activity called for in the intervention plan is within the skill repertoire of the consultee. Treatment integrity and acceptability (Gresham, 1989) depend on the consultee being able to do what is intended in the intervention; any deficits in skill must be clarified and remediated.

Most teachers are more skillful in areas of curriculum delivery than they are in areas of behavior management. This relative lack of skill can be attributed to at least two sources: poor teacher training in the area of behavior management (many teacher training programs devote only scant attention to this area, perhaps assuming behavior will be appropriate if the curriculum is delivered adequately); and a reluctance to be firm, perhaps due to a concern that students will rebel if held to high behavioral standards that are consistent. Because of the paramount need for consultants to be useful to teachers in this area, Chapter 6 is devoted to the causes, effects, and remedies for classroom behavior management problems.

Inadequate System Support   This is related to the concepts of "threat to role image" and "poor planning/delivery," but is specific to situations in which the consultee may want to participate in the desired intervention but believes that the system (school, district) will not support it for some reason. For example, consider a case in which systematic suspension for flagrant disruptive behavior is suggested. The teacher agrees, as does the principal, until it comes time for implementation. At this point, the principal decides to clear such a strong contingency with the assistant superintendent. Together they decide that the action is so important that the board of education had better support it before it is carried out. The board takes the suggestion under advisement and decides to consult with the county board lawyer, who promises to get back to the board with an opinion as soon as possible. Meanwhile, two months have gone by, and the disruptive behavior has gotten worse. Is this resistance or merely life in the bureaucracy? In any event, the scenario fits Wickstrom and Witt's (1993) conceptualization of a system factor that interferes with the achievement of goals established during consultative interactions. The moral of the story is that the consultant and the consultee should have other plans devised and ready to implement while waiting for the administration to make up its mind about policy.

The Principal's Office   If the building's main administrator doesn't believe in consultation, for whatever reason, the consultant will probably have a difficult time implementing ideas. Consultation success depends on administrative support at the building level as well as the district level. Huefner (1988) points out that administrators may resist consultation because they are leery of it. Consultation, until recently, had not established a sound foundation of method, philosophy, or treatment validity, so it should not be surprising that some local school administrators resist supporting it. Further, if a resource teacher, a counselor, or a school psychologist announces his desire and intention to engage in a consultation-based service delivery method, the principal may well wonder how the person's other work is going to get done. In other words, every change in activity involves a trade-off. Principals who are comfortable with the way things are may be reluctant to embrace a new system that may seem vague in its methods, or has not yet established a solid base of research support, or may upset the status quo.

Parsons and Meyers (1984) describe schools as either proactive or reactive. A proactive school is led by a principal who is familiar with cutting-edge philosophies and methods and, while not embracing anything blindly, is open-minded about studying newer ideas with a view toward incorporating them into the school. In contrast, the reactive principal usually only reacts under pressure; some outside force compels this person to take action, and it is taken reluctantly, with a negative affect coloring its implementation. School desegregation, under court order, was often handled in this way, as is, to a much lesser degree, full inclusion. In reactive systems, maintenance of the status quo is more important than the desire to seek ways to improve the system. Consultants working with reactive principals need to devote more time to establishing relationships, laying the groundwork, and explaining all steps of the process than do those working in more comfortable proactive sites. The new consultant, as well as an experienced member of a staff who now wishes to change her role and behaviors, needs to bond with the school principal into a team that has as its purpose the improvement of the school, particularly improvement in the ways in which education is presented to students who have learning or behavior/adjustment problems. New or experienced consultants who find themselves working with reactive principals should pay close attention to the material presented later in this section on ways of dealing with resistance. Working with proactive principals, however, should be a consultant's nirvana, since the opportunity for system improvement, if only at the school level, is ripe. An example of this situation is contained in the case study in Chapter 10, which shows how a proactive principal and staff together created a major system-level change. Idol (1997) has written extensively about ways of including the school principal in the planning for a collaborative effort. Two recent articles in *Educational Leadership,* a journal commonly read by principals, have focused on the role of the principal in fostering the collaborative ethic (Laud, 1998; Shen, 1998). A review of these articles or the Idol (1997) text may give the special educator or other ancillary staff some ideas for approaching a principal about collaboration.

A Functional Analysis of Causes for Resistance   Sugai and Tindal (1993) have provided an extended discussion of the causes for resistance (which they refer to as "roadblocks") taken from the behavioral perspective. They define a roadblock as "a situation or condition that interferes with the attainment of consultation goals or objectives" (p. 389). They prefer the term roadblock "because it infers less internalized motivation or intention, tends not to associate cause with a person, and places an emphasis on environmental explanations" (p. 389).

Sugai and Tindal identify four basic steps that should be considered in the assessment of roadblocks:

1. Determine that a roadblock condition exists and who is involved.
2. Identify the setting or context.
3. Conduct a functional analysis (or functional assessment; see Chapter 6).
4. Identify and define observable behaviors that indicate the presence of a roadblock.

Although they acknowledge that roadblocks can occur at the individual or systems level, they focus on the following factors that maintain roadblocks at the individual (that is, consultant or consultee) level:

1.   *Factors contributing to low rates of desired teacher behavior.*   Perhaps the consultee hasn't learned how to do the desired behavior, the situation doesn't allow for the intervention to be carried out in a powerful way, the consultee isn't able to be consistent for a variety of reasons, or the consultee isn't properly reinforced for engaging in the approved intervention behaviors.

2.   *Factors contributing to low rates of desired consultant behavior.*   The consultant may not be well trained, the system may demand too many other activities from the consultant (such as heavy teaching or assessment or IEP processing responsibilities), or the consultant may believe that his efforts are not appreciated; perhaps he perceives too much resistance from consultees or administrators. The consultee may also have a belief system, often unverbalized, that runs counter to the proposed interventions.

Strategies for dealing with these factors include skill training, provision for more appropriate reinforcement contingencies, removal of aversive consequences for engaging in consultation, and listening to the teacher to detect belief systems that may be interfering with the proposed interventions.

Gutkin and Hickman (1990) have studied the relationships among many types and sources of resistance to consultation. Using a case description questionnaire and an outcome questionnaire that was filled out by school psychologists who served as consultants, they determined that resistance was due to a complex set of reasons related to consultee, consultant, and organizational characteristics. Consultee characteristics associated with resistance included concerns about his problem-solving skills, classroom management skills, looking bad as a teacher, and self-confidence. Consultant characteristics related to consultee resistance included the consultant's limited experience in this role, confidence levels, and communication skills. Consultee resistance was also related to organizational factors such as the principal's attitude toward consultation, time allowed for consultation, and the organizational climate of the school.

ACTIVITY 3.11

In small groups, review the causes for resistance previously discussed. Are there others not mentioned in that material? In settings with which you are familiar, what seem to be the major causes for resistance? Develop at least one method for dealing with each of the methods previously discussed.

ACTIVITY 3.12

From your experiences in the schools, develop a behavioral chart like the one presented below and use it to analyze the ABCs of a resistance situation. An example is given:

Antecedents	Behaviors	Consequences
Consultant: "So we've decided to go with the nonverbal reminder when Lawanda speaks out loudly."	Teacher continues to loudly reprimand Lawanda.	Lawanda's behavior remains the same. Consultant makes a classroom observation.
Consultant: "What I observed was your reprimanding Lawanda instead of using the nonverbal reminder."	*Teacher:* "Yes, well, it's all she understands. That's the way these kids are raised." (Interfering belief)	*Consultant:* "Lawanda's behavior isn't improving. Would you be willing to implement another intervention?"

Resistance by Parent–Consultees

Most of what we have discussed applies to teachers as consultees, but, with some modification of focus, much of it could also apply to parent–consultees. Students who present with serious behavior/adjustment or learning challenges threaten the professional status and satisfaction of teachers, and these same behaviors or conditions also threaten and upset the personal lives of parents. The idea that an outsider (an individual representing the school) is asking to get involved in a family's life may have threatening connotations, especially for families that may already be somewhat dysfunctional or confused about how to deal with their child's school-related problems (Cobb & Medway, 1978; O'Shea, O'Shea, Algozzine, & Hammitte, 2001). Maital

(1996) has noted that parents may seek, and at the same time build defenses against, information and advice that they find uncomfortable.

There has been less study about the dynamics of parent resistance to consultation than about teacher resistance. Most of what is available is from the behavioral consultation school (Sheridan & Kratochwill, 1992) or has been borrowed from the family therapy literature (Chamberlain & Baldwin, 1988). In their 1988 article, Chamberlain and Baldwin give some suggestions for dealing with parental resistance, at least in a family therapy context:

- Develop a strong therapeutic alliance with the parents.
- Reframe suggestions made to parents to keep them consistent with the parents' preferred parenting style.
- Teach parents new parenting skills despite their possible disinterest.
- Develop a network of support for the therapist.

Liontos (1992) has delineated some of the sources of resistance to effective collaborations with families, including feelings of inadequacy; previous bad experiences with schools; suspicion about treatment from government institutions; limited knowledge about school policies, procedures, and ways to assist with schoolwork; and economic issues such as daycare, transportation, and other daily survival constraints. Educators may resist working with some families because of their own biases, lack of objectivity, or simple lack of knowledge of cultural differences.

Christenson (1995) has described a program (PEPS: Parent-Educator Problem Solving) consisting of a four-step procedure designed to include parents as integral members of a team whose purpose is to understand student adjustment and learning problems and to collaborate in solving them. Data indicate that this program has been related to improved home–school interactions and communications.

I hope that, as school-based consultants increasingly reach out to parents, a wider literature will develop in this area. For now, consultants confronted with resistance from parents should modify the following suggestions about overcoming resistance, which were originally intended to be used with teacher–consultees.

Overcoming Resistance

Once the sources and types of resistance are delineated, the consultant needs to determine methods for dealing with them. Included here are a number of ideas from the literature as well as suggestions derived from practice.

One possible way of overcoming resistance is to be certain that the idea of consultation is well defined to the staff when it is first used. Marks (1995) has discussed the DURABLE framework (originally developed by Maher and Bennett, 1984) for the introduction of consultation services to a school system. Each of the letters in the acronym stands for a step or process designed to clarify consultation as a service delivery mode and to ensure its success.

1. *Discussing.*   Consultation has to be discussed, explained, and promoted. It needs to be sold like any other new idea that involves a change in people's visions of their responsibilities.

2. *Understanding.*   Try to see that potential consultees grasp the purpose and nature of the consultative process and understand what some of its benefits can be. Some teachers may be interested in the research literature indicating that consultation often results in more effective teaching and behavior management approaches, in addition to lowering the incidence of referral for special education services (Bergan & Tombari, 1976; Rosenfield & Gravois, 1996; Villa, Thousand, Nevin, & Malgeri, 1996; Zins, 1992; Zins, Curtis, Graden, & Ponti, 1988; Zins & Ponti, 1987; see also the references in Chapter 1 about the effectiveness of consultation).

3. *Reinforcing.*   How does one support the collaborative efforts of others? By reinforcing them verbally and giving them recognition, by pointing out success and valid efforts, and by trying to locate and deliver tangible rewards from within or outside of the system.

4. *Adapting.*   A school system changing to a different way of delivering services to students needs to make adaptations in many ways. Perceptions of how things might be, paperwork, role shifts, expectations, reinforcements for new types of behavior, and so on generate systemic issues that need to be planned for and resolved if the changes are to work.

5. *Building.*   Marks (1995) suggests that efficacy of teachers and commitment of the whole staff need to be built before a new change can be successful. Just as Rome was not built in a day, a change to a consultation service delivery system won't happen overnight. Ponti, Zins, and Graden (1988) and Rosenfield and Gravois (1996) discuss steps they took to effect a change toward a consultation-based service delivery system at the district level. Chapter 10 of this text discusses some of the administrative considerations that need to go into making such a change.

6. *Learning.*   Joyce and Showers (1995) indicate that a sequence of model, practice, and feedback constitute the essential nature of all skill development. What to teach consultants and consultees about these roles has been addressed by a number of authors. Skill and knowledge competencies for consultants have been established by West et al. (1989). Dougherty (2000) lists seven areas of skill for consultants: communication, interpersonal, problem solving, professional and ethical, organizational knowledge, group work, and skills with culturally diverse populations. These skills may not have been taught in a consultant's previous training, so districts have to develop training programs to get these skills to their potential consultants. Also, skills as a consultee have never been presented to most current teachers since most of them were taught to believe that they would very likely be on their own in their classrooms and could expect little real help from others. Brown et al. (2001) have devoted a whole chapter of their book to the topic of the consultee as a variable in the consultation process. Chapter 1 of this book has information about the consultee as a learner and a collaborator.

7. *Evaluating.* There are many considerations here. We need to evaluate how well consultation is achieving its goals, how consultees value it, what effect it is having on referral rates, and so on. This calls for an a priori statement about goals and objectives that can be looked at as the change to a consultation-based system evolves. Without a set of goals and objectives, it will be difficult later to know what progress has been made. You have to know what progress will look like before you look for it.

Even after consultation has been introduced to a school staff as a valuable and desired activity, a school or a district may need to do other things to overcome resistance to it. Brown et al. (2001) suggest the following six ideas for dealing with resistance.

Reducing the Threat   Resistance may be tied to a possible loss of status or feelings of incompetence, a problem that the consultant needs to address. The primary way to do this is through the implementation of a collaborative approach in which the consultee is acknowledged as a co-equal in the consultation process. Since a collaboratively oriented consultant encourages the consultee to come up with her own solutions to problems, with the consultant serving as a facilitator for the consultee's ideas, the consultee holds a position of power in the relationship. In this approach, the strengths of the consultee are continually reinforced by the consultant. In cases in which the consultee has no ideas for intervention and feels threatened because of the expectation that he should, the consultant assists by suggesting ideas and waiting for the consultee to help in deciding which ones would work best in his classroom or home, or ways in which the home or classroom system might be changed in order for improvement to occur. These selected ideas are then refined by both parties, and the consultee implements them with the support and encouragement of the consultant.

Developing Positive Expectations   Consultants often believe that the consultee has the same degree of faith in the potential efficacy of the recommended intervention as does the consultant. Unfortunately, this may not be true. Sometimes a consultant has to lay some groundwork designed to affect the belief system of the consultee regarding the virtues of the intervention. This can be done by citing similar cases from your experience in which the intervention worked well, by having the consultee talk to other consultees who have had similar situations that were handled successfully, or by visiting programs in which interventions similar to the one recommended are being used successfully. Sometimes references to the literature can be useful, but it is best to provide a summary of this sort of information since the consultee may believe that having to read the literature simply adds to the burden of consultative efforts, thus adding to her resistance.

Incentives   An unfortunate reality of public schoolwork (and parenting) is that we have to seek our own reinforcers. In most states, all teachers with the same years of experience receive the same salary. There are very few other sources of reinforcement given to those who do an excellent job. For every "teacher of the year," there are hundreds of other teachers who do a wonderful job, unbeknownst to anybody except a few of their astute students and some parents and peers. For some teachers, the responsibility for engaging in consultative efforts to solve problems within their own classrooms may seem like yet another burden. Perhaps you, as the consultant, are the only one who knows what a teacher has done; therefore, you become the main source of reinforcement for that teacher. You can do this by informing the teacher that you are aware of his efforts, that his efforts are appreciated, and that through his efforts the student has a better chance for success than she would have had otherwise.

Brown et al. (2001) suggest that consultees should be afforded release time to participate in consultation. When I was employed as a school psychologist, I was fortunate in one of my schools to have an elementary principal who would take teachers' classes for 15-minute periods to provide time for consultation during the regular school day. Most principals simply don't have the time to do that, especially on a consistent basis.

The willingness to participate in consultation could become part of a teacher evaluation method. Teachers who have engaged in successful behavior-change projects could be written about in a newsletter or identified positively in some other manner to give them recognition for taking part in this valued activity. The case presented in Chapter 10 indicates how one school solved the problem of finding time to consult, which, in and of itself, can be a disincentive to utilize consultation services.

Establish a Clear Contract   Formal contracts are not usually expected in the everyday practice of school consultation projects. The agreement between the consultant and the consultee to work together to solve a student's behavior or learning problem is almost always informal and implicit. This reality has potential advantages and disadvantages. An advantage is that informality leads to flexibility and an easy give-and-take that allow participants to make changes as appropriate as long as communication remains open and treatment integrity is not threatened. A possible disadvantage of this informality is the lack of clear demarcation between each person's roles and responsibilities. Threats to treatment integrity may occur if parties to the informal agreement overstep their limits.

Possible elements of a clear contract might include the following:

1.   The consultant can offer a clear statement of her role:

My role as a consultant is to give you assistance in your efforts to work more effectively with this student. As such, I will be gathering information about the problem through interviews with you and observations of the classroom behavior of the student. I am not here to evaluate you. My job is to help you think through some possible ways of assisting the student to perform better in the classroom or on the playground.

2. The consultant can mention some specifics about the process of consultation, such as its give-and-take nature, its emphasis on collaboration, and the need for some data gathering and analysis. Early in their interaction, the consultant might tell the consultee:

> One of the ways in which I like to work with teachers is to encourage them to come up with their own ideas about how they would like to solve a student's problem. I have found that teachers have many good ideas but sometimes just need someone to discuss them with. Two heads are often better than one, and pooling our ideas can work better than if just one of us does all the work in generating ideas. Besides, we're talking about your classroom, and the fact is that you are the one who is going to be implementing most of the changes we will be discussing. Therefore, it makes sense that we work with your ideas, approaches with which you feel comfortable, rather than those of someone like myself who isn't going to be implementing them. Also, one of the activities I believe is most worthwhile is the gathering of information or data that will help us to know just how we're doing. In other words, we need to keep track of what the student is doing as we try different approaches to modifying her behavior or learning patterns. We'll try to make this data gathering as convenient as possible so as not to interfere with your teaching. Do you have any questions or comments about this approach?

Reduce the Consultee's Effort   Usually one of the effects of a consultative approach to problem solving is that the consultee has more work to do, at least initially, in behalf of one or more students than he had before the onset of the process. Time to consult, the need for data gathering, and thinking through new interventions are some examples of additional time investments. Ordinarily, when a referral for assistance is made, either directly to the school-based consultant or to the local SST, the teacher is already spending more time with the target student than with most students because of the nature of the presenting problems. The teacher hopes that through the referral process he will obtain some sort of relief. If he finds out that consultation results in more work rather than less, he may show resistance in the present case and also be unwilling to use the process again.

Depending on the case and the consultee involved, it may be a good idea for the consultant to be upfront about this reality and to point out that, at least initially, the consultation process may result in somewhat more effort on behalf of the student. If all goes well, the amount of effort will be reduced as the problem is resolved, and in the long run will be less than what would have been needed without the referral and the subsequent consultation. It is sometimes helpful to point out that the consultee is presently spending extra time with the target child and apparently isn't feeling that this expenditure of time is resolving the concerns. The new or different approaches generated through the consultation process may not cost the consultee any more time or trouble than the approaches he is now using.

Developing Multicultural Sensitivity   Understanding resistance to consultation in situations where there is a multicultural component is largely a matter of understanding facts and values. The facts one needs to consider have to do with differences in communication styles, preferred styles of interpersonal interactions, and traditional ways of dealing with problems and issues that arise in regard to dealing with children. The values may center around one's worldview, perspectives on the importance of individual achievement as compared to group cohesiveness, and the role of the family as compared to that of government institutions in decisons about students with disabilities. When a consultant and consultee come from different cultural backgrounds, it is necessary for the consultant to take the lead in negotiating the differences in opinion and approaches that may arise as a consequence of these cultural differences. Gibbs (1985), in her studies of African-American consultees, concluded that consultants would do well to attend to the importance of interpersonal relationships rather than task-issues at the onset of a consultative relationship. Behring and Ingraham (1998) review issues similar to these in their call for a multicultural emphasis in consultation which, if followed, would likely reduce some of the more subtle aspects of resistance that may occur in situations where constituents from differing cultural perspectives work together toward problem solving. In the field of counseling, where many of the communication, interpersonal, and problem-solving skills are very similar to those of consultation, Arredondo et al. (1996) have operationalized a set of multicultural competencies that apply equally well to consultation. Additional sources of relevant information can be found in Duncan (1995), Harris, Ingraham, and Lam (1994), Harris (1996), Jackson and Hayes (1993), Miranda (1993), and Tobias (1993).

ACTIVITY 3.13

Mr. SanFillipo, the Resource teacher at Grove Middle School, calls Ms. Phan, mother of a 13-year-old boy, Henry, who is having attendance, behavior, and achievement problems. Ms. Phan turns the phone over to her husband, who informs Mr. SanFillipo that they are not interested in discussing their son, and that they will take care of their own family's business. A month goes by and Henry shows no change in his behavior. What steps might a consultant take at this point?

ACTIVITY 3.14

Working in dyads, have one person act the role of the consultant, and the other a potential consultee. Assume that this is a first meeting between the two. Have the consultant introduce herself and explain the consultation process to the consultee. Have the consultee simply be accepting during this interchange. Repeat the process but have the consultee express doubts about the process based on the information you have learned about resistance, such as the extra amount of work, the need for data gathering, the implications of being observed, the belief that the referred student needs special education, and so on. In class, review strategies for dealing with these common forms of resistance.

Figure 3.4 presents a list of the important manifestations and causes of resistance in consultation, based on the acronym RESISTANCE. Also presented in Figure 3.4 is a list of some of the most useful approaches for dealing with resistance, following the acronym FACILITATE.

In summary, expect resistance, build in a plan for dealing with its most obvious causes, learn to recognize its symptoms, and realize that change is not easy for many people. Assuming that you, as either a self-selected or administratively appointed

Figure 3.4

Manifestations and causes of resistance, and methods for dealing with them

---

MANIFESTATIONS AND CAUSES OF RESISTANCE IN SCHOOL-BASED CONSULTATION

There are many ways that consultees can resist the consultation process. The following list uses the acronym "RESISTANCE" to remind us of the manifestations and causes of the insidious reality of resistance to consultation.

R   Refusal; active or passive
E   Expectations too high
S   Skill inadequacy
I   "I did it; it didn't work."
S   System lack of support; real or imagined
T   Threat to existing ecology of the classroom
A   Anxiety over being watched
N   Non-reinforcement for efforts
C   Confidence, lack of
E   Easier to insist that someone else (e.g., special ed.) do it

DEALING WITH RESISTANCE

Understanding resistance is one thing; dealing with it is quite another. The following is a brief list of suggestions based on the acronym for the key word in resistance-busting: "FACILITATE."

F   Facilitate
A   Assist in their thinking and plan building
C   Communicate both your support and ideas
I   Interpersonally relate
L   Live in their shoes
I   Inquire
T   Teach
A   Acknowledge their efforts
T   Tolerate their discrepant views, but don't allow inappropriate practices
E   Evaluate your collaborative efforts

---

consultant, believe in the value of this approach to dealing with students' learning or behavior-adjustment problems, do what you can to sell the idea to others, especially your consultees. Proceed only with administrative support, and gain the support of the influential teachers on the staff. A year after you have begun, evaluate yourself and your efforts. You will very likely be pleased.

INTERPERSONAL SKILLS

Ms. Baxter, the resource specialist–consultant, has been working with Mr. Cant, the woodshop teacher. They have reached an apparent stalemate over whether to try a stronger consequence for Sammy, their student, contingent on his careless behavior in the woodshop. Ms. Baxter says, "Well, I don't know. It's your baby. He's like so many of those kids from the East Side. It's pretty obvious that what you've been doing isn't right. Sometimes I don't know why we bother."

Imagine the same situation as in the previous scenario. Ms. Baxter says, "I realize that Sammy presents a real challenge. You've tried some very positive approaches with him, and I can sense your frustration with the situation. Let's take a look at what we've tried, perhaps think of some other issues we haven't thought about, and see if we can come up with another plan that might work. What do you think?"

It is easy to see a tremendous difference in approach between the first Ms. Baxter and the second Ms. Baxter. Who would want to deal with the former? She sounds negative, defeated, pessimistic, and biased. In the second case, Ms. Baxter makes an attempt to empathize, to be encouraging, to seek new ideas, and to involve the consultee in the ongoing problem-solving process. Which consultant would you want to deal with?

Consultation is essentially a problem-solving process that is dependent on effective communication and interpersonal skills. Communication skills can be successful only if delivered in the context of an interpersonal relationship that is positive and professional. This section reviews information and provides activities designed to improve a consultant's knowledge and skills in interpersonal relationships.

ACTIVITY 3.15

The following examples contrast positive and negative interpersonal traits and suggest comments that characterize them. The first example in each pair is a positive trait; the second is negative. After reading each pair of comments, create a different positive response that is appropriate for the trait.

Open: "I'm glad you could see me."
Closed: "You want to see me now? Well, I suppose."

Accepting: "I'm sure that you did what you felt was best."
Judgmental: "Why would you want to do it that way?"

Empathic: "It must really be difficult dealing with students who challenge us so often."
Callous: "What did you expect? That's what teaching here is all about."

Puts consultee at ease: "Tell me about your day."
Puts consultee on defensive: "Certainly there must be better ways to teach reading."

Stresses collaboration: "We can get together to mutually solve these problems."
Plays expert: "Oh, no, research clearly shows that doing it the other way is better. Trust me."

Professional approach: "Let's review to be sure I've heard you accurately."
Immature approach: "Billy? Did we discuss him already? What was our plan? Did we have one?"

Broad-minded: "Well, that's an interesting way to look at it. How might we use that idea?"
Narrow-minded: "Well, we've never tried that before. We'd better stick to the tried and true."

ACTIVITY 3.16

Think about the various kinds of relationships you have established with coworkers and supervisors over the past few years. Some, no doubt, were more positive than others. What were the interpersonal skills that some of these people manifested that made you enjoy working with and for them? What mannerisms (behaviors, traits) made you dislike or not want to work with others?

Desirable Interpersonal Characteristics and Skills

Your responses to Activity 3.15 and the list of positive traits presented in Activity 3.16 should make it clear that people generally respond more positively to, and are more likely to want to work with, consultants who manifest positive and professional interpersonal skills. Consultants who are open, constructive, caring, task-oriented, enthusiastic, calm, flexible, and respectful of others' points of view are more likely to have success than those who manifest the opposite traits. Schindler-Rainman (1985) points out that a positive personal outlook, a liking for creative approaches, and a willingness to take risks are valuable attributes. Others have found that consultants who exhibit warmth, understanding, and empathy are likely to have a positive and significant impact on their consultees (Schowengerdt, Fine, & Poggio, 1976).

Compared to the counseling literature, which has many studies of effective interpersonal skills (Herman, 1993), literature in the consultation field has not yet developed a wide base specifying the relationships among interpersonal traits and effectiveness in consultation. However, since counseling and consultation are similar in so many ways, it is likely that those interpersonal traits found effective for counselors will be similar to those which are effective for other consultants. For example, Bushe and Gibbs (1990) have found that a high degree of intuition and level of ego development are predictors of consultation success as measured by trainer and peer evaluations. Certainly these two variables also predict success in counseling. While research of this type is interesting, it is only suggestive since the dependent variable in the Bushe and Gibbs research was not actual success with problem resolution or consultee evaluations but the opinions of one's peers or trainers. Savelsbergh and Staebler (1995) have measured the interpersonal styles of 31 consultant teachers with the Myers-Briggs Type Indicator (Briggs Myers, 1976) and found that when these consultants were both data-based and outgoing (extroverted), they were perceived by their supervisors as being more effective.

Brown (1993) has presented a list of competencies needed for effective consultation that cover three main areas: knowledge base, skills, and judgmental competencies. Interpersonal competencies are found in each of Brown's three areas. For example, under *knowledge base,* he has listed conflict resolution, group dynamics, and theories of consultee resistance. Under *skills,* he includes developing collaborative relationships and synthesizing a personal model of consultation. His *judgmental competencies* list includes intervening in group process; developing an awareness of personal style and the ability to vary style based on the characteristics of the consultee; and providing successful consultation, as measured by consultee and client (student) variables, to teachers, parents, and other caregivers.

Idol, Nevin, and Paolucci-Whitcomb (2000) include in their collaborative consultation model three general areas of importance: *knowledge base; intrapersonal attitudes;* and *interpersonal communicative, interactive,* and *problem-solving skills.* They indicate that the interpersonal skills include the ability to work as a team member, to recognize individual differences, to be accepting of conflict and to know how to deal with it, and to be effective in using nonverbal communication.

Kurpius and Rozecki (1993) observe that effective working relationships depend on empathy, genuineness, and positive regard, which are the key characteristics of effective counselors (Egan, 1998). Maher (1993), referring to behaviors of successful consultants in the business world, has suggested that the essential factors in the interpersonal area may overlap those of the work ethic: commitment, persistence, desire to achieve, and desire to improve. A degree of risk seeking, similar to that of successful entrepreneurs, is also useful. This suggests a possible dilemma for school consultants: Public schools tend to be conservative and tradition-bound. Those who suggest risky approaches to problems had better be successful most of the time.

West et al. (1989) list thirty-six specific skills characteristic of successful collaborative consultants. Eight are identified as personal characteristics:

1. Possessing an internal frame of reference in order to be sensitive and concerned about how certain happenings affect others.
2. Establishing and maintaining rapport with all persons involved in the consultation process.
3. Identifying and implementing appropriate solutions to a problem.
4. Maintaining a positive self-concept throughout the consultation process.
5. Generating and maintaining enthusiasm throughout the consultation process.
6. Remaining open to others' ideas.
7. Encouraging progress by personally demonstrating flexibility and resilience.
8. Accepting and respecting divergent points of view.

The following is a list of interpersonal skills that are important for successful interactions in the schools, with suggestions for how a school consultant can manifest these skills.

Forging Positive Relationships   Although it isn't necessary to fall into the trap of believing that it is essential to be liked by all people at all times (Ellis, 1973), it is certainly the case that people are more willing to work with affable, outgoing, friendly people than with people who aren't.

Suggestions: Become one of the staff. Don't be aloof. Get out of your office or your own classroom. Make comments that indicate that you identify with your consultees rather than with any other group. Be the kind of person that consultees feel comfortable talking to. While maintaining your own professional identity (resource specialist, school psychologist, and so on), try to walk in your consultee's shoes. Learn the art of small talk and when to use it. For some consultees, five minutes of rapport building before serious talk begins is essential; for others, ten seconds of small talk is enough.

Conveying Competence and Confidence   Being friendly is essential, but consultees won't have any use for you if that's all you are.

Suggestions: Develop as many of the skills listed by West et al. (1989) and Brown (1993) as you can. School-based consultants first have to be competent in process; content knowledge comes with experience. When a situation arises for which you can't find any answer or solution and none is forthcoming from your consultee, admit that this is the case and then go out and find helpful information. Talk to your peers, search the literature for best practices, and review your experiences in other cases to see what you can come up with for your next meeting. Challenge your consultee to do the same.

Projecting the Idea That the Situation Is Going to Improve   A consultant can make a valuable contribution by being optimistic. Try to convey that the situation of concern will improve. Don't buy into the hopelessness you often hear from some consultees; provide an antidote to the defeatism that is so common, especially in inner-city schools. A good source of information about this phenomenon is Seligman's (1991) *Learned Optimism.*

Suggestions: Much of the defeatism that consultants hear in the schools is a function of stress and burnout. Teaching is a very difficult profession, and when a teacher's ego needs are thwarted by students who are disruptive or failing, the stresses begin to show. By the time the referral gets to the consultant, the teacher often wants relief in the form of the removal of the student or the implementation of some punishment plan.

When you perceive this degree of stress, remember the following:

- Be a good listener. Plan to spend some time allowing the teacher to vent frustrations.
- Reflect the emotional content of the consultee's message.
- Project the possibility that, by working together, you and the consultee can improve the situation.
- Demonstrate competent problem-solving skills (getting specifics, reviewing data), seek points of agreement, and stress the possibilities.
- Ask how you can help (short of removing the student from the teacher's responsibility).
- Set a time to meet again. This will show the consultee the ongoing nature of your commitment.

Following Through with Enthusiasm   One of the condemning definitions of consultants is that they "pop in, pop off, and pop out." Consultation as a service delivery method will be accepted as a viable, worthwhile model only if consultants demonstrate commitment manifested by timely follow-up, staying with the situation until it is resolved or until the consultee decides that she wants to let it develop on its own for awhile. Consultants need to follow through without becoming a nag or a pest.

Suggestions: Always set a time for a next meeting, and be there. Come prepared with a copy of the notes you wrote after your last meeting. (Examples of summary notes of consultation meetings were presented earlier in this chapter in Figures 3.2 and 3.3.) Be sure you have done the part of the plan assigned to you. Go beyond this if possible. Have some new ideas to discuss. Suggest some fresh perspective. Review current goals and interventions. Be prepared to praise efforts. Validate treatment integrity (i.e., whether the treatment is being done in the intended fashion). Be thorough without being overbearing. Respect your consultee's time constraints.

Developing and Maintaining Trust   Anyone who has been new to an organization knows that a period of time is necessary before trust is established. As the proverb says, it takes a lifetime to build trust but only a moment to lose it. Consultees need time to build an opinion of a new consultant, to see if that person is true to his word.

Similarly, consultants need time to build trust in those with whom they work. If a consultee says he has tried an intervention, has he? If a principal says she will provide support for a program, will she?

Suggestions: Be sure that you are honest and dependable in your dealings with others. Practice being a "high-trusting" person, one who expects others to do as they say, just as you do. If you find that you cannot follow through on some project as you said you would, be sure to inform your colleagues as soon as possible. Collaborative consultation is built on mutual trust, not just on hope.

POWER IN THE CONSULTATIVE RELATIONSHIP

Issues of power are always present when two or more people are involved in problem solving. The nature of consultation is such that power relationships can easily become problems if either or both parties aren't sensitive to this potential source of difficulty, or if one party believes that she needs to establish a power position over the other person.

One of the key concepts that underlies a collaborative approach to consultation is that of egalitarianism, or a non-hierarchical relationship between the consultant and the consultee. However, you cannot assume that the existence of this collaborative philosophy guarantees that power dynamics won't influence the relationship. It is best to understand power in interpersonal processes so that you can use it constructively.

French and Raven (1959) have discussed five forms of social power that can be influential in most types of interpersonal relationships. In the following examples, person A is usually (but not necessarily) in an authority position relative to person B.

- *Reward,* in which person A is able to bestow benefits, valued praise, or awards on person B.

- *Coercive,* in which person A can either dispense or withhold benefits from person B, or can legitimately confront person B.

- *Legitimate,* in which person B believes that person A has a legal or an authoritative ability to control person B.

- *Referent,* in which person B sees person A as similar to himself or holding like values and may therefore comply with suggestions from person A.

- *Expert,* in which person A is perceived as having knowledge or expertise not possessed by person B.

Later, Raven (1965) added a sixth source, *informational power,* in which the information has the power, not the expert (person A) who gives out the information. Martin (1978) and Harris and Cancelli (1991) point out that reward, coercive, and legitimate power should probably be reserved for supervisory or administrative personnel and that the power sources for a collaboratively inclined consultant should be referent, expert, and informational.

Referent Power

Caplan (1970) emphasizes referent power in the consultative relationship. The collegial nature of consultation, its non-hierarchical foundation, its voluntary status, and the use of indirect rather than direct confrontation tactics are all hallmarks of referent power. Consultees want to feel that you are one of them, or at least that you can see their problems from their points of view. Beginning school consultants (other than those who have served as special education teachers) are often asked, especially by veteran teachers, if they have had teaching experience. Since only about half of the school psychologists and about three-quarters of the school counselors in the United States have had teaching experience, the honest answer for many in those groups is "No." An ancillary staff consultant who must give this answer might next ask a consultee if the lack of teaching experience could get in the way of working together. If the consultee's answer is "Yes," the consultant should probably go back to rapport building before attempting to consult with this person.

Usually, however, even veteran teacher–consultees will wait to see if the consultative interaction shows that the consultant is someone who can empathize, see the problem from their perspective, join in the development of effective interventions, and be positive and professional in relationships with them. If they come to believe that the consultant has these positive characteristics, in addition to a solid knowledge base, they probably will accept him, no matter what his background is.

If, however, consultees believe that they cannot identify with the consultant, that he does not possess positive interpersonal characteristics and presumes to know more about the consultees' responsibilities than they know, consultees will reject him, and their efforts will collapse. In this case consultees will not see the consultant as having referent power and therefore may devalue his potentially useful contributions. Naturally, all of this could occur even if the consultant does have an extensive knowledge of curriculum, method, and behavior management, but simply doesn't know how to use this information as a source of *informational* power.

ACTIVITY 3.17

Assume that you are a special education teacher–consultant who has not taught in general education. A general education teacher–consultee subtly questions your ability to understand what teaching in general education classes is all about. How might you deal with this potential threat to your referent power base?

Expert Power

I have pointed out elsewhere that the expert model is not emphasized in this text because consultees in the human services field often reject it either overtly or subtly (Caplan & Caplan, 1993; Evans, 1980; Lippitt & Lippitt, 1986; West et al., 1989).

This is not to say that a consultant's expertise has no value in a collaborative model; it certainly does. Expertise in the *process* of consultation is essential. If a school consultant is not expert in the processes of consultation, she must seek help to become expert or abandon the enterprise. She should also be expert in the *content* of consultation (that is, specific information about learning and behavior problems and their amelioration and best practices in education), although such expertise is not always necessary in practice. It is, however, useful because it can assist the consultee in developing his ideas about what he would like to do about the referral problem. Collaborative consultation requires a non-hierarchical relationship between the consultant and consultee. When the consultant acts as the expert in the content area, the consultee can feel demeaned and may develop a dependency that spoils his ability to problem solve alone in future cases (Lippitt & Lippitt, 1986). Vernberg and Reppucci (1986) have commented that they see "expert" consultants as those who take over the problem-solving process, usually limiting their ideas to a few with which they are most familiar and thereby putting restrictions on the range of possible solutions. As an alternative, they suggest following the ideas generated by Rappaport (1981) which stress "empowerment," a term conceptually related to collaboration. One empowers consultees by listening to their ideas, developing interventions compatible with these ideas, and thereby strengthening the beliefs of the consultee that he can be an effective problem solver himself.

Naturally there are exceptions to these generalizations. Beginning teachers need the knowledge they gain from an experienced consultant, as do those with limited experience in specific settings. Insecure and passive consultees might also need to have specific ideas given to them, but these ideas should always be considered options that the consultee can consider and modify to suit her style and particular classroom contingencies.

Generally, however, it is best to encourage the consultee to come up with his own solutions based on his background, the goals for his class, his teaching style, and so on. Imposing ideas and values is a temptation that should be resisted. The consultant's expertise in both process and content should be used to help the consultee work out the details of his plans, to suggest ways to improve his ideas, and to list alternative steps or strategies from which he selects appropriate interventions based on his ideas about what he would like to do, as well as ideas from the consultant that are compatible with the consultee's expert judgments.

It is possible to get trapped into playing the expert and abandoning the collaborative model when under pressure from consultees to do so. The following scenario, along with the cases presented in Chapters 7 and 9, demonstrates how a collaboratively minded consultant avoids the expert trap. Note how the consultee continually tries to get the consultant, a school psychologist, to solve the problem and how the consultant "out-defers" the consultee (Conoley & Conoley, 1982).

Consultant:	Good morning, Mrs. H. How are you today?
Consultee:	Not so good. You know Sammy, of course. He's no better. When we had the SST meeting on him, you told me to get back to you if things didn't improve. Well, I'm back.
Consultant:	Sounds discouraging. Let's see if I remember the details. He's in your fourth grade, weak academically, a bit hyper,

Consultee:

Consultant:

off task. Right so far? You were going to gather some data on his work completion and out-of-seat behavior. We had also discussed using a contract. Is that right?

Consultee: Oh, you remember him all right. I tried the contract. It worked for a week or so. I really think he belongs full time in special ed. Why are we wasting time this way? Two periods of RSP aren't enough.

Consultant: Yes, the contract. I'm glad you were able to try it. Tell me about it.

Consultee: Well, you know, stay in your chair, finish some work for a change, and you can earn some free time. The usual sort of thing. He didn't know what to do with himself when he earned the free time (only twice, you know), so he seemed disinterested right away. What are you going to do about him?

Consultant: I'm not sure what we can do; it's kind of up to you. I'll be glad to help, but I really need to know more about what's been tried and where you'd like to go next with it. Also, I'd like to see the data regarding the two target behaviors.

Consultee: Well, the data sheets are in my room if you want to see them. They don't show any change since I started taking the data two weeks ago. If it is up to me, where I'd like to go next is back to SST, get a referral for assessment, and get on with full-time placement. That's what he needs. So should I put in another referral or what?

Consultant: No, that won't be necessary. We can bring it up at the next meeting for another look. But listen, have you got five minutes right now? Let's take a look at that data and then talk over some ideas about how to help Sammy.

Consultee: Well, five minutes, OK.

(Together they go to the consultee's room and review the data sheets.)

Consultee: Well, what should I do with him?

Consultant: Let's start with what has been tried and then see if some of those ideas are working and how we can build on what you've already tried with him.

Consultee: Well, as I say, nothing seems to work. I mean there is nothing I can do about his poor reading. If I stop to help him with every word, the group starts to moan.

Consultant: OK. Let's stay with that. The poor reading is a real problem, and we'll hope that his two periods a day in RSP are helpful to him. What has the RSP teacher said about it?

Consultee:	I haven't talked to her. It's so hard to find the time.
Consultant:	OK, that is something I can do. [Writes a note to himself to do this.] What are some ways you can get around his inability to read the books and still ensure his learning the content?
Consultee:	Well, I suppose if I could find a study-buddy for him whom he wouldn't clown around with so much. . . .
Consultant:	Good idea. Think about who your more serious students are; one of them would be a good role model for him. That's a good idea. What else have you thought about?
Consultee:	We did the contract, and it was a flop. What could I do with that? How should I do it? I wish you'd write one. Maybe I don't know how.
Consultant:	When you were using the contract, what ideas did you have about why it wasn't working? Why did it flop?
Consultee:	Well, as I told you, he didn't know how to take advantage of the reinforcer. He just wandered around the room and acted bored.
Consultant:	So he hasn't learned how to make good use of free time, even when he's earned it. Tell me about the reinforcer. Where did the idea of free time come from? Was it his choice?
Consultee:	No, it's what I always use. I took a course at the university, and that's what the teacher said: Use free time as a reinforcer because everybody likes it.
Consultant:	Well, what do you think of that now, I mean for Sammy?
Consultee:	Well, he's an exception. One for every rule, you know. What are you suggesting?
Consultant:	You know Sammy. What do you think he'd be willing to work for?
Consultee:	I don't know.
Consultant:	Have you seen the reinforcement survey some of the teachers use? It's that one-page questionnaire that gets at what kids like and are willing to work for. Many of the things listed aren't things you have at school; they're things their parents get or do with them. Do you think it might help to see how Sammy responds to this? Your contract idea might work after all if you're able to get a more specific set of reinforcers to use.
Consultee:	Yeah, well, maybe. Do you have a copy of it? I've seen it but haven't used it yet. And I need you to look at the contract before I try it again. It needs something to make it jazzier.

Consultant:	I'll be glad to. I'll get you some copies of the reinforcement survey, and after you've filled it out with Sammy, put it into my box and I'll come to see you about the contract wording and design. [Makes a few notes for himself.] Now, here's where we are now. I'll see the RSP teacher to get an update on Sammy's reading progress and to see if you and she can get together sometime to see how you two can coordinate your program for Sammy. Would that be all right? Good. I'll also get you some copies of the survey, and you'll return it to me and we'll meet then to develop another contract. I'll also put Sammy's name on the SST meeting agenda if you still want me to.
Consultee:	For sure.
Consultant:	Meanwhile, you'll be getting Sammy a good role model as a study-buddy, and what else would you like to try with him before we go to SST again?
Consultee:	I'm going to call his mom again. I had asked her to, well, you know, we talked about it at the last SST, getting him some books at his level from the library and sitting down with him every night to help him with his reading, writing, and spelling. I don't think she's done a thing about it.
Consultant:	You may be right. Could I make a suggestion? Perhaps you might put more focus on what Sammy's mother can do. Sometimes parents get overwhelmed when asked to work on too many things. What do you think?
Consultee:	Oh, I don't know. I think she can spend twenty minutes a night. They've only got one other child, and she has a husband at home. I'll feel her out about it. I gotta go. See you whenever. Get me that stuff. Say hello to your wife.

In this case, the consultee approaches the consultant feeling agitated and defeated. She has let her worst fears take over and has given up on her own ability to help the student. The consultant does not allow himself to fall into this trap of saving her by readily accepting her catastrophic reactions to what seems to be the result of a poorly designed contract, a poorly monitored study-buddy system, a failure in communication between the consultee and the RSP teacher, and a lack of follow-up on a plan that Sammy's mom was supposed to follow. In only five minutes or so, all of this is revealed, and steps are planned to remediate much of it. The consultant has assigned himself some tasks, and the consultee has some work to do. Since the consultee wants something official to happen, she is asking for another SST meeting. She knows that the SST is the forum where she can press her case for full-time special education for Sammy, and she may be able to talk the team into agreeing with her. The consultant hopes not, however, and he will continue to try to get all other sources of help for Sammy activated. Perhaps members of the SST will agree and make other suggestions that will further that aim.

Notice how often the consultee tries to get the consultant to do something: to take over responsibility for Sammy, or to activate a process of removing the problem from the consultee's doorstep. As you review how this consultant deflects these direct requests/demands, you should get some notion of how a collaboratively minded consultant works. It would have been very easy to do one (or both) of two things: give in and agree that full-time placement is needed, or act like the expert and tell the consultee just what she should do to deal with Sammy. When the consultee defers to the consultant's assumed expertise in solving all problems, the consultant out-defers her by getting her to think about what she has done and how she might improve it. When done well, this sort of verbal interchange between a consultee and a consultant exemplifies "the scientific art of collaborative consultation."

What forms of expert power did the consultant use? He was expert in his ability to maintain a calm demeanor, in his willingness to listen and integrate data, in his wanting to be helpful without taking over, and in setting a plan. These are all examples of process expertise. He did not tell the consultee how to teach reading or how to apply contingencies to Sammy's out-of-seat behavior. He might at some point, however, if the consultee asks about these problems and makes it clear that she doesn't know how to manage them.

ACTIVITY 3.18

Review the previous scenario. Rewrite the consultant's lines to make them reflect an expert's approach. Then rewrite the original again, making the consultant even more collaborative, if you can.

It is important to remember in collaborative relationships that expert power works both ways; the consultees also have this power (Martin, 1978). They make the ultimate decisions about which interventions will be tried and how the interventions will actually be implemented. They also have expertise in teaching or classroom behavior management that a consultant may not have. They know the curriculum, their students, and their own frame of reference regarding what is possible in their classrooms, what has worked for them in the past, and so on. Their knowledge base needs to be understood, respected, and used. Ignoring it threatens the consultative relationship and alienates teachers (Pugach & Johnson, 1989). The same comments apply to parents when they are serving as consultees (Brown et al., 2001).

Informational Power

According to Raven (1965), informational power derives from the fact that information based on scientific findings, or based on the experiences of people who know about the topic, is almost always recognized as valuable. Experts usually have informational power, but others do also. The source isn't as important as is the apparent usefulness of the information. One of the roles of the consultant discussed in

Chapter 2 is that of information giver. Consultees expect that school-based consultants have their positions because they have informational power in addition to some degree of expert power based on their experience, training, advanced degrees, and the ability to project themselves as experts.

Recent Thinking About Power Issues in Consultation

Raven (1992, 1993) has revisited the original French and Raven (1959) ideas about social power. In his current writings he introduces a power/interaction model of interpersonal influence. Factors to consider in using this model are one's motivation to influence (Just why does a consultant believe she should be involved in this situation?), an assessment of the availability of the power bases discussed above (Which ones can be accessed to advantage?), preparation of the influence attempt (How should the consultee be approached?), and the need to assess results (Just how will we know if our use of power was truly influential?). Erchul and Raven (1997) have discussed strategies for the use of this model.

O'Keefe and Medway (1997) have also taken a further look at the uses of power (which they refer to as *interpersonal influence*) in consultation. They believe that a major role for the school consultant is to try to influence the consultee to change his attitude and behavior toward the student without resorting to manipulative tactics. Petty, Heesacker, and Hughes (1997) have discussed the Elaboration Likelihood Model (ELM) of attitude change. This model posits the belief that intervention ideas that are developed collaboratively which consultees consider "reflectively" are more likely to be implemented and become a permanent part of the consultee's repertoire than are those considered "nonthoughtfully." A reflective consideration involves giving thought to the underlying assumptions that support the intervention, while a nonthoughtful adoption of an intervention is based on giving in to the alleged superior knowledge or experience of the consultant. Nonthoughtful adoptions tend not to be taken seriously. Petty et al. (1997) suggest that consultants try to make the interventions personally valued by the consultee, make the consultee's role explicit, be sure the consultee has the knowledge and skill to implement the interventions, and keep a positive emotional atmosphere throughout the consultation process. They also suggest that consultees are more likely to be reflective if they have collaborated about the design of the interventions, see the interventions as valuable from their perspective, and are congruent with their thinking about the problem. This model is very similar to the one utilized by Conoley et al. (1991) in which those researchers attempted to enhance consultation effectiveness by matching intervention recommendations to the consultee's perspective.

ACTIVITY 3.19

In dyads, have partner A invent a school-relevant problem and act very deferential toward the consultant (partner B). The consultant should practice deflecting this deference and urge the consultee to apply her own problem-solving skills to the problem.

SUMMARY

Dougherty (2000) describes seven areas of skills that consultants must have. The three most important are communication, interpersonal effectiveness, and problem solving. This chapter has presented information and activities pertaining to communication and interpersonal effectiveness, discussed resistance in consultation, and analyzed power functions in interpersonal relations. We will present a model for problem solving in Chapter 5.

Your ability to communicate and to deal positively and effectively with others often determines the success or failure of the consultative enterprise. Certainly anybody who believes that consultation is worth doing will need to study and master the skills referred to in this chapter. Feedback from a teacher or your peers regarding your skills in communication and interpersonal effectiveness can be very useful.

REFERENCES

Arredondo, P., Toporek, R., Brown, S. P., Jones, J., Locke, D. C., Sanchez, J., & Sadler, H. (1996). Operationalization of the multicultural counseling competencies. *Journal of Multicultural Counseling and Development, 24,* 42–78.

Babcock, N. L., & Pryzwansky, W. B. (1983). Models of consultation: Preferences of educational professionals at five stages of service delivery. *Journal of School Psychology, 21,* 359–366.

Behring, S., & Ingraham, C. L. (1998). Culture as a central component of consultation: A call to the field. *Journal of Educational and Psychological Consultation, 9,* 57–72.

Benes, K. M., Gutkin, T. B., & Kramer, J. J. (1991). Micro-analysis of consultant and consultee verbal and nonverbal behaviors. *Journal of Educational and Psychological Consultation, 2,* 133–149.

Benjamin, A. (1987). *The helping interview.* Boston: Houghton Mifflin.

Bergan, J. R. (1977). *Behavioral consultation.* Upper Saddle River, NJ: Merrill/Prentice Hall.

Bergan, J. R., & Kratochwill, T. R. (1990). *Behavioral consultation and therapy.* New York: Plenum Press.

Bergan, J. R., & Tombari, M. (1976). Consultant skill and efficiency and the implementation and outcomes of consultation. *Journal of School Psychology, 14,* 3–14.

Berne, E. (1964). *Games people play.* New York: Grove.

Bolton, R. (1986). *People skills: How to assert yourself, listen to others, and resolve conflicts.* New York: Simon & Schuster.

Briggs Myers, I. (1976). *Myers-Briggs Type Indicator.* Palo Alto, CA: Consulting Psychologists Press.

Brown, D. (1993). Training consultants: A call to action. *Journal of Counseling and Development, 72,* 139–143.

Brown, D., Pryzwansky, W., & Schulte, A. (2001). *Psychological consultation: Introduction to theory and practice* (5th ed.). Boston: Allyn & Bacon.

Bushe, G. R., & Gibbs, B. W. (1990). Predicting organizational development consultation competence from Myers-Briggs Type Indicator and stage of ego development. *Journal of Applied Behavioral Science, 26,* 337–357.

Caplan, G. (1970). *The theory and practice of mental health consultation.* New York: Basic Books.

Caplan, G., & Caplan, R. B. (1993). *Mental health consultation and collaboration.* San Francisco: Jossey-Bass.

Carkhuff, R. R. (1969). *Helping and human relations* (2 vols.). New York: Holt, Rinehart, & Winston.

Carkhuff, R. R., & Pierce, R. M. (1975). *The art of helping—Trainer's guide.* Amherst, MA: Human Resources Development Press.

Carner, L., & Alpert, J. (1995). Some guidelines for consultants revisited. *Journal of Educational and Psychological Consultation, 6,* 47–57.

Chamberlain, P., & Baldwin, D. V. (1988). Client resistance to parent training: Its therapeutic management. In T. R. Kratochwill (Ed.), *Advances in school psychology* (vol. 6, pp. 131–171). Hillsdale, NJ: Erlbaum.

Christenson, S. L. (1995). Families and schools: What is the role of the school psychologist? *School Psychology Quarterly, 10* (2), 118–132.

Cobb, D. E., & Medway, F. J. (1978). Determinants of effectiveness in parent consultation. *Journal of Community Psychology, 6,* 229–240.

Conoley, C. W., Conoley, J. C., Ivey, D. C., and Scheel, M. J. (1991). Enhancing consultation by matching the consultee's perspectives. *Journal of Counseling and Development, 69,* 546–549.

Conoley, J. C., & Conoley, C. W. (1982). *School consultation: A guide to practice and training.* New York: Pergamon.

Conoley, J. C., & Conoley, C. W. (1992). *School consultation: Practice and training.* New York: Pergamon.

Cormier, W., & Cormier, L. (1985). *Interviewing strategies for helpers: A guide to assessment, treatment, and evaluation.* Pacific Grove, CA: Brooks/Cole.

Daniels, T. D., & DeWine, S. (1991). Communication process as target and tool for consultancy intervention: Rethinking a hackneyed theme. *Journal of Educational and Psychological Consultation, 2,* 303–322.

DeForest, P. A., & Hughes, J. N. (1992). Effect of teacher involvement and teacher self-efficacy on ratings of consultant effectiveness and intervention acceptability. *Journal of Educational and Psychological Consultation, 3,* 301–316.

Dettmer, P., Dyck, N., & Thurston, L. (1999). , collaboration, and teamwork for students with special needs (3rd ed.). Boston: Allyn & Bacon.

Dougherty, A. (2000). *Psychological consultation and collaboration* (3rd ed.). Belmont, CA: Brooks/Cole.

Duncan, C. F. (1995). Cross-cultural school consultation. In C. Lee (Ed.), *Counseling for diversity* (pp. 129–139). Boston: Allyn & Bacon.

Egan, G. (1998). *The skilled helper* (6th ed.). Pacific Grove, CA: Brooks/Cole.

Ellis, A. (1973). *Humanistic psychotherapy: The rational emotive approach.* New York: Julian.

Erchul, W. P. (1987). A relational communication analysis of control in school consultation. *Professional School Psychology, 2,* 113–124.

Erchul, W. P. (1999). Two steps forward, one step back: Collaboration in school-based consultation. *Journal of School Psychology, 37,* 191–203.

Erchul, W. P., & Raven, B. H. (1997). Social power in consultation: A contemporary view of French and Raven's bases of social power. *Journal of School Psychology, 35,* 137–171.

Evans, S. B. (1980). The consultant role of the resource teacher. *Exceptional Children, 46,* 402–404.

French, J. R. P., & Raven, B. H. (1959). The basis of social power. In D. Cartwright (Ed.), *Studies in social power* (pp. 150–167). Ann Arbor: University of Michigan, Institute of Social Research.

Friend, M., & Cook, M. (2000). *Interactions: Collaboration skills for school professionals* (3rd ed.). White Plains, NY: Longman.

Gallesich, J. (1982). *The profession and practice of consultation.* San Francisco: Jossey-Bass.

Gibbs, J. T. (1985). Can we continue to be color-blind and class-bound? *The Counseling Psychologist, 13,* 426–435.

Ginott, H. (1972). *Teacher and child.* Upper Saddle River, NJ: Prentice Hall.

Gordon, T. (1974). *T.E.T.: Teacher effectiveness training.* New York: McKay.

Gresham, F. M. (1989). Assessment of treatment integrity in school consultation and prereferral intervention. *School Psychology Review, 18,* 37–50.

Gross, S. (1980). *Interpersonal threat as a basis for resistance in consultation.* Paper presented at the annual meeting of the American Psychological Association, Montreal.

Gutkin, T. B. (1999). Collaborative versus directive/prescriptive/expert school-based consultation: Reviewing and resolving a false dichotomy. *Journal of School Psychology, 37,* 161–190.

Gutkin, T. B., & Hickman, J. A. (1990). The relationship of consultant, consultee, and organizational characteristics to consultee resistance to school-based consultation: An empirical analysis. *Journal of Educational and Psychological Consultation, 1*(2), 111–122.

Hallahan, D. P., & Kauffman, J. M. (1995). *The illusion of full inclusion.* Austin, TX: Pro-Ed.

Harris, A. M., & Cancelli, A. A. (1991). Teachers as volunteer consultees: Enthusiastic, willing, or resistant participants. *Journal of Educational and Psychological Consultation, 2,* 217–238.

Harris, A. M., Ingraham, C. L., & Lam, M. K. (1994). Teacher expectations for female and male school-based consultants. *Journal of Educational and Psychological Consultation, 5,* 115–142.

Harris, K. C. (1996). Collaboration within a multicultural society. *Remedial and Special Education, 17,* 2–10.

Herman, K. C. (1993). Reassessing predictors of therapist competence. *Journal of Counseling and Development, 72,* 29–32.

Heward, W. L. (2000). *Exceptional children* (6th ed.). Upper Saddle River, NJ: Merrill/Prentice Hall.

Huefner, D. S. (1988). The consulting teacher model: Risks and opportunities. *Exceptional Children, 54*(5), 403–414.

Hughes, J. N., & DeForest, P. A. (1993). Consultant directiveness and support as predictors of consultation outcomes. *Journal of School Psychology, 31,* 355–373.

Idol, L. (1997). *Creating collaborative and inclusive schools.* Austin, TX: Eitel Press.

Idol, L., Nevin, A., & Paolucci-Whitcomb, P. (2000). *Collaborative consultation* (3rd ed.). Austin, TX: Pro-Ed.

Jackson, D.N., & Hayes, D. H. (1993). Multicultural issues in consultation. *Journal of Counseling and Development, 72,* 144–147.

Joyce, B., & Showers, B. (1995). *Student achievement through staff development: Fundamentals of school renewal* (2nd ed.). White Plains, NY: Longman.

Kauffman, J. M., Gerber, M. M., & Semmel, M. I. (1988). Arguable assumptions underlying the regular education initiative. *Journal of Learning Disabilities, 21,* 6–11.

Kratochwill, T. R., & Bergan, J. R. (1990). *Behavioral consultation in applied settings.* New York: Plenum.

Kratochwill, T. R., Sheridan, S., & Van Someren, K. (1988). Research in behavioral consultation: Current status and future directions. In J. F. West (Ed.), *School consultation: Interdisciplinary perspectives on theory, research, training, and practice* (pp. 77–102). Austin, TX: Association of Educational and Psychological Consultants.

Kurpius, D. J., & Rozecki, T. G. (1993). Strategies for improving interpersonal communication. In J. E. Zins, T. R. Kratochwill, & S. N. Elliott (Eds.), *Handbook of consultation services for children* (pp. 137–158). San Francisco: Jossey-Bass.

Laud, L. (1998). Changing the way we communicate. *Educational Leadership, 55* (7), 23–25.

Liontos, S. B. (1992). *At-risk families and schools: Becoming partners.* Eugene: ERIC Clearinghouse on Educational Management, College of Education, University of Oregon.

Lippitt, G., & Lippitt, R. (1986). *The consulting process in action.* (2nd ed.). San Diego, CA: University Associates.

Maher, C. A. (1993). Providing consultation services in business settings. In J. E. Zins, T. R. Kratochwill, & S. N. Elliott (Eds.), *Handbook of consultation services for children* (pp. 317–328). San Francisco: Jossey-Bass.

Maher, C. A., & Bennett, R. W. (1984). *Planning and evaluation in special education services.* Upper Saddle River, NJ: Prentice Hall.

Maital, S. L. (1996). Integration of behavioral and mental health consultation as a means of overcoming resistance. *Journal of Educational and Psychological Consultation, 7*(4), 291–303.

Maitland, R. E., Fine, M. J., & Tracy, D. B. (1985). The effects of an interpersonally based problem-solving process on consultation outcomes. *Journal of School Psychology, 23,* 337–345.

Marks, E. S. (1995). *Entry strategies for school consultation.* New York: Guilford.

Martens, B. K. (1993). A behavioral approach to consultation. In J. E. Zins, T. R. Kratochwill, & S. N. Elliott (Eds.), *Handbook of consultation services for children* (pp. 65–86). San Francisco: Jossey-Bass.

Martin, R. (1978). Expert and referent power: A framework for understanding and maximizing consultation effectiveness. *Journal of School Psychology, 16,* 49–55.

Maslach, C. (1982). *Burnout: The cost of caring.* Upper Saddle River, NJ: Prentice Hall.

Miller, D. F. (1996). *Positive child guidance* (2nd ed.). Albany, NY: Delmar.

Miranda, A. H. (1993). Consultation with culturally diverse families. *Journal of Educational and Psychological Consultation, 4,* 89–93.

O'Keefe, D. J., & Medway, F. J. (1997). The application of persuasion research to consultation in school psychology. *Journal of School Psychology, 35,* 173–193.

O'Shea, D., O'Shea, L., Algozzine, R., & Hammitte, D. (2001). *Families and teachers of individuals with disabilities.* Boston: Allyn & Bacon.

Parsons, R. D., & Meyers, J. (1984). *Developing consultation skills*. San Francisco: Jossey-Bass.

Petty, R., Heesacker, M., & Hughes, J. (1997). The elaboration likelihood model: Implications for the practice of school psychology. *Journal of School Psychology, 35,* 107–136.

Piersal, W., & Gutkin, T. (1983). Resistance to school-based consultation: A behavioral analysis of the problem. *Psychology in the Schools, 20,* 311–320.

Ponti, C. R., Zins, J. E., & Graden, J. L. (1988). Implementing a consultation-based service delivery system to decrease referrals for special education: A case study of organizational considerations. *School Psychology Review, 17*(1), 89–100.

Pugach, M. C., & Johnson, L. J. (1989). The challenge of implementing collaboration between general and special education. *Exceptional Children, 56,* 232–235.

Pugach, M. C., & Johnson, L. J. (1995) *Collaborative practitioners, collaborative schools*. Denver, CO: Love

Rappaport, J. (1981). In praise of paradox: A social policy of empowerment over prevention. *American Journal of Community Psychology, 9,* 1–25.

Raven, B. H. (1965). Social influence and power. In I. D. Steiner & M. Fishbein (Eds.), *Current studies in social psychology* (pp. 371–382). New York: Holt, Rinehart, & Winston.

Raven, B. H. (1992). A power/interaction model of interpersonal influence: French and Raven thirty years later. *Journal of Social Behavior and Personality, 7,* 217–244.

Raven, B. H. (1993). The bases of power: Origins and recent developments. *Journal of Social Issues, 49,* 227–251.

Resnick, H., & Patti, R. (Eds.). (1980). *Change from within*. Philadelphia: Temple University Press.

Rosenfield, S. A., & Gravois, T. A. (1996). *Instructional consultation teams: Collaborating for change*. New York: Guilford Press.

Safran, S. (1991). The communication process and school-based consultation: What does the research say? *Journal of Educational and Psychological Consultation, 2,* 343–370.

Sapolsky, R. (1994). *Why zebras don't get ulcers: A guide to stress, stress-related diseases, and coping*. New York: W. H. Freeman.

Savelsbergh, M., & Staebler, B. (1995). Investigating leadership styles, personality preferences, and

effective teacher consultation. *Journal of Educational and Psychological Consultation, 6,* 277–286.

Schindler-Rainman, E. (1985). Invited commentary: The modern consultant—a renaissance person. *Consultation, 4*(3), 264–267.

Schowengerdt, R. V., Fine, M. J., & Poggio, J. P. (1976). An examination of some bases of teacher satisfaction with school psychological services. *Psychology in the Schools, 13,* 269–275.

Seligman, M. (1991). *Learned optimism*. New York: Knopf.

Selye, H. (1993). History of the stress concept. In L. Goldberger and S. Brevitz (Eds.), *Handbook of stress* (2nd ed.). New York: Free Press.

Shen, J. (1998). Do teachers feel empowered? *Educational Leadership, 55*(7), 35–36.

Sheridan, S. M., & Kratochwill, T. R. (1992). Behavioral parent-teacher consultation: Conceptual and research considerations. *Journal of School Psychology, 30,* 117–139.

Smelter, R., Bradley, W. R., & Yudewitz, G. J. (1994). Thinking of inclusion for all special needs students? Better think again. *Phi Delta Kappan, 76,* 35–38.

Stainback, W., & Stainback, S. (1984). A rationale for the merger of special and regular education. *Exceptional Children, 51,* 102–111.

Sugai, G., & Tindal, G. (1993). *Effective school consultation*. Pacific Grove, CA: Brooks/Cole.

Thomas, C. C., Correa, V. I., & Morsink, C. V. (1995). *Interactive teaming: Consultation and collaboration in special programs*. Upper Saddle River, NJ: Merrill/Prentice Hall.

Tobias, R. (1993). Underlying cultural issues that effect sound consultant/school collaboratives in developing multicultural programs. *Journal of Educational and Psychological Consultation, 4,* 237–251.

Vernberg, E. M., & Reppucci, N. D. (1986). Behavioral consultation. In F. V. Mannino, E. J. Trickett, M. F. Shore, M. G. Kidder, & G. Levin (Eds.), *Handbook of mental health consultation* (DHHS Publication No. ADM 86-1466, pp. 49–80). Washington, DC: U. S. Government Printing Office.

Villa, R., Thousand, J., Nevin, A., & Malgeri, C. (1996). Instilling collaboration for inclusive schooling as a way of doing business in public schools. *Remedial and Special Education, 17,* 169–181.

Wagner, T. (1998). Change as collaborative inquiry: A constructivist methodology for reinventing schools. *Phi Delta Kappan, 79,* 512–517.

Webster's College Dictionary (2nd ed.). (1997). New York: Random House.

West, J., Idol, L., & Cannon, G. (1989). *Collaboration in the schools.* Austin, TX: Pro-Ed.

Wickstrom, K. F., & Witt, J. C. (1993). Resistance with school-based consultation. In J. E. Zins, T. R. Kratochwill, & S. N. Elliott (Eds.), *Handbook of consultation services for children* (pp. 159–178). San Francisco: Jossey-Bass.

Zins, J. E. (1992). Implementing school-based consultation services: An analysis of five years of practice. In R. K. Conyne & J. O'Neil (Eds.), *Organizational consultation: A casebook* (pp. 50–79). Newbury Park, CA: Sage.

Zins, J. E., Curtis, M. J., Graden, J. L., & Ponti, C. R. (1988). *Helping students succeed in the regular classroom: A guide for developing intervention assistance programs.* San Francisco: Jossey-Bass.

Zins, J. E., & Ponti, C. R. (1987). Prereferral consultation: A system to decrease special education referral and placement. *Community Psychologist, 20,* 10–12.

CHAPTER 4

Ethics and Advocacy in School Consultation

OBJECTIVES

1. Orient the reader to the nature of, and necessity for, ethical reasoning.

2. Summarize the major ethical principles that affect school consultation.

3. Indicate through the use of cases how ethical codes and standards of practice are applied in situations related to interactions among school personnel and students.

4. Delineate the role of the consultant in issues of advocacy for students and families.

5. Provide activities that readers can use to sensitize them to the ethical, standards of practice and advocacy issues that are discussed in this chapter.

Mr. Romero is the RSP teacher at Chavez Elementary School. He has been working with the general education staff to increase the amount and quality of services for students with disabilities in the general education classes. Lately he has been particularly concerned with the actions of Ms. Peterson, a second-grade teacher, who steadfastly refuses to make any accommodations for José, an eight-year-old with a moderate hearing loss. Since there is no "front of the classroom" as there had been when Mr. Romero was in school, Ms. Peterson's voice seems to come from all over and at varying degrees of volume. When Mr. Romero talked to her about it, Ms. Peterson just brushed him off, stating that she can't be going over to José all day long to repeat things to him in a louder voice. Mr. Romero sees this as a violation of the spirit of inclusion, in addition to a failure to provide the necessary accommodations for José. Is this a violation of ethical standards? What steps should Mr. Romero take to deal with this issue?

At Jackie Robinson High School, the teacher of students with moderate-to-severe disabilities, Mr. Struck continues to conduct his class as he did 30 years ago. He does mainstreaming reluctantly and only when he is directed to by IEPs. He seeks no collaborative relationships with general education classes. Is Mr. Struck violating any ethical principles with this attitude and behavior? What standards of practice or advocacy issues arise when a teacher acts like Mr. Struck?

THE PURPOSE AND IMPORTANCE OF ETHICAL REASONING

Professionals assuming the role of school consultants, whether internal or external, must be aware of and attend to ethical practices. As of this writing, there is no national association of consultants that has developed an ethical code, but fortunately other associations and organizations have. The codes provided by the Council on Exceptional Children (CEC) (1997), the American Psychological Association (APA) (1992), the American Counseling Association (ACA) (1995), and the National Association of School Psychologists (1992) give direction and guidance to school consultants. Ewing (2001); Gable, Arllen, and Cook (1993); Heron, Martz, and Margolis (1996); Howe and Miramontes (1991); Hughes (1986); Jacob-Timm (1999); Newman (1993); and Pryzwansky (1993) have also provided commentary and guidance. Howe and Miramontes (1992) and Jacob-Timm and Hartshorne (1998) have devoted texts to this subject, and Cook, Weintraub, and Morse (1995) have provided an interesting chapter on the ethical ramifications of restructuring in special education.

Attention to ethical responsibilities is important for at least the following reasons:

1. Consultants are dealing with the lives of other people, including minors who are relatively powerless to influence what happens to them in the schools.
2. Consultation implies influence and some degree of power.
3. Issues of confidentiality exist whenever consultants discuss students and their families.
4. These same issues exist when consultants discuss or observe teaching practices.
5. Any hint of unethical practices, whether validated or not, can destroy credibility and future efforts at consultation.

PRINCIPLES OF ETHICAL BEHAVIOR

Brown et al. (2001) provide six principles that summarize the contents of the APA and ACA codes as they apply to consultation.

Principle 1: Competence. No person should extend her services as a consultant unless she is competent to do so by training and experience. Unfortunately, it is not at all clear what competence means since consistency in standards of training is not common. Just exactly what sort of training and how much experience you should have is not clearly spelled out in codes of ethics, or in *standards of practice*, which are guidelines established to assist practitioners in the determination of appropriate practice. Professional responsibility often comes down to your own self-insight: If you don't feel competent to engage in a certain sort of professional activity, you probably aren't well trained and you shouldn't do it. Instead, explain your situation to your superior, and try to help the district find other persons to accomplish the task or seek additional training for yourself.

ACTIVITY 4.1

It has been mentioned in this text that the three primary competencies in consultation are communication, interpersonal skills, and problem solving. Discuss what it means to be competent in each of these three areas. What training or experience makes one competent to engage in the process of consultation? Additionally, what experience and training would be helpful in the overall area of content, such as knowledge of interventions and when to recommend them?

Principle 2: Protecting the welfare of clients. This is usually regarded as the most important ethical principle in human service work. In consultation it is necessary to regard both the consultee and the student as clients. Also, there may be multiple consultees and clients, so the welfare of all engaged parties becomes significant.

At the most obvious level, the development of interventions requires a constant interest in the welfare of the student(s) with whom the interventions(s) will be used. A student's welfare may be threatened through the use of assessment instruments that are not appropriate for that individual, the development of policies that may be biased against certain people, the encouragement of dependency on the consultant, and the use of interventions that are not well validated by empirical measures or through the personal experiences of either the consultee or consultant.

ACTIVITY 4.2

Discuss the concept of client (student) welfare. Give examples from your experience that indicate a positive example of meeting the welfare of the student, and a negative example. What steps can a school consultant take to ensure that the welfare of the student is the primary driving force behind interventions that are designed for, and carried out with, students?

Principle 3: Maintaining confidentiality. Whenever a consultation-based service delivery system is to be conducted in a school, confidentiality must be established at two levels: with the administration and with the individual consultees. A school principal should not ask a consultant to evaluate the performance of a teacher consultee, and the consultee should not have to fear that the consultant is talking to others about their conversations or the consultee's performance as a teacher.

There are limits to confidentiality, and these should also be explained to potential consultees. Abuse of other persons or threats to self or others need to be reported. Individual states may have laws excluding certain behaviors from the ordinary right to privileged communication. For example, sexual harassment between students at all ages is forbidden by law in some states, and knowledge of its occurrence must be reported to the local authorities.

ACTIVITY 4.3

Role-play an interview with a teacher–consultee with whom you have not consulted previously in which you explain your method of consultation and the fact of confidentiality in your proceedings, along with limitations to that confidentiality. Also, role-play giving a talk to all the teachers in the school about these same matters. How would you present your views to the principal before talking to all the teachers?

Principle 4: Responsibilities when making public statements. This usually applies to external consultants rather than to internal school-based consultants. An internal consultant needs to explain to potential employers and consultees the nature of consultation, how it will be conducted, and its limits. In the event an internal consultant has an occasion to speak to people from outside the school, especially the press, he should be careful not to disclose information obtained in confidence.

Principle 5: Social and moral responsibility. Consultants need to make sure that their behavior and statements are governed by the best interests of the constituents, not by their own needs or agendas. Backer and Glaser (1979; cited in Brown et al., 2001) have indicated numerous ways in which ethical conflicts can occur. Among them are creating unnecessary dependency on the part of the consultee, failing to recognize your own limitations, and imposing your own values on the consultee. Naturally, inappropriate physical or sexual behavior is always unethical and unprofessional.

Principle 6: Relationship with other consultants. In schools that have heavily invested in collaborative modes of problem solving and program building, numerous people may act in consultant roles from time to time. We need to respect the opinions of these individuals as well as those of external consultants while being sure to work with them in a positive manner, especially in situations when we may not agree with their approaches. It is sometimes surprising how many different people claim to speak for a given student. Each person believes she is advocating for the best interests of the student, but like the blind man and the elephant, some of them are perceiving only selected parts of the big picture. One of the roles and skills of high-functioning school-based consultants is to be able to meld these diverse ideas and personalities into a cohesive collaborative team. There is a more thorough discussion of advocacy issues at the end of this chapter.

In addition to these general principles elucidated by Brown et al. (2001), Howe and Miramontes (1992), and Jacob-Timm and Hartshorne (1998) have also contributed to this area. Gallesich (1982) has developed a list of twenty-eight guidelines for ethical behavior that she believes can serve as a code specifically designed for consultants. Among the most relevant for school consultants are these five:

1. Consultants avoid manipulating consultees.
2. Consultants strive to evaluate the outcomes of their services.
3. Consultants acquire the basic body of knowledge and skills of their profession.
4. Consultants know their professional strengths, weaknesses, and biases.
5. Consultants take active steps to maintain and increase their effectiveness.

A PROBLEM-SOLVING MODEL FOR DEALING WITH ETHICAL ISSUES

Jacob-Timm and Hartshorne (1998) summarize Keith-Spiegel and Koocher (1985), who have provided a problem-solving model designed to assist consultants and others in their efforts to determine if an ethical violation exists and how to deal with it. These steps, in addition to others suggested by Corey, Corey, and Callanan (1998), are as follows:

1. Identify the problem or situation.
2. Define the parameters of the situation.
3. Define the potential ethical–legal issues involved.
4. Consult legal–ethical guidelines.
5. Consult with trusted colleagues.
6. Evaluate the rights, responsibilities, and welfare of all affected parties.
7. Generate a list of alternative decisions possible for each issue.
8. Enumerate the consequences of making each decision.
9. Conduct a risk–benefit analysis.
10. Make the decision.

THE COUNCIL ON EXCEPTIONAL CHILDREN CODE OF ETHICS AND STANDARDS FOR PROFESSIONAL PRACTICE

The Council on Exceptional Children (CEC) (1997) has provided a very brief code of ethics and a more elaborate set of standards for professional practice. These are available on their web site at http://www.cec.sped.org/ps/code.html. This code of ethics requires a responsibility to members to:

A. Develop the highest educational and quality of life potential of individuals with exceptionalities.
B. Promote and maintain a high level of competence and integrity in practicing their profession.
C. Engage in professional activities which benefit individuals with exceptionalities, their families, other colleagues, students, or research subjects.
D. Exercise objective professional judgment in the practice of their profession.
E. Strive to advance their knowledge and skills regarding the education of individuals with exceptionalities.
F. Work within the standards and policies of their profession.
G. Uphold and improve where necessary the laws, regulations, and policies governing the delivery of special education and related services and the practice of their profession.
H. Not condone or participate in unethical or illegal acts, nor violate professional standards adopted by the Delegate Assembly of the CEC.

THREE EXAMPLE SITUATIONS

Each of the principles in the CEC Code of Ethics, along with the CEC Standards for Professional Practice, are used as the guidelines to help determine an appropriate course of action in each of the following three situations:

Situation 1

A special day-class teacher had referred a student with an emotional disturbance who presented with behavior-adjustment problems such as defiance toward teachers, physical assaults on other students, and inappropriate language. After a review of this situation and the development of specified interventions by the IEP team, and two individual consultations with the school psychologist, the teacher decided that what the student needed was a severe tongue-lashing in front of the class. This intervention had not been suggested by either the SST or the consultant. When the consultant followed up with the referring teacher, this teacher admitted what she had done, and indicated that the case was closed because the student had (at least for now) stopped his inappropriate behavior.

1. *Identify the problem:* The teacher has not followed the recommended interventions and has engaged in a behavior which might be detrimental to the target student.

2. *Define the parameters:* The teacher's questionable behavior occurred in the classroom in front of all the other students in that class.

3. *Define the potential ethical–legal issues involved:* At issue is whether the teacher's behavior violates ethical or legal principles. Is it acceptable and appropriate for a teacher to berate a student, either privately or, as in this case, in front of the student's peers? What alternative behavior might the teacher have engaged in?

4. *Consult legal–ethical guidelines:* It appears that guidelines A (quality of life), B (integrity of practice), C (activities which benefit individuals with exceptionalities), D (exercise of objective professional judgment), and F (work within the standards and policies of their profession) are being violated by the teacher's behavior. The primary standard of practice that is apparently violated is in the area of "management of behavior," which stipulates that special educators are to "apply only those disciplinary methods and behavioral principles which they have been instructed to use and

(continues)

which do not undermine the dignity of the individual . . ." (CEC Code of Ethics and Standards of Practice, 2000, Management of Behavior Section, number 1). The teacher may also be violating other aspects of this standard which are delineated in the CEC statement.

5. *Consult with trusted colleagues:* In this case the consultant had promised the teacher prior to the beginning of the consultations that he (the consultant) would hold all observations and discussions in confidence. The consultee, however, was informed that if the consultant became aware of behaviors that threatened or did harm to others, the confidentiality would be broken. The consultant decides to discuss this issue with two colleagues who, it turns out, have different views on this subject. One colleague says that the teacher did engage in behaviors that were "potentially dangerous to the student" and therefore should be informed that the consultant would be reporting this behavior to the principal. The other colleague said that the teacher's "being verbally firm with the student" was within her rights and did not constitute "probable harm."

6. *Evaluate the rights, responsibilities, and welfare of all concerned:* The teacher's right (and responsibility) is to manage her classroom and to deal with behavior challenges in a way that serves best to maintain a peaceful and productive classroom. The student's right is to be educated by individuals who have the student's welfare uppermost in their minds. As such, a student shouldn't have to endure hostile and (potentially) damaging verbalizations from his teachers. The student's parents have a right to expect that their son's teachers will maintain an atmosphere that conveys safety and concern for their child's welfare. It would appear in this case that the rights of the student and parent need to take precedence. The teacher does not seem to have acted in the best interests of the student, but rather seems to have given into frustration and (at least temporarily) lost her professional demeanor.

7. *Generate a list of alternative decisions:* The alternatives seem to be three: (a) do nothing; (b) talk to the teacher about her behavior and inform her that she is not allowed to talk to students that way and that she should desist from this behavior in the future; or (c) inform the principal, who will talk to the teacher about it and who may file an ethics violation against the teacher which, if sustained, will go into the teacher's personnel file.

8. *Enumerate the consequences of making each decision:* Choice (a) is clearly inappropriate; (b) may be acceptable, if you believe this behavior was an aberration and is not likely to happen again if you speak to the teacher about it; (c) seems to be the strongest remedy, and should probably be invoked if there is reason to think that this behavior has happened before and could happen again.

9. *Conduct a risk–benefit analysis:* The risk of utilizing choice (b) is that the teacher may not think the statement from the consultant is very meaningful, and may therefore be ignored the next time the teacher is feeling stressed by this student's, or any other student's, disruptive and disrespectful behavior. The benefit is that the teacher appreciates the faith the consultant has in her and, since she comes to think her behavior could have been damaging to the student because of what the consultant says to her about it, she vows to herself never to let it happen again. The risk involved in choice (c) is that the teacher may believe that her behavior was not out of line (she's witnessed other teachers berating their students and nothing was said to them about it) and therefore she's being unfairly discriminated against. Since she willingly took part in the consultation process, she now believes it was a mistake because none of this would have come up otherwise. She may interpret this to mean that the consultant cannot be trusted. The benefit of choice (c) is that it announces to all who come to know about it that this sort of behavior is unethical and will not be tolerated. It sends the strongest message to the teacher and to others who come to know about it.

10. *Make the decision:* Because the consultant is the only one who knows about the teacher's behavior, it is his decision among choices (a), (b), and (c) that will decide the disposition of the case. Of course, if he chooses option (c), the principal then becomes the leading decision maker regarding further disposition of the case.

The consultant decides to invoke option (b), based on his assessment of the seriousness of the offense, his knowledge of the teacher and her typical behavior, and his belief that this was likely to have been a professional lapse that will be corrected by his exercise of option (b). He talks to the teacher about it and she agrees that her behavior was excessive, certainly not typical of her, and she will not engage in that sort of behavior again.

ACTIVITY 4.4

Review the steps taken in the example above. Comment on the reasoning process the consultant goes through in trying to decide what to do. How would you have modified the process? Do you think there could have been other options? Do you agree with the final decision?

Situation 2

Ms. Abernathy (Ms. A), the RSP teacher–consultant in the Carter Elementary School (K–6), has been doing some co-teaching with Mr. Brandeis (Mr. B), a second-grade teacher. Mr. B has three students out of his twenty-six who have been identified as having learning disabilities. He believes three more also have learning disabilities, but he has not referred them as yet. He prefers to see if his new "APC: All Phonics Cure" method of teaching reading, which he has devised from a variety of sources, will bring these three, in addition to those already identified as having learning disabilities, up to grade level.

After watching and attempting to co-teach Mr. B's APC method for two weeks, Ms. A is very bothered by what she has observed. First, the method seems to be a poorly thought-out collection of ideas about phonemic awareness gathered during Mr. B's serious efforts to coalesce much of what is known about teaching phonetically into a unified approach, using the best of what various authorities have to say about these methods. Unfortunately, at least according to Ms. A, the result is a hodgepodge of ideas which are applied in a nonsystematic manner and which rely on a confusing mixture of material gathered from many different sources. Further, Mr. B is such an advocate of his phonics-based approach that he does nothing but phonics; whole language or other literature-based systems are discounted by him as useless, if not invalid. Ms. A is concerned that the students with learning disabilities, two of whom have been identified as having auditory processing problems, are being overwhelmed and confused by this barrage of auditory input. She can see them staring around the room and weakly mimicking the other students' rote responding to the hour-long phonic drills.

1. *Identify the problem or situation:* Ms. A believes that Mr. B is acting unethically—that is, not in the best interests of his students, especially those with learning disabilities.

2. *Define the parameters of the situation:* Mr. B is using an unproven, methodologically questionable method of teaching read-

ing in a situation where he has learners who need systematic, well-validated methods of teaching reading.

3. *Define the potential ethical–legal issues involved.* Two questions are involved: (a) Does a teacher have the right to use whatever methods he believes are appropriate? (b) Given the identified needs of the students with a learning disability, doesn't a teacher have to follow whatever interventions have been indicated by the IEP, or by the consultant?

4. *Consult legal–ethical guidelines:* Ms. A notes that each of the eight principles in the CEC code seem to apply to special educators. Mr. B is a general education teacher. Do these principles apply to him? Is there a code of ethics for general educators that should be consulted? Because Ms. A is confused about this, she goes to the next step in the ethical problem-solving model and consults with a colleague. Her colleague notes that the introduction to the eight principles from CEC indicates that the code applies to "educators of persons with exceptionalities." Together they agree that the code does apply to general educators who are, in inclusion or mainstreaming situations, "educators of persons with exceptionalities." They also review the Code of Ethics of the Education Profession promulgated by the National Education Association (1975). This document is not specific regarding the issue under scrutiny here. Returning to a consideration of the CEC principles and the standards of conduct, which are much more specific than the NEA Code, these two individuals are concerned that CEC ethical principles B (maintaining a high level of competence and integrity in practicing their profession), D (professionals exercise objective professional judgment), and F (professionals work within the standards and policies of their profession) are being violated. The questionable standard for practice in this situation is in the section on Instructional Responsibilities, where educators of students with disabilities are directed to "identify and use instructional methods and curricula that are appropriate . . . in meeting the educational needs of persons with exceptionalities."

5. *Consult with trusted colleagues:* Ms. A returns to her colleague and one other individual and they review the situation. All three agree that, in the absence of data to support Mr. B's unique teaching methods, he should be asked to desist from this method, if only for those students who seem to be confused by it.

(*continues*)

6. *Evaluate the rights, responsibilities, and welfare of all affected parties.* Mr. B's rights are to conduct his class in light of his understanding of the best practices in teaching and classroom management. His responsibility is to the standards for the teaching profession (for example, see California Department of Education, 1997) and to meet the educational, social, and emotional needs of his students. The rights of his students, among others, are to be taught in the most effective and efficient manner. Students with disabilities have additional rights spelled out in IDEA. Students' responsibilities are to conduct themselves in an appropriate manner so as to benefit from what the school has to offer. Their welfare is a key component in this ethical situation. Since they are to be educated in the least restrictive environment, and since the IEP team has decided that mainstreaming into a general education second-grade class is appropriate, it is necessary for the teacher in that class to meet the needs of those students, in addition to providing an appropriate education for all his students.

7. *Generate a list of all alternative decisions:* Ms. A and her colleagues believe four options are open to them: (a) do nothing; (b) remove special education students from Mr. B's class; (c) have Ms. A discuss their concerns with Mr. B and indicate their belief that his APC method is not appropriate for the students with learning disabilities, and may not be the best method for other students as well. They will also suggest some alternative and/or supplementary methods which they believe are more appropriate, and which Ms. A can help implement when she is engaged in her co-teaching efforts; or (d) inform the principal of their concerns, either as a first choice, or for certain if option (c) is chosen and rejected by Mr. B.

8. *Enumerate the consequences of making each decision:* Option (a) is useless; option (b) solves the problem of likely inappropriate methodology for the students with learning disabilities, but does nothing for the other students; option (c) seems best targeted for this situation. In the event that option (c) does not produce the desired result, option (d) will be used.

9. *Conduct a risk–benefit analysis:* The risks to option (c) are that Mr. B might believe that his autonomy as a teacher has been undermined. He might state that his methods are working very well for most of the students in his class (they might be; are they?) and since the students with disabilities are to be mainstreamed, he is providing them a real mainstreaming experience by expecting

them to learn in a method that is successful for students in the mainstream. Another possible risk is that he might accept option (c), try some of the modifications suggested, but because they are not his ideas, do them halfheartedly, or, perhaps, when Ms. A isn't in the room, not at all. The benefit would be that Mr. B might come to understand that mainstreaming doesn't mean that students with disabilities sink or swim with all others; it means that students with mild disabilities can find success in general education classes if the content and methods are adapted to their needs and abilities.

10. *Make the decision:*   Ms. A's decision is as expected: option (c). She meets with Mr. B, reviews her concerns and the options previously presented, and, with his approval, selects option (c). She thought he might select (b), but he surprised her by stating that he wants to prove that he can teach students with learning disabilities to read, even if his APC method may need to be adapted for them. Ms. A and Mr. B review some accommodations and modifications and return to their co-teaching as a much more collaborative team than they were before.

ACTIVITY 4.5

Respond to the same questions as in Activity 4.4. Also, discuss Mr. B's rights as a teacher in this situation.

Situation 3

Miss Sally Phillips (Ms. P) is a resource specialist–consultant in Hannibal High School. She was very pleased three years ago when her district decided to move toward more of a collaborative consultation mode of service delivery. She had long held the belief that her talents weren't being utilized while she was assigned the role of resource teacher and expected to teach students, primarily those with learning disabilities, all day. Because of her previous experience as both a math and science teacher at Hannibal High, she yearned to get back into the general education classrooms and assist teachers who were working with the same students with learning disabilities who

(continues)

were seeing her for one or two periods a day. She was convinced that she could offer many good ideas to content-area teachers if she only had the time to do consultation instead of teaching all day. Therefore, when the district decided to make the move toward a consultation-based system of service delivery for students with exceptionalities, she jumped at the chance. She's been acting as a consultant to the general education staff on a full-time basis for the past three years.

The problem is that she is very unpopular in her role. Specifically, general education teachers have complained to the principal that (1) she is pushy; she believes her ideas about accommodations and modifications are better than what the other teachers are doing, and she is quick to let them know that; (2) she is not a good listener; (3) when engaged in any form of cooperative teaching, she takes over as much as possible, and turns lessons into what she wants them to be; and (4) her concern for the needs of the mainstreamed students seems to have fallen by the wayside in favor of her using her position to impose her ideas on other teachers. Her recommended modifications and accommodations often seem to have no empirical foundation.

ACTIVITY 4.6

The class or study group should review this situation in light of the eight principles in the CEC code of ethics, and then follow the ten-step problem-solving method used in situations 1 and 2. Specifically, is there an ethical issue here? Which of the eight principles seem to be violated? Based on an analysis of this situation, what decision(s) seem(s) best?

AREAS OF POTENTIAL ETHICAL CONFLICT

Snow and Gersick (1986) have discussed five areas of potential ethical conflict. The first has to do with the nature of the consultation contract itself. In schools, there is rarely any formal contract established with internal consultants such as there might be with an external consultant. Internal consultants typically operate informally, but they certainly should be fairly explicit in explaining their role, their preferred method of interacting with the consultee, and confidentiality and its limits.

The second area concerns issues of loyalty and responsibility. In schools it often seems that consultants are serving many constituents at once: the teacher–consultee, the parent, the principal, possibly a higher-level administrator, and sometimes the sole interests of the student. Discussion of possible conflicts should occur between interested parties when it is clear that the different constituencies are at odds about how to proceed. It is sometimes not clear whose needs and interests should take precedence, although the student should be given top priority whenever possible.

The third area consists of value choices related to intervention techniques. Consultants and consultees may not agree, for a number of reasons, on what the interventions should be. Intervention choice is to some degree related to one's values, training, biases, and other variables that may not be made explicit. Again, discussion and compromise, hallmarks of a collaborative approach, are the best avenues to take if disputes occur. As a general rule, it is best to help the consultee develop his ideas since, for the most part, the consultee will be implementing them. Situation 3 included a good example of a consulting teacher who seemed to stand in direct violation of this ideal.

Snow and Gersick's fourth potential area of conflict is the use and limits of confidentiality. As I have previously mentioned, issues of confidentiality should be discussed and made clear before any sort of consultation work takes place. The discussion should start at the administrative level; be sure that your immediate supervisor knows your position regarding confidentiality. This should be shared with the local school principal and then with the teachers. School consultants starting a consultation service delivery system would do well to address the whole school staff to explain the process and review confidentiality issues. These should be reviewed with individual teachers the first time a consultant works with each of them. An example of how to present this to an individual consultee was presented in Chapter 1 in the material explaining the meaning of collaborative consultation.

The last area of potential conflict is the degree of responsibility for outcomes to be assumed by the consultant. In a collaborative mode, responsibility is shared, and accountability is the joint responsibility of all constituent parties. If plans don't work, the implementer has the responsibility to inform the other members of the problem-solving team, who will reconvene to assess the situation. If communication processes are working well, this should not be a serious issue (Friend & Cook, 2000; Pugach & Johnson, 1995). When communication seems to be breaking down, it may be appropriate for the consultant to look for possible sources and types of resistance or barriers to consultation, which are discussed in Chapter 3.

In the final analysis, school-based consultants need to be aware that they may come across situations in which there may be a violation of the ethical standards I have summarized. As professionals, when we believe a violation has occurred we are obligated to take some action, such as following the ten-step procedure previously described. As Jacob-Timm and Hartshorne (1998) point out, in the area of ethics, professionals have no rights, just responsibilities.

ADVOCACY

An advocate is a person who seeks to establish a certain condition for an individual client or group within a system. At its most elementary level, school consultation is all about advocacy; the consultant works (i.e., advocates) with the consultee(s) for the betterment of some condition for the client (student). In the most common case of a consultant working with a teacher to improve the learning of a student referred because of academic challenges, the consultant advocates for the student by assisting the teacher to take whatever steps are necessary to improve the learning environment for the student. In a more complex situation, a consultant might be working with a group of consultees (administrators, teachers, and playground aides) regarding issues of playground safety (i.e., freedom from harassment by others). They collaborate by using all the techniques described in Chapter 3 and together come up with a plan which makes good sense to the majority and has the commitment of the front-line staff (probably the playground aides). In even more impactive cases, consultants advocate for systems-change efforts where relatively large-scale projects may affect teaching or behavior management methods throughout the whole school or district. Chapter 10 presents a case demonstrating how the consultant worked with school personnel to affect a major change in service delivery for students with mild handicaps.

Given the seemingly straightforward positive aspects of an advocacy stance, a word of caution is in order. Some school consultants interpret advocacy in a somewhat stronger sense, that of taking a stand for a given position and doing everything it takes to see that the position comes to be accepted or adopted by all constituents of a problem, whether or not these other individuals are in favor of this position. For example, a behaviorally oriented consultant believes that the contingencies of reinforcement are the main driving forces behind students' behaviors. She advocates solely for all teachers to adopt this point of view, perhaps blurring some teacher's (or counselor's) efforts to understand students' behavior from alternative viewpoints, such as a counseling-communications–based system, or a psychoeducational approach, or, in selected cases, a neuropsychological approach (D'Amato & Rothlisberger, 1992). In situation 2 in this chapter, Mr. B was a strong advocate for his APC method of teaching reading. In his heart he believed that he was doing his best for his students. The resource teacher–consultant, Ms. A, thought it necessary to advocate for a different approach for at least some of the students in Mr. B's classes. Both individuals believed they were advocating for the best interests of students. Fortunately, a compromise was worked out, avoiding an ethics-based advocacy clash by these two constituents.

In a more detailed analysis of the concept of advocacy in consultation, Conoley and Conoley (1992) have described an advocacy model of consultation, characterized by individuals bringing ideas into an already existing structure in an effort to modify in some significant way how the structure deals with clients. Some of the more recent advocacy efforts have been in respect to acquiring permission for students to engage in prayer in schools, curriculum either for or against Darwinian evolution, the necessity for national standards, a voucher system, the purging of certain books from school libraries, clubs for gay and lesbian issues, and, in an area close to the heart of the content of this text, inclusion for students with disabilities. In each case an advocacy-minded individual or group believes that they are speaking for the rights of disenfranchised or relatively powerless groups (i.e., students) who cannot fight for these rights by themselves. Thus, advocacy consultation may find itself in a position of having to abandon the collaborative mode in favor of a more assertive stance, characterized by what the advocate believes is a higher value: the needs of students that may not be recognized or honored by the existing conditions of the school.

An example of advocates' successful efforts to impact on a culturally accepted situation is in the area of childrens' rights. Currently most people in this culture (and all over the world) believe that it is a right of children to be safe from harm. However, it wasn't until 1833 that child labor laws were enacted in England. These stated that children between the ages of 9 and 13 could not be required to work more than nine hours a day. In America, only 15 states had child labor laws by 1903, and it wasn't until 1938 that Congress passed the Fair Labor Standards Act, which generally set the minimum age at which children could be employed as 16. In regard to all forms of abuse, as recently as 1963 only 13 states had laws requiring the mandatory reporting of child maltreatment. We can see that it wasn't too many years ago that child labor and exploitation were common in America, as they still are in many places in the world (Sussman,1977). Only through the strong advocacy efforts of reformers did those practices get abolished, either by force of law or by the slow evolution of more enlightened thinking by most citizens.

In the case of the inclusion of students with disabilities, advocates have been fighting for this right in the halls of Congress and in the halls of public schools for at least 30 years. The first major breakthrough that resulted from advocacy for the rights of individuals was P.L. 94-142, passed in 1975. This ensured students with disabilities the right to a Free Appropriate Public Education (FAPE). In the ensuing years, advocates went to the next step, that of inclusion of those with disabilities into the Least Restrictive Environment (LRE), which was interpreted to mean the general education classroom whenever possible. Advocacy for these rights, including a clearer explication of the meaning of FAPE and LRE, continues.

In the final analysis, there is a place for advocacy, but it needs to be done in a collaborative style. Getting students' rights and needs met should be the primary basis for parenting and for working in the schools. In almost all instances, the ability to work together for these rights and needs will ensure a more harmonious work environment and a greater chance to have these rights and needs met than will the taking of strong advocacy positions that may be socially, scientifically, or politically inappropriate.

SUMMARY

This chapter has presented information about issues of ethics and advocacy. Ethical guidelines developed by professional groups were reviewed, and a set of guidelines based on the Council on Exceptional Children (1997) code and standards were used to determine how decisions can be made in cases of ethical concern. Advocacy was reviewed as an essential element in the consultative interaction, and one that requires considerable sensitivity in its application.

REFERENCES

American Counseling Association. (1995). *Code of ethics and standards of practice.* Alexandria, VA: Author.

American Psychological Association. (1992). *Ethical principles of psychologists and code of conduct.* Washington, DC: Author.

Backer, T. E., & Glaser, E. M. (1979). *Portraits of 17 organizational consultants.* Los Angeles: Human Interaction Research Institute.

Brown, D., Pryzwansky, W., & Schulte, A. (2001). *Psychological consultation* (5th ed.). Boston: Allyn & Bacon.

California Department of Education. (1997). *California standards for the teaching profession.* Sacramento, CA: Author.

Conoley, J. C., & Conoley, C. W. (1992). *School consultation: A guide to practice and training.* Needham Heights, MA: Allyn & Bacon.

Cook, L. H., Weintraub, F. J., & Morse, W. C. (1995). Ethical dilemmas in the restructuring of special education. In J. L. Paul, D. Evans, & H. Rosselli (Eds.), *Integrating school restructuring and special education reform* (pp. 119–139). Fort Worth, TX: Harcourt Brace.

Corey, G., Corey, M., & Callanan, P. (1998). *Issues and ethics in the helping professions* (5th ed.). Pacific Grove, CA: Brooks/Cole Publishing Co.

Council on Exceptional Children. (1997). *CEC code of ethics and standards of practice.* Reston, VA: Author.

CEC Code of Ethics and Standards of Practice. Retrieved December 21, 2000, from http://www. cec. sped.org/ps/code.html

D'Amato, R., & Rothlisberger, B. (1992). *Psychological perspectives on intervention.* New York: Longman.

Ewing, N. (2001). Teacher education: Ethics, power and privilege. *Teacher Education and Special Education, 24*(1), 13–24.

Friend, M., & Cook, L. (2000). *Interactions: Collaboration skills for school professionals* (3rd ed.). New York: Longman.

Gable, R. A., Arllen, N. L., & Cook, L. (1993). But—let's not overlook the ethics of collaboration. *Preventing School Failure, 37,* 32–36.

Gallesich, J. (1982). *The profession and practice of consultation: A handbook for consultants, trainers of consultants and consumers of consultation services.* San Francisco: Jossey-Bass.

Heron, T. E., Martz, S. A., & Margolis, H. (1996). Ethical and legal issues in consultation. *Remedial and Special Education, 17*(6), 377–385, 392.

Howe, K., & Miramontes, O. (1991). A framework for ethical deliberation in special education. *Journal of Special Education, 25*(1), 7–25.

Howe, K., & Miramontes, O. (1992). *The ethics of special education.* New York: Teachers College Press.

Hughes, J. (1986). Ethical issues in school consultation. *School Psychology Review, 15,* 489–499

Jacob-Timm, S. (1999). Ethically challenging situations encountered by school psychologists. *Psychology in the Schools, 36*(3), 205–217.

Jacob-Timm, S., & Hartshorne, T. (1998). *Law and ethics for school psychologists* (3rd ed.). Brandon, VT: CPPC.

Keith-Spiegel, P., & Koocher, G. P. (1985). *Ethics in psychology.* Hillsdale, NJ: Erlbaum.

National Education Association. (1975). *The Code of Ethics of the Education Profession.* Washington, DC: Author.

Newman, J. L. (1993). Ethical issues in consultation. *Journal of Counseling and Development, 72,* 148–156.

Pryzwansky, W. B. (1993). Ethical consultation practice. In J. E. Zins, T. R. Kratochwill, & S. N. Elliott (Eds.), *Handbook of consultation services for children* (pp. 329–350). San Francisco: Jossey-Bass.

Pugach, M. C., & Johnson, L. J. (1995). *Collaborative practitioners, collaborative schools.* Denver: Love Publishing.

Snow, D. L., & Gersick, K. E. (1986). Ethical and professional issues in mental health consultation. In F. V. Mannino, E. J. Trickett, M. F. Shore, M. G. Kidder, & G. Levin (Eds.), *Handbook of mental health consultation* (DHHS Publication No. ADM 86-1446) (pp. 393–431). Washington, DC: U.S. Government Printing Office.

Sussman, A. N. (1977). *The rights of young people: The basic ACLU guide to a young person's rights.* New York: Avon Books.

CHAPTER 5

The Process of Consultation

OBJECTIVES

1. Review the stages of the consultation process as presented by various writers.

2. Describe in detail the solutions-oriented consultation system (SOCS).

3. Provide guidance to assist consultants in developing solutions for the issues raised in each of the ten steps of the SOCS.

You are a resource specialist who has taken a strong interest in doing more consultation with the general education staff regarding both mainstreamed and at-risk students. You have read the material in the preceding chapters but aren't yet sure what process or steps to follow. Is there a systematic way of proceeding in consultation, or should you let events dictate what steps you follow?

You have been hired to present an inservice to a district that wants to improve its consultation service delivery system. The district has increased the amount of consultation that special education teachers and ancillary staff do, but staff members seem to be consulting, as the director of special services puts it, "by the seat of their pants." The director wants you to teach them how to structure their activities. What process should they follow?

As these vignettes indicate, how you go about consulting with others may be even more important than the actual content of the consultative activities (Dougherty, 2000). In this chapter we look at some generic processes for doing school consultation. Then we examine a highly structured approach known as the solutions-oriented consultation system (SOCS), which includes all the important steps a consultant needs to consider for effective consultation to take place.

ACTIVITY 5.1

Many readers have already engaged in some form of consultation activity, either as a consultant or a consultee. Recall the steps or stages you went through in the consultation process. Did they seem purposeful or random? Did you feel they made sense in light of the problem you were trying to solve?

ACTIVITY 5.2

Recall what you have learned from other college courses or life experiences about the problem-solving process. List the steps you believe are appropriate for a generic problem-solving model.

The problem-solving process that occurs in school consultation consists of the activities engaged in by both the consultant and the consultee as they work together to solve student learning and behavior problems or to improve teaching practices. In this chapter, we focus on how you go about being an internal consultant, someone who is employed on a (usually) full-time basis by a district or other educational entity, and whose title is not ordinarily that of "consultant," but is more likely to be a special education teacher, a school psychologist, a counselor, a mentor teacher, or a vice-principal. Almost all internal consultants have other responsibilities (e.g., to teach, to assess, to counsel, or to engage in administrative activities). Their consultation work has become an increasingly important part of what they do, particularly if they are special education teachers or school psychologists. External consultation is usually provided on a short-term basis by a professional person who is not regarded as a regular member of the school staff but who may be brought in to assist with specific cases, to direct system change efforts, or to lead staff development sessions. Activities and responsibilities of these external consultants are discussed by Brown, Pryzwansky, and Schulte (2001), Caplan and Caplan (1993), Dougherty (2000), and Erchul and Martens (1997).

STEPS TO FOLLOW IN THE CONSULTATION PROCESS

Numerous writers in the consultation field have described the consultation process. Terms such as *stages, steps, activities,* and *sequences* of consultation have been used synonymously with the more generic term *process.*

The best-known set of steps was initially presented by Bergan (1977): (1) problem identification, (2) problem analysis, (3) plan implementation, and (4) problem evaluation. Kratochwill and Bergan (1990) summarized much of the research that has been done using these steps as a model for the consultation process, and Bergan (1995) reviewed his belief that these four steps constitute the core of the consultation problem-solving process, which was reviewed in Chapter 2.

Brown, Pryzwansky, and Schulte (2001) define eight stages of consultation: (1) entry into an organization, (2) initiation of a consulting relationship, (3) assessment, (4) problem definition and goal setting, (5) strategy selection, (6) implementation, (7) evaluation, and (8) termination.

Dougherty (2000) discusses four stages—entry, diagnosis, implementation, and disengagement—with four phases embedded within each of these stages. Kurpius, Fuqua, and Rozecki (1993) describe six stages that they believe apply whether the consultation purpose is short-term individual or long-term organization-wide in scope: (1) preentry; (2) entry, problem exploration, and contracting; (3) information gathering, problem confirmation, and goal setting; (4) solution searching and intervention selection; (5) evaluation; and (6) termination. Like other authors, they note that this sequence is primarily intended to remind the consultant of the important steps but that considerable recycling among the steps is common.

Dettmer, Dyck, and Thurston (1999) specify ten steps in their recommended process: (1) preparing for the consultation, (2) initiating the consultation, (3) collecting information, (4) isolating the problem, (5) identifying concerns relevant to the problem, (6) generating solutions, (7) formulating a plan, (8) evaluating progress and process, (9) following up on the consultation, and (10) repeating consultation as necessary.

Redmon, Cullari, and Ferris (1985) have discussed the rationale for, and various stages of, the consultation process, and Marks (1995) has reviewed four different sets of steps emphasizing the relative importance of entry issues in the consultation process.

A GENERIC MODEL OF THE CONSULTATION PROCESS

Gutkin and Curtis (1999) refer to their current system of school consultation as *ecobehavioral consultation*. It blends their previously described problem-solving and behavioral models (Gutkin & Curtis, 1982) with the phrase they preferred in 1990, *ecological consultation* (Gutkin & Curtis, 1990). In their ecobehavioral model they utilize the four steps of the behavioral model which were previously described in Chapter 2 (Bergan & Kratochwill, 1990). I will describe the seven steps suggested by Gutkin and Curtis (1990) in some detail because they constitute a generic, representative set of steps common to those presented by the various sources previously listed. They indicate that cycling back and forth among the seven steps should be expected because of the shifting nature of realities as the process unfolds.

Define and Clarify the Problem

One of the most frequently cited references in the consultation literature is the Bergan and Tombari (1976) study that documents the significance of the problem identification stage of consultation. It is generally agreed that if this stage is successful, a positive outcome is more likely. Poor problem identification results in chaos because the consultant and the consultee are working on the wrong problem or two separate problems. This is not as unlikely as it sounds (Cleven & Gutkin, 1988; Lambert, 1976). One possible way that a problem may be poorly defined is in regard to the specification of the antecedents. A teacher may want to focus only on immediate (proximal) antecedents while the real source of a student's behavioral or learning difficulties may be the result of more distal antecedents (e.g., teacher tolerance, gang pressures, inadequate earlier schooling). Wilson, Gutkin, Hagen, and Oats (1998) have discussed the difficulties some teachers have in clarifying problems and selecting appropriate interventions. Some consultees need assistance in defining problems, and some consultants may need more training in how to elicit information from consultees to clarify problems. These are skills that subsume effective consultation and should not be taken for granted. Brown et al. (2001), in their chapter "The Consultee as a Variable," discuss the need for consultee training in problem identification. The skills discussed in this chapter, as well as in Chapter 3, should be of assistance to consultants.

The most common mistake in this step (other than incorrect problem identification) is to rush to solutions. Inexperienced consultants may feel pressured by the consultee's desire to get a quick solution to the problem. The consultee may expect the consultant to come up with a plan for solving the problem before it has been well defined. As is clear in the cases described in Chapters 7 and 9, consultants have to guard against this problem of premature strategy selection.

Analyze the Forces Impinging on the Problem

Here the consultant looks at the ecology of the student's life and the classroom to gather information about the problem, its possible sources, and their interrelationships within the context of classroom expectations. Following the reciprocal determinism ideas of Bandura (1978), which consist of an analysis of the relationships among the person, the behaviors of concern, and the environment, the consultant looks at the referred student's history and behavior as well as that of the behavior of the teacher, the possible influence of the student's parents, the classroom situation, the curriculum, sociocultural phenomena, and any other sources of influence that could be related to the behavior(s) of concern.

Brainstorm Alternative Strategies

Once the problem and its ecology are defined and understood, at least for the present, the consultant and the consultee should discuss some possible strategies to implement. Brainstorming as a method of freeing the mind to think of diverse possibilities is recommended, with the caution that this process has to be governed to some extent so that the participants don't waste time with ideas of no practical value. Pfeiffer and Jones (1974) include the following as three basic rules for the process of brainstorming:

- Do not evaluate strategies as they are being generated.
- Generate as many interventions as possible.
- Creativity and novelty are at a premium when generating a list of possible interventions.

What should come out of this exercise is a collection of ideas, collaboratively derived, that will form the basis for the next step.

Evaluate and Choose Among Alternative Strategies

It is common at this point for the consultee to ask the consultant to choose which strategy to use, once again deferring to the presumed expertise of the consultant. It is important to remember that the consultee should be the final judge of which strategy to select among those that seem most promising since the consultee will do most of the implementation. In doing this, the consultant is hoping to capitalize on *treatment acceptability*, a necessary characteristic of effective consultation. Without the teacher's (or parent's) acceptance of the intervention, it may very well not be implemented with the rigor required.

In complex problems a number of strategies may be selected at once, either for simultaneous implementation or to use as a quick substitute for the first strategy in the event of its obvious failure (for example, a plan to use extinction that results in an intolerable increase in the target behavior).

Strategy selection should be based on a mini–max principle: Select the strategy that will have the maximum impact for the minimal effort or intrusion into other classroom or family dynamics. Selecting a "can't miss" strategy that results in a chaotic classroom or turmoil among the client's siblings at home is self-defeating and should be avoided in favor of a more conservative strategy. Remember that one always has to be mindful of the ecological reality of a classroom or home. Any change in one aspect of that reality can have an unwanted influence on other aspects. The strategy of rewarding a deviant child with a preferred activity for short bursts of appropriate behavior may cause a revolt among your ordinarily well-behaved students who want equal preferred activity rewards for their ordinary good behavior. It also might be teaching the deviant student that he can be reinforced for only brief bits of good behavior. Sarason (1982) warns against the possibility of unintended negative consequences that may result from what seems to be a beneficial change for one aspect of the ecological whole. For example, a change in a method of presenting information may be beneficial to some students but have the reverse effect on others. In terms of a very large-scale intervention, the introduction of "whole-language" reading methods in California, Texas, and other states proved to be a boon to some adept readers, but much less so to many who needed structured instruction in phonetic analysis and synthesis (Stanovich, 2000).

Specify Consultant and Consultee Responsibilities

The "wh" questions—*who, what, when, where,* (and *how*)—come into play here. Consultation is much more likely to be successful when the consultant and the consultee settle these questions at the outset of the process of strategy implementation or shortly thereafter. The partners have to agree on responsibilities, or chaos may ensue. In an expert model it is likely that the consultant decides these issues, but in a collaborative model the consultant and the consultee need to work together and agree on details. For example, will the general education teacher or the consultant call the parent to discuss the current plan? What data gathering system will be used, the more comprehensive one suggested by the consultant or the simpler one preferred by the consultee? What are realistic goals for any given student? The cases in Chapters 7 and 9 give examples of how this process works and what a consultant should do if it begins to falter.

Implement the Chosen Strategy

If the process has worked well up to this point, the consultee should be eager to begin implementing the intervention(s). If it were always as simple as that, we could skip to the next step. Unfortunately, it doesn't always work that way for a number of possible reasons: (1) the problem itself shifts in focus somehow, and a revision is needed before the plan gets off the ground; (2) the consultee finds he doesn't have some material he will need to implement the plan, and you're both embarrassed that you didn't think of it in step 5; (3) the consultee finds that he can't really do the new behavior expected of him; and (4) the student reacts in some unanticipated way, and the consultee needs to return to an earlier step in the process, possibly even step 1, where a redefinition of the problem starts the process over again.

Implementation is the moment of truth in consultation. Here any previous weaknesses in the process come to light, and the strength of the consultant–consultee relationship is tested. The types of resistance discussed in Chapter 3 are also most likely to surface at this step.

Evaluate the Effectiveness of the Action and Recycle if Necessary

It is possible that the chosen and implemented strategy has worked very well and that the problem has been solved with no modifications needed. This, however, is unlikely. More likely is the possibility that modifications—mild, moderate, or extreme—will be needed. The consultant's role at this point is mainly twofold: monitoring the consultee's actions and assisting in collecting data that will serve as the basis for possible program changes. The consultant will also need to reinforce the consultee for efforts that often do not produce the hoped-for rapid results.

Eventually, one of the following or a variation will occur: (1) the project is a success, and you will present it as a triumph at your next staff meeting; (2) the project has some positive outcomes but still needs further work before both the consultant and the consultee are satisfied; (3) the project is minimally successful and requires a complete recycling through the sequence just described; or (4) the project is unsuccessful, and both the consultant and the consultee need to think about why.

If consultants follow the steps outlined by Gutkin and Curtis (1990) or those presented in the next section of this chapter (SOCS), it is probable that outcomes 1 and 2 will be the most likely scenarios.

SOLUTIONS-ORIENTED CONSULTATION SYSTEM (SOCS)

This section presents a format for school-based consultants to use when asked to consult about the behavior and learning problems of school-aged children. It is called the solutions-oriented consultation system (SOCS) because it emphasizes finding solutions to problems rather than merely studying them for classification or placement purposes. A list of *possible solutions* follows each step of the SOCS. These are intended to keep the reader (and practitioner) oriented toward solutions every step of the way through the SOCS. As you learn about this ten-step sequential process, you will also read about the many ways in which consultants can vary from these steps when necessary and appropriate. As I have indicated, consultation is rarely conducted in a lockstep, linear fashion. Consultants often find themselves moving through cases in creative ways, going back and forth among these steps. For those not yet experienced in consultation, it would be a good idea to follow these steps since they present a comprehensive and orderly way to go about the consultation process. However, remember that deviations may be appropriate, based on the experience level of the consultant and the characteristics of the consultee and the situation.

The steps described in this section will be illustrated in the extensive case studies in Chapters 7 (behavior problems) and 9 (academic learning problems). These cases demonstrate how the SOCS process can be used in a collaborative consultation program of assistance to parents and teachers.

Receipt of a Referral and Initial Thoughts About It

The process ordinarily starts with a teacher who needs assistance with educational planning for one or more of her students. She follows whatever steps are prescribed in her school, usually filling out and sending in a referral to a school consultant or the coordinator of the SST (see Figure 5.1). The consultant or coordinator reads the referral and forms an immediate impression based on at least the following:

- Is this regarding a student with a behavior or a learning problem, or both?
- Do I know this student or her family?
- Who is the teacher, and what does my knowledge of the teacher tell me about this referral?
- What should I do with this referral first: send it forward to SST, review with the teacher, or call the parents?

Figure 5.1

Consultation request information form

Teacher's name: _____ Date: _____

Student's name: _____ Grade: _____

Student's age: _____

Parents: _____

Referral concern: _____

History and/or other information about the problem: _____

_____

_____

Best time(s) to see me: _____

Depending on the nature of the case, any of these questions might be answered or dealt with first. Other initial thoughts involve priority (for example, responding immediately to suspected child abuse, hints of suicidal behavior, or behavior that threatens the safety of others); history of this student, if known; curricular and other classroom ecology factors; and, unfortunately, other time pressures.

Some practitioners may find Figure 5.1 too brief. Wouldn't a school-based consultant want to know a lot more before getting involved in a case? Yes, he would, but all of the additional information needed can be determined in the initial discussion with the consultee, which is the next step. The consultation request information form is simply an invitation from the teacher-consultee to the consultant or a relevant school-based team to discuss the consultee's problem. Sending this brief form indicates the consultee's willingness to get involved in the consultation process. A lengthy or cumbersome invitation might make the teacher reluctant to engage in the consultation process. An example of a more extensive referral form is available in Salvia & Ysseldyke (1998).

Possible solutions: At this time it is too soon to be generating specific solutions. However, the following ideas should be considered, just based on the nature of the referral:

- Given this teacher, this grade level, and other general considerations about the ecology of the situation, what general ideas come to mind?

- Should we take the time of the whole SST to discuss this referral, or would it be better to send it to an individual consultant to see if she can resolve it with the teacher and parent alone?

- Has this student been referred previously? If so, what interventions were tried, and with what degree of success? Perhaps one of these successful interventions should be tried again, if the current situation is compatible with that intervention.

Initial Discussion with the Teacher

Usually, the next step is for the referral to be sent to the SST or to a designated consultant to visit with the teacher who sent in the referral. (In the event your school sends initial referrals directly to the SST, you may want to skip to step 5 of the SOCS that deals directly with SST activities, and then return to steps 2, 3, and 4, perhaps as an SST designee, as appropriate.) In schools or systems that are changing to a consultative orientation, teachers have to resist the older habit of referring many cases to the psychologist or some other person for assessment for possible special education placement without first attempting other approaches. Under a consultation model, the older habit of requesting and expecting a hasty assessment for special education consideration should not be so common. Research data have been available for some time to support the belief that, among the mildly handicapped, a consultation approach results in a lower incidence of assessment and subsequent placement in special education classes (Curtis & Watson, 1980;

Gutkin, 1980; Medway & Updyke, 1985; Ponti, Zins, & Graden, 1988; Rosenfield & Gravois, 1996; Villa, Thousand, Nevin, & Malgeri, 1996).

Generally, it is best to visit with the referring teacher first for a number of reasons: (1) to verify receipt of the referral; (2) to acknowledge your concern about it; (3) to inform the teacher (in case he is someone with whom you have not previously worked) about your collaborative style of doing consultation and to discuss matters of confidentiality; (4) to get more information about the referral that will be helpful in determining your next steps; and (5) to begin or reestablish the rapport process.

Item 3 refers to the need to orient a consultee with whom you have not previously worked about your style and about confidentiality. This orientation should take place before discussion of the problem (Hughes, 1986). An example of this was given in Chapter 1 in the section on Useful Generalizations About Dealing with Consultees.

This initial meeting, as well as subsequent meetings, should take place during the referring teacher's natural break times rather than during an instructional period. With few exceptions, usually due to time pressures, it is best not to interrupt the teaching process to confer with teachers since teaching is the most important thing that happens in schools. Natural break times include planning periods, recess breaks, lunchtime, before and after school, and any other times when you can spend an uninterrupted ten minutes or so to gather information that will help you understand the problem and plan your strategy.

In the case of behavior problems, you will want to get some basics such as antecedents, severity, form, frequency, timing, and consequences of the behaviors of concern. In the case of academic learning problems, you will determine the areas of strength and weakness. For either type of problems, you will want to know what the consultee has done about the problem up to this point. Also, you will be forming a tentative hypothesis about the causes and possible solutions to the problem and, again, what steps you and the consultee should take next. It is important at this point to avoid the rush to solutions that is so tempting and that some consultees will want you to do. Although the SOCS is "solutions-oriented," that does not mean you should be impulsive about intervention selection.

The consultant should take notes during the initial and subsequent meetings. This has a number of purposes: (1) it indicates to the consultee that what he says is important enough to record accurately; (2) it helps you remember details (Given the large number of cases with which the average consultant is concerned, you will find it best to keep accurate data and to record it as soon as possible after it becomes known to you. Consultees don't like to have to repeat facts every time you consult with them. Your reference to accurate notes tells them that you are well organized and efficient.); and (3) it helps both the consultant and consultee keep track of what was discussed, both the facts of the case and the plans that you have made during each consultation.

Figures 3.2 and 3.3 show forms that a consultant completes after discussing the student with the consultee. The consultant uses the outline contained in these forms and fills them out based on the information provided by the consultee. The consultant gives a copy of this form to the teacher, and to the principal if appropriate. This serves as a reminder of what was discussed and serves as a starting point for future meetings. Because teachers have a limited amount of time available, 10-to-15 minutes is ideal for this meeting, although sometimes it takes longer, particularly the first meeting (Brown, Pryzwansky, & Schulte, 2001; Dougherty, 2000). Two sessions may be necessary just to cover the information listed in Figures 3.2 and 3.3. Busse and Beaver (2000) have presented a very detailed outline to follow for gathering information about the specifics of a behavioral problem referral. Using an outline of this complexity will ordinarily require at least two 15-minute sessions with the teacher. Given teachers' myriad activities, the consultant has to learn to be efficient. She has to come to a meeting prepared with a structured set of questions and must not give the impression that she's wasting or filling time.

Brown et al. (2001) discuss the 15-minute consultation as a realistic goal in school settings. In Chapter 2, the Sprick, Sprick, and Garrison (1994) 25-minute intervention development process was presented. Although their process is intended primarily for SSTs, it could easily be adapted for individual consultation purposes.

Some districts require the referring teacher to fill out additional information sheets, depending on the nature of the referral. If the referral concerns a student's behavior problems, the teacher may be required to fill out a behavior checklist (discussed below in step 6 and in Chapter 6). If the student has a learning problem, the form will elicit additional information about the exact nature of the learning problem. If the teacher has filled out any of these additional forms, the consultant will find this a good time to review them. Finish the discussion by telling the consultee what you will do next and, when appropriate, discuss what the consultee should do next.

Gutkin (1993a) has provided a problem-solving worksheet designed to give structure to the initial and subsequent interactions with the consultee. The steps in his problem-solving method are very similar to those in the SOCS formulation. Bergan and Kratochwill (1990) have also provided standardized consultation protocols designed to organize your approach to teacher or parent interviewing.

Possible solutions:

- Having gained a good idea of the teacher's perceptions of the referral, you can refine your thinking about the primary needs and concerns. This should give more focus to your beginning conceptualizations about the possibilities for interventions and probabilities for the success of some of these interventions.

- What types and degrees of support will this student and this teacher need? Is this a situation you can deal with yourself, or should it go to SST at this time?

- Begin to think about the most general categories of interventions that may be appropriate here. Suggestions for behavior problem referrals are contained in Chapter 6, while academic learning problem ideas are in Chapter 8.

- The most general type of solution at this time is to be supportive to the teacher or parent. They have come to you because the targeted student presents with challenges that are beyond their usual scope of interactions. They need to be helped through their feelings of discomfort, stress, and possibly even anger. The communication and interpersonal skills discussed in Chapter 3 will prove most useful to you at these early stages of the SOCS process.

Classroom Observation

Generally in the case of behavior problems, you will have already asked the teacher (in the previous step) about a good time to visit his classroom to make an observation. The purposes of observing are to verify the referral, to get an impression of the ecobehavioral dynamics that may be contributing to the referral, to study the teacher's style and methods, and to try to determine points of leverage when interventions may be useful. You have to be very careful to be supportive of the teacher. You must avoid giving the impression that you don't believe or trust the teacher or that you are going into his classroom with some hidden agenda. You must show the teachers in your schools that you are functioning like any scientist: You need to observe firsthand the nature of the problem or situation. Most teachers have no objection; in fact, they may be surprised if you don't ask to observe. In my experience, nearly all teachers ask when I'm coming in to observe, particularly if the referral is regarding a student with a behavior problem.

In the case of learning problems, a classroom observation may be considered optional, especially if you know how the teacher works and what the curriculum expectations and teaching methods are. The best practice is to visit the class regarding every referral, if time permits. Also, plan to visit at a time when the teacher believes you would have the best view of the referral problem. Lastly, since many learning problems are accompanied by a behavior problem (for example, distractibility or noncompliance), an observation may be warranted.

Brown et al. (2001) point out the need to have a definite purpose for the observation. You should not suggest doing it just to buy time. The observation should be designed to clarify the referral. It may turn out that the referral may be best dealt with by having the teacher deal with the referred student in a different way by using different methods, materials, or general classroom management tactics. You'll have a better sense of this after an observation.

Barkley (1988) believes that direct observation of the referred student in the natural environment (the classroom and the playground) should be an important part of student assessment, along with the use of checklists and teacher interviews. However, the picture the consultant gets of the referred student from teacher interviews or checklists may not be objective or accurate. Because the consultee is part of the ecology of the referral problem (the primary responder to the student's behaviors), it is easy to understand how nonobjectivity can creep into ratings or comments to the consultant during an interview or on a checklist.

There are a number of formal methods designed to assist an observer in making classroom observations. Barkley has developed the restricted academic situation (RAS) coding system (Barkley, 1990). Abikoff, Gittleman-Klein, and Klein (1977) have validated the classroom observation code, and Jacob, O'Leary, and Rosenblad (1978) have designed the hyperactivity behavior code. Reynolds and Kamphaus

(1992) have contributed their student observation system (SOS). In all of these systems, the observer, usually someone other than the teacher, codes behaviors into a variety of categories. The RAS, for example, uses eight codes in the in-school version of the instrument: off-task, fidgeting, vocalizing, talking to teacher/peer, playing with objects, out-of-seat, negative behavior, and teacher commands. All except the last category refer to target students; the eighth category codes teacher behaviors. Alessi and Kaye (1983) have provided a manual and videotape for training consultants in coding teacher behaviors such as prompts or reprimands.

The Reynolds and Kamphaus (1992) SOS is based on 15-minute observations of a targeted student using a time-sampling approach. The observer allows 27-second periods to go by, observes the student for 3 seconds, and then uses the next 27 seconds to record what was observed, repeating this process for a total of 30 observations in the 15-minute period. Up to 13 specific behavioral categories are recorded, such as the response to teacher/lesson, inappropriate movement, and aggression. Of the 13 categories, 9 are maladaptive behaviors and 4 are positive/adaptive. Obviously, you want to make repeated observations of a targeted student, particularly when the student is having behavioral difficulties as well as during periods in which the student adapts more positively.

The formal code-based observation systems are ordinarily used in research-based behavior change programs where interrater reliability and firm operational definitions are required. In the usual school consultation situation, however, the consultant has neither the time nor the necessary staff to do reliability checks or similar activities. Thus, most observation is more informal. Nevertheless, the consultant and the consultee do attempt to establish an operational definition of the target behavior(s). This step is essential and should be taken during the initial discussion with the teacher or after the first observation. Consultants soon discover that most consultees, unless they are used to describing behavior in operationally useful ways, need to be taught how to do so. There are numerous references available to help with this process. Alberto and Troutman (1999), Alessi (1988), Alessi and Kaye (1983), Gresham and Noell (1999), Hintze and Shapiro (1995), Mash and Terdal (1997), Shapiro (1987), Shapiro and Kratochwill (2000a, 2000b), and Ysseldyke and Christenson (1993) have all discussed methods for observing child classroom behavior. More detailed information about these methods is available in Chapter 6.

In the informal approach to observation, the consultant uses a wide variety of tactics depending on the particular classroom, teacher, type of referral problem, and time availability. At a minimum, the following questions need to be considered before starting an observation:

1. What time should the observation be done and for how long?

2. Exactly what information will be gathered and in what form?

3. While observing, should the consultant interact with the other students, the teacher, or neither?

4. What should the teacher tell the students about the consultant and the reason for his being in the room?

5. In addition to the targeted behaviors, should the consultant also record more general pieces of information, such as on-task versus off-task time?

6. To what extent should the teacher's behavior be noted?

Many of these questions and issues should have been mentioned and clarified during the initial discussion with the teacher.

Skinner, Rhymer, and McDaniel (2000) have described "naturalistic" observations as those that take place during ordinary classroom sessions. Narrative recording procedures are informal and primarily consist of a neutral observer recording what she sees in the classroom or playground. Since it is impossible, except with a wide-angle television camera, to record everything, the observer typically records only the antecedents and consequences of those behaviors that are being targeted, and does so in a narrative form. The following is an example of a narrative recording of a targeted behavior of a six-year-old boy referred for suspected ADHD:

Date: September 10, 2002

Time: 9:20

Setting: Reading follow-up activity; not teacher-led. Six other boys and girls doing a worksheet having to do with consonant substitutions.

Antecedents: Boy (Will) adjacent to Hans (targeted student) stuck his tongue out at Hans.

Behavior: Hans got up, walked over to the soft toys box, got out a "bopper," (a soft mallet, stuffed with cotton), and went to Will and proceeded to hit him with it.

Consequence(s): Others laughed. Teacher told Hans to desist. He did, but loudly proclaimed that he was mad because Will stuck out his tongue. Teacher said she would talk to Will and Hans about it at recess break. Hans continued to mutter at Will.

Possible Solutions:

• In the continued refinement of your knowledge base, developed as a result of the classroom observation, you may want to think in terms of supports needed by both the referred student and the teacher. Possible supports for the teacher would include simply taking time to talk to someone like yourself who can reinforce his efforts, lower his stress level about the situation, review what he has done up to this time about the problem, discuss the results of the classroom observation(s), and, of course, begin the process of developing interventions.

• Possible supports for the student would include interventions based on the student's levels of academic or social behavior, such as altered expectations, peer assistance, different instructional groupings, tutorial services, and so on. We may also want to consider assessment of the student's levels of functioning. Assessment is discussed in step 6 of this process.

Initial Discussion with Parents

The previous discussion regarding the first three SOCS steps has centered around referrals from teachers. Obviously referrals can also come directly from parents. In either event, the consultant will want to get parental input. The consultant has some choices to make about when a conference with the student's parents (or guardians) should take place, but there is no choice about whether or not such conferences should occur. *They must.* A positive home–school partnership is almost always the basis for improvement in behavior and learning problems, and this is true from preschool through adolescence (Brown, Pryzwansky, & Schulte, 2001; Christenson & Cleary, 1990; Christenson & Conoley, 1992; Dougherty, 2000; Dettmer, Dyck, & Thurston, 1999; Friend & Cook, 2000; O'Shea, O'Shea, Algozzine, & Hammitte, 2001). In addition to this common-sense reason, P. L. 105-97 (reauthorized IDEA) mandates parent involvement in all situations involving students with disabilities and those suspected of having disabilities.

In regard to when parents should be contacted, most school districts have adopted policies about the steps that must be taken before a teacher fills out a referral form. These steps often require the teacher to contact the parent to see if intervention at the parent–teacher level might be sufficient. Assuming the need for intervention beyond this level, the parent should also be told that the teacher is planning to ask for the assistance of the school-based consultant. In this way, the parent is already informed about the process and should be expecting some contact with the consultant in a timely manner.

The consultant may contact the parent before the initial consultation with the referring teacher, especially if the consultant already knows the parents and knows that this situation will require strong parental support. Conversely, the consultant may believe that it is best to wait until after he has conferred with the teacher and made at least one class observation before contacting the parent so as to have a better frame of reference from which to discuss the problem. Permission to administer a behavior checklist or an academic assessment device may have been obtained when the teacher talked to the parent; data from this might be helpful to have before consulting with the parent. In general, the consultant should have a fairly good understanding of the problem and some of the classroom dynamics before talking to the parent. Parents expect consultants to have a clear idea about what is going on at school and in the classroom in addition to having a plan for studying the problem. The detailed outline for conducting a teacher interview about a student who presents with a behavioral problem, presented by Busse and Beaver (2000), will give the consultant a very thorough knowledge of the dynamics of the problem. The Busse and Beaver outline would also be useful to follow if conducting an interview with a parent who is sensitive to the details surrounding his or her child's behavioral adjustment challenges.

It is important to remember that some parents are not going to welcome a phone call from the referring teacher or from the consultant. Nobody likes bad news. Even though we try to develop the idea that our intervention with parents and their child is intended to be helpful, it may not be interpreted as such. Dettmer et al. (1999) indicate that there may be five potential barriers in the early phases of help-offering interactions: teacher factors; lack of organizational and cultural competence; and family perceptual, attitudinal, and historical factors. Teacher factors include a range of approaches to parents from positive valuing to hostile disregard. If a teacher believes that a student's behavior is a function of the family's careless approach to the student's educational or social needs, the teacher may react to this belief by approaching the parent in a condemning or condescending fashion. However, the teacher may take the view that the family is doing the best they can in spite of whatever social or economic variables may be impacting on their lives, and therefore adopt a much more accepting and helpful stance. How each person perceives the problem often determines her reaction to it. If the parent believes her child is innocent of wrongdoing or would learn very well if the school would just treat him fairly, then her perception of this offer to help will probably be negative. Similarly, if the parent believes that the school is generally a hostile place, possibly because of her own remembered experiences of schools and teachers, she may project blame for the problem onto the school. An older sibling may have also had difficulty that the parent believes was due to a faulty approach by the school, so the parent greets this present referral as a likely repetition of that bad experience. This recollection of a historical event may need to be worked through with some parents before they are willing to join the school staff in a collaborative approach to the present problem.

One of the areas of difficulty between some homes and some school personnel concerns values. When people believe that they are talking to someone who holds values different from their own, they tend to become uncomfortable (Behring & Ingraham, 1998; Conoley & Conoley, 1992). For example, a parent may believe that corporal punishment is acceptable in child rearing, while the school (generally) does not. A teacher may state the opinion that each student should be held accountable for having her homework done every day, preferably proofed and signed by the parent. A single mother working a late shift may not have the time or energy to do this every day, and she may question the necessity of this value-driven requirement. Even more serious value issues, such as Afrocentrism, deserve to be heard and valued, although most public schools generally adhere to American or Euro-American ideas (Asante, 1987). A teacher may believe that democracy is a fine value for adults to live by, but he may practice strict autocracy in the classroom. The referred student, however, is being raised by parents who believe in a permissive style of child rearing, or, conversely, take the biblical injunction regarding rod sparing and child spoiling literally. School-based consultants often find themselves in the middle of value contrasts among the school staff and parents.

What about the consultant's own values? Especially when dealing with parents, the consultant has to recognize value differences for what they are, try not to let them interfere with a collaborative working relationship, and remember that winning agreements is more important than winning arguments.

Dettmer et al. (1999) have provided two self-rating questionnaires, one concerning your values as a consultant (1999, p. 109), the other concerning parents' attitudes, perceptions, and involvement in collaborative efforts (1999, p. 110). Consultants who complete these forms may find that they need to take a closer look at themselves if they expect to be successful in building productive relationships between home and school.

Numerous sources are available for detailed information about parent conferences (Breen & Altepeter, 1990; Conroy & Mayer, 1994; Nicoll, 1992; O'Shea, O'Shea, Algozzine, & Hammitte, 2001; Sattler, 1998; Turnbull & Turnbull, 1997). Christenson and Conoley (1992) have edited a text that details methods and implications of home–school collaboration. Sheridan, Kratochwill, and Bergan (1996) have described a conjoint behavioral consultation (CBC) model in which both parents and teachers are jointly the consultees in a collaborative approach to mutual problem solving that emphasizes the interconnectedness between home and school systems. When following this model, the consultant often meets with the teacher and parent(s) conjointly, expanding the contextual basis of the consultation while discussing cross-setting influences and the reciprocity within and between systems.

Brown et al. (2001) have provided an assessment outline useful for gathering information from parents, and Sonstegard (1964, quoted in Brown et al., 2001) presents an outline for interviewing parents who are concerned about the behavior problems of their children.

Possible Solutions:

- Now that you have talked with the parents and obtained their perspectives on the referral issues, it's a good time to put together the material gathered so far from the referral itself, the teacher interview, the classroom observation, and the parent interview to develop a fairly well-rounded picture of how relevant adults see the issues. The remaining piece of the puzzle may come from assessments of the student (step 6 of the SOCS). Try this outline to help you structure your knowledge up to this point:

    What are the behaviors of concern?

    What have people tried?

    How has the student responded to these interventions?

    What do the teacher and parent(s) believe would be the best intervention(s) to try at this point?

    What are your impressions of the situation, and about the interventions that have been suggested by the parent(s) and/or teacher?

    What supports and strategies for all constituents are emerging from these discussions?

    What ecological effects will any of these possible interventions have?

    What barriers or resistance may occur if any of these proposed interventions are tried?

- The references listed above contain many specific ideas for working with parents, including ideas that are practical and not difficult to implement. Two additional sources for specific assistance for parents are the book *Solve Your child's School-Related Problems,* edited by Martin and Waltman-Greenwood (1995) and *The Special Education Yellow Pages,* a list of Internet resources developed by Pierangelo and Crane (2000).

Getting Teachers and Parents Together: The SST Meeting

At this point you need to make a choice. Are you ready for, or do you need, an SST meeting? Does your system (local school or district) require an SST meeting, or does it leave that decision up to the individual to whom the referral was made? If your district's policy is to have the SST meeting early in the process, that meeting is likely to occur at this point, or before the consultant has observed in the classroom or talked with the teacher or the parent.

The structure, purposes, and methods of SSTs were discussed in Chapter 2. The information presented in this fifth step of the SOCS is designed to show the alignment of the SST process with the other SOCS steps, and to elucidate some specifics about how the SST contributes to case management for the consultant.

SSTs are general education functions that are primarily intended to be sources of assistance for general education teachers (Friend & Cook, 2000; Fuchs, Fuchs, Reeder, Gilman, Fernstrom, Bahr, & Moore, 1989; Huebner & Hahn, 1990). The makeup of an SST varies considerably across districts, as do the power relationships of members. Designated school consultants need to study the dynamics of these teams (as well as IEP teams) to be as effective as possible. As I have indicated, these teams exist in order to help teachers deal with students in the mainstream. Although not required by reauthorized IDEA, most states have adopted the stance that before a student can be referred for assessment to help determine if he is a child with exceptional needs, a multidisciplinary team must determine that the student's needs cannot be met with a modification of the regular education program. The various states have taken on the task of designing a means to ensure that this requirement is met. For example, Chapter 4 of Part 30 of the California Education Code (2001) states, "A pupil shall be referred for special educational instruction and services only after the resources of the regular education program have been considered and, where appropriate, utilized" (California Department of Education, 2001, sec. 56303). Given this requirement and other concerns in the special education field (such as an ever increasing number of students being labeled "disabled," especially "learning disabled"), states have increased their emphasis on the role of the SST as a monitoring device designed to make every effort to keep students in the mainstream while assuring that students who definitely need special education or related services are not denied them (Reschly, 1988; Reschly & Tilly, 1999).

School consultants need to be aware of the dynamics of multidisciplinary teams in the schools. Team members sometimes have agendas that, for various reasons, may not be in the best interest of the referred student. Part of the consultant's job is to keep the meeting focused on the relevant facts and the available data. In some schools there may be a feeling that if the teacher has referred a student, that is reason enough to go immediately to the assessment phase, which prompts a formal referral and subsequent federal guideline controls. If the parent agrees with this step, this establishes a legal agreement that an assessment will be conducted and an IEP scheduled within 50 days of the signing of the assessment plan. Once this step is taken, the case takes on a whole new perspective: Does the student have a disability that meets federal and state criteria? Unfortunately, this new emphasis may detract from the efforts of general educators who continue to assist the student in the regular track.

Although there are situations in which the development of an assessment plan may be the most appropriate thing to do, the team is still legally required (i.e., according to state guidelines, where applicable) to document the fact that modifications to the regular program have been made and that these modifications have not had a sufficiently positive effect. A common situation is the one in which the teacher has tried her preferred methods for dealing with behavior or learning problems but the student continues to present with difficulties. Most teachers want to keep their students; they develop a bond with them and only reluctantly want to discuss the possibility of considering the student for special education, especially in a self-contained class. What the teacher, and usually the parent, really want is assistance so that they can keep the student in the general education program. This is the situation where consultation assistance, either through individual efforts of consultants or through the SST, is most valuable.

The essential purpose of an SST is to do group problem solving. This implies that the group agrees, at least to some extent, on the nature of the problem, the kinds of data that are needed to understand the problem, and how to develop appropriate interventions. Just how any SST goes about this is a function of the style of the formal or informal group leader. The formal leader is often an administrator or a designee. An informal leader may be appointed or may simply emerge based on a variety of factors. Sometimes the student's parent may emerge as the informal SST leader by virtue of her forceful personality. Although school personnel are always nominally in charge, a parent may be the person who most strongly influences whatever decisions are made. In any event, the group leader may find that the process bogs down for a variety of reasons, such as disagreement about the nature of the problem, what should be done about it, or the role of the regular educator in the intervention process.

Meyers, Valentino, Meyers, Boretti, and Brent (1996) present data indicating that SSTs vary considerably in their approach to group problem solving. Since there are no federal government requirements or guidelines for the conduct of these meetings, each state is allowed to implement their use as it sees fit. Some states have no regulations or guidelines; hence, implementation becomes a local district or area issue. Obviously this leads to diversity in processes, goals, and outcomes. Three potential areas of difference across teams are their tendencies toward seeing problems from student-deficit or student-asset, teacher-skill or teacher-deficit, or student-need or system-need perspectives.

Dettmer et al. (1999) suggest a number of strategies that can be used in group problem solving. All are used extensively in the business world but may be underused in the education field. *Brainstorming* allows the free development and expression of ideas with a view toward loosening the thinking of participants to develop more creative solutions. I have mentioned that some school personnel may be uncomfortable with brainstorming if it seems to be taking participants too far afield or consuming precious time.

For those wishing to try brainstorming, Parsons and Meyers (1984) suggest some explicit steps to follow to ensure that the process does not deteriorate into chaos. First, clarify and agree on the general topic. Second, establish a time limit; they recommend five minutes. Third, try a warm-up activity, possibly brainstorming about an irrelevant topic or deliberately coming up with ridiculous ideas. Fourth, have the consultant act as recorder. Fifth, have participants list ideas: censor nothing; record them all. Sixth, after the time limit has elapsed, evaluate, clarify, and elaborate on ideas. People who haven't tried brainstorming are often amazed at the results and are often eager to try it again.

Lateral thinking can be contrasted with vertical thinking, which is the logic-oriented method favored by most people. In lateral thinking the group is asked to think of the problem from a different angle. According to Dettmer et al. (1999), a group using this approach might come up with the idea of having a student provide reinforcing comments for teachers who engage in more effective teaching practices rather than offering the ordinary recommendation that the teacher should provide all the reinforcement.

Concept mapping is now commonly used by some teachers as an alternative to outlining. With this method individuals express ideas about the problem and its solution. These are drawn on sheets of paper with lines connecting them as appropriate. Ordinarily, major concepts emerge, and each will have connected themes, impressions, or facts. This helps sort out ideas and allows major concepts to dominate subordinate ones.

Idea checklists consist of premade lists of intervention ideas or sources of assistance that may come in handy when people are feeling stuck. For behavior and learning problems, the lists of ideas (that is, possible interventions) offered by Choate (1993), Cummins (1988), McCarney and Cummins (1998), McCarney and McCain (1995), Rathvon (1999), and Sprick and Howard (1995) have proven to be quite useful in some SSTs.

Radius and Lesniak (1988) suggest eight steps that the SST leader or a designee can use to structure meetings held to discuss individual students referred for learning or adjustment problems. First, the student's *strengths* are listed. This puts the group in a positive frame of mind about the student. Second, *known information* about the student's school background, family composition, health, and current performance levels is reviewed. Third, *modifications* that have been tried are noted. Fourth, the team's *concerns* are prioritized. Typically, these may include academics, behavior, physical issues, attendance, family concerns, and so on. Fifth, the group lists *questions* for which the answers are not yet known, such as the student's cognitive abilities or what will happen if a certain intervention is tried. Sixth, the group *brainstorms* ideas for action. In steps seven and eight, the best of these are *selected*, and *assignments* are made in terms of who will do what and when it will be done. At subsequent meetings, usually within two to four weeks, this information is reviewed and modified as appropriate. Additional sources of information about the conduct of SSTs are in Fuchs, Fuchs, and Bahr (1990), Meyers et al., (1996), Rosenfield (1992), Safran and Safran (1996), and Zins, Curtis, Graden, and Ponti (1988).

Possible Solutions:

- Having (possibly) held the SST, in which the team has agreed on possible interventions, the consultee should now feel that the referral issue has been given serious consideration and that viable interventions have been developed. The consultant will want to review these possibilities with the consultee as soon as possible after the SST meeting to ensure the following:

  Has the consultee understood the proposed interventions?

  Does he agree with them?

  Is he able to implement them?

  What are some possible implications for the ecology of the classroom?

- Too often, following the SST, there is a brief feeling of elation, since the group and, hopefully, the consultee, have come to believe that progress has been made, if only at the conceptual (i.e., practical ideas, not yet implemented) level. If this initial enthusiasm is not followed up by personal consultation with the consultee, a number of things can occur:

  The consultee immediately gets busy with the ordinary rigors of teaching (or parenting) and does not quickly utilize the interventions.

  Habit strength operates as a barrier to rapid change of a teacher's or parent's response style.

  The consultee starts to have second thoughts (buyer's remorse) about the proposed interventions, and may decide not to implement them, or to do so in a fashion with somewhat less treatment validity than the SST had in mind.

  Some combination of the various types of resistance discussed in Chapter 3 begins to appear.

- All of these possibilities point to the necessity of close monitoring of the intervention program that has been established. Therefore, the primary solutions to which the consultant should be oriented at this time are *support* and *monitoring*. As mentioned previously, the time for the consultee to implement the interventions is the moment of truth in consultation. Either the consultant will be available and helpful at this stage, or the whole process may disintegrate.

Assessment of the Referred Student

The consultant is always engaged in some degree of assessment while engaging in all the previous steps, especially ecological assessment while doing the classroom observation, previously discussed in step 3. In this sixth step, I spell out some more aspects of assessment which may occur in individual assessment sessions conducted by school personnel or outside agencies, or which might occur in the classroom or playground.

Learning Problem Assessment Here the task of the school consultant largely depends on his profession and the nature of the learning problem. Since a consultant might be a resource specialist teacher, a school psychologist or a counselor, a speech and language therapist, a learning or behavior specialist, or a mentor teacher, his approach may vary as a function of his training and experiences. Each of these professional staff members is expected to have training specific to his field of expertise. The exceptions may be learning or behavioral specialists or mentor teachers, who may be former regular education teachers who assist other regular education teachers with in-class modifications of methods and materials but who may never have been trained in assessment methodology beyond that given to all regular education teachers. Given the possible differences among these people, the argument for team consultation becomes more convincing.

If a referral indicates that the primary concern is academic, the referring teacher (or the local system) needs to decide to whom the referral should be directed. In these cases, it is probably best to direct the referral to the SST and let that team decide how to proceed. Team members should select the specialists based on the assessment needs, but only if assessment beyond what the regular education referring teacher can provide is deemed necessary. As I have mentioned, all consultants have to monitor the SST to be sure that a recommendation for assessment is valid, not made just to buy time or to avoid having to modify the regular program. Remember also that time spent in assessment and report writing takes time away from remediation, counseling, or consultation with parents and teachers, services that can have more impact on children's lives than does gathering test scores. Chapter 8 details the diagnosis/analysis process used in cases of academic learning problems.

Behavior Problem Assessment: Functional Assessment of Behavior This process is primarily used with students referred because of behavior problems. Here the behaviorally oriented consultant tries to see what affects the behavior; what drives it, maintains it, and prompts it; and what makes it potentially valuable or appropriate from the standpoint of the student. In other words, the consultant needs to get inside the reasoning of the student in order to determine the causes of the behavior. Actually, the behaviorally oriented consultant has been engaged in this sort of detective work ever since receiving the referral, at least on an informal basis. Her solutions-oriented thinking is further refined during the initial discussions with the teacher(s) and parent(s), both of whom should be her consultees, and her observation(s) in the classroom. The referral issue is then reconceptualized following the classroom observation(s).

Essentially, functional assessment (sometimes called applied behavioral analysis) considers antecedents, behaviors, and consequences, and how they interact (Alessi & Kaye, 1983; Shapiro, 1987; Shapiro & Kratochwill, 2000a, 2000b). These key concepts, and the terms and specific behavioral referents subsumed under them, were mentioned in previous steps and in Chapter 2.

Antecedent events (themselves often behaviors of teachers or others) might include teacher's directions, earthquake drills, noises by other children, an upcoming social event, and, most important, the client's entire developmental history. Added to this list, especially by cognitively oriented behaviorists, are the student's expectancies and self-monitoring functions. What a student thinks about a situation adds immeasurably to her reaction to it (Hughes, 1988).

Consequences are events that follow the target behavior and influence its future probability of occurrence. We ordinarily think of positive reinforcement, extinction (planned ignoring), and punishment as three major classes of consequences that are used, wittingly or otherwise, by behavior modifiers.

Gresham (1991) believes that some behaviorists do not attend sufficiently to the potential influences of distal antecedents (see Chapter 2). He also suggests that behaviorists tend to focus excessively on the controlling influences of the consequences of behavior, sometimes ignoring the powerful potential of antecedent manipulation.

It is very important to remember that people who practice behavior modification do not directly modify or change behavior. Although these people are regarded by others (and themselves) as behavior change specialists, they realize that the behavior of a student is a function of the antecedents and consequences that surround it. What can really be controlled or manipulated (at least, hopefully) are the antecedents and consequences, not the student's behavior itself. In other words, behaviorists manipulate these antecedent and consequent factors and then see what effects these manipulations have on the target behavior. It isn't the behaviorist or teacher who's changing the student's behavior; it's the student who changes it (or doesn't) depending on how the antecedents and consequences are altered by the adults who, by and large, control these contingencies.

This point is important to stress to parents and teachers, who sometimes believe that behaviorists have mysterious powers that allow them to change the behaviors of students without altering anything the parent or the teacher is doing. For some people, the bad news about behavior modification comes when they find out that there are no mysterious methods. If behavior is going to change, it will best happen when those who control the antecedents and consequences are willing to change the way in which they set up or deliver antecedent and consequent events. In the case of cognitive behavior modification, the student tries to self-manipulate the antecedents (for example, thoughts) and consequences (such as self-reinforcement) that control behavior.

At the end of a functional assessment, the following groups of questions should have at least tentative answers:

1. What exactly is the behavior of concern? What does it look like, how long does it last, how often does it occur, who else is involved with it, what purpose does it serve, and how serious is it?

2.   What seems to prompt it? Does it occur because of some readily identifiable cause or antecedent? Does it seem to be driven by internal events (perhaps hunger or anger)? Have you asked the student why he does it? What does this tell you?

3.   What happens after the target behavior that may have a functional relationship to the occurrence of the behavior? Does the student seem to get what he wants as a function of the behavior? In short, what purpose (function) did the behavior seem to have? If no readily discernable consequent event can be determined, do you believe that the reinforcement for the behavior is internal—that is, satisfying in and of itself without any external events needed to justify (reinforce) its future occurrence?

It should be clear that answers to these questions may not always be obvious. In fact, many of them may never be answered. Psychology, since its beginnings as a science, has been trying to solve the intriguing questions regarding motivation. Philosophers likewise have debated the notion of causes of behavior and the possible role of determinism since Aristotle's time (Edwards & Pap, 1973). Traditional behaviorists such as Skinner (1971) have argued for a hard determinism. Cognitive behaviorists are not inclined to take such a rigid stance, preferring to acknowledge our inability to understand the wellsprings of human behavior. Is everything we do caused by our learning history, or does our free will allow us to rise above (or fall below) the contingencies that have been previously established in our learning history?

Psychodynamic, Ecological, and Biophysical Approaches   Psychodynamic approaches are those that rely on interpretations of the meaning of behavior, and to the influences of one's "internal" life and thoughts. The roots of this perspective go back to Freud (Chethik, 1989). Although there are variations, most psychodynamicists believe that people's behavior is to some extent an effort to deal with unresolved conflicts that manifest themselves as symptoms of emotional disturbance, and to satisfy intrapersonal needs and drives. The symptoms, or surface behaviors, are merely "the tip of the iceberg" with the driving forces behind these symptoms lying beneath the surface. Behavior problems, and learning problems, are treated through psychotherapy or counseling, with little attention given to contingencies of reinforcement, academic remediation, or other activities that focus on the observable behaviors.

Counselors, psychologists, and psychiatrists are the primary referral personnel to consider when a consultant believes there may be a strong psychodynamic factor behind the behavior or learning problems. Educational applications of these psychoanalytic/psychodynamic approaches are sometimes referred to as psychoeducational, an approach which blends interest in both the inner life and external behavior of students. Resources that are helpful in this area are Long and Morse (1996) and Redl (1972).

Ecological assessment does not deal directly with the student but focuses more on classroom and playground dynamics: what these environments look like, what teachers do, what the expectations are, what the formal and unwritten rules are, and how all of these factors influence behavior and learning. How students act is in some part attributable to how others around them act. The consultant needs to be aware that a classroom observation is just that: an observation of what is going on in the classroom that could be affecting the behavior of the targeted student(s). Chapters 6 and 8 contain more information about this approach to the understanding of behavior and learning problems.

Biophysical problems include poor health, inadequate vision and hearing, poor nutrition, or any of a host of other internal factors that could be causing a child to behave or learn in a less-than-expected manner. These factors are explored in more depth in Chapters 6 and 8, as they apply to behavior and learning problems.

What is most important at this point is that the consultant and consultee(s) agree about the nature of the problems and their mutual goals. Raiffia (1968) discusses the Type III error: solving the wrong problem. This can occur when participants talk past each other, don't fully disclose their perceptions, or haven't sufficiently assessed the problem. In order to avoid this, they must take a thorough look at the many possible contributing factors (for example, age, ethnicity, family dynamics, ability level, motivation, school history, health factors, and expectations). Agreement about the nature and the sources of the problem is then established, as are mutually determined goals and objectives. Carrying out these steps logically leads to the seventh step of the SOCS, *planning interventions*, and also suggests measurable objectives that will be useful when it comes time to evaluate the success of this consultation.

Possible Solutions:

- Now that we have added the student assessment piece of the puzzle, we should be able to focus in on the most important features of the referral problem. Certainly if the assessment has detected learning difficulties that indicate possible eligibility for special education and related services, the SST will discuss this issue with the parent and, most likely, develop a formal assessment plan, one that meets federal and state guidelines. Once the parent has signed approval of this assessment plan, the district has 50 days to conduct the assessment and hold an Individualized Education Plan meeting to discuss the results and prepare a plan for the special education of the student, if appropriate.

- If, however, it does not seem appropriate to refer the student for a formal assessment, the consultant and consultee, usually along with the parent, should review all the data and determine the areas of intervention needed. They may use the following outline as a guide:

Academic area needs:

Reading	Readiness skills
	Word recognition skills
	Comprehension skills
Math	Number facts
	Basic computation
	Word problems

Written expression	Printing or cursive letter formation
	Punctuation, capitalization, and spelling
	Grammar
	Connected discourse
Content areas	Appropriate study skills and habits
	Content review

Behavioral/social needs:

Acquisition and	Social skills training
performance skills	Anger management and conflict reduction skills
	Contingency plans
Personal counseling	Individual or small group
	Family based

Planning Interventions

At this point the consultant has reviewed the referral, studied the pertinent records, talked with the consultees (teachers and the parents), probably observed the client and the classroom, possibly engaged in discussion about the client at an SST meeting, done a functional assessment or a diagnosis/analysis of the learning problem, and has considered causes of the problem and possible steps to take toward a solution. When determining what plan should be followed, I recommend a collaborative approach: The intervention ideas are primarily determined by the consultee, with the consultant facilitating and developing them as needed. Expert consultation (ideas generated only by the consultant) should only be used when collaboration is not producing a good result or in an emergency.

Collaboration as a primary mode of plan determination is recommended for the following reasons:

1.   Plans that are thought of and supported by the consultee are more likely to be followed than are those that are primarily the ideas of the consultant.

2.   Since the consultee will probably do most of the instructional modification or behavior change work in the classroom, the plan should be one she can be comfortable with. Plans developed by outsiders may not fit the consultee's situation well. This applies especially well if the parent-consultee is also involved in the behavior change project.

3.   By emphasizing the collaborative model, consultants avoid the dependency relationships that can so easily develop when using an expert model. When teachers find that they become their own primary problem solvers, they feel more empowered to solve future problems themselves or with only minimal help from an outsider (Friend & Cook, 2000; Graden, 1989; Rosenfield, 1987).

Given this emphasis on collaborative approaches, just how does the consultant work with the consultee to develop an effective plan? The first step is to realize that both of them have contributions to make. However, the teacher-consultee is the one who is going to be carrying out most of the plan. Therefore, he should have both the first and last words about what the plan will consist of. Most teachers, who are unfamiliar with this point of view, may expect the consultant to take over the case and to provide expert advice about how to proceed. Conoley and Conoley (1992) discuss this deferential attitude and suggest that the collaboratively minded consultant meet deference with deference. Consultants who take the point of view that consultees have within themselves a number of good ideas that probably will need support and development will not get trapped into accepting the consultee's initial stance of helplessness as a signal to play the expert role.

The consultant's job is to elicit from the consultee what he wants to do, given the situation, and then to encourage and facilitate these plans. The consultant will probably need to help the consultee think through the possible consequences of whatever approach he has suggested and to add refinements. This is the collaborative part, which defines the consultant as an expert in the process of consultation but not necessarily in the content. Between the two of them (or three or more depending on parental or SST involvement), they will probably come up with a better plan than either of them would have alone.

Curtis and Meyers (1988) have listed characteristics of the collaborative model that make it distinctly different from the expert model: (1) it implies coordinate status, (2) the consultee is involved in the process throughout, (3) the consultee has the right to accept or reject strategies, and (4) the consultation is voluntary. Further information about, and rationale for, the collaborative approach to consultation can be found in Chapter 1.

As the cases presented in later chapters will demonstrate, the collaborative approach is a challenging and rewarding activity for school-based consultants. The challenge comes primarily from having to rein in your own tendencies to tell other professionals and parents what to do and in convincing these same professionals that they have good ideas to implement. The rewards come when the students start to improve their learning or behavior and the consultees have a feeling of pride and empowerment because they made such a significant contribution to both the design and implementation of the interventions.

Factors to Consider in Designing Interventions The plan that the consultant and the consultee agree on should meet at least the following criteria:

1. It makes sense in light of the referral.
2. It is objective-driven rather than casually thought through.
3. It is not labor intensive; the consultee should not feel that he has been given an undue burden to carry.
4. All constituents or stakeholders are involved in, and supportive of, the plan.
5. It has some form of evaluation built in with checkpoints established.
6. It meets the KISS standard: *keep it simple and sensible.*
7. It meets the five standards for treatments mentioned in Chapter 1: *acceptability, validity,* and *ethics* need to be considered in the design of the interventions, *integrity* needs to be considered in the carrying out of the

intervention, and *effectiveness*, which will be determined as the interventions are carried out, becomes the final standard to be met.

Given the singular significance of the choice of interventions, it would be comforting to know that there is a research base to direct us in matters of intervention selection. Unfortunately, research into this complicated question has only recently begun to emerge; there is not yet a scientific foundation for intervention selection that makes it easy. At least four reasons (factors) account for this situation, which Elliott (1988) has identified as consultant, consultee, treatment, and client (student). *Consultant* factors include consultant communication, interpersonal and problem-solving skills, such as how he conceptualizes problems and explains his ideas to the consultees. *Consultee* factors include amount of experience (with more experienced consultees tending to be more critical of others' treatment plans [Witt, 1986]), their knowledge of remedial or behavioral techniques, and their degree of self-confidence. *Treatment* variables include the amount of time required to implement the intervention and the type of treatment. Briefly, interventions that take little time and are positive tend to be preferred. *Client (student)* variables include type of problem (acting out versus acting in) and severity of problem.

Reimers, Wacker, and Koeppl (1987) discuss a model in which high treatment acceptability (that is, a treatment favored by the consultee) should be related to high treatment effectiveness. Indeed, acceptability may have much to do with effectiveness. More research on this relationship is needed. Conoley, Conoley, Ivey, and Scheel (1991) have also contributed information about the importance of interventions matching the consultee's perspectives.

In lieu of a scientific basis for matching treatments with Elliott's (1988) four variables, consultants have to rely on their experience with people; with learning and behavior problems; and with the norms and expectancies of schools, teachers, and parents. They must also have a firm grasp of what is available in the research literature (Mastropieri & Scruggs, 2000; Morrow & Woo, 2001; Slavin & Madden, 1989; Stanovich, 2000; Wang, Haertel, & Walberg, 1993) and keep an eye toward interventions that are practical, time-efficient, and positive. Classrooms are not clinics; what is acceptable to a counselor working one-on-one with students who are disruptive or a tutor working in a similar way with a student who reads poorly may be quite unacceptable to a teacher with 30 students who is expected to maintain control and move the curriculum forward for all of her students.

Our responsibility as school consultants is to listen carefully to teachers, watch them work, absorb their world, and then try to get them to come up with plans they think may work given their perceptions of the problem's causes and dynamics and to help them think through these plans and implement them. Brown et al. (2001) suggest the following four consultant skills:

1. Assessing consultee's values and worldview to determine which types of intervention are likely to be most acceptable.
2. Having a working knowledge of numerous interventions related to the problems that the consultant is likely to encounter.

3. Being able to communicate the nature of an intervention as it relates to consultee's/(student's) problems and, if necessary, teaching the intervention to the consultee.

4. With the consultee, monitoring the efficacy of the intervention and redesigning it as necessary. (p. 177)

Acceptance can be seen as passive or active. Passive acceptance commonly occurs in the expert model of consultation, where the consultant more or less tells the consultee what to do and the consultee believes she is supposed to do it. Whether she does or not or how well she does it is often questionable. Active acceptance refers to the consultee's belief that the intervention is really worth doing, that it was at least partly derived from her perspective, that it meets the standards just discussed, and that she can't wait to try it. Witt and Elliott (1985) have developed an Intervention Rating Profile (IRP) which can be used to assess treatment acceptability. Four of the fifteen items on the IRP measure the suitability of intervention, willingness to use it in the classroom, appropriateness, and reasonability. In a study utilizing the IRP, Wilkinson (1997) found teachers highly accepting of a standard contingency management program, which was generally successful with primary grade students. One of the teacher-consultees, however, was unable to faithfully carry out the treatment plan, and the student in her classroom did not profit as much from the plan as did the students in the other classrooms.

Another form for rating treatment acceptability and intervention effectiveness is the Behavior Intervention Rating Scale (BIRS; Van Brock & Elliott, 1987). This scale has three factors: acceptability (which is the same as the 15-item IRP previously mentioned), effectiveness (an additional 7 items), and rate of effect (2 items). The BIRS and an additional Children's Intervention Rating Scale (CIRP) are available in Elliott, Witt, and Kratochwill (1991, pp. 108 and 109). A treatment integrity scale is also available in the same source (p. 127).

Elliott and Busse (1993) echo the generalizations of Brown et al. (2001) by pointing out the crucial role of consultee acceptance of the treatment plan. The research they review suggests the following:

1. Professional jargon is not appreciated, and may serve as a detriment to treatment acceptability.

2. Teachers prefer treatments that require minimal consultant involvement.

3. Positive treatments are considered more acceptable than are negative treatments.

4. What a teacher will accept depends on the severity of the problem. The more severe the problem, the greater the latitude of acceptance.

5. The more teachers know about behavioral principles, the greater their latitude in accepting behavioral plans.

6. There is an inverse relationship between teacher experience and her acceptance of behavioral plans.

Pugach and Johnson (1987, 1995) have demonstrated that peer collaboration seems to have a powerful positive effect on treatment acceptability. In an effort to determine the functional utility of recommendations delivered in a peer collaborative method, Johnson and Pugach (1996) used the following 15 categories of interventions in actual classroom situations:

1. *Academic adjustment.* Teacher changes methods, expectations, materials, and so on.
2. *Charting/self-monitoring.* Teacher, aide, or student keeps track of behavior frequencies.
3. *Seat change.* Teacher moves the target student or others for specified periods.
4. *Management adjustment.* Teacher changes his methods of classroom behavior management.
5. *Positive reinforcement.* Teacher uses social, activity, or material reinforcers.
6. *Assignment clarification.* Teacher emphasizes homework clarification and follow-through.
7. *Immediate assistance.* Teacher works with a targeted student to prepare her for a new assignment and to ensure that she proceeds appropriately after getting a direction or assignment.
8. *Curtail negative teacher response.* Teacher is prepared for negative student behavior and plans a positive or neutral communication style.
9. *Increase communication with parents.* Teacher believes that the parents can be influential and plans to support them in their efforts.
10. *Daily notes.* This is related to item 9 as a specific tactic.
11. *Restructure peer interaction.* This is related to items 1, 3, and 4; the teacher uses grouping to capitalize on modeling effects.
12. *Peer tutoring.* Teacher uses peer tutoring within or between classes.
13. *Contracts.* Teacher makes goals explicit, usually in writing.
14. *Clarification of tasks and expectations.* Teacher uses task analysis: breaking down difficult assignments into manageable parts.
15. *Other.* Teacher uses specialized techniques such as time-out, suspension, referral to others, and so on.

Using these relatively standard interventions in a process in which teachers assisted each other in thinking through referral problems, Johnson and Pugach (1996) found that 86 percent of 70 problems discussed by their peer-collaborative teams were reported to be either much improved or improved. It is difficult to know whether the apparent simplicity of these interventions rendered them acceptable and successful or whether the influence of a peer collaborator was the primary determinant in their successful use. In any event, this study demonstrates that relatively common, uncomplicated interventions can result in a high success rate. It also points to a potentially valuable model of consultation service delivery: peer collaboration (Bay, Bryan, & O'Connor, 1994). Chapters 6 and 8 present other lists of interventions that are widely known and generally have strong treatment acceptability. The cases presented in Chapters 7 and 9 demonstrate the crucial role of treatment acceptability in the consultation process. We will see in these cases how consultees' failure to buy into treatments can stall the consultation process. This failure to accept treatment recommendations is discussed also in the material on resistance in Chapter 3.

Zins and Erchul (1995) have provided six valuable guidelines for selecting interventions:

1. In general, implement positive interventions before resorting to behavioral suppression or reduction techniques.
2. Choose the least complex and intrusive interventions possible. Modifying existing practices rather than learning new skills is generally easier for consultees.
3. When a new skill must be learned by a consultee, design it to fit into current organizational (classroom) structure and routines as much as possible.
4. Promote interventions that require less time, are not ecologically intrusive, and are seen by consultees as (likely to be) effective.
5. As a long-term strategy, help consultees access existing resources or develop new ones in their own organizations.
6. Focus intervention efforts on promoting change at the highest organizational level possible.

As the cases in the later chapters demonstrate, our ability to understand and solve referral problems may lie in our understanding of the psychodynamics, ecological influences, or biophysical factors that can have a strong effect on behavior and academic learning. Also, our own philosophical beliefs influence how we approach referrals. Some people look to psychodynamics almost exclusively. Others are wedded to curriculum-based measurement to the exclusion of other assessment considerations. Others prefer rational–emotive behavior therapy (Ellis, 1995) or behavior modification or process training. I hope that consultants will keep an open mind regarding causes and assistive strategies and will not become overly restrictive in their views. To show how different techniques may be used to understand and deal with school learning and behavior problems, D'Amato and Rothlisberg (1992) have provided an extensive case study of a student, followed by explanations of how this student's case would be handled by practitioners representing eight different approaches.

Possible Solutions:

One way of designing interventions is to conceptualize them in large groupings and then develop specific interventions within each of the large categories. The following is a list of five large categories, with some possible interventions that might logically be utilized within each category.

- Prevention

  Rearrange the classroom so the students find it easier to get around. This may reduce noise, confusion, and the accidental bumping of each other as they move about the classroom.

  Set up class rules and consequences that may serve to forestall possible conflicts or confusion in procedures. State these rules positively.

  Separate students who may not be able to resist the temptation to be unproductively sociable or provocative toward each other.

- Communication

  Develop a habit and system of talking with students about their behaviors of concern, as well as behaviors you wish to reinforce.

  Organize times in the classroom for students to talk about the classroom arrangements, curriculum, methods, and behavioral standards (Glasser, 1969; Nelson, Lott, & Glenn, 1997).

  Utilize the services of the school counselor to talk with students with whom you find it difficult to communicate.

- Contingencies

  Establish a reinforcement menu of activities, tangibles, and other reinforcers you are willing to dispense, contingent on students reaching predetermined positive goals.

  Develop contracts to specify the relationships between behaviors and reinforcers or other contingencies. All contracts should be written in a positive fashion (Allen, Howard, Sweeney, & McLaughlin, 1993; Miller & Kelley, 1994).

- Competency Training

  Academic:

  Determine the student's levels of achievement in relevant areas; try to arrange classroom situations where the student is able to get assistance when materials are too difficult.

  Also, arrange for remedial help through whatever resources are available.

  Behavioral/Social:

  Assist the student to recognize the behaviors that are not acceptable and teach alternative behaviors.

  Use contingency plans as previously discussed.

  Arrange for out-of-classroom assistance with a counselor in school, or through an outside agency.

- Biochemical

  Arrange for a health evaluation by the school nurse or an outside agency.

  Encourage parents to consult with a medical practitioner regarding medical approaches to behavioral/adjustment difficulties or for health/hygiene instruction for the family.

Implementing Interventions

Once the plan is agreed on, the consultee is ready to start the implementation process. At this point the actions and reactions of the consultee and the student are of major importance. Ordinarily the consultee does most of the implementation, while the consultant monitors and advises as the implementation unfolds. Exceptions might occur in the case of a collaborative arrangement between the consultant and consultee when the consultant carries a noticeable share of the responsibility for direct intervention implementation. Co-teaching is an example of this (Dettmer et al., 1999; Friend & Cook, 2000), and would be a fairly common activity for resource teachers to engage in.

As I have mentioned, the student is, as always, a key player in this drama because her reactions to the plan determine the plan's future. In traditional behavior modification systems the student was often not informed that a plan was being implemented. Researchers believed that if the student knew how the teachers were trying to manipulate the situation in the class, she might find some way of thwarting their efforts. In the newer cognitive behavior modification modes, and in the development of contracts, the student is very likely a key contributor to both plan determination and plan implementation. Cases presented later in this text demonstrate how each person involved in the plan is given his role.

Of course, implementation may involve multiple students and consultees. Other children in the class, parents, additional teachers, and counselors all may have a part to play. The more people that are involved, the more important it is that each person understand what her roles are. Equally important is the consultant's concern about the skill levels of all these people. The primary roles of the consultant in plan development and implementation are to ensure that each of the participants has the skills to carry out the plan, and that they are carrying out the interventions faithfully (with integrity, or fidelity). Neither of these criteria can be taken for granted. Consultants often find that what they thought was a simple plan to implement (for example, smile at the student when he gives you eye contact) may be something the consultee is not used to doing or doesn't do easily. The best way to know if the skill levels are in place is to ask the consultees (and students, when appropriate) if they feel comfortable doing what the plan requires of them, and then watch them doing it. In this way, the consultant works to ensure both treatment acceptability and integrity, which are essential if a plan is to be successful (Lentz, Allen, & Erhardt, 1996; Noell & Gresham, 1993; Witt, 1990).

The necessity of insuring integrity derives from the common observation that interventions are not always carried out in the way in which they were intended. When this occurs, we are in the position of the chemist who discovers contaminants in her test tubes. Public school classrooms, playgrounds, and family-home realities often constrain the valid implementation of consultation plans. Difficulties in providing the timely provision of reinforcement; the impracticality of shifting activities when needed; and the control of variables such as mood, behavior of other students, fire drills, students coming and going (sometimes to receive needed ancillary services), and hunger are examples of problems that can affect treatment integrity.

Gresham (1989) suggested the following conclusions based on his review of the research literature:

1. Simpler suggestions (interventions) tend to be more faithfully followed than do more complex interventions.
2. Interventions that take more time, materials, and resources tend not to be as carefully implemented as briefer or less involved interventions.
3. The more people involved in the intervention, the less faithfully it will be implemented.
4. The consultee's belief in the validity of the treatment enhances treatment integrity.
5. The higher the motivation of the consultee, the more likely the treatment will be carried out accurately.

The probability of treatment integrity increases as a function of continuing consultant involvement. One of the real tragedies of excessive consultant–consultee caseloads is the inability of the consultant to carefully monitor each case. Be sure, when acting as a consultant, that you have reviewed the facts about each case before seeing the consultee for a follow-up session or before making a classroom observation so that you can remember the details of the background and of the treatment plan. This inspires the consultee's confidence in you and in the process, and it enables you to determine if the treatment is being carried out with integrity.

Skills the classroom teacher-consultees typically may not have are data keeping, operationally defining behaviors, skill in reacting in certain specified ways (for example, extinction), contingency contract development, instructional modifications, and listening and reflecting skills. The role of the consultant is to assist the consultee (and students, when appropriate) in the development of the skills necessary for the treatment to be successful. Numerous sources designed to help the consultant teach these skills to consultees are available (Benjamin, 1987; Kanfer & Goldstein, 1986; Mastropieri & Scruggs, 2000; Morrow & Woo, 2001; Shapiro & Kratochwill, 1988, 2000a, 2000b; Walker & Shea, 1999; Zins, 1993; Zirpoli & Melloy, 2001).

Brown et al. (2001) point out that consultees have certain expectations and preferences in regard to the consultation process. These beliefs and attitudes are brought to the consultative interaction and can have a strong effect on the process. They were discussed in Chapter 1.

Sometimes a plan cannot be implemented without materials that are not readily at hand, such as material reinforcers, computer-assisted instructional programs, event counters, curricular materials, award certificates, and so on. The consultant should try to obtain them quickly. Plans that involve cumbersome apparatus or curricular materials that are not easily available or are too costly should probably be avoided except in the most extreme circumstances.

Monitoring a plan as it begins and progresses is the most important role of the consultant in the plan implementation phase. The consultee's efforts to carry out the plan and the student's reactions to the plan are of equal importance. It is very common, for several reasons, to modify plans after they are implemented. Perhaps the consultee isn't willing or able to carry out the plan as prescribed. The student may change his behavior in an unanticipated way, which may be either positive or negative. Unanticipated events from the outside may have an unwanted influence on the plan. Positive or negative changes in the student's behavior or learning patterns may also occur so rapidly that a major change in the program seems warranted. It is necessary for the consultant to have sufficient time to monitor these possible events in order to talk with the various consultees involved and to make changes when needed.

Some itinerant consultants may be at a site only once a week. When their availability is stretched this thin, they find it very difficult to carry out this monitoring function. In these cases it is even more important that the consultee be well trained in what to look for and what to do, given various changes in the data. The collaborative philosophy is especially appropriate for this kind of situation because the consultee will have been included as an equal partner since the onset of the consultation, and therefore should feel competent in the area of program modification. Such a possibility might not occur to a more dependent consultee in an expert model of consultation.

If the plan the consultant and the consultee(s) have decided on requires specified student actions, which is common in a cognitively oriented behavior modification or skill-learning program, the consultant and the consultee need to be sure that the student is willing and able to play his role. For example, not all students are able to keep their own data or provide their own reinforcement in the manner intended by the plan. Again, the consultant needs to think of these planned-for student actions as skills that may need to be taught, rehearsed, and monitored (Hughes, 1988).

Possible Solutions:

- The interventions ("solutions") are underway. The primary needs of consultees at this point are to be supported and to know that if there are problems in the implementation of the interventions they can get fairly rapid assistance from the consultant. To that end, in an ideal world the consultant would be able to monitor the initial steps of the plan, possibly by being in the classroom in the earliest phases of the intervention. Due to the many other responsibilities of an internal school consultant, this is rarely the case. A second, more realistic option is for the consultant to make contact with the consultee shortly after the plan's implementation to discuss treatment integrity and continued acceptance of the plan.

- Some consultees expect quick results from well-planned interventions. Assuming the referral was for a fairly significant problem, it is unrealistic to expect a rapid turnaround of a student's performance, either academic or behavioral. An experienced consultant needs to help the consultee understand the nature of habit strength in the perpetuation of behaviors. Long-standing habits cause people to persist in, or return to, behaviors that may have been inefficient or self-defeating. Students' approaches to their schoolwork, to their social interactions, and to their negative self-talk may be ingrained because these behaviors have served a defensive purpose for these students. Asking or expecting students to give up inefficient or inappropriate behaviors very quickly, possibly to engage in behaviors with which they are not comfortable, is asking a lot. The incapacitating nature of academic learning problems leads some students to resist most remedial efforts because they fear yet another failure. Why work hard to improve when efforts to do so have never worked before? The "learned optimism" of Seligman (1990) isn't learned easily by students accustomed to failure.

Monitoring Interventions

As I have mentioned, consultation usually does not follow the linear steps that I am describing here. The process is much more circular: One may need to go back at any time to earlier steps, repeat some steps a number of times, and sometimes take leaps forward. The number of variables affecting this circularity is infinite and include at least the following: (1) the skill levels of the participants, (2) the complexity of the situation, (3) hidden agendas that may not seem evident at the onset of the consultative relationship, and (4) naturally occuring changes in classroom ecology or in the targeted student's life that necessitate changes in the interventions.

One step that is always included, sometimes repeatedly, is ongoing consultation with the consultee(s) throughout the process. In some cases the consultant may have to meet with the consultee(s) a number of times before rapport is established; in other cases, it takes a long time before the consultee(s) has established the confidence it takes to implement a new program. At other times, a program may be started the day after the first meeting between the consultant and consultee only to end in disaster the following day and not start again until more meetings have taken place. Suffice it to say that effective consultation rarely occurs as a result of one brief visit between a consultee and consultant.

During the ongoing discussions the consultant will be involved in answering questions, dealing with resistance, gathering data, suggesting modifications, dealing with consultees' feelings of vulnerability, and trying to reassure consultees in order to ensure a successful project.

Questions that come up vary from the profound to the mundane. For example, in behavior-change programs there are questions of children's rights, bribery, long-term consequences of treatments, and the relative importance of all aspects of the program, among others. In academic learning problem cases, there will be concerns about allowing poor achievers easier assignments, grading on effort rather than achievement, and the time necessary for instructional modifications. It is easy to get sidetracked by some of these questions, and the consultant needs to weigh each one in light of the goals of the project that have been mutually decided on. This is another argument in favor of the collaborative approach to consultation. If the consultant and the consultee have been working as a team throughout the project, the mutual respect developed between them will ensure goal-directed questions and concerns rather than those that often develop when people are not in sync with each other (Friend & Cook, 2000). Excessive questioning of every aspect of the program plan and its implementation is a good sign that the consultant and the consultee have not reached that level of rapport or trust that mutuality requires. It may be necessary at times to "call the game": to back away from the content of the questions to find out about the relationship itself. Reassurance may be all that is needed, especially with consultees with whom you are working for the first time, but you may also find that you are dealing with some of the more serious forms of resistance.

Resistance is to be expected in consultation. The idea that two professionals working collaboratively on student-related issues are always going to agree and carry out interventions as one has envisioned them is not realistic. Disagreements are going to occur, and resistance to the plan has to be recognized and dealt with. Sources and types of resistance were discussed in Chapter 3.

The main methods for dealing with resistance are to uncover its roots, deal realistically with them, look for ways to modify the plan or a consultee's responsibilities, provide reassurances, emphasize the rewards that may accrue if the plan is carried out, seek help from other sources of support such as a principal or a mentor teacher, and, if necessary, call a halt to the project for awhile. Given the intensity of some of the situations that call for consultation, it is sometimes necessary to take time out from plan building. When you return to it, people are sometimes more willing to progress. In any case, do not take resistance personally. The difficulty may be in the consultant's relationship with the consultee, or it may be that the plan simply isn't effective. In either case, treat resistance as an objective problem that can be worked out. Taking it personally, getting defensive, or, in the worst case, complaining to others about the consultee's lack of effort or professionalism only jeopardizes your relationship with the consultee and may tarnish your reputation in the school and the district.

Another function of ongoing consultation is data gathering and sharing. Data-driven decisions should be the hallmark of program modification. In addition to gathering baseline data before starting your intervention, you and the consultee must come up with a plan for how further data will be gathered. Will the consultee do it? How? Will the consultant have sufficient time to observe and gather data? This is usually not the case in the schools; time does not permit it, at least on an on going basis. If the responsibility will primarily be the consultee's, she is going to have to be trained well and, of course, willing to do it.

Consultees, particularly those for whom the consultation process is new, often feel vulnerable. This needs to be considered throughout the consultation process. Since teaching is such an isolated profession, with most teachers working by themselves behind closed doors (very little cooperative teaching occurs in most districts), it is not surprising that not all teachers welcome the collaborative efforts of an outsider. The idea of being observed on a regular basis, the possibility that the consultant may be talking to others about what he sees in classrooms (which, of course is an egregious violation of ethical standards), and the fact that teachers may have to change their own behavior according to some plan, no matter how collaboratively designed, can easily make some consultees feel very vulnerable. Again, the consultant needs to be sensitive to this possibility, put herself in the consultee's shoes, and make sure that she gives all the support she can to the consultee in this difficult process.

Possible Solutions:

- If the interventions are going according to plan and they seem to be effective, no further solutions are needed; stay the course. By all means, don't disturb interventions that are working well just to appease your own curiosity. Informed modifications are appropriate; frivolous tinkering is not.

- If, however, any of the possible reasons for plan failure are occurring (e.g., the plan itself is ineffective; proposed reinforcers are not available or do not have an impact on targeted behaviors; resistance; inability to monitor the plan because of too many other commitments), review these with the consultee and work out solutions. Poorly conducted interventions lead to failure and increased resistance to further consultative assistance. Be proactive, or all your preliminary work is for naught.

Evaluation and Closure

The process of evaluation is an effort to find or determine the value of something. Patton (1986) describes it as a systematic method of collecting information about activities and outcomes in consultation that inform the evaluator about how consultation is proceeding and its effects.

Evaluation should be both ongoing (formative) and cumulative (summative). It is primarily based on an effort to determine if the goals of the consultation project are being met. Therefore, the consultant and the consultees must agree at the outset what the goals of the consultation project are. Though this seems to be obvious, it sometimes isn't. Consultation projects are often started without a clear agreement about what the goal(s) are. The consultee may believe, for example, that the goal of a behavior-change project is simply to give the consultant enough data so that the consultant can refer the student back to the SST for special education consideration. The consultant, however, is convinced that if the consultee would carry out the plan effectively, the student would never have to be considered for special education. In another case, the consultant may believe that if a student who uses foul language could reduce his swearing by half, the project would be successful; the student's mother, however, believes that nothing less than a complete stop to all swearing is an appropriate goal. If these questions aren't resolved at the outset or shortly thereafter, there may be some angry participants at the conclusion of these consultative efforts.

Establishing the goals of the consultation gives direction to the evaluation and to the types of data to be gathered. Depending on the focus of the project, you may want to use objective data, such as that obtained by counting frequencies or durations of behaviors or by using questionnaires, rating scales, or check sheets. You may also gather anecdotal impressions (possibly using narrative recording procedures [Skinner et al., 2000] which you may have utilized in step 3 of the SOCS) or summarize interviews with the consultees. Another source of data might be to make pre- and post-consultation videotapes of the student engaging in the targeted behaviors.

The goal of ongoing evaluation is to provide data that can be used to modify the program. The purpose of the final evaluation is to summarize what took place and to determine its effectiveness. Dougherty (2000, p. 126) suggests the following questions to guide the evaluation process:

To what degree has behavior in the student (or system) changed in the desired direction? A response to this question requires clearly stated goals and some method for measuring intervention effects as they are occurring.

To what degree was the consultant able to enter the system psychologically? Dougherty refers here to the process in which a consultant goes beyond merely entering a situation physically; psychological entry occurs when the consultee accepts the consultant and has a positive regard for the consultative process.

In what ways has the organization changed as a result of consultation? Consultative efforts influence what Dougherty refers to as the "client-system," which for our purposes is usually the local school or district. Successful consultative efforts get people, especially administrators, talking about the possibility of applying lessons learned from the consultation to other settings. Herein lies the real power of the consultative model: If the consultant can show school or district-level personnel that a different way of approaching problems can be successful and can get the local teacher (consultee) and the principal to talk about it outside of its local confines, the change process is facilitated.

To what degree have the goals established in the contract been met? By "contract," Dougherty refers to either the formal contract that an outside consultant might establish with the employing district or to the informal or the implicit contract established when an internally based consultant and consultee agree to work together. To the extent that the goal of the contract is a change in the student's behavior, this question is similar to the question about the degree of behavior change in the student. If the goal was behavior change in a specified direction, and it has been achieved, then the contract has been fulfilled. Some degree of behavioral change on the part of the consultee is ordinarily undiscussed but clearly necessary in some behavior-change programs. As indicated in the SOCS and in Chapter 2, changes in antecedents and consequences require consultee behaviors that are not the same as they were before the intervention was implemented. These changes can be documented along with the changes observed in the student's behavior.

To what degree have established timetables been met? School consultants rarely set firm timetables when the focus of the consultative project is a student with a behavior or learning problem. Because of the complexity of some of these problems, it is unrealistic to state at the outset that the project will be completed or successful in a given amount of time. Sometimes the consultant is pleasantly surprised when his initial consultation with a teacher results in some dramatic change in the target behavior. More common, however, is the reality that many different tactics have to be tried before the successful combination is found. In some cases, success has been achieved when the consultee simply learns to accept a troublesome behavior, even though it still exists. In this case, although the goals of the contract may not have been met, the consultee may still feel that it was successful simply because his comfort level is now higher. External consultants, brought in under a contract in which they are paid by the hour or day, may be under the greater pressure to produce a successful outcome by a certain time. This can be unfortunate since the goals(s) may not be achieved by the deadline date. Although the consultation may be moving along adequately, key breakthroughs may not occur before the funds expire, and the project may die for lack of leadership when the consultant is no longer available.

How successfully has a given intervention been carried out? One of the fascinating aspects of doing consultation is that one is always learning something new about human interactions. What sometimes occurs is that the consultee implements an intervention "incorrectly" only to have it work splendidly. Given the complexity of the dynamics involved in students' behavior and learning problems, it should not be surprising (except to consultants with rigidly held theoretical positions) that our best-laid plans sometimes don't work while some curious misapplication of our plans or our theoretical positions does the job very well. We can rationalize all we want, but a better stance is to acknowledge the success we've observed and learn from it. Experience indicates that true collaboration occurs when the consultee feels free to apply treatments in a way that makes sense to her without violating treatment integrity (Caplan & Caplan, 1993; Petty, Heesacker, & Hughes, 1997). What is most important is that the consultant knows how the consultee is applying the treatment so that the results can be attributed to the actual treatment instead of what was planned on paper but never really done.

How effectively has the consultant established an effective working relationship with the consultee? I have emphasized throughout this text that consultation depends on effective relationships. This is especially true if you follow a collaborative mode of functioning. It is possible that a successful consultation can occur without a positive relationship; after all, it isn't necessary that people working together like each other. It is not likely, however, that success will occur if the relationship isn't effective. Effectiveness implies mutual respect—the willingness to work cooperatively, communicate honestly, and know when to give in and when to be firm. Sometimes the consultant and the consultee may disagree on the diagnosis or treatment. How they work out these conflicts determines if the project will be successful.

To what degree has consultation been worth the cost in time, effort, and money? The criteria of time, money, and effort are subjective. It depends on how much of these three criteria has been expended, what the results are, and how people value them. To the parent of a student who has a severe disability, a year's effort to get the student to comply with requests is well worth it. An outsider who is unfamiliar with the problem might consider this expenditure too costly in terms of staff involvement. Throughout recent years there has been an increase in tolerance for dealing with students who exhibit extreme behaviors, which was unheard of in public school classrooms only a few decades ago. The current trend toward full inclusion of all students in the regular track may mean that a disproportionate amount of resources is funneled in this direction. Whether it is worth it or not is a value question that a broad array of individuals need to consider.

Brown et al. (2001) have provided many examples of forms and questionnaires that can be used for evaluating the consultation process throughout its various stages, as well as the preferences and actions of consultees. Conoley and Conoley (1992) have presented a similar array of forms that could easily be adapted for one's own specific purposes. Parsons and Meyers (1984) have developed a consultee satisfaction form that asks the consultee to rate the consultant and the process of consultation in five different areas: efficacy of consultation, consultant expertise, consultant's administrative abilities, interpersonal style, and general comments. Gallesich (1982) offers a consultation evaluation survey designed to determine the consultee's perceptions of the skill and the efficacy of the consultant. Thirty-four items cover the areas of interpersonal, communication, and problem-solving skills, asking the consultee to rate the consultant on a seven-point Likert scale.

Although it is not necessary to use any of these forms or variations of them in every case, it is useful and professionally appropriate for the consultant to seek information about his efforts from his consumers—the teacher or parent-consultees with whom he works.

Dettmer et al. (1999, pp. 221–236) conceptualize evaluation according to three purposes and as both formative and summative. The first purpose is *context*, in which the focus is on the success of the consultation program per se. Here is a formative question deriving from this purpose: "What program aspects should be changed to fit this school and community?" Here is a summative question: "Should the consultation program be continued next year?"

The second purpose is *process*, in which the focus is on the skills of the consultant. A formative question is "What interpersonal management skills need to be changed?" A summative question is "Do I have the skills to be an effective consultant?"

The third purpose is *content;* the focus here is on student progress. A formative question is "Are achievement and behavior improving?" A summative question is "Does this client need more or less restrictive service?"

You can find further in-depth discussions of the evaluation process as applied to consultative services in Attkisson, Hargreaves, Horowitz, and Sorensen (1978); Bell and Nadler (1979); Bergan and Kratochwill (1990); Galloway and Sheridan (1994); Gresham and Noell (1993); Gutkin (1993b); and Suchman (1967).

Closure occurs when the consultant and the consultee agree that the consultative effort ought to be terminated, at least for the present. It is also possible that a case may be closed because the relationship between the consultant and the consultee has deteriorated. In this case one or the other party simply provides his own closure even though the case is not resolved. Fortunately, this is not common. A more common observation is that some consultation cases never seem to end; certain students need assistance throughout their school careers. Most cases, however, do reach at least a tentative conclusion, although the time it takes to do so is not easily predictable. Probably the best rule of thumb is to say that consultation ends when the consultee feels it should, assuming the student's needs are being met. Since the consultee has referred the student, she is in the best position to know when the consultation should end. We hope this coincides with the project's success.

Dougherty, Tack, Fullam, and Hammer (1996) have discussed the closure process, preferring to use the term *disengagement*. They point out that this is probably the most neglected aspect of the consultation process, at least in the consultation literature. Dougherty (2000) discusses this issue at some length in Chapter 6 of his text.

SUMMARY

In this chapter I have reviewed both generic problem-solving processes suitable for school-based consultants and SOCS, a ten-step method for conducting an individual student consultation. The steps are logically and sequentially organized. As I have mentioned, however, consultation rarely evolves in the linear fashion suggested by these steps. Variations will occur, and the competent consultant will learn when and how to allow for, or encourage, deviations. Trying to keep a complex human enterprise such as consultation flowing in a lockstep fashion is like trying to herd cats. Relax and enjoy the deviations.

REFERENCES

Abikoff, H., Gittleman-Klein, R., & Klein, D. (1977). Validation of a classroom observation code for hyperactive children. *Journal of Consulting and Clinical Psychology, 45,* 772–783.

Alberto, P. A., & Troutman, A. C. (1999). *Applied behavioral analysis for teachers* (5th ed.). Upper Saddle River, NJ: Merrill/Prentice Hall.

Alessi, G. (1988). Direct observation methods for emotional/behavioral problems. In E. S. Shapiro & T. R. Kratochwill (Eds.), *Behavioral assessment in schools: Conceptual foundations and practical applications* (pp. 14–75). New York: Guilford Press.

Alessi, G., & Kaye, J. (1983). *Behavior assessment for school psychologists.* Kent, OH: National Association of School Psychologists.

Allen, L. J., Howard, V. F., Sweeney, W. J., & McLaughlin, T. F. (1993). Use of contingency contracting to increase on-task behavior with primary students. *Psychological Reports, 72,* 905–906.

Asante, M. K. (1987). *The Afrocentric idea.* Philadelphia: Temple University Press.

Attkisson, C. C., Hargreaves, W. A., Horowitz, M. J., & Sorensen, J. E. (Eds.). (1978). *Evaluation of human service programs.* New York: Academic Press.

Bandura, A. (1978). The self-system in reciprocal determinism. *American Psychologist, 33,* 344–358.

Barkley, R. A. (1988). Child behavior rating scales and checklists. In M. Rutter, A. H. Tuma, & I. S. Lann (Eds.), *Assessment and diagnosis in child psychopathology* (pp. 113–155). New York: Guilford Press.

Barkley, R. A. (1990). *Attention deficit–hyperactivity disorder: A handbook for diagnosis and treatment.* New York: Guilford Press.

Bay, M., Bryan, T., & O'Connor, R. (1994). Teachers assisting teachers: A prereferral model for urban educators. *Teacher Education and Special Education, 17,* 10–21.

Behring, S. T., & Ingraham, C. L. (1998). Culture as a central component to consultation: A call to the field. *Journal of Educational and Psychological Consultation, 9*(1), 57–72.

Bell, C. R., & Nadler, L. (Eds.). (1979). *The client-consultant handbook.* Houston: Gulf.

Benjamin, A. (1987). *The helping interview.* Boston: Houghton Mifflin.

Bergan, J. R. (1977). *Behavioral consultation.* Columbus, OH: Merrill.

Bergan, J. R. (1995). Evolution of a problem-solving model of consultation. *Journal of Educational and Psychological Consultation, 6,* 111–124.

Bergan, J. R., & Kratochwill, T. R. (1990). *Behavioral consultation and therapy.* New York: Plenum.

Bergan, J. R., & Tombari, M. L. (1976). Consultant skill and efficiency and the implementation and outcomes of consultation. *Journal of School Psychology, 14,* 3–14.

Breen, M., & Altepeter, T. (1990). *Disruptive behavior disorders in children.* New York: Guilford Press.

Brown, D., Pryzwansky, W. B., & Schulte, A. (2001). *Psychological consultation: Introduction to theory and practice* (5th ed.). Boston: Allyn & Bacon.

Busse, R. T., & Beaver, B. R. (2000). Informant report: Parent and teacher interviews. In E. S. Shapiro & T. R. Kratochwill (Eds.), *Conducting school-based assessments of child and adolescent behavior* (pp. 235–273). New York: Guilford Press.

California Department of Education. (2001). *California special education programs: A composite of laws.* Sacramento: Author.

Caplan, G., & Caplan, R. (1993). *Mental health consultation and collaboration.* San Francisco: Jossey-Bass.

Charles, C. R. (1992). *Building classroom discipline* (4th ed.). White Plains, NY: Longman.

Chethik, M. (1989). *Techniques of child therapy.* New York: Guilford Press.

Choate, J. C. (1993). *Successful mainstreaming.* Boston: Allyn & Bacon.

Christenson, S. L., & Cleary, M. (1990). Consultation and the parent-educator partnership: A perspective. *Journal of Educational and Psychological Consultation, 1*(3), 219–241.

Christenson, S. L., & Conoley, J. C. (1992). *Home-school collaboration: Enhancing children's academic and social competence.* Silver Springs, MD: NASP.

Cleven, C. A., & Gutkin, T. B. (1988). Cognitive modeling of consultation processes: A means for improving consultees' problem definition skills. *Journal of School Psychology, 26,* 379–389.

Conoley, J., & Conoley, C. (1992). *School consultation: Practice and training* (2nd ed.). Boston: Allyn & Bacon.

Conoley, C., Conoley, J., Ivey, D., & Scheel, M. (1991). Enhancing consultation by matching the consultees' perspective. *Journal of Counseling and Development, 69,* 546–549.

Conroy, E., & Mayer, S. (1994). Strategies for consulting with parents. *Elementary School Guidance and Counseling, 29,* 60–66.

Cummins, K. (1988). *The teacher's guide to behavioral interventions.* Columbus, MO: Hawthorn Educational Services.

Curtis, M., & Meyers, J. (1988). Consultation: A foundation for alternative services in the schools. In J. Graden, J. Zins, & M. Curtis (Eds.), *Alternative educational delivery systems: Enhancing instructional options for all students* (pp. 35–48). Washington: NASP.

Curtis, M. J., & Watson, K. (1980). Changes in consultee problem clarification skills following consultation. *Journal of School Psychology, 18,* 210–221.

D'Amato, R. C., & Rothlisberg, B. A. (1992). *Psychological perspectives on intervention.* New York: Longman.

Dettmer, P., Dyck, N., & Thurston, L. P. (1999). *Consultation, collaboration and teamwork for students with special needs* (3rd ed.). Boston: Allyn & Bacon.

Dougherty, A. M. (2000). *Consultation: Practice and perspectives* (3rd ed.). Belmont, CA: Brooks/Cole.

Dougherty, A. M., Tack, F. E., Fullam, C. B., & Hammer, L. A. (1996). Disengagement: A neglected aspect of the consultation process. *Journal of Educational and Psychological Consultation, 7*(3), 259–274.

Edwards, P., & Pap, A. (Eds.). (1973). *A modern introduction to philosophy.* New York: Free Press.

Elliott, S. N. (1988). Acceptability of behavioral treatments: Review of variables that influence treatment selection. *Professional Psychology, 19,* 68–80.

Elliott, S. N., & Busse, R. T. (1993). Effective treatments with behavioral consultation. In J. E. Zins, T. R. Kratochwill, & S. N. Elliott (Eds.), *Handbook of consultation services for children* (pp. 179–203). San Francisco: Jossey-Bass.

Elliott, S. N., Witt, J. C., & Kratochwill, T. R. (1991). Selecting, implementing, and evaluating classroom interventions. In G. Stoner, M. Shinn, & H. Walker (Eds.), *Interventions for Achievement and behavior problems.* Silver Spring, MD: NASP.

Ellis, A. (1995). Changing rational-emotive therapy to rational-emotive behavior therapy. *Journal of Rational–Emotive and Cognitive–Behavior Therapy, 13,* 85–90.

Erchul, W. P., & Martens, B. K. (1997). *School consultation: Conceptual and empirical bases of practice*. New York: Plenum.

Friend, M., & Cook, L. (2000). *Interactions: Collaboration skills for school professionals* (3rd ed.). New York: Longman.

Fuchs, D., Fuchs, L. S., & Bahr, M. (1990). Mainstream assistance teams: A scientific basis for the art of consultation. *Exceptional Children, 37,* 128–139.

Fuchs, D., Fuchs, L. S., Reeder, P., Gilman, S., Fernstrom, P., Bahr, M., & Moore, P. (1989). *Mainstream assistance teams: A handbook on prereferral intervention*. Nashville, TN: Peabody College of Vanderbilt University.

Gallesich, J. H. (1982). *The profession and practice of consultation*. New York: Jossey-Bass.

Galloway, J., & Sheridan, S. M. (1994). Scientific practitioner: Implementing scientific practices through case studies: Examples using home-school interventions and consultation. *Journal of School Psychology, 32* (4), 385–410.

Glasser, W. (1969). *Schools without failure*. New York: Harper and Row.

Graden, J. L. (1989). Reactions to school consultation: Some considerations from a problem-solving perspective. *Professional School Psychology, 4,* 29–35.

Gresham, F. M. (1989). Assessment of treatment integrity in school consultation and prereferral intervention. *School Psychology Review, 18,* 37–50.

Gresham, F. M. (1991). Moving beyond statistical significance in reporting consultation outcome research. *Journal of Educational and Psychological Consultation, 2,* 1–13.

Gresham, F. M., & Noell, G. H. (1993). Documenting the effectiveness of consultation outcomes. In J. Zins, T. Kratochwill, & S. Elliott (Eds.), *Handbook of consultation services for children* (pp. 249–276). San Francisco: Jossey-Bass.

Gresham, F. M., & Noell, G. H. (1999). Functional analysis assessment as a cornerstone for noncategorical special education. In D. J. Reschley, W. D. Tilly, & J. P. Grimes (Eds.), *Special education in transition: Functional assessment and noncategorical programming* (pp. 49–80). Longmont, CO: Sopris West.

Gresham, F. M., & Witt, J. (1987, October). *Practical considerations in the implementation of classroom interventions*. Paper presented at the annual meeting of the Oregon School Psychological Association, Eugene.

Gutkin, T. B. (1980). Teacher perceptions of consultation services provided by school psychologists. *Professional Psychology, 11,* 637–642.

Gutkin, T. B. (1993a). Cognitive modeling: A means for achieving prevention in school-based consultation. *Journal of Educational and Psychological Consultation, 4*(2), 179–183.

Gutkin, T. B. (1993b). Conducting consultation research. In J. Zins, T. Kratochwill, & S. Elliott (Eds.), *Handbook of consultation services for children* (pp. 227–248). San Francisco: Jossey-Bass.

Gutkin, T. B., & Curtis, M. (1982). School-based consultation: Theory and techniques. In C. R. Reynolds & T. B. Gutkin (Eds.), *The handbook of school psychology* (pp. 796–828). New York: Wiley.

Gutkin, T. B., & Curtis, M. (1990). School-based consultation: Theory, techniques, and research. In C. R. Reynolds & T. B. Gutkin (Eds.), *The handbook of school psychology* (2nd ed., pp. 577–611). New York: Wiley.

Gutkin, T.B., & Curtis, M. (1999). School-based consultation theory and practice: The art and science of indirect service delivery. In C. R. Reynolds & T. B. Gutkin (Eds.), *The handbook of school psychology* (3rd ed., pp. 598-637). New York: Wiley.

Hintze, J. M., & Shapiro, E. S. (1995). Systematic observation of classroom behavior. In A. Thomas & J. Grimes (Eds.), *Best practices in school psychology—III* (pp. 651–660). Washington, DC: NASP.

Huebner, E., & Hahn, B. (1990). Best practices in coordinating multidisciplinary teams. In A. Thomas & J. Grimes (Eds.), *Best practices in school psychology—II* (pp. 235–246). Washington, DC: NASP.

Hughes, J. (1986). Ethical issues in school consultation. *School Psychology Review, 15,* 489–499.

Hughes, J. (1988). *Cognitive behavior therapy with children in schools*. New York: Pergamon.

Hyman, I. A. (1997). *School discipline and school violence: The teacher variance approach*. Boston: Allyn & Bacon.

Jacob, R. G., O'Leary, K. D., & Rosenblad, C. (1978). Formal and informal classroom settings: Effects on hyperactivity. *Journal of Abnormal Child Psychology, 6,* 47–59.

Johnson, L. J., & Pugach, M. C. (1996). Role of collaborative dialogue in teachers' conceptions of appropriate practice for students at risk. *Journal of Educational and Psychological Consultation, 7*(1), 9–24.

Kampwirth, T. (1981). Diagnosing poor learning: Some considerations. *Journal for Special Educators, 17,* 142–149.

Kanfer, F. H., & Goldstein, A. P. (Eds.). (1986). *Helping people change.* New York: Pergamon.

Kramer, J. (1990). Training parents as behavior change agents: Successes, failures, and suggestions for school psychologists. In T. B. Gutkin & C. Reynolds (Eds.), *The handbook of school psychology* (2nd ed., pp. 685–702). New York: Wiley.

Kratochwill, T., & Bergan, J. (1990). *Behavioral consultation in applied settings: An individual guide.* New York: Plenum.

Kurpius, D., Fuqua, D., & Rozecki, T. (1993). The consulting process: A multidimensional approach. *Journal of Counseling and Development, 71,* 601–606.

Lambert, N. M. (1976). Children's problems and classroom interventions from the perspective of classroom teachers. *Professional Psychology, 7,* 507–517.

Lentz, F. E., Allen, S. J., & Erhardt, K. E. (1996). The conceptual elements of strong interventions in school settings. *School Psychology Quarterly, 11*(2), 118-136.

Long, N., & Morse, W. (1996). *Conflict in the classroom.* Austin, TX: Pro-Ed.

McCarney, S. B., & Cummins, K. (1998). *The prereferral intervention manual* (2nd ed.). Columbus, MO: Hawthorne Educational Services.

McCarney, S. B., & McCain, B. R. (1995). *The behavior dimensions intervention manual.* Columbia, MO: Hawthorne Educational Services.

Marks, E. S. (1995). *Entry strategies for school consultation.* New York: Guilford Press.

Martin, M., & Waltman-Greenwood, C. (Eds.). (1995). *Solve your child's school-related problems.* New York: HarperPerennial/NASP.

Mash, E. J., & Terdal, L. G. (Eds.). (1997). *Assessment of childhood disorders* (3rd ed.). New York: Guilford Press.

Mastropieri, M. A., & Scruggs, T. E. (2000). *The inclusive classroom: Strategies for effective instruction.* Upper Saddle River, NJ: Merrill/Prentice Hall.

Medway, F. J., & Updyke, J. F. (1985). Meta-analysis of consultation outcome studies. *American Journal of Community Psychology, 13,* 489–505.

Meyers, B., Valentino, C. T., Meyers, J., Boretti, M., & Brent, D. (1996). Implementing prereferral intervention teams as an approach to school-based consultation in an urban school system. *Journal of Educational and Psychological Consultation, 7*(2), 119–149.

Miller, D. L., & Kelley, M. L. (1994). The use of goal setting and contingency contracting for improving children's homework performance. *Journal of Applied Behavioral Analysis, 27,* 73–84.

Morrow, L. M., & Woo, D. G. (Eds.). (2001). *Tutoring programs for struggling readers.* New York: Guilford Press.

Nelson, J. R., Lott, L., & Glenn, H. (1997). *Positive discipline in the classroom* (2nd ed.). Rocklin, CA: Prima.

Nicoll, W. (1992). A family counseling and consultation model for school counselors. *School Counselor, 39,* 351–361.

Noell, G. H., & Gresham, F. M. (1993). Functional outcome analysis: Do the benefits of consultation and prereferral intervention justify the costs? *School Psychology Quarterly, 8,* 200–226.

O'Shea, D., O'Shea, L., Algozzine, R., & Hammitte, D. (2001). *Families and teachers of individuals with disabilities.* Boston: Allyn & Bacon.

Parsons, R. D., & Meyers, J. (1984). *Developing consultation skills: A guide to training, development and assessment for human services professionals.* San Francisco: Jossey-Bass.

Patton, M. Q. (1986). *Utilization-focused evaluation.* Beverly Hills, CA: Sage.

Petty, R., Heesacker, M., & Hughes, J. (1997). The elaboration liklihood model: Implications for the practice of school psychology. *Journal of School Psychology, 35,* 107–136.

Pfeiffer, J. W., & Jones, J. E. (Eds.). (1974). *A handbook for structured human relations training* (Vol. 3). La Jolla, CA: University Associates.

Pierangelo, R., & Crane, R. (2000). *The special education yellow pages.* Upper Saddle River, NJ: Merrill/Prentice Hall.

Ponti, C. R., Zins, J. E., & Graden, J. L. (1988). Implementing a consultation-based service delivery system to decrease referrals for special education: A case study of organizational considerations. *School Psychology Review, 17*(1), 89–100.

Pugach, M. C., & Johnson, L. J. (1987). Peer collaboration. *Teaching Exceptional Children, 20,* 75–77.

Pugach, M. C., & Johnson, L. J. (1995). Unlocking the expertise among classroom teachers through structured dialogue: Extending the research on peer collaboration. *Exceptional Children, 62,* 101–110.

Radius, M., & Lesniak, P. (1988). *Student study teams: A resource manual.* Sacramento, CA: RISE.

Raiffia, H. (1968). *Decision analysis.* Reading, MA: Addison-Wesley.

Rathvon, N. (1999). *Effective school interventions.* New York: Guilford Press.

Redl, F. (1972). *When we deal with children.* New York: Free Press.

Redmon, W. K., Cullari, S., & Ferris, H. E. (1985). An analysis of some important tasks and phases in consultation. *Journal of Community Psychology, 13,* 375–386.

Reimers, T. M., Wacker, D. P., & Koeppl, G. (1987). Acceptability of behavioral treatments: A review of the literature. *School Psychology Review, 16,* 212–227.

Reschly, D. (1988). Alternative delivery systems: Legal and ethical implications. In J. Graden, J. Zins, & M. Curtis (Eds.), *Alternative educational delivery systems: Enhancing instructional options for all students* (pp. 525–552). Washington, DC: NASP.

Reschly, D., & Tilly, D. (1999). Reform trends and system design alternatives. In D. J. Reschly, W. D. Tilly, & J. P. Grimes (Eds.), *Special education in transition.* Longmont, CO: Sopris West.

Reynolds, C. R., & Kamphaus, R. W. (1992). *Behavior assessment system for children (BASC).* Circle Pines, MN: American Guidance Services.

Rosenfield, S. (1987). *Instructional consultation.* Hillsdale, NJ: Erlbaum.

Rosenfield, S. (1992). Developing school-based consultation teams: A design for organizational change. *School Psychology Quarterly, 7,* 27–46.

Rosenfield, S., & Gravois, T. (1996). *Instructional consultation teams.* New York: Guilford Press.

Safran, S., & Safran, J. (1996). Intervention assistance programs and prereferral teams: Directions for the twenty-first century. *Remedial and Special Education, 17,* 363–369.

Sarason, S. B. (1982). *The culture of the school and the problem of change* (2nd ed.). Boston: Allyn & Bacon.

Salvia, J., & Ysseldyke, J. (1998). *Assessment* (6th ed.) Boston: Houghton-Mifflin.

Sattler, J. M. (1998). *Clinical and forensic interviewing of children and families: Guidelines for the mental health, education, pediatric, and child maltreatment fields.* San Diego, CA: Author.

Seligman, M. (1990). *Learned optimism.* New York: Pocket Books.

Shapiro, E. (1987). *Behavioral assessment in school psychology.* Hillsdale, NJ: Erlbaum.

Shapiro, E. S., & Kratochwill, T. R. (Eds.). (1988). *Behavioral assessment in schools.* New York: Guilford Press.

Shapiro, E. S., & Kratochwill, T. R. (2000a). *Conducting school-based assessments of children and adolescent behavior.* New York: Guilford Press.

Shapiro, E. S., & Kratochwill, T. R. (2000b). *Behavioral assessment in schools: Theory, research and clinical foundations.* (2nd ed.). New York: Guilford Press.

Sheridan, S. M., Kratochwill, T. R., & Bergan, J. R. (1996). *Conjoint behavioral consultation: A procedural manual.* New York: Plenum.

Skinner, B. (1971). *Beyond freedom and dignity.* New York: Knopf.

Skinner, C. H., Rhymer, K. N., & McDaniel, E. C. (2000). Naturalistic direct observation in educational settings. In E. S. Shapiro & T. R. Kratochwill (Eds.), *Conducting school-based assessment of children and adolescent behavior* (pp. 21–54). New York: Guilford Press.

Slavin, R. E., & Madden, N. A. (1989). What works for students at risk?: A research synthesis. *Educational Leadership, 46,* 1–8.

Sonstegard, M. (1964). A rationale for interviewing parents. *School Counselor, 12,* 72–76.

Sprick, R., & Howard, L. M. (1995). *The teacher's encyclopedia of behavior management.* Longmont, CO: Sopris West.

Sprick, R., Sprick, M., & Garrison, M. (1994). *Interventions.* Longmont, CO: Sopris West.

Stanovich, K. E. (2000). *Progress in understanding reading: Scientific foundations and new frontiers.* New York: Guilford Press.

Suchman, E. A. (1967). *Evaluative research: Principles and practices in public service and social action programs.* New York: Sage.

Turnbull, A. P., & Turnbull, H. R. (1997). *Families, professionals, and exceptionality: A special partnership* (3rd ed.). Upper Saddle River, NJ: Merrill/Prentice Hall.

Ullmann, L., & Krasner, L. (1965). *Case studies in behavior modification*. New York: Holt, Rinehart, & Winston.

Van Brock, M., & Elliott, S. (1987). The influence of treatment effectiveness information on the acceptability of classroom interventions. *Journal of School Psychology, 25,* 131–144.

Villa, R., Thousand, J., Nevin, A., & Malgeri, C. (1996). Instilling collaboration for inclusive schooling as a way of doing business in public schools. *Remedial and Special Education, 17,* 169–181.

Walker, J. E., & Shea, T. M. (1999). *Behavior management: A practical approach for educators* (7th ed.). Upper Saddle River, NJ: Merrill/Prentice Hall.

Wang, M. C., Haertel, G. D., & Walberg, H. J. (1993). Toward a knowledge base for school learning. *Review of Educational Research, 63,* 249–294.

Wilkinson, L. A. (1997). School-based behavioral consultation: Delivering treatment for children's externalizing behavior in the classroom. *Journal of Educational and Psychological Consultation, 8* (3), 255-276.

Wilson, C. P., Gutkin, T. B., Hagen, K. M., & Oats, R. G. (1998). General education teachers' knowledge and self-reported use of classroom interventions for working with difficult-to-teach students: Implications for consultation, prereferral intervention and inclusive services. *School Psychology Quarterly, 13,* 45–62.

Witt, J. (1986). Teachers' resistance to the use of school-based interventions. *Journal of School Psychology, 24,* 37–44.

Witt, J. (1990). Collaboration in school-based consultation: Myth in need of data. *Journal of Educational and Psychological Consultation, 1,* 367–368.

Witt, J. C., & Elliott, S. N. (1985). Acceptability of classroom management strategies. In T. R. Kratochwill (Ed.), *Advances in school psychology* (Vol. 4, pp. 251–288). Hillsdale, NJ: Lawrence Erlbaum Associates, Inc.

Ysseldyke, J., & Christenson, S. (1993). *The instructional environment system—II.* Longmont, CO: Sopris West.

Zins, J. E. (1993). Enhancing consultee problem-solving skills in consultative interactions. *Journal of Counseling and Development, 72,* 185–190.

Zins, J., Curtis, M., Graden, J., & Ponti, C. (1988). *Helping students succeed in the regular classroom.* San Francisco: Jossey-Bass.

Zins, J. E. & Erchul, W. P. (1995). Best practices in school consultation. In A. Thomas & J. Grimes (Eds.), *Best practices in school psychology—III* (pp. 609–623). Washington, DC: National Association of School Psychologists.

Zirpoli, T., & Melloy, K. (2001). *Behavior management applications for teachers.* Upper Saddle River, NJ: Merrill/Prentice Hall.

CHAPTER 6

Consulting About Students With Behavior Problems

OBJECTIVES

1. Present a list of common reasons for behavior problems.

2. Review descriptive terminology regarding behavior problems.

3. Establish a basis for making decisions about when, where, and how to intervene in regard to behavior problems.

4. Present information about diagnostic methods useful to consultants that are in accord with IDEA '97 provisions.

5. Provide numerous general and specific ideas about generating and selecting interventions.

Mr. Jacobs is an English teacher. In his opinion, his tenth-grade class is his worst class of the day because of the presence of three boys who always seem to be doing something to irritate him. They are mildly defiant, just enough to get a small laugh from some of the others, and they always seem to be talking to somebody. Their work is careless and sometimes contains suggestive comments. He has separated them and once sent one of them to the vice-principal's office, but he is reluctant to do more, hoping they will soon see that their behavior is self-defeating and leading to poor grades. He sees you, the school-based consultant, in the teacher's lounge in November and asks you for some advice. How might you respond to Mr. Jacobs's request?

Miss Peterson, an experienced primary-grade teacher, has been assigned a student in her third-grade regular education class who presents with severe handicaps (Down syndrome and acting-out behaviors). She is not pleased with this placement, which she feels was forced on her by a too-compliant administrator. During the first week in her class, this student has caused major disruptions. She has sent you an SOS requesting your immediate consultation. How might you, the RSP/consulting teacher, respond to this request?

AN ORIENTATION TO THE NATURE OF BEHAVIOR PROBLEMS

School-based consultants may be asked to assist consultees who are concerned about behavior problems in the classroom. In this chapter, I use the phrase *behavior problems* very broadly to refer to any student action that is intended to disturb, or has the effect of disturbing, the learning process of the student or other students. In the language of IDEA '97 (P.L. 105-17), any student who is identified as disabled under the provisions of that legislation, and whose behavior "impedes his or her learning or that of others" (IDEA, section 614, (d) (3) (B) (i)) must have a *functional behavioral assessment* conducted and a *behavior intervention plan* written for him. The teacher or another school authority is responsible for determining the existence of a behavior problem. It therefore follows that any given behavior is or is not a problem depending on the beliefs of the classroom teacher or other school authorities.

ACTIVITY 6.1

Recall situations from your own childhood or your school-based professional experience in which similar behaviors were regarded as, or treated as, problems depending on the teacher or on another aspect of the classroom ecology, such as class size, type of class, presence of an aide, or philosophy of the school administration. What caused the same behaviors to be treated as a problem in one situation but not in another?

In general, the purpose or function of any voluntary behavior is to get something, avoid something, or both. In the case of a classroom behavior problem, you may often find it quite easy to determine whether the student is trying to get something (such as teacher attention, peer attention, power, or revenge), avoid something (such as completing work, being harassed by others, personal discomfort, or boredom), or both (perhaps peer attention as an alternative to boredom, or disruptively seeking the attention of the teacher as a means of avoiding having to think and work independently). Evans and Meyer (1985) frame the issue of purposes in terms of three functions that a behavior may serve: (1) *social communicative*, where a student, either verbally or nonverbally, indicates a communicative intent, such as saying or implying "Leave me alone!"; (2) *self-regulatory*, where a student responds to a physical state such as hunger or overstimulation and her behavior is an effort to deal with or alter this physical state; and (3) *self-entertainment (play)*, where a student believes that school is a place for social interaction and he seeks it out at every opportunity, even when others are not interested in it.

A second generalization is that most behavior problems have multiple determinants. It is rare that a student has only one reason for her poor classroom behavior (Kazdin, 1985). This is important since the treatment you apply needs to be tailored to the many causes that may operate in a case. Typically, causes are both external (for example, gang influences) and internal (such as a desire for power; physical conditions such as health, hunger, or neurological impairment; or self-talk). Cause may be related to a distal antecedent: anything that has happened in the student's past to have predisposed him to a given pattern of behavior or responding, such as child-rearing practices; or it may be related to a proximal antecedent, which occurs close to the target behavior and is presumed to have been the most immediate prompt to that behavior, such as one student calling another a derogatory name. However, it may be multifaceted, influenced by two or more reasons. If a student tells herself that others want to hurt her, and someone looks at her in a way that she perceives to be threatening, she may react to this stimulus by yelling at or hitting the other student. External antecedents are easier to detect: one child provokes another; the teacher raises her voice; the principal appears on the playground; or the building shakes violently from an earthquake, causing some students (and teachers) to panic.

Two particular types of behavior problems are *internalizing behaviors,* which may be manifested by the student's withdrawal or anxiety, and *externalizing behaviors,* which are characterized by acting out, disruption, and disobedience.

COMMON REASONS FOR BEHAVIOR PROBLEMS

Eleven reasons are presented for the presence of both externalizing and internalizing behavior problems. This list is not intended to be exhaustive, but it does contain those reasons that should be considered by consultants when students manifesting behavioral challenges are referred to them. Additional perspectives on causes for behavior problems are given by Charles (1999) and Alberto and Troutman (1999).

Attention from Others

The specifics of how this process operates are complicated, depending on the age of the student, the receptivity of the audience, the target of the attention seeking, and the intentionality of the behavior that gets attention. For example, some behaviors, such as wearing odd clothing or speaking inarticulately, may gain attention even though the student may not want the kind of attention they get. Dreikurs (1968) and Dreikurs and Gray (1995) cite attention-seeking as one of the four "mistaken goals" of students with behavior problems, the other three being power-seeking, revenge, and withdrawal. According to Dreikurs, the student who seeks attention does so because he believes he is not getting enough attention, or at least the attention he desires. Getting positive attention from others is a powerful human need and shouldn't be denied in the proper context. Unfortunately, students identified as having behavior problems mainly seek attention in disruptive or obtrusive ways, so the attention they get is very often negative rather than positive. Oddly, for some students, any attention, positive or negative, is better than the feeling of being ignored.

ACTIVITY 6.2

Give some examples of attention-seeking behaviors that are disruptive to the learning process. In groups of three, analyze these behaviors and develop some tentative plans for dealing with them.

Child-Rearing Practices

This may be both a distal antecedent (these practices may have occurred years ago but still have an influence) or a proximal antecedent (as in the case of a student who comes from a home where he sees conflict, confusion, and negativity every morning before leaving for school). There are many ways in which parents can fail to provide the kind of emotional and physical stability needed for a student's feeling of well-being and emotional security, including divorce (or the threat of it), laxness, inconsistency, harshness, demeaning comments, coercive control, and so on. Patterson, Chamberlain, and Reid (1982) have identified five positive parenting practices that are important in this regard: (1) fair, timely, and consistent discipline; (2) close monitoring of the activities, whereabouts, and affiliations of their children; (3) positive behavior management techniques that show children that they are valued, encouraged, and supported; (4) involvement in a child's activities, such as Scouts, sports, and entertainment; and (5) problem-solving and crisis-management skills that help the child resolve conflicts. Patterson et al. (1982) have taught these skills to parents with very positive results.

ACTIVITY 6.3

Have class members role-play some ineffective parental practices and discuss how a consultant might approach parents in an effort to have them change these practices. For example, two students could role-play a coercive interaction (Patterson, Reid, Jones, & Conger, 1975) characterized by the parental figure giving a command, the child whining or demanding her way out of it, and the parent either escalating or giving in. Review how this interaction might be improved. Do this also for ineffective teacher practices.

Classroom Management Practices

Even to casual observers, including parents, it seems clear that some teachers need more training in classroom behavior management. They lack either the will or the skill to take behavior management seriously. Their classes are marked by disorganization, noise (not the productive noise of busy students but the noise of talking out inappropriately, arguing, moving about unnecessarily, and so on), and a general lack of evidence about who is in control. Students in these classes are often more hyperactive, louder, more disrespectful, and more unproductive than are students in other classrooms. Often students who misbehave in these classrooms do not do so in classes under better management. Kampwirth (1988) has developed a list of questions that consultants can use to assist them in evaluating classrooms marked by many behavior problems in order to determine teacher behaviors or classroom arrangement variables that may contribute to these problems. Some of these questions are related to preventive aspects, such as the quality of the classroom's physical appearance (neat, attractive, functional), whether rules are clearly displayed or otherwise conveyed, whether students have knowledge of the consequences for both appropriate and inappropriate behavior, and evidence of an organized plan for teaching. Teachers also need to pre-plan a sequence of interventions which they can use in the event of misbehavior.

There are a number of excellent texts that provide a wide range of ideas about, and methods for, dealing with issues of classroom behavior management (Alberto & Troutman, 1999; Bauer & Sapona, 1991; Charles, 1999; Emmer, Evertson, Sanford, Clements, & Worsham, 1989; Evertson, Emmer, Clements, Sanford, & Worsham, 1989; Jones & Jones, 1998; Walker & Shea, 1999; Zirpoli & Melloy, 2001).

ACTIVITY 6.4

Students should interview teachers they know in order to get ideas about their behavior management techniques. What do teachers who are skilled at behavior management do about relatively common behavior management problems such as talking out, bothering one's neighbor, engaging in off-task behavior, and so on?

Anti-Authoritarianism

Many Americans are ambivalent about authority figures. Historically, America was founded during a rebellion against the authority of the English crown, and its Constitution begins with a rationale for a revolution: "When in the course of human events." On the one hand, most people respect authority figures (such as police officers and teachers) because they recognize that someone must be in control so that the needs and rights of all people will be respected equally. On the other hand, an increasing number of people are recognizing that authority figures are not always right, fair, or honest, and that ordinary citizens have a right and a duty to monitor the behavior of authority figures even as they monitor ours. This ambivalence extends to the classroom. Teachers and researchers report that students today are considerably less impressed with the authority of teachers than they were a few decades ago (Charles, 1999). Teachers report that they currently spend more time just trying to get their classes under control so that they can teach. Teachers need to prove that they can control the class and that they have the authority to do so. In some inner-city urban areas, teachers are paid an extra stipend for teaching in some schools because the stress of unruly classes drives teachers away from these areas.

For some students, the desire for power in interpersonal relationships extends to their relationships with the teacher. They overtly or subtly test teachers to see who will win a power struggle. For others, revenge against past hurts which are real, imagined, or projected onto the schools from their home situations is a primary, though often unverbalized, reason for misbehavior. Dreikurs (1968) has discussed the phenomena of power and revenge along with attention and withdrawal, the four behaviors or activities that he has identified as the mistaken goals of misbehavior.

The general heading of anti-authoritarianism includes the influence of gangs, ethnic conflict, and the sense of alienation from the schools that are realities for some students. Gangs reject schools and influence their members to avoid school or to be disruptive when there. Other students, who may or may not be under gang influence, sense that they are not accepted by school personnel. As a result, they become alienated from the school's educative and socializing influence, often in the same way that they feel alienated from their own parents. Glasser (1992) believes that schools have traditionally practiced coercive practices with students, especially those who feel alienated from these institutions. Instead of having the effect of drawing these students toward the goals of the school, these practices usually have the opposite effect. In his book he lists many examples of how schools can become less characterized by "boss-management" and more characterized by "lead-management."

If a student is also caught up in conflicts between social or ethnic groups in school, this distracts him from academic efforts. His ability to focus psychic energy on learning is disrupted in favor of self-protective efforts that sometimes involve the use of weapons.

ACTIVITY 6.5

Discuss gang-influenced or other sources of anti-authoritarian behaviors class members have observed in the schools. What are schools doing about these behaviors? What ideas do students have about different approaches to these behaviors? Mathews (1992) discusses a "Pro-Youth" strategy for confronting and dealing with gang issues in the schools.

Media Influence

The modeling influence of current media, particularly movies and television, is related to anti-authoritarianism. Lieberman (1994) believes that primarily the visual media, but also recorded music geared toward teens, has desensitized our culture to violence and anti-authoritarianism to the point where violence and hostility are portrayed as culturally normative. The American Psychological Association report *Violence and Youth* (1994) has come to similar conclusions. Predictably, media representatives tend to deny any causative relationship between portrayed violence and its increase in our society, claiming that their portrayals merely reflect society, not govern it, in spite of considerable evidence to the contrary (Lieberman, 1994). Video games commonly display aggressive behaviors which often result in severe injury or death to numerous characters; killing is casual and results in no grief, mortification, or apparent long-term effects on any of the remaining game characters. Hughes and Hasbrouck (1996) review the scientific data available on this issue and point out that the effects of violence portrayed on TV and other media are conditioned by other factors but that, in general, TV violence does contribute to the level of aggression and subsequent violence and criminality among children and teens.

ACTIVITY 6.6

Stage a debate between students acting as educators and others acting as media representatives on the topic: "Does media violence influence the behavior of schoolchildren?"

Wanting to Have Fun or Alleviate Boredom

"Kids just wanna have fun!" For some students, the desire to enjoy themselves is more important than any other agenda the teacher may have. Glasser (1992) believes that having fun is a student need that schools ignore or try to repress at great cost. He states that this need is as important as three others he discusses: belonging, power, and freedom. Often, students' efforts to have fun are benign and tolerable, but sometimes they seriously intrude on the teacher's efforts to keep all students productive and on task, after which the teacher has to intervene. Jones (1987) points out that most misbehavior simply consists of students' efforts to be sociable with each other, usually in a positive, fun-oriented way. This socializing is done for two reasons: people are gregarious, and schoolwork is often not very interesting. Jones's observations of classrooms led him to conclude that most behavior problems are simply massive time wasting, consisting of students chatting with each other, passing notes, moving about the room socializing, and generally goofing off. Some of the teachers he observed lost almost 50 percent of their teaching time to correcting these minor but real irritants.

ACTIVITY 6.7

In small groups, discuss the role of "fun" in learning. What can teachers do to meet students' needs (or desires) to have fun while learning?

Disruptive Behaviors as Psychiatric Diagnoses

Attention deficit (hyperactivity) disorder (ADHD), conduct disorder (CD), and oppositional defiant disorder (ODD) are three diagnostic categories in the *Diagnostic and Statistical Manual* (*DSM*-IV) of the American Psychiatric Association (1994). They constitute three of the most common labels given to children who exhibit a wide variety of behaviors considered inimical to the learning process. Although behaviorally oriented consultants probably consider these terms to have communicative rather than explanatory value, we often hear them used as causative entities—for example, "Of course she can't sit still; she has ADHD." (The next section of this chapter discusses this issue further.) In addition to these three disruptive behaviors, the *DSM*-IV lists anxiety, depression, somatization, schizophrenia, and other internalizing disorders, all of which may be used to label children, and to give a putative cause for the behaviors of concern.

ACTIVITY 6.8

Class members should review the *DSM*-IV criteria for the various diagnoses related to childrens' behavior disorders. These criteria should be compared to the criteria established in IDEA for the determination of the categories of "Emotional Disturbance" and "ADHD."

Poor Health

Some students have allergies that affect their ability to concentrate on schoolwork. Others may have a poor diet that leads to hypoglycemic-type behavior marked by irritability and uncooperativeness. Some students may have other undetected medical conditions (such as poor vision or hearing, Tourette's disorder, and so on) that can influence their behavior. Hill (1999) provides a more detailed discussion of health issues that can influence behavior.

Communication Skill Deficits

Teachers often report that students with behavior disorders often don't seem to understand the class rules, expectations, or consequences. Sometimes the reasons for this possibility are obvious: English language learners and students with hearing impairments may not fully understand what teachers or other students are saying. More subtle, though, is the possibility that a student may have an information processing dysfunction that impairs her ability to understand some or all of what is being conveyed to her, either verbally or through nonverbal cues that most students understand easily. Receptive language problems may appear to be simple inattention or distractibility, but may be due to a slowness or insecurity in processing language symbols. Students with this kind of disorder often have learning disabilities, especially in the language arts areas (Lerner, 2000). Referral to a speech and language specialist may be appropriate in these cases.

ACTIVITY 6.9

From their experience, have students discuss symptoms and causes for apparent communication problems that may be related to either behavior or learning problems.

Differences in Temperamental Traits

Some students seem inherently more impulsive and irritable than others. Inborn differences in activity levels, adaptability, and mood may be strongly interacting with environmental variables to produce the behaviors we observe. Chess and Thomas (1996) have discussed nine different dimensions of behavioral style: activity level, adaptability, approach/withdrawal, attention span and persistence, distractibility, intensity of reaction, rhythm, threshold of responsiveness, and quality of mood. They have grouped children into three clusters ("slow to warm up," "difficult," and "easy") based on the apparently inherent behavioral styles that these students exhibit at an early age. Buss and Plomin (1984) conceptualize temperament as a set of genetically determined personality traits or dispositions: *activity* (tempo and vigor), *emotionality* (emotional and behavioral arousal), and *sociability* (preference for others). There is little doubt these inborn traits, which are manifested well before preschool, can have powerful effects on how students respond to stimuli. Understanding them can provide useful approaches to the analysis of some forms of problem behavior in students. Carey and Jablow (1997) have provided some valuable suggestions for methods of approaching students who manifest different temperamental traits. Carey (1998) provides an interesting perspective on the diagnosis of ADHD, which may be incorrect if temperamental traits have not been taken into consideration.

ACTIVITY 6.10

Class members can consider and describe their own temperamental traits or those of someone they know well. They might also indicate how these traits were useful or detrimental in their own educational or vocational experiences.

Events as Antecedents in Specific Settings

The potential for disruptive behavior exists in any situation in which students are gathered. Some students will look for opportunities to irritate their peers, and they usually know who will react. Some "accidentally" bump into others, knock things off tables, make unacceptable noises, or simply exist, which in itself irritates others and leads to problems. Sometimes teachers give confusing information that leads to murmuring, loss of concentration, and escape behaviors.

Some teachers need to be helped to understand that these seemingly random antecedents inevitably occur among students, with certain students apparently destined to contribute more spice to the behavioral stew of a classroom than others. Consultants who have a firm grasp of the causes of behavior problems can help teachers understand these causes and possible solutions. At the end of this chapter, the section "General Ideas for Modifying Classroom Behavior" offers numerous suggestions that can be modified to suit different situations and teacher styles.

ACTIVITY 6.11

Class members should observe a class of students and look for the "little things" that often make a difference, such as those suggested above. What seemingly innocuous behaviors of some students, or the teacher, resulted in an escalation of maladaptive behavior in the classroom or playground?

TERMINOLOGY/CATEGORIZATION: THE *DSM-IV* APPROACH

When asked to define *behavior problem*, most people immediately think of children who disrupt the classroom for a variety of reasons, such as those I have just mentioned. Others think of spoiled or poorly raised children who only need a firm hand

(Valentine, 1987). Others emphasize categories described in the *DSM*-IV (American Psychiatric Association, 1994), such as conduct disorder, oppositional defiant disorder, or attention deficit disorder (usually the hyperactive-impulsive or combined types). Still other people, particularly those making eligibility decisions on IEP teams, interpret behavior problems strictly from the perspectives of either Public Law 105-17, which defines the categories of Emotional Disturbance or Other Health Impaired, or Section 504 of the Vocational Rehabilitation Act of 1973, which allows children found to have ADHD to be afforded services or accommodations in the general education program as needed. Although criteria vary from state to state, these laws define the behaviors needed in order to find students eligible for special education or related services.

The *DSM*-IV approach is the predominant method used by clinical psychologists, psychiatrists, and others outside the public school system. Some school psychologists and counselors may also use this system. *DSM*-IV essentially relies on a rating-scale approach. For example, to define a student as having a conduct disorder (CD), the clinician determines (not necessarily relying on specific objective criteria) that the student exhibits at least three of the behaviors listed in Figure 6.1.

Achenbach and McConaughy (1996) indicate that the list of behaviors presented in Figure 6.1 constitute only the most current version of a CD; previous *DSM* versions are different. Thus, depending on which version of the manual is used, a child might or might not have a CD. Obviously this continual shift in the meaning of CD has treatment and placement implications, and the same can be said for many other *DSM*-IV diagnoses, especially ADHD.

If the clinician thinks that the student exhibits (or has exhibited) the required number of behaviors, then the student is diagnosed as having a CD. It is not clear if this determination is an effort to label a disease entity that causes the delinquent behavior or simply an attempt to categorize. Regarding the *DSM*-IV, Knopf (1995) says:

> In summary, there are few if any compelling reasons why school psychologists need to use the *DSM* system. While some may feel that their ability to label a referred problem means that they understand it and are ready to successfully resolve it, this has never been empirically demonstrated. (p. 854)

An issue of the *School Psychology Review* (National Association of School Psychologists, 1996) was devoted to the *DSM*-IV and its utility in the practice of school psychology and counseling, including issues concerning diagnoses and special education decision making. The authors of the various articles indicated some of the strengths of the *DSM*-IV (for example, a fairly comprehensive list of the commonly accepted symptoms that constitute clinical diagnoses, guidelines regarding behaviors that may predict future adjustment problems, and suggested explanations for behavioral syndromes). They also mentioned some concerns, such as a lack of specification about how behaviors are to be measured or who constitutes a valid informant, a similar lack of specification regarding the degree of symptom strength needed for inclusion in a child's protocol, failure to account for situational specificity of syndromes, no gender or age differences in criteria, and diagnosed conditions being

Figure 6.1

DSM-IV criteria for a conduct disorder

A. A repetitive and persistent pattern of behavior in which the basic rights of others or major age-appropriate societal norms or rules are violated, as manifested by the presence of three (or more) of the following criteria in the past twelve months, with at least one criterion present in the past six months.

Aggression to people or animals

(1) Often bullies, threatens, or intimidates others.

(2) Often initiates physical fights.

(3) Has used a weapon that can cause serious physical harm to others (e.g., a bat, brick, broken bottle, knife, gun).

(4) Has been physically cruel to people.

(5) Has been physically cruel to animals.

(6) Has stolen while confronting a victim (e.g., mugging, purse snatching, extortion, armed robbery).

(7) Has forced someone into sexual activity.

Destruction of property

(8) Has deliberately engaged in fire setting with the intention of causing serious damage.

(9) Has deliberately destroyed others' property (other than by fire setting).

Deceitfulness or theft

(10) Has broken into someone else's house, building, or car.

(11) Often lies to obtain goods or favors or to avoid obligations (i.e., "cons" others).

(12) Has stolen items of nontrivial value without confronting a victim (e.g., shoplifting, but without breaking and entering; forgery).

Serious violation of rules

(13) Often stays out at night despite parental prohibitions, beginning before age 13 years.

(14) Has run away from home overnight at least twice while living in parental or parental surrogate home (or once without returning for a lengthy period).

(15) Is often truant from school, beginning before age 13 years.

B. The disturbance in behavior causes clinically significant impairment in social, academic, or occupational functioning.

C. If the individual is age 18 or older, the criteria are not met for Antisocial Personality Disorder.

Source: Reprinted with permission from the *Diagnostic and Statistical Manual of Mental Disorders,* 4th Edition. Copyright 1994 American Psychiatric Association.

either present or absent based on an absolute number of minimum behaviors needed. Gresham and Gansle (1992) have also commented that the *DSM*, along with other classification systems, are not linked directly to interventions and do not lead to treatment plans that are useful. They, along with most others who view behaviors from a school-based behavioral intervention standpoint, regard *functional assessment and functional analysis* to be the approach of choice for dealing with the social/behavioral/emotional problems of children (Chandler & Dahlquist, 2002; Shapiro & Kratochwill, 2000). This approach will be discussed further later in this chapter.

At an IEP meeting, special education eligibility criteria are the primary source of the diagnoses or categories by which students are found to be eligible for special education and related services. However, P.L. 105-17, which lists standards for eligibility for emotional disturbance (ED), is written in such a way that many students could be classified as having ED depending on factors other than their actual behavior or degree of emotional disturbance (Kauffman, 1982). Nevertheless, in spite of this apparent opportunity for laxness in the interpretation of the criteria, fewer than 1 percent of students in American public schools are classified with this disability (U.S. Department of Education, 2000).

NON–*DSM*-IV CATEGORY SYSTEMS

Achenbach and McConaughy (1997) have reviewed empirically based assessment systems for delineating types of emotional/behavioral disorders. They have categorized behavior problems along the continuum mentioned above: internalizing–externalizing. *Externalizing* is some combination of the three disruptive behaviors: attention deficit (hyperactivity) disorder, conduct disorder, and oppositional defiant disorder. *Internalizing* is characterized by depression, anxiety, obsessive-compulsive tendencies, overcontrolled behavior, suicidal ideation or attempts, and somatization. Students who manifest these internalizing problems are characterized as being overcontrolled. Their symptoms can easily go unnoticed since these students do not act out, intrude on others, or defy classroom rules as do those students whose behaviors are classified as externalizing. It is important to understand that these internalizing conditions are potentially more serious for the long-term mental health of students than are the externalizing behaviors that more readily command our attention. An edition of *School Psychology Review* (National Association of School Psychologists, 1990) was devoted to internalizing problems in school-aged students.

Quay and Peterson (1996) have identified six major categories of behavior problems: conduct disorders, anxious-withdrawn, immaturity, psychotic behavior, motor excess, and socialized aggressive.

These various categorization systems have been described and researched at length (Reynolds & Kamphaus, 1990; Shapiro & Kratochwill, 2000), and each is favored by some theorists and school personnel. Some of these systems have been operationalized through rating scales or interview formats, most of which are commercially available (Achenbach & McConaughy, 1996; Connors, 1997; McConaughy & Ritter, 1995; Quay & Peterson, 1996; Reynolds & Kamphaus, 1992).

Other than for their use in eligibility/placement decisions, most school-based consultants usually do not emphasize or rely on these traditional category systems of diagnosis. They believe a behavioral or functional approach to assessment to be more practical. Hartmann, Roper, and Bradford (1979) have listed the differences between the traditional and behavioral approaches, which demonstrate why the behavioral approach is more appropriate for school purposes. Table 6.1 presents important elements of those differences.

As Table 6.1 indicates, the behavioral approach differs in significant ways from the traditional, or categorization, approach. The behavioral approach looks at the function of behavior, while the traditional approach regards behavior as symptomatic of an underlying condition that produces the behavior. For example, if a student is disruptive, defiant, and uncooperative toward a teacher, the behaviorist looks at the student's learning history and the contingencies currently operative in the classroom. Personality constructs such as "oppositional" are merely used as descriptors for communication purposes, or perhaps can be used to define a "trait" if the behavior is consistent across many settings, but not as explanatory constructs. The traditionalist probably would diagnose the disruptive, defiant student as having a conduct disorder since the student's behaviors match those listed in *DSM*-IV under that category (see Figure 6.1). Such a diagnosis runs the risk of confusing the cause with the symptom, so that one might be led to believe that the condition "conduct disorder" causes the described behaviors. This belief in the process of reification, or giving categories a life of their own, along with the subsequent power to produce symptoms, has been a major stumbling block in any rapprochement between behaviorists and traditionalists (Deitz, 1982). There have been some attempts to integrate the traditional and behavioral models.

Thus, while both behaviorists and traditionalists are interested in the causes of behavior, they look at different sources for those causes. The behaviorist looks at current functions that the behavior is attempting to serve and the contingencies that

Table 6.1

Selected differences between behavioral and traditional approaches to assessment

Behavioral	Traditional
Current contingencies maintain behavior.	Behavior is a function of intrapsychic determinants.
Behavior must be carefully delineated since it will constitute the main focus of change.	Behavior is a symptom of underlying conflict.
Antecedents and consequences are important maintaining variables.	Behavior is used to determine diagnostic labels.
Direct observations of behavior are most important.	Interviews, projective tests, and self-reports yield important diagnostic data.

support the behavior, while the traditionalist looks at past history or internal events that have led to the disease or disability (that is, the category), which in turn leads to the observed behaviors.

It is interesting to note that behaviorists are forced by the current legal bases for special education (and, in the case of hospital or clinic treatment, by the insurance industry) to use a category system based on fairly traditional nosological systems (such as the *DSM*-IV) in order to provide the settings or resources for their treatment approaches. Thus, a student has to be labeled something before treatment can be provided. In spite of two decades of argument against a categorical system of funding special education and related services in the schools (Hunt & Marshall, 1999; Prasse & Schrag, 1999; Ysseldyke & Marston, 1999), the system is still being used, and even more categories are being developed every few years. ADHD and traumatic brain injury (TBI) are among the latest to be added: ADHD under Section 504 of the Vocational Rehabilitation Act of 1973 and TBI under IDEA, which currently lists 13 eligibility categories.

BEHAVIORAL DIAGNOSTIC METHODS

No matter their theoretical predilections, all authorities agree that some systematic method of diagnosis is necessary prior to the instigation of interventions (Alberto & Troutman, 1999; Reynolds & Kamphaus, 1990). Behaviorists, in their emphasis on behavioral referents, utilize *behavioral assessment*, which has been defined as "the identification of meaningful response units and their controlling variables for the purposes of understanding and altering behavior" (Hayes, Nelson, & Jarrett, 1986, p. 464). Currently there is an emphasis on the use of *functional assessment*, a method now required by IDEA for understanding the purposes of behaviors that impede learning. Functional assessment is a process of "gathering information on the events and other variables associated with the occurrence of a targeted behavior" (McComas, Hoch, & Mace, 2000, p. 80). One of the important variables to be determined on the basis of a functional assessment is the function or purpose of the student's behavior. Those conducting a functional assessment directly observe behavior and ecological influences and record these observations using charts or anecdotal notes. On the basis of this information they determine whether the student's behavior is an effort to obtain something (e.g., positive reinforcement) or to avoid something (e.g., some environmental or personal event perceived as being aversive). After behaviorists have assessed behavior and determined its functions, they engage in a *functional analysis*, which is the deliberate manipulation of variables believed to be controlling or influencing the behavior, in order to see what effects these manipulations have on the behavior. Chandler and Dahlquist (2002) discuss the differences between functional analysis conducted in a natural setting (i.e., a classroom or playground) and that which is done in *analogue* settings, separate areas where strict control can be placed over all contributing variables. McComas et al. (2000) state that a "functional analysis involves systematic manipulation of events within a single-case design and results in the identification of the behavior-environmental relations, or behavioral mechanisms, that maintain the problem behavior" (p. 80). In practical terms, functional assessment is useful because it allows the observer to make better predictions about the relationships among the student and the antecedent conditions, the probable effect of known reinforcers, and other variables that may influence the probability that a given behavior will occur. To be able to determine such probabilities, the consultant needs to interview the teacher or parent-consultee very carefully about the details that surround the occurrence of the target behavior(s) in addition to observing the interactions among the consultee, the student, and the student's peers in the classroom or playground.

One possible result of such interviewing and observing is that assumptions about functional relationships may be contradicted by the data. For example, the consultant may believe that a given behavior is controlled by a reinforcement system that she feels is inadequate. Functional assessment may reveal that some antecedent, either distal or proximal, may be controlling the behavior. Gresham and Witt (1987) present evidence in support of the idea that inappropriately arranged antecedents result in more referrals than do inadequate reinforcement (consequent) systems.

When the functional assessment is completed, and the evaluator believes she has a good idea of the function of the behavior, she will engage in a set of interventions designed to test the hypotheses about these functions. Data resulting from these interventions should verify or falsify the hypothesized functions of the target behaviors.

Functional assessment and analysis, carefully done, take considerable time and effort. Someone other than the teacher (who is ordinarily too busy teaching) must be the objective observer in the classroom. This person has to be trained to record antecedents, behavior, consequences, setting events, and other aspects of the classroom ecology that may be influencing the target behavior(s), and to give guidance to the teacher in his efforts to apply interventions designed for functional analysis. Although school-based consultants are probably the ideal people for this task, they usually do not have the time to devote to it over an extended period. It is usually necessary to train a paraprofessional to do the functional assessment observations, if such a person is available. If not, the consultant may need to select times when he can do the observations, relying on the teacher (the consultee) to do the rest. Admittedly, this is not the ideal way to conduct a functional assessment, but it is often the best that can be done given the limited resources available in the schools.

Figure 6.2 gives an example of a functional behavioral assessment done by a resource teacher-consultant and the referred student's teacher. Note the attention to the search for causes (functions) of the student's behavior, in addition to efforts to answer the "wh" questions: What is the behavior? When does it happen? Where does it happen? Who is involved? Antecedents and consequences are also addressed in this assessment.

Excellent sources of further information about functional assessment are Alberto and Troutman (1999), Carr (1994), Chandler and Dahlquist (2002), Gresham and Noell (1999), Kaplan (2000), O'Neil, Horner, Albin, Storey, and Sprague (1990), Shapiro and Kratochwill (2000), and Wright and Gurman (1998).

Figure 6.2

Functional behavioral assessment example

The following FBA was conducted by a school-based resource specialist with a special education teacher-consultee, whose responses are often represented here.

FUNCTIONAL BEHAVIORAL ASSESSMENT
CONSISTENT WITH IDEA MANDATES

Student: Johnny BeGood   **DOB**: 11-11-89   **C.A.** 10-4

School: ABC   **Number of students in class**: 12

Teacher(s): Mr. Johnson   **Aide**: Ms. Smith

Setting: Special education; special day class

Target behavior(s): Johnny is noncompliant; he does very little schoolwork; he pesters others (i.e., threatens, bullies, extorts money).

What is the current frequency/intensity/duration of the behavior? (1) Johnny refuses to follow teacher directives between five and ten times a day. If teacher repeats the request he will often become verbally abusive. This refusal/escalation may last between five and fifty minutes. (2) Johnny turns in only about 20 percent of the work assigned; this is mostly math, his best subject. (3) He pesters others with verbal insults and threats between five and twenty times a day, largely depending on the reactions of the other students or Mr. Johnson or Ms. Smith. He may persist until he is timed-out; sometimes he just stops, especially if he gets no reaction.

When, and during what activities, does the target behavior occur? Pretty much throughout the day, with fewer problems occurring during math. During recess he is usually against the wall because of these behaviors.

What actions or behaviors of the targeted student or others typically precede the behavior? Teachers have not seen anything the others do to provoke Johnny. They are intimidated by him, and try to avoid doing or saying anything to him. If he sees others getting attention for good student behaviors, he will sometimes insult them for that. Otherwise, it just seems to arise with no specific identifiable antecedent.

What are the typical consequences of the behavior, planned or otherwise? (*Teacher's response*): I usually ask him to desist, and both Ms. Smith and I try to do it positively (e.g., "Johnny, remember our rules about politeness in class. I need you to do your own work at this time"). Sometimes when I'm sick of it, I'll be stronger in my correction ("Johnny, stop insulting/pestering Billy. Mind your business, which is your work"). I never know which correction will or won't work. He seems fairly oblivious to my interventions.

Are there known health issues that could be affecting his behavior? He seems physically healthy. Vision and hearing are apparently OK. The nurse has tried to get

(*continues*)

Figure 6.2 *continued*

a more detailed history, but Mrs. BeGood just says there is nothing wrong with him, and refuses to answer more detailed questions. Certainly (I believe) he is emotionally unhealthy.

What are some desired reinforcers for this student? Free time works somewhat, but he usually winds up losing it because he uses it unwisely. He seems not to know what to do with himself if he isn't commanding attention by being a nuisance. Teacher has tried stickers, points toward bigger prizes (models, Pokemon cards), but he has earned these only once, and he didn't seem impressed by it. He usually seems to like positive attention. At times, he tells us to "get lost" when we give him verbal reinforcement.

What is the function of the behavior? What is the student trying to get or avoid? Teacher believes he's trying to get attention. We also believe he's trying to avoid doing schoolwork, except math. I think he's seeking power, or maybe revenge. I don't know what for.

What are the desired replacement behaviors? Compliance to task requests; nonhostile behavior toward others; increase in academic output.

Under what conditions/situations are replacement behaviors exhibited? When and where does the student behave well? He's at his best during math. He'll stop provoking (sometimes) when teachers request it. He'll sometimes stop if he gets no reaction from the others.

What has been successful in managing (i.e., replacing) the target behavior(s)? Nothing has been really successful. Perhaps a full day of math would help!? So far, nothing has worked really well.

What has been unsuccessful? Pretty much everything listed above. Success is slippery with him. Sometimes Mr. Johnson thinks he's done or said something that gets to him, but then it doesn't seem to work the next day.

Have there been any recent changes in the school or home environment, daily schedule, medications, and so on? The home environment is characterized by inconsistent discipline; threats are common, as is ignoring deviant behavior, as reported by Mrs. BeGood. Mr. Johnson reports little follow-through regarding schoolwork or notes home. He's not on any medications we know about.

Describe the behavior of others that may be influencing the student's behavior. Other than that of his parents (see above), we don't know what it is. His peers try to avoid him. Could that be it?

Other comments or ideas about the nature or causes of the target behavior(s). Johnny is a very unhappy boy. He has a large chip on his shoulder. He feels responsible to no one, especially when he is upset.

ACTIVITY 6.12

Discuss the functional assessment conducted on Johnny BeGood (Figure 6.2). Answer the following questions:

What are some antecedents to Johnny's behavior?

What consequences are presently operating?

What are some likely functions of Johnny's behavior?

What strategies and supports should the teacher/school/home implement in order to improve Johnny's behavior?

Develop a positive behavioral intervention plan that will address Johnny's needs in the least restrictive environment.

The next section discusses the various diagnostic methods used in *behavioral assessment*, such as charting methods, rating scales, self-report questionnaires, and interviews of teachers and parents.

Charting Methods

When the consultant agrees to observe a particular student or to have someone else do the observation, she needs to obtain a fairly comprehensive description of the behaviors of concern from the teacher. Variables to consider include the type of behavior, frequency, setting events (when it occurs, under what conditions, and so on), duration, intensity, and any other information that will help the observer know what to look for (Alberto & Troutman, 1999; Shapiro and Kratochwill, 2000; Walker & Shea, 1999). The consultant will often need to assist a teacher in carefully defining behaviors of concern. Some teachers have a difficult time being "behavioral"; they tend to describe their concerns in terms of value judgments (such as "bad," "disruptive," or "provocative") rather than in terms of observable actions.

There is a wide literature on methods of recording (charting) data as it occurs in the classroom or playground (Alberto & Troutman, 1999; Alessi & Kaye, 1983; Kratochwill, 1982; Reynolds & Kamphaus, 1992; Skinner, Rhymer, & McDaniel, 2000). Alessi and Kaye (1983) have provided a videotape to accompany their manual. It demonstrates a method for making inter-individual student comparisons (that is, comparing a targeted, referred student to others in the same class or setting) rather than the traditional intra-individual comparisons (in which a targeted student continually serves as his own comparison subject). Alessi (1988) points out that there may be some validity problems with inter-individual analyses, such as observing the students while they are behaving well, not getting a valid description of the behaviors of concern from the teacher, and selecting as a comparison student another student who may have problems similar to those of the student referred but who hasn't been identified by the teacher for a wide variety of reasons.

ACTIVITY 6.13

A teacher asks you to observe a girl in her seventh-grade class who she says is aggressive. What questions might you ask the teacher to help clarify what she means by *aggressive?* Your goal should be to convert what may be a value judgment into a set of observable behaviors.

ACTIVITY 6.14

In pairs of two, have one partner play the role of a teacher who has referred a student for what he calls excessive disruptiveness. The other partner plays the role of the consultant, who tries to get the teacher to be specific about the behavior of concern and to get answers to questions about possible antecedents and consequents, including classroom dynamics and results of interventions the teacher has tried.

The most common method of charting behavior is probably *event recording.* Here the observer has determined in advance what the behaviors of concern are and then indicates with a mark on a predesigned form every occurrence of them for a specified period of time. It is also necessary to record duration if they are continuous behaviors in which length of time is an important variable, as in tantrums or time on task. A rate of occurrence can be computed by dividing the number of times the behavior occurred (for discrete behaviors such as cursing) or the total length of time the behaviors occurred (as with tantrums) by the length of the observation period. This provides data against which you can compare treatment effects. When the observer is using the inter-individual comparison method discussed previously (Alessi & Kaye, 1983), computing a rate of occurrence allows him to compare two or more nontarget students with the target student. Figure 6.3 shows a typical event recording form with tallies indicating the occurrence of discrete behaviors and time periods during which continuous behaviors occurred.

Naturally, forms could be designed with multiple behaviors listed. Alberto and Troutman (1999) and Hintze and Shapiro (1995) give examples of forms that allow for a variety of event recording purposes.

Time sampling is a special case of event recording in which the observer records behaviors if they occur during specified brief periods of time. For example, the observer would note that a behavior occurred if it did so at least once during a specified 15-second interval, using the following 5 seconds to record the note on the form. This process would continue for a given length of time, possibly a half hour, during the same period of time each day for two weeks or so. The student observation system form included in the BASC system (Reynolds & Kamphaus, 1992) uses a time-sampling method; it was previously described in Chapter 5.

Figure 6.3

Event recording form

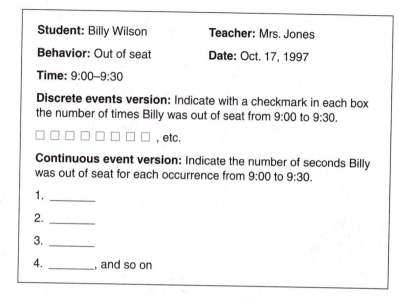

Further refinements in recording behaviors can be found in Alberto and Trout-man (1999), Sattler (2001a), Shapiro and Kratochwill (2000), Sugai and Tindal (1993), and Sulzer-Azaroff and Mayer (1986). Some of these methods require sophisticated approaches and the availability of personnel whose only responsibility is to record behaviors, but most can be adapted for use by a teacher or aide.

The reality in the public schools is that ordinarily there is no one available to do extensive or sophisticated behavior charting. The three people with the interest and potential sophistication to do this sort of work are the teacher, the teacher's aide (presuming the existence of such a person, a rarity in general education classes), and the school consultant. As I have mentioned, all three persons are busy and cannot devote sole attention to specific disruptive students in order to accurately tally their behaviors and the behaviors of the teachers. The best we can usually hope for is that the teacher or aide will maintain some sort of tally sheet and will make a conscientious effort to tally behavior for at least brief periods of the day. As potentially unscientific as this may be, it is better than nothing. In my experience as a school consultant, I have often assisted teachers by showing them how to tally behaviors, but rarely have I had the time to sit in a classroom on a regular basis and record behaviors. Often teachers tire of this data-gathering activity after a few days, especially if they are tallying behaviors to gather baseline information. Teachers want to get on with the interventions and deal with the behaviors rather than count what they feel they already know exists. The consultant has to decide in each case how best to deal with these potential problems.

These realities, among others, mean that trying to do behavior modification in the classroom is not simple. Your results may not be as scientifically defensible as those in the journals devoted to tightly controlled studies (for example, the *Journal of Applied Behavior Analysis*). The authors of articles in this and other journals usually have a staff of graduate students to act as observers/recorders in the classrooms in which their experiments take place. However, knowing this limitation should not deter us from doing what we can. Clearly, somewhat imperfect data are better than no data at all as long as the imperfect data are not invalid.

The consultant's role isn't the same as the scientist's. The consultant has the more mundane, but crucial, responsibility of helping teachers deal with complicated situations in ways that enhance the school experience for all the students in the class. In the process, the consultant may have to leave some of the niceties of experimental rigor to those with the resources to do so.

ACTIVITY 6.15

Take a behavioral description from a teacher and then construct a charting method based on the teacher's concerns. To make this chart useful for classroom observation, be sure that it has clear definitions of the behaviors of concern, a method for recording each incidence and length of the behavioral episodes (if appropriate to the referral concern), time of day when behaviors occur, and a method for indicating probable antecedents and consequences to the behavior. Also, indicate possible replacement behaviors and a method for recording them. Figure 6.4 gives an example of such a chart, which was custom-designed for a given situation. Describe the behaviors of concern, a recording method, possible antecedents, consequences, the student's reaction to consequences, and other relevant information.

Rating Scales

Another method for determining the type and severity of behavior problems is to have the teacher or parent fill out a rating scale. Several examples include the Child Behavior Checklist (CBC) (Achenbach, 1991a; Martin, Hooper, & Snow, 1986), the Teacher's Report Form (Achenbach, 1991b), the Behavior Disorders Identification Scale (Wright, 1988b), the Emotional or Behavioral Disorder Scale (McCarney, 1992), the Connors Teacher Rating Scale (Connors, 1997), the Behavior Assessment System for Children (Reynolds & Kamphaus, 1992), the Children's Attention and Adjustment Survey (Lambert, Hartsough, & Sandoval, 1990), the Devereux Behavior Rating Scale (Naglieri, LeBuffe, & Pfeiffer, 1993), and the Revised Behavior Problem Checklist (Quay & Peterson, 1996). These scales provide a basis for determining behaviors on which to focus. The rater judges the student's behavior according to the separate items and rates the student on a three-, five-, or seven-point Likert-type scale, depending on the severity of the behavior.

For example, an item on the Behavior Disorders Identification Scale (Wright, 1988b) is "[student] becomes upset when a suggestion or constructive criticism is given." The teacher (rater) indicates the extent to which this behavior is exhibited

Figure 6.4

Event sampling, with examples

Behavior 1: off task, defined as no apparent progress toward assigned task for at least one minute

Time: 9:04

Possible antecedents: reading; he seemed bored

Consequences: teacher prompt

Student's reaction: brief return to reading

Other information: teacher kept track of number of prompts

Possible replacement behavior: Time on task, defined as number of words read or questions answered

Behavior 2: rude verbal comments, defined as comments made to others with the apparent purpose of upsetting them

Time: 9:18

Possible antecedents: Chang bumped him

Consequences: reminder to desist by teacher

Student's reaction: blamed Chang; told teacher to watch Chang instead of him

Other information: conflict has been growing for a few weeks

Possible replacement behaviors: increase in prosocial statements to peers

Note: In regard to behavior 2, rude verbal comments, there will be an escalating set of consequences. Student will be given a reminder to desist from this behavior the first time it occurs. The second time it occurs, the student will be required to meet with the teacher after school to complete a writing task. The third time it happens, the student will be sent to the principal's office and assigned to detention. For each half day of no rude comments to others, the teacher may provide a check mark and a positive comment. Check marks may be turned into a material or activity reinforcer after a predetermined number of points have been accumulated.

---

by giving from one point ("Behavior not exhibited in my presence") to seven points ("Behavior occurs more than once per hour"). In this way, the consultant gets a good idea of the behaviors of concern and their severity. Having more than one teacher rate the child (when appropriate) gives an idea of the situational specificity of the behaviors: A disruptive or withdrawn student may be showing different patterns of behaviors in different settings. This particular instrument also has a home version (Wright, 1988a). There are numerous other home-based rating scales available, such as the Child Behavior Checklist, Parent's Report Form (Achenbach, 1991a), the Connors Parent Rating Scale (Connors, 1997), a section of the Behavior Assessment System for Children (Reynolds & Kamphaus, 1992), and the Children's Attention and Adjustment Survey (Lambert et al., 1990).

Scales specialized for particular diagnostic categories, such as social skills and ADHD, have also been developed. The Social Skills Rating System (Gresham & Elliott, 1990) measures five social behaviors (cooperation, assertion, responsibility, empathy, and self-control) along with three problem behaviors (externalizing, internalizing, and hyperactivity). There are forms for the parent, the teacher, and the referred student to fill out. The social behaviors are measured on a three-point scale of frequency and importance; the problem behaviors are measured on frequency only. Another rating scale used for social skills measurement is the Walker-McConnell Scale of Social Competence and School Adjustment (Walker & McConnell, 1995), which is connected to a social skills training program developed by Walker, Todis, Holmes, and Horton (1995). Another choice is the Matson Evaluation of Social Skills with Youngsters (MESSY) (Matson, Ratatori, & Helsel, 1983). This has both self-report and parent/teacher forms. Other available rating scales include the Attention Deficit Disorders Evaluation Scale—School Version (McCarney, 1995), the SNAP Rating Scale (Atkins, Pelham, & Light, 1985), and subscales of the instruments already mentioned (e.g. the Child Behavior Checklist and the Quay-Peterson).

As handy and seemingly valid as these rating scales are, there are some disadvantages to their use (McConaughy & Ritter, 1995; Martin et al., 1986; Merrill, 1999). First, the rater may be biased one way or another, and this can affect the way in which he rates the child. Second, it is common for persons reviewing a rating scale or checklist to focus on certain items that seem very important. Remember that individual items usually do not have high reliability, especially when compared to that of the whole test. Given these possible limitations, it is best to use these scales only in conjunction with the other diagnostic methods discussed in this chapter.

Self-Report Rating Scales   The rating scales just discussed are all filled out by an informant other than the target student, usually a teacher or parent. It is often very useful to have the student complete one or two of the numerous self-report instruments that are available. As with all structured instruments used in assessment, the consultant has to be aware of the psychometric and developmental characteristics of these instruments. Developmentally immature youngsters may not be able to either read or understand the meaning of the items. Further, they may respond defensively rather than admit to certain behaviors or thoughts. With these caveats in mind, the consultant may have the student fill out a self-report questionnaire and then compare the results to other sources of information. The consultant might also use the student's responses to generate discussion about how the student perceives situations. These discussions might best be conducted by school counselors or school psychologists.

Among the instruments that have respectable norming data are the Children's Personality Questionnaire (Porter & Cattell, 1979); the MMPI (Hathaway & Monachesi, 1963); the Millon Adolescent Personality Inventory (Millon, Green, & Meagher, 1982); the Children's Behavior Checklist, Youth Self-Report Form (Achenbach, 1991c); the Behavior Rating Profile (Brown & Hammill, 1990); the Revised Children's Manifest Anxiety Scale (Reynolds & Richmond, 1985), the Children's Depression

Inventory (Kovacs, 1992); the Self-Esteem Inventory (Coopersmith, 1984), the Piers-Harris Self-Concept Scale (Piers, 1996); the Reynolds Adolescent Adjustment Screening Inventory (Reynolds, 2001); the Reynolds Adolescent Psychopathology Scale (Reynolds, 1998); the Behavior Assessment System for Children (Reynolds & Kamphaus, 1992); and the Children's Inventory of Anger (Nelson & Finch, 1973).

On these self-report scales, the student typically responds either "yes" or "no" or in some Likert-like manner. A recent review of 36 self-report instruments is available in Witt, Heffer, and Pfeiffer (1990). Merrill (1999) also provides a review of many of these instruments.

Classroom Observations

A most valuable assessment method is observation of the behaviors in the classroom or playground as they occur. Chapter 5 has a section on methods for conducting classroom observations, which is step 3 of the SOCS.

Interviews

The art of interviewing requires all the skills discussed in Chapter 3 and presented in further depth by Benjamin (1987), Egan (1994), Lentz and Wehmann (1995), Merrill (1999), and Sattler (1998). I cannot overstress the need to be an effective interviewer in order to be successful as a school consultant. What happens during the interview, both in terms of information transmission and interpersonal bonding between the consultant and the consultee, provides the foundation on which consultation rests. Kratochwill, Van Someren, and Sheridan (1989) have developed a competency-based model for training school-based consultants in the interview skills that are necessary in order to function in a behavioral model of consultation.

There are three primary sources of interview data: the teacher(s), the parent, and the referred student. The consultant may interview all three concerned personnel, depending on the case and time availability. Certainly the most concerned teacher(s) should be interviewed, as should the parents. The amount of time devoted to the parent interview depends somewhat on the age of the student; the younger the student, the more necessary it is to involve the parent in the assessment and treatment process. Interviewing the student can be very useful in terms of understanding her perspective, discussing antecedents and consequences to her behaviors, getting to know her self-perceptions, and reviewing possible reinforcers.

Teacher Interview Step 5 of the SOCS in Chapter 5 deals briefly with the initial discussion (interview) with the teacher, which may occur either before or during an SST meeting, and step 9 of the SOCS reviews ongoing case monitoring efforts, which are largely interview-centered. Rating scales, discussed previously, may be used during an interview, with the rating scale constituting an outline and data-recording system for the interview.

When it becomes clear that you need to interview the teacher(s) about a student who presents with a behavior problem, it is useful to consider at the least the following:

1. What is the problem?
2. What do I want to know?
3. How can I get the most out of the interview?
4. What can I do to make the teacher believe that the interview was worthwhile?

Basic information about the problem has probably come to you in some abbreviated way through the use of a referral form, directed either to you or to the SST. The following are typical questions/comments that the consultant might use in order to elicit information about the problems and classroom context in which they occur:

- Tell me more about your concerns about the student.
- Give me an example of this behavior. What is it like, typically? Who else is involved in it?
- What seems to bring it on? What causes it? What circumstances are occurring when it happens?
- What do you typically do when it occurs? What has been your response in the past and currently? What is the response of the other students? What has been the result of these responses?
- You've described settings in which it occurs. Are there times when it does not occur in the same settings? If so, what seems to determine whether or not it occurs?
- What is your goal with this student and these behaviors? How do you want this student to behave? (This may seem like an odd question. Won't the consultee always say, "Like she should; like the other students"? Or "I want her to stop acting this way and start acting like she should"? If the consultee responds in this fashion, tell him that the purpose of the question was to give the two of you a goal for this student. How do the two of you want this student to behave? In other words, what behaviors of the student will you reinforce, and what behaviors will you ignore or discourage?)
- Given what you know about this behavior and what you've tried up to now, what do you believe would be a good approach to take at this time? What do you believe is the best thing to do at this time?

Be aware that when teachers are asked these questions they may come up with one of two responses other than what you intended. The first is an attempt to put the burden on you to solve the problem unilaterally—for example, "That's why I referred the student to you. What do you think I should do?" The implication here is that you are the expert and the teacher will do whatever you tell her, or will at least consider it. The second type of response is designed to put the problem in somebody else's lap by requesting that the student be referred to special education (assuming that the student is not already identified as a student with a disability) or at least be removed a few hours a week for counseling. In this case the teacher sees you as the gatekeeper who needs to be convinced that the student's behavior is so difficult that only special education (or counseling) can deal with it. In both cases it is important to keep the focus on the consultee and the student as a part of the classroom. The simulated conversation between a teacher and a consultant presented in Chapter 3 gives an example of how a consultant can encourage this focus. The cases in Chapters 7 and 9 also contain examples of how the consultant can deal with these sorts of reactions, which will remain common as long as the teachers with whom you are working see you as either an expert or a gatekeeper. Consultants who stress a collaborative approach to problem solving will notice a decrease in this sort of dependency as their style becomes familiar to the teachers with whom they consult (Allen & Graden, 1995; Davison, 1990; Friend & Cook, 2000). Chapter 3 discusses teacher responses that indicate resistance to the consultation process and ways of dealing with this resistance.

Parent Interview   Other than a call from the school to report that their child has been injured, there is probably no phone call parents fear more than the one that says that their child is causing serious behavior problems. The usual message that follows is that the parents need to talk to their child about it, come to the school to discuss it, or allow school personnel to come to their home to discuss it.

This phone call (or written note) causes a number of different reactions among parents. School personnel need to be aware of the following possible reactions:

1.   *Anger.*   The parents may be angry at their child, at the school, or at the teacher in particular. They may also project blame onto others, often onto other students, or even accuse the teacher (directly or indirectly) of poor teaching or inadequate behavior management.

2.   *Denial.*   The parents may simply deny that there is a problem or try to minimize it, attempting to convince you that it's a temporary thing and will soon go away, even though it may have been noted for years.

3.   *Acceptance.*   Here the parents are well aware of the disruptions their child causes, they agree that these problems are serious, and they want to know what they can do to help. Obviously this is the reaction the teacher or the consultant is hoping for, but it may take some time to appear.

Parents naturally tend to be protective of their children. The goal of school personnel is to work with this tendency, to use it to their advantage by projecting the impression that they, too, are on the side of the child and that they want to work as a team with parents to develop their child's strengths and ability to interact well with others in the classroom.

When either anger or denial is predominant, you need to approach a parent in the same way a counselor does when faced with an angry or confrontive student:

stay calm, don't take the reaction personally, be a good listener, reflect feelings, and take time to develop rapport (Benjamin, 1987). Confrontation early in the proceedings will only strengthen the parents' defenses; arguing leads to a win-win mentality that stifles the give-and-take that is often necessary in the beginning stages of an interview with a defensive person.

ACTIVITY 6.16

In dyads, one person plays the part of a teacher calling a parent about his child's disruptive behavior. The other person plays the part of the parent, who acts defiant or hostile to the teacher.

In a second scenario (partners switch roles), the parent maintains a denial position; he asserts that his child would not engage in such behavior and that the teacher must be mistaken.

Teachers and consultants need to have a plan in mind before the parents are called or interviewed face to face. They need to have their facts well organized and must be in a positive, helpful frame of mind. This is not always easy, especially for the teacher who has just finished a difficult day with the target student. Here are some issues to think through and plan for before dialing the parents or meeting with them after school, along with some strategies for keeping the interview positive and problem-centered.

1.   Explain your reason for concern. After spending a few moments building rapport, which always includes some comments about the target student's strengths, the consultee (or the consultant) will spell out the behaviors that need to be discussed. Keep your discussion of both the strengths and the behaviors of concern objective and data-oriented. This impresses the parent positively and indicates a professional approach to observation of the child.

2.   Review efforts made to deal with the problem. Tell the parent what school personnel have tried and what results they have had. Generally, you haven't had good results; otherwise, you probably wouldn't be having this interview. Try, however, to indicate some areas of improvement in order to set a positive tone for the discussion.

3.   Ask for the parent's opinion of the situation. Does she see this behavior at home? What does she think causes it? What does she (or would she) do about it at home?

4.   At this point you may ask the parent what she thinks the school ought to do about the behavior, or you can suggest a plan for discussion. Remember the suggestion that was presented in Chapter 3: Your goal is to get an agreement, not to win an argument. Try not to debate with the parent about every point in your plan; be ready to compromise on small points in order to develop a plan both of you can agree on. Think of the discussion as "win-win" in purpose. Negotiate toward yes

(Fisher & Brown, 1988; Fisher & Ury, 1981). Strive to achieve Gordon's (1974) Method III ("no lose") results.

5. Having arrived at some goal-oriented, positive plan that involves action on the part of the school and the home, summarize it to see if there are any further questions or comments that the parent wishes to make. Then set a date when you will call the parent to review the plan, usually in a week or so. Of course, be sure to follow through on this promise.

ACTIVITY 6.17

It is worthwhile to do many role plays of parent–consultant interviews. As a group, discuss the kinds of situations that could come up during a parent interview, review possible strategies for dealing with them, and then take turns role playing these situations. Also, practice with three persons involved: the teacher, the parent, and the consultant.

Further information about the communication skills necessary to interview parents are contained in Chapters 3 and 5. Procedures for interviewing students are discussed later in this chapter in the section on communication methods.

DETERMINING PRIORITIES FOR INTERVENTION

It is common for a teacher to refer a student for a wide variety of behavior problems. Students with behavior problems are rarely displaying only one circumscribed behavior of concern. Depending on the circumstances, it may be best, at least at first, to only work on certain behaviors rather than all the concerns the teacher has expressed. Prioritizing which behaviors to work on is a necessary early step in the consultation process. Cooper, Heron, and Heward (1987) list nine factors that should be considered when prioritizing target behaviors. The consultant should determine:

1. If the behavior is of danger to the individual or to others.
2. If the frequency of the behavior or, in the case of a new behavior, the opportunities to use the behavior warrant intervention.
3. The duration of the problem or, in the case of a new behavior, how long the individual's need for the new behavior has existed.
4. If the behavior will produce a higher level of reinforcement for the individual than other behaviors under consideration. Generally, behaviors that produce a high level of reinforcement take priority over behaviors that produce a low level of reinforcement.
5. The impact of the behavior on the individual's skill development and independence.

6. If learning the (substitute) behavior will reduce the negative attention that the individual receives.

7. If learning the (substitute) behavior will increase reinforcement for others in the individual's environment.

8. The difficulty (time and energy) to be expended to change the behavior.

9. The cost involved in changing the behavior.

It is not always easy to determine what should be involved in the conceptualization of these factors, particularly in the early stages of discussing and observing the target behaviors. Among the variables that make certitude difficult are the behaviors of the other students (Do they wittingly or unwittingly provide reinforcement for the problem behaviors?), the ability and willingness of the teacher to implement change; the strength of the behaviors (that is, the value that the student ascribes to these behaviors in her efforts to either obtain reinforcers or avoid aversive situations, or in her belief that these behaviors will support her self-concept and self-perceived role in the classroom), and the degree of parental and cultural support for the desired change.

The decision about which behaviors to focus on and how to prioritize your efforts should be the result of a discussion between you, as the consultant, and the teacher, with input from the student's parents and others (e.g., SST) as appropriate. Consultants always need to remember that the consultee will be doing most of the in-class intervention work; therefore, the consultee should take the lead in determining priorities for that setting. The consultant, however, should determine priorities for other settings, such as parent work, the need for medical intervention, school-based counseling, or other outside referrals.

It may be best, depending on the situation, to delay the determination of priorities until the consultant has interviewed the consultee, observed the behaviors of concern, and gathered information through the charting methods or rating scales previously discussed.

GENERAL IDEAS FOR MODIFYING CLASSROOM BEHAVIOR

This section presents some ideas that consultants should be aware of when consulting about students who demonstrate inappropriate classroom behavior. This information is relatively brief and is intended only to outline general notions that can be adapted to particular cases. Interested readers can find a wide array of literature in this area, much of which is indicated in this chapter's references. This discussion is limited to classroom rules, contingency management, contracting, non-contingency related interventions, social skills training, communication methods, and general comments.

Classroom Rules

It is a truism that no one has taught school for more than ten minutes without recognizing the need for rules to govern the classroom. All experienced teachers have a set of rules, which are usually characterized by the following:

1. They are brief, both in the way each one is written and in the total number of rules.
2. They are usually positive.
3. They are reasonable.
4. They are clear and are usually behaviorally stated.
5. They are capable of being enforced in a firm, fair, and consistent manner.

Alberto and Troutman (1999) suggest the following "rules about rules":

1. Be specific about what is expected.
2. Make as few rules as possible.
3. Be explicit about the relationship between rules and consequences (p. 466).

Sulzer-Azaroff and Mayer (1986) have provided some additional guidelines for developing classroom rules. They also give examples of negatively stated classroom rules and some positive alternatives to each one. Here are three:

Negative: Don't be late to class.
Positive: Be in your seat *when the tardy* bell rings.

Negative: Don't waste time.
Positive: Complete your assignments on time.

Negative: Don't touch, hit, or kick others or throw objects.
Positive: Keep your hands, feet, and objects to yourself.

Typical examples of positive rules include the following, which were found on the front wall of a third-grade class:

1. Be polite to each other.
2. Be prepared to follow directions and do your best work.
3. Leave your seat only for schoolwork purposes.
4. Respect everybody's property.

ACTIVITY 6.18

In small groups, discuss methods for establishing classroom rules. Have a group devise appropriate rules for primary, middle, junior high, and senior high classes. Review these in light of the criteria for the development of the class rules just given.

Some teachers have a set of rules that they have found to be effective, and they simply announce them the first day of class. Sometimes they give examples of what the rules mean and rehearse examples of their meaning and violations of them. Other teachers believe that students should assist in developing their own class rules. While helping the students to make up their own rules, teachers may subtly direct the students' thinking toward rules they have already considered or previously used. In this way the students feel that they have had a voice in the development of the rules, and the teachers succeed in getting the rules they feel comfortable with.

Rules need to be accompanied by consequences. These can also be stated in writing, although this is not common; teachers often prefer to be able to establish consequences depending on the factors surrounding each rule infraction, a practice that can, unfortunately, lead to inconsistency and bias. Here is a set of rules followed by a brief list of examples of violations and a set of predetermined consequences:

Rule	Examples of Violations	Consequences
Be polite	Hitting, pushing, saying mean things	Teacher reprimand, time out, loss of recess
Be prepared to follow directions and do your best work	Not paying attention, turning in poor work	Being asked to repeat directions

Kampwirth (1988) has suggested a list of interventions for rule violations, ranging from mild through moderate, severe, and profound in the degree of intrusiveness. As a general rule, the mildest interventions should be used until it is clear that something more intrusive needs to be tried. Sprick and Howard (1995) have presented a list of 100 behavior problems, with 500 plans for solving them. Their method is to start with the simplest plan to use and then escalate the degree of involvement as the problem proves to be more difficult.

ACTIVITY 6.19

In small groups, arranged according to grade levels from preschool through high school, design lists of consequences that range from the mildest to the most severe. Review each group's list, noting the different consequences that are believed to be appropriate at the different grade levels. A sequenced set of activities for dealing with behavior problems, called the "BEST" procedure, is presented at the end of this chapter. "BEST" is an acronym for Basic, Elaborated, Serious, and Total School.

The school-based consultant needs to be aware of the rules the consultee is using and how they are being enforced. Some behavior problems are the result of inappropriate rules or inconsistently enforced rules. This latter problem is especially possible and troublesome in overcrowded classrooms where there are a number of students exhibiting behavior problems simultaneously. Consultees may need help in thinking through their rules and applications. Some students need to know that the rules are meant for them; sometimes a review of the rules with the consultee and the student done in the context of the communication (conference) methods discussed below can clarify misunderstandings.

Contingency Management

Contingency management refers to the application of the ABC model of behavioral sequences. The *A* stands for "antecedents"—those behaviors, situations, or events that precede, and are presumed to be causally related to, the *B* ("behavior") that follows them. This behavior is the overt act that the actor or others can judge to be positive, neutral, or negative in effect. The *C* stands for "consequence," the stimulus that follows the behavior in time. It can be positive, neutral, or negative (aversive) from the perspective of either the student who engages in the target behavior or those in the environment who react to it, such as a teacher, a parent, or peers. Of course, a consequence may occur from natural circumstances: if a child kicks a chair, she may get a broken toe; this is what Dreikurs (1968) calls a natural consequence.

As simple as the ABC conceptualization may sound on the surface, further study indicates that it can be very complex. It is not always easy to determine which kind or combination of antecedents may be prompting the behaviors we see, which is why a functional assessment needs to be done. The consultant needs to gather information about a given student from a wide variety of sources in order to accurately determine what the antecedents and consequences may be. Steps 2, 3, and 4 of the SOCS process (discussed in Chapter 5), consisting of interviewing and observing, are the keys to determining antecedents, consequences, and the purposes of the student's behavior.

Another way to conceptualize the nature of contingency management in the classroom is in terms of the "if . . . then" rules that the teacher has established: When a student engages in a target behavior, a certain contingency will apply. This implies that there are classroom rules and preestablished, usually negative, consequences for students who fail to obey the rules. Conversely, there are positive consequences for appropriate prosocial behavior. Grading systems are commonly built on "if . . . then" propositions, although they may not be explicitly spelled out. Contingencies tend to be more explicit in special education classrooms because the students in these classes usually need the structure of knowing exactly what the consequences for their behavior, either positive or aversive, will be. Here are some examples of contingency management:

Ms. Rivera has noticed that her fourth-grade students start getting noisy and more active as recess approaches. This behavior has been increasing over the last week. Ms. Rivera tells her students that she has noticed the increase, gives examples of what she means, elicits examples from the students, and then tells them that she will delay their recess for two minutes if she notices it again. She has to apply this contingency only once during the following week; the students are no longer behaving inappropriately before recess.

Mr. Smith, a junior high shop teacher, has decided to modify his grading procedures to emphasize neatness in the work space. He tells his students that every now and again he will give a signal, which means that all students should back away from their work stations and projects while he walks through the classroom giving bonus points to those students who have a neat work area and deducting points for a messy area. After he has done this twice, only one boy persists in being messy, and Mr. Smith counsels with him individually. This contingency change has produced a positive effect.

Mrs. Mellow, who teaches a senior high advanced English class, has decided to talk with her students about their apparent boredom and the carelessness in some of their assignments. Her students give her some ideas about ways to make the class materials and discussion more interesting, including a greater effort to relate the older plays and stories they are studying to contemporary problems. She gives each of the three groups the challenge of modifying Shakespeare's *Richard III* to make it more contemporary. Each group should develop its own modifications. Also, students agree as a class to determine the criteria for grading each other's efforts. These changed contingencies regarding student involvement result in a very lively set of activities that make *Richard III* come alive for these bright seniors.

These examples could be multiplied a hundredfold by those who study classroom practices (Cooper, 1999; Metcalf, 1999). The consultant needs to study the contingency practices of teachers who have excellent classes as well as those who have difficulty with behavior management and motivation. One of the goals of observing a class in action should be trying to find ways in which the teacher may be better able to manage the behavior and instructional presentation to enhance learning and improve the socioemotional climate of the room. The Student Observation System from the BASC (Reynolds & Kamphaus, 1992) and the TIES-II (Ysseldyke & Christenson, 1993) would be good starting points to give direction to classroom observation relative to a consultee's use of contingency management, as well as many other aspects of student and teacher behaviors.

Contracting

A contract is a specific form of a contingency management system, an agreement between a teacher or parent and a student that is based on the "if . . . then" proposition mentioned above. In a simple contract, the consultee may say to a student, "If you finish your work, then you can go outside." If the student agrees to this statement, the contract exists. If the student does not agree, no contract has been made since contracting implies mutual agreement. Teachers base most behavior management on a rather informal style of contracting. They often make "if . . . then" statements, though they do not always ask for, or expect, any verbal agreement from the students. Agreement is often assumed since the teacher, operating as a benevolent autocrat, as most teachers do, is giving a directive that he expects students to follow.

Teachers are often bothered by the fact that a referred student doesn't follow the implicit contracts that the teacher has been establishing. Because uncooperative students usually do not follow implicit contracts, they may need more explicit contracts that involve more than verbal statements or apparent verbal agreement; the agreement may need to be in writing.

Consultants are often asked to help consultees write contracts until the consultees develop some experience with them. This is an appropriate task for a school-based consultant and one she should welcome, particularly with an inexperienced teacher or a parent. Here are some general guidelines for establishing formal (written, explicit) contracts:

1. Keep the contract simple. It should be no more complicated or cumbersome than necessary. Most abandoned contracts met that fate because they were too time- or cost-intensive for the consultee.

2. Tasks and rewards need to be very specific. Spell out exactly what the student is to do, or stop doing, and exactly what the consequences will be.

3. Specify time constraints; for example, when will the contract go into effect, how long will it last, and when must an assignment be completed?

4. Avoid tasks that are too difficult for the student. At first, it is a good idea to make the contract easy for the student to fulfill. In that way the student will become attracted to the idea of contracting; then you can escalate the expectations.

5. Formal contracts are signed by both parties and often witnessed by another teacher, the consultant, the parent, or the principal.

6. Be prepared to have some students fail to carry out the contract. Discuss the reasons for failure with the student and then try again.

Homme (1970) describes a method of transferring control of the contract from the consultee to the student over a period of time. When this occurs, the student tends to become more involved in the contract because she owns more responsibility for it. More details about writing effective contracts can be found in Homme (1970), Gallagher (1988), Krumboltz and Thoresen (1969), and Walker and Shea (1999). Kaplan and Hoffman (1990) have produced a book with many examples of contracts that are visually appealing to students. Figure 6.5 gives an example of a contract written for a fifth-grade girl designed to increase her use of prosocial comments to other students.

Non–Contingency-Related Interventions

Most of the previous discussion regarding behavior problem intervention has been presented from a behavioral point of view because most of the behavior change literature is presented from that perspective and most research data have been provided by the behavioral school (Bergan, 1977; Bergan & Kratochwill, 1990). This is not to say that other perspectives have no use and should be discounted. The literature contains numerous references to behavior change procedures that have nothing to do with behavior modification as such (Charles, 1999; Hyman, 1997; Kanfer &

Figure 6.5

Behavior contract between a student and a teacher

```
AGREEMENT

Here's a good deal for both of us!!

Ms. Portelo (teacher) agrees to give Sylvia (student) one bonus point for each time
Ms. Portelo hears Sylvia make a positive comment to another student. Sylvia can
earn up to four bonus points per day for this behavior. Good luck, Sylvia!!

This contract begins on: December 11, 2001 at 9:00 a.m.

This contract will be reviewed on: December 20, 2001 at 2:30 p.m.

Signed: _____
        MRS. PORTELO        SYLVIA        SYLVIA'S MOM        DATE
```

Goldstein, 1986; Walker & Shea, 1999). These can be classified as psychodynamic (counseling, including the use of media such as puppets, art, and music), ecological (changing situations or events within the client's environment, either within or outside the classroom), or biophysical (medication, diet, or megavitamin therapy). Behaviorists may argue that many of these treatments have behavioral components: For example, changing an ecological component may be interpreted as antecedent manipulation; medication may be seen as an effort to treat symptoms only rather than some underlying cause. However, most people see them as distinctly different, primarily because they derive from a philosophical position that treats behaviors as symptoms of underlying disorders, not as the disorder itself, which is a hallmark of behavioral thinking (Ullmann & Krasner, 1965).

Social Skills Training

Over the past decade, researchers have become increasingly aware that deficits in social skills are correlated with behavior problems. Indeed, many behavior problems may be seen as symptomatic of a lack of social skills or a failure to apply them. Parker and Asher (1987) have found poor peer relations to be correlated with dropping out of school, crime, and the diagnoses of psychopathology. Some *DSM*-IV disruptive behavior categories may not be caused so much by internal psychopathologies as by failure to learn more appropriate behavior. Trower, Bryant, and Argyle (1978) have observed that psychiatric disorders such as anxiety, conduct disorder, personality disorder, and mood disorders are all characterized by limited or ineffective social skills.

Goldstein, Spafkin, Gershaw, and Klein (1983) list six general sets of social skills:

1. Beginning social skills (such as listening and saying "Thank you").
2. Advanced social skills (such as joining in constructively and apologizing).
3. Skills for dealing with feelings (such as expressing one's feelings and understanding the feelings of others).
4. Skill alternatives to aggression (such as negotiating and using self-control).
5. Skills for dealing with stress (such as getting ready for a potentially difficult situation and standing up for a friend).
6. Planning skills (such as gathering information and deciding what caused a problem).

A review of the nature of behavior problem referrals indicates that many of these problems are due either to a social skills acquisition deficit or to a social skills performance deficit. An *acquisition deficit* is the absence of, or failure to have learned, particular social skills, while a *performance deficit* is the failure to perform these skills at the right time and to an appropriate degree (Gresham, 1995).

Assessment instruments for the measurement of social skills are primarily rating scales, which I mentioned earlier in this chapter. Anecdotal records, as presented in Figure 6.3 as recordings of events, are useful for keeping track of specific examples of social skill deficits. Numerous sources of information and complete curricula in social skills training have recently been developed. Among the sources for this information are Walker et al. (1995), Elliott and Gresham (1992), and Goldstein (1999), whose *The Prepare Curriculum* consists of three major emphases: aggression reduction, stress reduction, and prejudice reduction. Magg (1992) has presented a useful model for integrating consultation service delivery into social skills training in the schools. Sheridan and Elliott (1991) describe how the behavioral model of consultation can be used in the assessment and treatment of social skills, and Colton and Sheridan (1998) demonstrated that a combination of conjoint (i.e., parents and teachers working together) behavioral consultation and social skills training improved the cooperative behavior of elementary-aged boys who were diagnosed with ADHD.

Communication (Conferencing) Methods

This group of methods is characterized by teachers' efforts to talk with students who present behavior problems about these behaviors, their effects, and their possible consequences. These methods also emphasize efforts to invite cooperation from these students. By using these relatively mild and unobtrusive techniques, teachers hope that they won't have to resort to any of the more serious consequences discussed in the sections on contracts and contingency management.

Consider this scenario. Jason, a sixth-grader, has been passing notes, whispering, and irritating others over the past few weeks. His teacher, Mr. Jacobs, has told him, in front of the whole class, to desist. This has had a temporary effect each time, but overall Jason's behavior problems are increasing. Mr. Jacobs decides he needs to conference with Jason about this situation. How should he do it?

This is another referral that school consultants should welcome. It gives the consultant a chance to assist a consultee at the primary and secondary prevention stages of problem solving rather than the tertiary stage, when the consultee has become very irritated with a student. Intervening at the earlier stages might cause the situation to de-escalate. Communication that can be effective at these stages often consists of the relatively benign methods explained by Ginott (1971), Gordon (1989), and Glasser (1990), and as the milder forms of interventions suggested by Sprick and Howard (1995).

Haim Ginott (1971), in *Teacher and Child,* points out that teachers need to exert self-discipline. Otherwise, they may create or escalate the negative interaction between themselves and the student. In other words, "When the children act like children, the adults need to act like adults." This is often easier said than done, particularly when a student's disruptiveness is spoiling the teacher's efforts to teach or when repeated requests of "Behave yourself" have been ignored. According to Ginott, teachers who have lost their self-discipline tend to attack the student instead of focusing on the behavior and its causes, demand rather than invite cooperation, deny students' feelings, use labels and other pejorative comments, lecture excessively, and ignore the student's opinions and feelings. Ginott emphasizes "sane messages" (statements that address the situation without attacking a student's character) and "congruent communications" (when the teacher's statements to a student match the student's feelings about the situation and about himself). In his various books, Ginott gives many examples of interactions between adults and students that exemplify his soft approach to inviting cooperation in the classroom.

Thomas Gordon's *Teacher Effectiveness Training* (1974) was an attempt to develop the concept of "win-win" discussions between teachers and students who were in dispute over some issue. Gordon discussed three methods of discussion. Method I was characterized by teacher domination: teacher wins, student loses. This is, unfortunately, probably the most common model in teacher–student conferences, particularly with difficult students. In this model, the teacher lays down the law, argues with the student if the student disagrees, and ends the discussion when the student indicates a willingness to comply. In Method II, the student subtly or overtly takes over the power position in the conversation, and the teacher gives in: student wins, teacher loses. This is especially likely to happen when teachers are confronted by aggressive students who have a threatening demeanor or by manipulative students who know how to get around the teacher's concerns, talk their way out of responsibility, and con the teacher. Students soon learn which teachers are vulnerable to a Method II attack.

In Methods I and II, power is the key ingredient. The teacher has it in I; the student has it in II. In Method III, the parties in a conflict-of-needs situation join together in a search for a solution that is acceptable to both given the confines of public school expectations. In this method, the teacher relies on I-messages and active listening. In an *I-message,* the teacher (or the student) states needs or perceptions of the situation. *Active listening* involves an interpretive process in which the listener (the teacher) tries to detect the emotion or feeling behind the student's statements and directs the student's response to these feelings as well as to the overt content of the message. When teachers do this, they defuse potential conflict, indicate to the students that they are interested in getting to the feelings behind the content, and thereby avoid the power-based interactions inherent in Methods I and II.

Gordon has analyzed communication patterns between parties, one of whom is ostensibly in charge (such as parents and teachers), the other of whom is in a subservient position (typically the student). He has identified 12 roadblocks to communication that authority figures often use to dominate, bully, condescend to, or simply infuriate the subservient person. (These were presented in Chapter 3.) Gordon's books are rich in examples of his techniques.

William Glasser, a psychiatrist, was originally trained in psychodynamic methods of understanding human socioemotional problems. He took a position at a California detention facility for girls and came to a conclusion that many of the young women with whom he worked lacked personal responsibility for their actions. He determined that they had made some bad choices and that it didn't do them or anybody else any good to blame other people or situations for their own behavior; they chose to act the way they did, which was why they were in trouble with the law. His earliest writings demonstrated methods of talking with individual students and whole classes. For example, Chapter 10 of *Schools Without Failure* (Glasser, 1969) presents a model for classwide discussions of problem situations based on a rational problem-solving method stressing individual responsibility and plan building. Glasser inferred that teachers were able to do this and were generally good at it.

In his later books, Glasser presents a different view of school life for students. He takes schools to task for failures to make an effort to really stimulate students to be the best they can be. He seems to agree with students that schools, particularly high schools, are boring. He points out that students need belonging, power, fun, and freedom. In *The Quality School: Managing Students Without Coercion* (1992), he shows how teachers can evolve from the "boss-teacher" model, which he feels dominates most public school discourse between teachers and students, to a "lead-teacher" approach. In answer to the question "How do we talk with students who are disrupting the educational process?", he suggests a review of the behaviors of concern (such as "What were you doing when I asked you to stop?"), reminders of class rules, and the development of a plan to prevent future occurrences. The purpose of the conference is to find solutions, not to assign blame.

Ginott, Gordon, and Glasser all rely on the following communicative behavior prerequisites: teachers must take a pro-student stance in their conversations with students; they need to be good listeners, not good lecturers; and they need to understand that students will be defensive and will deny responsibility and project blame onto others. None of these reactions should deter teachers from focusing on the behavior, its consequences, and a plan for dealing with it that meets both the teacher's and the student's needs.

ACTIVITY 6.20

After considering the communication-based approaches just summarized, discuss their pros and cons. When would these approaches be appropriate for a consultee to use? When would they be inappropriate?

Here are some general guidelines for consultees when they are planning to confer with students about their behavior:

1. It is best to have conferences when no other students are around and you can devote five minutes or so to the student without being interrupted.

2. Don't sit behind your desk; trappings of authority are likely to increase defensiveness or forced compliance.

3. Strive to listen more than you talk. Tape-record your conferences from time to time to determine the ratio of your talking compared to the student's. Also try to determine the sources of breakdown in communications that sometimes happen.

4. Use open-ended questions more than closed questions, especially when discussing the student's feelings about her classroom experience. (Chapter 3 gives examples of these types of questions.)

5. Avoid asking why the student has engaged in a deviant behavior. Generally, students will say they don't know, or they will give you some socially acceptable reason that they hope will satisfy you and won't get them in further trouble.

6. Try to get the student to take the initiative in coming up with a plan to solve the problem. Realize that her plan may reflect her degree of immaturity, so you may need to facilitate the process of working out the details. This parallels the process of collaborative consultation.

7. If the student is reluctant or cannot come up with a plan, suggest some ideas that are acceptable to you and encourage commitment from the student. Sometimes you may have to wait a day or so before deciding on a plan.

8. Never argue with a student. Arguments often turn into heated exchanges and are detrimental to rational problem solving.

9. Note the student's emotions; these often give clues to her feelings. Avoid trapping the child in a logical or emotional corner. Leave an escape route by suggesting options.

10. If you suspect that the student is emotionally distressed beyond what you would expect in the circumstances, you may want to make a referral to the school-based consultant (that is, the psychologist or the counselor) or to the student's parent who may wish to seek his or her own resources for direct service (counseling) or other assistance in understanding the student.

SEVEN GENERALIZATIONS ABOUT BEHAVIOR MANAGEMENT IN THE CLASSROOM

1. Classrooms with good behavioral management are rule-governed. With a few exceptions (such as a highly charismatic or greatly feared teacher), there is a high correlation between rules enforcement and good behavioral control. Students will test new or inconsistent teachers to determine if the rules mean what they say and under what circumstances.

2. Good behavior managers demonstrate a high ratio of positive to negative statements to students.

3. Students need to perceive that teachers have power and are not afraid to use it.

4. Ignoring misbehavior is risky. Using extinction as a sole method for dealing with disruptive behavior may be catastrophic. This method needs to be supported by positive contingencies for appropriate behavior and possibly negative contingencies for disruptive behavior. Since reinforcement for most misbehaviors lies in the reactions of the other students, a teacher who simply ignores the behavior may see a rapid escalation of it.

5. The major determinant of teacher–student interactions is the relationship between them. A positive relationship coupled with a good curriculum and effective motivational techniques goes a long way toward controlling a student's tendency to engage in off-target disruptive behaviors.

6. Power in the classroom can be obtained by either the teacher or the students. It needs to be earned. Gordon's Method III (win-win) is based on the subtle power of the teacher to control a conference with a student so that the student feels heard, not demeaned, and believes he has the power to change his own behavior.

7. The teacher is the ultimate reinforcer. If the teacher's favor or approval is reinforcing and she capitalizes on this fact, little else is needed (assuming the emotional and neurological integrity of the student). If the teacher's favor is not reinforcing, the student will need an enticing curriculum, effective motivational techniques, self-discipline, or external controls (fear of aversive consequences).

ACTIVITY 6.21

In dyads, with one person being a teacher-consultee and the other a school-based consultant, role-play discussions in which the teacher wants advice about how to deal with behavior problems in the classroom.

THE "BEST" APPROACH

The following is an example of an approach to assist school-based consultants delivering information to teachers about a sequenced method of intervening with behavior problems. It is modeled after the system developed by Sprick and Howard in their book *Teacher's Encyclopedia of Behavior Management* (1995). "BEST" is an acronym for the four levels of intervention that are presented here: Basic, Elaborated, Serious, and Total School. The consultant can develop material like the example in Figure 6.6 which reviews selected aspects of the most common behavior problems that cause students to be referred to SST or other school disciplinary teams. The consultant may wish to work through a team to develop materials like this example. This material can be presented either in the context of teacher inservice meetings, or individually with selected teachers.

Figure 6.6

Dealing with challenging behaviors

BEHAVIOR: Disrespect or defiance toward adults.

Definition: This is an intentional verbal or nonverbal (e.g., hand-signs; facial movements) behavior *intended* to demean or insult an adult or his/her authority. An observer infers *intention* by the presence of such behaviors as tone of voice (mocking, falsetto, mimicry, and so on), body language, type of response to directives, and the actual words used by the student. Disrespect and defiance are often characterized by arguing, rudeness, or other behaviors indicative of a lack of respect for the adult. Defiant students refuse to comply with ordinary expectations of adults and directly or indirectly challenge adults to respond to the defiance.

Causes: Students engage in these behaviors for a variety of reasons. Usually there is a power component, since disrespecting or being defiant toward adults hopefully would lower their power base, thereby increasing that of the offending student. These behaviors may have been modeled for the offending students by others with whom they live or associate, such as a parent or sibling, or peers, including gang members. It may also be that the student believes the teacher has been disrespectful toward the student, and is simply retaliating. In situations where the disrespect or defiance is associated with extreme anger or rage behavior there may be no readily identifiable model or power motive. The behavior stems from the student's desire to lash out as a reaction to perceived stressors or insults.

General Comments

1. Disrespectful, defiant students are very difficult to deal with because they attack teachers and parents in a way that is both unexpected and a direct violation of the social contract that exists in the relationship between students and adults in all cultures throughout the world. We expect some of this behavior from the "terrible twos" because of their lack of socialization and their limited cognitive development. By school age, we don't expect much of this behavior, unless the student has been put under extreme stress and is overreacting with aberrant behavior, as in a rage, or unless the student has been raised in an environment where this sort of behavior by others is common or tolerated. During the elementary grades we are surprised and distressed by this behavior. Those who engage in it are usually referred for counseling and/or assigned to special education settings.

   As students get into the junior high grades, we tend to see an increase in this behavior and, with some exceptions, it is predictive of difficulties in this regard throughout adolescence. This is true more for males than females, but certainly not exclusively so. Students over 16 tend to be in better control of their emotions due to socialization and the further development of the cerebral cortex, which affords them better reasoning power, the ability to see things from a broader perspective, and less of an egocentric view of life.

2. Disrespectful and defiant behaviors can be very similar or very different. They are presented together because they often occur simultaneously. The previous definitions indicate the ways they are not the same. The disrespectful student tries to demean the teacher but, if mildly reminded of the inappropriateness of his behavior, may give in and follow directives, although with a sneer. Students tend to maintain this smoldering resistance to compliance in everything they do. They tend to be passive, while the defiant student is active. Mild reminders to comply are met by defiant students with increased resistance and an "in your face" demeanor. The challenge for the teacher to take action is stronger in the case of defiance. It is here that the teacher must be strongest in her resolve to follow one of the cardinal rules in classroom behavior management: When the children act like children, the adults have to act like adults. Easily said.

3. Here are some examples of disrespectful behavior:

Example 1:

Teacher: "Students, we need to put away our art materials. We need to work on our social studies projects today."

Student: "We need to do this, we need to do that. What we want to do is finish our art. Why can't we do what we want for a change?"

Example 2:

Teacher: "Billy, you need to stop bothering José and get back to your own work."

Student: "Hey, I'm not bothering anybody. Just calm down."

In both cases the teacher has presented a directive, either to the whole class or to a targeted student. In the first case, the student has decided to answer for the whole class and to let the teacher know that her directive is unwelcome and should be argued with. In the second case, the teacher's directive is for one student only, and he challenges the teacher to, essentially, mind her own business (as if classroom management is not the teacher's business).

4. Here are some examples of defiant behavior:

Example 1:

Teacher: "Students, we need to put away our art materials. We need to work on our social studies projects today."

Student: "Hey, we're just getting into this art work. Forget that boring social studies; we want to work some more on art."

Example 2:

Teacher: "Billy, you need to stop bothering José and get back to your own work."

Student: "Hey, butt out. You need to stop bothering me. If I want to talk with my friend, I will. So, like, MYOB."

In both of these cases of defiance, the teacher has given the same directives as above. Here, however, the student responds in a way that cannot easily be ignored, or treated only with a look of disdain. The teacher must take action, or chaos will ensue. Direct threats to authority cannot be tolerated in a classroom.

(continues)

Figure 6.6 *continued*

5. In most cases of disrespect or defiance the teacher will react with some sort of immediate response. Hopefully it will be something in line with the seriousness of the offense, given the classroom dynamics at the time of the offense. Here is a series of BEST responses that the teacher will want to consider:

BASIC: The teacher has to keep the class group moving along with the curriculum. Proceed with the rest of the class as if the student didn't just say what he did. Then either go over to the student or call him to you and talk with him about what he just said. Try to remain neutral and objective. In the case of defiance, you may need to take some deep breaths before you talk with the student, because you may be very upset about what you just heard.

At this level of intervention, the teacher is considering the offense to be unexpected, not common, and coming from a student who is not well known for this kind of response. The teacher should respond in kind, treating the offense as an uncommon aberration, and one that should be handled privately. In the examples previously cited, the teacher might say something like the following:

"(Student), I'm surprised by what you just said. I do not expect students to argue with me, or be disrespectful toward me when I give a direction. Do you understand that?"

Assuming the student responds to this with some sort of apology or recognition of the error of his ways, this might end the situation, hopefully forever.

If the student decides to argue further, tell the student you will need to speak with him at a later time, during which time you will get into a further discussion of the incident, and teach the offending student better ways of responding, requiring the student to practice these responses, such as the following:

Follow the directive without comment.
Say: "Teacher, please, one more minute for art?"
Say: "When will we be able to finish our art?"
Say: "Sorry, I didn't know I was bothering anyone."

You may want to try a "role-reversal" technique, where the student plays the part of the teacher, and vice versa. The student (acting as the teacher) gives a directive to the teacher (acting as the student), and the teacher gives a disrespectful or defiant response. Sometimes, seeing what a defiant response feels like by having someone else do it to you can have a strong impact. Also, you may need to prompt some students to think about what their reactions should be when the teacher will need to make some unwanted comment to them. It might look like this:

Teacher: "Billy, I want to talk to you about your playground behavior. Before I do, I want you to remember to respond to me in a respectful manner, even if you don't like what I say to you. Remember to think first before responding."

Finally, at this BASIC level, be sure you are giving positive reinforcement (R+) for compliance to directions and respectful behavior. Teachers are generally very good at doing this for a whole class; in the case of a student who tends toward these behaviors, the teacher may want to individualize this positive reinforcement on a daily basis.

ELABORATED: The teacher moves to this level when it is apparent that the student did not benefit from the soft approach presented in BASIC, and continues to respond in a disrespectful/defiant manner. Here the teacher will want to keep a log of examples of these behaviors in anecdotal form. When a few examples have been noted, discuss these with the student. Help him to see what is offensive and unacceptable about them. You might want to explore possible reasons for these behaviors, other than what is on the surface. It might be best to consult with a counselor, school psychologist, or administrator before proceeding further. Some common reasons that prompt these behaviors are three discussed by Dreikurs (1968): attention-seeking, power, and revenge. It is also necessary at this point to inform the student's parents about this behavior. Sometimes a strong message from a parent takes care of behaviors like these.

If it is clear that the behavior is prompted by power (i.e., the power the student gets from entertaining his peers and showing off with anti-authority posturing), the student should be asked about this motivation. Some students crave power. It may be possible to give the student some degree of legitimate power within the classroom or school through prosocial behaviors. Teachers and schools should try to identify what activities could be assigned to students that might meet their desires to gain prestige by demonstrating their competence.

In the case where these behaviors continue or escalate, the teacher will need to institute some consequences. Schools vary in their procedures regarding these consequences; consult with your administrator before deciding on out-of-the-class consequences that your school may not support. In-class consequences would include time-out in some restricted part of the room, moving the student's desk away from a likely peer who may be prompting and/or reinforcing this behavior, restricting recess time or activity, or having the student copy out some of the preferred responses previously mentioned in the BASIC section.

The positive reinforcement mentioned in the BASIC material should be enhanced here. While keeping track of offending behaviors, try also to keep track of instances of respectful, compliant behavior. Assuming you have mentioned this problem to the student's parents, it is always a good idea to inform the parents of any improvements you have observed. Surprise the student by letting her know that you have observed these behaviors. Perhaps a further surprise to the whole class could come in the form of a whole-class positive reinforcer earned because of an increase (perhaps disguised as "seen throughout the class," rather than focused on a single student) in respectful behavior.

SERIOUS: This level should be reserved for instances of the targeted behaviors that are constant, unremitting, and/or are observed among a number of students in the class. The implementation of this level assumes that the previous two levels have not produced the desired results. Chronic disrespect and defiance require parental and administrative involvement. Review the instances of these behaviors with your administrator and follow her advice. At this level, parent involvement is required. It is likely that the administrator will call for a parent–teacher conference, which may also involve a counselor, school psychologist, and, possibly, the student. It is best if the school personnel can get together before the meeting to discuss their strategies.

The basic point to be made at this conference is that these behaviors cannot be tolerated. Options for consequences, in the event that the behaviors continue, are suspension, movement to a different campus, or possible referral to whatever programs may exist outside of the regular education program. Although special education is not likely, unless it is determined that the student meets the eligibility standards for Emotional Disturbance, the district may have some arrangement with a county office of education to provide alternative education services for students whose disruptive, defiant behavior is chronic.

If it is determined that the student is to remain in the regular school, counseling efforts should be arranged, either within the school or through an outside clinic. Strong contingencies for these behaviors need to be enforced in the classroom. Of course, positive reinforcement for instances of appropriate behavior should also be evident.

(*continues*)

Figure 6.6   *continued*

TOTAL SCHOOL: If it is clear that disrespect and defiance are a widespread problem in the school, a school-wide program of remediation needs to be instituted. A committee of concerned teachers, counselors, school psychologists, student representatives, community members, and administrators should review the problem, study what efforts have been made so far to deal with it, try to find examples of programs that have been tried elsewhere, and then come up with a plan, which may need to be unique to the local school.

ACTIVITY 6.22

Working in groups by grade-level interest (pre-K, K-3, 4-6, 7-9, 10-12), develop a "BEST" plan for dealing with a common behavior problem other than disrespect or defiance, which is the example above. Focus particularly on a sequence of interventions that are practical, have some research support, and show respect for the student. Discuss your plans with other class members.

SUMMARY

This chapter has presented information about dealing with students who have classroom behavior problems. We reviewed methods of classifying these problems, diagnostic approaches (rating scales, observations, interviews), and general strategies for dealing with the problems. The next chapter presents two cases in which behavior problems are the main concern. You will see how the SOCS approach (Chapter 5) and the information presented in this chapter helped school consultants assist school personnel and parents in these cases.

REFERENCES

Achenbach, T. M. (1991a). *Manual for the child behavior checklist and revised child behavior profile.* Burlington: University of Vermont, Department of Psychiatry.

Achenbach, T. M. (1991b). *Manual for the teacher's report form and 1991 profile.* Burlington: University of Vermont, Department of Psychiatry.

Achenbach, T. M. (1991c). *Manual for the youth self-report and 1991 profile.* Burlington: University of Vermont, Department of Psychiatry.

Achenbach, T. M., & McConaughy, S. H. (1996). Relations between *DSM-IV* and empirically based assessment. *School Psychology Review, 25*(3), 329–341.

Achenbach, T. M., & McConaughy, S. H. (1997). *Empirically based assessment of child and adolescent behavior: Practical applications* (2nd ed.). Newbury Park, CA: Sage.

Alberto, P. A., & Troutman, A. C. (1999). *Applied behavior analysis for teachers* (5th ed.). Upper Saddle River, NJ: Merrill/Prentice Hall.

Alessi, G. (1988). Direct observation network for emotional/behavioral problems. In E. S. Shapiro & T. R. Kratochwill (Eds.), *Behavioral assessment in schools: Conceptual foundations and practical applications* (pp. 14–75). New York: Guilford Press.

Alessi, G., & Kaye, J. (1983). *Behavior assessment for school psychologists.* Kent, OH: NASP.

Allen, S. J., & Graden, J. L. (1995). Best practices in collaborative problem solving for intervention design. In A. Thomas & J. Grimes (Eds.), *Best practices in school psychology—III* (pp. 667–678). Washington, DC: NASP.

American Psychiatric Association. (1994). *Diagnostic and statistical manual of mental disorders* (4th ed.). Washington, DC: Author.

American Psychological Association. (1994). *Violence and youth: Psychology's response*. Washington, DC: Author.

Atkins, M. S., Pelham, W. E., & Light, M. (1985). A comparison of objective classroom measures and teacher ratings of attention deficit disorder. *Journal of Abnormal Child Psychology, 13,* 155–167.

Bauer, A. M., & Sapona, R. H. (1991). *Managing classrooms to facilitate learning*. Boston: Allyn & Bacon.

Benjamin, A. (1987). *The helping interview*. Boston: Houghton Mifflin.

Bergan, J. (1977). *Behavioral consultation*. Columbus, OH: Merrill.

Bergan, J. & Kratochwill, T. (1990). *Behavioral consultation & therapy*. New York: Plenum.

Brown, L. L., & Hammill, D. D. (1990). *Behavior rating profile*. Austin, TX: Pro-Ed.

Buss, A. H., & Plomin, R. (1984). *Temperament: Early developing personality traits*. Hillsdale, NJ: Erlbaum.

Carey, W. B. (1998). Temperament and behavior problems in the classroom. *School Psychology Review, 27,* 522–533.

Carey, W. B., & Jablow, M. M. (1997). *Understanding your child's temperament*. New York: Macmillan.

Carr, E. G. (1993). Behavior analysis is not ultimately about behavior. *Behavior Analyst, 16,* 47-49.

Carr, E. G. (1994). Emerging themes in the functional analysis of problem behavior. *Journal of Applied Behavioral Analysis, 27,* 393–399.

Chandler, L., & Dahlquist, C. (2002). *Functional assessment: Strategies to prevent and remediate challenging behavior in school settings*. Upper Saddle River, NJ: Merrill/Prentice Hall.

Charles, C. M. (1999). *Building classroom discipline* (6th ed.). White Plains, NY: Longman.

Chess, S., & Thomas, A. (1996). *Know your child*. New Brunswick, NJ: Jason Aronson.

Colton, D. L., & Sheridan, S. M. (1998). Conjoint behavioral consultation and social skills training: Enhancing the play behavior of boys with attention deficit hyperactivity disorder. *Journal of Educational and Psychological Consultation, 9,* 3–28.

Connors, C. K. (1997). *Connors rating scale—revised technical manual*. Toronto: Multi-Health Systems.

Cooper, J. (Ed.). (1999). *Classroom teaching skills*. Boston: Houghton-Mifflin.

Cooper, J., Heron, T., & Heward, W. (1987). *Applied behavior analysis*. Upper Saddle River, NJ: Merrill/Prentice Hall.

Coopersmith, S. (1984). *Self-esteem inventories*. Palo Alto, CA: Consulting Psychologists Press.

Davison, J. (1990). The process of school consultation: Give and take. In E. Cole & J. Siegel (Eds.), *Effective consultation in school psychology* (pp. 53–70). Toronto: Hogrefe & Huber.

Deitz, S. (1982). Defining applied behavioral analysis: An historical analogy. *Behavior Analyst, 5*(1), 53–64.

Dreikurs, R. (1968). *Psychology in the classroom*. New York: Harper & Row.

Dreikurs, R., & Gray, L. (1995). *Logical consequences*. New York; Penguin-NAL.

Egan, G. (1994). *The skilled helper*. Boston: Houghton Mifflin.

Elliott, S. N., & Gresham, F. M. (1992). *Social skills intervention guide*. Circle Pines, MN: American Guidance Service.

Emmer, E. T., Evertson, C. M., Sanford, J. P., Clements, B. S., & Worsham, M. E. (1989). *Classroom management for secondary teachers*. Boston: Allyn & Bacon.

Evans, I. M., & Meyer, L. H. (1985). *An educative approach to behavior problems: A practical decision model for interventions with severely handicapped learners*. Baltimore, MD: Brookes.

Evertson, C. M., Emmer, E. T., Clements, B. S., Sanford, J. P., & Worsham, M. E. (1989). *Classroom management for elementary teachers*. Upper Saddle River, NJ: Merrill/Prentice Hall.

Fisher, R., & Brown, S. (1988). *Getting together*. Boston: Houghton Mifflin.

Fisher, R., & Ury, W. (1981). *Getting to yes: Negotiating agreement without giving in*. Boston: Houghton Mifflin.

Friend, M., & Cook, L. (2000). *Interactions: Collaboration skills for school professionals* (3rd ed.). New York: Longman.

Gallagher, P. (1988). *Teaching students with behavior disorders*. Denver: Love Publishing.

Ginott, H. (1971). *Teacher and child.* New York: Macmillan.

Glasser, W. (1969). *Schools without failure.* New York: Harper & Row.

Glasser, W. (1992). *The quality school: Managing students without coercion* (2nd ed.). New York: Harper & Row.

Goldstein, A. P. (1999). *The prepare curriculum.* Champaign, IL: Research Press.

Goldstein, A. P., Spafkin, R. P., Gershaw, N. J., and Klein, P. (1983). Structures learning: A psychoeducational approach for teaching social competencies. *Behavioral Disorders, 8*(3), 161-162.

Gordon, T. (1974). *Teacher effectiveness training.* New York: McKay.

Gordon, T. (1989). *Discipline that works.* New York: Random House.

Gresham, F. M. (1991). Whatever happened to functional analysis in behavioral consultation? *Journal of Educational and Psychological Consultation, 2*(4), 387–392.

Gresham, F. M. (1995). Best practices in social skills training. In A. Thomas & J. Grimes (Eds.), *Best practices in school psychology—III* (pp. 1,021–1,030). Washington, DC: NASP.

Gresham, F. M., & Elliott, S. (1990). *Social skills rating system.* Circle Pines, MN: American Guidance Service.

Gresham, F., & Gansle, K. (1992). Misguided assumptions of *DSM* III-R: Implications for school psychological practice. *School Psychology Quarterly, 7,* 79–95.

Gresham, F. M., & Noell, G. H. (1999). Functional analysis assessment as a cornerstone for noncategorical special education. In D. J. Reschly, W. D. Tilly, and J. P. Grimes (Eds.), *Special education in transition* (pp. 49–80). Longmont, CO: Sopris West.

Gresham, F. M., & Witt, J. C. (1987, October). *Practical considerations in the implementation of classroom interventions.* Paper presented at the annual meeting of the Oregon School Psychological Association, Eugene.

Hartmann, D., Roper, B., & Bradford, D. (1979). Some relationships between behavioral and traditional assessment. *Journal of Behavioral Assessment, 1,* 3–21.

Hathaway S. R., & Monachesi, E. D. (1963). *Adolescent personality and behavior: MMPI patterns of normal delinquent, dropout and other outcomes.* Minneapolis: University of Minnesota Press.

Hayes, S., Nelson, R., & Jarrett, R. (1986). Evaluating the quality of behavioral assessment. In R. Nelson & S. Hayes (Eds.), *Conceptual foundations of behavioral assessment* (pp 463–503). New York: Guildford Press.

Haynes, S., & O'Brien, W. (1990). Functional analysis in behavior therapy. *Clinical Psychology Review, 10,* 664–668.

Hill, J. L. (1999). *Meeting the needs of students with special physical and health care needs.* Upper Saddle River, NJ: Merrill/Prentice Hall.

Hintze, J. M., & Shapiro, E. S. (1995). Systematic observation of classroom behavior. In A. Thomas & J. Grimes (Eds.), *Best practices in school psychology—III* (pp. 651–660). Washington, DC: NASP.

Homme, L. (1970). *How to use contingency contracting in the classroom.* Champaign, IL: Research Press.

Hughes, J. N., & Hasbrouck, J. E. (1996). Television violence: Implications for violence prevention. *School Psychology Review, 25*(2), 134–151.

Hunt, N., & Marshall, K. (1999). *Exceptional children and youth.* Boston: Houghton Mifflin.

Hyman, I. (1997). *School discipline and school violence: The teacher variance approach.* Boston: Allyn & Bacon.

Jones, F. (1987). *Positive classroom discipline.* New York: McGraw-Hill.

Jones, V. J., & Jones, L. S. (1998). *Comprehensive classroom management: Creating communities of support and solving problems* (5th ed.). Boston: Allyn & Bacon.

Kampwirth, T. J. (1988). Behavior management in the classroom. *Education and Treatment of Children, 11*(3), 286–293.

Kanfer, F. & Goldstein, A. (Eds.). (1986). *Helping people change: A textbook of methods.* New York: Pergamon.

Kaplan, J. S. (2000). *Beyond functional assessment.* Austin, TX: Pro-Ed.

Kaplan, P. G., & Hoffman, A. G. (1990). *It's absolutely groovy.* Denver: Love Publishing.

Kauffman, J. (1982). Social policy issues in special education and related services for emotionally disturbed children and youth. In M. M. Noel & N. G. Haring (Eds.), *Progress of change: Issues in educat-*

ing the emotionally disturbed. Vol. 1: *Identification and program planning* (pp. 1–10). Seattle: University of Washington Press.

Kazdin, A. (Ed.). (1985). *Treatment of antisocial behavior in children and adolescents*. Pacific Grove, CA: Brooks/Cole.

Knopf, H. (1995). Best practices in personality assessment. In A. Thomas & J. Grimes (Eds.), *Best practices in school psychology—III*. Washington, DC: NASP.

Kovacs, M. (1992). *Children's depression inventory*. Los Angeles: Multi-Health Systems.

Kovacs, M., & Beck, A. T. (1977). An empirical-clinical approach toward a definition of childhood depression. In J. C. Shulterbrandt & A. Raskin (Eds.), *Depression in childhood: Diagnosis, treatment, and conceptual models* (pp. 1–25). New York: Raven.

Kratochwill, T. R. (1982). Advances in behavioral assessment. In C. R. Reynolds & T. R. Gutkin (Eds.), *Handbook of school psychology* (pp. 314–350). New York: Wiley.

Kratochwill, T. R., Van Someren, K. R., & Sheridan, S. M. (1989). Training professional consultants: A competency-based model to teach interview skills. *Professional School Psychology, 4,* 41–58.

Krumboltz, J., & Thoresen, C. (1969). *Behavioral counseling*. New York: Holt, Rinehart, & Winston.

Lambert, N., Hartsough, C., & Sandoval, J. (1990). *Children's attention and adjustment survey*. Circle Pines, MN: American Guidance Services.

Lentz, F. E., & Wehmann, B. (1995). Best practices in interviewing. In A. Thomas & J. Grimes (Eds.), *Best practices in school psychology—III*. Washington, DC: NASP.

Lerner, J. (2000). *Learning disabilities* (8th ed.). Boston: Houghton-Mifflin.

Lieberman, C. (1994). *Television and violence*. Paper presented at the Council of State Governments Conference on School Violence, Westlake Village, CA.

McCarney, S. B. (1992). *Emotional or behavior disorder scale*. Columbus, MO: Hawthorne Educational Services.

McCarney, S. B. (1995). *Attention deficit disorders evaluation scale—School version*. Columbus, MO: Hawthorne Educational Services.

McComas, J. J., Hoch, H., & Mace, F. C. (2000). Functional analysis. In E. S. Shapiro & T. R. Kratochwill (Eds.), *Conducting school-based assessments of*

child and adolescent behavior (pp. 78–120). New York: Guilford Press.

McConaughy, S. H., & Ritter, D. R. (1995). Best practices in multidimensional assessment of emotional or behavioral disorders. In A. Thomas & J. Grimes (Eds.), *Best practices in school psychology—III* (pp. 865–877). Washington, DC: NASP.

Magg, J. W. (1992). Integrating consultation into social skills training: Implications for practice. *Journal of Educational and Psychological Consultation, 3*(3), 233–258.

Martin, R., Hooper, S., & Snow, J. (1986). Behavior rating scale approaches to personality assessment in children and adolescents. In H. M. Knoff (Ed.), *The assessment of child and adolescent personality* (pp. 309–351). New York: Guilford Press.

Mathews, F. (1992). Re-framing gang violence: A pro-youth strategy. *The Journal of Emotional and Behavioral Problems, 1*(3), 221–230.

Matson, J., Ratatori, A., & Helsel, W. (1983). Development of a rating scale to measure social skills in children: The Matson Evaluation of Social Skills with Youngsters (MESSY). *Behaviour Research and Therapy, 21,* 335–340.

Merrill, K. W. (1999). *Behavioral, social, and emotional assessment of children and adolescents*. Mahwah, NJ: Erlbaum.

Metcalf, L. (1999). *Teaching toward solutions*. West Nyack, New York: The Center for Applied Research in Education.

Millon, T., Green, C. J., & Meagher, R. B. (1982). *Millon adolescent personality interview manual*. Minneapolis: National Computer Systems.

Naglieri, J. A., LeBuffe, P. A., & Pfeiffer, S. I. (1993). *Devereux behavior rating scale—School form*. San Antonio, TX: Psychological Corporation.

National Association of School Psychologists. (1990). *School Psychology Review, 19*(2), whole issue.

National Association of School Psychologists. (1996). *School Psychology Review, 25*(3), whole issue.

Nelson, W. M., III, & Finch, A. J., Jr. (1973). *The children's inventory of anger*. Unpublished manuscript, Xavier University. Cincinatti, OH.

O'Neil, R. E., Horner, R. H., Albin, R. A., Storey, J., & Sprague, J. (1990). *Functional analysis: A practical guide*. Baltimore: Brookes.

Parker, J. G., & Asher, S. R. (1987). Peer relations and later personal adjustment: Are low-accepted children at risk? *Psychological Bulletin, 102,* 357–389.

Patterson, G. R., Chamberlain, P., & Reid, J. (1982). A comparative evaluation of parent training procedures. *Behavior Therapy, 13,* 638–650.

Patterson, G. R., Reid, J. B., Jones, R. R., & Conger, R. E. (1975). *A social learning approach to family intervention.* Eugene, OR: Castalia.

Piers, E. V. (1996). *Revised manual for the Piers-Harris children's self-concept scale.* Los Angeles: Western Psychological Services.

Porter, R. B., & Cattell, R. B. (1979). *What you do and what you think.* Champaign, IL: Institute for Personality and Ability Testing.

Prassy, D., & Schrag, J. (1999). Providing noncategorical, functional, classroom-based supports for students with disabilities: Legal parameters. In D. Reschly, W. Tilly, & J. Grimes (Eds.), *Special Education in transition.* Longmont, CD: Sopris West.

Quay, H. C., & Peterson, D. R. (1996). *Manual for the revised behavior problem checklist—PAR version.* Odessa, FL: Psychological Assessment Resources.

Reynolds, W. M. (1998). *Adolescent psychopathology scale (APS).* Odessa, FL: Psychological Assessment Resources, Inc.

Reynolds, W. M. (2001). *Reynolds adolescent adjustment screening inventory (RAASI).* Odessa, FL: Psychological Assessment Resources, Inc.

Reynolds, C. R., & Kamphaus, R. W. (1990). *Handbook of psychological and educational assessment of children: Personality, behavior, and context.* New York: Guilford Press.

Reynolds, C. R., & Kamphaus, R. W. (1992). *Behavior assessment system for children (BASC).* Circle Pines, MN: American Guidance Service.

Reynolds, C. R., & Richmond, B. O. (1985). *Revised children's manifest anxiety scale (RCMAS).* Los Angeles: Western Psychological Services.

Sattler, J. (1998). *Clinical and forensic interviewing of children and families.* San Diego, CA: Sattler Press.

Sattler, J. (2001a). *Assessment of children: Behavioral and clinical applications* (4th ed.). San Diego: Sattler Press.

Sattler, J. (2001b). *Assessment of children: Cognitive applications* (4th ed.). San Diego: Sattler Press.

Shapiro, E., & Kratochwill, T. (Eds.). (2000). *Conducting school-based assessments of child and adolescent behavior.* New York: Guilford Press.

Sheridan, S. M., & Elliott, S. N. (1991). Behavioral consultation as a process for linking the assessment and treatment of social skills. *Journal of Educational and Psychological Consultation, 2* (2), 151–173.

Skinner, C. H., Rhymer, K. N., & McDaniel, E. C. (2000). Naturalistic direct observation in educational settings. In E. S. Shapiro and T.R. Kratochwill (Eds.), *Conducting school-based assessment of child and adolescent behavior.* New York: Guilford Press.

Sprick, R., & Howard, L. (1995). *Teacher's encyclopedia of behavior management.* Longmont, CO: Sopris West.

Sugai, G., & Tindal, G. (1993). *Effective school consultation.* Pacific Grove, CA: Brooks/Cole.

Sulzer-Azaroff, B., & Mayer, G. (1986). *Achieving educational excellence.* New York: Holt, Rinehart, & Winston.

Trower, F., Bryant, B., & Argyle, M. (1978). *Social skills and mental health.* Pittsburgh, PA: University of Pittsburgh Press.

Ullmann, L. & Krasner, L. (1965). *Case studies in behavior modification.* New York: Holt, Rinehart, & Winston.

U.S. Department of Education. (2000). *Twenty-second annual report to Congress on the implementation of the Education of the Handicapped Act.* Washington, DC: Author.

Valentine, M. (1987). *How to deal with discipline problems in the schools.* Austin, TX: Educational Directions.

Walker, H., & McConnell, S. (1995). *The Walker-McConnell scale of social competence and school adjustment.* Austin, TX: Pro-Ed.

Walker, H., Todis, B., Holmes, D., & Horton, G. (1995). *The Walker social skills curriculum: The ACCESS program.* Austin, TX: Pro-Ed.

Walker, J., & Shea, T. (1999). *Behavior management: A practical approach for educators* (7th ed.). Upper Saddle River, NJ: Merrill/Prentice Hall.

Witt, J. C., Heffer, R. W., & Pfeiffer, J. (1990). Structured rating scales: A review of self-report and informant rating processes, procedures and issues. In C. R. Reynolds & R. W. Kamphaus (Eds.), *Handbook of psychological and educational assessment of children: Personality, behavior and context* (pp. 364–394). New York: Guilford Press.

Wright, D. B., & Gurman, H. B. (1998). *Positive intervention for serious behavior problems* (2nd ed.). Sacramento, CA: RISE.

Wright, F. (1988a). *Behavior disorders identification scale: Home version.* Columbia, MO: Hawthorne Educational Services.

Wright, F. (1988b). *Behavior disorders identification scale: School version.* Columbia, MO: Hawthorne Educational Services.

Ysseldyke, J., & Christenson, S. (1993). *The instructional environment system—II.* Longmont, CO: Sopris West.

Ysseldyke, J., & Marston, D. (1999). Origins of categorical special education services in schools and a rationale for changing them. In D. Reschly, W. Tilly, & J. Grimes (Eds.), *Special education in transition.* Longmont, CO: Sopris West.

Zirpoli, T., & Melloy, K. (2001). *Behavior management: Applications for teachers* (3rd ed.). Upper Saddle River, NJ: Merrill/Prentice Hall.

CHAPTER 7

Case Studies in Consultation: Behavior Problems in the Classroom

OBJECTIVES

1. Present two cases utilizing the SOCS approach where the primary concerns are behavior problems exhibited by students at two different grade levels.

2. Ask the readers a set of questions about the process and interventions used by the consultants and consultees in these cases.

3. Reflect on the content of previous chapters, especially Chapters 5 (where the outline for these case studies, SOCS, was presented) and 6 (which discussed issues in consultation regarding behavior problems), and demonstrate how a consultant can use the ideas and information presented in these chapters.

ORIENTATION TO THE CASES

The SOCS system helps the consultant and the consultee follow an organized system designed to generate solutions for referrals and to persist in consultative activities until the situation has improved to a reasonable degree.

The following two cases, along with the two cases on learning problems presented in Chapter 9, are not presented as perfect examples of how consultation should be done. Depending on one's theoretical orientation, and the process one chooses to follow, it is certainly possible that these cases could have been handled quite differently with different possible results. What I have tried to do is follow a set of steps (SOCS) primarily embedded in a behavioral approach and to represent typical realities in schools, including both positive and negative aspects of these realities. The cases were gleaned from my experiences as a special education teacher and a school consultant. None of the names of the students or any other participants are real; think of them as composites of students and school personnel who could very well be in the schools you are, or will soon be, working in.

Sequential numbers in brackets within the cases refer to questions or comments designed to stimulate discussion about the consultative process. The reader is encouraged to respond to these questions and comments in light of his or her own perceptions of these cases and others with which he or she may be familiar.

The first case in this chapter seems relatively simple. At the time of referral, the client (Tyrone) presents with some irritating teasing behaviors. However, the special education teacher-consultant's work reveals a more complicated picture. Despite those complications, the collaborative process brings the situation to a fairly satisfactory conclusion.

In the second case (Todd), we have a stronger referral statement. Here the consultant, a school counselor, combines her consultative work with some counseling of Todd. Again there is some degree of success, though perhaps not as much as she and the teacher might have hoped for.

Case A   Hostile Teasing

Tyrone is well-known in the Jackson Elementary School. He has been here since kindergarten, and every year he has given each of his teachers a lot to be concerned about. The problem isn't just that he's mean, loud, often off task, or simply another underachiever in our school. The problem is that he is all of these things, sometimes only mildly but often noticeably. Each of his previous four teachers (grades K–3) referred him to the SST for assistance in dealing with his disruptiveness and poor achievement with varying degrees of success. Now it is November of Tyrone's fourth-grade year, and this year's teacher, Mrs. Hoyt, is determined to turn Tyrone around, as she says, "before it's too late." She has therefore filled out the required referral form and put it into my box. My task, among others, is to serve as the coordinator of the SST.

RECEIPT OF A REFERRAL AND INITIAL THOUGHTS ABOUT IT

My name is Ms. Allen. I'm the resource specialist here at Jackson, and have been for the past five years. Tyrone has been seeing me one period a day for a learning disability in reading since last year. I'm not surprised by this referral; as soon as I knew that Tyrone was going to be in Mrs. Hoyt's fourth-grade class, I said to the principal, "How much do you want to bet Tyrone will be referred before Thanksgiving?" He just smiled and nodded his head, saying, "Kids like Tyrone start this way and then wind up in full-time special education when it all just gets to be too much. I think this year we ought to quit hoping things are going to get better and instead put together a solid behavioral support plan of some sort. Otherwise, we may have to consider ED [P.L. 105-17, emotionally disturbed]." Although I thought the possibility of ED was extreme, I did agree that when the referral came, we would need to do our best to support the teacher and Tyrone. I would especially like to see the principal's prediction regarding ED not come true.

This is Tyrone's fifth year with us and his fifth referral. Each year we have come up with some sort of behavior management plan based on the proclivities of that year's teacher and SST, and each year some sort of resolution of the problem has occurred. Second grade was probably the best for Tyrone and his teacher. That teacher seemed more able to roll with his punches; she actually seemed to enjoy him. While in second grade the rate of physical aggression was cut in half, talking out decreased about 33 percent, and task compliance increased about 50 percent. Not surprisingly, Tyrone's mom liked her best of all his teachers. Last year's SST, believing that Tyrone had turned the corner on behavior, focused on his problems in reading, and found him eligible for one hour a day of resource help, which I provide.

Tyrone lives with his mom and one younger brother, now in second grade. The younger sibling is doing well in school. He seems to have an altogether different approach to life; more easygoing and happy, I'd say. Tyrone's parents have been divorced for four years now; the divorce took place about the time Tyrone was

Figure 7.1

Consultation request information form

Consultee (teacher): Mrs. Hoyt

Grade: 4   **Room:** 12

Consultant: Ms. Allen

Student referred: Tyrone Washington

Student's birthdate: February 2, 1992

Date: November 10, 2001

School: Jackson

Parent: Mrs. Washington

Age: 9-8

Reason for referral: Failure to complete tasks (especially reading comprehension and writing), poor spelling, teasing, taunting of others, noncompliance.

Background information: Tyrone has a long history of verbally negative behavior and poor achievement. He's been referred before. He lives with his mother (divorced) and one younger brother. Dad lives elsewhere. We need to do something about this problem before it's too late. What about medication? Special education?

Best time to see me: Before school (or lunch).

---

starting kindergarten. Tyrone's father lives in another state and rarely makes contact with the family.

Figure 7.1 shows Mrs. Hoyt's completed consultation request information form, with only the basic information needed at that point. I get a copy, as does the principal, and Mrs. Hoyt keeps one.

My first step will be to call Mrs. Hoyt (the consultee) and to acknowledge the referral. Before putting it on the SST calendar, however, I'll try dealing with it myself. This often works just as well as letting it go to the SST and saves all the other team members a lot of time [1]. Besides, I know Tyrone quite well, and I know what we've tried in the past and what's worked.

Before issuing a referral form to a teacher, the district requires the teacher to contact the parent. Therefore, it isn't necessary for me to call Mrs. Washington, Tyrone's mom, before discussion with the teacher. I'll do so after I've consulted with Mrs. Hoyt. Mrs. Washington will be expecting my call; we've talked many times before. I'll also be sending a copy of this referral to Mr. Pruzek, our school psychologist. He handled Tyrone's referral in grades one, two, and three. I indicated to Mr. Pruzek that I'll initiate the handling of this case.

INITIAL DISCUSSION WITH THE TEACHER

I was able to see Mrs. Hoyt on Wednesday afternoon after school. She and I get along just fine. She's experienced, a good teacher, firm, but also fair and consistent. She expects maturity from her fourth-graders. She often reminds them during the first week of school that they have to leave their primary-grade behaviors at home or out in the playground because the fourth-grade classroom is for grown-up boys and girls. For the most part the students buy into her ideas. They see her as a teacher who doesn't put up with much. She has her rules and her consequences, and she sticks to them. By this time of the year, her class is usually productive, under good control, and in many ways seems to be ideal. Nevertheless, I still had a hunch that Tyrone would be referred before Thanksgiving [2].

Mrs. Hoyt said that she was aware of Tyrone's behavior from her previous service on the SST, the information in the cumulative folder, my anecdotal reports, and the behavior plans developed by Mr. Pruzek and Tyrone's previous teachers. She said that she had tried some of the activities that others had tried with Tyrone, especially having him keep a daily record of his own behaviors and providing his own reinforcements in the form of notes home to his mother, extra computer time, and cleaning the chalk off the blackboard. All of these approaches seemed to have a palliative effect: short-lived, and ultimately discouraging for both Mrs. Hoyt and Tyrone. I asked her what she thought would be the best approach at this time. She suggested medication to control his hyperactivity since it had worked so well with the other children she had had. Also, she wondered why Tyrone hadn't been considered for the full-time special education program; she remembered suggesting this idea in a previous SST meeting when Tyrone was beginning the third grade. I commented that both of these ideas would certainly be considered, but I wondered what she believed she could do to manage his behavior in the classroom. She smiled and informed me that if she knew the answer to that she would have done it and not put in a referral.

This is a crucial point in every consultant's experience. In this case, Mrs. Hoyt has tried some ordinarily useful tactics with the student, and she therefore feels it is appropriate to turn the case over for an "expert" or "pair-of-hands" solution (Block, 1981). As discussed in previous chapters, this is a seductive trap for a consultant because the consultee behaves as if your value at this point is in your ability to recommend a solution, preferably one that is foolproof and not labor-intensive, prior to any careful analysis of the current realities. Let's see how the situation unfolds [3].

I decided to get a clearer picture of the current situation in Mrs. Hoyt's class, so I reviewed the consultation request information form (Figure 7.1) with her. I found that her specific referral concerns at this time included Tyrone's failure to complete tasks, especially in reading comprehension and writing; poor spelling; and verbal off-task (teasing) behaviors. She added that other students were poorer in their academics but that he was her most disruptive student, largely because of his teasing of other students. The history of the problem has already been stated. The family situation remains stable; Mom works, and the two boys are in the care of an afterschool sitter (a high school girl). Mrs. Hoyt reviewed the steps she had taken to date (mentioned previously), but in this retelling she seemed to soften her earlier stance, when she claimed that none of these interventions worked. It is

possible, she hinted, that the promise of being allowed to help with classroom chores (cleaning the blackboard, feeding the fish) might serve as a reinforcer. Of course, many other well-behaved students wanted to do these things, too, Mrs. Hoyt reminded me [4].

During this discussion, Mrs. Hoyt reiterated her request to have Tyrone referred to a pediatrician for medication and asked if I would discuss the idea with Mrs. Washington. I said that this discussion was certainly possible but that I preferred to see what we might be able to do with a behavioral approach before recommending a biophysical approach. However, I added, what is most important is the teacher's willingness to work with me in developing such a program. Between the two of us, I believed, we could come up with ways of helping Tyrone that would turn him around.

Mrs. Hoyt looked at me with a mixture of disgust and pity. After exhaling deeply and closing her eyes for a few seconds, she said, "Yes, well, I suppose we must, if only to prove to you that none of this behavior modification stuff will work. So what am I supposed to do?" The following conversation ensued:

Consultant: The first thing I want you to do is to forget that medication exists and to work together with me to solve your and Tyrone's problems.

Mrs. Hoyt: (Looking at me askance) I can forget the medication, but what makes you think Tyrone's problems are mine?

Consultant: In my experience, I have found that teachers want every student to succeed. When they don't, teachers, especially the better ones, get bothered by it and find themselves worrying about it, reacting more strongly than they might want to and possibly letting these problems spoil their teaching effectiveness. Tyrone's behaviors become your problem in the sense that you are forced to deal with them, to the detriment of the smooth running of your classroom.

Mrs. Hoyt: Well, I can agree with you about his ability to bother me, never mind the other students, with his teasing and all. We might as well get busy with this. I just want you to understand that it isn't me who has the problem; it's Tyrone. So, what should I do?

Consultant: I'd like to start with your ideas about interventions. What steps do you feel you might be able to take in regard to any one of Tyrone's troublesome behaviors? Let's pick one behavior that you'd like to start on.

Mrs. Hoyt: I suppose the thing that bugs me most, and I know it irritates the other students, is his teasing behavior. I think I can motivate him to do the schoolwork, but his teasing is too much. Why does he do that?

Consultant: Well, so far I don't know. Why do children tease each other? What ideas do you have?

Mrs. Hoyt: I suppose he thinks it's funny. He does get some of the other kids to laugh. You know, if you pick on one child, some of the others

always find that funny, and then it starts to spread. I'm afraid he (Tyrone) is going to turn into one of these bullies you hear about. Do you think it has to do with his not having a father at home?

Consultant: That's possible. [Should I point out that there are other children in the class who tease and who have fathers at home? Of course, there are also children who don't have fathers at home who do not tease. No, I won't mention either fact. I'm not trying to win debating points.] Let's focus on this teasing behavior. What have you been doing about it?

Mrs. Hoyt: Mild reprimands, mainly. I've also put him off to the side on the playground, and I've asked the other playground monitors to do the same thing. When it happens in the classroom, I give him "the look," which usually stops him. Then I've talked to him about it a number of times. He always promises to stop the teasing, but it always comes back a day or two later, one way or another.

Consultant: Well, I guess I'm lucky. He doesn't do that in the resource room, at least not that I've noticed. I should keep an eye out for it. Would you agree to get some data on this? Don't tell Tyrone yet; just do the same as you have been doing about it. Keep track of how often it happens, with whom, and the form it takes [5]. You know, like what he says and to whom. Could you do that for a week? What I'll do is call Mrs. Washington and get a fix on the family situation. Maybe I can get some insight into your question about the teasing being related to Mr. Washington's not being in the home. Is there anything else you'd like me to review with Mrs. Washington?

Mrs. Hoyt: You want me to keep track of his mean talk for a week? I can tell you right now what he says and to whom. (Pauses; I say nothing.) Alright, I'll try. And when you talk to Mrs. Washington tell her how important it is that Tyrone complete every paper he brings home. She's got to insist on it, or he won't bother.

Consultant: OK. So, under "today's plan" (on the consultation notes form; see Figure 7.2) I'll indicate that you'll keep track of the teasing and I'll discuss the family situation and ask Mrs. Washington to be firm about the homework. Is this morning break a good time to talk? Good. Let's meet again next week, same time, same day, and we'll review what we've got.

I think that was a very good first meeting. Although the consultee came prepared to argue for medication and special education, she turned out to be agreeable about putting those issues on the back burner until other steps had been tried. Sometimes this discussion is moot because the consultee has already suggested medication to the parent. Some districts allow this; others tell their staff to let that sort of recommendation come from the SST or from the psychologist, the counselor, or the nurse.

Figure 7.2
Consultant notes form

Consultee (teacher): Mrs. Hoyt   **Date:** November 15, 2001

Grade: 4   **Room:** 12   **School:** Jackson

Consultant: Ms. Allen   **Parent:** Mrs. Washington

Student referred: Tyrone Washington   **Age:** 9-8

Student's birthdate: February 2, 1992

Reason for referral: (See Figure 7.1.)

Background information: (See Figure 7.1.)

Solutions that have been tried and results: For teasing of others: mild reprimands, time-out on playground, discussions with Tyrone, keeping a daily record of his teasing and of his prosocial behaviors, with a reinforcement program attached to these. So far, no dramatic results. The behavior continues as before. Since this was Mrs. Hoyt's primary concern at this time, this was the only behavior discussed.

Tentative ideas that were discussed: Use of medication, special education, continuance of current positive reinforcement system, addition of other incentives.

Today's plan: Mrs. Hoyt will continue her positive reinforcement plan, and will keep a written record of Tyrone's teasing behaviors. Ms. Allen will contact Tyrone's mother, Mrs. Washington, and review our concerns with her.

Next meeting date: November 22

Each school-based consultant has to establish a framework or a philosophy about recommending a biophysical approach (which, ideally, is not a recommendation for medication but a suggestion that the parent may wish to refer the child to a medical practitioner to see if a medical approach to the child's behavior might be appropriate). We are not in the business of recommending medication or other biophysical approaches; this is rightfully the province of the medical professionals. Our expertise is in behavioral approaches, insight-oriented or ego-supportive counseling, or other psychoeducational interventions; and we ought to be using these until we are convinced that a medical approach is required. In Tyrone's case, we haven't reached that point yet and may never reach it [6].

CLASSROOM OBSERVATION

The format described in SOCS shows that a classroom observation follows the initial discussion with the teacher. However, the format is not always followed step by step. In this case, since I have asked the consultee to gather more information herself, I'll move to another activity.

INITIAL DISCUSSION WITH THE PARENT

I called Mrs. Washington at work later that same day. She could only talk briefly. She knew about the referral and was not happy. She thought Mrs. Hoyt was too fast on the draw in referring Tyrone in November; he hadn't been given a chance to adjust to a new teacher and the greater expectations of fourth-graders. (Given Tyrone's previous record, I thought the referral may have been somewhat slow in coming, but I kept this opinion to myself.) Mrs. Washington wanted to know what she could do, and I mentioned the need to follow up on uncompleted papers and homework. I also mentioned our concern about the teasing. She said that she is so tired when she comes home after work that she (and Tyrone) don't need the hassle of fighting over homework or his school behavior. (This is a serious, and increasingly common, reality in the schools. A single mom who works all day comes home for some quality time with her children and doesn't want to have to deal with homework.) I sympathized and then asked her what ideas she had for dealing with Tyrone's difficulties with task completion. After a moment's silence, she said she didn't know; what would I suggest? I said that I thought it might be a good idea to meet with Mrs. Hoyt so that the three of us could talk about it together. (I know Mrs. Hoyt; she'll welcome the meeting. I ordinarily wouldn't suggest such a meeting without clearing it with the teacher first.) I also indicated that I wanted to review the progress Tyrone was making in the resource room program. We agreed on a before-work meeting and decided that Tyrone should also attend the meeting. We'll meet a week from today at 8:00 in the morning.

What was accomplished in this five-minute phone call?

1. Our relationship was reestablished.
2. We got past at least some of the blame issues, though probably not all of them.
3. I did not allow the parent-consultee to become dependent on me by telling her what to do.
4. I've given Mrs. Washington a week to think about her initial stance of not being willing to help with the homework assignments or her reluctance to talk about the teasing. Most parents will soften that sort of defensiveness within a week.

I left a note in Mrs. Hoyt's box telling her about the parent conference next week, suggesting that we meet at 7:50 to review her baseline data on the teasing and to discuss a strategy for the 8:00 meeting.

GETTING TEACHER AND PARENT TOGETHER: THE SST MEETING

At this point, I decided not to bring Tyrone's case to the SST just yet. I based my decision on what had occurred so far and on an understanding that I've forged with the school principal regarding discretion in case management. I'm aware that not all districts or schools give this much independence to their consultative special education staff. You should strive to get it, however. Autonomy, in the hands of competent, experienced people, leads to creative problem solving (Jayanthi & Friend, 1992). It also saves the SST's time, which should be reserved for more serious cases. Let's hope this case doesn't turn into one.

A week later, at 7:50, Mrs. Hoyt and I looked over her "teasing" data. She had defined teasing as verbal comments made to others that had the purpose of upsetting them. These included comments about one student's weight, another's body odor, another's sister who is developmentally delayed, another's being a teacher's pet, and so on. These comments often resulted in an argument and sometimes pushing and threats made between Tyrone and the student he was teasing. Mrs. Hoyt had recorded five of these incidents per day on the average over the past week. No observable antecedents were noticed; the drive to tease seemed internal to Tyrone. I said we'd meet at our originally planned time today to discuss an intervention. Then we talked about the impending parent conference. We decided to accept Mrs. Washington's feelings but to try to enlist her support concerning the importance of the homework issue. "What can we offer her as a plan?" I inquired. Mrs. Hoyt suggested a daily home–school homework reminder sheet. I reinforced this idea just as Mrs. Washington arrived [7].

Mrs. Washington was, like so many parents and teachers, rushed. She had to leave for work in ten minutes. How could she help? We stressed two points. First, we'd like her support in the area of homework monitoring. She balked mildly but acknowledged that she knew it was important. How should she do it? Mrs. Hoyt said she would be willing to train Tyrone on how to fill out a daily report form that evaluated his efforts for the day on a 1 to 5 rating scale and to list work to be completed at home. Mrs. Washington's job was to require the form every day, to reinforce Tyrone for a good report, and to see that he completed the work listed. We realized that we should have provided more structure but, given our limited time, we had to let the issue go at this point, with a promise that I would call Mrs. Washington in a week to see how the monitoring was going. Tyrone was asked to comment on this approach. He looked cowed and said it was fine with him. At that point we asked Tyrone to go to the playground because we wanted to discuss the teasing behavior and data, but Mrs. Hoyt and I thought it was best to lay the groundwork with Tyrone privately rather than bring it up in to him and Mrs. Washington together without some better explanation about it to Tyrone.

We explained the teasing briefly and showed Mrs. Washington the data. She acknowledged that Tyrone and his brother were constantly at each other with this sort of thing and that Tyrone dominated the situation to the point of bringing his brother to tears a couple of times a week. She thought he picked it up from TV sitcoms, especially from the cartoon characters who routinely insult each other. What did we recommend? I asked her what she was doing about it now. She said, "I'll tell them to stop it or they are both going to their rooms. They wind up in their rooms, at least Tyrone does, about once a week because of it." I asked her what she would like to do about it. She thought restricting TV would be a good idea. I said I thought that was a good idea. (As far as I'm concerned, it always is. Kids spend more time, annually, in front of the TV than they do at school. But just restricting TV doesn't mean that Tyrone is going to learn to curb his hostile verbal interactions. Something positive is needed.) I suggested that while the TV was off, Mrs. Washington and the boys might want to work on some family projects like baking cookies or making decorations or just reading together. She looked at me and said, "You know, we don't do much of that. I wonder if it would work."

Time was up. I wrote in my plan book that I was to call Mrs. Washington in a week about the homework issue and less TV and more family activities [8]. I also needed to discuss how she might talk to Tyrone about teasing his brother. Perhaps Mr. Pruzek might share this task with me.

In reviewing this conference, Mrs. Hoyt and I agreed that it, unfortunately, was typical of school-based consultation: little time to develop themes or issues, some rough-and-ready solutions thrown out, and meetings terminating before the participants feel as if they have had a chance to really explore the issues. I wish that it wasn't this way, but everyone who works in the schools is familiar, if not pleased, with this scenario. Consultants have to strive for a balance between dispensing general ideas (such as those presented at the end of Chapter 6, and those previously discussed) and becoming specific with plans before the problem and the current dynamics have been explored. This problem is equally true in the SST process. A major complaint of teachers is that they feel that they do not get the opportunity to express their ideas or concerns, or to specify details of referral problems, at either the SST or IEP meetings. Parents often say the same thing (Kaiser & Woodman, 1985; McKellar, 1991; Maher & Yoshida, 1985). This is especially true in multicultural contexts (Winzer & Mazurek, 1998).

ASSESSMENT OF THE REFERRED STUDENT

Learning Problem Assessment

A thorough assessment of Tyrone's academic difficulties was conducted last year when he was placed in special education because of a learning disability in the area of reading. His other language arts areas are also weak. No assessment of these areas was done in response to this present referral because the primary focus at this time is on his behavior and his reluctance to complete assignments that are within his range of competence.

Functional Assessment of Behavior

When I met with Mrs. Hoyt later that morning, we focused on the components of teasing. The rate of teasing was three to seven times a day. It was directed mainly at three other students, two of whom were easy targets because they were social isolates, verbally below average, and often deficient in their schoolwork. The teasing occurred when Tyrone apparently thought that Mrs. Hoyt wasn't observing him. Examples of the teasing included "God, you're a gook. You can't even spell"; "You're the biggest nerd around and a crybaby, too. I'll get you after school"; and "I'll bet you don't even know who your dad is. He's probably one of those berry pickers." The content of these comments suggested Tyrone's own problems: He wasn't a good student, and his parents were divorced, which might account for the comment about parentage. What had gone wrong to cause his father to rarely contact him and his brother [9]?

Given these data and my faith in the consultee's ability to accurately describe and record behaviors, I decided I didn't have to make a separate observation of the behaviors, which I commonly do in the case of behavior problems. We thought we ought to move ahead to clarify specific details of the interventions, assuming that the antecedents were primarily internal and the consequences were probably enhanced feelings of strength derived from successfully putting down another child. We felt that the treatment ought to be mild confrontation and counseling by Mrs. Holt, with assistance from Mr. Pruzek. After reviewing some possibilities, Mrs. Holt decided that she would see Tyrone privately and enlist his help in a project concerning some students who needed additional help with their work, either in her class or in the third grade. She would encourage him to be a study-buddy for one of the children he had been teasing. In line with that, she would mention that she was concerned about some of the comments that she had heard him make to a few of the children and that she was confident that he could learn some more helpful things to say, along with being a study-buddy helper. Lastly, she would be firmer with him regarding the work-completion issue and explain the daily report form that she would be starting that day. She would also ask Tyrone for his ideas about both the problems and possible solutions. There's no reason why our client can't collaborate also [10]!

Additional Areas of Assessment: Psychodynamic, Ecological, and Biophysical Factors

A possible psychodynamic explanation for Tyrone's hurtful teasing, extracted from the few teasing comments the consultee has heard, is his father's absence. We have to be very careful here; generating conclusions from limited data is risky in any area, especially in human motivations. A counselor might possibly be able to give a more refined view of a client's psychodynamics, but here, as is so often the case, we don't have the luxury of waiting for that refinement. A review of our plan with Mr. Pruzek may give us added insights; I'll send him a note about it.

Ecological factors play into our hunch about Tyrone's inferiority feelings due to his living in a fatherless home and his being a poor achiever in a class where most of the students achieve better than he does. We are hoping to turn around his self-image with these simple teacher-oriented procedures. We may decide later that a more intrusive procedure, such as formal individual or group counseling, is needed.

Biophysical factors don't seem relevant here. Tyrone appears to be healthy, and he doesn't appear to be ADHD. Interestingly, since coming up with the plan just described (largely Mrs. Hoyt's idea), she hasn't brought up the idea of medication again. Maybe it will surface later if this plan doesn't work. Some people seem to equate ADHD with medication without evaluating the many possible explanations for daydreaming or restless behavior. Hunger, boredom, anxiety, or temperamental traits could be causing this behavior. Child rearing may account for some of the hyperactive/impulsive behaviors that are often treated with stimulant medications such as Ritalin. Emotional disturbance may carry symptoms of ADHD. One study found 69 different characteristics supposedly being part of an ADHD complex, with 38 proposed causes for the condition (Goodman & Poillion, 1992). School personnel need to be cautious in making referrals to medical personnel based simply on a teacher's opinion; behavior modification or counseling approaches may be more appropriate than medication (Barkley, 1998).

PLANNING INTERVENTIONS

I have already described our original plan, which we will stick with for now. In this case, the teacher was able to devise a simple school–home daily report form; in other cases, if the consultee is unfamiliar with how to do this, I may have to help her. Also, Mrs. Hoyt felt confident about talking with Tyrone about the teasing behavior; other consultees might feel better if I do it, or if Mr. Pruzek does it. If a teacher asks, I will usually talk to the student (with the teacher observing), hoping that the consultee may feel like doing it himself next time. Modeling this simple surface behavior counseling interaction is the sort of skill building that is a valuable function of consultation in the schools [11]. I asked Mrs. Hoyt about her other concerns, such as poor academic achievement and noncompliance, but she said she thought it was enough to work on these two problems: teasing and failure to complete homework. I agreed with her. Working on too many problems at once can be exhausting and confusing. Besides, it is interesting how often an improvement in one problem seems to lead to improvements in other areas without any special plan for those areas.

IMPLEMENTING INTERVENTIONS

The following week three new referrals were in my box, along with a reminder of the need to do three-year workups on two special education students and assorted notes to call certain people and be sure to stop by and see three teachers. All in a day's work. Nothing, however, from either Mrs. Hoyt or Mrs. Washington. Good news or bad? We'll see.

A few days later I heard from Mrs. Hoyt, who had good news. Her conference with Tyrone went very well. He denied teasing, but not strongly. His denial doesn't really matter; all we want is a change in behavior. And a change has occurred, along with his eager acceptance of the role of tutor to two peers. Mrs. Hoyt wisely didn't just select Tyrone; she announced as a general policy for her class that she would be doing more cooperative learning and that a number of students would be working together on assignments. She observed (overheard) only two instances of teasing from Tyrone during the previous four days, and each time she simply said to him, "Remember what we talked about." His eyes darted around each time, but he didn't deny anything. She'll continue this plan for another week. In the area of completed tasks, she has seen mild progress in class but good progress with the home–school note system. Tyrone has been cooperative, saying, "My mom says I gotta do it." Good.

I called Mrs. Washington. She was very upbeat about things. Apparently she gave Tyrone a stern lecture, along with tears on both sides, about the teasing behavior, and she has been strict about the home–school notes. She said she was upset about his difficulty with schoolwork and wanted to know why the school hadn't informed her earlier about it. I chose not to point out that it had been discussed with her during previous SST meetings in addition to the last two years during teacher-conference week. I decided instead to focus on our current plan. I asked if there were any way we could help her with her efforts to work with Tyrone on his schoolwork, and she said she'd appreciate knowing more about how she could help, other than nagging. I told her I would ask Mrs. Hoyt if she would call her about it. I think she will; if not, I'll do it. It reminded me of one of the projects I hope to get started some day: a homework-helper workshop for parents. I've got to talk to the principal about it [12].

MONITORING INTERVENTIONS

This case lasted two more weeks. The consultee successfully instituted her cooperative learning plan and was modifying it as needed. Other teachers were asking her about the plan because they had heard the two of us talking about it in the lounge. Tyrone's work productivity had increased; teasing was down but not out. Mrs. Washington had met with Mrs. Hoyt to review Tyrone's work, and the meeting went well. Our principal, cagey administrator that she is, asked me to organize the homework-helper workshop for next semester but, of course, to show her the plans before implementing anything! This sort of responsibility-without-authority dynamic is the royal road to stress, but it comes with the territory in the schools. I'll do it.

EVALUATION AND CLOSURE

The goals of this project were to reduce Tyrone's teasing behavior and increase his work completion. Although data on teasing were not kept after the third week, the consultee felt that the problem had been dealt with in two ways: She and Mrs. Washington told Tyrone that they didn't want him to tease, and Mrs. Hoyt gave Tyrone a sense of responsibility in the classroom through her cooperative learning scheme. From time to time he continues to tease or provoke others, but it isn't common and doesn't bother her anymore. The issues of medication and special education referral have also gone away. This often happens when a teacher learns to like a child more because she is having more success with him [13].

On the home front, Mrs. Washington is generally consistent about following through with the home–school report form, missing it only about once a week. Some days, she says, she just can't get to it. I'll keep calling her once a week for a few more

weeks to encourage her; she'll let me know if she needs any more help. We talked briefly about Tyrone's father. She informed me that "the less said about him, the better." I decided to let it be. We also talked about the possibility of counseling, but she wasn't interested unless it was with Tyrone only at school. Mr. Pruzek, upon reviewing our progress to date, suggested that we seemed to have a positive, growth-oriented program for Tyrone, and we should carry on with this plan and consult with him in a month to make any further determination regarding counseling for Tyrone. He pointed out that many students on his waiting list were more seriously needy than Tyrone. He agreed to call Mrs. Washington to discuss Tyrone's teasing interactions with his brother. For the present, we'll continue with the interventions as described, and touch base with each other as needed.

NOTES AND COMMENTS ON CASE I

Overall, this was a relatively simple and successful case. The consultant was able to give positive direction to both the teacher and the parent-consultee, and their efforts had a beneficial effect on the student's behavior.

In this case, as in all others, there were a number of choice points: times when the consultant needed to make a strategy or tactic decision. Although not all of these decisions are equally important, some can influence the course of the consultation in very dramatic ways, both philosophically and practically.

Following is a list of questions and comments derived from the various events in this case, indicated by the bracketed numbers in the narrative.

1.   The consultant decides to deal with the case herself instead of putting it through the SST. When is this a good idea? What are some criteria to follow to determine whether a case should go to the SST or be referred directly to a specialist or an administrator?

2.   What are the characteristics of effective teachers at the lower middle-grade level? What are some teacher behaviors you look for when visiting a class at this level? How could you evaluate a class to determine factors that might be causative or contributive to behavior or learning problems?

3.   Is the consultant overreacting to the consultee's comments? Is it possible that the consultee just wants some assistance, not a pat answer? The issue may not be the consultee's direct request. Consultants sometimes believe that they have to provide the expertise of content. The consultee, however, always appreciates the expertise of process but only sometimes that of content. What guidelines might you follow when giving advice?

4.   When the issue of activity reinforcers comes up, consultees may reject this idea because they believe it isn't fair to give these favored activities to bad-acting students as reinforcers for good behavior when students who are ordinarily well

behaved do not get these privileges. How would you respond to a consultee who makes this objection?

5.   Here the consultant is assuming that the consultee knows how to keep data on this teasing behavior. Has the consultee been given enough direction? What might happen if nothing more specific is said about what the data should look like?

6.   Does your district have a policy on recommending medical referral or even medication? Interview psychologists, nurses, administrators, counselors, and others to see how they deal with this issue. Since there is the possibility of ADHD, should Mrs. Hoyt (and Mrs. Washington) be asked to fill out an ADHD rating scale? This issue is discussed further in the section on psychodynamic, ecological, and bio-physical factors (p. 300).

7.   A daily home–school homework reminder sheet is fairly common, especially in the middle and junior high grades. Many students can't or won't bother to keep track of their homework responsibilities during these years, and this system works well for many of them. You might ask people working at the middle or junior high level their opinions about this intervention.

8.   It's interesting to see how the consultant turned a question about sibling battles into a discussion about turning off the TV and engaging in cooperative family activities. Of course, it was Mrs. Washington who had already used a reduction of TV watching, spurred by her concerns about the effects of sitcom interactions. The consultant was quick to pick up on this and to suggest ways of filling the evenings with cooperative activities. Some families find this very hard to do. Working parents often comment that they are too tired when they get home from work; TV is the activity of choice. How might a consultant bring up the possibility of a TV-free hour or so every school night? What suggestions do you have for how parents might fill that time?

9.   Why doesn't Tyrone's father spend any time with his children? To what extent should a school-based consultant explore this question? It involves delving into the core of this family's dynamics, which can be a dangerous process if not handled sensitively. If this school had a counselor with the time to engage in this sort of case exploration other than the very part-time psychologist, Mr. Pruzek, it would be worth doing. More likely, it is the sort of issue usually referred to a family-service or child-guidance clinic, with hopes that the parents will follow through with the referral. As we will see later, Mrs. Washington is currently against bringing up the topic of Mr. Washington.

10.   What do you think of these interventions? What alternatives or additional interventions would you suggest? Remember, we also have activated Tyrone's mother in the process with the home–school report system.

11.   In Chapter 2, you learned about the mental health model of consultation. Recall the Caplans' four "lacks": skill, knowledge, confidence, and objectivity (Caplan & Caplan, 1993). In working with teacher and parent-consultees, you will confront situations where these lacks are evident. It is the consultant's responsibility to work toward reducing these lacks through direct instruction and personal support

(in the case of lack of confidence). Modeling, role playing, coaching, and so on are all appropriate methods to employ in providing assistance to teacher and parent-consultees who need help in areas crucial to intervention success. What other lacks have you observed in those who work directly with students?

12.   One of the fascinating offshoots of consultation work is the number of ideas that come to mind about ways of improving the schools, especially for at-risk students. Hardly a conference goes by without the consultant saying, if only to herself, "What if . . . ?" or "Wouldn't it be great if. . . . ?" In this case, the consultant raises the question of a set of workshops for parents regarding homework. What does your school do about communicating with parents about homework and ways in which parents can assist with it? Some helpful references are Hoover-Dempsey, Bassler, and Burow (1995), Keith (1987), Lombana (1983), and Swap (1987). Recently, Cooper, Valentine, Nye, and Lindsay (1999) have presented data indicating that students who do more homework have higher grades. In their study, this was true across gender, grade, ethnicity, and SES.

13.   Sometimes when school-based consultants evaluate a situation in which a student is referred, they find out that the referred student does not have as serious a problem as do other students in the same class. For some reason, however, she is picked by the teacher for referral. Barring parental pressure or other reasons, it is sometimes the case that the referring teacher and the referred student have failed to bond, which causes the teacher to select this student not so much to seek assistance for the student but in hopes of having the student transferred somewhere else, either to special education or to someone else's class. When you suspect this might be the case, what can you do to improve the bond between the teacher and the student? Caplan and Caplan (1993) discuss this as a lack of objectivity; the referring teacher sees something in the targeted student that prompts a referral. The teacher somehow doesn't see it in others. Zins, Curtis, Graden, and Ponti (1988) are a good resource for dealing with teacher–student interactions and discovering ways of assisting teachers to develop better interpersonal relations with their students. There are also many related ideas in Stoner, Shinn, and Walker (1991).

Case B   Defiance

Todd, who is now 14 years, two months of age, was referred in November of his seventh-grade year because of his defiant behavior, particularly toward his social studies and English teachers, who "have had it up to here with him." A review of the referral with his other teachers revealed that he was a fair student with them, not an academic star but not a big problem. They would not have referred him.

Two years ago, Todd's fifth-grade teacher noticed this problem. She suspended him twice, referred him to the school counselor, and also referred him to SST. Todd was somewhat better in grade six, where he was under the thumb of a particularly forceful male teacher. Now in the seventh grade, Todd has six different teachers and reacts differently to each of them, being particularly difficult in the classrooms of the two referring teachers, Mrs. Hansen and Ms. Jones.

Todd was retained in grade one. In grade three he was referred for learning disability placement but was not found eligible under his district's strict guidelines. The district has no other funded source of help for poor achievers, so parents are advised to find whatever tutoring they can on their own. Todd apparently did get some tutoring during grade three, and his reading and writing skills improved. However, he has remained a poor academic student, typically earning Cs and Ds [1].

Todd is the younger of two children in an intact family. His father is a machinist, steadily employed, and his mother works full time as a department store clerk. Todd's older brother, now 18, dropped out of high school in his junior year and is employed for 20 hours a week at McDonald's. He has gang affiliations but has not been arrested. Todd admits to not liking his brother; in fact, he may be afraid of him.

Todd's mother, Mrs. Blanca, states that Todd has been increasingly defiant toward her, also. He is not this way toward his father. Mrs. Blanca would like help in dealing with Todd, since she is afraid he will turn out like his older brother if somebody doesn't do something about it soon.

RECEIPT OF A REFERRAL AND INITIAL THOUGHTS ABOUT IT

My name is Bobbi Casey. I'm the counselor for the seventh grade at Kennedy Junior High, which has 1,000 students in grades seven, eight, and nine. At Kennedy we use a consultation-based service delivery model, which means that we try to work collaboratively with one another to help solve the learning or behavior problems of our students. All initial referrals come to the grade-level counselor, who decides how to deal with them. Learning problem referrals are usually sent to the SST or the RSP teacher-consultant, but behavior or adjustment problems may stay in my office unless the referring teacher or a school administrator believes they should go to the SST for some reason. I sometimes refer cases to the school psychologist or to the SST.

I learned about Todd last May when I took my annual trip to the K–6 feeder school to consult with its counselor about "red flag" students, whom we are now calling "at risk." Of the 60 students coming from that school, Todd's name was among the 5 identified as potential dropouts based on his fifth- and sixth-grade teachers' comments and the fact that his older brother had dropped out. Our procedure is to call all at-risk students into our office during the first week of the semester and get to know them. I remember Todd from that meeting; in my notes I wrote that he was sullen and uncommunicative, very defensive, and eager to get out of my office. I meant to get back to him again but got too busy with everything else. When the referral came last week, I wasn't surprised [2].

Our teachers are asked to try to define their concerns behaviorally: to give concrete examples and to avoid inferences. Mrs. Hansen and Ms. Jones put in the referral together since their lunchroom conversation convinced them that Todd was acting the same way in each of their rooms. His other teachers say he is a poor student but not a big problem.

My initial impressions are that Todd is too old (too mature physically) for seventh grade (the ghost of first-grade retention has come back to haunt us), that he seeks out nice (weak, defenseless) women to humiliate, and that he feels that his main chance at recognition is to act the role of a rebellious teen and to lead his less-mature peers into the joys of adolescent nonconformity. The referring teachers may have different views. Let's see [3].

INITIAL DISCUSSION WITH THE TEACHERS

Both consultees came to see me at lunchtime today. I've known each of them for at least three years. They are both competent; Mrs. Hansen tends to be much less outgoing than Ms. Jones. After brief pleasantries we got into our discussion. They defined Todd's problems (behaviors of concern) as refusal to follow directions, verbally provoking others, and talking back to both teachers with an attitude that says, "Hey, Teach, make me." Both have spoken to him about these concerns; he acts disinterested, bored, and condescending. Both have called home. Mrs. Hansen talked to Mr. Blanca, who told her that she has to be firm with him. Ms. Jones talked to Mrs. Blanca, who said that she would talk to Todd about it but was putting up with the same behavior herself.

I asked both consultees to demonstrate for me what he did, while I played the part of a teacher. They were quite forthcoming in their portrayal of an arrogant pop-off, the kind you're glad isn't your child. I then asked about their reactions to him. They agreed that it varied depending on the situation, but usually they gave him a frown of disapproval, asked him to apologize, or threatened to send him to the office. Mrs. Hansen had sent him twice, but Ms. Jones hadn't, pending advice from me. I asked them about the frequency of these defiant behaviors. They estimated that they occurred once or twice a day, depending on their need to interact directly with him. His behavior toward the other students tended to be bullying. He's bigger than almost everybody else, seems sexually more mature, and flaunts it. He probably says suggestive things to some of the girls because they are often heard telling him to shut up. All in all, he isn't liked, but he is given a rather wide berth. In short, Todd is an unpopular student who is increasing the behaviors that make him unpopular. He seems to be the kind of student that Dreikurs, Grunwald, and Pepper (1982) had in mind for the category "power seekers." If you use the *DSM*-IV, you might say that he has an oppositional defiant disorder; according to Quay's (1986) system, Todd would be classified as having a conduct disorder [4].

With time being short as usual, we decided to keep track of the client's defiant behavior for one week, during which I would call him into my office and discuss the problem with him. Mrs. Hansen said she wanted to do more; she was burning out fast. I asked her what she had in mind. She suggested detention contingent on his refusal to follow her directions, if only to get his attention. Ms. Jones readily agreed but was concerned that detention might make him worse. What did I think? I said that each of them had the right to invoke the detention contingency; it was available. However, the school principal and the counseling staff discouraged its use, preferring to deal with disruptive behavior in nonpunitive ways.

The teachers each decided to keep track of Todd's defiant acts and then, after class every day, have him stay long enough for them to tell him what they had observed. I asked them to consider telling him about any positive things he might have done, but they both looked at me as if to say "You haven't been paying attention." Then they both rushed off to class [5].

CLASSROOM OBSERVATION

Ordinarily I try to do classroom observations, especially if I don't know the teacher very well, if the teacher asks me to, or if the behavior is so strange that it has to be seen. In this case I thought I knew what I would see in both classes. After all, I had seen other students, both boys and girls, play this sort of game in the past. I decided to forego the visit and instead have Todd come in to see me.

I hoped that by going to a direct-service approach with the client instead of the usual indirect approach of consultation I would be able to get a deeper understanding of the dynamics that might account for Todd's behavior. I wanted to confront him with its importance, just as the consultees were doing. This was about to become Todd's week on the hot seat [6].

INITIAL DISCUSSION WITH THE PARENTS

I reached Mrs. Blanca by phone at work for one of those one-minute phone calls that are often all you can get with working people. I reviewed our concerns; she understood. I asked her how we might be able to help. She said she thought he needed to be dealt with firmly. She wasn't able to be firm with him because "He is my baby." A customer was waiting; she explained. What time could she call me? Tomorrow between 8:30 and 9:00? I agreed. Good, she'd call. Good-bye [7].

GETTING TEACHERS AND PARENTS TOGETHER: THE SST MEETING

As I have indicated, I rarely go to the SST with a behavior problem unless it is very severe and is definitely impeding academic progress. It is possible, of course, that SST members might come up with some ideas beyond what my consultees and I can come up with, but in this case I didn't think so. Rather than take members' time at this point, I opted to skip the SST; perhaps we'll come back to it later.

ASSESSMENT OF THE REFERRED STUDENT

Learning Problem Assessment

As implied earlier, Todd is not strong academically, but his achievement, according to the group tests, is not seriously deficient. He can hold his own academically when he chooses to do so. I did not plan for any further academic assessment at this time.

Functional Assessment of Behavior

I decided that I could better engage in this activity after I met with Todd and heard again from the teachers. Todd and I met for 15 minutes the next morning. Initially he acted like he had done before: closed-mouthed, sullen, mildly hostile, and generally uncooperative. I tried all my reflective techniques, but there wasn't much forthcoming from him except denial and apparent distortion. Here is a transcript of our conversation:

Consultant: Todd, I've asked you to come in to see me again because I'm concerned about your relationship with two of your teachers, Mrs. Hansen and Ms. Jones.

Todd: What're you talking about? I didn't do nothing.

Consultant: What these two teachers have told me is that you sometimes refuse to follow their directions, you provoke others and get them angry with you, and you talk back to these teachers.

Todd: [silence]

Consultant: [after 20 seconds] I've hit you with some pretty bad news. I'm wondering what you think about what I've said.

Todd: Yeah, well, they're like picking on me, you know. There's plenty of guys screwing off in there, and I'm the one who's in trouble.

Consultant: You're concerned that they're picking on you and you're in some sort of trouble for it?

Todd: Yeah.

Consultant: You're probably right that there are some others who also give the teachers grief, and you may also be right about being in some trouble with your teachers. After all, they don't like it when students don't behave well in class. Do you see how they could be bothered by your behavior?

Todd: Yeah, but they're always bugging me about, you know, like, "Do this, do that." I do my work. The other teachers ain't complaining, are they?

Consultant: I'm glad you brought that up. You're right. I've asked all your other teachers, and they tell me you're doing OK in their classes. So obviously you're not a troublemaker. What is it about these two classes? That's what I'd like to know.

Todd: They're a drag. The stuff's boring. Who cares about history anyway? And in English we only write and listen to everybody read. What a bore.

Consultant: Not all of your work is exciting to you. What subjects do you like this semester?

Todd: Phys ed, home ec; math's a drag, but Mr. Simpson's cool. Shop's got too many rules. They're all OK, I guess. I gotta get back to class now.

Consultant: I realize this sort of conversation isn't your favorite thing to do, but I need you to stay longer. We still haven't worked out this problem with Ms. Jones and Mrs. Hansen. Let me tell you what is going to be happening this week. Mrs. Hansen and Ms. Jones are going to be keeping notes on your behavior, and they're—

Todd: [interrupting] Yeah, yeah. Mrs. Hansen already bugged me about it. She's all like going to send me to Club Med [the students' name for detention]. You tell her to do that?

Consultant: No, but if she or Ms. Jones decides to do it, I would support them. I'm feeling that you don't realize what impact your behavior has on them.

Todd: [grinning] Yeah, I bug 'em a little. It's no big deal. What're you telling me? I gotta like kiss up to 'em?

Consultant: Kissing up is one thing I don't think I could talk you into. You're not that kind of guy. I'm more concerned about what we can do to make your time with these teachers more interesting so you won't feel the need to bug them. What I'd like you to be thinking about, and what I'll be thinking about also, are ways that we could make your time in their rooms more enjoyable for everybody, without this business of bugging people being such a big part [8].

Todd: Hey, I think if everybody just got off my back and didn't make such a big deal about a little teasing we'd get along just fine. Can I go back to class now?

Consultant: I know this isn't comfortable for you, but we need to come to some sort of agreement on a plan. What I'd like to do is meet with you again next week after the teachers have shown me their data for this week. In the meantime I'll be thinking of some ways to make your experience in their classes better for everybody, and I'd like you to be doing the same. What do you say, partner?

Todd: Huh? Yeah, OK, I dunno. They gonna be showing you all the stuff they're writing down?

Consultant: Yes, I asked them to so that I would have a better idea of what their concerns are. What I'd like you to do is to be thinking about some ideas about how these classes can be better for you and for everybody.

Todd: Yeah, all right. Maybe I should be writing down what they do. When will I see you again?

Consultant: You know, that's not such a bad idea, you writing down what they do. Why don't you, as long as it doesn't get in the way of your assignments? I'll call for you next week, probably during a different period. What don't you want to miss?

Todd: Phys ed.

Consultant: OK. Before you go, is there anything else you'd like to talk to me about?

Todd: Nah.

Consultant: OK. I'll see you in a week. Bye.

As the week went by, I saw Todd in the hallway a couple of times. He didn't look at me.

The teacher-consultees met with me at the agreed-on time and showed me their data. In both cases there had been a dramatic decrease in the rate of defiance relative to their memory of preceding weeks. One problem of starting an intervention before getting solid baseline data is that it is sometimes difficult to know if you are making any headway. In this case, as in many others in the schools, teacher-consultees do not want to put off interventions pending solid baseline data; their classes are often being ruined by these behaviors. They know about how often the behaviors occur, so they will often start intervening with or without your approval. In this case, they were determined to do something, so they did.

Their treatment, as I have mentioned, was to keep a record of Todd's transgressions and to inform him of them after each period. I asked that they also inform him of good behaviors they had observed, and both thought I was putting them on: after all, Todd never did anything right. As it turned out, they were both surprised to find that not only had his defiance calmed down, but they were actually able to point out something nice he had done in both classes. He helped a slow learner correct his spelling in English, and he commented positively on a nice map-coloring job a student had done in social studies. They wondered what magic I had performed in my meeting with him. So did I, but I deflected the praise to their strategy, while also wondering if the threat of Club Med may have been influential. It seemed almost too good to be true. I suggested that we decide how to proceed. They wanted to drop the written record of his negative behaviors because he seemed to have learned his lesson and also because it was tiresome. So what should we do?

This sort of decision point is very common in consultation. The consultant has established good rapport with the consultees, they are eager to start an intervention, and within a week they are singing your praises because the intervention seems to be working. You're often amazed yourself. But your experience tells you to be aware of the honeymoon phenomenon. Todd's behavior has a long history;

to expect it to be extinguished in favor of more prosocial behavior on the basis of a few interventions is asking for too much too soon. What very often happens, especially if you believe the problems are solved and therefore terminate with the consultees or agree to put the issue on the back burner, is that the consultees call you back in another few weeks to tell you that the student has regressed to his old self.

In terms of a functional assessment of Todd's behavior, I see the major driving forces (positive consequences) being power and attention (Dreikurs et al., 1982). With his bullying tactics he is able to gain a sense of control over others and also gain whatever prestige there is in being defiant to adults. This is the way he has established his role, his identity, and the desperate sort of self-esteem that derives from this position. He receives a lot of negative attention (primarily from teachers, but also from his peers) for his defiant acts, which seems to be what he wants. Until recently (since this last intervention), he never seemed to seek attention for being positive, only for being negative. The antecedents were directions from the teacher or another student telling him to do something, or something internal that prompted him to defy convention. The consequences were usually twofold: He made an impression on others for his defiance, and he got into trouble with the teachers. This dual response (positive because Todd got the hoped-for, and presumably pleasurable, result of watching others be mad at or afraid of him; negative because he got disapproval) is very common in the case of defiance and other forms of behavior problems. One has to assume that the pleasure gained from attention getting and power struggling outweigh the pain. Otherwise, what's the point?

Additional Areas of Assessment: Psychodynamic, Ecological, and Biophysical Factors

We know that Todd comes from a home in which the disciplinary power seems to belong primarily to the father; his mother admits this. We have also learned that Todd has an older brother who had school difficulties and possibly engages in antisocial behaviors. Although Todd does not seem to identify strongly with his brother, he is at a stage in which he may resort to a lowest common denominator as a temporary model. Clearly his mother is concerned about this. One wonders if she hasn't made reference to Todd about his turning out like his brother, a future scenario that she fears.

In an effort to understand the dynamics that support and drive Todd's behavior and to suggest ways in which Mr. and Mrs. Blanca might be able to work together in helping Todd through his adolescence, I decided to arrange a meeting with one or, preferably, both parents along with Todd. Pending that meeting, I reviewed with the two consultees what I thought were the dynamics so far and mentioned my concerns about stopping their apparently successful intervention after only a week. They agreed to continue with the present plan, probably because they sensed that I wanted them to.

Mr. and Mrs. Blanca agreed to come to the school at 7:30 the following morning. We could have 15 minutes together. I asked them to bring Todd with them [9]. When they arrived, we spent a few minutes with small-talk rapport building and then got into our mutual interests. When I talked about the concerns of both consultees, Mrs. Blanca nodded a lot, and Mr. Blanca looked very unhappy, glancing first at me and then at Todd. I also revealed the latest turnaround that the consultees had reported, emphasizing Todd's prosocial actions. This gained a smile from everybody except, unfortunately, Mr. Blanca. Deciding to focus on the negative only, he pinned Todd down with an angry look and told him he won't have that sort of behavior and this is the last he wants to hear of it. (Wouldn't it be nice if that's all it took, I thought!) Mr. Blanca didn't comment on the prosocial part. Todd's response was that he was doing fine in all the other classes; these two were just boring. To my surprise, Mrs. Blanca said that if that was true, couldn't Todd be moved out of those classes? I thought all of these comments were telling in regard to the family dynamics: Mr. Blanca gives an order and focuses on the negative, and Mrs. Blanca makes an excuse and seeks an escape route for Todd. I responded by saying that Todd and I were discussing his behavior in social studies and English. I felt that we had made some good progress over the past week and that we should continue to try to have Todd meet his responsibilities in all his classes since I felt confident that he could. I asked Todd what he thought, and he said, "Yeah, I guess." I thought that answer kept him OK in the sight of both parents: He's passively promising to behave to satisfy his father, and he's leaving the door open for continued complaints about these boring classes in case he needs to use this ploy again with his mother. I suggested that we talk about ways in which Todd's parents could help him with his schoolwork, and both parents sat up to listen. Todd looked bored.

I mentioned the following four ways that parents can help:

1. Set aside a homework time.
2. Ask to see what the assignments are before and after they are done.
3. Give help and encouragement as needed.
4. Check periodically with Todd's teachers to see how he is doing.

I gave them the teachers' room phone numbers and the time of each teacher's free period. (They had been sent this information at the beginning of the year, but they couldn't remember it.) We concluded the conference by reassuring each other that Todd could do well and that we would work together closely to see that he does [10].

The biophysical possibilities were not brought up at this meeting because there was no reason to suspect that Todd has any difficulty in this area. He has always been healthy, he's never shown any of the symptoms of ADHD, and his vision and hearing are normal. In this case there does not seem to be any significant biophysical contributors to his behaviors.

I asked both consultees to meet with me after school for ten minutes to review the conference. They were both pleased with me for taking the time to have the conference, and they felt that things looked good. We briefly discussed the classroom situation (demands, class format, seating arrangements, grouping, and so on) and any ways we could think of to change Todd's role image in the classroom. We had already decided to continue monitoring his defiance and to give him daily feedback. Now we decided to put more emphasis on whatever prosocial things we see him doing. I said I would find an excuse for getting him to help me on some task in my office and to chat with him while he was doing it.

PLANNING INTERVENTIONS

In this case, the plan (that is, the set of steps the consultees will take to correct the problem) has already been in effect for more than a week. As I have mentioned, violating the sequential nature of the steps in the SOCS process described in Chapter 5 is common. Consultees are anxious to try something, and they will do so, if only unwittingly. Remember that when the consultee refers a student to the consultant, a plan is already in effect. It probably isn't working—hence, the referral. Given this reality, it might be more accurate to call this section of the process "plan modification" rather than "implementation." In any event, at this point we take all the information we have and decide what to do.

The collaboratively derived plan we adopted consists of keeping track of defiant episodes and prosocial behaviors and reviewing them with Todd at the end of each social studies and English period. This requires some time investment from the teachers, but so far they have accepted it. At the same time they are not reprimanding Todd when he is defiant but are treating his behavior with benign neglect. Of course, this reaction can have its limits: Todd may push his behavior to a point where the consultee is required to take stronger steps in order to keep classroom decorum. Fortunately, this hasn't happened yet. The purpose of this approach is to let Todd know, with only a slight delay of feedback, what he is doing that irritates others and what prosocial behaviors have been observed. Hopefully he will get the point and give up the irritating behaviors.

Why should Todd give up this behavior? It has been his calling card, his identity, for a long time and has certain gains associated with it. Why risk giving that up when there is no assurance that its substitute will yield the same gains? One possible answer comes from the Dreikurs et al. (1982) notions of power and attention. Dreikurs et al. refer to these as "mistaken goals of behavior," activities a student engages in when "he has lost his belief that he can find the belonging and recognition that he desires, and erroneously believes that he will find acceptance through provocative behavior by pursuing the mistaken goals of behavior" (p. 14). The appropriate method suggested is to give the student the attention he seeks when he engages in prosocial behavior (as when the behaviorist rewards good behavior while ignoring inappropriate behavior; Alberto & Troutman, 1999; Walker & Shea, 1999), to avoid power struggles by not confronting the student who is trying to pull you into one, and to find some way to give the student a prosocial power base. In cases of both attention seeking and power, the consultee must let the student know what the purpose of the behavior is: to be noticed, and to be part of the social group by negative rather than by positive means. (For further suggestions about this technique, see Albert, 1996; and Ferguson, 1995.) The consultee must also suggest how the child can have his needs for attention and power met in ways that do not disrupt the rights of others to learn.

My concern at this point is threefold: (1) Will it work? (2) If it does, how do we phase it out? (3) If it doesn't, what's next? Also, I'm wondering what sort of stress these new expectations are having on Todd. We're asking him to change a behavior of long duration; how does he deal with the temptation to revert to his old self, especially if provoked by someone? One way to assist a client with a behavioral transition is to use some "stop and think" cognitive behavior modification techniques (Brigham, 1989; Durrant, 1995; Hughes, 1988; Kendall & Braswell, 1985; Larson, 1992; Larson & McBride, 1990; Murphy & Duncan, 1997). Essentially, these techniques consist of getting a cooperative client to analyze his thought processes in order to see where anger or irrational thinking (Robinson, Smith, Miller, & Brownell, 1999) or mistaken goal problems (Dreikurs et al., 1982) can get him into trouble.

Who has the time or skill to provide such training? In the best of all possible worlds, it would be readily available at the school, in a local clinic, or through a cooperative arrangement with some mental health treatment source. Going outside the school requires major parental commitment and possibly some financial resources. Would Todd's parents think this was worth the investment? I didn't ask, so I never found out. Instead, I thought I'd start with a resource right here: our own school psychologist, Ms. Marks. I'd ask her if she might be interested in this problem.

She was. Not only did she see this as a very good use of her time; but since she knew of at least five other students who could benefit from the same sort of training, she decided to start a group for cognitive behavior modification centering on aggressive, defiant behaviors. Wow! What a stroke of luck! It's amazing what you can come up with right on your own staff if you look for it. She wrote a brief description of what she wanted to do with the group based on the Kendall and Braswell (1985) model, called the parents of the six boys she had in mind (including Todd's parents), got phone approval from all six, and sent official permission forms to them the same day. Five were returned, and she started with these five the next week. Ms. Marks does not waste time.

IMPLEMENTING INTERVENTIONS

Because of the usual round of crises in the life of a junior high counselor, I lost touch with Todd for a week. Mrs. Hansen stopped by to see me and asked what had happened. I showed her my desk full of pink slips (calls to be returned), career information materials to be distributed, and so on, and she understood. She said that Todd was slipping somewhat. He had smarted-off to her that morning and she wondered what we were doing about it. At that point, so did I.

I called a meeting of the two consultees and our school psychologist, Ms. Marks. We spent some time reviewing what had happened over the past week or so, what was going on in the group counseling with Ms. Marks, and what we should do at this point. Ms. Jones reflected some frustration: The honeymoon of our initial treatment plan seemed to have ended. Why? Was this common? Is all this effort worth it? She was showing signs of depression, somewhat seconded by Mrs. Hansen. They were in the mood for revenge. Ms. Jones suggested that we proceed with detention.

Students like Todd often have this effect on teachers. Todd's defiance flies in the face of everything teachers stand for. Students who flaunt their ability to spoil teachers' efforts are very challenging. Consultants need to be aware of this. Teachers have their ego needs satisfied by teaching, watching students progress, and feeling that they are making a valuable contribution to society through their efforts. They are achieving Maslow's (1968) stage of self-actualization when they are teaching well; students who get in the way of that achievement frustrate teachers and can cause them to regress in their behavior in the classroom. They need an objective outsider who can work with their feelings of discouragement, help them to see what role the defiant student is playing, and help them cope with that role and (we hope) successfully turn it around. This is an excellent opportunity for a school-based consultant.

One of the first things that consultees need to understand is that behavior problems are rarely remediated in a short period of time. They usually have a long reinforcement history; they have been meeting the client's needs at some level, and for a student to give them up may require the application of resources and influences not entirely controlled by the school. A review of the reasons for poor behavior (see Chapter 6) shows some of the issues important in creating and sustaining a behavior problem that may require the assistance of nonschool personnel: parents, medical practitioners, and counselors who have time to engage in relatively long-term therapy. But let's see what our team has to say.

Ms. Marks, our psychologist, reported that Todd came to the counseling group and tried to jeopardize it. He was silly, wouldn't take part in the activities, and said he wanted to quit. Ms. Marks kept him after the others had gone and listened to his concerns. He was afraid of being identified as a crazy who had to see a shrink. He saw no point in taking part in the group since his behavior had improved. Ms. Marks explained that the purpose of the group was to help youngsters learn to understand themselves and why they react the way they do. She reminded Todd of his long history of defiance, what effect it had on others, and its likely long-term consequences. Apparently Todd softened and agreed to come back to the group. Ms. Marks described Todd as having a hard-shell finish but a much softer interior [11].

Mrs. Hansen wants to have an after-school conference with Todd and lay down the law to him. She will use after-school detention the next time he smarts off and have him call his parents in her presence so he can explain to them (preferably the father) why he got detention. That's it. She's had it.

Both consultees want to drop the daily monitoring. It's a bother, and Todd doesn't seem to care about it. Ms. Jones was able to report some good news, however. In her social studies class, Todd hadn't really been a problem for the past week. He had been doing his work adequately and had turned in a project report that he had done at home. She was favorably impressed. She complimented Todd on it, and he said that his parents were on him about his homework, so he had to do it. Ms. Jones sensed, however, that he really was proud of himself for having done a job on time. I made a note to call Todd's mom and to reinforce her efforts in the homework area.

We discussed the problem further and decided on the following:

1. I would call Todd in to review where we were, compliment him on his behavior in Ms. Jones's class and on getting the paper in on time, and get some commitments from him regarding the issues we have discussed.
2. Ms. Marks would continue her counseling group with him.
3. Mrs. Hansen would see him after school and tell him that she would be calling his dad and sending Todd to after-school detention if he refused to obey requests or used any defiant language toward her.
4. Ms. Jones would keep her fingers crossed, hoping that his cooperative behavior in her room wasn't just a fluke. She would also find ways to make him feel part of the group whenever she could.

My conversation with Todd went very well. He apologized to me for giving Mrs. Hansen a hard time; he won't apologize to her, however, because he doesn't like her. He says she's too bossy. We discussed ways in which he could make himself a useful contributor in Ms. Jones's class, such as volunteering to help another child or just learning to keep his hostile comments to himself. He said that he was working on that in Ms. Marks's group. He was learning to put a roadblock between his brain and his mouth and to count to three before responding whenever he thought he was going to say something somebody wouldn't like. He enjoys it! I commented that it must feel good to know that he is able to control himself when he wants to. He smiled and said that he was having fun learning how to talk to himself about his emotions. He didn't know he could do that. He thought his father ought to take some lessons, and his brother, too! I went on to tell him that Ms. Jones had told me about his good behavior in her room and that she was impressed that he had gotten his paper in on time. Todd told me that seven kids were late with theirs. I had the sense that he was proud to be on the good side for a change.

Mrs. Hansen had her conference with him. Surprisingly, he did apologize to her, even before she had a chance to tell him about the consequences he would suffer if he was defiant with her. She did anyway, not trusting him to turn over a new leaf without some punishment consequence attached to it. She may be right, given his attitude toward her. She really doesn't deserve his hostility. She's upset with his negative behavior and has allowed herself to be pulled into a power play with him. I think that is what Todd means by calling her bossy. She's been burned enough. When he left the conference with her, he said that she wouldn't get a chance to send him to detention "even if she wanted to." We didn't know what to make of that comment.

I called Todd's mom at work and had about one minute to boost her spirits by reporting the good news. She was ecstatic, of course. I also complimented her on being sure that Todd had done his social studies homework. She said that Mr. Blanca had stepped in and insisted that Todd do homework from 6:30 to 8:00 in the evening, whether he had any or not. This simple intervention apparently has sent a message to Todd that we all agree that he will have to become a real student rather than a hanger-on, a troublemaker. I think the Blancas' experience with their older son has taught them a lesson; they aren't going to let Todd slip away, too.

MONITORING INTERVENTIONS

I decided to put Todd's case on the back burner for awhile. Two weeks later, Mrs. Hansen was in to see me about another boy in her class, and I asked about Todd. She said he was much improved. She had to send him to detention only once, and he handled it very well. She expected an angry outburst from him but got none. I told her to mention the matter to Ms. Marks; she said she would. I haven't heard from Ms. Jones, but I think things are going well in there. I'll check in another week or so. Ms. Marks is bursting her buttons over her success with her group, Todd included. While she was in such a good mood, I brought up a continual problem, which is very significant for first-time parents of teenagers: communicating with teens. Anybody who has had teens or worked with them knows what they can be like. She took an immediate interest and said that she would like to try the STEP-Teen program with a small pilot group. Who would I recommend? I suggested that we put a notice in the school–home newsletter and announce it, including a clip-out sheet interested parents could return. We should offer it once during the daytime hours and again during an evening for working parents, about four sessions each. OK? Good, Ms. Marks commented. She'll talk to the newsletter editor about it. I plan to make a personal call to Mrs. Blanca and a few others I'm aware of to personally invite them to attend.

EVALUATION AND CLOSURE

I did not do any formal evaluation. We had gathered no real data; the exact dates of the different types of interventions were not accurately recalled, and so many interventions were going on at the same time that it didn't seem as if the project could be formally evaluated. Who knows what effect the daily record keeping, the threats from Mrs. Hansen and Mr. Blanca, and the group counseling program had on the behavior? Further, in the ordinary school counselor day, there is no time for anything but the most cursory record keeping. I'm not a laboratory with tightly controlled procedures.

All constituents agree that this is a successful case, at least so far. Todd has dropped his defiant act, he's more cooperative, and he's doing more academically. As an interesting spin off, we will soon be starting two parent groups titled "Talking with Your Teen." I plan to sit in on the daytime one.

As you learned in Chapter 5, evaluation has as its goal the determination of the value of something. I think this consultation project was very valuable for all concerned. Although our goals were only loosely set (reduction in defiant acts and verbalizations; increase in academic work production), I think it's fair to say we met them. Some day, when the pink slips are only an inch thick and I don't have oodles of test scores to record and . . . well, you know what a counselor's office is like, I'd like to do one of those tightly designed studies we used to read about in grad school. However, right now, I have to see Mrs. Overdue about a gang problem in her class.

NOTES AND COMMENTS ON CASE 2

This was a generally successful case characterized by a considerable amount of collaboration among the various consultees. From a scientific point of view, the results are difficult to discuss because not much attention was devoted to the analysis of discrete data. In the everyday hubbub of activities that constitute the work of school counselors and other school consultants, careful data analysis is a luxury.

The following is a list of questions and comments derived from the various events in this case, indicated by the bracketed numbers in the narrative.

1. Except for special education, Todd's school has no source of help for students who manifest academic problems. What other kinds of resource programs for assistance are present in the schools with which you are familiar? If you were asked to develop such a resource, how might you go about it?

2. Each school-based consultant has to develop a plan for dealing with at-risk students, however they are locally defined. These students are typically considered unlikely to graduate from high school because of a higher-than-normal number of dropout indicators, such as dysfunctional families, learning problems, antisocial behavior, truancy, and a history of dropping out among older siblings (Walker, Colvin, & Ramsey, 1995). It is very easy to let our good intentions in this regard get lost in the everyday shuffle of students and papers. Generation of an "at-risk committee" headed by an assertive person who is committed to this problem is a first step toward dealing with it. How does your junior high or high school deal with this issue?

3. The question of the value of grade-level retention has been discussed for many years. What is the research evidence concerning this topic? If there are generalizations that result from the research, how might they lead to some guidelines a school could use to decide its own grade-level retention policy? (See Jimerson, Carlson, Rotert, Egeland, & Sroufe, 1997.)

4.   Does the use of these labels help anything? Do they explain why the student engages in the target behaviors, or are they just a convenient way for professionals to communicate with each other? These questions are more than rhetorical. As discussed in Chapter 6, the mental health and special education fields have always had lively discussions about the purpose and usefulness of labeling or diagnosing (Bratten, Kauffman, Bratten, Polsgrove, & Nelson, 1988; Reynolds, Wang, & Walberg, 1987; Ysseldyke, Algozzine, & Thurlow, 1992). It appears that there will always be people who think they know more about a student if a label has been attached. Other people stick to the behaviors. Does a student have ADHD because she doesn't like to sit still for long, is very inquisitive, and often seems lost in the classroom? Or do we simply call her ADHD because the label is needed in order to get special education assistance, accommodations under Section 504 of the Vocational Rehabilitation Act, medical intervention, or insurance reimbursement?

5.   What do you think of this intervention? The point is to alert the student to the fact that the teacher is paying attention to the student's behaviors (to positive behaviors also, we hope) and to encourage the student to curb the negative behaviors. What might you do to encourage teachers to try this relatively simple approach?

6.   The image of the hot seat seems possibly negative. The consultant is responding to a sense of urgency from the teachers and has arranged so far for two interventions: the teachers' daily reporting to Todd about their observations, and time with the counselor, which will be followed with a parent conference by phone. How might you structure this discussion with Todd? Remember that this case could be dealt with by any of a number of school-based consultants. How might a resource teacher deal with the situation at this point?

7.   Although less than ideal, this sort of rushed conference is often the best a consultant can get. We hope that all concerned parties will have more time later to sit down and have a thorough conference. This should be the goal of all collaborative consultants.

8.   Note the counselor's effort to bring Todd into the planning process. Instead of using only interventions done to students, it makes good sense to bring students into the planning to give them a sense of self-determination and control over what happens to them. Students, like consultees, are much more likely to follow plans that they have had a voice in determining. How might you structure this process of student self-determination for Todd to be sure it has a good chance of working?

9.   Once again, the consultant has decided to bring Todd into the discussion, this time with his parents. This is a potentially difficult situation for all parties. Do you think it was a good idea to include Todd at this point, or should more groundwork have been done with the parents before including Todd?

10.   This conference seems to have gone well. School personnel are sometimes concerned about having conferences with parents because they fear being rejected, ignored, or subtly threatened. Develop a list of hopes and fears that teachers have for a conference; do the same for parents. Discuss ways of ensuring that our hopes

are realized (through effective planning, for example) and that our fears can be managed (for instance, by converting negative thoughts to positive).

Negative: The parents may scowl throughout the conference.

Positive: Scowling indicates their discomfort, not their evaluation of me. I have to try to make them more comfortable.

Chapter 5 presents ideas about conferencing with parents, as do Christenson (1992), O'Shea, O'Shea, Algozzine, and Hammitte (2001), Sheridan, Kratochwill, and Bergan (1996), and Turnbull and Turnbull (1997).

11.   The consultant was very pleased that the school psychologist had this conference with Todd and worked through this crisis. It would have been easy for the psychologist to dismiss Todd from the group. Nobody would have been surprised that Todd acted the way he did in the group; that's the way he is. What needs of Todd's are being met by this behavior? How might his needs be met in ways other than the ones he's now using?

REFERENCES

Albert, L. (1996). *A teacher's guide to cooperative discipline.* (Rev. ed.) Circle Pines, MN: American Guidance Service.

Alberto, P., & Troutman, A. (1999). *Applied behavior analysis for teachers.* Upper Saddle River, NJ: Merrill/Prentice Hall.

Barkley, R. A. (1998). *Attention deficit hyperactivity disorder: A handbook for diagnosis and treatment.* New York: Guilford Press.

Block, P. (1981). *Flawless consultation.* Austin, TX: Learning Concepts.

Bratten, S., Kauffman, J., Bratten, B., Polsgrove, L., & Nelson, C. (1988). The Regular Education Initiative (REI): Patent medicine for behavioral disorders. *Exceptional Children, 55,* 21–27.

Brigham, T. (1989). *Self-management for adolescents: A skills-training program.* New York: Guilford Press.

Caplan, G., & Caplan, R. (1993). *Mental health consultation and collaboration.* San Francisco: Jossey-Bass.

Chethik, M. (1985). *Techniques of child therapy.* New York: Guilford Press.

Christenson, S. L. (1992). *Home-school collaboration.* Washington: NASP.

Cooper, H., Valentine, J., Nye, B., & Lindsay, J. (1999). Relationships between five after-school activities and academic achievement. *Journal of Educational Psychology, 91,* 369–383.

Dreikurs, R., Grunwald, B. B., & Pepper, F. C. (1982). *Maintaining sanity in the classroom: Classroom management techniques.* New York: Harper & Row.

Durrant, M. (1995). *Creative strategies for school problems.* New York: Norton.

Ferguson, E. (1995). *Adlerian theory: An introduction.* Chicago: Adler School of Professional Psychology.

Fink, A. (1998). The psychoeducational philosophy: Programming implications for students with behavior disorders. *Behavior in Our Schools, 2*(2), 8–13.

Goodman, G., & Poillion, M. (1992). ADD: Acronym for any dysfunction or difficulty. *Journal of Special Education, 26,* 37–56.

Hoover-Dempsey, K., Bassler, O., & Burow, R. (1995). Parents' reported involvement in students' homework: Strategies and practices. *The Elementary School Journal, 95,* 435–450.

Hughes, J. (1988). *Cognitive behavior therapy with children in schools.* New York: Pergamon.

Jayanthi, M., & Friend, M. (1992). Interpersonal problem solving: A selected literature review to guide practice. *Journal of Educational and Psychological Consultation, 3,* 147–152.

Jimerson, S., Carlson, E., Rotert, M., Egeland, B., & Sroufe, L. A. (1997). A prospective, longitudinal study of the correlates and consequences of early grade retention. *Journal of School Psychology, 35,* 3–25.

Kaiser, S. M., & Woodman, R. W. (1985). Multidiscipli-
nary teams and group decision-making techniques:
Possible solutions to decision-making problems.
School Psychology Review, 14, 457–470.

Keith, T. Z. (1987). Children and homework. In A.
Thomas (Ed.), *Children's needs: Psychological perspectives.* Washington: NASP.

Kendall, P., & Braswell, L. (1985). *Cognitive behavioral
therapy for children.* New York: Guilford Press.

Larson, S. (1992). Anger and aggression management
techniques utilizing the Think First curriculum.
Journal of Offender Rehabilitation, 18, 101–117.

Larson, S., & McBride, S. (1990). *Think First: anger and
aggression management for secondary level students.* VHS tape. Milwaukee, WI: Milwaukee Board
of School Directors.

Lombana, J. (1983). *Home-school partnerships: Guidelines and strategies for educators.* New York: Grune
& Stratton.

Long, N., & Morse, W. (1996). *Conflict in the classroom*
(5th ed.). Austin, TX: PRO-ED.

McKellar, N. A. (1991). Enhancing the IEP process
through consultation. *Journal of Educational and
Psychological Consultation, 2,* 175–187.

Maher, C. A., & Yoshida, R. K. (1985). Multidisciplinary
teams in the schools: Current status and future possibilities. In T. R. Kratochwill (Ed.), *Advances in
school psychology* (Vol. 4, pp. 13–44). Hillsdale, NJ:
Erlbaum.

Maslow, A. (1968). *Toward a psychology of being* (2nd
ed.). Princeton, NJ: Van Nostrand.

Murphy, J. & Duncan, B. (1997). *Brief intervention for
school problems.* New York: Guilford.

O'Shea, D., O'Shea, L., Algozzine, R., & Hammitte, D.
(2001). *Families and teachers of individuals with
disabilities.* Boston: Allyn & Bacon.

Quay, H. (1986). Classification. In H. C. Quay & J. S.
Weery (Eds.), *Psychopathological disorders of childhood* (3rd ed., pp. 35–72). New York: Wiley.

Redl, F. (1972). *When we deal with children.* New York:
Free Press.

Reynolds, M., Wang, M., & Walberg, H. (1987). The
necessary restructuring of special and regular education. *Exceptional Children, 53,* 391–398.

Robinson, T., Smith, S., Miller, M., & Brownell, M.
(1999). Cognitive behavior modification of hyper-
activity/impulsivity and aggression: A meta-analysis
of school-based studies. *Journal of Educational
Psychology, 91,* 195–203.

Sheridan, S. M., Kratochwill, T. R., & Bergan, J. R.
(1996). *Conjoint behavioral consultation: A procedural manual.* New York: Plenum.

Stoner, G., Shinn, M., & Walker, H. (Eds.). (1991).
*Interventions for achievement and behavior prob-
lems.* Silver Spring, MD: NASP.

Swap, S. (1987). *Enhancing parent involvement in
schools: A manual for parents and teachers.* New
York: Teachers College Press.

Turnbull, A., & Turnbull, H. (1997). *Families, professionals, and exceptionality: A special partnership.*
Upper Saddle River, NJ: Merrill/Prentice Hall.

Walker, H., Colvin, G., & Ramsey, E. (1995). *Antisocial
behavior in school: Strategies and best practices.*
Pacific Grove, CA: Brooks/Cole.

Walker, J. E., & Shea, T. M. (1999). *Behavior management: A practical approach for educators* (7th ed.).
Upper Saddle River, NJ: Merrill/Prentice Hall.

Winzer, M., & Mazurek, K. (1998). *Special education
in multicultural contexts.* Upper Saddle River, NJ:
Merrill/Prentice Hall.

Ysseldyke, J., Algozzine, B., & Thurlow, M. (1992).
Critical issues in special education. Boston:
Houghton Mifflin.

Zins, J., Curtis, M., Graden, J., & Ponti, C. (1988).
Helping students succeed in the regular classroom.
San Francisco: Jossey-Bass.

CHAPTER 8

Consulting About Students with Academic Learning Problems

OBJECTIVES

1. Delineate important variables in school learning.

2. Review the most important reasons for poor learning.

3. Discuss methods of assessing problems in learning.

4. Develop an understanding of the scope and sequence of the curriculum.

5. Review the nature of consultation regarding instructional procedures.

6. Present two brief examples of consulting about problems in learning.

7. List numerous general and specific ideas for interventions in the area of problems in learning.

It is December, and Mrs. Kim, the third-grade teacher, is very concerned about the lack of academic success of four of her students, three boys and a girl. She knows that referring students for poor learning is not encouraged in her district, and she believes that referring all four would be a poor reflection on her. She decides to refer them one at a time, probably one per month for the next four months. How should she decide whom to refer first? What factors come into play when a teacher decides to make a referral for poor learning?

Ms. Lopez, the principal at Crossroads Middle School, asks you to talk with her about what she calls the crazy patchwork of learning-problem referrals to SST. Some teachers refer many students, some never refer any, some referrals seem to be for solid reasons, and others seem unnecessary. She wants some guidelines developed so that teachers will better understand what constitutes a good referral for learning (skill attainment) problems as opposed to underachievement (performance; accomplishment of work). How might you, as a school-based consultant, assist Ms. Lopez?

INTRODUCTION

The term *academic learning problems* is used in a broad sense to refer to any student deficit in academic production that concerns the teacher. From a practical point of view, it is usually the teacher (but sometimes a parent) who determines whether or not a learning problem exists. Given the wide variations in achievement patterns among U.S. schools, it is quite possible that one teacher could be very concerned about a child who earns a percentile of 40 on a nationally normed test, whereas another teacher could be very pleased with students who earn that score. Parents, of course, have an important role to play in the referral process, and their influence can determine whether or not a student is referred. There are communities in the United States in which a meeting of the local board of education would be swamped with phone calls from concerned parents if the annual achievement scores reported in the local newspaper indicated a slight drop. In other neighborhoods, however, this level of concern would not be evident. Does this imply that there are more learning problems in the former school district than in the latter? Hardly. It is merely a reflection of the sensitivity of some parents to these issues compared with the more casual, perhaps even defeatist, approach found in other communities.

This chapter reviews information about variables that contribute to school learning, possible causes for academic learning problems, suggestions for how school-based consultants can help teachers and parents understand these problems, and ideas for what can be done about them, particularly within general education classrooms.

IMPORTANT VARIABLES IN SCHOOL LEARNING

School-based consultants need to be aware of the research that delineates the important variables in school learning. What factors really make a difference in whether students learn well or not? Consultees and other school personnel expect consultants to be able to answer their questions about the evidence base for applying one treatment (intervention, remediation) rather than another. Unfortunately, because of the complexity of classroom learning, which is based on the interaction of complicated variables such as students' ability levels, developmental needs, class size, prior achievement, motivation, home support, teaching methods and materials, and so on, you should not expect that any one method of intervention is sure to be better than another in any given case, assuming that both methods have some rational relationship to the needs of the situation. However, a body of literature does inform us about some of the more important variables and suggests which ones should be considered when trying to determine intervention plans.

Wang, Haertel, and Walberg (1993) used three methods—content analysis, expert ratings, and results from meta-analyses—to quantify the importance and consistency of variables that influence learning. Borrowing from the "effective schools" literature (Edmonds, 1979; Purkey & Smith, 1983), Wang et al. (1993) looked at the effects of distal variables (such as school restructuring, types of school organization, and state and local policies) and proximal variables (such as instructional strategies and practices, as well as student aptitudes). In general, their three methods of analysis suggest that the following six theoretical constructs account for the greatest effects on school learning, from most influential to least influential:

1. Student characteristics.
2. Classroom practices.
3. Home and community educational contexts.
4. Design and delivery of curriculum and instruction.
5. School demographics, culture, climate, policies, and practices.
6. State and district governance and organization.

It is clear that proximal variables (numbers 1, 2, and 3) are more important contributors to school success than are distal variables (numbers 4, 5, and 6).

Cohen (cited in Brandt, 1991) maintains that schools should begin restructuring to solve problems by addressing proximal variables, such as curriculum, instruction, and assessment, that emphasize student outcomes. Wang et al. (1993) would certainly agree. These problems are commonly brought to the attention of the school-based consultant, although at the initial referral they may not seem to be involved. Consider this referral statement: "This student has a learning disability. He needs to be in special education." Once the consultant sorts through this statement, she discovers that it is essentially a request for assistance in curriculum, instruction, and assessment. What is needed is an evaluation of the learning environment, along with an assessment of the student's needs. When the results of both pieces of information are available, the consultant, the consultee, and the school can best assess the consultee's statement that the student needs to be in special education.

According to Wang et al. (1993), the key proximal variables that influence student learning are psychological, instructional, and home environment. *Psychological* variables include aptitudes such as cognitive, metacognitive, motivational, and affective. *Instructional* variables include classroom management techniques and the amount and quality of teacher–learner academic and social interactions. Significant *home environment* variables are parent attitudes and activities that support school learning and behavior, participation in school activities, and high expectations for student success. The authors summarize their findings by emphasizing the significance of the proximal variables:

> Two major findings from the present review suggest important policy implications: the actions of students, teachers and parents matter most to student learning; policies at the program, school, district, state and federal levels have limited effect compared to the day-to-day efforts of the people who are most involved in students' lives. Knowing that proximal variables have a greater impact on school learning than distal ones, educators, when formulating policies, should be mindful of where they can make the biggest difference in terms of the student, the classroom and the home. (p. 279)

ASSESSING REASONS FOR POOR SCHOOL ACHIEVEMENT

The goals of assessing an academic problem are to determine the reasons for the problem and to suggest remedial strategies. There is extensive literature on the reasons for school failure (Bloom, 1964; Glaser, 1977; Good & Brophy, 1984; Gordon, 1984; Kampwirth, 1981; Kelly, 1999; Messick & Associates, 1976; Oakes, 1999; Rosenfield, 1987). Nine reasons are presented as to why some students do poorly in school. Consultants should consider each reason as they listen to the consultee and other specialists discuss the student's learning problem and as they progress through the consultation process. Usually more than one of the reasons are responsible for, or related to, the referral problem. Following each of the nine reasons are suggested interventions that may assist consultees in dealing with these reasons.

Diminished Mental Ability

It has been long established that individuals differ in their ability to perform the cognitive skills related to academic achievement (Gustafsson & Undheim, 1996). Further, it has been demonstrated for some time that cognitive ability and school achievement are strongly, though not perfectly, related (Brody, 1997). Correlations of 0.6 to 0.7 are commonly found when comprehensive intelligence tests are compared to academic achievement (Salvia & Ysseldyke, 1998; Sattler, 2001). Obviously other factors also play a part in school achievement (Neisser, Boodoo, Bouchard, Boykin, Ceci, Halpern, Loehlen, Perloff, Sternberg, & Urbina, 1996), but the level of mental ability, as measured by well-normed intelligence tests, is a fairly dependable predictor of academic achievement (and school grades and school completion) across all socioeconomic groups (Reynolds & Kaiser, 1990; Sattler, 2001). This is not to imply that there are not problems with the use of I.Q. tests; their limitations are freely acknowledged in the literature (Figueroa, 1990; Neisser et al., 1996; Reschly & Grimes, 1995; Sattler, 2001; Valde & Figueroa, 1994). Suffice it to say, for the purposes of this discussion, that knowing a student's level of mental ability, whether measured by standard, norm-based instruments or by any of a number of alternative assessment methods (Lidz, 1987; Reschly, 1979; Reschly & Grimes, 1995), helps us to understand one possible cause for academic difficulties and may be useful in planning for that student.

Suggested interventions:

- Simplify verbal instructions.
- Use manipulatives, visuals, and concrete aides.
- Increase "wait time," the span of time given to students to respond before moving on to another student.
- Remind students of their past knowledge.
- Model all responses before expecting students to respond.

Health and Sensory Factors

Poor vision, hearing, or general health should certainly be looked at as possible contributors to academic deficiencies. The screenings done by school nurses should detect these problems, but in some cases a more thorough evaluation needs to be done. If the consultant believes the academic problem may be related to these factors, a physical evaluation of the student should be conducted by qualified personnel.

Suggested interventions:

- Refer to school nurse.
- Inform parents.
- Accommodate seating and other variables for the student.
- Inquire about food for students who are nutritionally deprived.

Motivation

Some students don't do well in school because they are not interested in the curriculum or in the way it is presented. All of us can remember how an inspired teacher made us take an interest in a subject we thought was going to be boring. We can also remember another teacher who took what we thought was going to be an interesting subject and ruined it with a stultifying presentation.

Our public schools are not just for students who are interested in schooling; they are for everybody. It is therefore necessary for every teacher to make the curriculum interesting for all students, not just those who are naturally attracted to the subject matter. However, teachers often find students who seem disinterested, no matter how well the material is presented; they seem immune to good teaching. Because they are not interested, these students put in the minimal amount of effort and soon are failing. Some teachers are reluctant to refer students whom they feel are failing because of motivation problems, possibly because they believe this may reflect on their teaching abilities. However, this is usually not the case, since most of the students in their classes are achieving adequately, indicating generally appropriate teaching methods.

There are numerous reasons for poor motivation:

- Diminished mental ability, resulting in difficulty keeping up with the material and a subsequent desire to quit attending to material that seems overwhelming.
- Poor models at home; parents or siblings who show little or no interest in school achievement.
- Poor teaching (discussed later in this section).
- Depression (discussed later in this section).
- A poor match between the student's inherent interests and the required curriculum.
- Personal distaste for schooling in general or for particular subjects or teachers.
- Little perceived reinforcement for success.

This last reason for poor motivation has been very influential in the thinking of behaviorists, who take the view that behavior is a function of its antecedents and consequences: If there is little learning, it might be because there is either an inadequate set of antecedent conditions (i.e., curriculum, method, review of previously learned material, encouragement, goal setting, and so on) or no effective reinforcement for it (i.e., meaningful success, acknowledgement for work well done, sensible grading policies, goal attainment, and so on). If the learner does not believe that the consequences of learning are strong enough or immediate enough, she may produce poorer quality work and have less success. Poorer work leads to even less reinforcement, and so the cycle continues. Behaviorally oriented theorists often believe that the reinforcement system needs to be made richer, perhaps with an extrinsic reinforcement system that goes beyond grades (which are rarely encouraging for the poorly motivated students), teacher or parent praise (which may be on a very thin reinforcement schedule), or success with academic tasks (which isn't common). Contracts, material rewards, and special activities contingent on increased academic productivity or accuracy are sometimes associated with an apparent increase in motivation, if only temporarily. Whether or not these tactics actually improve motivation is moot; if the tasks are being completed, we are free to enjoy an increase in achievement. Perhaps an increase in intrinsic motivation will follow these academic successes.

When education is looked at from a student-centered point of view, an important area of inquiry is this: What motivates the students to do the work? Why do some do it and others don't? The usual explanation is that there is an inherent human tendency to want to master the environment, which is the result of a natural curiosity about the ways of the world that can only be satisfied by the accumulation of facts and skills. The expression "Curiosity killed the cat," which is sometimes used to squelch students' desires to understand their world, has a redeeming retort: "But satisfaction brought it back." Further, most students are encouraged by their parents to do well in school; indeed, this seems to be a fairly reliable cultural–developmental expectation that students accept (McLoyd, 1998). Lastly, many teachers have observed a crowd instinct in classrooms: If they can get the class leaders to do the assignments, many other students follow their lead. In other words, some students do schoolwork only because others are doing it. Being gregarious, children tend to do what their peers are doing. For teachers in some schools, the secret to effective work production is to figure out which students hold power among their peers and to get this group to work with them in terms of effort and behavior; then the rest will follow. When these sources of motivation do not seem operative, the teacher may have to resort to the kinds of extrinsic reinforcers just mentioned.

Suggested interventions:

- Review the subject matter and teaching methods with the student to determine if there is an apparent problem in either area from the student's point of view.

- Find ways of getting students involved in the learning tasks; in what ways could the tasks be more meaningful?

- Provide a variety of interesting visual material to accompany the ordinary auditory–verbal discussion.

- Provide for cooperative and other group-oriented learning experiences.

- Frequently reinforce efforts, possibly with extrinsic (activity, social) reinforcers.

- If you believe that your failing students are attributing the failures to external causes (e.g., bad luck, teacher discrimination) or to internal causes (e.g., low ability, ethnic heritage), talk to them about these mistaken notions (Marsh & Craven, 1997). Your school counselor may be able to conduct group sessions with underachievers to help them explore their reasons for poor achievement.

- Teach study skills and learning strategies.

- Try to balance the use of anxiety: Some anxiety spurs efforts; too much discourages people from trying.

Ineffective Teaching Practices

One of the reasons for poor motivation (see above) is what some students regard as poor teaching. If a student comes to school with a poor foundation for learning because his parents either didn't care to, or were unable to, provide a good set of preschool experiences at home or in a formal preschool, that student will probably get off to a poor start and may have difficulty catching up with the other students. That student is going to need very good teachers if he is to avoid the "cumulative deficit" phenomenon that so often affects underachievers. Further, some students learn well only when being very carefully taught. This was the whole basis for the separate special education system that dominated the education of students with disabilities for many decades (Smith, 2001). It was believed that if children weren't learning well in the general program, they would do better if they had a modified curriculum, specially trained teachers, and, if necessary, special equipment. Now, however, many leaders in the special education field are saying quite the opposite: The thrust is to keep all children in the regular education program and to require regular and special educators to collaboratively design and carry out effective programs in the general education setting (Smith, 2001; Stainback & Stainback, 1987). The implications are tremendous: Excellent teaching of all students will now be required, and those who need modifications will no longer be assigned to either self-contained or part-time special education classes. General education teachers will be expected to keep students with learning problems in their classrooms. How will they learn to be successful with them? We hope these teachers will learn through changes in preservice education and a wider acceptance of consultants, who can assist them in finding ways to modify their curriculum, expectations, and methods (Dettmer, Dyck, & Thurston, 1999; Friend & Cook, 2000; Idol, Nevin, & Paolucci-Whitcomb, 2000; Mayen, Vergason, & Whelan, 1996; Rosenfield & Gravois, 1996; Salend, 1998). Whether the student is in general or special education, what she will get from the experience depends on the skills and knowledge base of the teachers. In addition to knowing their content areas and child–adolescent development, teachers need to be aware of and utilize effective teaching practices. Darling-Hammond (1996) has summarized seven necessary practices of good teachers:

1. Provide work that is regarded as meaningful to the students.
2. Give students choices that are within the limits of the curriculum goals and behavioral constraints of the classroom.
3. Give equal thought to student output as well as teacher input.
4. Assess, monitor, teach to the student's strengths, and review.
5. Utilize learning experiences that scaffold or mediate students' learning.
6. Build strong relationships to students and their families.
7. Develop student's confidence.

At the level of the individual lesson, Slavin (1997) recommends the following steps:

1. State learning objectives and orient students to the lesson.

2. Review prerequisites.

3. Present new material.

4. Conduct learning probes (i.e., pose questions to students to assess their level of comprehension and to modify your presentation accordingly).

5. Provide independent practice.

6. Assess performance and provide feedback.

7. Provide distributed practice and review.

Suggested interventions:

- Assist the teacher by reviewing his methods, materials, and goals.

- Introduce the teacher to a variety of good ideas that are relatively simple to use.

- Assist the teacher by modeling lessons or engaging in cooperative activities with the teacher or through collaborations with other teachers.

- Consider obtaining the assistance of others, such as the principal, mentor teachers, or a curriculum specialist.

Inability to Concentrate

Attention deficit disorder, with or without hyperactivity as one of its components, is increasingly recognized as a valid and relevant psychoeducational diagnosis (Barkley, 1998). Although experts and practitioners may disagree about numerous aspects of this condition (Armstrong, 1995), there is little doubt that most educators and psychologists agree that there are some students who don't do well in school because they find it very hard to concentrate and to focus attention on the relevant stimuli in the classroom. This condition is certainly not new. Many years ago the phrase *Strauss syndrome* was applied to students who were thought to have a brain injury because they could not relax and concentrate in school. A physician, Alfred Strauss, had noted that this behavior was common among students who had sustained head trauma. He generalized that students who exhibited similar symptoms must also have sustained brain injury, even though there may not have been any history to verify it. During the 1950s and 1960s, the phrase *minimal cerebral dysfunction* was used to explain why some students couldn't concentrate in school and also why they had learning disabilities. Again, hard evidence of brain injury was usually not required for the diagnosis; if the student had a certain complex of symptoms, such as an inability to concentrate, hyperactivity, or impulsiveness, brain injury was assumed to be the cause. In 1980, the American Psychiatric Association (APA), in the third edition of its *Diagnostic and Statistical Manual,* decided to call this symptom complex *attention deficit disorder.* Since then, in what may seem to be a confusing sequence of switchbacks in terminology, the APA has changed its system twice. In the current edition, *DSM-IV,* a diagnosis in this area may result in one of three possibilities: a predominantly inattentive type, a predominantly hyperactive-impulsive type, or a combined type (American Psychiatric Association, 1994).

Whatever the current fads in terminology, everyone agrees that there are some students in every class who engage in the behaviors just described. They do not learn well because they aren't attending to the curriculum or classroom expectations. Whether they are able to attend and simply choose not to, perhaps because they would rather be somewhere else (motivational problems), must be decided by those who know the student best and have seen her in a variety of learning situations. If the student appears unable to attend or to remain calm enough to profit from instruction even after modifications to the regular program have been attempted, she should be referred for a medical evaluation, preferably to a pediatrician familiar with the ADD complex. Perhaps a medical approach to this problem is appropriate and would be the most effective strategy to take after in-class modifications have been tried.

Suggested interventions:

- Place students in environments where there are a minimum of distractions.
- Keep the lessons highly structured.
- Use materials that draw attention to the relevant stimuli.
- Have students repeat instructions before getting started on assignments.
- Assign highly distractible or inattentive students to study-buddies who can assist in keeping them on task.
- Find activities that will give hyperactive students something to do, within the confines of task expectations.
- Teach organizational and study skills.
- Try organizing the material into smaller chunks, if feasible.
- Use technology that serves an instructional purpose and doesn't become yet another source of distraction.
- Reinforce all efforts at concentrated work.

Emotional Disturbance

Emotional disturbance has been codified as a category of exceptionality (IDEA, P.L. 105-17). As a category, it requires that a student be identified as eligible for special education and related services only when the IEP team believes that the condition is quite severe and adversely affects educational performance. Emotional disturbance is the one category of exceptionality that almost everybody can relate to because by the time we reach adolescence most of us have had experiences that make us emotionally upset, at least temporarily. Parents die, relationships dissolve, or we suffer some form of trauma that at the time seems devastating. Fortunately for most of us, these are transient occurrences, the significance of which passes with time. We are able to mobilize our resources and get on with our lives. Some people, however, due to their constitutional makeup and the circumstances they have endured, seem consistently upset, depressed, or angry with specific people or situations or with the world in general (Bauer & Shea, 1999; Costenbader & Buntaine, 1999; Kauffman, 2001; Long & Morse, 1996; Quay & Werry, 1986; Wicks-Nelson & Israel, 2000). This student typically does not do well in school. He is unable to focus his energies on learning since he is so obsessed by whatever is bothering him. Abused and neglected students, those experiencing the trauma of family conflict and possible divorce, and those being raised by parents who have passed on their own disturbed view of the world to their children are all at risk for school failure (Erickson, 1998; Kauffman, 2001).

It is important to note that emotional disturbance, like so many other conditions, exists on a continuum. Most students who exhibit some degree of emotional disturbance do so to a limited degree or in a transient fashion and should not need special education services.

Suggested interventions:

- Try to maintain a conflict-free classroom; do not let students bully others.
- The teacher may need to find ways of giving a disturbed student a non-punitive time-out from whatever stress is causing the student to become agitated or withdrawn.
- Refer the student to a school counselor, school psychologist, or perhaps to a local mental health agency.
- Chapter 6 contains many other suggested interventions for students who exhibit behavior disorders.

Poor Study Skills

When teachers are asked why they think certain students aren't doing well academically, they often respond, "Well, if she'd just study, she'd do fine." Failure to apply oneself through study, or possibly not knowing how to study, has been identified as a major reason for poor academic production, particularly as students enter junior and senior high school (Barron & Associates, 1983; Gleason, Herr, & Archer, 1988; Mintzes, Wandersee, & Novak, 1997; Perkins, 1995). Some study problems may be due to ADD, poor motivation, or emotional disturbance, as previously indicated. School-based consultants need to include some study of a referred student's study methods and habits in order to determine the extent to which problems in this area could be contributing to academic learning difficulties.

Suggested interventions:

- Along with teaching content, all teachers should be teaching students *how to study* the content to ensure integration and retention.
- Note-taking is a skill that is both poorly understood and poorly practiced among underachievers. Kiewra (1991) provides a set of suggestions, including providing skeletal notes before a lecture or chapter reading.

- Have students underline (or copy down) the one or two most important sentences in a body of content. Also, have them write down, after every paragraph or so, one sentence that summarizes what they have just read.
- Stress the necessity of finding a quiet place for home study. This emphasis should also be made to your students' parents.
- Teach your students the *PQ4R* method (Anderson, 1995; Thomas & Robinson, 1972), which is an update of the SQ3R method. The PQ4R method (preview, question, read, reflect, recite, and review) is a valuable aid to those whose approach to textual or note content is generally disorganized. Friend and Bursick (1999) also recommend the *KWL Plus*, which is a method for helping students think through an assignment based on what they already *know*, what they *want* to know, and, at the end of an assignment, what they have *learned*.

Cultural, Socioeconomic, and Linguistic Differences

It is a commonplace observation that students from many culturally or linguistically different backgrounds do poorly in most American schools, while Eurocentric and Asian students generally do better. Students from minority backgrounds, particularly those who are English language learners, usually have more difficulty with academic achievement than do Eurocentric students (Grossman, 1995; Knapp, 1995; McLoyd, 1998; Mullis, Dossey, Foertsch, Jones, & Gentile, 1991). Even here, however, there are exceptions (Baruth & Manning, 1992). Gleitman, Fridlund, and Reisberg (1999) have shown when students from different ethnicities and racial groups are compared across SES, their scores are much more similar. There is some evidence that some of the commonly observed differences exist because the instruction given to minority students is not compatible with their cultural backgrounds (Boykin, 1994; Vasquez, 1993). McLoyd (1998) suggests that the following factors are related to poor academic achievement:

- Poor health care.
- Low expectations—low self-esteem.
- Learned helplessness.
- Peer influences and resistance cultures.
- Tracking.
- Child-rearing styles.
- Home environment and resources.

Trueba, Jacobs, and Kirton (1990) have shown that high school teachers of English have low expectations of Latino students. Their study shows that these students were quite capable of higher-level work when they saw the connection between the assignments and their out-of-school lives. In some inner cities, more than half of the minority students drop out of high school (Rumberger, 1995). Asian-American students are the major exception to generalizations about the lower achievement of minority students; they typically achieve better than all other minority groups in American schools (Levine & Havighurst, 1989).

Data for Caucasian, African-American, and Latino students gathered from the National Assessment of Educational Progress (NAEP, 1990, cited in Byrnes, 1996 pp. 265–267) for nine-, thirteen-, and seventeen-year-olds found reading scores to be 8 to 15 percent higher for Caucasians than for minorities. In writing, scores were 7 to 20 percent higher, while in math (using SAT data) Caucasian students were 13 percent ahead of Latinos and 22 percent ahead of African-Americans. The NAEP data were similar in science and social studies to those obtained for reading and writing. All of these results were, to some extent, correlated with socioeconomic status, with middle-class minority students in all ethnic groups doing better than their counterparts from lower socioeconomic groups. Data on reading from the 1994 NAEP looked at similar results from a different perspective. The 1994 data indicated that only 31 percent of African-American students and 36 percent of Hispanic students in fourth grade could read at a "basic level," while 71 percent of the Eurocentric students could read at that level (Campbell, Donahue, Reese, & Phillips, 1996). Most recently, the U. S. Department of Education secretary, Rod Paige, expressed his dismay at the widening gap between the best and worst fourth-grade readers based on the NAEP results for the year 2000, which indicated that virtually no change has been made in the scores of the poorest readers, who tend to be African-Americans and Hispanics. These results prompted Secretary Paige to say, "After spending $125 billion (of assistance to schools in the area of remedial reading) . . . over 25 years, we have virtually nothing to show for it" (Helfand & Groves, 2001).

Byrnes (1996) contrasts three groups of theories about these differences: cognitive-deficit, contextual, and cultural incongruity. Each of these views has a wide range of theoretical, if not empirical, support that derives from diverse sources such as nutrition studies, the role of stimulation, values, and communication patterns. If they are to be successful, consultees who teach students from cultural/ethnic groups different from their own need to determine ways that teachers can use to capitalize on the diverse ways in which their students prefer to learn. Nieto (1996) discusses some culture-specific educational accommodations, such as using groups of the same sex with Navajo children, developing more interactive as opposed to didactic methods with African-American students, and developing collective responsibility and using peer tutoring and mentoring among Latino youths.

Suggested interventions:

- When working with English Language Learners (ELL), make sure that oral presentations to them are comprehensible. Repeat key phrases and emphasize important vocabulary. Increase wait time.
- Increase the use of visual aids.
- Adapt materials as appropriate.
- Accept answers based on content, not perfection of English grammar.
- Use examples from all the different racial and ethnic groups represented in the classroom.

- Avoid tracking, which can lead to resegregation (Schofield, 1995; Slavin, 1995).

- Use cooperative learning as often as possible. It can lead to greater participation of minority students.

- When grouping students from different racial and ethnic groups for classwork, provide a structure and common goals that will require the various groups to work together. Proximity alone does not ensure social harmony (Slavin, 1997).

Learning Disabilities

Of all the reasons for poor learning in school, learning disabilities is probably the best known reason and the one most often cited. Interestingly, this reason was nonexistent, or at least nonlabeled, until Samuel Kirk first used the phrase *learning disabilities* (LD) in 1963 while giving a talk to parents of children who weren't doing well in school but weren't retarded, emotionally disturbed, or sensorially impaired. He used the phrase to include that group of children who heretofore had been assumed to be merely slow, lazy, or to have some form of minimal brain injury. He thought that an educationally relevant phrase would be more practical than an etiology-based phrase, such as "brain damaged" (Lerner, 2000). Since Kirk first used the phrase, it has not only gained acceptance, but children identified as LD have now reached up to 5.5 percent of the total school population (with a range of 2.9 percent in Georgia to 9.2 percent in Massachusetts) and make up more than 50 percent of all U.S. children identified as having disabilities (U.S. Department of Education, 1998). Growth patterns like this suggest that many children who aren't doing well in school may be considered for, and found to have, a learning disability (Heward, 2000; Lerner, 2000). Advocates for the learning disabled are pleased with this growth because they see it as a recognition of the reality of the condition and an acknowledgement of the needs of these children. Others, however, see special education for children with these mild sorts of learning problems as a convenient escape route for regular educators (Salvia & Ysseldyke, 1998; Skrtic, 1991).

There doesn't seem to be any argument about the existence of learning disabilities; the bigger questions today concern their diagnosis, whether or not there is an increase in this diagnosis for social or political reasons, and how and where students with these disabilities should be educated (Baker & Zigmond, 1990; Lerner, 2000; Will, 1986; Zins, Curtis, Graden, & Ponti, 1988).

Some specialists in the learning disabilities field assume that students with these disorders have a degree of neurological impairment. The current definition proposed by the National Joint Committee on Learning Disabilities states that learning disabilities are "presumed to be due to central nervous system dysfunction" (NJCLD, 1997). The Interagency Committee on Learning Disabilities, a committee commissioned by the U.S. Congress, also takes this view (ICLD, 1997). Naturally, if a school-based consultant believes that a student referred because of learning (or behavior) problems may have a neurological impairment that needs to be established for diagnostic or treatment purposes, he should encourage a referral for such a diagnosis. Clearly, most students, even those with learning and behavior problems, do not have any significant degree of neurological impairment detectable by current technology. Those who do may profit from a compensatory approach as opposed to a developmental or remedial approach (Lerner, 2000; Rosner, 1999; Teeter, 1989).

In this book I am not concerned with the numerous questions and issues that surround the learning disabilities concept, nor do I present refined techniques for diagnosis. There are numerous other sources that are valuable in that area (Bos & Vaughn, 1998; Lerner, 2000; Mercer, 1997; Swanson, 1991).

Suggested interventions:

- Modify the curriculum to adapt to the student's particular style of learning and responding, to whatever extent this is feasible. Break down tasks, use visual aids, use mnemonics, try study-buddies, apply technology, utilize advance organizers, consider opportunities for cultural infusion, and individualize whenever possible.

- Utilize peer assistance, cooperative groupings, and non–special education school programs designed to remediate learning problems (e.g., Project Read, Reading Recovery).

- Review your concerns with the student's parents and encourage them to assist their child in highly structured ways.

- Reinforce approximations to complete success; don't require perfect papers from those for whom this goal is stress inducing.

- After the faithful implementation and failure of interventions designed to ameliorate or compensate for a student's academic learning problems, the teacher, consultant, or parent should make a formal referral for assessment in order to determine if the student meets the eligibility criteria for the category of learning disabilities.

The school consultant looks at these nine somewhat overlapping reasons for poor learning to see what possible contribution they may be having to the referral problem. As the cases in Chapters 7 and 9 demonstrate, our ability to understand referral problems and ameliorate them may lie in our understanding of the interplay of these reasons, as well as the influences of psychodynamic, ecological, or biophysical factors that can have a strong effect on behavior and academic learning. Also, our own philosophical beliefs influence how we approach referrals. Some people look to psychodynamics almost exclusively. Others are wedded to curriculum-based measurement to the exclusion of other assessment considerations. Others prefer rational-emotive behavior therapy (Ellis, 1995) or behavior modification or process training. I hope that school-based consultants will keep an open mind regarding causes and assistive strategies and will not become overly restrictive in their views. To show how different techniques may be used to understand and deal with school learning and behavior problems, D'Amato and Rothlisberg (1992) have provided an extensive case study of a student followed by explanations of how this student's case would be handled by practitioners representing eight different approaches.

ACTIVITY 8.1

The reasons given previously may not cover all possible reasons for poor learning. Readers may be aware of others that are not included or implied above. What are some other reasons for poor school achievement?

THE ROLE OF THE SCHOOL CONSULTANT

The role of the consultant largely depends on her profession and the nature of the learning problem. Since the consultant might be a special education teacher, a school psychologist, a counselor, a speech and language specialist, or a mentor teacher, she may bring a perspective to her consultation approach that is slightly different from the viewpoint of another professional. Each of these staff members is expected to have training in assessment that is relatively specific to her profession, with the possible exception of the mentor teacher, who may not have specific assessment training.

If a referral indicates that the primary concern is academic, the referring teacher (or the local system) needs to decide to whom the referral should be directed. It may go directly to a consultant. In some cases it is best to direct it to the SST (or an equivalent group) and let the team decide how to proceed. The team should select the specialists based on the assessment needs, if assessment beyond what the teacher can provide is deemed necessary. As I mentioned in my discussion of SOCS (Chapter 5), the consultant has to monitor the SST to be sure that a recommendation for assessment is valid, not made just to buy time or to avoid the need for further accommodations in the general education class. Remember also that the time spent on assessment and report writing is time away from remediation, counseling, or consultation with teachers and parents, services that can have more impact than does the gathering of test scores.

Together, the consultant, teachers, and parents of the referred student evaluate the reasons for poor learning, which vary considerably across students. For example, consider referrals from a third-grade teacher who has two students of the same age with reading problems. (The standard scores for these two students are about 85, in a school in which the average standard score is about 100.) The consultant may find that, in one case, the student is of somewhat limited mental ability (verbal and nonverbal I.Q.s are both about 85), demonstrates a moderate and uncorrected hearing loss in both ears, achieves poorly in all academic areas, and comes from a home in which neither parent graduated from high school and neither worries too much about academic success since everyday problems of economic coping have a higher priority. In the second case, the student has an I.Q. of about 115 (verbal 100, performance 130), is hyperactive and impulsive, does very well in math and art, but shows some signs of language confusion. His parents, both college graduates, have insisted on no special education assistance for their boy since the first grade.

ACTIVITY 8.2

How might a school-based consultant approach each of the two situations just described? What other information would he need before he could help the SST and the parents deal with each child's below-grade-level reading achievement?

Chapter 1 discusses the consultee as a variable in the consultation process. I pointed out that consultees manifest both expectations and preferences (Brown, Pryzwansky, & Schulte, 2001). When working on cases involving academic problems, the consultant needs to consider the preferences of the consultees. De Mesquita and Zollman (1995) discuss possible intervention strategies in mathematics and indicate that some consultees prefer one or a combination of instructional interventions. One possibility they studied with primary grade teachers was a cognitive approach (having the student use manipulatives, engaging in self-talk, using real-world props, and so on). Another was a behavioral approach (largely manifested by manipulation of reinforcers: material, activity, or social). A third was a cooperative/peer learning approach (grouping arrangements, peer assistance). In contrast to consultation for behavior/adjustment problems, in which behavioral approaches are generally favored, consultee preferences about academic problems in this study were primarily for cognitive and cooperative/peer learning approaches. Although much work has been done regarding consultee preferences for dealing with behavioral problems, we need more research evidence for consultee preferences about academic problems (Johnson & Pugach, 1996; Rosenfield, 1987).

INSTRUCTIONAL CONSULTATION

Instructional consultation has gained increased interest since the publication of Sylvia Rosenfield's (1987) *Instructional Consultation* and her subsequent *Instructional Consultation Teams* (Rosenfield & Gravois, 1996). Rosenfield believes that mismatches between the learner's capabilities and the curriculum constitute the basis for most learning problem referrals. Rather than viewing the problem as one inherent to the student (such as LD, or minority status), she believes it is more useful to examine the dynamic interaction of the learner, the setting, teaching methods, and the curriculum. As such, this is primarily an ecologically oriented approach to assessment and intervention. She stresses classroom observation and curriculum-based assessment as opposed to extensive norm-based assessment, which often seems designed to find the problem within the referred student. Her teacher interview style is similar to Bergan and Kratochwill's (1990). The tasks that are collaboratively designed and carried out by the teacher and the consultant are task analysis, process analysis, error analysis, designing instructional interventions, and managing the learning environment for the student.

Rosenfield and Gravois (1996) review the general guidelines indicated in Rosenfield's earlier book and go on to demonstrate how teams of school-based professionals (for example, resource teachers, administrators, school psychologists, and so on) work collaboratively to solve learning and behavior/adjustment problems, usually within the confines of the regular classroom. There are three stages of team development. At *initiation*, a school or a system commits to developing and using an instructional teams model. During *implementation*, the team actually tries out the system and works out the technical problems. At *institutionalization*, the system adopts an instructional consultation team approach as a regular part of its service-delivery system. Some of the newer topics that are currently being developed by Rosenfield and her associates are training modules for school-based consultants (particularly in multicultural sensitivity), coordination of family and community services with the school team, and issues related to secondary school use of instructional consultation teams. In regard to this last area, Rosenfield suggests grade-level teams as a focus point for either individual students or larger issues of curricular delivery.

An approach compatible with Rosenfield's is that of Vacca and Padak (1990), who provide some guidelines to assist consultants in the evaluation of the possible sources of academic problems of both individual students and whole classes. Rather than simply evaluate the products of students' learning with, for example, a norm-based, CBM, or work sample, the consultant may help the consultee evaluate the process of learning as it goes on in the classroom. Questions to be looked at here might include the following:

- What are the students doing during instructional time? What demands or expectations does the teacher have for their performance? How do they communicate their understanding of the material?

- When teaching is not teacher-directed, what are the students doing, individually or with others? What keeps them on task? What can be done when they are off task?

- What does the classroom look like? Are child products prominently displayed? Are there many different prompts or motivators for reading? Are activity areas kept fresh and inviting?

Ysseldyke and Christenson (1993) have developed the Instructional Environment System—II (TIES—II), which can serve as a framework for studying the interaction between a student and her learning environment. Their system includes 12 instructional–environmental components and 5 home-support-for-learning components, which are described in detail later in this chapter. A review of the impact of each of these components can facilitate the development of instructional plans.

Other sources of evaluative data might be incidental. Just listening to a child interpret text or hearing two or more students discuss what they have read tells the teacher how the students are generating hypotheses about their reading efforts and thereby helps the teacher know why some students have trouble making valid inferences about the text they are trying to interpret.

ASSESSMENT OF PROBLEMS IN LEARNING: THE RIOT

RIOT is an acronym that stands for:

Records review: The consultant often starts an analysis of a referral with a look at the cumulative folder, and the special education folder if there is one. These documents should give some indication of the student's past history of grades, standardized test scores, and teacher comments. In the case of a student assigned to special education, there may be documentation of functional behavioral assessments and positive behavioral intervention plans.

Interview with the consultee and others who have observed the student's efforts at learning, including the student himself: Interviewing consultees and other adults was discussed in Chapter 3. A student referred for difficulties in learning and/or achievement can also contribute to the database regarding causes, symptoms, and possible interventions by providing information through a structured or informal interview. Figure 8.1 indicates some possible questions that might be asked in the case of an achievement problem. Sattler (1998) provides an extensive interview format for children and adolescents with learning problems (pp. 942–944), as well as a sentence completion technique for generating hypotheses about students' feelings about their academic work (p. 410).

Observation of the student's efforts at work completion and the whole class atmosphere for learning: The referring teacher(s) can provide samples of the student's work. These are particularly helpful if an historical pattern can be generated. Schools' increasing use of portfolios should be a rich sort of archival data for students as they progress through the grades. The consultant will also want to make one or more classroom observations in order to see the referred student as she goes through her efforts to accommodate to expectations. The observation is also intended to give the consultant a picture of the ecological aspects of the classroom setting. The TIES–II instrument, discussed below, is an excellent tool for giving structure to this aspect of assessment.

Testing, both formal and informal: Although it is entirely possible that a referral for a learning problem may be resolved without test data, it is not common. Usually all parties will need to know specifics about a student's achievement levels, specific skill deficits, and approaches to academic tasks before being able to generate effective interventions. A blend of norm-based and informal (e.g., informal reading inventories, curriculum-based assessments) methods may be chosen, depending on the situation. Details about testing procedures can be found in Cohen, Swerdlik, and Smith (1992), Salvia and Ysseldyke (1998), Sattler (2001), Shapiro (1989), and Shinn (1998).

Figure 8.1

Sample interview questions for a student referred because of an achievement problem

---

Hello_____; my name is_____.

I am the _____ here at _____school.

I'd like to talk to you about school, especially about ways that we can help you get better at some of your schoolwork.

If I ask you a question that you don't understand or can't answer, tell me and I'll try to ask it in another way.

Tell me about school in general. What are some of the parts of school that you like the best?

What are some subjects you don't like so well? What is it you don't like about_____?

(Focusing on the referral areas): What happens when you try_____?

What are some of the parts of _____that seem difficult for you?

What are some things people have done to help you with _____?

Do you feel they helped you?

What are some ways you have found that makes _____ go better or easier for you?

What would you like us at school to do to help you with _____?

Are there any questions you wanted to ask me about school?

Here is an outline of questions and suggestions for conducting the RIOT assessment, which may apply to either a learning or a behavior/adjustment problem.

1. Refine the reason for referral. What do the consultees really want to find out? What exactly are the learning or behavior adjustment problems? Get diagnostic information (for example, typical in-class behaviors; typical behavioral difficulties) from the referring party.

2. Is this referral a three-year reevaluation? If so, update the progress of the student in the special education program that has been provided during the last year and since the last complete evaluation. Use an interview plus a review of the student's records and whatever testing data are necessary.

3. What are the goals of this assessment? These are usually the goals of the referring person and other interested parties (the parent, yourself, the student). Some

systems put goal statements in their reports—for example, "The purpose of this assessment is to determine the reasons for the student's slow reading progress" or "One of the purposes of this assessment is to determine the effectiveness of the RSP pullout program in improving the student's math ability." These goal statements add focus to the assessment.

4. Once you've determined what the problems and goals are, determine sources of information that will clarify the problems and achieve the goals. Again, use all four aspects of the RIOT.

5. You probably should start with some observation of the student in an important area without letting the student know you are observing her. Discuss with the teacher how he wants you to observe in his classroom. If he has no preference, observe as a participant: circulate around the room, observing how all the students react to the materials. This gives you a frame of reference against which to judge the behavior/responses of the referred student.

If possible, try to get the teacher to show you what is being done currently to deal with the student's learning problem. Again, try to have this done unobtrusively.

Be sure to have something positive to say to the teacher about his work after every observation. This requires you to become a good observer of what people are doing well. Be sincere, of course.

6. Discuss your observations with the teacher. Was this a typical day? If not, what is? How is the current intervention working? If not well, how does the teacher want to change it? What else is needed?

7. Presumably the referral (if original, not a three-year) is made because the student isn't progressing adequately. This stimulates questions:

 a. What are the interventions the teacher is trying?

 b. How well are they being done?

 c. How might they be improved?

 d. Is the teacher amenable to assistance? Is she willing to try things?

 e. What can you offer? This is the point at which consultation often spins off from assessment and becomes the collaborative problem-solving process described throughout this text.

UNDERSTANDING THE SCOPE AND SEQUENCE OF THE CURRICULUM

All school-based consultants need to be aware of what students are being taught: the scope and sequence of the curriculum. Scope and sequence refer to the content of the curriculum and the order in which it is taught. Richardson and Anders (1998) comment that the curriculum may be looked at from three perspectives: the explicit curriculum (the one passed down from the state); the hidden curriculum (the one the teachers actually teach); and the absent curriculum (the one teachers do not teach). Elkind (1976) describes three types of curricula, all of which occur simultaneously:

1. The official school curriculum, which is the material that the state requires schools to teach because it is considered to be most appropriate for the transmission of the culture and the development of requisite skills (for example, history, reading, math, and so on).

2. A personal curriculum, which is designed by each individual learner and based on his own needs, interests, attitudes, and other factors that determine his willingness to participate in the schools' offerings.

3. A developmental curriculum, which is based on fundamental skills (processes) that are prerequisite to school success, such as the ability to attend, to reason, to remember, to organize information, and so on.

Elkind notes that the role of the school-based consultant is to assist teachers in promoting the official curriculum, often by studying students or situations in which students are not doing well with this curriculum. When a student isn't successful with the official curriculum, the consultant institutes a study of that student's developmental and personal abilities and interests (that is, the other two curricula) in order to determine the source of the student's school (official curriculum) failures.

Although state boards of education and local district boards develop official curriculum guidelines which may vary from broad to highly specific (such as California's Standards, a set of highly specific goals for each subject and grade level), it sometimes appears that textbook publishers actually have the final word about scope and sequence. Most teachers rely heavily on the assigned texts and their accompanying manuals (Doll, 1989). The advantage of this approach is that the teacher is given structure and ideas about how to teach and assess students' progress. A possible disadvantage is that teachers may become dependent on the textbook authors' ideas, which are generally geared to the average and above-average learner. There may not be sufficient consideration given to the needs of students at risk for school failure. One of the functions of a school consultant is to work with the classroom teacher-consultee in creating ways of making the general education core curriculum accessible to students with learning difficulties. This is not an easy task. It has been made all the more difficult in this era of educational reform, which seems largely to be an effort to make the curriculum more rigorous, and to substitute excessive annual achievement testing for real reform. Consultants must be willing to take the time to study the curriculum in order to help the teacher in an informed way. Of course, it also requires a teacher-consultee who is willing to try methods and develop materials that go beyond what is available in the teacher's manuals.

A second way of understanding curriculum is to study a teacher's expectations and methods of teaching and evaluating her students. Expectations may be referred to as goals or objectives; in special education, these are developed through the IEP process. In general education classes, teachers should have developed fairly explicit ideas about their goals, which may derive from state guidelines or text authors. Gickling and Havertape (1982) provide the following guidelines to help you interpret expectations and methods at the level of the lesson or task:

1. The teacher's intention in assigning the task.
2. How that intention was manifested in the particular task set.
3. How the task was presented and specified (task analysis).
4. The pupil's perceptions of #3.
5. The materials available for the task.
6. The pupil's task performance, including interactions with the teachers and other pupils.
7. An assessment of short-term learning outcomes immediately following the task.
8. An assessment of longer-term learning outcomes, for instance, at the end of each term, in order to evaluate development and retention of learning over a series of learning tasks (pp. 10–11).

All of these guidelines can be observed directly, except number 4, which somewhat reflects Elkind's (1976) developmental or personal curricula. The consultant, having gained entry and established rapport, may wish to observe a teacher presenting a number of lessons in order to get a broad picture of the methods, materials, and style used by the teacher. Information gathered from these observations is invaluable in understanding the teacher's objectives, the students' reactions to the teacher, the materials and the expectations, and the interaction of these variables.

ACTIVITY 8.3

Compare the Gickling and Havertape guidelines (above) with those of Slavin (presented in the section on "Ineffective Teaching Practices"). Blend the two lists to make one comprehensive list which would be useful to a consultant when observing a teacher giving a lesson. You might also want to use elements from Ysseldyke and Christenson's TIES—II.

TIES-II

Ysseldyke and Christenson's *The Instructional Environment System—II* (1993) has been mentioned as a useful tool for structuring classroom observations. In this system, the consultant uses a set of interview and observation forms designed to gather information on 12 instructional environment components and 5 home-support-for-learning components.

Instructional Environment Components:

- *Instructional match.* Is instruction matched to the results of an instructional diagnosis? Does it meet the student's needs?
- *Teacher expectations.* They should be high but realistic and well communicated to the student.
- *Classroom environment.* Behavior management is positive and supportive; there is appropriate use of instructional time.
- *Instructional presentation.* Instruction is clear and effective; the students understand what they need to do; there are periodic checks of their understanding.
- *Cognitive emphasis.* Students understand how to think about the content. Strategies for learning are explicitly taught.
- *Motivational strategies.* Students' interest is heightened.
- *Relevant practice.* Skills taught are practiced to ensure a high degree of success.
- *Informed feedback.* Students receive quick and specific feedback on their performance or behavior; errors in performance are corrected.
- *Academic engaged time.* Students are expected to keep involved with the tasks; teacher monitors students to ensure task engagement.
- *Adaptive instruction.* When the instruction does not seem to be effective, it is modified.
- *Progress evaluation.* Direct and frequent measurement of students' progress is used to plan future instruction.
- *Student understanding.* Students demonstrate that they understand the content of the lesson.

Home-Support-for-Learning Components:

- *Expectations and attributions.* The value of hard work at school is emphasized.
- *Discipline orientation.* Parents monitor the student's behavior in an authoritative (not authoritarian) manner.
- *Effective home environment.* The relationship between the child and the parent is positive.
- *Parent participation.* The home environment supports schooling.
- *Structure for learning.* Daily routines that support school learning are established.

The result of a TIES—II evaluation is a set of statements about the extent to which the student is being exposed to an effective and supportive instructional system. It results in a global picture of what is happening at school and home to assist the student's learning. Ysseldyke, Christenson, and Kovaleski (1994) have demonstrated the use of the TIES—II in actual classroom situations.

Somewhat similar to TIES—II is the EBASS system (Greenwood, Carta, Kamps, & Delquadri, 1995), which uses a computer-assisted system to record specific behaviors of teachers and students and provides a printout indicating the frequency and percentage of time that different behaviors of the teacher and the child were observed. The recorder indicates, usually on a laptop computer, the occurrence of predetermined behaviors of teachers and students in ten-second intervals for varying lengths of time (perhaps one hour or all day) and then obtains a printout of these data. This results in a much more molecular analysis of the teacher–student interaction than one gets from the TIES—II system.

CONSULTATION ABOUT ACADEMIC PROBLEMS: TWO EXAMPLES

Chapter 9 contains two extensive case studies demonstrating how a school-based consultant might deal with complicated cases of academic problems using the SOCS format (see Chapter 5). Here are two brief examples demonstrating how consultants can help teachers in simpler and more typical referrals.

Example A Third Grade; Poor Reading

The teacher-consultee, Ms. DeSousa, refers a boy, Ahmed, to the school SST in October because he is lagging in his reading development. The coordinator of the SST refers the case to Mr. Lee, the resource specialist, and appoints him to be the case manager (consultant). In this district, the case manager attempts to solve the case without having to refer it to the whole SST but will refer back to the team when it is clear that he cannot solve it without assistance.

Mr. Lee visits with Ms. DeSousa and reviews the facts. Ahmed has always been near the bottom of his class (cumulative folder information). He was given some Reading Recovery assistance in first grade, which seemed to help, but no other help since. Now he is in the bottom of Ms. DeSousa's three groups and is not doing well. He is becoming reluctant to read. Together, the consultant and the consultee decide that Mr. Lee will do an informal reading assessment (IRI, CBA, and a phonics survey) and a review of Ahmed's health and family status.

Mr. Lee finds that Ahmed knows most of his phonics facts but seems slow at blending known sounds. He is at a frustration level of 3.1 and an instructional level of 2.1, about a year behind his age expectancy. He is considered to be of about average ability (based on the conversation with him and his math achievement) and has no sensory or other health problems. His family is intact and concerned.

Based on this information, the consultant does not suspect a learning disability but believes that Ahmed may be what Stanovich (2000) refers to as a "garden-variety poor reader," one who has a developmental delay that will most likely remit

with age and extra attention but does not constitute a serious problem requiring special education. The consultant (Mr. Lee) and consultee (Ms. DeSousa) decide to try the following:

1. Specify the phonics rules still unmastered, locate materials for teaching them, and enlist the aide of a cross-age tutor to spend 15 minutes a day three times a week with Ahmed (and two others who need similar help) in Mr. Lee's room.

2. Review the referral and Mr. Lee's findings with Ahmed's parents and enlist their aid with structured reading practice at home using books at Ahmed's instructional level (Christenson & Conoley, 1992; Swap, 1993). Appropriate books can be determined from a list provided by Ms. Carlo and are available either from the local library or from her (Monson, 1985). Mr. Lee will work with Ahmed's mother on methods for assisting the child at home. Ahmed's dad works the evening shift but agrees to help on the weekend with this problem.

3. Ms. DeSousa agrees to find materials with which her lowest group can be more successful—for example, stories geared toward a beginning second-grade level. She is put in contact with the district curriculum director for assistance with this task. She also appoints one of her more mature students, who is a good reader, to monitor the seatwork activities of this low group while Ms. DeSousa is working with her other groups. One of the tasks of this monitor is to keep a record of all the words this group has trouble with. These are then put on flashcards, and Ms. DeSousa designs a series of games to reinforce the practice of these words (Ekwall, 1988; Lerner, 2000). The monitor and the cross-age tutor play the games with the group.

Two months later, the parents, the teacher, and Ahmed all report that there has been much improvement. Most of the members of the low group have increased their reading levels and speeds. The cross-age tutor is assigned to another classroom, the low group monitors itself, parents continue helping at home and provide weekly library trips, and the consultant writes a summary statement for Ahmed's cumulative folder and reports to the SST coordinator that this case is on hold for now. No further interventions are planned.

Example B   Seventh Grade; Dysgraphia

Shelley, a seventh-grade girl, is referred by Mr. Jefferson, her English teacher (the consultee), because of her very poor writing skills. Shelley rarely turns in any written work. When she does, it is usually very poorly done. Because of this, she is failing

English. Mr. Jefferson believes that Shelley's problems in writing may be due to a learning disability, which he has heard is called "dysgraphia." He believes that Shelley should get help from the resource specialist (special education) teacher during her English period. Mr. Jefferson has advised Shelley's mother, Ms. Birdsong, to make a referral for assessment since he believes this will expedite the process of her daughter's receiving special education services.

The SST coordinator asks to see Mr. Jefferson for a conference. She reviews the district policy regarding requests for assistance with learning and behavior/adjustment problems and reminds Mr. Jefferson that the policy calls for referrals to be made through the SST process. Although administrators hope that parents will become aware of their children's problems, they do not recommend telling parents to insist on an assessment before the SST tries to apply prereferral modifications to the regular education program. Some parents get the idea from teachers and advocacy groups that they have a right to, and therefore should insist on, a formal referral for complete assessment before more parsimonious steps have been taken. In 1989, about 68 percent of the states required that districts engage in prereferral interventions before proceeding to formal referral for assessment (Carter & Sugai, 1989). This has increased recently to include about 75 percent of the states and is intended to reduce referrals for testing and subsequent overidentification of students for special education services (Salvia & Ysseldyke, 1998).

Because Mr. Jefferson has already called Shelley's mother and told her to request an assessment, the SST coordinator asks him to call Ms. Birdsong and explain the district policy, asking her to reconsider her request for a full assessment until the local school attempts prereferral interventions. Ms. Birdsong agrees to do so but wants to be kept abreast of the SST's progress to know if Shelley has dysgraphia or not.

The SST coordinator has intended to refer this case to the school resource specialist teacher, Mr. Levy, asking him to act as the case manager (consultant). However, because of Ms. Birdsong's heightened concern, the coordinator asks the whole SST to discuss the case first. The SST comes up with the following ideas:

1. Mr. Levy will take Shelley from her class and administer both an informal test of writing (for example, generate a 200-word theme on "My Favorite Place" or something similar) and a formal test (the Test of Written Language—3 [Hammill & Larson, 1996] or subtest 5 of the Detroit Tests of Learning Aptitude—4 [Hammill, 1998]). Since both of these tests are norm-based, the school asks Shelley's mother to sign a permission form; it is policy in this district to have parents approve the administration of any norm-based test, even if it is not part of a formal referral for special education eligibility.

2. Based on the results of these tests and work samples from Shelley's classes, the SST will decide what steps to take.

Mr. Levy reported that, overall, Shelley writes at about the third-grade level in all areas except handwriting skill; she forms letters well, and everything she writes is legible. However, her sentence construction is limited to four- to seven-word sentences, her punctuation and capitalization suggest that she hasn't internalized any rules but randomly tries various forms, and her stories are disorganized. She admits that she doesn't like to write, except for notes to her friends. She says she has no use for writing outside of school. No one in her family writes letters, nor do they have a computer for writing or using e-mail, although all her friends do.

Mr. Levy reinforces what Mr. Jefferson has told Shelley. He says, "You are failing English because of the poor quality of your written work. We are concerned about it and would like to find ways to help you improve your writing skills."

Shelley seems reluctant to try anything new or different; she gives the impression of either not caring or having given up. She knows she's no good at writing, and "That's that."

The SST reviews these findings and impressions, discusses different ways of helping Shelley, and decides to try the following:

1. Have a conference with Shelley, Mr. Levy, and Mr. Jefferson to review Shelley's current grades for this marking period and to encourage her to apply herself to the remedial steps the SST has discussed.

2. Follow this conference with a parent–teacher–student meeting indicating the school's desire to have Shelley's parents help her and the staff by monitoring her homework in English up to the next marking period, when everyone will meet again to discuss their progress.

3. Develop some individualized materials to help Shelley review capitalization and punctuation rules and to provide practice.

4. Have Shelley work with a study-buddy from her English class who will agree to proofread her written assignments and help her improve her first drafts.

5. Give extra help with outlining, using materials provided by Mr. Levy.

6. Require that every night Shelley must write at least 100 words on a topic of her choosing in a format she prefers (for example, as a letter to a friend or a movie star, a report for another class, or a poem or short story). This assignment will be monitored by her parents and turned in to her teacher. Very well-written papers will earn some extra credit.

7. Locate a writing program on the school's computer system and encourage Shelley to use this system, especially when making final copies either for class or any other reason.

Shelley balks at all of this; she says it is too much to do. Mr. Jefferson and her parents stress the extra credit possibility, and her parents inform her that she is required to do the 100 words every night, "period."

After about two weeks, Shelley agrees to do the punctuation and capitalization worksheets in class. Why? Because Mr. Jefferson discovers six other students who could also benefit from the work and divides his class into "specific skills" practice days two days a week.

About a month later, Ms. Birdsong calls to say that she is very pleased with the improvement in Shelley's papers and in her grades in English. Shelley refused to do the writing one night, so her parents restricted her activities, cutting off her phone and TV privileges. She hasn't refused since then.

The SST decides to terminate this case; the dysgraphia is apparently remitting.

GENERAL IDEAS ABOUT INTERVENTIONS FOR PROBLEMS IN ACADEMIC LEARNING

The school-based consultant is often asked to assist consultees in planning programs for students who are at risk for academic failure. Some of these students are in regular education classes and have never been referred for disabilities or recognized as having them. Others are students who have been identified and are now being mainstreamed or included in regular education classes. And still others are in special education settings, either full or part time, and are not doing as well as expected there. No matter the setting or circumstance, these students are not doing well academically relative to their peers or their own expected levels of performance based on estimated ability levels. The hope is that their teachers will ask for help from the school-based consultant and work collaboratively with her, the SST, or other service delivery personnel or systems to ensure the development of new approaches for these students.

Ideas that consultants have found useful in their work with consultees who are working with underachieving students are listed below. These ideas have been taken from a wide variety of sources (Batche & Knoff, 1995; Bos & Vaughn, 1998; Choate, 1993; Fisher, Schumaker, & Deshler, 1996; Jones, 1987; McCarney & Cummins, 1988; Mayen, Vergason, & Whelan, 1996; Munson, 1987; Rathvon, 1999; Salend, 1998; Stoner, Shinn, & Walker, 1991; Zins, Curtis, Graden, & Ponti, 1988).

Curricular Modifications:

1. Select content that matches the interests and needs of the students.
2. Clarify daily, weekly, and monthly goals.
3. Use enrichment activities designed to heighten interest.
4. Design expectations so that students can be successful 70 to 100 percent of the time.
5. Avoid reading material that is at the students' frustration level unless others (for example, peer-assisted learning, cooperative groups, and so on) are able to assist them.
6. While holding high standards, avoid overwhelming at-risk students with work requirements that appear too difficult or too much.

Modifications of the Method:

1.   Try to increase what is variously known as academic engaged time, academic learning time, or time on task (TOT). These phrases all refer to the necessity of keeping students actively engaged with the curriculum. One way of ensuring increased TOT is close monitoring of what the students are doing. Greenwood (1996) and Gettinger (1995) have found that high rates of monitoring correlate well with academic achievement in all grades.

2.   Focus attention on the relevant stimuli. Teach at-risk students the LISTEN approach (Bauwens & Hourcade, 1989): When the teacher says, "Listen, please," the students should do the following:

Listen to the teacher.

Idle their motor.

Sit up straight.

Turn toward the teacher.

Engage their brain.

Now . . . [follow instructions and so on].

3.   Give a strong focus to what is most relevant. Use outlines, semantic organizers, webs, highlighted materials, think–pair–share, visual aids, interactive methods, and so on (Cooper, 1999).

4.   Provide taped lessons, calculators, computer-assisted instructional materials, overheads, and other technology as available.

5.   Provide easy access to cues (for example, *there* = a place (usually); *their* = ownership).

6.   Give more examples before starting work (for example, "For those ready to begin, go ahead; if you want more examples, LISTEN").

7.   Think of concrete examples and ask the students for examples.

8.   Alter your voice to emphasize points. When students get noisy, speak in a quiet voice; this often (but not always) encourages students to quiet down.

9.   Demonstrate (model) correct responding; have students do the same.

10.   Always use at least two modalities (for example, visual and auditory) and, when appropriate, others. For example, when teaching about the colonial states, tell the students about them, show them on a map, and then have different students represent different states and stand together (kinesthetic modality) to show their geographical relationship to one another.

11.   Give students more time to respond. In some cultures, rapid responding is not a value. Also, remember that many learning disabled students process information slowly; don't rush them. Further, students who are anxious tend to block when they feel rushed. Give them time to respond. Tobin (1987) reviewed the findings on wait time, the time that elapses between a teacher's questions and a student's opportunity to respond. Teachers who require at least a three-second wait time receive

more thorough answers and get more students to respond. The answers also tend to be correct more often and be more sophisticated.

12.   Allow many ways to report information: oral, written, acted out, conveyed through another person, multiple choice, essay, tape-recorded, computer-generated, and so on.

13.   Be explicit in the use of reinforcement. Tie it to specific actions and identify the actions. For example, "I like the way you were careful with your paper heading. It looks good. Would you like to show it to the rest of the class?" Remember, accept a "no" answer; not all students like to show off their work.

14.   Many poor learners lack the meta-skills that seem to automatically occur among good learners: for example, study skills, attending to relevant stimuli, keeping on task, being organized, having materials, proofreading, skimming, identifying important information, using reference skills, and so on. These need to be identified and, very often, directly taught.

15.   Task-analyze your expectations; process-analyze your students' efforts.

16.   Design the classroom to avoid traffic problems and enhance your ability to get from one part of the class to another to provide support and avoid behavioral problems.

17.   Use cooperative learning whenever possible, especially in the content areas of social studies, science, and English. There is considerable evidence indicating the benefits of this approach (Dugan, Kamps, Leonard, Watkins, Rheinberger, & Stackhaus, 1995; Fantuzzo, King, & Heller, 1992; Haynes & Gebreyesus, 1992; Nastasi & Clements, 1991; Slavin, 1995).

Placement Options:

1.   Always consider the general education class ideal unless proven otherwise.

2.   Special education should be conceived of as a philosophy, a need for "special" education, a signal that the possible range of methods used in the general education program are probably not enough, and an acknowledgement that what suits many students does not suit them all. It should not be conceived of as a place for those unable to profit from "general" (that is, ordinary) education. The IEP team may admit a student to special education with the full intention of continuing his education in a general setting with collaborative consultative help from a school consultant.

3.   Grade-level retention does not have a good track record. Usually, students held back a year do not do any better academically than students of equal achievement levels who are promoted. Often, retained students do more poorly socially than do their promoted peers, especially in the junior high years (McCoy & Reynolds, 1999; Rafoth & Carey, 1995).

4.   Short-term pullout remedial programs seem beneficial for some students but not for others. It is not clear why this is so. For any student who manifests skill deficiencies, these programs (for example, Reading Recovery, Project Read, Language) are worth trying, but at-risk students also need to receive the benefit of many of the curricular and methodological modifications mentioned in this chapter.

SUMMARY

Nearly every day, a school-based consultant receives requests from consultees for assistance with students who are not doing well academically. Traditionally, when a request of this type was made, there was an implicit assumption that something was wrong with the student; perhaps she had a learning disability, an emotional disturbance, or was "just plain slow." We have moved forward in our philosophy of education to the point where many educators now interpret these problems from a systems or ecological perspective. Now we look at the mismatch between the student and the teacher's expectations, which may be caused by curricular inappropriateness, teaching methods that don't match the student's needs, motivational lacks other than intrachild ones, and a host of other possibilities. Our assessment of the problem should not rely on pulling the child from the classroom and administering (primarily) norm-based tests, writing psychometrically oriented reports, labeling the student with some pseudo-explanatory disorder, admiring the complexity of the problem, placing the student somewhere else, and then moving on to other cases, of which there are no shortages. Instead, we are moving into an era of broad-based assessment: reviewing previous progress; interviewing significant individuals in the student's life; observing the student, especially in areas she finds difficult; and, if needed, administering tests designed to pinpoint the areas of need. Expected as part of this newer model of assessment is a constant interchange with the student's teachers and parents carried out in a non-hierarchical, collaborative fashion.

This chapter has reviewed some of the variables (for example, psychological, instructional, and home environment) that interact to influence students' academic status. Also reviewed were reasons for poor learning, the role of the school-based consultant when dealing with referrals for poor learning, the sources and nature of the curriculum, and instructional environment and home support components. Two brief examples of instructional consultation were presented, and the chapter concluded with a list of recommendations that school-based consultants will find useful.

REFERENCES

American Psychiatric Association. (1994). *Diagnostic and statistical manual* (4th ed.). Washington, DC: Author.

Anderson, J. (1995). *Cognitive psychology and its implications* (4th ed.). New York: Freeman.

Armstrong, T. (1995). *The myth of the ADD child*. New York: Dutton.

Baker, J., Zigmond, N. (1990). Are regular education classes equipped to accommodate students with learning disabilities? *Exceptional Children, 56,* 515–526.

Barkley, R. (1998). *Attention-deficit hyperactivity disorder: A handbook for diagnosis and treatment.* New York: Guilford Press.

Barron, B. G., & Associates. (1983). Study skills: A new look. *Reading Improvement, 20,* 329–332.

Baruth, L. G., & Manning, M. L. (1992). *Multicultural education of children and adolescents*. Boston: Allyn & Bacon.

Batche, G. M., & Knoff, H. M. (1995). Linking assessment to intervention. In A. Thomas & J. Grimes (Eds.), *Best practices in school psychology—III* (pp. 569–586). Washington, DC: NASP.

Bauer, A., & Shea, T. (1999). *Learners with emotional and behavioral disorders*. Upper Saddle River, NJ: Merrill/Prentice Hall.

Bauwens, J., & Hourcade, J. J. (1989). Hey, would you just listen? *Teaching Exceptional Children, 21,* 61.

Bergan, J. R., & Kratochwill, T. R. (1990). *Behavioral consultation and therapy*. New York: Plenum.

Bloom, B. (1964). *Human characteristics and school learning*. New York: Wiley.

Bos, C., & Vaughn, S. (1998). *Teaching students with learning and behavior problems* (4th ed.). Boston: Allyn & Bacon.

Boykin, A. (1994). Harvesting culture and talent: African American children and educational reform. In R. Rossi (Ed.), *Schools and students at risk* (pp. 116–130). New York: Teachers College Press.

Brandt, R. (1991). On restructuring schools: A conversation with Mike Cohen. *Educational Leadership, 48*(8), 54–58.

Brody, N. (1997). Intelligence, schooling, and society. *American Psychologist, 52,* 1,046–1,050.

Brown, D., Pryzwansky, W. B., & Schulte, A. C. (2001). *Psychological consultation: Introduction to theory and practice* (5th ed.). Boston: Allyn & Bacon.

Byrnes, J. P. (1996). *Cognitive learning and development in instructional contexts*. Boston: Allyn & Bacon.

Campbell, J., Donahue, P., Reese, C., & Phillips, G. (1996). *NAEP 1994 reading report card for the nation and the states*. Washington, DC: U.S. Department of Education, National Center for Educational Statistics.

Carter, J., & Sugai, G. (1989). Survey on prereferral practices: Responses from state departments of education. *Exceptional Children, 55,* 298–302

Choate, J. (1993). *Successful mainstreaming: Proven ways to detect and correct special needs*. Boston: Allyn & Bacon.

Christenson, S. L., & Conoley, J. C. (Eds.). (1992). *Home-school collaboration: Enhancing children's academic and social competence*. Silver Spring, MD: NASP.

Cohen, R., Swerdlik, M., & Smith, D. (1992). Psychological testing and assessment. Mountain View, CA: Mayfield Publishing Company.

Cooper, J. (Ed.). (1999). *Classroom teaching skills*. Boston: Houghton Mifflin Company.

Costenbader, V., & Buntaine, R. (1999). Diagnostic discrimination between social maladjustment and emotional disturbance. *Journal of Emotional and Behavioral Disorders, 7,* 2–10.

D'Amato, R. C. (1990). A neuropsychological approach to school psychology. *School Psychology Quarterly, 5,* 141–160.

D'Amato, R., & Rothlisberg, B. (1992). *Psychological perspectives on intervention*. New York: Longman.

Darling–Hammond, L. (1996). The right to learn and the advancement of teaching: Research, policy of practice for democratic education. *Educational Researcher, 25,* 5–17.

De Mesquita, P. B., & Zollman, A. (1995). Teachers' preferences for academic intervention strategies in mathematics: Implications for instructional consultation. *Journal of Educational and Psychological Consultation, 6*(2), 159–174.

Deno, E. N. (1970). Special education as developmental capital. *Exceptional Children, 37,* 229–237.

Dettmer, P., Dyck, N., & Thurston, L. (1999). *Consultation, collaboration, and teamwork for students with special needs*. Boston: Allyn & Bacon.

Doll, R. C. (1989). *Curriculum improvement: Decision making and process* (7th ed.). Boston: Allyn & Bacon.

Dugan, E., Kamps, D., Leonard, B., Watkins, N., Rheinberger, A., & Stackhaus, J. (1995). Effects of cooperative learning groups during social studies for students with autism and fourth grade peers. *Journal of Applied Behavioral Analysis, 28,* 175–188.

Edmonds, R. (1979). Effective schools for the urban poor. *Educational Leadership, 37*(1), 15–27.

Ekwall, E. (1988). *Locating and correcting reading difficulties* (5th ed.). Columbus, OH: Merrill.

Elkind, D. (1976). Child development in educational settings. *Educational Psychologist, 12,* 49–58.

Ellis, A. (1995). Changing rational-emotive therapy to rational-emotive behavioral therapy. *Journal of Rational-Emotive and Cognitive-Behavioral Therapy, 13,* 85–90.

Erickson, M. (1998). *Behavior disorders of children and adolescents*. Upper Saddle River, NJ: Prentice Hall.

Evans, S. S., Evans, W. H., & Mercer, C. D. (1986). *Assessment for instruction*. Boston: Allyn & Bacon.

Fantuzzo, J., King, J., & Heller, L. (1992). Effects of reciprocal peer tutoring on mathematics and school adjustment: A component analysis. *Journal of Educational Psychology, 84,* 331–339.

Figueroa, R. A. (1990). Best practices in assessment of bilingual children. In A. Thomas & J. Grimes (Eds.), *Best practices in school psychology—II* (pp. 93–106). Washington, DC: NASP.

Fisher, J. B., Schumaker, J. B., & Deshler, D. D. (1996). Searching for validated inclusive practices: A review of the literature. In E. L. Meyen, G. A. Vergason, & R. J. Whelan (Eds.), *Strategies for teaching exceptional children in inclusive settings* (pp. 123–154). Denver, CO: Love Publishing.

Friend, M., & Bursick, W. (1999). *Including students with special needs: A practical guide for classroom teachers* (2nd ed.). Boston: Allyn & Bacon.

Friend, M., & Cook, L. (2000). *Interactions: Collaboration skills for school professionals.* New York: Longman.

Fuchs, D., & Fuchs, L. S. (1991). Framing the REI debate: Abolitionists versus conservationists. In J. W. Lloyd, N. N. Singh, & A. C. Repp (Eds.), *The regular education initiative: Alternative perspectives on concepts, issues and models* (pp. 241–255). Sycamore, IL: Sycamore.

Gettinger, M. (1995). Best practices for increasing academic learning time. In A. Thomas & J. Grimes (Eds.), *Best practices in school psychology—III* (pp. 943–954). Washington, DC: National Association of School Psychologists.

Gickling, E., & Havertape, J. (1982). *Curriculum-based assessment* [self-study format, C. Righi & F. Rubinson (Eds.)]. Minneapolis: National School Psychology Inservice Training Network.

Glaser, R. (1977). *Adaptive education: Individual diversity and learning.* New York: Holt, Rinehart, & Winston.

Gleason, M., Herr, C., & Archer, A. (1988, Spring). Study skills: Teaching study skills. *Teaching Exceptional Children,* 52–57.

Gleitman, H., Fridlund, A., & Reisberg, D. (1999). *Psychology* (5th ed.). New York: Norton.

Good, T. L., & Brophy, J. E. (1984). *Looking in classrooms* (3rd ed.). New York: Harper & Row.

Gordon, E. W. (1984). *Human diversity and pedagogy.* Pomona, NY: Ambergris Family Press.

Greenwood, C. (1996). The case for performance-based instructional models. *School Psychology Quarterly, 11,* 283–296.

Greenwood, C. R., Carta, J. J., Kamps, D., & Delquadri, J. (1995). *Ecobehavioral Assessment System Software.* Kansas City, KS: Juniper Gardens Children's Center.

Grossman, H. (1995). *Teaching in a diverse society.* Boston: Allyn & Bacon.

Gustafsson, J., & Undheim, J. (1996). Individual differences in cognitive functioning. In D. C. Berliner & R. C. Calfee (Eds.), *Handbook of educational psychology.* New York: MacMillan.

Hammill, D. (1998). *Detroit tests of learning aptitude—4.* Austin, TX: PRO-ED.

Hammill, D. D., & Larson, S. (1996). *The test of written language—3.* Austin, TX: PRO-ED.

Haynes, N., & Gebreyesus, S. (1992). Cooperative learning: A case for African-American children. *School Psychology Review, 21,* 577–585.

Helfand, D. & Groves, M. (2001). *Poor readers have gotten worse, U.S. study shows.* Los Angeles, CA: Los Angeles Times.

Heward, W. (2000). *Exceptional children* (6th ed.). Upper Saddle River, NJ: Merrill/Prentice Hall.

Hynd, G. W., & Obrzut, J. E. (Eds.). (1981). *Neuropsychological assessment and the school-aged child.* New York: Grune & Stratton.

Idol, L., Nevin, A., & Paolucci-Whitcomb, P. (2000). *Collaborative consultation* (3rd ed.). Austin, TX: PRO-ED.

Interagency Committee on Learning Disabilities (Ed.), (1997). Learning disabilities: A report to the U.S. Congress. Washington, DC: U.S. Government Printing Office.

Johnson, L., & Pugach, M. (1996). Role of collaborative dialogue in teachers' conceptions of appropriate practice for students at risk. *Journal of Educational and Psychological Consultation, 7,* 9–24.

Jones, F. (1987). *Positive classroom instruction.* New York: McGraw-Hill.

Kampwirth, T. J. (1981). Diagnosing poor learning: Some considerations. *Journal for Special Educators, 17*(2), 142–149.

Kauffman, J. (2001). *Characteristics of emotional and behavioral disorders of childhood and youth* (7th ed.). Upper Saddle River, NJ: Merrill/Prentice Hall.

Kauffman, J. M., & Hallahan, D. P. (Eds.). (1995). *The illusion of full inclusion.* Austin, TX: PRO-ED.

Kelly, K. (1999). Retention vs. social promotion: Schools search for alternatives. *Harvard Educational Letter, 15*(1), 1–3.

Kiewra, K. (1991). Aids to lecture learning. *Educational Psychologist, 26,* 37–53.

Knapp, M. (1995). *Teaching for meaning in high poverty classrooms.* New York: Teachers College Press.

Lerner, J. (2000). *Learning disabilities* (8th ed.). Boston: Houghton Mifflin.

Levine, D. V., & Havighurst, R. S. (1989). *Society and education* (7th ed.). Boston: Allyn & Bacon.

Lidz, C. S. (Ed.). (1987). *Dynamic assessment: An interactional approach to evaluating learning potential.* New York: Guilford Press.

Long, N., & Morse, W. (1996). *Conflict in the classroom* (5th ed.). Austin, TX: PRO-ED.

McCarney, S. B., & Cummins, K. K. (1988). *The pre-referral intervention manual.* Columbia, MO: Hawthorne Educational Services.

McCoy, A., & Reynolds, A. (1999). Grade retention and school performance: An extended investigation. *Journal of School Psychology, 37,* 273–298.

McLoyd, V. (1998). Socioeconomic disadvantage and child development. *American Psychologist, 53,* 185–204.

Marsh, H., & Craven, R. (1997). Academic self-concept: Beyond the dustbowl. In G. D. Phye (Ed.), *Handbook of classroom assessment: Learning, achievement and adjustment.* San Diego: Academic Press.

Mayen, E., Vergason, G., & Whelan, R. (1996). *Strategies for teaching exceptional children in inclusive settings.* Denver, CO: Love Publishing.

Mercer, C. D. (1997). *Students with learning disabilities* (5th ed.). Upper Saddle River, NJ: Merrill/Prentice Hall.

Messick, S., & Associates. (1976). *Individuality and learning.* San Francisco: Jossey-Bass.

Mintzes, J., Wandersee, J., & Novak, J. (1997). Meaningful learning in science: The human constructivist perspective. In G. D. Phye (Ed.), *Handbook of academic learning: Construction of knowledge.* San Diego: Academic Press.

Monson, D. L. (Ed.). (1985). *Adventuring with books: A booklist for pre-K–grade 6.* Urbana, IL: National Council of Teachers of English.

Mullis, I., Dossey, J., Foertsch, M., Jones, L., & Gentile, C. (1991). *Trends in academic progress.* Washington, DC: U.S. Department of Education, National Center for Educational Statistics.

Munson, S. M. (1987). Regular education teacher modifications for mainstreamed mildly handicapped students. *Journal of Special Education, 20*(4), 489–502.

Myers, P. I., & Hammill, D. D. (1990). *Learning disabilities: Basic concepts, assessment practices, and instructional strategies* (4th ed.). Austin, TX: PRO-ED.

Nastasi, B., & Clements, D. (1991). Research on cooperative learning: Implications for practice. *School Psychology Review, 20,* 110–131.

National Joint Committee on Learning Disabilities (NJCLD). (1997). *Letter from NJCLD to member organizations. Topic: Modifications to the NJCLD*

definition of learning disabilities. Baltimore: Orton Dyslexia Society.

Neisser, U., Boodoo, G., Bouchard, T., Boykin, A., Ceci, S., Halpern, D., Loehlen, J., Perloff, R., Sternberg, R., & Urbina, S. (1996). Intelligence: Knowns and unknowns. *American Psychologist, 51,* 77–101.

Nieto, S. (1996). *Affirming diversity: The sociopolitical context of multicultural education* (2nd ed.). White Plains, NY: Longman.

Oakes, J. (1999). Promotion or retention: Which one is social? *Harvard Education Letter, 15*(1), 8.

Perkins, D. (1995). *Outsmarting I.Q.: The emerging science of learnable intelligence.* New York: Free Press.

Pike, K., Compain, R., & Mumper, J. *New connections: An integrated approach to literacy.* New York: HarperCollins.

Pressley, M., Yokoi, L., Van Meter, P., Van Etten, S., & Freebern, G. (1997). Some of the reasons why preparing for exams is so hard: What can be done to make it easier? *Educational Psychology Review, 9,* 1–38.

Purkey, S. C., & Smith, M. S. (1983). Effective schools: A review. *Elementary School Journal, 83,* 427–452.

Quay, H. C., & Werry, J. S. (Eds.). (1986). *Psychopathological disorders of childhood* (3rd ed.). New York: Wiley.

Rafoth, M. A., & Carey, K. (1995). Best practices in assisting with promotion and retention decisions. In A. Thomas & J. Grimes (Eds.), *Best practices in school psychology—III* (pp. 413–420). Washington, DC: NASP.

Rathvon, N. (1999). *Effective school interventions.* New York: Guilford Press.

Reschly, D. (1979). Nonbiased assessment. In G. Phye & D. Reschly (Eds.), *School psychology: Perspectives and issues* (pp. 215–273). New York: Academic Press.

Reschly, D. J., & Grimes, J. P. (1995). Intellectual assessment. In A. Thomas & J. P. Grimes (Eds.), *Best practices in school psychology—III* (pp. 763–773). Washington, DC: NASP.

Reynolds, C. R., & Kaiser, S. M. (1990). Bias in assessment of aptitude. In C. R. Reynolds & R. W. Kamphaus (Eds.), *Handbook of psychological and educational assessment of children: Intelligence and achievement* (pp. 611–663). New York: Guilford Press.

Richardson, V., & Anders, P. (1998). A view from across the Grand Canyon. *Learning Disabilities Quarterly, 21*(1), 85–97.

Rosenfield, S. (1987). *Instructional consultation.* Hillsdale, NJ: Erlbaum.

Rosenfield, S. A., & Gravois, T. A. (1996). *Instructional consultation teams.* New York: Guilford Press.

Rosenshine, B., & Stevens, R. (1986). Teaching functions. In M. C. Wittrock (Ed.), *Handbook of research on teaching* (3rd ed., pp. 376–391). Upper Saddle River, NJ: Prentice Hall.

Rosner, J. (1999). *Helping children overcome learning difficulties.* New York: Walker & Co.

Rumberger, R. (1995). Dropping out of middle school: A multilevel analysis of students and schools. *American Educational Research Journal, 32,* 583–626.

Salend, S. (1998). *Effective mainstreaming: Creating inclusive classrooms.* Upper Saddle River, NJ: Merrill/Prentice Hall.

Salvia, J., & Hughes, C. (1990). *Curriculum-based assessment.* Upper Saddle River, NJ: Prentice Hall.

Salvia, J., & Ysseldyke, J. E. (1998). *Assessment* (7th ed.). Boston: Houghton Mifflin.

Sattler, J. (1998). *Clinical and forensic interviewing of children and families.* San Diego: Sattler Publishing.

Sattler, J. M. (2001). *Assessment of children* (4th ed.). San Diego: Sattler Publishing.

Schofield, J. (1995). Promoting positive intergroup relations in school settings. In W. D. Hawley & A. W. Jackson (Eds.), *Toward a common destiny: Improving race and ethnic relations in America.* San Francisco: Jossey-Bass.

Shapiro, E. (1989). *Academic skills problems: Direct assessment and intervention.* New York: Guilford Press.

Shaywitz, S. E., & Shaywitz, B. A. (1991). Introduction to the special series on attention deficit disorder. *Journal of Learning Disabilities, 24,* 68–71.

Shinn, M. (Ed.). (1998). *Advanced applications of curriculum-based measurement.* New York: Macmillan.

Skrtic, T. M. (1991). The special education paradox: Equity as the way to excellence. *Harvard Educational Review, 61,* 148–206.

Slavin, R. (1995). *Cooperative learning: Theory, research and practice.* Boston: Allyn & Bacon.

Slavin, R. (1997). *Educational psychology: Theory and practice.* Boston: Allyn & Bacon.

Smith, D. (2001). *Introduction to special education.* Boston: Allyn & Bacon.

Stainback, W., & Stainback, S. (1987). Educating all students in regular education. *TASH Newsletter, 13*(4), 1–7.

Stanovich, K. (2000). *Progress in understanding reading: Scientific foundations and new frontiers.* New York: Guilford Press.

Stanovich, K. E., Nathan, R. G., & Zolman, J. E. (1988). The developmental lag hypothesis in reading: Longitudinal and matched reading-level comparisons. *Child Development, 59,* 71–86.

Stoner, G., Shinn, M. R., & Walker, H. M. (1991). *Interventions for achievement and behavior problems.* Silver Spring, MD: NASP.

Swanson, H. (1991). *Handbook on the assessment of learning disabilities.* Austin, TX: PRO-ED.

Swap, S. M. (1993). *Developing home-school partnerships: From concepts to practice.* New York: Teachers College Press.

Teeter, P. A. (1989). Neuropsychological approaches to the remediation of educational deficits. In C. R. Reynolds & E. Fletcher-Janzen (Eds.), *Handbook of clinical child neuropsychology* (pp. 357–376). New York: Plenum.

Thomas, E., & Robinson, H. (1972). *Improving reading in every class: A sourcebook for teachers.* Boston: Allyn & Bacon.

Tobin, K. G. (1987). The role of wait-time in higher-cognitive-level learning. *Review of Educational Research, 57,* 69–95.

Trueba, H., Jacobs, L., & Kirton, E. (1990). *Cultural conflict and adaptation.* New York: Falmer.

U.S. Department of Education. (1998). *Twentieth annual report to Congress on the implementation of the Education of All Handicapped Act.* Washington, DC: Author.

Vacca, J. L., & Padak, N. D. (1990). Reading consultants as classroom collaborators: An emerging role. *Journal of Educational and Psychological Consultation, 1*(1), 99–107.

Valde, G., & Figueroa, R. (1994). *Bilingualism and testing: A special case of bias.* Norwood, NJ: Ablex.

Vasquez, J. (1993). Teaching to the distinctive traits of minority students. In K. M. Cauley, F. Linder, & J. McMillan (Eds.), *Annual editions: Educational psy-*

chology 93/94. Guilford, CT: The Dushkin Publishing Group.

Wang, M. C., Haertel, G. D., & Walberg, H. J. (1993). Toward a knowledge base for school learning. *Review of Educational Leadership, 63*(3), 249–294.

Wicks-Nelson, R., & Israel, A. (2000). *Behavior disorders of childhood.* Upper Saddle River, NJ: Prentice Hall.

Will, M. (1986). *Educating students with learning problems: A shared responsibility.* Washington, DC: U.S. Department of Education.

Ysseldyke, J., & Christenson, S. (1993). *The instructional environment system—II.* Longmont, CO: Sopris West.

Ysseldyke, J., Christenson, S., & Kovaleski, J. (1994). Identifying students' instructional needs in the context of classroom and home environments. *Teaching Exceptional Children, 26*(3), 37–41.

Zins, J. E., Curtis, M. J., Graden, J. L., & Ponti, C. (1988). *Helping students succeed in the regular classroom.* San Francisco: Jossey-Bass.

Case Studies in Consultation: Academic Learning Problems in the Classroom

OBJECTIVES

1. Present two cases utilizing the SOCS approach where the primary concerns are learning problems exhibited by students at two different grade levels.

2. Ask the readers a set of questions about the process and interventions used by the consultants and consultees in these cases.

3. Reflect on the content of previous chapters, especially Chapter 8, to demonstrate how the consultant used the information presented in these chapters.

This chapter is similar in structure to Chapter 7, which presents two cases demonstrating how the SOCS process was applied to classroom behavior problems. In this chapter, the focus is on academic learning problems.

As in Chapter 7, questions and comments about the cases appear at the end of each case. Once again, these cases are not designed to represent examples of perfectly engineered consultation efforts. Each represents typical situations encountered by school-based consultants. Some readers may not agree with the appropriateness of the steps taken by the consultants who conducted these cases; in consultation, many options can be taken, and competent school-based consultants may disagree about the sequence or importance of procedures. Consider these cases as they are intended: for class discussion or private reflection. Each case is a composite of many cases in which I have been involved. As in Chapter 7, none of the names of people or settings are real.

Case 3 | Learning Disability

Hello, my name is Brian Lee; I'm the resource teacher here at ABC School. We've been back to school for two weeks now, and we're as busy as ever. I've taken on some new challenges over the past year that I'm still getting used to. I've been a resource teacher for five years. Last year we decided to move to a collaborative consultation model of service delivery. Making a long story short, the change hasn't been easy. Despite the objections of some of our more traditional teachers, we've decided to move even further into the collaborative model this year. The case I'm going to share with you demonstrates some of the problems and solutions that are possible in this model. Although I'm sure we've made mistakes, I think it is a good example of how this model can function when people decide to work together. In any event, it's a good case to learn from.

Here are the basics. Pete Jackson, one of our fifth-graders, was referred during the second week of school for these reasons: "Pete can't read any of our textbooks. I think he has a very serious reading disability. Naturally, he can't spell or write, either.

I think he needs special education." Pete is ten years, three months old at the time of referral. He is the second of four children from an intact, middle-class background. His reading problems have been noted since first grade. He was referred in grade three and was assessed by the school psychologist but found not eligible for special education as a student with a learning disability because he did not have the required discrepancy between ability and achievement. His WISC-III verbal I.Q. was 95, his performance was 102, his achievement standard scores in reading and spelling were about 82, and math was 95, computation only. He has no behavior problems. In fourth grade he apparently went into hiding, or else began practicing those compensatory tactics so often spontaneously developed by those with learning problems; his teacher said he was doing OK. Now he has a new teacher, Mr. Mendoza (our consultee), who wrote the referral opinions you've just read. He has alerted the parents, who have also called the school principal. It looks like this will be a front-burner case for awhile.

RECEIPT OF A REFERRAL AND INITIAL THOUGHTS ABOUT IT

I know Pete only from seeing him on the playground. None of his siblings have come to my attention either through SST or otherwise. I remember when we talked about him two years ago. Someone on the SST (Was it me?) commented that we'd only have to wait another year or two; then the discrepancy between ability and achievement would grow to the point that we would feel obligated to determine his eligibility for special education services as a student with a learning disability. Until then he'd just have to bide his time. Our school doesn't have any other form of assistance for poor achievers; it's left up to the parents to provide whatever help they can. Some teachers utilize in-class peer assistance, cross-age tutoring, and cooperative groups to assist the slower students.

Here's what I want to know:

- What are Pete's levels of achievement relative to the other students in his grade?
- What have his parents done about his problems?
- Given the fact that he can't read the fifth-grade books, what can he read, and how can we deliver the curriculum to him without his being able to read the books?
- Does he have specific skill deficits, and how can they be remediated?
- What resources can the school or parents bring to bear on this case and others like it?
- What system changes or improvements need to be made to prevent cases like this in the future?

To get answers to some of these questions, I'll start with a conference with Pete's teacher, Mr. Al Mendoza [1].

INITIAL DISCUSSION WITH THE TEACHER

I meet with Mr. Mendoza during our mutual lunch break. He is quite forthcoming in his opinions: Pete needs help, more than a regular classroom teacher has time to give, and special education should be useful to him. Biting my tongue, I ask for some background information. "Simple enough," Mr. Mendoza says. "Pete's a nice kid, no behavior problems, seems well adjusted, tries to do assignments but turns in pretty much illegible stuff. Spelling? Forget it; anything beyond three or four letters is likely to be wrong. I know he's not just a slow learner; his math skills are good. Let's go to SST and get the assessment papers developed; Pete's parents are waiting" [2].

It sounds like Pete has some serious learning problems in the language arts area. I ask, "What adjustments have you made in the classroom so far, and what ideas do you have for how to help Pete?"

Mr. Mendoza looks at me as if to say, "Are you deaf?" He doesn't say that, however. Instead, he patiently points out to me that he has 28 fifth-graders, many of whom have problems, and he just doesn't have time to make all sorts of adjustments. Besides, what is special education for anyway?

Trying to think of a way to remind Mr. Mendoza that special education isn't a place so much as it is a service that can occur in any classroom, I say, "It's possible that Pete will get some direct service from me in my resource room [I still see students two periods a day], but we are always interested in bringing help as close to the general education program as possible."

I tell Mr. Mendoza that I would like to work with him in discovering ways in which he can help Pete in the general education classroom. He sighs, not wanting to hear this, but says that he can assign another boy as a study-buddy to help Pete with some work, and asks if that's OK.

This is the kind of response I was hoping for. Without any more convincing, the consultee has come up with a very good idea, something that doesn't always work but is worth a try. I say, "I think it's an excellent way to start the helping process. One of my roles in our new system is to work with teachers to find effective ways to help students in the general education classroom. I will be glad to work out some details of the study-buddy program or any other ideas that you have about how to help Pete or any of your other students who are having difficulty."

I still shake internally whenever I make this offer since I know there are teachers who will overwhelm me with referrals if they think I'll take over for them. I'm still working through this role confusion that has developed since we started using the collaborative model (see Chapter 10 for more discussion of this topic) [3].

I tell Mr. Mendoza that I am coming into his class on Tuesday morning of next week to observe Pete. I ask, "When would be a good time?" I also say that I'll put Pete's name on the SST agenda for next Thursday, so Mr. Mendoza should plan to come to that meeting. We part, still friends.

CLASSROOM OBSERVATION

Let me fill you in a little about our consultee. Mr. Mendoza has been a teacher in the elementary grades for about 20 years. He is regarded as dependable, likable, and traditional. He teaches now in pretty much the same way he did 20 years ago. The major change is probably that now he does more cooperative learning activities with his students. The kids like him; he maintains good classroom discipline in a positive way. He apparently has no ambitions to move upward in the school hierarchy. He likes what he is doing, and he's pretty good at it. When you visit his class, however, it feels somewhat like going back in time. The desks are still in straight rows, although they are moved occasionally. His room environment is basic. He doesn't believe in anything flashy. He maintains a calm demeanor, works from a very predictable schedule, and expects standards to be upheld, which they usually are.

I visit Mr. Mendoza's room on Tuesday morning from 9:00 to 9:45. It is language arts time, and the students are reading a story, taking turns as he directs them by asking questions about it as they go along. After they finish the story, they respond to some questions about it and then, in small groups, mutually review their answers and come up with an idea for a jointly written story similar to the one they have just read. I have never heard of this idea, but I can see its possibilities.

Pete isn't asked to read out loud, but he does try to read some of the printed questions along with his study-buddy, who seems to be a neat kid who takes his role seriously. He helps Pete pronounce about every third word of the question: "Describe the atmosphere of the Johnson household when Lori announced that she was going to buy a horse." I wander around the room looking at the students' efforts at writing answers to these questions and, in general, I am favorably impressed. It's great to get out into the general education classes and see what the students who are normally learning are able to do. Being in a resource room for most of your career makes you think nobody learns easily anymore!

Before I leave the room I ask Mr. Mendoza to put together a portfolio of Pete's typical work so we can review it at the SST meeting. Our teachers are used to this now, so it is no problem for him. I say, "I think the study-buddy system seems to be working well." Mr. Mendoza agrees but points out that Pete still needs to learn to read. I agree.

INITIAL DISCUSSION WITH THE PARENTS

As noted in Chapter 5, parent input is necessary in all cases of school-based collaborative consultation work. It may come either before or after consultation with the teacher or before the SST meeting to which the parents will be invited. In our school, SST is optional, depending on the case. In this case, we are going to bring Pete to the SST because of the severity of his language arts learning problems. I think it's best to contact Pete's parents before the meeting to let them know about our concern and to solicit their input. Parents always feel more at home during an SST meeting if they know the people there, if only by phone.

I talk with Mrs. Jackson. She says that Pete is showing signs of beginning to dislike school because he feels like a fool if he ever has to read out loud or show anybody what he has written. Whatever he writes in class gets back to him full of corrections, mostly spelling errors, and he hates it. Both she and her husband are very concerned about Pete's problem; why hasn't the school done anything about it?

I try to explain our limitations in being able to fund positions designed to provide help outside of special education. She says, "I think that's nonsense," and tells me that she intends to call a school board member about it.

I reply, "The opinions of parents are often taken seriously by board members." I hope this will prompt her to carry through with the phone call.

Mrs. Jackson tells me that she and her husband try to help Pete with his reading but don't know what to do. Once they thought he was just slow to get started and would catch up, but now both parents are really worried that he might never catch up. She asks, "Can he be learning disabled? Does he have dyslexia? His Uncle Bob has that; I doubt he can read the newspaper."

I can sense her growing despair about the situation. I tell her that Pete is now working with a study-buddy in the classroom, which she says that she knows. I ask, "What do you think should happen?"

She replies, "I'd like any kind of special help the school can offer."

I mention the possibility of special education, since it is the only formal special assistance program we have, and she balks somewhat. Pete has told her that he doesn't want to go to what he refers to as the "dummies' room." I inform her that being identified as a student with a disability doesn't necessarily mean going to a special room; we try to bring services to the students in the regular classes. In any event, we haven't decided anything yet. The purpose of the SST is to explore ideas about how to help. She says that she is anxious to get started [4].

GETTING TEACHERS AND PARENTS TOGETHER: THE SST MEETING

We are going to SST now because of the pressure to get something started, although my preference would have been to wait until we had gathered some objective data about Pete's academic skill levels. The meeting should be quick; we'll probably all agree that his functioning is too low to expect any real progress in his deficit areas without some special intervention. Classroom-based assistance probably won't be sufficient [5].

In attendance at the SST are the principal, Mr. Mendoza; Pete's mom, Mrs. Jackson; our school psychologist, Mr. Huff; Ms. Billow, our school nurse; and myself. Our school psychologist coordinates these meetings, at the principal's request. We start with a review by Mr. Mendoza, who editorializes that he thinks special education is necessary because Pete has dyslexia. Mr. Huff practically becomes unglued; our SST members should know not to diagnose or suggest placement at an initial meeting. Mr. Huff handles it well, however. (After the meeting, our principal takes Mr. Mendoza aside and reviews these protocol matters with him.)

Mrs. Jackson says that she is very upset that the school hasn't provided help sooner. She asks, "Why don't you have a system to help kids before they need special education?" Good question. Our principal responds in terms of budget realities. There is simply no money to hire anyone to do this sort of work [see note 1]. Mrs. Jackson goes on to say that Pete is worried that we are going to put him in special education; he wants no part of it.

Mr. Huff says that no decision has been made yet, but if we as a team, including the parents, decide that special education is the best thing to do, we will help Pete work through his feelings about it. Other students have balked at the same thing only to find out that they like the special education room after they have been in there for awhile. "Remember," he says, "we aren't talking about a full-time placement—possibly only a period or two a day. But it's too soon to say."

I say, "I think we need specifics about Pete's academic levels," and everyone agrees. I offer to do testing in reading, spelling, and writing. Pete's math computation is fair; he just can't read the word problems. The nurse will do a vision and hearing screening. We decide to talk about what we can do in the interim.

The study-buddy system is working well; our principal will call the study-buddy to the office and reinforce his efforts with a call home to his parents while the student is in the office. The idea of a cross-age tutor, possibly a seventh-grader, is mentioned. I'll get someone from our list of trained cross-age tutors and coach the tutor about how to do it. We've done only a little bit in this area, usually successfully. Mr. Mendoza agrees to accept oral work instead of written work whenever possible.

Mrs. Jackson says that she and her husband will be glad to spend time helping Pete. However, she's gotten the idea that she might make him worse because she doesn't know anything about how to teach reading. I tell her that we will be glad to give her some assistance in this area but mention that I think we should wait until the test data are available, at which point we will know better what to do. I inquire about a computer with a word-processing program at home; she says they have one. I suggest that she might want to have Pete practice his spelling and other written work on the word processor. She says that they have tried this but that Pete was not interested [6].

At this point we have agreed on many things and are ready to get started on the next phase: assessment by myself and the nurse, cross-age tutoring, continued study-buddy help, acceptance of oral rather than written work whenever possible, and home-based computer use for spelling and writing.

ASSESSMENT OF THE REFERRED STUDENT

Learning Problem Assessment

I start my assessment of Pete's learning problem with a review of his cumulative folder. His last group achievement test was at the end of grade three, when he had standard scores of about 80 in reading and grammar/writing. Math computation was at 100.

I have him come to my resource room the next day, where I review the SST meeting. He tells me that his mother has also reviewed it with him and that now he is going to get some new reading, spelling, and writing "games" for their computer. He says that his mother also promised to let him play some fun games on the computer after he does his work.

I start the assessment with the Woodcock-Johnson Achievement Battery-III (Woodcock, McGrew, & Mather, 2001) Letter–Word Identification Test. Pete's standard score is 80. I then have him read a grade-level 2-2 reader to see how many words he can read in one minute. He reads 68 with five errors. I go on to a 3-1 reader; he reads 35 words per minute with six errors. I believe we need to stay with second-grade material. I also pick up the following specific skill deficiencies: consonant blends and digraphs, vowel sounds, vowel digraphs and diphthongs, and blending. My feeling is that Pete is not seriously impaired in his reading (i.e., dyslexic) but certainly does have a reading disability. I think that with some concentrated remedial work he can move quickly.

His spelling is weakly phonetic: *mowth* for *mouth*, *talst* for *tallest*, and *tabel* for *table*. He knows they are wrong, suggesting that his visual memory is not bad but certainly not reliable. His spelling score on the W-J is at a standard score of 77; writing samples are 79. I have him write for two minutes about his favorite TV show. He produces 18 words, 6 of them misspelled. The cursive handwriting is fair for his age and gender.

I think Pete is eligible for special education services as a learning disabled student. I need to get back to Mr. Huff to see what we can come up with as a processing disorder, which is required in this state. He'll probably need to do more testing to find something. That could take awhile. In the meantime, I know what to suggest to the cross-age tutor and to Mrs. Jackson. Assuming that Mr. Huff finds a processing disorder (which is usually not too difficult, given the apparent lack of national or local standards for what constitutes a processing problem), I think the SST will agree that we can serve Pete in special education. What I want, however, is to give him only one period a day (I hope for no more than one year) and to include him and Mr. Mendoza in an in-class consultation-based service delivery system starting ASAP. But before we get to the next SST meeting or take any other immediate action, let's look at some other possible factors.

Functional Assessment of Behavior

As noted, Pete doesn't have any behavior problems of any significance. His behavior during academic lessons is characterized by good effort, but little success. He doesn't do anything to jeopardize his success.

Additional Areas of Assessment: Psychodynamic, Ecological, and Biophysical Factors

Mrs. Jackson informs me that Pete seems to be a well-adjusted boy. He gets along with everybody, has the usual squabbles with his siblings, but generally is blessed with an easygoing personality. He is currently bothered by his failure to achieve in school and wants to hide his reading difficulties from his family and friends. Although he has expressed some concerns about special education placement, he probably will be willing to try it and will most likely adjust to it easily. Mrs. Jackson does not think that an emotional problem is related to his failure to read.

Comments about the ecology of Pete's classroom were previously made. Mr. Mendoza is a traditionalist, with some leanings toward more modern ideas (cooperative groupings; cross-age tutoring). There really isn't anything that goes on in the classroom that contributes to Pete's academic problems except a kind of benign neglect (that may have been going on all last year), which is being corrected by this referral.

In the biophysical area, Pete is in good health and always has been. He has never been hyperactive. His attention wanders a bit when he's bored, but he seems normal otherwise. There seems to be no reason to suspect any medical cause for his problem. Our nurse hasn't yet seen him for the vision and hearing workup, but neither Mrs. Jackson nor I suspect he has any problem in either area.

PLANNING INTERVENTIONS

I call Mrs. Jackson to review my assessment results and opinions. I tell her that I will be working with the cross-age tutor and that I'd like to meet with her and/or Mr. Jackson to suggest some specific ways in which they can help Pete at home. What I have in mind are a series of high-interest, low-vocabulary books that she can start with at the second-grade level and a phonics workbook that he can use along with some games, a review of the computer materials they have obtained, and a progress-monitoring system. Within a week we have most of what we need to finalize a plan to review at next week's SST meeting. Given the discrepancy between Pete's cognitive ability scores two years ago and his present achievement standard scores, along with the processing dysfunction (assuming that Mr. Huff can find one), we should be able to find Pete eligible for special education as a student with a learning disability. My plan is to give him one period a day of special help, primarily on phonics skills, and to work with Mr. Mendoza to adjust his classroom expectations to allow for Pete's disability. I need to see Mr. Mendoza about this.

I see him a few days later, when we reserve about 15 minutes of uninterrupted time together. I present the test results I have obtained, and he isn't surprised. I ask, "How do you think we should proceed?"

He says, "So what's wrong with special education? He looks eligible, and he'll get a lot more from you and your small-group class than I can give him."

I reply, "I agree that he needs some concentrated remedial work in phonics, which I can give him in the resource room, and a lot of confidence building, which I think we're both good at." Then I emphasize our school's philosophy of maintaining students in the general education classroom as much as possible. "How is the study-buddy program going?" I ask, "and what else can we do to help Pete in your class?"

Mr. Mendoza reluctantly acknowledges the school's general education commitment toward inclusion and reports that the study-buddy project is good; he has started it with two other students in his room. He is also doing more oral examining of a few other students who are very poor at written work, which reminds him of two children he wants to refer! I bypass that comment but ask for some details on the other study-buddy combinations. (Brainstorming to myself, I wonder if many students should have study-buddies. I'll think more about that later.)

Mr. Mendoza seems stuck at this point, so I probe further into exactly what prevents Pete from learning the content of the fifth-grade class. Mr. Mendoza repeats his concern about the reading deficit. He then asks about Mrs. Jackson's offer to help.

"How might you be able to use this offer?" I ask.

He says he can meet with her and review the weekly plan of what is going to be read in the class and see if she can go over this material with Pete at home. I tell him that's a great idea since we are going to follow up on her offer to help. I say that I'm also going to review my test data with her in addition to suggesting some high-interest, low-vocabulary books. I point out that I will suggest one period of resource room help for Pete at the SST meeting next week.

What about Pete's involvement in all this? Since he is the central person in these efforts and certainly has a stake in them, I decide to feel him out about his views. He tells me he has sensed that something is going on; all this testing, the cross-age tutor, the study-buddy, and Mr. Mendoza's changes in the classroom must mean something. "Am I going to be sent to special education?" he asks, fighting back tears.

I tell him that we are trying to find the best ways and places to give him help in getting caught up to where he wants to be. He argues that he is doing OK and is getting enough help already, especially at home. I agree that there are a lot of things going on with him now. "What do you think we should do?" I ask.

He says he is getting better and doesn't need any special education. I decide not to push that possibility, but instead compliment him on his efforts and tell him that the teachers and his parents will talk about him soon and let him know what we think when we have all our information gathered.

Mr. Huff reports that he has found a processing difficulty just where I expected he would—in auditory processing, specifically Incomplete Words and Sound Blending subtests from the Woodcock-Johnson Cognitive Battery-III. The nurse, Ms. Billow, reports no problems in hearing or vision. We are ready to go back to the SST, which will now act as an IEP team since Pete is to be recommended as a potential special education student.

The team meets the following week. All the major players are in attendance except for Pete, at his parents' request, since they don't want him hearing about the special education possibility until after we have decided on it for sure. Then they will tell him if necessary. The team agrees on the following:

1. Pete is eligible for special education as a student with a learning disability. He will receive one period a day of direct service in the RSP room and will be assisted in his classroom through a consultation model, with myself and Mr. Huff serving as the consultants. (When we got started on this model a year ago, we used to make these agreements only to find that, without something more definite, they often didn't happen. Now when I come to an IEP team expecting that we might go to consultation for service delivery, I bring my

schedule book with me to see when I'm going to be able to deliver the time to which I'm committing myself.) In this case, we agree on Wednesday mornings from 9:00 to 9:30. I'll come into Mr. Mendoza's class, monitor what Pete is doing, review his progress, and decide when to meet with Mr. Mendoza if we aren't seeing progress [7].

2. In the resource room, I'll be working directly on the phonic weaknesses we've detected. My long-term goal will be to increase Pete's reading two grade levels during this coming year, from an instructional level of mid-second grade to mid-fourth. My short-term objective is to solidify Pete's phonetic-attack skills. Though this task is not spelled out on the IEP form, I plan to review all unknown words on the Ekwell Basic Sight Word List (Ekwell & Shanker, 1988) and all words in the second- and third-grade readers we use. Then I'll have Pete read these books and others at these levels using a guided practice method, repeated readings, shadow reading, and story twisting (that is, having the child make up something different about each story, dictating that difference, and then reading his different version). I'll also be reviewing the content of the curriculum in Mr. Mendoza's room so Pete will have a good conceptual grasp of the material for discussion purposes.

3. Mr. Mendoza says he will continue the study-buddy plan and will call Mrs. Jackson weekly to review classwork with her so she can continue to help at home.

4. Mr. Huff says that he will meet with Pete soon to talk about our decision to give him assistance in the resource room during one period a day. Since Pete has expressed concern about this possible placement, we all need to be supportive. Mrs. Jackson says she will tell Pete about it tonight. She knows that Mr. Jackson will agree with the plan. She also mentions that Pete is really taking to the word processor now that he has learned how to use it. She wonders where he can get keyboarding lessons. Good question; we aren't teaching this at school. (Our computer resources have not been extensive up to this year. We hope to have all students on the computers every day by next year.) Mrs. Jackson's last question concerns a vague promise I made at the last SST meeting about giving her some help on how to help Pete; specifically, what should and shouldn't she do when she works with him in reading? I tell her I will talk to her right after the meeting about it.

What I tell her are these general tips:

  a. Make reading as enjoyable as possible.

  b. Work together at a specified time at least four times a week.

  c. Stay with relatively easy material.

  d. Keep a record of all reading errors (miscallings of words) and review them in a gamelike format.

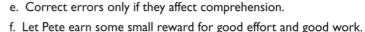

  e. Correct errors only if they affect comprehension.

  f. Let Pete earn some small reward for good effort and good work.

  g. Expect bad days; reading is not easy or rewarding for Pete yet, so there will be some regressions. Don't get discouraged, or he will, too.

IMPLEMENTING INTERVENTIONS

Four weeks have gone by. I find Pete to be a pleasure to work with. He seems to be one of those poor readers who somehow just doesn't get reading easily and who falls deeper between the cracks every year. His deficits have finally accumulated to the point where he has given up trying, gets good at hiding the problem, and hopes it will all go away. Sometimes we don't catch these problems until junior high. Then remediation really gets tough because the students have reached a point of serious discouragement multiplied by the problems of early adolescence.

  While working with me, Pete asks if he can be a cross-age tutor for some of the younger students I see. I think that is a wonderful idea and will get his parents' permission. Perhaps he can tutor during part of our time together.

  My bigger challenge comes in working with Mr. Mendoza, who seemed to lose interest in Pete's problems once he knew Pete was going into special education. He does talk with me about how Pete is doing, but I see little evidence that he is trying to be accommodating. When I notice how this pattern is developing, I arrange a meeting after school with him to review where we are.

  One of the persistent problems in consultation is keeping up some degree of enthusiasm for the process, or belief in the value of the interventions. Consultation regarding difficult problems requires a relatively long-term commitment, the strength of which waxes and wanes as the process proceeds. In school-based consultation, an IEP meeting tends to be a major or climactic event; after the client is placed (if so), it is very easy to assume that the problem is solved and to put it on the back burner or terminate our interest in what happens to the client in the general education classroom. Now that we are emphasizing a consultation-based model of service delivery to our mildly handicapped youngsters, in addition to all other at-risk students, we have found that our real work often begins after the IEP team meeting. That should be true in this case. Not only do I, in my resource room, have to try to get Pete closer to grade level by working on his specific skill deficits, but, I also have to access Mr. Mendoza's room and help him be a better teacher for Pete. What if Mr. Mendoza doesn't want to? What if he thinks the problem has been solved with the decision to go to special education? What will he think about my showing up in his classroom every Wednesday morning?

  During our first year of this model, we found that not all teachers welcome this type of help. In fact, some of them told us outright that they didn't want us to come into their classrooms since "It was too disruptive." Generally, we have gotten past those initial obstacles, but not entirely. Some teachers will probably never buy into this model, and we will have to tread lightly with them. But how about Mr. Mendoza?

I ask him during our meeting how it's going with all the changes over the last month. He thinks it's going well. He's been thinking about how he used to deal with slow learners in previous years, about how he referred all of them for special education. If they didn't get in, he hoped they would be able to keep up, but he never really changed anything for them. He was regarded as a tough teacher, and that meant that the students had to sink or swim; it was up to them. Now, since he has been doing so much of the buddy-system method, he's finding that a number of his slower students are keeping up better than he thought they would. He wonders what I think of his expanding this "new cooperative learning approach" that so many of the other teachers seem so pleased with. Won't it just make the slower kids dependent on the faster ones? Whatever happened to independent effort?

Our staff went through an inservice some time ago about cooperative learning, study teams, team teaching, co-teaching, and other alternative teaching modes. Mr. Mendoza apparently wasn't ready for it at the time, but now he is. Can we credit his turnaround to this case? It seems that way.

I tell him, "Mr. Peterson, our district learning specialist, is the person to see about these things. Our principal can also help. Your friend on the teaching staff, Ms. Osprey, is very good at all of these techniques; perhaps our principal can arrange a time for you to visit her class." Mr. Mendoza seems genuinely interested in pursuing the idea.

Our discussion turns to the broader picture of what we, as a whole school, can do to help our poorer learners. Together we come up with three ideas:

1. Emphasize discussion as an alternative to reading as the primary mode of information input and processing.
2. Talk to our principal about a volunteer parents-as-tutors program.
3. Develop a more systematic cross-age tutoring program throughout the school.

We decide to review these ideas with the principal before bringing them up at a faculty meeting.

MONITORING INTERVENTIONS

I ask Mr. Mendoza how the emphasis on discussion as a learning tool, as opposed to reading only, is working out. He says that he likes it, that it makes the class more lively, but that certain students aren't very good at it. They aren't all verbally expressive, and some students rarely contribute anything. I point out that no one modality is best for all of us. For Pete, specifically, it seems quite good. He likes to talk and always seems to know what the content is about even though he still doesn't read it very well. I mention that I am giving him help in the resource room so that he can do more grade-level reading, as is his mother at home. Mr. Mendoza has been giving him a lot of reinforcement in the classroom for his oral discussion strengths as well as for his efforts to keep up with the class when they do read. All in all, it seems to be going smoothly. All my worries seem misplaced; the consulta-tion model seems to be working quite well because Mr. Mendoza has decided to go along.

Our meeting with the principal went well; at least, we were asked to bring these ideas up to the faculty at the next meeting and to ask for volunteers to put together a substantive proposal that all the faculty can agree on. I was hoping for more leader-ship from our principal, but at least it's a start. I can't tell you how surprised some of the old guard were to hear Mr. Mendoza leading this discussion. They thought they were witnessing a spiritual conversion; in some ways they were.

Pete's doing well with me and with his parents. He is much more involved with his schoolwork both in class and at home. He's becoming a computer fan and is now bugging his parents to buy the latest updates of everything. On a very positive note, his idea of being a cross-age tutor has been implemented; he volunteered to give up his afternoon recess to tutor a third-grade boy who is reading at the first-grade level. As usually happens in these cases, I expect the tutor will gain more than the tutee, and that's fine.

EVALUATION AND CLOSURE

As you learned in Chapter 5, evaluation should be directed toward determining the degree to which the goals of the consultation were or are being met. The goals were to develop a plan of action that would get Pete some academic help and to do it in a way that would keep him as close to the general education program as possible. He was found to be eligible for special education, which allows us to give him an hour a day of concentrated help, and we have been able to effect some changes in his class-room that are enabling him, along with others, to learn well in spite of their reading and writing limitations. At this point we can only look at the ongoing goals since we do not know if our implicit final goal of bringing Pete up to grade level is going to be achieved.

As I stated at the outset, I think this case is interesting because it demonstrates some of the problems and solutions that are possible when using a collaborative consultation-based model. You have seen that we did use a one-period-a-day resource room remedy as a partial solution, and I also hope you noted that the more powerful treatment effects are likely to be those brought about by Mr. Mendoza's changes in the regular classroom. Here we were dealing with a traditional teacher, one who had been operating from a comfortable and successful frame of reference for about 20 years. He was known as tough, which is sometimes a euphemism for "You learn it my way or else." What was most exciting for me was that he initiated his own move-ment toward modern practices with the study-buddy method. My job had been to reinforce his ideas and to facilitate his thinking (without telling him what to do) as he explores other ways to meet his goals and make learning easier for his students. He proved worthy of the risk inherent in the nonexpert stance taken by collaboratively minded consultants. As I think back on what happened with Mr. Mendoza, I am happy to say none of his ideas came from me; at least, I never found myself having to tell

him what to do. I may have buffed and polished his ideas somewhat, but he gets all the credit. I think that explains his zeal when he asked me about instructional reform at the last faculty meeting. Perhaps this case could lead to some sort of systems change around here. When it comes from the grassroots, it often grows well. Personal commitment makes the difference.

NOTES AND COMMENTS ON CASE 3

1.   What other questions might you ask at this time? What resources does your school have for poor learners who aren't eligible for special education? This school does have a cross-age peer-tutoring system but nothing else. Many schools have Title I monies or provide remedial work through systems such as Reading Recovery (Clay, 1985). How might you start the process of getting your school to provide remedial instruction?

2.   Before reading ahead, how would you respond to what the consultee has just said?

3.   The resource teacher/consultant states that he is still working through this role confusion that has developed since his school has changed to a collaborative consultation model. What does he mean by role confusion? How have schools dealt with this problem? Roles of school-based consultants are discussed in Chapter 2 of this text. See also Chapter 1 of Dettmer, Dyck, and Thurston (1999).

4.   What might you say in response to the "dummies' room" comment attributed to Pete?

5.   This school may be in a time warp. Almost all schools now require some degree of documented evidence that in-class interventions (modifications; adjustments of methods, materials, or expectations) have been made before or concurrent with the student's being brought to the SST. What is the procedure at your school? Chapter 2 discusses the roles and procedures for SST meetings. Also, the consultant doesn't believe that in-class assistance through consultation alone will be sufficient. What criteria might he be using in making this decision? What are some of the factors to be considered in deciding whether a student can be fully assisted in the regular class or if he should be removed for at least part of the day for assistance elsewhere?

6.   Increasingly, many parents have computers at home. They need guidance in how to use a computer to assist their children. What assistance might your school offer parents in this regard? What software programs might be helpful for Pete?

7.   This school's consultation-based service delivery program has not yet evolved to the point where pullout programs are obsolete. Our RSP/consultant is not yet doing much co-teaching, team teaching, or other "pull-in" collaborations currently popular throughout the country. Many of these strategies are discussed in Cooper (1999); Meyen, Vergason, and Whelan (1996); and Salend (1997).

Case 4   Student at Risk

Maria does not care for school. In fact, if her parents didn't insist that she go, she wouldn't. She is 15 now and a sophomore in the general education program at Carter Senior High. Credit-wise, she's still a freshman. At the rate she is going, it will take her another three years to graduate. I doubt she will last that long.

Maria is presently taking math fundamentals, social studies (American history), general science (for the second time), family studies (home economics), and P.E. She is failing the first three and barely passing the other two. It is November, and her teachers are very worried about her. Her social studies (history) teacher put in the referral.

RECEIPT OF A REFERRAL AND INITIAL THOUGHTS ABOUT IT

My name is Ms. Suiter, and I have an interesting split position here at Carter High. In the mornings I am one of two RSP teachers; in the afternoons I serve as the counselor for half the sophomores. I've been here for seven years. During that time I've seen our school population change from primarily a college-bound white middle-class student body to a much more diverse population. Whereas seven years ago 75 percent of our students went on to some sort of postsecondary education, that figure is now down to about 40 percent, and almost all of these students are community college bound. Also, our dropout percentage has risen from about 15 percent to 32 percent.

Maria seems, in many ways, typical of these changes; she comes from a home where neither parent graduated from high school. Her one older brother transferred from here to our continuation school a year ago. Maria's family is bilingual. Her parents were born in the United States; her grandparents immigrated from Mexico about 50 years ago. Maria and her family make occasional visits to Mexico to visit their relatives. Maria and her brother are fluent in both Spanish and English.

Our teachers vary in their reactions to our current realities. Some of the older teachers still act as if nothing has changed, and they teach as they did a decade ago: largely verbal lectures, not many class activities, and written assignments that are expected to look like college-level work. They believe their job is to separate the chaff from the wheat and let the chips fall. Other teachers, many of them younger and some (fortunately) from cultural and linguistic backgrounds similar to those of our newer students, have a mission to work with the students where they are and to present materials in a way that provides for much more student involvement. You can see why these differences among our teachers result in some heated discussions. However, even with these differences, we as a faculty generally get along, at least as long as no one makes too much out of the contrasting methods and philosophies [1].

Over the past seven years I've implemented a consultation-based service delivery system from my unique dual position. In our system, the teachers send all referrals to the assistant principal (AP), but they indicate on the referral the specialist to whom they really want it to go. The AP screens them and decides whether to send them to the position or person indicated or to send them elsewhere. Maria's referral came from her history teacher and was directed to me. Since it seems like a motivation problem that may have special education implications, I think having this referral sent to me makes sense.

When I get a referral like this, my first thought is: "What do I know about this student?" Next I decide who to talk to about it. In this case, I think it's best to get all of Maria's teachers together since there seem to be problems in many of her classes. I know Maria because I called her in a month ago when her teachers sent me the names of students who were failing after the first six weeks. My visit with her at that time was rushed, as usual, because I had received notices regarding 74 students! In my six minutes with her, I got the usual noncommittal responses, a vague promise to do better, and a shy smile with a "Thank you" at the end. My notes said, "At risk."

INITIAL DISCUSSION WITH THE TEACHERS

Since I know Maria is in academic trouble in more than just her history class, I decide to hold a case conference and invite all five of her teachers to come. All five come to the meeting and inform me that she is failing math, history, and science and barely passing family studies and P.E. My question to each is "Why is she failing?" Her history teacher (Mr. Petrullo, a great old guy who loves kids and loves history, and who will be my main teacher-consultee) says it's simple: Maria is often absent, and when she's there, she may as well not be since she hasn't read anything and doesn't know what chapter they're on. His efforts to get her involved have been met "with a twisted head and excessive nail picking." The math teacher laughs and says, "Ditto." The science teacher says that Maria has failed every test she has taken this semester and acts as if she couldn't care less. He thinks she is depressed, obsessed with boys, and will probably be a dropout. Family studies gives a slightly better report, as does P.E. Both of these last two teachers are female, but so is the science teacher. All five want me to see her and find out what's going on. Should they bother with her or not? How can they motivate her when she appears to be so indifferent? Of course, she's not the only student like that, they unnecessarily inform me. They want to know if I care to hear about some others. I suggest we focus on Maria. What we learn from her may help us deal with the others.

I ask them to answer their own questions about motivation. What do they think will make a difference with her? What is there about their subjects that might be of interest to her? What methods have they found that work with other low-motivation students? Answers are not forthcoming. Mr. Petrullo says that he is trying to get close to her when she is in class, but she has erected a barrier and he doesn't have time in class to get around it. The science and math teachers inform me that they didn't come to the meeting to be asked to try harder. They see her as a future dropout, and it is up to her to turn herself around. Can't I counsel her into trying harder? [2].

"What about special education?" the teachers ask.

I respond that the records indicate that Maria was assessed two years ago and found not eligible. I would be glad to review the idea with the school psychologist, Ms. Yates, who wasn't able to come to the meeting, but I personally don't see this as a special education possibility or responsibility. I think we all see it as motivational. How can we deal with that problem? Again, answers are not forthcoming. The teachers wonder, "Aren't counseling and special education the only approaches?"

Time is running out and we aren't getting anywhere. I ask the teachers to think about this question of motivation. I will focus on one teacher, Mr. Petrullo, to begin with and see where we go from there.

Obviously, this has not been a very productive or successful meeting. I have noticed that group meetings such as this case conference are often frustrating. I don't know how to get a group of teachers to come up with ideas. They almost invariably get tied up in some group conspiracy of either silence or "It's us versus them, and we have standards to uphold." As I have indicated, this reluctance to accommodate nontraditional learners, multiplied by the nonacademic orientation of many of our current students, seems to be at the core of an increasing number of referrals [3].

The questions I believe I need to answer in this case are in two categories: immediate concerns about Maria, and long-term questions about how this school and the faculty need to come up with solutions designed to keep up with the shifting demographics. Regarding Maria specifically, I have the following questions and concerns:

1. What is she like as a person, and how does this affect her schoolwork?
2. What are her academic levels? Is she able to read the tenth-grade texts?
3. What happens in her classrooms to either encourage or discourage her participation?
4. Should we make program changes that will be more appropriate for her? What does *appropriate* mean?

CLASSROOM OBSERVATION

I ask Mr. Petrullo when he would like me to visit. He thinks that the second half of a period would be best because that is when the discussion usually gets lively. I tell him I can't wait to make the visit, knowing how much fun he and his students seem to have when freewheeling about historical issues and their current relevance. We decide on next Tuesday, assuming that Maria is at school. She has missed about 50 percent of the Mondays this semester and some Tuesdays also.

The students at Carter, especially the sophomores, know me, so my visiting a classroom is not regarded as remarkable or suspicious. Sad to say, it would have been perceived that way about four years ago when we had a major drug abuse problem and ancillary staff were continually sniffing around in hallways and classrooms looking for suspicious activities. We don't do that much anymore, even though we know there is still quite a bit of drug activity. Another sign of resignation to forces beyond our control? I hope not.

Mr. Petrullo's classes are always fun. He has a lot of energy, and his classes are characterized by lively interactions, brave arguments, and the kind of enthusiasm that is characteristic of turned-on adolescents. His style has earned him accolades from a variety of sources over the years. He's a bit of a ham, and it works. He used to dress up like Lincoln and other famous figures, but he doesn't do that anymore. Still, if I were a student, I'd like to be in his class. Students rarely complain that he is boring. I worry about those who do.

On Tuesday, Maria is very uninvolved with the discussion on tariffs. Mr. Petrullo calls on her once (probably for my sake), and one of her friends tries to get her involved in the discussion, but she demurs. After class Mr. Petrullo puts his big paw around her shoulder (we don't do that much anymore, but Mr. Petrullo sometimes forgets) and says he wants to see her after school. No problem, just a brief talk about her work. She agrees. I ask if I can sit in, and they both agree. When she leaves, I ask Mr. Petrullo if he can see me before the afternoon meeting. He agrees.

INITIAL DISCUSSION WITH THE PARENTS
Before the afterschool meeting I call Maria's mom, Mrs. Fuentes. She is at home. She works three days a week as a domestic and is able (and eager) to come to school to discuss Maria. She is glad I have called since she and her husband are both very worried about Maria. Mr. Fuentes works as an auto mechanic all day and can't come to a daytime meeting, but she will be glad to come in on Thursday at 11:10, Mr. Petrullo's free period. I'll inform him of the meeting.

GETTING TEACHERS AND PARENTS TOGETHER: THE SST MEETING
At this point I think it's best to keep the case simple and not to involve the SST until I know how the team can help. I decide to follow up my initial discussions with Mr. Petrullo to see what he thinks. When we meet, I ask him what might be effective in getting Maria more involved with his class. He says he has been thinking about the problem since our last meeting and wants to run three ideas past me:

1. Contact her parents and see what they can do about it.
2. Set up some sort of contract with her that spells out very clearly what she has to do to earn a passing grade.
3. See her after school today and tomorrow to review the material with her and give her some sort of boost.

I tell him that every one of his ideas has merit and is worth pursuing; in fact, I've moved forward on his first idea already by arranging the parent meeting. He's pleased by this. He then asks for some ideas about how he might develop a contract that will meet her needs and to which she will respond. I ask what has worked for him in the past. He says he has only used a few, which spelled out how work was to be done and what grades would be given. "Nothing fancy," he says.

I suggest, "We are talking about a student whose present level of involvement is so low that we probably ought to stick to very basic 'acting like a student' behaviors such as attendance, having requisite materials, and responding at least once per period." He agrees and says we should talk to Maria about it after school [4].

I ask him what his goals are for the after-school meeting. He mainly wants to let Maria know that he cares about her, that he is concerned for her when she doesn't come to class, and that he wants to see if there is anything that he can do to help her with what might be bothering her. I say that I think those are excellent goals. He is apparently trying to meet Maria where she is emotionally rather than act out the role of the angry, demanding teacher, which would almost certainly turn her away. You can see what sort of person Mr. Petrullo is: caring, empathetic, and fatherly. I say that I want to be at the meeting because I need to get to know Maria better but that Mr. Petrullo should do most of the interacting.

I've learned how to do this job better over the past few years. Before, I used to take over meetings like this and thereby give the impression that I was the main person there and that it was all right for the teacher to take a back seat and let me do all the work. Now I make it clear that the meeting is between the teacher and the child (and/or parent). I monitor and facilitate as necessary, but I'm in a secondary role.

I close our meeting by asking Mr. Petrullo if he feels OK about the contract or wants to discuss it further. He says he is ready to go with it, so we part company until the after-school meeting with Maria. Note that I'm not telling him how to write the contract. I could, and I used to. Now if teachers say they can do it, I let them. I'm not always thrilled by what they do, but that's all right. It's all part of my effort to empower teachers by staying out of the decision-making process as often as possible and letting them try things their way. Of course, if I see that they are very far off base, I'll make suggestions, and I'll give them some examples, but only if necessary.

The after-school meeting goes as I expect. Mr. Petrullo is very friendly, encouraging, and enthusiastic. Maria is reticent, quiet, and compliant, but generally noncommittal. She denies that there is any real problem, then says that the work is too hard, and then asks to get out of math and science. At this point Mr. Petrullo looks at me for help.

I say that we are here to start a process of helping Maria be successful in her classes that is going to involve her teachers, myself, her parents (she looks at me with astonishment and concern when I mention her parents), and especially herself. Is she willing to work with us to help her be more successful in school? This can be a risky question. Some children will say no or talk around the question. I gamble with Maria because she seems to be basically compliant. I am right.

Maria says that she is willing but doesn't know why her parents have to be involved. Mr. Petrullo replies, "We always try to get parents involved, even if the student is a senior. You're lucky to have parents who want to get involved."

Maria looks dark; I think she sees this business of getting her parents involved as a dirty trick on our part.

Mr. Petrullo says that for now he wants Maria to look at the contract that he has handwritten during his prep period. If she agrees, she can sign it.

CONTRACT

I, Maria Fuentes, agree to come to class each day (unless excused for illness by my parents). I will be sure to have my book and a notebook and a pencil for taking notes. I will also make at least one relevant comment or answer at least one question during each class period. I will study the material and do my best on the weekly exam on Thursdays.

Each week, on Friday, Mr. Petrullo will give me a weekly report card based on these behaviors. I will bring it home and have my parents read and sign it. I will return it to Mr. Petrullo on the following Monday.

For every signed form Mr. Petrullo receives, I will receive five bonus points toward my next class grade.

Signed: Mr. Petrullo _____

Maria Fuentes _____

Ms. Suiter (witness) _____

It's funny about contracts. You never know how students are going to respond to them. I've had students who act like courthouse lawyers; they want to haggle with me over every word. I've had other students agree to everything and do nothing that the contract stipulated. And I've seen simple ideas like this one turn students around when I thought the contract wasn't going to be effective. Much of the literature on contracting seems to be written for younger students. Most high school teachers are not about to ask a student what she would like to earn for being a good student. Grades and mild praise are the reinforcers in high school for those who are not invested in learning as a goal in itself. So Mr. Petrullo has stuck with grades as his reinforcer in this case, and I see no reason to object. I'll discuss it later with Maria when I see her myself [5].

Maria seems pleased with the contract. I believe she thought it was going to be something awful, but it isn't. She signs it and then wants to know what we are going to talk about with her mother. Mr. Petrullo tells her that we are going to ask her to talk with Maria every day about her schoolwork, ask her what her homework is, see to it that Maria has a good place to do her homework, verify that she actually does it, and review and sign the weekly contract. We will give a copy of the contract to Mrs. Fuentes on Thursday, and it will go into effect the following Monday.

Mr. Petrullo then asks Maria why she misses school so often on Monday. She says she is sick a lot. He suggests that she come to school even if she isn't feeling like it, that we want her here and that we will talk to her mother about it. She then says that sometimes she goes with her mother on Mondays to help clean a really big house. She doesn't want us to tell her mother that she told us that, but that's the way it is. Besides, Maria gets 15 dollars for the job, and she needs the money. We say that we will keep the confidence but that we will encourage Mrs. Fuentes to be sure that Maria is in school every day. The meeting ends [6].

Mr. Petrullo and I have no time to meet before Mrs. Fuentes comes in on Thursday. Since we have only about 15 minutes for this conference, my main goal is to keep the discussion solutions-oriented. Mrs. Fuentes admits that Maria is becoming more difficult to deal with at home. Defiance and noncompliance are on the rise, just as they are with Maria's older brother. I mention that our local child guidance clinic has a family counselor who is very helpful to parents dealing with exactly that sort of behavior. I say that I would be glad to get the clinic's number for Mrs. Fuentes. She wants it, though she doubts if Mr. Fuentes will approve of their going to the clinic.

Mr. Petrullo is anxious to get on with the contract, so he brings it out and gives Mrs. Fuentes a copy. She says that Maria has shown it to her and that she thinks it's fine. She wants Maria to finish regular high school and will support anything we want. We mention to her about talking every day with Maria about her work, checking the homework, and so on.

"What about the absences?" I ask. Mrs. Fuentes says that she often gives in to Maria when she says she is too sick to go to school. Sometimes Mrs. Fuentes has to go to work early and doesn't know until she gets home that Maria hasn't gone to school.

Two years ago, our school instituted a computerized home-calling system that informed parents that their children were absent. Unfortunately, many of our parents didn't get the calls because they either weren't home and didn't have an answering machine or because their children answered the phone or intercepted the answering machine message and the message got lost. Now, if the parents don't call back, the call is repeated in the evening, which works better.

Nothing is said by either party about Maria's allegation that she helps her mother at her job instead of coming to school on Mondays. We're hoping that we'll never have to mention it and that Maria's attendance will improve on the basis of what we're currently doing. The meeting ends with each side vowing to support the other.

ASSESSMENT OF THE REFERRED STUDENT

Learning Problem Assessment

Strictly speaking, I don't know that we have a learning problem here in the sense of a learning disability that prevents the student from doing well academically. My feeling is that this is more of a production deficit: resistance to school tasks because of boredom, a reluctance to invest oneself in learning tasks, or a sense of futility. Possibly it's a symptom of learned helplessness (Maier & Seligman, 1976). However, I think it's best to check with the school psychologist who did the evaluation a few years ago.

We meet in her office for ten minutes, and she reviews her report. She gave Maria the WISC—III, on which Maria earned a verbal I.Q. of 83, performance of 92, and full-scale of 87. Ms. Yates's notes indicate that she offered to have Maria tested in Spanish but that Maria said she preferred English. The WISC—III scores were regarded as valid—that is, not contaminated by health, motivational, or primary-secondary language issues. At that time her achievement standard scores on the Woodcock-Johnson were all in the mid-80s. Essentially, she was doing about as well as the I.Q. tests predicted.

I'm sure we could get into a discussion about the meaning of all this for students like Maria, but I simply want to know if Ms. Yates thinks Maria can read and comprehend the tenth-grade texts she is expected to read. Ms. Yates answers, "She probably could, but not well—probably somewhere between the instructional and frustration levels. She would probably be reading very slowly, with somewhat below-average comprehension." That's what I was afraid of.

Ms. Yates goes on to say that this situation is becoming the norm for our sophomores. She is appalled at how many of our faculty still haven't accommodated themselves to this reality. She says she has talked with the principal about it but feels like she hasn't made much impact. She asks, "Would you be willing to help bring our administration and faculty to the realization that the old days are gone and that we need to make curricular and teaching method changes if we are to provide our current students with the kind of school experiences that will be meaningful to them?"

Wow! That's quite a statement! I tell her that I, along with many others on the faculty, have been sensitive to this problem. Then I set a time with her for next week to discuss it. Who knows? Maria could be a catalyst for some meaningful changes around here.

Ms. Yates goes on to caution me that there is not always a one-to-one correspondence between test results and actual textbook competence. This is especially likely to be true with test data that are two years old. What I really should do is see Maria and listen to her read aloud from her books. This will give me a better grasp of her current abilities to succeed. In addition, Ms. Yates suggests having Maria bring in her recent schoolwork and reviewing it with her. Her teachers might also have some things to show me. In our district, the idea of portfolio-based assessment has recently begun in the elementary schools but so far has been avoided at the high school level by a very reluctant staff. We'll get to that next year, maybe.

Ms. Yates's comments prompt me to have Maria come in to see me about her schoolwork, the contract, and for general counseling assistance. I ask her to bring her social studies and science books for her appointment tomorrow. She passively agrees.

Unfortunately, Maria's ability to read and comprehend the two texts she brings with her is somewhat less than Ms. Yates predicted. Maria reads slowly, doesn't recognize about every eighth word, and doesn't seem to know how to organize what she reads into comprehensible information. She reads these books at about frustration level; she can get through them, but it's not easy or enjoyable. It's not surprising that she doesn't read them very much. And if she doesn't read the material, how can she engage in the classroom discussions? Some students do, especially those who pick up context clues from the other students and are basically interested in the material. Others, like Maria, who seems to be moving into the learned helplessness syndrome, simply avoid the discussions, especially if they are whole-class interactions.

While Maria is with me, I ask about the contract and how it is going. She says her parents have been on her case about it and keep bugging her to do her homework and show it to them. I silently thank them for showing this concern and say, "I think that's a sign of their concern for you." She passively agrees and then adds that she isn't going to be allowed to go on the Monday job from now on until her grades get better, all because of the contract. (They usually don't have that much impact!)

I review my concerns about Maria's reading limitations with her and wonder if there is someone at home who can help her with her reading. She says her brother reads well, but she knows he won't want to help her. "He's too stuck up," she says.

I gamble, asking if she thinks he might agree to help if I ask him. I knew her brother, Rudi. He left us a year ago to go to the continuation school, but I remember him as a neat kid who just might help out if asked. She declines, I think for matters of personal pride. Too much sibling stuff, I'm afraid. I inquire about either of her parents helping. She thinks maybe her mother; her father doesn't read much. She's not sure he can, "At least not tenth-grade books," she says with a sigh.

"So," I say, "shall we [meaning you] approach your mother and ask her to sit with you for a half hour every night and go over your schoolwork with you?"

"Yeah, OK, I'll ask her," says Maria.

Great! I say to myself.

When Maria leaves, I make a note to call Mrs. Fuentes and tell her of our new plan and to encourage her involvement in it. I'm somewhat concerned that Maria has been going along with this plan just to get me off her case. I really don't get a strong feeling of any serious commitment on Maria's part to improving her schoolwork as yet. I do think that Mrs. Fuentes will be very cooperative, however, because I think she'll see this as having a positive potential for a number of reasons. It will get her closer to Maria, whom she feels she is losing to the alienation of adolescence; it will give her something constructive to do to help her daughter; and it will relieve some of the guilt she feels about having Rudi drop out of the regular high school.

Functional Assessment of Behavior

The functions of Maria's school behavior seem to be (1) to avoid engaging in academic work because it is too difficult for her; (2) to substitute social interests for academic pursuits; and (3) to put in one's time, as if school is a jail sentence, until she is old enough to leave, at which point she can get on with important and less-threatening activities. The reinforcers that keep this behavior alive seem to be (1) negativity toward school makes teachers avoid you and expect little from you; (2) an occasional piece of luck in getting somebody else to do some assignments for you; and (3) the belief that every day she becomes more attractive to the boys, so who needs school?

These largely belief-system (internal) reinforcers have arisen from years of listening to older, poorly achieving girls, and her need to have some goals other than success in school.

Additional Areas of Assessment: Psychodynamic, Ecological, and Biophysical Factors

I don't profess to be an expert in any of these three areas, but I think I understand enough of the surface behavior and events to make some good judgments about what is going on with Maria and her situation. At the psychodynamic level, based on my conversations with her, I believe Maria sees herself as nonacademic. She's eager to leave school and get on with her life, which she sees as work- and boyfriend-oriented. She plans to be a mother, probably in her early twenties. I hope not earlier, but if it happens, it will be accepted. She does not plan on a career since her husband will support her. She does not plan to go on to college, but it will be nice if her children do. A dream deferred. Should we interrupt this image for her? Making a potentially long story short, I'll say yes. Maria's boyfriend and future husband will just have to wait his turn. I want to ENABL Maria: education *now* and babies *later*.

Let's look at the ecology question from two perspectives: home and school. Her home and community tend not to give education as high a priority as they give family issues. A view too often expressed is that a girl like Maria who isn't very good at school shouldn't worry about it; there are more important things. A high school diploma would be nice, but, after all, most of the adults in the community didn't graduate, and they are doing all right.

But there is something else in Maria's family: a mother who says she will help. I find this out when I call to ask about the plan just described. Mrs. Fuentes says she would have started doing this a long time ago if she thought she knew enough to help. But she thought parents weren't supposed to interfere. She doesn't really know what they do in school, and her children haven't been very forthcoming ever since fifth or sixth grade. I say that the main purpose of this plan is to ensure that Maria reads the material and to assist her with both word recognition and comprehension. Mrs. Fuentes laughs, saying that she hopes she understands it herself; after all, she never finished high school.

I say, "I think you'll do very well. The main thing is your interest and your willingness to show Maria that you feel that education is very important."

Mrs. Fuentes says she'll try. We thank each other and promise to check back in a few weeks to see how everything is going.

Can cultural expectations be changed one case at a time? Maria and her mother will help us find out [7].

The school ecology has already been mentioned somewhat. Essentially, I see our task as one of changing both attitudes and methods. My plan is to work with Ms. Yates and the others (faculty, administrators, parents, and students) who have a stake in this problem to organize a study group to analyze the changes in our student body and our community. What can we do to turn around the steadily declining success rate that we have witnessed over the past decade? It isn't just our faculty and administrators who need to take a look at themselves; it's our students, too. We are becoming used to students who are trying to convince us that the educational process is a sham. They float through without any real commitment and claim that school has only a minimal impact on them. I'm sure there is literature out there that describes programs that make a difference to the educationally alienated, and I'm sure that our students and faculty have ideas about how we might restructure our school to meet the needs of our students. Pie in the sky? Maybe, but no more so than every other good idea that people think can't work because . . . well, because [8].

I don't believe there are any important biophysical factors that have an impact on this case. I'm fairly certain now that Maria's absences are not due to any health problem. Her vision and hearing are fine, and she's in good health.

PLANNING INTERVENTIONS

We've identified six overlapping, related problem areas, some having to do directly with Maria and her behavior, and some that influence her due to the behavior of others or the nature of the system. Listed here are the six areas and some possible interventions.

Maria Is Failing in Three Subjects   Interventions:

1. *Conference with Maria.*   We've already done this, apparently with good preliminary results.
2. *Provide some sort of tutoring, at school or at home.*   Mrs. Fuentes's agreement to monitor Maria's work might not be considered tutoring, but it is a solid step in the right direction. Other than special education, our high school doesn't have a formal system of tutoring designed to remediate specific deficiencies in basic skills. We could use a cross-age tutor. Who, when, where, using what materials? This is a problem we haven't faced historically, so we need to talk about this when we have our hoped-for discussions with the school administrators about reforming our system for today's students.

Maria Manifests a Serious Motivational Problem   Interventions:

1. *Conference with Maria.*   We need to talk about her lack of interest and effort. We know that uninvolved teens have their minds elsewhere. Perhaps she'll have some discussions with me while I'm wearing my counselor hat. (Due to too many pressures, I can only give her about ten minutes twice a week. However, I think I will give her the time for maybe three or four weeks.) Among the things we'll discuss are study skills, time management, and her self-talk regarding her status as a student.
2. *Child guidance clinic.*   I hope Mr. and Mrs. Fuentes will follow through on this. We'll see.

3. *Contract.*   Mr. Petrullo's contract may boost Maria's efforts to participate.

4. *Improve reading.*   Sometimes motivation is connected to a student's perception of her ability to be successful. We know that Maria's reading skills are poor. Perhaps if we can improve her reading, she will show more interest in being productive.

5. *Study-buddy system.*   A study-buddy system is used in some classes at different times. Perhaps this would help in some of Maria's classes.

6. *Change her self-concept.*   Try to change Maria's self-concept as a silent, know-nothing student by giving her answers before a question-and-answer time and then calling on her to answer these questions. If she will cooperate, this plan could nudge her out of her general reticence to speak in class.

7. *Written record.*   Have Maria keep a written record of her assignments, due dates, and so on in an effort to get her more structured and aware of her responsibilities. This record will need to be checked often at first. Will the teachers accept this responsibility?

8. *Plan for success.*   Try to find at least one way every day that Maria can be successful in every class. Again, will the teachers be cooperative about this?

9. *Modify presentations.*   Emphasize the possible use of cooperative learning strategies and other alternatives to the lecture-discussion method that still dominates our content-area methods.

Maria May Be Depressed   We hear the word *depression* a lot in regard to teens nowadays. I don't know if this is just a fashionable way of saying that teens are sometimes down in the dumps due to the numerous pressures of social relationships, sex, school expectations, parent–child dynamics, and extracurricular activities, which has always been true, or if there may really be an increase in clinical depression due to the complexities of modern life. In any event, Maria often seems down, at least at school. Her parents haven't noticed it at home. Or are they, like many parents, apt to deny it even when it seems obvious to others?

Interventions: I hope I will be able to make a determination about depression when I see Maria for counseling. If I believe she truly is depressed, not just down because she sees little hope or need for school, then I will encourage her parents to bring her to the child guidance clinic.

Maria Is Often Absent   Interventions:

1. We'll try to find out what the reasons are, other than her helping her mother on Mondays. It's probably her general antipathy toward school. I'll talk to her about it during counseling.

2. Being present in class is written into Mr. Petrullo's contract. We'll see if that helps.

3. If the problem persists, we will discuss with Maria and her parents our policy on excessive absences.

4. Is it possible that Maria may respond to a "wake-up buddy" system, in which a peer (a friend, preferably) comes to her house every morning to get her up and out the door for school? This has been successful elsewhere.

Teachers Project the Blame onto Maria and Believe the Best Solution Is Counseling   Interventions:

1. I plan to hold another meeting with Maria's teachers to discuss these possible solutions. When doing so, I hope they will see that part of the solution lies with them. If they will make Maria a priority among all the students they are concerned about, I believe she will start to take notice and reciprocate by being more attentive and responsive in class.

2. I will review my counseling goals with the teachers and indicate how they have a part, also. Counseling by itself rarely solves a multifaceted problem such as this one.

Teachers Are Not Adapting to Our School Population   Maria is just one of many students for whom the curriculum, expectations, and resources are inappropriate. Interventions:

1. Discuss the issue with staff members and get their ideas about what is needed to meet these realities.

2. Put together a staff interest group to plan how to present this concern to the principal.

3. Review this situation with the principal, listing problems and possible solutions.

4. With the support of the principal and key staff members, develop a committee to discuss the situation and devise a plan for dealing with it.

A few days later I meet with Mr. Petrullo. We talk only briefly about Maria because I want to present the ideas I've just listed. As I expect, he is in favor of the items concerning staff adaptation to the school population, and he mentions three other faculty members who are also interested. We are on our way to developing a systems-improvement plan. However, let's not forget Maria. We still need to follow through on her.

IMPLEMENTING INTERVENTIONS

I start to see Maria twice a week to implement the plans I've just discussed. She is reluctant to come with me at first, but I am assertive with her and also lean on my parent support system. Mr. and Mrs. Fuentes tell her to see me, so she does. It is interesting to note that Maria may have given both me and her parents more resistance if we had been operating independently about her. Now that she knows we are working collaboratively, she is more compliant. Also, when she sees that I'm not a shrink planning to delve into her innermost secrets, she is relieved. Most students and parents don't know that in high schools there is no time for in-depth counseling of any length; my seeing her for two sessions a week is very much the exception.

Mr. Petrullo reports that the contract is successful. Maria is producing more work of better quality, and her attendance is now almost 100 percent. Her Thursday exam grades are now at the C level for the first time this year. Mr. Petrullo has so far sent home three weekly report cards, all of which have been signed and returned, twice by both parents. With the bonus points they have agreed to, Maria could earn a B for this quarter. Mr. Petrullo says that he is willing to share his results with Maria's other teachers. Perhaps we can come up with a contract that will be useful in all classes.

I've talked to Mrs. Fuentes only once in the past two weeks. She is holding firm on the homework monitoring. She has even received support from an unlikely source, her son, who tells Mrs. Fuentes that she should have made him do his home-work when he was in regular school. She's not sure if he's serious or not. So far she and her husband are still thinking about the referral to the child guidance clinic. They want to see if things get better without taking that step.

A hallway conversation with Maria's math fundamentals teacher results in a cur-sory review of our progress with Maria and a promise to organize another staff meet-ing on her. It also develops this teacher's interest in the study-buddy idea and a desire to know more about how to structure it. I say we'll discuss everybody's experience with this sort of grouping as well as other cooperative-teaching methodologies, along with our interest in doing more of these strategies schoolwide. The teacher says she is interested in joining these discussions. She also notes that since Maria is showing up more often now, she finds herself attending to her more readily. Still, Maria has fundamental skill deficits in arithmetic that somebody ought to do something about.

"What about special education?" the teacher asks.

I explain the criteria for that program and tell her that Maria doesn't meet them. I say, "We're thinking this is more of a motivation problem."

The teacher laughs. "If you want to see a motivation problem, just come to my class sometime."

I don't find her comment so funny, and it's just another example of the need for some form of system improvement.

MONITORING INTERVENTIONS

A month after our initial staff meeting on Maria, I call another meeting to review our progress. Mr. Petrullo gives an enthusiastic summary of his efforts; I review my coun-seling goals (our sessions have now ended) and discuss the role of Maria's parents. The math and science teachers report that Maria is now doing better, largely because she is coming to school and, for some reason, seems more involved. She is also turn-ing in some homework, although it is often wrong. She is showing concomitant improvements in family studies and P.E.

I explain that I want to spend the rest of our 15-minute meeting on the subject of cooperative learning and other alternative methods of teaching, just to get their opinions. I review, briefly, material I have learned from classes, workshops, and the literature. I also bring up the notion of culturally appropriate materials. As expected, I am reminded of the Cinco de Mayo celebration and black history month. We need to move forward in this area, past the celebrations approach to multiculturalism.

But how? I don't have the time or expertise to restructure our school. As I have indicated, we need to get at least part of the staff to draw up some tentative plans, tell the principal of our resolve, and move forward. I believe we are going to need some outside expertise in this area, and that means spending money. In today's budget realities it may be a real obstacle. But there I go again; my budget crisis conditioning needs to be reversed. I need to give up my learned depression and exchange it for learned optimism (Seligman, 1991).

EVALUATION AND CLOSURE

As you can tell, I'm not a data-oriented person. I haven't presented graphs showing how each of our behavioral objectives were met. I could, but who has the time to prepare these things? In the high school I work in, simply finding the time to deal with a noncrisis student such as Maria is a luxury. As for graphing data, asking swamped teachers to do the same, and applying statistical tests to these data, forget it; let the university researchers do that [9].

For my part, I'm happy with our efforts for the following reasons:

1. Maria is now coming to school more. Since data about attendance are easy to come by, courtesy of our office staff and computers, we know that she has increased her attendance 27 percent over the past month. That's great.

2. She is doing more work in class, especially history, and is turning in more assignments and more homework in all classes. That's also great. We have not yet made much progress on remediating her deficit skills; that will be next month's target.

3. We have established a strong working relationship with Maria's parents, and it has paid off very well in terms of attendance and homework monitoring.

4. We have stirred up interest in school reform here at Carter, at least among some of the staff. I have already heard the negative rumors about this: I should have moved forward more quickly with the plan development and consultation with our principal. I'll work on that next week.

In general, I believe this collaborative consultation effort has been very effective. We have not yet solved some of the basic problems that underlie the development of a student like Maria in our schools, but I think we have helped her and her family and have been able to use her case as a springboard for making some fundamental changes in how we do business here at Carter. I have no idea what we'll look like a

year from now or, more likely, three years from now since these restructuring efforts, if serious, take about that long to work their way into an entrenched system (Rosenfield & Gravois, 1996; Zins, Curtis, Graden, & Ponti, 1988; Zins & Illback, 1995). I know we are in for some tough times. Giving birth to new ways of doing things is not easy; resistance is going to occur. It's either that or stagnation. I'll start by reviewing the references that follow the notes for this case.

NOTES AND COMMENTS ON CASE 4

1. What are the implications for dealing with a changing school population? How does this influence teaching styles, class size, support services, staff development needs, and so on?

2. It is interesting that some of these teachers believe that a counseling approach is the way to improve academic achievement. Is there a counseling approach or technique that will increase academic motivation? What are some other ways of improving motivation toward academic improvement? See Ames and Ames (1990), Dweck (1986), Maehr and Meyer (1997), Stipek (1996), Urdan and Maehr (1995), and Wentzel and Wigfield (1998).

3. What are some methods for getting teachers to generate ideas at an SST meeting or case conference? Why might they be resistant to doing so? Chapter 5 reviews some strategies for generating ideas within SST meetings. See also Bay, Bryan, and O'Connor (1994); Evans (1990); Gutkin and Nemeth (1997); Margolis, Fish, and Wepner (1990); Meyers, Valentino, Meyers, Boretti, and Brent (1996); Powers (2001); Ross (1995); Thomas, Correa, and Morsink (1995); and Whitten and Dicker (1995).

4. Chapter 5 has information about contracting. Remember that a common problem with contracting is the tendency to make the contract either too complicated or too labor-intensive for the teacher. Either of these concerns is especially true for high school teachers. How might you develop an inservice meeting to review contracting to make it appealing to teachers? Epanchin, Townsend, and Stoddard (1994); Maher (1987); and Miller and Kelley (1994) suggest some useful techniques for implementing contracting in classrooms.

5. In pairs, devise a learning problem for which a contract might be useful. Then draft a simple positive contingency contract. Discuss these contracts in class.

6. If this Monday-absence pattern continues, what should the school do about it? What systems do your local schools use to deal with excessive absences?

7. Is there a potential cultural clash developing here? The school is trying to create some discomfort within Maria and her family by encouraging Maria to change her perspective and encouraging her parents (especially her mother) to change the family's approach to schooling by insisting on homework, checking weekly reports, and requiring Monday school attendance. Could these changes exacerbate the rift

already developing between Maria and her parents? Or might these changes heal that rift and pull the parents and child closer together?

8. What programs for dealing with schoolwide underachievement, particularly at the high school level, have been found successful? See Bergerud, Lovitt, and Horton (1988); Bossert (1985); Epstein, Jackson, Salinas, and Associates (1991); Horton and Lovitt (1989); Lenz, Alley, and Schumaker (1987); and Teddlie and Stringfield (1993). Teddlie and Stringfield report the following six characteristics associated with effectiveness in low-SES schools: (1) promotion of high educational expectations; (2) hiring of principals who are initiators and innovators; (3) increasing the external reward structure for academic achievement; (4) focusing on basic skills; (5) evaluating the effects of the community on achievement—if the community doesn't support it, try to buffer the school from the effects of the community; and (6) hire younger, possibly more idealistic teachers.

9. What do you think of the consultant's stance regarding the possibility or necessity of gathering data? Are there ways to do this that are not obtrusive and burdensome? How might you gather some objective data, other than the attendance data, in this case?

REFERENCES

Ames, R., & Ames, C. (1990). *Research on motivation in education* (vol. 3). New York: Academic Press.

Bay, M., Bryan, T., & O'Connor, R. (1994). Teachers assisting teachers: A prereferral model for urban educators. *Teacher Education and Special Education, 17,* 10–21.

Bergerud, D., Lovitt, T. C., & Horton, S. V. (1988). The effectiveness of textbook adaptations in life science for high school students with learning disabilities. *Journal of Learning Disabilities, 21*(2), 70–76.

Bossert, S. (1985). Effective elementary schools. In R. M. J. Kyle (Ed.), *Reaching for excellence: An effective schools sourcebook.* Washington, DC: E. H. White.

Clay, M. M. (1985). *The early detection of reading difficulties.* Auckland, NZ: Heinemann.

Cooper, J. (Ed.). (1999). *Classroom teaching skills.* Boston: Houghton-Mifflin Co.

Dettmer, P. A., Dyck, N. T., & Thurston, L. P. (1999). *Consultation, collaboration, and teamwork for students with special needs* (3rd ed.). Boston: Allyn & Bacon.

Dweck, C. S. (1986). Motivational processes affecting learning. *American Psychologist, 41,* 1,040–1,048.

Ekwell, E. E., & Shanker, J. L. (1988). *Diagnosis and remediation of the disabled reader.* Boston: Allyn & Bacon.

Epanchin, B. C., Townsend, B., & Stoddard, K. (1994). *Constructive classroom management: Strategies for creating positive learning environments.* Pacific Grove, CA: Brooks/Cole.

Epstein, J. L., Jackson, V. E., Salinas, K. C., & Associates. (1991). *Manual for teachers: Teachers involve parents in schoolwork (TIPS).* Baltimore: Johns Hopkins University, Center on Families, Communities, Schools, and Children's Learning.

Evans, R. (1990). Making mainstreaming work through prereferral interventions. *Educational Leadership, 47,* 73–77.

Friend, M., and Cook, L. (2000). *Interactions: Collaboration skills for school professionals.* New York: Longman.

Gutkin, T., and Nemeth, C. (1997). Selected factors impacting decision making in prereferral intervention and other school-based teams: Exploring the intersection between school and social psychology. *Journal of School Psychology, 35,* 195–216.

Horton, S. V., & Lovitt, T. C. (1989). Construction and implementation of graphic organizers for academically handicapped and regular secondary students. *Academic Therapy, 24*(5), 625–641.

Lenz, B. K., Alley, G. R., & Schumaker, J. B. (1987). Activating the inactive learner: Advanced organizers in the secondary content classroom. *Learning Disability Quarterly, 10,* 53–67.

Maehr, M., & Meyer, H. (1997). Understanding motivation and schooling: Where we've been, where we are, and where we need to go. *Educational Psychology Review, 9,* 371–409.

Maher, C. (1987). Involving behaviorally disordered adolescents in instructional planning: Effectiveness of the GOAL procedures. *Journal of Child and Adolescent Psychotherapy, 4,* 204–210.

Maier, S., & Seligman, M. (1976). Learned helplessness: Theory and evidence. *Journal of Experimental Psychology: General, 105,* 3-46.

Margolis, H., Fish, M., & Wepner, S. (1990). Overcoming resistance to prereferral classroom interventions. *Special Services in the Schools, 6,* 167–187.

Meyen, E. L., Vergason, G. A., & Whelan, R. J. (1996). *Strategies for teaching exceptional children in inclusive settings.* Denver, CO: Love Publishing.

Meyers, B., Valentino, C. T., Meyers, J., Boretti, M., & Brent, D. (1996). Implementing prereferral intervention teams as an approach to school-based consultation in an urban setting. *Journal of Educational and Psychological Consultation, 7*(2), 119–149.

Miller, D., & Kelley, M. (1994). The use of goal setting and contingency contracting for improving children's homework performance. *Journal of Applied Behavior Analysis, 27,* 73–84.

Powers, K. (2001). Problem solving student support teams. *The California School Psychologist, 6,* 19–30.

Rosenfield, S., & Gravois, T. (1996). *Instructional consultation teams.* New York: Guilford Press.

Ross, R. P. (1995). Best practices in implementing intervention assistance teams. In A. Thomas & J. Grimes (Eds.), *Best practices in school psychology—III* (pp. 627–637). Washington, DC: NASP.

Salend, S. J. (1997). *Effective mainstreaming: Creating inclusive classrooms.* Upper Saddle River, NJ: Merrill/Prentice Hall.

Seligman, M. E. P. (1991). *Learned optimism.* New York: Knopf.

Sizer, T. R. (1984). *Horace's follies: The dilemma of the American high school.* Boston: Houghton Mifflin.

Stipek, D. (1996). Motivation and instruction. In D. C. Berliner & R. C. Calfee (Eds.), *Handbook of educational psychology.* New York: Macmillan.

Teddlie, C., & Stringfield, S. (1993). *Schools make a difference: Lessons learned from a 10-year study of school effects.* New York: Teachers College Press.

Thomas, C. C., Correa, V. I., & Morsink, C. V. (1995). *Interactive teaming: Consultation and collaboration in special programs.* Upper Saddle River, NJ: Merrill/Prentice Hall.

Urdan, T. C., & Maehr, M. L. (1995). Beyond a two-goal theory of motivation and achievement: A case for social goals. *Review of Educational Research, 65,* 213–243.

Wentzel, K., & Wigfield, A. (1998). Academic and social motivational influences on students' academic performance. *Educational Psychology Review, 10,* 155–175.

Whitten, E., & Dicker, L. (1995). Intervention assistance teams: A broader vision. *Preventing School Failure, 40,* 41-45.

Woodcock, R., McGrew, K., & Mather, N. (2001). *Woodcock-Johnson III. Tests of Cognitive Abilities and Tests of Achievement.* Itasca, IL: Riverside Press.

Zins, J., Curtis, M., Graden, J., & Ponti, C. (1988). *Helping students succeed in the regular classroom: A guide to developing intervention assistance programs.* San Francisco: Jossey-Bass.

Zins, J., & Illback, R. (1995). Consulting to facilitate planned change in schools. *Journal of Educational and Psychological Consultation, 6*(3), 237–245.

CHAPTER 10

Systems-Level Consultation: The Organization as the Target of Change

1. Orient the reader to the basic concepts involved in organizing changes within a school or school system.

2. Delineate the factors that influence change efforts.

3. List the steps to guide the implementation of systems change efforts.

4. Provide a case study demonstrating how one school prepared for and carried out a change regarding its special education service delivery system.

WHY SYSTEMS-LEVEL CONSULTATION?

The previous nine chapters of this book have mainly been concerned with consultation involving individuals or small groups of students, with teachers and parents as the consultees. This is appropriate since most of the work of school consultants centers around referrals by consultees who wish to obtain some assistance in dealing with students who manifest difficulties in behavior, adjustment, or academic achievement. I hope that the material in the first nine chapters will help you deal with everyday important issues that affect the futures of the referred students and let you assist teachers in achieving their goals for all students.

When consulting about individual cases, the school consultant will often encounter situations in which it is apparent that something about the way the individual school or the whole district deals with persistent problems in the delivery of its services to students may be contributing to these problems. Examples are presented in the case studies in Chapters 7 and 9. Because of the issues raised in the case of Tyrone in Chapter 7, suggestions were made for the development of a homework helper program, as well as a program to reduce teasing (bullying) behavior. With Todd, the counselor indicated that the school would be starting parent discussion groups. In Chapter 9, the case of Pete stimulated interest in developing a volunteer parents-as-tutors program, a cross-age tutoring program, and a closer look at instructional practices. Maria's situation centered around the same issue of instructional practices in a school where the demographics have changed dramatically. Rather than plod through change efforts teacher by teacher, wouldn't it be better if the whole school could agree on and adopt an educational approach geared closer to the needs and interests of its current student body?

Although any of the changes (improvements, additions) listed above may seem small relative to a bigger picture of total school or district reform or restructuring, they are all steps in that direction. An accumulation of small successes not only improves service delivery, but prompts people to look for more ways to keep the spirit of improvement moving along.

In this chapter we examine the reasons why a school consultant needs to be aware that the learning and adjustment of students is a systems-wide issue. Student difficulties do not reside only within the students themselves or because of the nature of their classrooms or homes. Although not nearly as influential as the actions of individual teachers and parents, the policies that emanate from large government entities, local school boards, and district and school levels do affect student learning and behavior (Wang, Haertel, & Walberg, 1993). These policies and beliefs can influence the decisions that classroom teachers and schools make regarding curriculum, methods, class size, and other important variables. The newly mandated reality of annual nationwide assessments of achievement has school districts reassessing how the instructional day should be spent, given the high-stakes nature of these assessments.

We will then examine the influence of the school or district organization on teachers, parents, and students. We limit our scope primarily to the district level as opposed to studying the influences of the county, state, or federal government. Then we discuss the systems change process and steps to guide this process. Finally, I present a format for the study of systems change, along with a case study demonstrating how a school-based consultant brought one school through the process of changing to a consultation-based service delivery system.

WHY SYSTEMS–LEVEL CONSULTATION?

School districts and individual schools operate under a set of explicit and implicit rules not all that different from the rules teachers establish for their classes. Employees are expected to be at work on time, to carry out their responsibilities, to cooperate, and to strive toward achieving the mission of the district or school. These global expectations, readily understood by all employees, are certainly a good starting point for the kind of mutuality of purpose that is essential for organizational health (Illback & Zins, 1995; Schmuck, 1990). However, when people are expected to adhere to the details that stem from these global rules, which may involve interpretation of, and cooperation with, the mission, problems can arise. Here are four common scenarios, along with a question that derives from each and that indicates the need for some degree of consultation:

ABC School has a rule that says, "No fighting on the playground." One teacher, Ms. Viera, believes this means serious fist-throwing battles between (usually) boys. Another teacher, Mr. Wu, interprets it to mean any touching not done in fair play in a game or any verbal comments that another child might interpret as unwanted (e.g., bullying). Whose view of the meaning of "no fighting" should be used, or how might a compromise be reached?

At Marshall Junior High there has been an increase in ganglike attire among the students, particularly among those who live on the other side of State Street. Half the teachers think no gang attire should be allowed, while the other half believes that clothing is just a symptom and that we should go after the root causes of behavior and forget the clothing. What should the school do about the issue of a dress code?

The district superintendent has noticed a general decline in achievement over the past five years. The more people she talks to, the more ideas she gets about causes and cures. She appoints two people, the school psychologist and the special education teacher, as co-chairs of a task force to look into possible ways of dealing with this issue of declining achievement. How should these two proceed?

The district director of special education has issued a call for more inclusion of special education students in the regular classes. Most, but not all, of the special education teachers support this idea; the general education staff is split about 50–50 on the issue, favoring inclusion for the mildly/moderately disabled, but drawing the line strongly on inclusion for students with more severe disabilities. What should the district do to clarify the meaning of the legal, philosophical, and practical issues involved in inclusion? How should they seek support for it?.

ACTIVITY 10.1

Analyze the four scenarios just presented and indicate how an internal school consultant might approach each of them. What are some issues to consider in entry (How can you get started?) and diagnosis (How should you go about getting information to analyze the problem?)?

DISTRICT/SCHOOL ORGANIZATION FACTORS THAT INFLUENCE CHANGE EFFORTS

Knoff (1995, adapted from Egan, 1995) describes four characteristics of an operating school district that contribute to an understanding of the dynamics of districts and individual schools. These four characteristics operate in a holistic and ecological condition of interdependency.

The Receiving System

The traditional receivers of service were K–12 students. Recently, however, schools have expanded their service base to include preschoolers and families through the innovation of full-service schools. Since these service receivers are our clients, we need to address their needs. What do they want from the schools? What are their goals? How can we integrate their unique interests with the accepted tradition that dictates policy from more distant sources such as the government and boards of education?

The Performance System

Five elements define the performance system: a mission statement, goals that derive from the mission statement, activities that lead toward the goals, materials and resources needed, and specific outcomes compatible with the goals and the mission statement.

A mission statement gives overall guidance to the whole educational enterprise and sets the tone for everything that follows. Goals, activities, the need for resources, and specific outcomes can be specified within time frames. The achievement of broadly defined goals (such as the reduction in dropouts from 40 percent to 10 percent or an increase in achievement from the 30th percentile to the 50th) may take five years to accomplish. Toward the achievement of these broad and optimistic goals, a school might set annual goals that are more modest but headed in the intended direction. These should be stated in behavioral, observable terms and, of course, should be derived from the collaborative input of all constituencies, including the receiving system.

ACTIVITY 10.2

Does your school or district have a mission statement? If so, what long-term or short-term goals can be derived from that statement? Consider something in your school that needs improvement (e.g., attendance, reading achievement, playground behavior, "morale"). Devise a long-term goal that addresses this need.

The Human Resources and People System

This system includes the entire staff: teachers, aides, administrators, specialists, cooks, secretaries, bus drivers, campus security, and so on. A major goal of this system is to hire excellent people at the outset. However, this is not always possible. In times of personnel shortages, districts may need to hire some people that they would not have otherwise hired. This may be particularly true during teacher shortages, which many states are currently experiencing. Once hired, people need to be developed: inservice, mentoring, coaching, encouraging, and team building are all activities that can contribute to development. The need for a constant renewal of skills, knowledge, attitudes, and enthusiasm is recognized by every well-functioning school system. Assuming that the staff will always keep up professionally without being prompted to do so may be naïve (Basham, Appleton, & Dykeman, 2000; Sparks & Hirsh, 1997).

Knoff (1995) points out that your title (i.e., resource specialist, psychologist) shouldn't restrict you from performing activities that may not be traditionally associated with that title. In school consultation, any person with the skills and knowledge to serve in this capacity should be encouraged and allowed to do so. A resource teacher, for example, may be the best person to assist a new teacher in matters of classroom management; a team of three people, two ancillary and one regular-grade teacher, may be the best group to plan an evaluation program for the school; a psychologist may be in the best position to offer staff development in the area of conflict management, anger management, and social skills training, all of which are designed to improve the school climate.

ACTIVITY 10.3

What are some areas in which a resource teacher, special day class teacher, counselor, or school psychologist could have an impact on a whole school, other than through direct contact with students and IEP functions? Review the material in Chapter 3 on inservice staff development, then put together an inservice program for meeting an identified need.

The Pervasive System Variables

Building, district, and community influences are considered to be macro-level variables that can have positive or negative influences on service delivery. Knoff (1995) identifies six specific variables that are, to some extent, controlled at the macro level:

Incentive and Reward Factors   Just why do teachers and other school personnel do the best job they can? Certainly personal pride should be the primary determinant of this, but other, more extrinsic variables can also be influential. Salary, contract negotiations, building or district-level recognition, and released time for professional development activities are some of the specific ways in which districts provide incentives. How each is handled can affect morale and the desire to do one's best.

Quality of Life and Climate Factors   How do people feel about the school? Do they want to be there? Is it a good place for children? The answer to these questions varies immensely across schools and districts in the United States. To get a taste of some situations that detract from high quality in some neighborhoods, one should read Kozol's (1991) *Savage Inequalities*, an exposé of the dreadful conditions that exist in some schools in inner cities.

These quality-of-life and climate factors are both tangible and intangible. Certainly books and other materials need to be provided, but teachers and students need to know that the environment is safe, welcoming, and encourages high achievement. Parent involvement and support that lead to student involvement are essential, as are dedicated teacher efforts and harmonious race relations.

Environmental Factors   Environmental factors include a wide variety of influences that are community-based (for example, socioeconomic status, government and police support, and neighborhood conditions) and those that are related to the natural environment, especially when the environment becomes threatening (for example, during hurricanes, earthquakes, terrorist threats or attacks, or floods). A series of adverse environmental events can depress the ability of citizens to perform to their best potential.

Political Factors   This includes the potential impact of leaders at all ends of the spectrum, from the federal government to the local school board. Business leaders, the PTA, and other influential groups can become willing and valuable partners in reform efforts if you make an effort to include them.

Cultural Factors   These factors include the values, beliefs, assumptions, norms, and so on that can affect the productivity of a school or a district. Shifting demographics, new personnel, new dictums from the state department of education, and other events have an impact and may cause subtle or serious changes in how people relate to each other and to their jobs. Reform efforts that fail to consider the cultural norms of a school are likely to be given a poor reception (Brubacher, Case, & Reagan, 1994; Fullan, 1991).

Nonrational Factors   Systems resist change, just as people do. People develop a vested interest in what they are doing and how they are doing it and often resist change even when they see the need for it. Reformers need to understand that change does not happen overnight, even when the participants seem interested; habits die hard. All the factors mentioned in Chapter 3 about resistance to individual consultation can apply to reform efforts. Kampwirth (1996; see also Chapter 3) presents a list of causes, manifestations, and possible remedies for resistance both at the individual consultee and whole system levels. Friend and Cook (2000) and Dougherty (2000) have also contributed information about the causes for resistance and strategies for minimizing the influence of resistance.

WHO INITIATES SYSTEMS CHANGE?
WHERE DOES IT COME FROM?

In the typical school, as in other organizations, the formal leaders are generally expected to decide what changes are needed and how the school or organization should implement them. Although this older model of paternalistic leadership is still honored, the trend over the past few decades has been toward a decentralization of power and authority. Murphy (1991) reviews the history of some of these efforts to reform the public schools. He notes that the first wave of reform in the 1980s took the position that reform had to come from the established leadership of the schools. These included centralized control and higher standards. The second wave, starting in the later 1980s, deemphasized central control and began to utilize the benefits of local school restructuring. Today both the formal leaders (superintendents, principals, and so on) and other constituency groups (teachers, parents, and so on) have powerful voices, if not equal ones, in matters of organization, philosophy, method, and goals (Fullan, 1991). This change follows the spirit of collaboration that has been stressed throughout this text.

Given the current model of dispersed authority, it is common for the impetus for change to come directly and strongly from those people who are closest to the problem, the constituents who sense a need for a different approach to conceptualizing and solving the everyday problems that arise in schools' efforts to deal with *A Nation at Risk* (National Commission on Excellence in Education, 1983). This grassroots impetus has arisen from two divergent strands: (1) there is a growing understanding that change is needed and may best be generated from those closest to the problems, and (2) change that emanates from the top down is often subtly if not overtly rejected by those closest to the problems because these individuals don't feel that they were a part of the problem-solving process. Since they often have had no ownership of the solutions, they may not have personally needed to see that these solutions were carried out correctly or successfully (Heifitz & Laurie, 1997; Safran & Safran, 1997).

Considering the use of prereferral teams (i.e., SST, TAT, IAT, and so on; see Chapter 2) as examples of specific tactics in the overall strategy to reduce the number of students removed from the general education track, Meyers, Valentino,

Meyers, Boretti, and Brent (1996), using extensive interview and survey data, indicate that some prereferral teams are ineffectual because of insufficient teacher involvement/participation in the team process or because some teams or team members don't respect teachers. Among the authors' suggestions for the improvement of prereferral teams are the following three ideas, which speak to the importance of including teachers in this systems-change process:

1. Increase teacher involvement on teams.
2. Increase respect for teachers.
3. Provide information and training for teachers/team members.

Henning-Stout, Lucas, and McCary (1993); Powers (2001); Rosenfield (1992); and Rosenfield and Gravois (1999) give good examples of how to make prereferral teams more effective.

Teachers, as constituents of a change process, have considerable power in determining whether or not a given change is sustained beyond some mandated (that is, funded) lifetime. McLaughlin and Marsh (1978) find that federally funded innovative programs remain part of the school routine only when teachers believe that the innovation has made a difference in the lives of the most difficult children.

But teachers are not the only ones who decide what works, what stays, and what disappears. Hall, Rutherford, Hord, and Huling (1984) look at the role and style of the local school principal in the determination of the staying power of an innovation. In doing so they categorize principals as *responders*, those who do as the district office says; *managers*, those who adapt innovations to their own schools; and *initiators*, those who design their approaches to change around the interests, skills, and needs of their schools. Hall et al. find that change is more common and of higher quality in schools led by initiators.

An interest in change, therefore, can come from a variety of sources and for a variety of reasons. *A Nation at Risk* (National Commission on Excellence in Education, 1983) spurred American educators to think about the need for change, although it did not necessarily result in a wide unanimity of beliefs about the direction or extent of changes. What that report did was remind us that we, as a nation, had somehow lost the gains that seemed to occur after the U.S.S.R.'s launch of *Sputnik* in 1957 prompted us to bolster our science and math teaching. After the key trigger event of *Sputnik*, the federal government poured unprecedented amounts of money into the schools with some impressive, though temporary, results. Unfortunately, scores on the SAT and ACT continued to decline in the 1970s. This led to more calls for reform, culminating in GOALS 2000. GOALS 2000 served as a trigger event on the national scale because it informed the states and districts that the federal government was once more committed to making a massive effort to reform or revitalize public education. More recently the federal government has passed the No Child Left Behind Act, which was signed by President Bush in January 2002. This act will provide the states with the largest increase in history of federal aid to school districts. It will require annual testing of students in grades 3 through 8 in reading and math, starting no later than the year 2005. A sizable percentage of these additional funds will be targeted for schools with low achievement, with the funds intended to help these schools to improve their test scores. Schools not showing improvement over a period of years could be subject to consequences. Thus, for the first time, the federal government is not only offering carrots, it is also threatening with sticks. Whether the lofty goals of these federal government efforts can or will be achieved will depend on the efforts of local individuals working at the grassroots level. As I have implied, these people are likely to embrace reforms if they feel that they have been part of the reform process and that their ideas have been heard and valued. Otherwise, the reform movement may fail, predictably, as Sarason (1990) says, for at least the following reasons (Knoff, 1995):

1. Many reform enthusiasts and plan developers do not work in the schools or they have positions that are only distally related to classroom realities. They do not understand what it takes to effect change; they do not consult collaboratively.

2. America's educational problems are far too complex to be fixed with quick fixes. The diversity of the school population creates realities that require input from a variety of nonstandard sources: parents, community leaders, teachers, and even students.

3. Reform leaders need to understand the difference between power and influence. Because of their positions, those in charge of many reforms have the power to establish reform policies and to fund them, but they may not know how to, or be able to, influence those who need to carry out the policies at the classroom level.

4. True collaboration and shared decision making require a massive change in the existing traditional power structure and relationships among the various constituencies: administration, teachers, ancillary staff, parents, and so on. Although we have seen evidence that this change can occur, it is now more the exception than the rule.

5. As long as those most responsible for the needed changes at the student–teacher level feel powerless about their roles in the reform process, they will tend to avoid a serious implementation of handed-down ideas, they will engage in the process in minimal ways, and they will avoid real change. Habit, after all, is comforting. The desire to change emerges best from within. As McAdams (1997) indicates, "Convincing a critical mass of teachers to adopt a major reform project, especially one directly affecting instruction, is a time-consuming process fraught with practical and political difficulties" (p. 140).

In summary, change can arise from anyone who has an idea and is willing to put it forward. It comes from the warnings issued by national studies and from thoughtful persons who see a need for system improvement (reform) and want to respond to it. The form that change takes will depend on a host of variables, some tangible (money, facilities, personnel) and some intangible (felt needs, zeal, comfort level, need for achievement or power, resistance, and so on).

STEPS TO GUIDE THE IMPLEMENTATION OF SYSTEMS CHANGE: THE DECIDE APPROACH

Welch (1999) has provided a set of general guidelines to assist schools or districts to make decisions and to problem solve in order to improve a system's ability to provide effective service delivery to all schoolchildren. Welch uses the acronym DECIDE to remind consumers of the steps in this method, which, in modified form, are outlined below with examples and activities to help clarify the steps.

D: Define the Situation

1. What is currently taking place? Are you concerned about achievement scores? About a rise in the incidence of bullying behaviors? Describe in behavioral terms what the problem/issue/challenge is.

2. Who is involved? Who are the constituents of this issue? Who are the stakeholders? In addition to those who are obvious (students, teachers) include here groups that may be somewhat peripheral, but who still may have an impact on the issue, such as grandparents, bus drivers, ancillary staff, and so on.

3. When and where does it occur? Does it occur in the classroom, playground, from home to school, or during assemblies or athletic events?

4. History/dynamics. What do people know about where and when this issue became of concern? What have people done about it so far? With what results? What seems to make the behaviors of concern more or less noticeable?

5. Don't rush to solutions. Since educators tend to be action oriented, some may wish to develop interventions without following the next steps in the DECIDE system.

ACTIVITY 10.4

Define an issue of concern to your school staff. It can be in the areas of student relationships, achievement, groupings, curriculum, parent relations, and so on. Follow all the points listed above.

E: Examine the Environment

1. The focus here is on the "where" questions, but the other questions (what, who, when, why, and how) may resurface when the environment in which the behaviors of concern appear is studied.

2. An ecological analysis should be done at this point. What is there about the surroundings in which the behaviors of concern occur that could be contributing to these behaviors?

ACTIVITY 10.5

Focus on one problem area: student underachievement. Reflect on one classroom or a composite of classrooms where there is a problem of underachievement. Delineate the factors that may be contributive to the poor achievement.

C: Create a Goal Statement

1. Give this statement (include as many as may be necessary) focus and specificity, since it (they) will drive the rest of the decision-making process. Welch (1999) reminds us that all goal statements should be positive (i.e., not "dead men" behaviors, those activities that just as well could be done by a dead person, such as, "José will sit quietly in his chair all day"). The goal statements essentially consist of four components:

   a. *Behavior:* Use descriptors of objects, actions, and events that are concrete, observable, and measurable (Alberto & Troutman, 1999).

   b. *Condition:* Where and under what circumstances will the behavior occur?

   c. *Criterion:* Include a requirement for acceptability by setting a level or standard that the behavior must meet.

   d. *Duration:* For how long must the behavior be carried out? If the student meets the goal for one day, is that acceptable?

ACTIVITY 10.6

Create a goal statement regarding the situation you described in Activity 10.5. Be sure to include information about the four components discussed above.

I: Invent an Intervention Plan

1. This is where the emphasis shifts from process (how something is done) to content (what will be done, under what conditions, by whom, when, how, and where).

2. Welch (1999) suggests five subareas to be considered in the development of the plan:

   a. *Brainstorming:* This was discussed in Chapter 5; it consists of getting stakeholders to generate ideas in a freewheeling, noncritical atmosphere. Egan (1998), Friend and Cook (2000), and Welch and Sheridan (1995) give suggestions for the proper conduct of brainstorming.

   b. *Resource allocation:* There are five types of resources to be considered when developing an intervention plan. These are *human* (Who can and will carry out the plan?); *informational* (Where does information about the issue and its possible solution come from? What laws or regulations may impact on intervention design?); *technological* (What technological tools could be used to help solve the problem? Are they available?); *physical* (Where will the interventions be carried out? Might your school need a separate "study room" for students who are unable to maintain their behavior during ordinary lessons? Where will it be located?); and *financial* (Will there be a cost associated with the intervention? Is the money for this allocated already? Where might it come from if not readily available?). Another resource not mentioned by Welch (1999) but which needs to be considered is *time*. If the intervention takes someone's time, what will be given up in order to have the time to engage in the intervention? As mentioned in numerous contexts throughout this book, time is a major problem in the delivery of collaborative consultation in the schools; it may also be a major problem in the delivery of complicated interventions. In *Prisoners of Time* (1994), the National Education Commission on Time and Learning notes that time is a crucial element in the determination of the success of any school reform or restructuring effort.

c. *Time lines:* When will the various steps begin, for how long will they be operative, and when will they end?

d. *Cost-benefit analysis:* It may be necessary to attempt to determine if the benefit associated with this change will be worth the costs of the change. Difficult as it is to answer questions of value when it comes to human services, there may be times when the intervention planning team will need to face some hard realities: Not all interventions can be fiscally supported.

e. *Cross-referencing the goal and action plan:* In the development of the intervention plan, it is necessary to go back one more time to determine if there is a close alignment between the original goal statement and the current version of the intervention plan. Sometimes, after the brainstorming and consideration of all the factors listed above, the plan that emerges may not have a good chance of achieving the original goal statement. If not, it's back to the drawing board to revise the plan. Finally, the team must take a look ahead at the final step in the DECIDE system, *evaluation*, to determine how and when to do formative evaluations of the plan.

ACTIVITY 10.7

In small groups, engage in a brainstorming session on what to do about a schoolwide problem, such as dangerous and abusive playground behavior. Select a few possible interventions for this problem. Then determine how each of the six resources previously discussed would be used to implement the interventions. What problems might arise from a plan to use a designated "time-out" room for students demonstrating abusive or dangerous behavior on the playground?

D: Deliver the Action Plan

1. This is the moment of truth in consultation regarding individual or small groups of students, and in systems improvement efforts as well. All of the steps outlined above are used to provide guidance as the intervention team implements the intervention(s).

2. Again, the important questions must be answered: Who will do what, when, where, how, and, if still necessary, why?

3. As mentioned above, time must be set aside for the conduct of the formative evaluation procedures.

4. Regrettably, formative evaluation sometimes informs us that the intervention isn't working. This alerts the team to review the situation, revise the plan as appropriate, and begin again.

ACTIVITY 10.8

The case study in this chapter involves a school that decides to modify its method of inclusion of students with mild-to-moderate disabilities. Assume the plan isn't working. Isolate an aspect of the intervention plan that may not be working, and determine an alternative plan that would meet the criteria discussed above.

E: Evaluate the Intervention Action Plan

1. What is your formative evaluation telling you? Where are the bottlenecks or breakdowns in delivery of the intervention? Are the consultees and other involved personnel implementing the interventions correctly? Are the reactions of those whose behavior is the target of the intervention appropriate for the goal? Are the planned-for resources available and being used advantageously?

2. Welch (1999) suggests that formative evaluation helps the team to "take its own pulse." This refers to analyzing how the team is working together. Communication, interpersonal, and problem-solving skills are being put to the test; just how is the partnership working?

3. The final step of DECIDE is a summative evaluation. To what extent was the goal actually met? Since the purpose of an evaluation is to determine the value of an intervention, what was the value of the activities taken by everyone in the name of systems improvement? What was learned from this experience?

ACTIVITY 10.9

Review the literature in special education, school psychology, or counseling to find some articles that discuss how change efforts in the schools were evaluated. Was the evaluation plan determined before the project was started? Were objective (behavioral) criteria used as data sources? What were the results of the evaluation?

Consultants might think that these steps could easily be applied to one-on-one consultation efforts as well as whole-school or whole-system reform. This is true; problem-solving steps are fairly generic. Zins and Illback (1995) point out that any systems-change process is usually conceptualized as consisting of the following phases: *diagnosis, planning, initiation, implementation,* and *institutionalization.* Chapter 5 contains information about other ways of conceptualizing the stages or phases of the change process. Although Chapter 5 emphasizes individual consultee and client situations, the change process is fairly similar in the case of systems change, with the exception of the need for more group interactions and the possible need for greater resources (e.g., money) in the latter case.

Hall and Hord (1987) present a Concerns Based Adoption Model (CBAM) that is designed to clarify issues in systems change. They refer to their stages of concern as *developmental* because they occur in a (more or less) sequential order:

- *Awareness.* This stage is somewhat mistitled since most constituents have only the slightest knowledge of the proposed change.

- *Informational.* Constituents are hearing more about a proposed change but have not yet internalized its potential impact on them.

- *Personal.* Concern is starting to develop: Constituents are beginning to wonder how this possible change will affect them personally.

- *Management.* The change process is moving along more rapidly. Questions about the details of resources, time commitments, and changed job descriptions are raised.

- *Consequence.* Serious questions about student impact are now being discussed.

- *Collaboration.* It is now apparent that all involved constituents need to be included in future planning.

- *Refocusing.* Modifications and elaborations of the original plans are examined in light of what has occurred so far.

In light of the ideas expressed in this text, the author wonders if the *collaboration* step shouldn't follow *personal,* since the involvement of constituents would be helpful in dealing with the issues raised in *management.*

In their large-scale systems-change projects, Rosenfield and Gravois (1996) demonstrate how the CBAM stages of concern are observed. Kuralt (1990) used the CBAM to determine that the instructional consultation model (Rosenfield, 1992) resulted in reduced placements in special education and improvements in targeted students' reading comprehension.

FORMAT OF THE SYSTEMS-CHANGE CASE STUDY

The case study you will read at the end of this section follows a series of stages that give coherence and order to the change process. These stages are different from those that applied to the individual cases in Chapters 7 and 9 and are modifications of those presented by Brown, Pryzwansky, and Schulte (2001) and Parsons (1996). They consist of the following:

1. A problem statement.
2. A brief history of the concern that has developed around this problem.
3. A list of the concerned parties.
4. A statement about key trigger incidents that prompted action.
5. Developing initial plans for change.
6. A description of a fermentation period when issues and concerns were dealt with.
7. A list of the specific interventions agreed on.
8. The implementation of the interventions.
9. Monitoring and evaluation of the interventions.

In the following subsection, I describe each stage in some detail.

Problem Statement

Systems change (reform, renewal, restructuring) starts with an identified problem. Although some people ignore the old saying "If it ain't broke, don't fix it," most people consider it to be sage advice. Naturally, unless you define the terms, most old sayings don't mean much. What exactly is "broke" when it comes to interpersonal affairs, the functioning of a system, or the achievement of students? In some schools and geographic areas, underachievement according to national standards is and has been the norm for so long that no one considers it a problem anymore. It isn't "broke" because people are used to it being that way. In such desperate cases, it is difficult to know at what point underachievement would be considered a problem.

For our purposes, a situation becomes a problem to be solved when someone in authority decides that it (the situation) is impeding her goals for the system. Although there may be many situations that someone is unhappy about, it is not likely that any strong, organized effort to fix them will occur until someone with the authority to command resources, direct people, and focus energy decides to do so. For example, federal issues such as welfare, education, defense, infrastructure, crime, and sundry other areas have problems connected with them that become candidates for intervention only when people in authority decide to focus on them. Each administration and Congress decide what is most important and consider the various constituencies involved, as well as the political ramifications of dealing with the selected areas; these become the problems that are dealt with. Most Americans are well aware of the phenomenon that occurs every four years when candidates for the presidency make exaggerated promises about their plans for the next four years, if elected. After the election, the real priorities are decided, and some of the promises go begging.

In the public schools there are many issues that can be dealt with as potential or real problems at any given time: underachievement, discipline, social unrest, diversity, curriculum modifications, groupings of students, infusion of technology, and so on. Although all of these problems receive varying degrees of attention, occasionally one of them rises to the fore as the current "crisis" (sometimes referred to as an "opportunity") that attracts considerable attention and results in a dedicated effort to deal with it. This issue may have been identified by a number of constituents for a long time. When officially recognized as a problem to be solved by those in authority, it becomes the focus of formal change efforts.

ACTIVITY 10.10

List some problems in the schools with which you are familiar, and indicate the amount of effort that has gone into improving them. What happened to make the reality become a problem (opportunity) that people felt deserved attention?

History of Concern

Every problem has a history. Problems don't just spring up out of nowhere, though some may strike us that way (e.g., gang killings, terrorist attacks). As I have implied, a problem may exist for some time (gangs often threaten each other; terrorists are probably always planning new attacks) but not draw sufficient attention to itself for a variety of reasons; thus, it remains unattended to. At some point the situation grows in size or severity and affects more people, some of whom are important or vocal. Or some outside influence (a new law or court judgment; a real terrorist attack) comes to bear on it, and people in authority take notice. Typically they will discuss it among themselves, call in those close to the problem to discuss it, possibly generate a task force to study it, and then perhaps commit to doing something about it.

ACTIVITY 10.11

For one of the problem areas mentioned in Activity 10.10, recall the history of the problem. When did it seem to start, how did it develop, when did people really begin to take notice of it, and how did they start the process of problem resolution?

Concerned Parties

Also known as *constituents, stakeholders,* or *parties at interest,* concerned parties are individuals who are affected by the problem or who will be affected by changes to the situation. For example, at the highest reaches of government, stakeholders in the situation called *corporate welfare* are policy makers, accountants, political leaders, stockholders, and advocates for the cause of the corporations. However, regarding welfare for families who live in or near the poverty level, stakeholders are also the children involved, their parents, those who collect rent from these parents, those who sell food to them, and so on. All of these people could be affected by any change in the welfare structure. In the schools, a change in the dress code affects the parents, the stores who specialize in the latest fashions, stores that sell uniforms, and the students and their behavior at school.

ACTIVITY 10.12

Alpha School has experienced a steady decline in achievement scores over the past decade. Who are the constituents of this problem? Who will be affected by any change in policy or practice vis-à-vis the students' achievement efforts?

Key Trigger Incidents

These incidents are usually environmental events that cause influential people to take notice of the situation and decide that it is a problem. The event can be dramatic, such as a student committing suicide, which prompts the school principal to organize a crisis response team and to consider hiring another school counselor. Or it might be the state's announcement of a serious drop in math scores, prompting the board of education to order a review of the math curriculum. Or it could be a massive gang fight on the playground, prompting parents to require the school to do something about interpersonal relationships among students. The September 11, 2001, terrorist attacks in the United States caused the president to put all his focus on the apprehension of the terrorists and their supporters. Some trigger events simply happen in the minds of influential people; these people decide on their own, usually after information about a situation has been brought to their attention, that something should be done about it. It is then officially a problem (or opportunity or challenge).

Sometimes the trigger event is a series of incidents that coalesce to bring a situation to the minds of influential people. For example, in California in the summer of 1996, the governor discovered that his state had an abundance of money that it had to spend on the schools because of a previous legislative fiat. He decided to lower the class size in grades K–3 to 20 students per class. (They had been at about 29 per class.) In doing so, he was following the lead of Tennessee and some other states that had been engaged in a lower-class-size effort for some years.

In California, almost all districts decided to lower their class sizes and to obtain the extra money offered by hiring new teachers and finding room for these classes. These changes had strong impacts in the schools. There was a great influx of new, largely inexperienced teachers in classes at all levels, partly because some upper-grade teachers decided to teach in the primary grades to take advantage of the lower class sizes. Some of these new teachers had not had teacher training or done student teaching. Districts and teacher-training institutions responded in various ways to this challenge. One response was to introduce an intern-teacher corps consisting of people with a bachelor's degree who had not been trained in teaching techniques but who indicated an interest in teaching. They were hired with the stipulation that they would immediately embark on a program of certification training, some of which was to be done by the district and some by the teacher-training institutions of higher education. In one district near San Diego, the district and the teachers' union decided to release three experienced teachers to act as consultants (mentors, advisors, but not evaluators) to the 15 new teachers in the district to help these inexperienced teachers learn the fundamentals and further refinements of teaching. This approach appears to have been a success: all 15 new teachers were still on the job into the second semester, whereas in other districts many had resigned by that time.

Most trigger incidents are not so dramatic, nor do they require such impressive degrees of cooperative planning as did the California situation. More likely, the trigger incident is some event that occurs amid a growing awareness that a situation should be examined. Once influential people seize it as a challenge, the time is ripe for applying the principles of systems change discussed herein.

ACTIVITY 10.13

There have been many trigger incidents in the brief history of the full inclusion movement. At the national level, these incidents have consisted of statements from leaders in the field and court judgments. At the local level, they typically have consisted of a parent requesting that her child who is disabled be enrolled in the regular education classes for all or most of the school day. Since the courts have generally supported this request, districts needed to react when these requests (trigger events) were made. When this phenomenon first began to occur, many districts were not ready, and they reacted in a wide variety of ways.

Recall how your district reacted to these requests for full inclusion when they first started to develop and how the district policy toward future requests has evolved. How has your district responded to this challenge?

Developing Initial Plans for Change

Although the source for initial plan development can vary, usually the local school administration or district-level personnel develop the framework for this stage in the systems-change process. There is a wide literature that they can follow in their efforts to develop a rational approach to this and all other stages of the process (Adelman & Taylor, 1997; Bacharach, 1990; Borgelt & Conoley, 1999; Egan, 1998; Miles & Lewis, 1990; Sarason, 1990; Snapp, Hickman, & Conoley, 1990; Valentine, 1991; Wehlage, Smith, & Lipman, 1992). Fashola and Slavin (1998) present a summary of reform models and discuss commonalities among those that have been successful.

When you perceive a problem but do not have a firm grasp on its dimensions or attributes, you may find yourself running in all directions. This danger can be partly avoided by gathering information from the constituents. Whoever is developing the initial plans probably will want to start with a needs assessment (Harvey, 1990; Illback, Zins, & Maher, 1999; Nagle, 1996), with "need" being defined as a discrepancy between a current unsatisfactory situation and a more desirable one. Just how do the constituents see this problem? What do they think should be done about it? Block (1981) suggests the following four steps.

Deciding to Proceed   Here the interested parties get together and review what they know about the problem. They then attempt to conceptualize it in a problem-solving format and agree that it is worth studying and solving.

Selecting Dimensions   The committee needs to decide just what it will study. Members should avoid cluttering the study with issues that are not relevant or that will not result in the development of focused data or effective interventions.

Deciding Who Will Be Involved in the Data Collection   As a general rule, a needs assessment should gather information from all relevant constituents. An exception may be a situation in which it is not sensible to stir things up prematurely by asking questions and getting information from some constituents before really deciding to effect a change. Some constituents may feel threatened at the thought of a change and may respond with information designed to protect whatever they feel is being threatened. Thus, the committee needs to decide just how far to spread its net of data gathering at this early stage. It might be better to wait until a firmer decision is made to move toward a change.

Selecting the Data-Collection Methods   The usual methods for gathering information are questionnaires, surveys, interviews, and record reviews. With a questionnaire, a blend of closed and open-ended questions can be used. A committee of interested personnel representing all the stakeholders can put together a questionnaire or an interview form to assist in gathering the information. Once the information is gathered, the committee can review the information and interpret it.

ACTIVITY 10.14

Imagine that your district has decided to explore the possibility of changing from a pullout RSP special education service delivery model to one based on a collaborative consultation model. How do you think the district might go about exploring the possibility and potential of this newer model? Who would the constituents be? What methods of initial data gathering might they use?

Fermentation Period

During this period there will be discussions about various dimensions of the problem, data gathering will proceed, and other activities designed to define the problem will take place. In poorly organized or immature systems, there will be suggestions for quick fixes; reliance on old, previously used remedies; efforts to bury the problem; or the generation of excuses about why nothing can be done. Resistance within the system can occur at this time; those who see the possible solutions as a threat may want to deny the reality of the problem.

If the system recognizes the situation as a challenge and is mature enough to want to move forward to a solution, it will start the inquiry process. Constituents will be interviewed, records will be reviewed, task-specific groups will consider what is known, and tentative plans will be discussed. Stop-gap measures may be put into place if the situation calls for some rapid response (for example, an increase in gang violence on campus), but the goal should be to come up with a long-term plan that will deal with the problem in an effective and growth-oriented fashion. The purpose of the plan is to improve the way in which the system operates vis-à-vis the problem now and in the foreseeable future.

The fermentation period allows people to take the time to look at the problem from a broad perspective. Very often what seems like a localized problem has ramifications that were not considered initially. The gang violence problem, for example, reveals a need to examine closer ties to the community and its leaders (including the police, social welfare agencies, and the parents), gang members in the student body, drug and weapons traffic, dress codes, the counseling program, and so on.

At the end of the fermentation period, the study groups will have reported to the authorities, and together they can decide on implementation plans.

ACTIVITY 10.15

Imagine that your school has decided to strengthen its prereferral intervention process in an effort to slow the placement rate of students in special education programs. A committee of interested special and regular education teachers, administrators, and ancillary staff develops some possible methods. The committee presents these to the whole school for consideration. What problems or issues might be raised that will extend the fermentation period?

Specific Interventions

This part of the process consists of listing the interventions to be used; their sequential order (if appropriate); who is responsible for what parts of the plan; how the plan will be accomplished; where it will occur; and other details such as how it will be paid for, if that is a consideration. If the planned changes cannot be funded, the team studying the problem needs to apply pressure to get it paid for, seek outside funding, or rethink the plan.

This is often the period in a change process that generates the most enthusiasm. Anger and confusion about the problem have passed, potential difficulties about developing a plan have been resolved, and now the group has agreed on specifics. As long as there are no funding problems, energy and a sense of purpose should be at a peak.

ACTIVITY 10.16

Imagine that in your high school two major reform efforts have been developing concurrently. One has to do with a move toward implementing the General Education Initiative by giving support to regular education class teachers in their efforts to mainstream or include students with disabilities. The other has to do with modifying the structure of the day so that more flexible times can be given to subject areas as the semester progresses. What possible problems could arise as a result of trying to implement both of these reform efforts at the same time?

Implementation of Interventions

Under the direction of the appropriate administrator or designee, the program begins. Some beginnings may not directly affect the targeted students or the problem itself but may consist of activities that are preliminary to the main or major events that will influence the problem more directly. For example, before some changes can occur, systems may need staff development, physical plant changes, new kinds of recruitment (for example, volunteer tutors), new materials, or a new pupil monitoring system. Since these activities are directly tied to the systems-change project, they must be successfully accomplished in a timely fashion, or the project could be delayed. Delays cause discouragement and a loss of enthusiasm. They should be avoided.

After the preliminary activities are successfully accomplished, the more direct systems-change activities begin. If planning has been competent and if the change participants carry out their assigned duties, there is reason to expect some degree of initial success. This success creates a honeymoon effect: Participants believe that the plan is perfect and that nothing can go wrong. Such perfection hardly ever happens, however, in any comprehensive systems-change process; there are simply too many factors that can intrude and lessen enthusiasm during a middle period of the implementation process.

Monitoring and Evaluating the Interventions

The degree to which these problems are worked out determines the fate of the remainder of the process. Some of the problems may be mechanical (equipment breaks down), financial (other demands intrude, state funding decreases, inflation increases), personal (resistance becomes evident when the plan is finally implemented), or administrative (the administration decides that another problem is more important and decides to pull back its support). The characteristics of the system, described previously in this chapter, exert their influence at this point. The hope is that the system is strong enough to withstand these potentially destructive factors and can proceed with a successful change effort.

Other possibilities include the fact that the interventions are being implemented correctly but are not having the desired effect. Your formative evaluation suggests that some aspects of the interventions need to be changed. This is often very discouraging to those who designed and/or are implementing the interventions. Getting past the all-too-common finding that plans need to be changed in midstream is a major challenge to those who are personally involved in wanting to see the interventions be successful. If the planners and implementers are willing to change the interventions, you may hope to see an improved product.

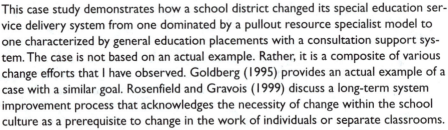

Case 5   Changing to a Consultation-Based System of Service Delivery for General/Special Education

This case study demonstrates how a school district changed its special education service delivery system from one dominated by a pullout resource specialist model to one characterized by general education placements with a consultation support system. The case is not based on an actual example. Rather, it is a composite of various change efforts that I have observed. Goldberg (1995) provides an actual example of a case with a similar goal. Rosenfield and Gravois (1999) discuss a long-term system improvement process that acknowledges the necessity of change within the school culture as a prerequisite to change in the work of individuals or separate classrooms.

In this case the process of effecting change is not easy or quick. The various stages of systems change (mentioned previously) are all observed, though not in the well-regulated fashion implied by those who develop such stages. As in the cases in Chapters 7 and 9, the change process does not unfold in a lock-step, sequential fashion. The process may best be described as linear circularity. While it generally moves forward, it does so in a recursive, circular fashion; for every two steps forward, there may be one or one-and-a-half steps backward or sideways.

PROBLEM STATEMENT
At King Elementary, a K–6 school in the Middletown School District, 6 percent of the 900 students have been identified as having a specific learning disability (SLD), predominantly in the area of reading and written language. About 90 percent of these students are served for up to three periods a day in one of the two resource rooms in the school. None of these students is placed full time in a special day class; students with more severe learning disabilities, or other disabilities who have been determined to need this type of placement, are educated in a different district school.

King School has the services of a speech and language specialist three days a week, an elementary counselor full time, and a school psychologist two days a week. The principal, Ms. Jacobs, is assisted by a vice-principal, Mr. Hashimoto.

King is in many ways a typical elementary school. It is located in an urban neighborhood consisting mainly of working-class people. Of its students, 62 percent are Anglo-American, 24 percent are Latino, 10 percent are African-American, and the remainder are primarily Asian-American or Middle Eastern-American. Of the teachers, 80 percent are Anglo-American females; there are two Latino males and one African-American female. Of the 54 students identified as learning disabled, 55 percent are Anglo-American, 30 percent are Latino, and 12 percent are black.

Scheduling is the problem first brought up in a teacher staff meeting. Some teachers think the students with SLD are missing too much of what goes on in their general education classes because of their part-time placements in the resource room. Though unverbalized in that meeting, there have also been conversations among some teachers, including one of the two RSP teachers, that maybe this pullout program isn't in the best interests of the identified students. Some of these students don't seem to profit much from their placements based on their annual test scores, and others seem not to transfer much of what they learn in the RSP room to the demands of the general education classes. Some of the older students in the RSP actively dislike the special education class because they feel it stigmatizes them. Over the past few years, some parents have pulled their children out of this program, largely because their children dislike being identified as "special education."

HISTORY OF CONCERN

Schools, like all well-established large institutions, have a culture, a set of norms and habits that guide their everyday activities. In the U.S. public schools for the past 50 years or so, a special education system that consists largely of pullout and special day class programs has been part of that culture—and, by and large, a comforting part. People have expected the system to provide some extra, or "special," education for students with disabilities and assume that the nature of this education requires special settings. At the same time, there have always been voices within the system that have questioned the value of this form of special education (Dunn, 1968; Howe & Miramontes, 1992). Over the last decade, the number and strength of the voices questioning the status quo in special education have grown steadily (Goodlad & Lovitt, 1993; Lewis & Doorlag, 1999; Lloyd, Singh, & Repp, 1991; Salend, 1998; Stainback & Stainback, 1996).

The history of the concern at King School is based only somewhat on these national concerns about special education as a separate system. The school staff members at King are more concerned about their own students than about national agendas. They feel that students attending the RSP are missing out on the general education curriculum and may not be making enough gains in the RSP classes to justify the continued existence of this program.

CONCERNED PARTIES

Any change in service delivery affects both general and special education. Thus, it is no exaggeration to say that all persons concerned with the school will be potentially affected by a change in this area. Naturally the students will be affected, as will their parents. All teachers and ancillary staff can expect a significant change in how they work. For example, general education teachers used to the idea that there is a program "out there" for dealing with students who manifest learning (and possibly behavior) problems need to consider the fact that these students may no longer go "out there" but will stay in the general education classes. The teacher will be expected to deal with the students' learning problems with the help of a collaborating staff of administrators, special education teachers (who no longer have a classroom of their own), and ancillary staff. If this plan is to be successful, these ancillary staff (school psychologists, counselors, and speech and language specialists) will also experience a major change in their expected daily activities. The thought of all this change, based on what many consider to be an unsubstantiated premise—that students with SLD will do better in the mainstream if given accomodations and modifications—seems overwhelming to some staff but has great potential to others.

KEY TRIGGER INCIDENT

As is often the case, a number of small incidents seem to occur almost simultaneously. Alone, none may have been significant, but together they constitute a collective trigger that prompts the school to begin serious discussions of the issue.

Three incidents occurred simultaneously and together served as a trigger for this systems-change project:

1. The principal attended a district workshop in which the idea of implementing the General Education Initiative was briefly discussed.
2. The school psychologist attended a national convention in which she heard about changes in special education and became interested in how that might work at King School.
3. A small group of teachers, including one of the RSP teachers, brought up the issue at a staff meeting.

In a few weeks, an idea once regarded as unlikely to flourish rapidly became a hot topic. The impetus for change has formed.

DEVELOPING INITIAL PLANS FOR CHANGE

Within a week the word has spread through the school and outside to the parents that a change in the special education system is being discussed. Once this happens, the leaders of a change movement must take control, or the rumor mill will take over and cause chaos. In this case the principal, Ms. Jacobs, calls a meeting with the two special education teachers, the district director of special education, the ancillary staff, and a representative teacher from each of the grade levels. This committee of 12 is asked for input. Although a few people on the committee seem skeptical of the idea, it is generally greeted with enthusiasm. Following are some of the questions at the meeting and (at least tentative) answers:

This new model calls for "collaborating." Who exactly is going to do the collaborating? Will it be others in addition to the two RSP teachers? Anybody with the expertise to be helpful in a case can collaborate. This might include the ancillary staff, the general education class teachers, or administrators.

How will it be decided who will collaborate? The decision will take place largely through an expanded SST system. Questions will change from a focus on eligibility and placement to a focus on needs and ways in which to accommodate them in the general education classrooms.

What about those learning disabled students who are probably somewhat ADHD and manifest behavior problems? They have a very difficult time maintaining themselves for five hours in a general education class. How will not giving them an "escape valve" (that is, the special education room) be helpful to them? This question is one of the most sensitive since it is difficult to know if the general education teacher who asks it is expressing her own need for an "escape valve" from students who are difficult to manage and teach. Two different kinds of answers are offered:

1. With the collaboration process in place, the consultants will help the general education teachers deal with the wide variety of learning and behavior problems presented by these students.

2. If these students can feel more successful in general education classes, they may not engage in disruptive, off-target behaviors. Their self-concepts as students should improve as they start to see themselves as successful in the general education classes.

There are 30 classes at King School. How are these two RSP teachers going to be able to serve 15 classes each? Aren't they going to be spread too thin? Remember that the RSP teachers are responsible for meeting the goals and objectives of the (roughly) 27 students currently assigned to each one. These students are likely to be spread among 15 classes. One way to deal with this is to put more students with SLD in certain classes, have a smaller teacher–pupil ratio in those classes, and cut down the number of teachers to consult with to 10 or so. Also, the RSP teachers are not the only ones serving as consultants in this effort. Ancillary and general education teachers may also serve, although their time in classes may be limited by their other responsibilities. The collaborative consultation model does not depend on the consultant's presence in the classroom of the targeted student; much consultation can be done outside of the classroom.

This raises the question of time. Just when are the general education teachers going to find the time to do the out-of-class collaborating? Finding time may be the biggest single problem in the schools (National Education Commission on Time and Learning, 1994). There never seems to be enough time to do what needs to be done. At King School, like most elementary schools, teachers do not have a planning period, so this leaves before school, after school, recess breaks, and lunch time (when the teachers are not on duty). Some consulting can be done while the consultant is in the regular classroom; however, in order to plan well, more 15- and 30-minute blocks of time would help. One tentative solution is the hiring of an additional teacher who can cover classes while out-of-class collaboration takes place. Will the district fund this person? Can the King budget afford it? Can the district and King split the costs of such a position? Ms. Jacobs says she will look into it.

What about the parents of the identified students? Aren't they going to be bothered when they hear that their children aren't going to be getting special education anymore? Ms. Jacobs says that this has already happened; she has received two phone calls from parents demanding to know why their children are being sent back to the general education classes without the benefit of an IEP meeting to change the service delivery system spelled out in the IEP, which is for RSP services. Ms. Jacobs informed them that their children will not be dismissed from special education, that our discussions only concern alternative ways of delivering the needed services, that no decisions have yet been made, and that parents will be fully informed before any changes take place. She also says that she has started to put together a letter informing all parents of students in the RSP program of the discussions relative to this possible change and telling them that they will be invited to participate if this committee decides that there is support for the proposal at the school and district levels. She also will ask parents to indicate their interest in being part of the planning committee if planning goes beyond the present informal discussions. The committee supports her responses to the parents and the generation of the letter.

There is no way to prevent this sort of rumor. Once some teachers hear of any impending change in the school system, they are quick to let their friends in the community know about it. Depending on how parents interpret the rumors, either positively ("Our children are going to be served in the general education classes.") or negatively ("They are putting our children back in the general education classes, which will overwhelm them. That's not what I call special education!"), they can strongly influence the change process. This can have a damaging effect on planning because the rumors that spread may not only be wrong but may be difficult to correct later. The district director of special education says he will inform the superintendent to be ready for questions about these discussions at the next meeting of the board of education.

Based on the questions asked and suggestions given, the committee decides that the idea is worth pursuing. Another meeting will be held in two weeks. By then the letters to the parents will have been received, and some parents will have responded; also, the board of education will have met, and some questions may come up at their meeting. (The superintendent has briefed the board. Their response to questions from citizens is that a new service delivery system is being studied but that it is only in the preliminary stages; no decisions have yet been made.)

FERMENTATION PERIOD

This is that period between official meetings when people air their views in the lunchroom, the hallway, the parking lot, and the neighborhood. Three different groups are developing: one in favor of the inclusion of all students with SLD into the regular program with consultative support to the general education teachers, one opposed to it, and a small offshoot of "middle-road" people who think that inclusion might be good for some of the students with SLD but not for all of them. The questions and problems just mentioned are discussed, with each group answering the questions from its point of view. Each group claims to be advocating for the best interests of the children; and, like the blind man and the elephant, each takes its position from its own perspective, unable or unwilling to admit that the other side might have a better perspective. It is clearly time for the leaders to take control, clarify issues, and seek consensus. Otherwise, the groups will continue to polarize, and the proposal will die.

Two weeks after its initial meeting, the committee—now expanded to include any interested staff member and three parents who want to be included (requiring the meeting to be held in the evening, distressing some of the teacher members)—convenes again for a two-hour meeting that is structured and coordinated by a small subcommittee (consisting of two teachers, two parents, and Ms. Jacobs) organized by the principal. Here is the agenda for the meeting:

1. Welcome and introductions by Mr. Hashimoto, vice-principal (10 minutes).
2. Overview of the proposal for full inclusion of all students with SLD by Ms. Jacobs, principal (10 minutes).
3. Questions from the audience, to be answered by a panel consisting of Ms. Jacobs; the two RSP teachers; Mr. Lopez, school psychologist; and Dr. Jackson, district director of special education (15 minutes).
4. Small-group discussions of questions and answers already presented (10 minutes).
5. Brief (2-minute) summaries from each group (10 minutes).
6. Break; open discussion (15 minutes).
7. Small-group discussion on each of the following focused topics (15 minutes).
   a. Effects on students with SLD.
   b. Effects on everyday classroom life.
   c. Additional resources needed.
   d. Solutions to the time problem.
   e. Solutions to other potential problems.
   f. Potential benefits of this proposal.
8. 3-minute summaries from each group (18 minutes).
9. Summary and description of future plans by Ms. Jacobs (10 minutes).

The meeting lasts two hours. At the end, after summarizing what she heard, Ms. Jacobs asks for a straw vote from the group. She asks, "Should we pursue this proposal further or continue providing service in our current model?"

The vote is 16 to 5 in favor of moving forward with the proposal. Ms. Jacobs says that she is prepared to move ahead to the plan-development stage, with September of the following year as the target date of implementation. She asks for volunteers to serve on the planning committee; eight people, including two parents, volunteer.

All things considered, this is a very effective meeting. Although there is not complete unanimity (there rarely is in public education), there is enough support to encourage the principal to go forward.

Now the real work begins, consisting of at least the following elements:

1. Plan the logistics: job descriptions, possible time allocations, possibility of additional staff time, materials purchasing, and so on.
2. Contact all constituents with information on an ongoing basis.
3. Hold IEPs this academic year for all involved students to indicate that services will be provided in the regular classroom with consultative assistance to the regular teacher.
4. Create a series of staff development workshops on inclusion issues.
5. Contact the special education department of the local state college to see if the faculty is interested in working collaboratively on this project.
6. Network with other districts to see which have moved toward a collaborative model; find out how they did it.
7. Seek possible outside funding to cover anticipated costs.

ACTIVITY 10.17

Comment on the steps taken during the fermentation period. What effective things happened? What might have been done differently? What potential problems have not been dealt with adequately?

SPECIFIC INTERVENTIONS

During the remainder of the academic year, the committee, with some changes in composition and now usually including five concerned parents, meets monthly to put the final touches on the plan scheduled to start in the fall of the next school year. All parents of students with SLD are asked to attend an IEP meeting about their child. There the following philosophy and plan for full inclusion with consultative help is outlined to them:

1. We believe we can meet the needs of your child without having to remove her from her peers in the general education class. We can do this by having the special education teachers and other staff assist the general education teachers with ways of accommodating the curriculum and other classroom expectations to the ability level of your child in those subject areas affected by your child's SLD. In this way, your child's special education needs will be met, and she will not be required to miss the program of core curriculum studies given to all other students in her grade. Our general education and special education teaching staff are determined to see that whatever stigma may have been attached to having to leave the general education class to go to the special education room will no longer exist.

2. Your child's regular education teacher will be assisted by anyone on staff who has the expertise to provide consultation (assistance, advice, specific skills) to the general education teacher. Although this person will usually be one of the special education teachers, consultants may also include the school counselor, school psychologist, or other general education teachers. As the parent, you are invited to take part in whatever consultative services you want from our staff (such as homework hints, discipline, ways of supporting your child, and so on).

3. Your child's specific program will be determined by the general education teacher in consultation with the individuals just mentioned and with the student study team (SST). These people will meet at least monthly to discuss your child's progress, more often as needed. You will be given a copy of the plan for your child's special education program on a monthly basis. Of course, you will be invited to these SST meetings when they are held.

4. We anticipate that we will be able to hire two more floating aides to assist us in implementing some of the accommodations necessary for some students. We are also going to hire a teacher who will act as a substitute teacher in classes when your child's teacher needs to attend a meeting (SST or otherwise) concerning our inclusion program.

IMPLEMENTATION

The program as just outlined is implemented in September. All but three parents support the new plan. The IEPs on the students whose parents support the change are modified the previous spring to reflect the children's full inclusion with consultative assistance on a regular basis. The three parents who refuse this change are offered a transfer to a more traditional pullout program in another school, but all three refuse it. Their children are being seen individually by one of the RSP teachers or the special education aide three times a week for two hours each. This is an unfortunate drain on the time of the personnel, but staff members hope that in time these parents will decide in favor of the full inclusion plan. All newly identified students with SLD will be offered either the full inclusion plan or services in a different school since King School will no longer have a pullout RSP for students with SLD.

The 51 students identified for special education services in general education classes (54 are actually identified, but 3 are to be served in a traditional way) are distributed throughout the classes as follows:

Grade one: 5 students, all in one teacher's room.

Grade two: 8 students, 4 each in two teachers' rooms.

Grade three: 12 children, 6 each in two teachers' rooms.

Grade four: 10 children, 5 each in two teachers' rooms.

Grade five: 8 children, 4 each in two teachers' rooms.

Grade six: 8 children, 4 each in two teachers' rooms.

There are 18 teachers in grades one, two, and three at King School. Each of these classes averages 25 students. In grades four, five, and six there are 15 teachers, each with an average of 30 students. Teachers who show an interest in this project are asked if they are willing to be an inclusion class. Those who agree receive the in-class services of one of the RSP teachers, now called "consulting teachers" (CTs), for one hour (or 45 minutes in grades four, five, and six) five days a week, with one of those days being set aside for individual conferences between the CT and the general education teacher while the floating substitute teacher takes the class. These teachers also receive an additional period for independent planning, again being relieved by the floating sub. There are more than enough volunteers at each grade level; each of the participating teachers is chosen by random drawing. For example, one of the six first-grade teachers is selected (four teachers want to do it) and therefore has the CT in her class five days a week from 9:00 to 10:00, with Friday set aside for a conference time between these teachers and other consultants as available while the floating sub-stitute teacher takes the class.

The plan calls for CT 1 to be assigned to grades one, two, and three. She will be in the first-grade class from 9:00 to 10:00 every day, in one of the two second-grade classes (class 2A) from 12:30 to 1:30, in the other second-grade class (2B) from 10:00 to 11:00, in one of the third-grade classes (3A) from 11:00 to 12:00, and in the other third-grade class (3B) from 1:30 to 2:30. Collaborative planning times occur on Friday for grade one, on Tuesdays for grade 2A, on Thursdays for grade 2B, on Wednesdays for grade 3A, and on Fridays for grade 3B. These times were selected in a joint conference with all concerned staff. The schedule for the floating aide is coordinated with the plans set by these teachers and by the plans and needs of the teachers in grades four, five, and six. A corresponding weekly planning schedule for the upper-grade teachers who use CT 2 is also devised.

Additional scheduled activities include the time from 2:30 to 3:00, Wednesday through Friday, which is used for planning between the CT and her aide. Parent conferences, primarily by phone as needed, are done at 3:00, Wednesday through Friday. SST meetings for new referrals are held on Mondays and Tuesdays from 2:30 to 3:30.

The SST meetings designed to formalize the plans for each currently identified student are held Monday through Thursday from 8:00 to 8:45, with three students discussed at each meeting. Although the structure of these 15-minute sessions varies somewhat depending on needs, the general plan is to devote 5 minutes to a review of the current plan and 10 minutes to the development of a new monthly plan, copies of which are sent home to the parents. This allows for all 51 students to have their plans reviewed monthly. If more students enter the program, or the population of identified students goes down, this schedule can be adjusted.

During the time the CT is meeting individually with the general education teacher, he may be either planning modifications and accommodations for the identified students or discussing ways of making the curriculum more accessible for these students and others who are having difficulty with the assignments. He may also choose to use some of this time to co-teach lessons, with the floating sub assisting, or may use the time to train student peer tutors. How this time can be used most effectively has not been dictated; staff believe they need this first implementation year to try various activities to see what works and what they need to do during these times.

Once every two months, during a student-free day, the inclusion program staff take part in inservice activities related to inclusion for half the day. For the rest of the day, they get together and share success stories and discuss problems under the leadership of a local university faculty member who is knowledgeable about inclusive programs.

The question of plan evaluation has been discussed throughout the plan's development. Teachers and parents are concerned about the following:

1. Will students with SLD profit academically as much from an inclusion program as they will from the traditional pullout program?
2. How well accepted will students with SLD be when fully integrated into general education classes?
3. How will included students feel about themselves when they are in the general education classes full time? How do these feelings compare to those they held about themselves when they were in the pullout program?

To answer question 1, staff members give all students with SLD achievement tests, both norm-based and curriculum-based, in reading, writing, and math in January and June of the planning year. These data are used as a baseline growth rate and are to be compared to data gathered during the same two months during the first year of the plan's implementation.

Question 2 is to be answered using a sociometric measure in which children are asked to select students they would most like to work on school projects with and would be most likely to invite to a party. Gresham and Elliott (1989) have reviewed the use of these techniques with students with SLD.

Question 3 has two parts. The first is measured by a simple questionnaire to be administered to all included students and an equal number of non-disabled students from the same classes asking for opinions about their acceptance in classes. The second part in question 3 requires that the included students be given a self-report questionnaire modified from Piers and Harris (1996) during the last six months of the planning year and then again a year later when they are fully included. The district director of research is consulted about appropriate minimally intrusive procedures to use and is responsible for data analysis.

ACTIVITY 10.18

Review the plan just described. How effective do you think it will be? What are some possible problems that may arise? How might you design a program differently?

SUMMARY

This chapter has reviewed some general considerations for consultants and others in the schools who are interested in systems change (reform). It is crucial that the constituents of the problem are involved at every step beyond initial discussions so that they will feel some ownership of the solutions that are determined to be the best for the local situation.

The case presented in this chapter indicates how a school, under the direction of a strong leader and a cooperative staff, was able to develop a plan for the termination of a resource program based on the pullout model and replace it with an inclusion model that returned almost all identified students who have learning disabilities to age-appropriate general education classes. It also allowed for planning time, collaborative efforts, and continued staff development. The primary hurdles overcome by the staff were (1) the typical resistance that accompanies any change effort, (2) concern about the ability to find the funds for hiring a floating substitute teacher, and (3) getting agreement from parents who may have become comfortable with the pullout program. A brief description of a plan for program evaluation was also provided.

REFERENCES

Adelman, H. S., & Taylor, L. (1997). Toward a scale-up model for replicating new approaches to schooling. *Journal of Educational and Psychological Consultation, 8*(2), 197–230.

Alberto, P. A., & Troutman, A. C. (1999). *Applied behavioral analysis for teachers* (5th ed.). Upper Saddle River, NJ: Merrill/Prentice Hall.

Bacharach, S. B. (1990). *Educational reform: Making sense of it all.* Boston: Allyn & Bacon.

Basham, A., Appleton, V., & Dykeman, C. (2000). *Team building in education.* Denver, CO: Love Publishing.

Block, P. (1981). *Flawless consultation.* San Diego, CA: Pfeiffer.

Borgelt, C., & Conoley, J. (1999). Psychology in the schools: Systems intervention case examples. In C. R. Reynolds & T. B. Gutkin (Eds.), *The handbook of school psychology* (pp. 1,056–1,076). New York: John Wiley.

Brown, D., Pryzwansky, W. B., & Schulte, A. C. (2001). *Psychological consultation: Introduction to theory and practice* (5th ed.). Boston: Allyn & Bacon.

Brubacher, J., Case, C., & Reagan, T. (1994). *Becoming a reflective educator.* Thousand Oaks, CA: Corwin.

Dougherty, A. M. (2000). *Psychological consultation and collaboration.* Belmont, CA: Wadsworth/Thompson Learning.

Dunn, L. M. (1968). Special education for the mildly retarded: Is much of it justified? *Exceptional Children, 35,* 5–24.

Egan, G. (1985). *Change agent skills in helping and human service settings.* Monterey, CA: Brooks/Cole.

Egan, G. (1998). *The skilled helper* (6th ed.). Monterey, CA: Brooks/Cole.

Fashola, O., & Slavin, R. (1998). Schoolwide reform models: What works? *Phi Delta Kappan, 79,* 370–379.

Friend, M., & Cook, L. (2000). *Interactions: Collaboration skills for school professionals.* New York: Longman.

Fullan, M. (1991). *The new meaning of educational change.* New York: Teachers College Press.

Goldberg, I. (1995). Implementing the consultant teacher model: Interfacing multiple linking relationships and roles with systemic conditions. *Journal of Educational and Psychological Consultation, 6*(2), 175–190.

Goodlad, J. I., & Lovitt, T. C. (Eds.). (1993). *Integrating general and special education.* Upper Saddle River, NJ: Merrill/Prentice Hall.

Gresham, F. M., & Elliott, S. N. (1989). Social skills assessment technology for LD students. *Learning Disability Quarterly, 12,* 141–152.

Hall, G. E., & Hord, S. M. (1987). *Change in schools: Facilitating the process.* Albany, NY: State University of New York Press.

Hall, G. E., Rutherford, W., Hord, S., & Huling, L. (1984). Effects of three principal styles on school improvement. *Educational Leadership, 41*(5), 22–31.

Harvey, T. R. (1990). *Checklist for change: A pragmatic approach to creating and controlling change.* Boston: Allyn & Bacon.

Heifitz, R., & Laurie, D. L. (1997). The work of leadership. *Harvard Business Review,* 124–134.

Henning-Stout, M., Lucas, D. A., & McCary, V. L. (1993). Alternative instruction in the regular classroom: A case illustration and evaluation. *School Psychology Review, 22,* 81–97.

Howe, K. R., & Miramontes, O. B. (1992). *The ethics of special education.* New York: Teachers College Press.

Illback, R., & Zins, J. (1995). Organizational interventions in educational settings. *Journal of Educational and Psychological Consultation, 6*(3), 217–236.

Illback, R. J., Zins, J. E., & Maher, C. A. (1999). Program planning and evaluation: Principles, procedures, and planned change. In C. Reynolds & T. Gutkin (Eds.), *Handbook of school psychology* (pp. 907–932). New York: John Wiley.

Kampwirth, T. (1996, Fall). Dealing with barriers and resistance in school-based consultation. *CASP Today,* 10–12.

Knoff, H. M. (1995). Best practices in facilitating school-based organizational change and strategic planning. In A. Thomas & J. Grimes (Eds.), *Best practices in school psychology—III* (pp. 239–252). Washington, DC: NASP.

Kozol, J. (1991). *Savage inequalities: Children in America's schools.* New York: Crown.

Kuralt, S. (1990, August). *Classroom collaboration: Implementing consultation-based interventions in five multidisciplinary teams.* Paper presented at the annual meeting of the American Psychological Association, Boston.

Lewis, R. B., & Doorlag, D. H. (1999). *Teaching special students in general education classrooms.* Upper Saddle River, NJ: Merrill/Prentice Hall.

Lloyd, J. W., Singh, N. N., & Repp, A. C. (Eds.). (1991). *The regular Education Initiative: Alternative perspectives on concepts, issues, and models.* Sycamore, IL: Sycamore.

McAdams, R. P. (1997). A systems approach to school reform. *Phi Delta Kappan,* 138–142.

McLaughlin, M., & Marsh, D. (1978). Staff development and school change. *Teacher's College Record, 80,* 70–95.

Meyers, B., Valentino, C. T., Meyers, J., Boretti, M., & Brent, D. (1996). Implementing prereferral intervention teams as an approach to school-based consultation in an urban school system. *Journal of Educational and Psychological Consultation, 7*(2), 119–149.

Miles, M. B., & Lewis, K. S. (1990). Mustering the will and skill for change: The findings from a four-year study of high schools that are experiencing real improvement offer insights into successful change. *Educational Leadership, 47,* 57–61.

Murphy, J. (1991). *Restructuring schools: Capturing and assessing the phenomena.* New York: Teachers College Press.

Nagle, R. J. (1996). Best practices in conducting needs assessments. In A. Thomas & J. Grimes (Eds.), *Best practices in school psychology—III* (pp. 421–430). Washington, DC: NASP.

National Commission on Excellence in Education. (1983). *A nation at risk: The imperative for educational reform.* Washington, DC: U.S. Government Printing Office.

National Education Commission on Time and Learning. (1994). *Prisoners of time.* Washington, DC: U.S. Government Printing Office.

Parsons, R. D. (1996). *The skilled consultant.* Boston: Allyn & Bacon.

Piers, E. V., & Harris, D. B. (1996). *The Piers-Harris Children's Self-Concept Scale.* Los Angeles: Western Psychological Services.

Powers, K. (2001). Problem solving student support teams. *The California School Psychologist, 6,* 19–30.

Pugach, M. C., & Johnson, L. J. (1995). *Collaborative practitioners, collaborative schools.* Denver, CO: Love Publishing.

Rosenfield, S. A. (1992). Developing school-based consultation teams: A design for organizational change. *School Psychology Quarterly, 7,* 27-46.

Rosenfield, S. A., & Gravois, T. A. (1996). *Instructional consultation teams: Collaborating for change.* New York: Guilford Press.

Rosenfield, S. A., & Gravois, T. A. (1999). Working with teams in the school. In C. Reynolds & T. Gutkin (Eds.), *The handbook of school psychology* (3rd ed., pp. 1,025–1,040). New York: John Wiley.

Safran, S. P., & Safran, J. S. (1997). Prereferral consultation and intervention assistance teams revisited: Some new food for thought. *Journal of Educational and Psychological Consultation, 8*(1), 93–100.

Salend, S. J. (1998). *Effective mainstreaming: Creating inclusive classrooms.* Upper Saddle River, NJ: Merrill/Prentice Hall.

Sarason, S. B. (1990). *The predictable failure of educational reform: Can we change before it's too late?* San Francisco: Jossey-Bass.

Schmuck, R. A. (1990). Organization development in schools: Contemporary concepts and practices. In T. B. Gutkin & C. R. Reynolds (Eds.), *The handbook of school psychology* (2nd ed., pp. 901–921). New York: Wiley.

Snapp, M., Hickman, J. A., & Conoley, J. C. (1990). Systems intervention in school settings. In T. B. Gutkin & C. R. Reynolds (Eds.), *The handbook of school psychology* (2nd ed., pp. 922–936). New York: Wiley.

Sparks, D., & Hirsh, S. (1997). *A new vision for staff development.* Alexandria, VA: Association for Curriculum and Development.

Stainback, W., & Stainback, S. (Eds.). (1996). *Controversial issues confronting special education: Divergent perspectives* (2nd ed.). Boston: Allyn & Bacon.

Valentine, E. P. (1991). *Strategic management in education: A focus on strategic planning.* Boston: Allyn & Bacon.

Wang, M. C., Haertel, G. D., & Walberg, H. J. (1993). Toward a knowledge base for school learning. *Review of Educational Leadership, 63*(3), 249–294.

Wehlage, G., Smith, G., & Lipman, P. (1992). Restructuring urban schools: The new futures experience. *American Educational Research Journal, 29,* 51–93.

Welch, M. (1999). The DECIDE strategy for decision making and problem solving: A workshop template for preparing professionals for educational partnerships. *Journal of Educational and Psychological Consultation, 10*(4), 363–377.

Welch, M., & Sheridan, S. (1995). *Educational Partnerships: Serving Students at Risk.* Fort Worth, TX: Harcourt Brace.

Zins, J. E., & Illback, R. J. (1995). Consulting to facilitate planned organizational change in schools. *Journal of Educational and Psychological Consultation, 6*(3), 237–245.

Index